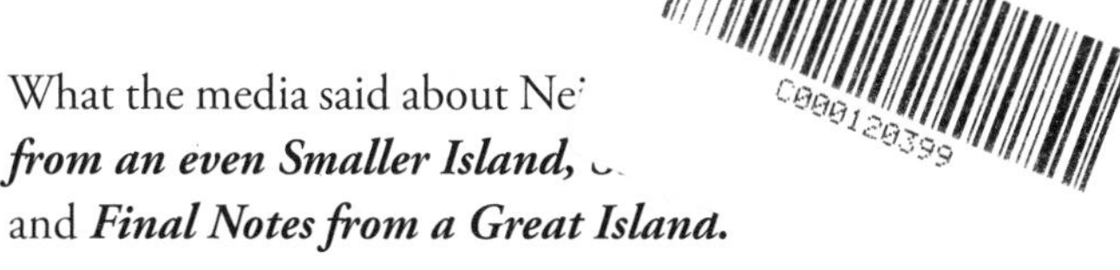


What the media said about Ne'
***from an even Smaller Island,*** ...
and ***Final Notes from a Great Island.***

## Final Notes from a Great Island

"Neil Humphreys gives readers a wonderful inside look at Singapore from an outsider's point of view. And it's all written in an honest and humorous way. As soon as I started reading, it felt like I was in Singapore and actually visiting the places Humphreys talks about. He describes the people, places and the city in such vivid detail."

—*Galaxie Magazine* (Malaysia)

"*Final Notes from a Great Island* is a great read because it's full of little scenarios that we can relate to in our daily lives. Far from trying to tackle the big issues, Humphreys is adept at capturing those tiny idiosyncrasies that make us who we are as a people."

—*IS Magazine*

"Chock full of witty anecdotes, *Final Notes from A Great Island: A Farewell Tour of Singapore* should be made a mandatory History text for all Singaporean students. See Singapore through the eyes of a true-blue *ang moh* as he puts a fresh twist on stuff you thought was boring...like the Merlion."

—*LIME*

## Scribbles from the Same Island

"Some of his observations are so bitingly spot-on, you don't know whether to laugh or just hit him over the head."

—*Her World*

"He is that voice in your conscience that you wish will go away and let you be that *kiasu, kaypoh* and uptight Singaporean that you've become."

—*TODAY*

"That's Humphreys's specialty—coaxing humorous thoughts from otherwise conservative minds, and making liberal thinkers guffaw mindlessly."

—*Sunday Mail* (Malaysia)

**Notes from an even Smaller Island**

"The book presents a warts-and-all view of the city-state and celebrates many of the things most often criticised."

—*BBC World*

"A thoroughly enjoyable read on the virtues (or hazards) of living in Singapore through the eyes of a 6-foot-4-inch Briton whose style is so disarmingly honest, you will laugh at the things you once considered the bane of your existence...Decidedly Singapore, distinctly British."

—*Singapore FHM*

"He pokes fun at Singaporeans ... but rather than bristle at his observations, you are likely to twitch with mirth. The ribbing is always cushioned by good-natured quips often sprinkled with hilarious anecdotes."

—*The Sunday Times*

"Blatant prejudices are chewed on, digested and spat out with an equal measure of candour and tongue-in-cheek."

—*Singapore Seventeen*

# Complete Notes From Singapore

# NEIL HUMPHREYS

# Complete Notes From Singapore

THE OMNIBUS EDITION

This edition with new cover published in 2008

Published by Marshall Cavendish Editions
An imprint of Marshall Cavendish International
1 New Industrial Road, Singapore 536196

Photo on page ix by: Gerald Gay, Copyright 2002-2007
www.TalkingCock.com. Used with permission.

Cover and illustrations by Lock Hong Liang



Other Marshall Cavendish Offices:
Marshall Cavendish Ltd. 5th Floor, 32–38 Saffron Hill, London ECIN 8FH, UK • Marshall Cavendish Corporation. 99 White Plains Road, Tarrytown NY 10591-9001, USA • Marshall Cavendish International (Thailand) Co Ltd. 253 Asoke, 12th Flr, Sukhumvit 21 Road, Klongtoey Nua, Wattana, Bangkok 10110, Thailand • Marshall Cavendish (Malaysia) Sdn Bhd, Times Subang, Lot 46, Subang Hi-Tech Industrial Park, Batu Tiga, 40000 Shah Alam, Selangor Darul Ehsan, Malaysia



**National Library Board Singapore Cataloguing in Publication Data**
Humphreys, Neil.
Complete notes from Singapore : the omnibus edition / Neil Humphreys. – Singapore : Marshall Cavendish Editions, c2007.
p. cm.
ISBN-13 : 978-981-261-661-6
ISBN-10 : 981-261-661-6

1. Singapore – Anecdotes. 2. Singapore – Humor. I. Title.

DS609

959.57 — dc22 SLS2007020706

Printed in Singapore by KepMedia International Pte Ltd

*For the women in my life*

# ACKNOWLEDGEMENTS

I should recognise the persistence of the gang at Marshall Cavendish and Pansing. They insisted that an omnibus edition was the way to go. I had reservations. I wasn't sure what an omnibus was. But I agreed when they allowed me to include pictures of semi-naked women.

Puay Koon drew those naked women with an accuracy that was altogether rather alarming and Colin Goh found the time to make up some kind words and produce a remarkable Singapore movie in the same year (*Singapore Dreaming*, go see it).

My old mates, Scott and David, made invaluable contributions to all three volumes and I'm genuinely grateful that they're still talking to me.

Tracy will begin divorce proceedings if I do not acknowledge that she took the photograph that graces this omnibus edition. She took the cover photograph on my first book, received no credit and went as far as contacting a solicitor. Thanks for the photo. Thanks for not divorcing me. Thanks for always being there.

Going through the three books again, I notice that one character crops up more than any other. It's extraordinary. She lives in England, yet still manages to pop up all over the pages to discuss her nurse's underwear and kangaroo cemeteries. So I dedicate this special edition to a special woman. Thanks mum, for contributing to every chapter of my Singapore story.

# FOREWORD

Looking back, I don't know exactly what it was that made us cast Neil Humphreys as Sir Thomas Stamford Raffles, the founder of modern-day Singapore, in our low-budget, low-brow comedy film, *TalkingCock the Movie.*

Firstly, he looked nothing like Raffles, and secondly, he had an unusual accent. Although he was an Englishman, he didn't speak like he had a potato stuffed in his mouth like Raffles probably did. While I recognised traces of Cockney in his accent, more than anything, he sounded, well, Singaporean. And not in that fake, condescending way that many expatriates do whenever they try to speak Singlish, the local creole. This man knew the difference between a *lah, leh* and a *hor.*

Perhaps we found it appealingly subversive to cast someone so post-colonial as Singapore's biggest colonial bigwig. Or maybe it was just Neil's infectious sense of humour and obliging manner that made him so much fun to have on set. Or perhaps it was because he was willing to work cheap, just like the rest of us.

Whatever the reason, now, whenever I think of Sir Stamford Raffles, the image I see in my head is not the Singapore Tourism Board-approved statue that stands outside the Victoria Theatre, but rather, Neil in his muddy track shoes, white knickerbocker trousers, and an ill-fitting black jacket that calls to mind an organ grinder's monkey.

And why not? Neil spent more time in Singapore (over 10 years) than Raffles ever did (around 5 years, and even then with lots of travelling in between), and probably mingled far more with the locals. Also, while Raffles drafted Singapore's first constitution, I dare say it is nowhere near as entertaining as what you're about to read.

With the clear affection he's demonstrated for Singapore in his writings, and judging by the popularity of his books, Neil is definitely the front-runner for the title of Singapore's favourite *ang moh* (literally: 'red-haired one', meaning 'Caucasian' in the Southern Chinese Hokkien dialect).

There are, however, some narrow-minded detractors who would seek to deny Neil this singular honour by pointing to his recent departure from Singapore for Australia. To them I say: what could possibly be more Singaporean than emigrating to Australia?

Good luck, Neil. And be careful not to *ji seow* the dingos too much, *hor.*

Colin Goh
Founding Editor
www.TalkingCock.com
Singapore's most popular satirical website

# INTRODUCTION

WHEN I found myself peering down at my elderly landlady's exposed breasts, I can honestly say I never thought, "Over ten years from now, I'll be introducing an omnibus edition of my books with those two swingers." But there you go. It's been 11 years since my old Singaporean landlady flashed me. Yet I still get asked if she really did perform 'the twin potato sack routine' every Saturday. Three books have subsequently been written, hundreds of columns have left the laptop and I've moved to another continent, but Singaporeans still want to discuss two things—the landlady's boobs and the midnight funeral. Without a doubt, those two events will be carved onto my tombstone: Here lies Neil Humphreys. He nearly got a nipple in the eye from his deranged, elderly landlady. And on his first night in Singapore, he visited the most bizarre coffee shop the Asian city-state has ever known.

Not that I'm ungrateful. On the contrary, those two daft encounters changed my career and, at the risk of sounding melodramatic, my life. I was working as a speech and drama teacher for my dear 'Singapore godmother', Juliet McCully, when I began telling those two stories to the young women in reception in a desperate attempt to sound exotic and engaging. I accomplished neither, but they did laugh. I shared the stories with some of my upper secondary students and they also laughed. It appeared that Singaporeans were listening to the governing powers; they were taking this business of a sense of humour seriously at last. Indeed, I watched, fascinated, as the students took the piss out of each other, not in a vicious, personal attack but in an often self-deprecating fashion. The humour was often more intelligent and perceptive than the puerile rubbish that usually passed for comedy on Singapore television. Still, being a relative newcomer to the country in the 1990s, I began to recognise a glaring contradiction. At a certain level, the message was constantly being advocated and stressed: Singaporeans cannot laugh at themselves. They just can't. It was a cultural thing. An Asian values thing. A filial piety thing. A Singaporean thing. Whatever it was, it was a 'thing' and many Singaporeans had been afflicted by it, apparently.

But I didn't seem to know too many. Where were these people who supposedly couldn't laugh at themselves? I eventually found them, of course. They appeared to be using 'Asian values' as a get-out clause, a buffer to hold off unwelcome criticism. It's like when the guy in the movies says, "Don't hit me! I'm wearing glasses!" In Singapore, it was a case of, "Don't satirise me! Asian values!" And the impenetrable shield came down. Recalling those attitudes now reminds me of the current climate in Australia in many ways. When a dissenting voice offers an alternative view, it is often dismissed as 'un-Australian', which is the new buzzword Down Under. Lampoon, ridicule or mock here and it can be labelled, put down and brushed aside as 'un-Australian'. In Singapore, it can be considered as going against 'Asian values' and therefore unacceptable. Singaporeans simply just can't afford to lose face, I was told, on so many tedious occasions.

It didn't take long to realise that the people who instructed me in the ways of face-saving were 'talking cock'. It was nonsense, a convenient fallacy. Singapore was changing—rapidly. As a teacher, I noticed that students were increasingly distracted, bored even. Their trains ran on time, their streets were safe and spotless and their upgraded apartments were modern—all genuinely commendable achievements (neither England nor Australia could make a similar claim)—but it was no longer enough. There was a growing sense of restlessness. They wanted to 'talk cock', discuss alternatives and poke a satirical finger at themselves and their Singapore way of life. I'd like to think that the East Asian currency crisis of 1997 (combined with the 2002 Sars outbreak) forced some younger Singaporeans to accept that their economy was not infallible and question the notion that the pursuit of material wealth had to be all-consuming. There was room to lighten up a bit and maybe add a touch of irreverence to the dusty bookshelves marked 'Singapore collection', which brought me back to my landlady with the big boobies …

But I was apprehensive. The Singapore literary scene was markedly different in the 1990s. It appeared to take itself rather seriously. The importance of being earnest seemed to be the average Singapore author's motto. There were coffee-table books galore on the Fall of Singapore in 1942, the struggle for independence and Lee Kuan Yew's speeches. All commendable stuff but hardly recommended literature for a newcomer like myself, who just wanted to understand the quirks and foibles of his adopted country. I could find academic tomes on Stamford Raffles, the British East India Company and the rise of the People's Action Party but very little on the country's most important and relevant subject: its people.

That's not to say Singapore's range of published work wasn't an eclectic mix. Quite the opposite in fact. If I was in the market for angst-ridden poetry about suicidal, sex-starved, gender-confused, oppressed young adults, I was spoilt for choice. And if I ever fancied spending a little money on a little honey with a Southeast Asian lady of the night, I need look no further than a local bookshelf to find titillating facts on price and performance, and discover which racial groups had the biggest 'cuckoo birds'.

But there appeared to be this gaping hole where the middle ground should have been. The shelves had weighty political and economic tomes on one side and prostitutes and bit-part actresses on the other. Yet none of my Singaporean friends were really reading these books. They were reading Nick Hornby and buying Bill Bryson's travel books on Australia and the United States. One of Bryson's best-selling books—even in Singapore—was *Notes from a Small Island*, a book about Britain by an American writer. Written by an outsider with an insider's perspective, the book was shifting so many copies, it was almost single-handedly filling that literary middle ground back in Britain. Now, that sounded like a good idea ...

I visualised *Notes from an even Smaller Island* being like Bryson's *Notes from a Small Island* but younger and 'harder'. That's Essex Man parlance for 'more aggressive', in a streetwise *ah beng* sense, rather than a powerful, emotive literary sense. Yes, I was naïve and a bit of a prat. My original title was the truly lame *A Young Englishman in Singapore*. I thought it was a trendy riff on Sting's 'An Englishman in New York', which told the true story of Quentin Crisp, a gay writer struggling to be accepted in London and New York. The song encapsulated that outsider-trying-to-fit-in stuff. That'll give my book a street-cred cachet, I thought. But my publisher pointed out, quite rightly, that the title had a post-colonial whiff about it and conjured images of me in a white suit and a panama hat, sipping a pink gin at the Singapore Cricket Club. In my defence, I only did that for the first year. I had to do something with my Monday nights.

Eventually, we settled on the current title because it was a cheeky pun on Bryson's classic, my original inspiration, and provided an immediate hint of its contents and tone. I joked at the time that if Bryson ever decided to sue me, at least I'd get to meet my literary hero in court. But the more I was asked if I was concerned that Bryson's publisher would sue me, the more worried I became that Bryson's publisher would sue me (in case you're wondering, the answer is, of course not. No one has copyright over the English language. So if you fancy writing *Notes from an even Smaller Island still: A tour of Sentosa,* go for it.) In subsequent editions, the title was extended. It now reads *Notes from an even Smaller Island: Singapore through a young Brit's eyes,* thanks to a little research by my publisher, who concluded that the Top Ten lists for travel books are often dominated by lengthy titles, thus making it easier for them to pop up when readers conduct online searches. In other words, if someone did a Google search for a Singapore book before the title extension, *Notes* wouldn't come up. Now it would. Bearing that fact in mind, my next book will be called *Notes from Down Under: A youngish Dagenham-born Brit-who-used-to-live-in-Singapore's tour of Australia, where there are free amateur porn clips available for downloading 24 hours a day*. That should ensure the title pops up on most search engines for the next 20 years.

There is an interesting postscript to the first book's title. I recently met Bill Bryson at a book talk in Melbourne (his, not mine, don't get carried away) and he vaguely knew of me and my Singapore books, but he made no reference to the book titles or a pending court appearance. But then, considering I was dribbling and jabbering away like a traumatised groupie at the time, he was probably eager to get rid of me.

But the publisher, though enthusiastic, had reservations. That's a publisher's job—to have reservations; and, on this occasion, they were justified. When I initially pitched my idea around the offices at *The Straits Times*, where I was working at the time, I was met with understandable scepticism. "It's a funny social observation book about my experiences in heartland Singapore," I said. "It's an expat's travel book; it's been done before," they said. "No, this is different. Expats will read it, but it's not a book for expats," I said. "It's not a travel book—it's social analysis. I'm not a Singaporean, but it's a book primarily for Singaporeans. It's not a weighty, academic tome, but it's not throwaway fluff either. It's funny, but it's not a comic book for the humour section." You can see where I might have had problems marketing the idea.

So I just started writing the damn thing. The landlady's boobs story. The midnight coffee shop story. The frog in the toilet bowl story. They all went in, along with a few vignettes from my working-class council house childhood in Dagenham, England, for purposes of socio-economic comparison, general merriment and personal therapy. Most importantly—and most worryingly for my publisher—the book took the piss. Out of me. Out of my childhood. Out of my travelling companion Scott. Out of my family. And out of Singapore and Singaporeans. The first four were fair game, although my mother constantly calls me to ask, "Did I really say that? You make it sound like I've spent my entire life doing nothing but fucking swear." And to protect his identity, I sometimes think I should've used a false name for Scott. Although when I met him in Wales a day before his wedding and informed him of my intentions to share our Singapore story, he replied, "Write what you bloody like." So I did. And when he finally read the finished book about a year later, he said, "It's a load of bollocks."

But the Singapore part was tricky. *Notes from an even Smaller Island* was a slight publishing risk because I, the naïve, idealistic, first-time author, refused to compromise. Today, every man and his blog attacks the Singapore 'gahmen', its political policies, *kiasuism* and the island's societal flaws, but it certainly wasn't commonplace at the end of the 1990s. And I wasn't even Singaporean! The general consensus within the publisher's shortly before the book's release was that it might have a chance with expats and rebellious teenagers. But there was a perceptible concern that the average Singaporean could say: "This *dumpwee* guy is telling us how we live our lives. Who does this patronising *ang moh* bastard think he is?"

Then I saw the cover. And I was immediately convinced that its design was the commercial kiss of death. Now, just to clarify, I never intended to put myself on the cover. I always visualised a quirky, colourful illustration of a generic young western traveller wandering across a map of Singapore. But the publisher asked for a few publicity shots of me, in full backpacker mode, standing in front of various historic landmarks. I had reservations. First, I was adamant that *Notes from an even Smaller Island* was not a backpacker's book. And second, Singapore doesn't have many historic landmarks. Besides, the book wasn't a coffee-table, picture postcard look at the island anyway. Nevertheless, this dutiful—and somewhat desperate—first-time author dragged his poor wife around City Hall, Raffles Hotel and the Padang, places that we seldom visited, to capture the 'lost backpacker searching for the elusive Singapore soul' look. But I am no model. And my wife is no photographer. After three hours, we wanted to kill each other. So, naturally, at the moment we were about to snap, she snaps, and that photograph ends up on the cover of my first book. I was unshaven, sweaty and inadvertently holding the city map upside down. The first fresh-faced shots taken that day said: "Man just stepped off yacht at Raffles Marina." This shot said: "Man just stepped in dung." With the patchy, goatee beard, I looked like an extra from *Blackadder* (a nice 80s pop culture reference that no one under 20 is going to get). I'll never forget Scott's reaction. When I sent him the book, he said, "Who the fuck put Sir Francis Drake on the cover?" Fortunately, the original cover was subsequently replaced in later editions. Thank heavens that title sold, otherwise Dagenham's D'Artagnan would still be popping up on musty bookshelves.

There are a couple of things I must point out about each of the book covers. Yes, it really is the same shirt on all three covers. On the reprinted *Notes from an even Smaller Island*, it is pink. On *Scribbles from the Same Island*, it is blue and on *Final Notes from a Great Island,* it is yellow. But it is the same shirt. I wore it for the *Scribbles* photo shoot and, to save a few bucks, the publisher changed its colour and the angle and threw it onto the reprinted *Notes*. So, to bring closure to the ritual, I wore it one more time for *Final Notes* and then we burnt it in a solemn ritual at Clifford Pier with close friends, representatives from the publisher's and a few confused tourists from China who thought I was passing the shirt on to a dead relative. The shirt's original colour? See *Scribbles*.

I do think each cover is a slight improvement on the previous one except for one glaring flaw: They look like a weight-watchers campaign in reverse! The scrawny, bearded bloke on the first cover had disappeared by the second book, probably because the heftier chap on the final cover had eaten him. I wasn't just travelling across Singapore, I was eating my way around the island. Inherited from my father, my bowels had always moved quicker than a shot from a canon. In over 20 years of eating saturated fat and chips, washed down with lashings of cold calories, nothing could stick to me until I was introduced to the wonders of suppertime eating in Toa Payoh. Singapore cuisine, take a well deserved bow. You broke me.

*Notes from an even Smaller Island* hit the bookshelves and I was quite content to leave Singapore and try my luck elsewhere. We'd had a great run, I'd left my job at *The Straits Times* to promote the book and my mum could tell the world that she had produced an author. (Which she did. Quite literally. I introduced her to the Internet and the cost-effectiveness of online messaging. She introduced herself to the world. Should you ever venture into a chat room to share your personal problems and an inquisitive auntie offers support and some maternal advice, it's probably my mother.) But the book kept selling. And selling. And selling. *Notes* popped in and out of the best-seller list for over five years. It had to be reprinted within a couple of months, six times within the first two years and it's now in its twelfth reprint. In a country not known for its ability to shift English language books in vast quantities (an author once told me that Singapore was a first world economy with a third world publishing industry—an opinion not too far off the mark in the late 1990s), *Notes* has never quite run out of legs. Tourists and expats did read it but, most importantly for me, Singaporeans made up most of the readership and they were certainly an eclectic mix. Students and teenagers took it to school, English teachers discussed it in class and the National University of Singapore stuck it on its recommended reading list. (That still tickles me. I read books about the rise of working class radicalism in Britain and the differences between Nazism and Stalinism when I was at university. Singapore students get to read books about naked landladies in Toa Payoh. Lucky bastards.) But it was the aunties that made me the most proud. Although I champion the country's pioneers in all three books, I never expected the aunties to actually read them. I assumed they would find the ripe, colourful language offensive. But they turned up by the dozen at book talks, told me I was a cheeky chap, patted me on the head and asked me to sign copies for their friends. One memorable auntie asked my wife to sign the particular page where she first appears in the book. But it didn't stop with aunties. PAP politicians read the book—some even liked it—embassies and high commissions recommended *Notes* to incoming staff and *TODAY* newspaper asked me to join them and write a weekly humour column in a similar vein. I even found myself talking to my mother about my Singaporean escapades, via the BBC World Service airwaves.

So a second book was a no-brainer, right? Yes and no. *Notes from an even Smaller Island* didn't lend itself to a natural sequel. It was complete. I was happy with it and, more importantly, didn't have anything else to say really. But the *TODAY* column took off and good old-fashioned hubris intervened. Readers were kind enough to write in and say they enjoyed the column and asked when the second book was coming out. That was flattering. Then there were readers who wrote in and said they enjoyed the column and suggested I write a book. My first book. That was a little disconcerting. So I decided to slap together all my *TODAY* columns, throw in a few new, racy ones not fit for general consumption and cheekily called it *Scribbles from the Same Island*, a great title that my wife came up with. Singapore journalists cobble together their newspaper columns all the time so I thought they could shuffle along a bit and make some room for me to jump on the bandwagon.

Line for line, page for page, *Scribbles from the Same Island* is probably the funniest of the three books because it's a compilation of humour columns. It also brought together two audiences—those who bought the first book and those who read the *TODAY* column. Interestingly, some of the latter prefer *Scribbles* because they read it before they knew a first book existed. Initially, *Scribbles* did better than *Notes* and was launched across the region. But there is the obvious risk that weekly humour columns can get repetitive when they are separated not by seven days but by a single page. *Scribbles* does work but only in short doses.

Now ... the hubris. In *Notes*, I devoted a chapter to tackling the contentious subject of the 'conmen' within Singapore's expatriate community—the fakers who get by on their fast-talking mother tongue, bluff and bullshit. Naturally, I got away with it because I'm a fellow Caucasian westerner and therefore I can play the race card and therefore I have no skeletons in my closet and therefore I have carte blanche and so on. Naturally, most Singaporeans lapped it up, particularly Singapore males around my age. I heard anecdotal stories of some of my articles on Sarong Party Girls, the Pinkerton Syndrome and the persistent, post-colonial White is Right mentality being pasted on dormitory walls by national servicemen and, never one for allowing objectivity to get in the way of one's ego, I let it go to my head. So in *Scribbles*, I wasn't merely writing; I was crusading. So I went on the rampage, chopping down the *ang moh* 'conmen' with my literary parang and toppling the unjust expatriate bias that has allowed foreign mediocrity to disguise itself as foreign talent and slip through immigration's cracks.

It took about six months to step back far enough to see I'd gone a tad too far. Constantly paranoid that the foreign talent 'conmen' would tar me with the same brush, I now risked doing precisely that to others by being so overtly critical of the expatriate population. Moreover, in the post-Nick Leeson world of currency crises, recessions and Sars, the foreign talent/expatriate package phenomenon was becoming passé. Many had already gone and the ones that stayed had often done so out of a genuine love for the country. At the launch of my third book, a middle-aged Caucasian lady took off her hat and quietly said: "Not every westerner in Singapore is here to rip off the country. There are some who want to give something back."

She was bald. Along with her husband, she had shaved her head for a local cancer charity and had raised thousands of dollars. She wasn't critical. Indeed, she was rather complimentary and a wonderfully warm-hearted woman, but I was suitably humbled.

*Scribbles from the Same Island* was irreverent, daft and contained one of my favourite chapters in all three books ('The Freak'), but I was never entirely satisfied. Besides, the best things always come in threes: Star Wars, condoms, *roti prata*. Even the Singapore Prime Minister's Office was stressing that you shouldn't stop at two. No, it had to be a trilogy and when my wife and I decided it was time to hunt echidnas Down Under, I was determined to pen a more appropriate send-off. But my wife had reservations, initially. What else did I have left to say about such a tiny island? On this occasion? Plenty. I planned to write a stand-alone travel book that would venture beyond Orchard Road and repudiate those travel guides that insisted that Singapore merited little more than a three-day shopping spree and a trip to the Night Safari. That's why *Final Notes from a Great Island: A Farewell Tour of Singapore* will always be my favourite of the three books. At times, it's an unashamedly sentimental tribute to the country, but honesty had at least taken the place of all that hubris.

*Final Notes* surpassed the efforts of its predecessors, going straight in at No. 1 on the best-seller lists in Singapore and refused to budge for several months. The book seemed to be everywhere: on supermarket shelves, at the Sentosa Cable Car station and even the Jurong Bird Park. Singaporeans and expatriates didn't just read about my tour—they *did* the tour. Ivy Singh-Lim, who runs the Poison Ivy bistro mentioned in the book, contacted me after its publication to tell me people were turning up at her restaurant in the remote Kranji countryside, equipped with nothing more than a copy of *Final Notes*. Bloggers referred to their trips to the TreeTop Walk at the MacRitchie Reservoir Park and the farms around Lim Chu Kang. Even Haw Par Villa saw a massive surge in its daily admissions. Yeah, all right. I made that last one up. But the reach of *Final Notes* continues to amaze me. Students at the University of Hong Kong study the book in their Southeast Asian writing course; a parent told me her son was reading excerpts in the national public speaking finals (I hope he skipped the Hokkien bits) and an MP asked, only half-jokingly, if I'd ever considered joining the People's Action Party. It was around that time that I decided it was probably time to leave.

And here we are over 10 years later, right back where we started: introducing a book that includes a formidable, semi-naked landlady. The only difference is there are now three titles in one volume. It's the *dumpwee* box set. With an omnibus edition, one can be compelled to do a George Lucas and create a director's cut by beefing up the funny bits and deleting all the crap bits. I did toy with the possibility of replacing me on the cover with a CGI character. But I knew the publisher would almost certainly turn me into Jar Jar Binks. So I've left well alone. Some of the writing, particularly in the first two books, is raw and occasionally flawed and I do appear to be inexplicably infatuated with the word 'fuck' in *Scribbles*. But Singapore moves so fast that each of these books has become a product of its time. Indeed, some of the references to events and landmarks in *Notes from an even Smaller Island* are so dated, the book feels like a time capsule. I now think that's a good thing. That's why I haven't changed a single word. The books represent my Singapore at the time each was written and that's how they'll stay. In a country where constant change is the norm and people and places are rarely afforded the opportunity to stand still and reflect, it is imperative to preserve anything that is associated with the evolving city-state.

And why would I want to edit stories involving midnight funerals, 'cuckoo birds' and murderous dogs anyway?

Neil Humphreys
Geelong, Australia, 2007

SINGAPORE'S NATIONAL BEST-SELLER

# NEIL HUMPHREYS

# Notes From an Even Smaller Island

## *Acknowledgements*

Some people say that writing a book is a torturous experience and, my God, I would have to agree with them. However, there are many masochistic individuals who helped the process along with their support, encouragement and the occasional blow to the head.

I will always be grateful to my publisher for being brave enough to take a risk with this work when others would not. I would also like to thank my editor. There was a lot of blood, sweat and tears along the way but she just wiped them all off the manuscript and we carried on.

This book would not have been possible without my dear friend David, who brought me to Singapore in the first place, and Scott, my old travelling partner. David gave me a goddaughter, Scott gave me an excuse to swear a lot. I will always be grateful for both.

For inspiration, I must acknowledge the people of Singapore (and Dagenham!). I hope they will still speak to me after this.

The support of my wonderful family has been vital and I thank my mother for always being there and for being a 'real woman'.

But I dedicate this book to the one person who stood over my shoulder every day to remind me that my writing was utter crap.

This one is for my best mate, Tracy, for always being my best mate.

# *Prologue*

There is nothing like being mugged twice to make you want to leave a country and head for a tiny equatorial island in Asia.

But that is exactly what happened.

The first time was farcical. When I was seventeen, a couple of friends and I were going to a nightclub called Fifth Avenue, which was full of young girls with too much make-up and pushed-up cleavages. Tacky, but teenage heaven. Naive and about as subtle as a kick in the head, we wore our Sunday best and all the jewellery we could lay our hands on and headed out. We looked like a mugger's pension scheme as we went into a hamburger place opposite the club.

Considering I was less streetwise than Harry Potter back then, it did not register that the only people in the restaurant were a gang of youths standing near the counter. We strolled up to the counter, waving £10 notes and jangling jewellery like a pawnbroker.

A boy came up to me and asked if I could give him fifty pence. Alarm bells were not yet ringing, as the young lad looked as if he had only just moved onto solids. Momentarily stunned, he hit me with a line that now seems spectacularly hilarious.

'Come on,' he said, 'give me fifty pence or I'll kill you.'

'What?' I asked in disbelief, still failing to take this surreal situation seriously. Then he sat down next to us and magically produced a knife. Surely this was not happening. Ironically, a police patrol car was parked directly outside the front of the restaurant.

'Now, don't fuck about. Give me fifty pence now,' my new companion continued.

Then I audaciously attempted a ploy that still tickles me. I haggled.

'How about I give you thirty pence?'

'I want fucking fifty.'

'Look mate, I'll give you thirty as I need to get the bus home.' I still was not taking my eleven-year-old mugger seriously.

'Those blokes over there are all with me and they're watching me, so don't fuck me off.'

This revelation unequivocally altered the odds. There were between eight and ten guys standing just behind the boy, monitoring his 'progress'. I strongly suspect their young protégé lost his cherry with us. What else could we do? They were all in their early twenties and looked like they should be playing basketball in the NBA.

I lost thirty pence but my other friend, who naively opened his wallet in front of the apprentice mugger, was relieved of £10 and a watch. We hurriedly left the restaurant, walked past the oblivious policemen parked outside and dejectedly went home. My deteriorating view of law and order in Britain took another downward turn. Surely there had to be a more suitable alternative to this?

Four years later, I found myself sitting in a stockbroker's office in London earning obscene amounts of money. I had just graduated from the University of Manchester and needed money quickly as I intended to travel. I worked in the static-data department, yet, to this day, I still cannot fathom the value of what I did, what the purpose of my job was and who benefited from it. What did I do? Well, I took a set of figures from one computer column and transferred them to another. Then at the end of my first week working there, everything became clear. A payslip landed on my desk. It was my first since I had left university and I decided on the spot that I wanted to be a static-data man for the rest of my life.

As the numbers mounted on my in tray, so too did the figures in my bankbook. I had long entertained the prospect of exotic travel and now I had the wad of notes to do it. At university, I had met a man, as you do, called David. David was Chinese Singaporean and had invited me to stay with him in Singapore. My reply was 'sure', wondering where it was in China.

That is disgraceful, I hear you cry. Such geographical ignorance borne out of years of jingoistic sentiment. The sad fact is that you would be right. Large sections of the British population hold a rather simplistic view of geography and demography that has been cultivated by their educators – the tabloid media – for several decades and it goes like this. Decent white people come from Britain, loud white people come from Australia and loud, arrogant white people come from the United States. Darker white people with silly accents come from Europe, which is approximately fifty thousand miles away, and brown people come from Pakistan, a country that is quite good at cricket and its natives come to England to set up corner shops. Black people come from Africa, which is where Sir David Attenborough goes to make his wildlife programmes. Yellow-skinned people come from China, where they spend their days bowing and eating with chopsticks. China, by the way, is in the Far East, which is just off the coast of Mars and has something to do with communism. This, in turn, has something to do with a man called Lenin. Or is it Lennon? Something to do with the working classes, anyway. All of these 'foreigners', who, of course, cannot speak a word of the Queen's English (well, not proper English like what we do), come to England periodically to take everybody's jobs and claim social security benefits. Hell, it is enough to make you bang your chest, wave a Union Jack and sing *God Save the Queen* while standing on a silver jubilee tea tray.

However, I digress. As I was saying, I promised to visit my friend in Singapore while muttering to myself, 'I will visit your sacred land the day Lord Horatio Nelson gets his eye back and Gibraltar is returned to Spain.' I needed to be convinced further that my future lay on an island smaller than Greater London. I needed to be mugged again.

I am a diehard fan of the rock group Oasis. I know all about their childish arrogance and abhorrent attitudes but I just love their music. So when I heard that those belligerent brothers from Manchester were going to stage the two biggest gigs that Europe had ever seen at Knebworth in the summer of 1996, I knew I would be there.

On the eve of the gig, my friends and I had a little drink to celebrate the occasion. From what I remember, the night was a classic. Being friends with the landlord, we had 'afters', which meant we could drink into the small hours of the morning. Around 2 a.m., we reached the moral dilemma shared by pub drinkers everywhere to quote the famous Clash song: 'Should I stay or should I go now?' And the conversation, as always, went like this:

Sensible one: 'Drink up! We've got just enough money between us to get a taxi.'

Danny: 'Bollocks! I'm not going anywhere while there is still un-drunk Guinness left on the table.'

Most intoxicated one (me): 'What's all the fuss about? We're going to see Oasis tomorrow. Besides, it's your round Danny so sod off up the bar.'

Danny: 'Bollocks! I'm not going anywhere while there is still un-drunk Guinness left on the table.'

Me: (singing) '...And after all, you're my wonderwall.'

Sensible: 'I'm tired and you two have to be up in five hours for the gig.'

Me: 'Relax, we'll sleep on the train. Everything's fine. Danny get the drinks in.'

Danny: 'Bollocks! I'm not going anywhere while... shit, it's all gone. Right, I'm off to get a pint of Guinness. Who wants one?'

And so we stayed. To this day, though, I wish we had retained just a shred of common sense and taken a taxi. We had to walk three miles home and, as we clumsily climbed a fence into a dark local park to take a short cut, we were asking for trouble.

Public parks are a strange phenomenon in suburban England. During the day, they welcome senior citizens walking their dogs while children laugh as their wheezing fathers push them on the swings. When the parks close for the day, however, they transform themselves under the cover of darkness into a den of sleaze. A place used only by gangs, drug addicts and young teenagers so desperate to have sex that they are willing to suffer sub-zero temperatures and risk catching frostbite on the bum.

Into this illicit cauldron stumbled three young drunks, for whom the real London world of crime and violence had stopped existing about five pints ago. Their world was one of Lewis Carroll: a world of giggling and nonsensical language. It was always on a collision course with London's depressing reality. It was a red rag to a bull.

I heard some noises in the background that sounded like young boys fooling around. So, because I was drunk and because I am mentally subnormal when I am drunk, I shouted out 'fuck off'. The rustling sounds of bodies moving in the distance were swiftly followed by fast-moving footsteps. In that split second, I sobered up and realised I had done something seriously stupid.

The frustrating thing was that we almost made it. Danny and I ran like racing greyhounds and we had almost reached the park's gateway. I could see the streetlights and passing cars drawing closer, signs of life that would make a public kicking less likely. Then I heard the 'sensible one' scream. His scream stopped Danny and me dead in our tracks.

'Come back! Neil! Danny! Please come back!' he cried.

Danny and I looked at each other with a rational soberness that was instantaneous. Believe me, there is no medical potion in the world that sobers you up quicker than fear.

We turned and walked back with all the enthusiasm of a pallbearer. When the sensible one emerged from the darkness, the first thing I saw was the six-inch-long blade held to his throat, which, and I know this sounds terribly pretentious, actually reflected the moonlight. It was being held by a guy whose first impression immediately substantiated my belief in Darwinism. He was so stoned I could have got high from his breath. He was flanked by two morons who wielded neither a weapon nor a brain and were clearly the sheep in this operation.

The knife man wanted to know which one of us had shouted out 'fuck off'.

Nothing can accurately describe how I felt or how my body reacted. At that moment, I hated the world for all its bitter ironies. With plans to travel the world in the near future and on the very day I intended to see Oasis perform, I was going to either die or, at the very least, spend the rest of my life with a face resembling the London Underground map. There was only one thing to do: lie my arse off.

'I said it. I shouted it out to some blokes who were in front of us, giving us verbal. That's who we were chasing.'

'Don't lie to me. Don't fucking lie to me. Do you think I'm a cunt or something?' asked knife man. Answering this question truthfully would have really dropped us in it.

'Look mate,' I said, 'we don't want any aggravation. We don't want to fuck about. We're just on our way home.'

In a way, this put knife man in a difficult situation. He had only gone out that night to get stoned. He certainly did not want to commit first-degree murder. I mean, that could really spoil your weekend, couldn't it? He also had to contend with his two young protégés who were observing his every move. Knife man had to do something quickly.

'Give me all your money,' he said, delighted with his powers of improvisation.

We handed over our wallets like naughty kids in a playground. I also had to forfeit a gold ring and the sensible one had to hand over his watch before he was released and we were sent on our way. We called the police, who knew we were drunk and refused to take us seriously. But at least we realised that the world's most intelligent thieves had made off with the princely sum of fifty pence. Clearly not enough to pay their annual subscriptions to Mensa. So that cheered us up a bit.

Meanwhile, my dear friend David sent me a letter kindly informing me that if I still intended to travel, there would always be a spare bed for me at his apartment.

With no hesitation whatsoever, I left for Singapore three months later.

My good friend Fran swears this story is true. He lives in Bukit Batok in the western part of Singapore and was late for work one day so he hailed a taxi. The taxi pulled over to the kerb and Fran got in. He was greeted by a middle-aged Chinese Singaporean in perpetual motion, suggesting that he might explode if he stopped moving. His English was a little broken and the brief exchange that followed will stay with me forever.

'Hallo, where you go?' began the taxi driver breezily enough.

'Somerset Road, please.'

'East Coast, you go East Coast?' asked the taxi driver excitably.

The East Coast is a popular beach area among locals and tourists. I like the place but it is nowhere near Somerset Road, which is in the centre of town. In Singaporean terms, where you can be just about anywhere in 20 minutes, it is a million light years away from the East Coast.

'No, thank you,' continued Fran, 'I want to go to Somerset Road.'

'Yeah loh, East Coast, very nice. East Coast very pretty, what.'

'No. I would like to go to Somerset Road, please.'

'Oh... don't want East Coast?'

'No.'

'But East Coast nice. You go East Coast.'

'Somerset Road, please.'

'Yah, East Coast, you go East Coast.' The taxi driver was now having difficulty containing his excitement.

'Look, Somerset Road, I have to go to Somerset Road,' said Fran impatiently.

'East Coast, nice place, what.'

'Oh, fuck it.' With that, my friend bid the near-hysterical man a fond farewell, strangled him and hunted for a saner taxi driver, which is by no means an easy task.

What is the point of mentioning this alongside my two muggings? Well, I believe that each incident provides a neat microcosm of both England and Singapore, or at least they do for me. Of course, not everybody who lives in or visits England will become a mugging victim and not every cab driver in Singapore is half-demented but it goes much further than that.

England had and continues to have a vibrant arts scene that I, as a young Englishman, miss terribly. I could give a million reasons why Oasis will never play in Singapore. All of them, like fans needing to get permission to stand up and dance, would be depressing. I miss having a few beers with friends without having to mortgage my house first and, most of all, I miss the country's piss-taking sense of humour.

Nevertheless, Singapore gives me the one thing that I now cherish more than anything else – safety. Before people start thinking 'Oh, here we go again', I am not about to preach about the virtues of law and order. I agree that Singapore still has a long way to go in many respects and there are things about both the country and its people that drive me to distraction but I do feel that people here take their well-being for granted. Just think about those English and Singaporean incidents. The first gives an indication of the exciting freedom that a youth in England can have and the hedonism that money can buy. Make no mistake, sex, drugs and rock 'n' roll were readily available to me as a teenager and pursuing all three can be great fun. It is not a big deal. However, following that path almost culminated in one of my friends being carved up by a drug addict. That is a big deal.

That is why I prefer the Singaporean story. In essence, it is irritating, impatient and, to some, may even be downright annoying but it is also quite humorous and, most importantly, comparatively harmless. This is how I view Singapore right now. I know that I will return to England because I miss my family but for me, right here, right now, this city-state in Southeast Asia is a wonderful place to be.

# *Chapter One*

In Singapore, a food court is called a hawker centre and I did not experience one on my very first night in the country. After a twenty-hour journey, I had arrived with my good friend Scott, a promising young architect from Yorkshire, at Changi Airport earlier in the day. Now anyone who lands at Changi Airport and fails to be impressed is either a liar or Helen Keller. It is a staggering example of what modern architecture and human efficiency can achieve. For those seeking a contrast, visit Malaga Airport in Spain and, after fighting your way through loud, sunburnt British families in matching shell suits, take a casual look around. Be enthralled by the countless non air-conditioned buildings, the sweaty armpits and the delayed flights. Then return to Changi. You will consider it no longer an airport but a Mecca for seasoned travellers. Enjoy the pleasurable sensation when you are struck with an irrepressible desire to bend down and kiss the spotless carpets. Although I attempted to do just this, I was promptly told to get up by a police officer wielding a very large gun. I tried to explain the whole Mecca thing but I could tell he was not really interested.

Anyway, Scott and I waltzed through customs (that raised a few eyebrows) and then we met David. Lots of embracing followed before we stepped out into the November sunshine. Thwack! Unlike Greece or Egypt, where the heat gently strolls up and tickles you under the arms, the Singaporean humidity positively head-butts you. Scott was raining sweat and I was seriously blushing. In fact, things could have got pretty tricky if we had not removed our coats and scarves when we did.

On the way to his car, David said, 'Did you bring umbrellas? There's going to be heavy rain today.'

I could not see a single cloud in the stunningly clear blue sky. 'Good one, Dave,' I said, 'you're still as funny as a migraine.'

Five minutes into the journey and I thought we had got caught in the middle of a marble throwing tournament. I cannot say that it started to rain because it did not. It just rained. Sun. Rain. Sun. Then rain again. Welcome to the Singaporean monsoon season.

Like the impending visit of the Inland Revenue, there is no warning. It just happens. Clouds appear, the deluge hits you and you are left wondering for the one thousandth time how those old women living along your corridor instinctively know when to bring in their washing. Then, just as you have manoeuvred your life raft into position, the Sun comes out, the miraculous drainage system has cleared the water and you are left looking a fool in the middle of Orchard Road holding a pair of oars.

We reached David's apartment in Toa Payoh, which is in central Singapore, shortly after. When he dropped off our two jet-lagged bodies into his apartment, he said there was a hawker centre opposite the apartment block if we got peckish.

Speaking to us as if we were mentally ill, David explained that a hawker centre is essentially a food court that contains a series of food stalls, each specialising in an Asian culinary delight. We simply go in, sit at one of the tables and wait for the person selling drinks to take our drink order. We then go to a stall, tell the hawker seller what we want and then retake our seats. Now what could be easier? At around 11 p.m., two tired young Englishmen set off on their first Asian adventure.

Following David's instructions, we crossed the road and spotted lots of tables with matching chairs. People were sitting around these tables eating various dishes and talking quietly: so far so good. With a boyish eagerness, we found an empty table, sat down and waited for the drinks seller to come round. Time passed and we noticed that we were attracting some strange looks. I would not say that these looks were aggressive but rather shocked and puzzled. I assumed it was because we were in the heart of the Toa Payoh community, one of the oldest housing estates in Singapore. It is not every day that two Caucasians, one standing at 6 feet, 4 inches and the other just over five feet, walk into a hawker centre.

After about five minutes, the staring had intensified and the drinks seller still had not appeared. Suddenly, Scott, who is not usually known for his eloquence, exclaimed, 'Fucking hell! There's a fucking dead body over there.'

'Where?'

'There! Fucking there. The one who is lying down and not fucking breathing.'

'Oh, shit. What are we going to do?'

'Well, I'm not fucking staying here if that's what the food does to you.'

We stood up with an indescribable sense of urgency, leaving our numerous observers open-mouthed, and fled the scene wondering what the hell went on in this bizarre country. I mean, I have eaten at places where you pick out the fish you want before it is cooked but this was something else. Had we inadvertently stumbled upon some satanic cannibalistic ceremony, where 'dishes' were carefully displayed and chosen? Were we to be the next course on the menu à la steamed 'ang moh'?

Of course not. We had simply walked into a funeral ceremony. If anyone who knew the deceased remembers two crazy jet-lagged white men treating the funeral service of their loved one like a restaurant, then I can only apologise. Having spent some time in the country, I now realise that funerals are often held at the bottom of apartment blocks in an area called the void deck. Should I now pass a funeral, I nod respectfully to those in attendance. But you have to admit that those wooden tables and red chairs are remarkably similar to the ones used in hawker centres.

We ended up having instant noodles before collapsing into bed where we proceeded not to sleep for almost six hours. The room had no air-conditioning so two exhausted Englishman, who had left brisk November temperatures of around 5–10°C, tried unsuccessfully to ignore the sweltering humidity and were forced to watch the Asian Sun rise.

We had heard about the ferocity of the local mosquitoes but being on the thirteenth floor, we had assumed that unless the flying pests were armed with rocket packs, we would be beyond their reach. We could not have been more wrong. Looking in the mirror the next day, we looked like we had spent a night in the village of the damned. The pulsating bites on Scott's legs were so big that he had to go to the doctor for fear of having one of his calf muscles burst.

As our flesh began to resemble a plate of beans on toast, I asked David out of desperation what we could do.

'Nothing,' he laughed, 'they only bite tourists.'

I have since concluded that he is right. I am not a doctor but I am sure that your immune system builds up some sort of defence to the 'mossies' as I seldom get bitten now. I have trekked through Bukit Timah Nature Reserve and I have cycled around the rustic island of Pulau Ubin. Each time, I have returned without so much as a peck on the cheek from our flying bloodsucking friends. So if you visit a new country and you spot one heading for the jugular, sing that country's national anthem or greet the mosquito in the local language. This should confuse and disorientate him and he will fly off in search of a new tourist.

Thankfully, though, my first impressions of Singapore went beyond the psychological habits of the mosquito and I soon detected a trend that enabled me to make a profound observation: size does matter. In everything. Everywhere.

Genetically speaking, Asians are not as tall as Westerners. Men are usually short and stocky while women are shorter and more petite. Of course, these are very general descriptions. Singapore has a population that is rapidly racing past four million. The Chinese, at 77 per cent, make up the majority while 14 per cent are Malay and just over 7 per cent are Indian. Foreign workers, like myself, make up the rest. Hence, it would be ignorant to suggest that the average Singaporean is of a certain height or build. However, it would be fair to say that I have yet to meet a Singaporean who is just over 1.92 metres tall, long-legged and has size 12 feet. Yet that figure stands before me in the mirror every morning. It also followed a dear old Chinese lady into a lift on the ground floor of an apartment block in Toa Payoh one afternoon. She looked at me, muttered something in Chinese and got out of the lift as fast as her little legs could carry her. The lift was still on the ground floor. I wanted to chase after her and say that I had just moved in but I figured that a lanky Caucasian chasing after a little old Chinese lady in flip-flops might cause a bit of a scene to passers-by.

Nevertheless, it must be said that if Singapore is guilty of any kind of 'ism', it has to be 'heightism'. I was once standing in a mini-mart, having a chat with the owners, when I felt a fly brush past my trouser leg. Thinking nothing of it, I swiped the fly away with my hand and carried on talking. Collecting my change, I felt the brushing sensation below my left knee again, only this time it felt more like a tug. I looked down to find the cutest little Chinese boy fiddling with my trouser leg with his right hand as he held his mother's hand with the other. He could have been no more than two years old but he had balls the size of watermelons. He made eye contact with me by craning his head so far back that it was almost at right angles with his spine. He then pointed up at me and bellowed in an astonishingly loud voice, 'Wah, so tall ah!' Looking exceedingly pleased with himself, he then started to giggle. I resisted the temptation to launch him into orbit with a swift dropkick and found myself laughing with him. His mother's red-faced apologies only made me laugh even more.

There was another incident in the same shop that not only shows the problems I have suffered with my height here but also demonstrates what a complete prat I am. I was once again being served and as I moved my arm suddenly to reach for my wallet I felt a dull thud against my right elbow, followed quickly by a distinct 'ooh' sound. Looking round, I saw a frail old Chinese woman rubbing her chin while repeatedly muttering 'ooh'. Quickly calculating her height and recalling the circular motion of my arm, I realised I had socked the poor woman on the jaw. I felt terrible. I mean it was an awful situation that was not helped when I spotted two schoolboys over her shoulder turning purple in their efforts not to explode with laughter. Anyone who has ever been in such a situation knows the predicament I was in. The episode was not without humour, to say the least, and laughter is contagious. Had those boys erupted (and the shopkeeper was not far behind), I would have followed and I know that laughing in the old dear's face would not have been the appropriate reaction. My precarious position was made worse by her apparent inability to say anything other than 'ooh'.

Biting my lip, I said, 'Auntie, I'm really, really sorry.'

'Ooh,' she replied, rubbing her chin.

'I don't know what to say. It was an accident.'

'Ooh,' came the reply once again.

The rubbing gathered momentum as the auntie adopted this endearing, puzzled expression that suggested she still was not quite sure what had happened. I wish I could lie but I had caught her squarely on the jaw and, to this day, I am amazed she remained on her feet. Eventually, she generously accepted my apology and I helped this wonderful woman, who was still 'oohing' and rubbing, out of the shop. If I am ever about to reach for my wallet now, I get the coastguard to conduct a thorough search first. I have also realised that laughing at old ladies who have been smacked on the jaw shows a complete lack of emotional intelligence. But, my God, it was funny.

It took me about a week to realise that Singapore does not cater for tall people at all. Admittedly because it does not have that many. When travelling on the Mass Rapid Transit (MRT) underground train system, the annoying handgrips that are suspended from the roof of each carriage have dealt me many a deft blow. On several occasions, I have had my pleasant daydreaming shattered by one of those stupid things smacking me on the back of the bloody head. Is it essential for these handles to wobble? It makes no difference to balance. I hold the fixed steel pole from which the handles hang and I have not fallen over yet. No, I believe the handles are deliberately made to be flexible by geeky engineers who thought it would be a titteringly-good idea to watch unsuspecting commuters get bludgeoned with them.

Additionally, I have no choice but to make a spectacle of myself every time I alight from a train. It is a real chore. When I am focused, I stoop slightly as the doors open so the sight of a tall, skinny hunchback greets everyone on the platform. That is fine. When, however, I am half-asleep, I get my head taken off by the low doorframe and it is extremely painful. That is most certainly not fine. When this happens, the doors open and those waiting on the platform are greeted by a lanky Caucasian rubbing his head and shouting, 'For fuck's sake!' Yes, it is that painful.

It does not stop there. Lift buttons, doorframes, rotating fan blades, off-the-peg clothing, shoes and urinals in public toilets – my height and build has caused problems in all these areas. In fact, ceiling fans are a particular nuisance.

My first job here was as a speech and drama teacher. At a pre-school one day, I was teaching a young class of toddlers the song "If you're happy and you know it, clap your hands". Noticing it was time to end the class, I sang, 'If you're happy and you know it, wave goodbye.' I then threw my hands up in the air. The rotating fan blades above swiftly brought them back down again. I was lucky enough to escape with a bad cut on my left hand. I thanked my lucky stars, though, because the kids enjoyed piggyback rides. The idea of receiving the death sentence for decapitating a pre-school child did not seem too appealing. I taught in that room for a year and no matter how much the sweat poured from the foreheads of those poor children, the fan was never switched on. The children might have lost a few kilos but they left the room in one piece.

To give an indication of the height and weight differences between me and the average Singaporean, I recently spent six hours scouring Orchard Road to find a collared shirt. I was not looking for a Ralph Lauren or a Hugo Boss but more of a Neil Humphreys, i.e., a shirt that fitted. There proved to be just one shop that had shirt sleeve lengths that matched my own. Consequently, I have devised a new shopping technique to save on the unnecessary preamble. On entering, I immediately ask the shop assistant to measure my arm length to see if they stock anything that matches it, usually something that Ah Meng, the orang-utan at Singapore Zoo, might have grown bored with. This process, save the assistant's giggling, takes about 30 seconds and I am soon sent on my way with the cry, 'Try Mr Frankenstein's tailors on the corner, you freak!' It may be humiliating but it does save time.

By the way, I do enjoy the frankness of the average Singaporean shop assistant. It is so refreshing. When I finally bought some shirts, I was delighted to find a shop that stocked clothes in my size in a variety of styles and colours. Usually, I get something along the lines of 'Yes, we do have one shirt that will fit you. I believe it was ordered by a Mr Cuthbert Nathaniel Smythe during those wildly excessive colonial days. This neon khaki safari shirt is a little dusty but I'm sure if I knock 10 per cent off, we'll say no more about it.'

So while I was paying for my purchases, I was eager to express my gratitude. 'I'm so glad to have found something that fits me. I've been looking for six hours.'

'That's because you're too long, lah,' said the young cashier who was folding my clothes.

'Am I?'

'Of course, what. You're so tall and your arms are really long. You'll never get clothes in Singapore.'

Fighting back the tears, I retorted, 'But I just have, haven't I?'

'Yeah lah, but only because we have European stocks and you've taken the biggest. I think you're too long for Singapore.'

'Oh, you don't fucking say.' Okay, I did not say the last part but I did collect my receipt in a rather hurried fashion. I also steadfastly refused to flirt with the young waif, even though I suspect she found me damned attractive with my ready wit and Neanderthal measurements.

Yet her in-your-face serving style is an example of one of my first impressions of Singapore. Its people can usually speak two or three languages and can write in at least two, an accomplishment that is extremely impressive to a man who is still struggling with his native tongue. How well each language is spoken depends, obviously, on age, education and socioeconomic background, all of which makes for some entertaining customer services.

When Scott and I began to eat in hawker centres, we found our early experiences terrifying. Men in black wellington boots would stand behind their respective stalls and if we ventured close enough would bellow, 'Wha' you want?' And when I say bellow, I mean bellow. This voice would slap you in the face and perforate your eardrums. Before you knew it, you were ordering things like boiled squid just so you would not get shouted at again. Then the woman who sold drinks would come to the table and take our order. She would never write anything down, yet she would go back to the drinks stall and collect the already waiting drinks. How did she do it? It is very simple. Female drink stall operators in Singapore have the loudest voices in the universe.

No matter which hawker centre you go to, the drinks seller will approach your table and eloquently ask, 'Want drink or not?'

To which you reply, 'Two cokes, please.'

Then it begins. She lifts her chin and points it towards the general direction of the drinks stall, which could be up to 25 metres away, with fifty talking customers in between. Opening her mouth to reveal a chasm that could easily fill Changi Airport, she stands up straight and, like Mount Vesuvius with a queasy tummy, erupts, 'T-W-O C-O-K-E-S, O-N-E C-O-F-F-E-E A-N-D T-W-O S-P-R-I-T-E.'

Scott and I jumped under the table the first time it happened. Never had I heard such a sound produced by a human being. Imagine standing on an airport runway as a Boeing 747 takes off, clearing your head by just a few metres. Think about the sound that those four engines make as they roar past. Now pretend they are saying 'Two cokes, one coffee and two sprite' and you will have some idea of what a female drinks seller in a hawker centre sounds like. Thirty seconds later, the same woman does it all over again, yet I have not come across a drinks seller who sounded hoarse.

Of course, I find hawker centres and their employees particularly endearing because I used to work in a café that was owned by my uncle in Bromley-by-Bow, an industrial area in East London. Our daily clientele consisted of enormous construction workers or lorry drivers, who used to grunt their orders, bitch about the prices and display their vast, greasy backsides while they ate. And I, a fourteen-year-old skinny teenager with zero confidence, was expected to serve them. No matter what I did, it was always wrong. How I used to wish that, for just one day, I was big enough to stand up to them and tell them all to fuck off. Now I wish I could have sent them 'hawker-centre woman'. Yes, sent 'hawkerwoman', the new crime fighter, to the heart of male-dominated, chauvinistic working-class East London to bring justice back to the world. Just one blast from her volcanic mouth would have scared the little shits witless. And should they have decided to pursue the matter, hawkerwoman would then have produced the chopper that the Hainanese chicken rice guy uses and decapitated each and every one of the bastards. Oh, you have got to have a dream.

One thing I have noticed since I have been here is the steady evolution from hawker centre to food court. Naturally, when friends visit from England, they extol the virtues of the bright, clean and efficient food courts. They remark that the food courts are much more hygienic than those grubby little hawker centres, which should all be swept away. I am not so sure. I have always believed that hawker centres do need radical face lifts. A country that strives for a knowledge-based economy could at least produce an eating establishment that was not littered with cigarette butts, used tissues and dropped food. However, without fail, hawker centres always produce good, cheap food. Food courts with their higher overheads cannot but, for whatever reason, they do not seem to be able to reproduce the quality of food produced in hawker centres either. If I am going to pay S$3.50 for a plate of chicken rice, then, at the very least, it must be as tasty as a S$2 plate from a hawker centre. But it is not.

So we are left, on the one hand, with modern food courts that are mediocre and overpriced and, on the other, hawker centres that still earn a small profit but not enough to undergo the essential renovations needed to compete in the new millennium. I just hope that when the sad day comes and the last hawker centre is swept away, I can still call upon hawkerwoman to save the day when I need her. Like I said, you have got to have a dream, haven't you?

# Chapter 2

There is a song written by Robbie Williams called 'Millennium' that I believe could be an anthem for Singaporean 'aunties'. Whenever I hear the song, which contains the line 'Come and have a go, if you think you are hard enough', Singaporean aunties immediately spring to mind. To borrow from London terminology, I have yet to meet anyone who is 'harder' than a Singaporean auntie. Believe me, they are rock solid and their resolute attitude and lust for life is something that the younger, greedier generation can learn from.

A Singaporean auntie or uncle can be anyone who is from the older generations, like an English old age pensioner (OAP), and the term is used out of affection and respect. In a country where so much emphasis is placed upon the family unit and respecting your elders, it is only right that the elderly are held in such high esteem.

When the Japanese invaded and occupied Singapore, then a British Crown colony, in February 1942, these people endured terrible hardships. Under the constant surveillance of the *kempeitai* (the Japanese military police), many were imprisoned, tortured and even executed. Nevertheless, underground resistance groups still flourished until the war ended. When Singapore began its transformation from Crown colony to a leading Asian economic city-state, these hardworking people were the backbone. Far be it from me to deny the importance of the political direction of the Lee Kuan Yew-led People's Action Party to achieve prosperity but I am certain that modern-day Singapore owes everything to its aunties and uncles. So every time I see students and young executives brushing past them as if they were invisible to get on a bus or train, I really want to throttle the impatient little bastards.

Unfortunately, the same attitude exists in Dagenham, my home town, only it is much worse. Dagenham is in Essex, the county to the east of London. Built in the 1920s to take families away from the overcrowded London slums, Dagenham became home to the world's largest public housing estate almost overnight. Covering just 4 square miles, the town has a population of 90,000. However, the residents who first occupied its red-bricked boxes and made it a more homely place to live are now treated with contempt. When they are not being mugged, Dagenham's elderly are often abused in the high street by little parasites who would not be there if it was not for them. It is rare to hear a teenager in Dagenham addressing an elderly stranger with a term as respectful as 'auntie' or 'uncle' whereas it is still commonplace in Singapore. You have to be devoid of all respect and compassion to look an auntie in the eye and forcibly steal her purse but it happens in my tiny home town all the time.

I would like to lighten the mood a little, if I may, and talk about the wonderful aunties and uncles who make up over 6.5 per cent of Singapore's population (well, the ones over 65 do). I love 'em. However, the first thing a foreigner seeking to make a good impression must do is calculate whether a person actually qualifies for auntie or uncle status. Whatever you do, do not make the near fatal mistake of assuming that anyone older than yourself automatically qualifies to be an auntie or uncle.

Let's stick with the ladies to demonstrate this point as they tend to be more vociferous. When I was a teacher, a well-to-do parent covered in jewellery approached me at the end of a lesson for an update on her child's progress.

I said, 'Yes, of course. Your boy is doing very well, auntie. His vowel sounds are much more distinct and...'

'Auntie?' she shrilled. 'Did you just call me auntie? How old do you think I am?'

Like a bullet in the brain, my dad's two pearls of wisdom hit me. Never wear white socks with trousers and never, ever try to guess a woman's age. I am particularly poor at this exceedingly dull game and usually end up saying something like 'Ooh, you must be about eleven', which only serves to irritate everybody.

'Well, I'm sorry. I didn't mean to...'

'You can't call me auntie. I'm not old. You can only call old women "auntie". If my mother was here, you could call her auntie.'

What a conversation this was turning out to be. First, she wanted me to 'guess that age in five', then she wanted me to play 'happy families'.

'I understand and I'm really sorry if I...'

'Do you know, I've never been called auntie before. I'm only thirty-three. I've got two children. He's my elder son and he's only seven. You must be really careful who you call auntie, especially if it's a woman.' I wanted to disagree and say that surely I must be more careful of calling someone auntie if it were a man, but I thought better of it.

'Just remember that it can be rude to call a young woman auntie. She might turn around and scold you.'

As opposed to the friendly little chitchat that we have just had, I thought.

I cannot understand why she was so upset apart from the fact that I had aged her by at least twenty years. She should have been flattered that I had grouped her with Singapore's elite A-team. It would be like someone in England mistaking me for a member of the SAS Commando Unit, which happens all the time actually. I would be chuffed and you would be, too. The Singaporean aunties and uncles are a unique breed and they know it.

I remember complaining about the heat while waiting for a number 238 feeder bus in Toa Payoh one day. When it arrived, I lumbered towards it only to realise it was a non air-conditioned bus. About to unleash another pitiful whine, I was stopped in my tracks by the sight of my first Singaporean auntie in action. Wearing a trademark auntie pyjama suit, she marched determinedly towards the bus. Now I am not one to exaggerate but she had fifteen shopping bags in each hand while carefully balancing a grandchild on each shoulder. Without missing a step, she waltzed past me (and it just so happened that I was at the front of the queue) and got on the bus. To my astonishment, the old woman, who must have been in her late sixties and barely 1.2 metres in height, then managed to produce her farecard and insert it into the machine without dropping a single bag or grandchild.

The adventures of an auntie on a bus do not stop there. Should you be close enough to hear two aunties chatting, which is basically anywhere on a bus, you are guaranteed an entertaining journey. You see, aunties cannot converse quietly. When I first travelled on a bus here, I thought the elderly were wired up to a PA system. They usually sit directly opposite each other on the seats that face one another at the front of the bus and natter away.

I remember two wonderful aunties involved in an animated conversation on the number 54 bus. It was packed and I was one of the many people who had to stand. Yet right in front of me were two seated aunties who had slipped their shoes off to put their feet up on the seat facing them. They were making more noise than a chain saw felling a tree. It was marvellous. The two women jabbered away in what I think was Hokkien, one of the many Chinese dialects, and when they laughed, they roared. No one told the aunties to keep it down and no one asked them to make room for others to sit down. They certainly did not offer anyone else a seat and why the hell should they?

I am not saying that the elderly in Singapore are rude because generally they are not. Nor am I saying that British pensioners are without character or humour because that too would be a gross exaggeration. My own grandmother has left me doubled up with laughter more times than I care to remember. She is now in her eighties but until recently she used to perform her unique brand of Hawaiian dancing for guests. Weighing in at over 200 lbs, she would wiggle her hips ever so slightly while nonchalantly flicking her fingers out to the side. If you listened carefully enough, you might just catch the word 'Hawaii' escape from her lips. Moreover, she also enjoyed showing my girlfriends that she could not only still do the can-can but could also 'show her bloomers (knickers) with the best of them'. And she did.

Basically, all I am suggesting is that Singaporean aunties and uncles 'have got balls' as the Mafia would say. They are both resilient and fearless.

Take the Chinese auntie who cooked at a private pre-school that I used to teach at. She is a real woman whom I admire very much. If she ever decided to keep a diary, I know I would enjoy it more than those written by Bridget Jones, that fictional neurotic middle-class prat who took the British literary world by storm. Auntie was a real woman. Even performing the most mundane of tasks like travelling to school showed how hard she really was. Needing to prepare the schoolchildren's breakfasts, auntie would arrive shortly before me on her husband's motorbike. Walking to school, I would hear their large motorbike bringing up the rear. Wearing matching white crash helmets, they would go roaring past like two giant table tennis balls. Carrying her customary ten shopping bags of meat, fish and vegetables, I never once saw auntie hold onto her husband, no matter how fast the bike was going. Yet without fail, she would always raise one of her bag-laden hands and wave enthusiastically, causing the bike to wobble on several occasions, which, in turn, caused the driver to shout expletives at his demented wife. It was quite wonderful.

The school grounds were set in one of the few remaining rural parts of Singapore. The area was also home to some of the republic's more exotic species of animals such as monitor lizards and black-spitting cobras. On one memorable occasion, an enterprising cobra had slipped into one of the classrooms to seek a little sanctuary from the damp rainy conditions outside. Unsurprisingly, it was not long before the class was full of screaming children and teachers. In fact, one of the teachers jumped onto the table and became quite hysterical. As the smoke cleared, auntie appeared in the doorway with her sleeves rolled up, holding a broom in one hand and a bucket in the other. After being told that the snake was behind one of the shelves, she sprung into action. Moving the shelves, she thrashed around like a crazed psychopath. Fortunately, for the snake at least, it slithered through a hole and into the garden. The police eventually arrived and captured it. It is not often you sympathise with a black-spitting cobra but, knowing what it was capable of and knowing what auntie was capable of, I did.

However, I am delighted to report that she is neither the exception nor the queen of Singaporean aunties. No, the queen of Singaporean aunties would have to be Saudita – the major inspiration for writing this book.

Saudita is an elderly Indian woman who weighs about 250 lbs and has a tongue filthier than a drunken sailor. She could speak three languages: Tamil, Malay and swear. This mountain of a woman could strike fear into any man, woman or child who dared to cross her path. And she was my live-in landlady, from whom I rented a room for a year. To be honest, I am surprised that I am still here to tell some of her tales.

In twelve months, she must have sworn at me in every language except English, which she hardly knew. Indeed, her lack of spoken English led to many surreal telephone calls. First of all, she could not pronounce my name properly. It was always 'Neeoooh' with the pitch rising dramatically on the 'ooh'. I would be sitting in my locked bedroom when I would hear her cry 'Neeoooh!' Seeing me walk towards the phone, she would merely grunt and point at the receiver. Every time I picked up the phone, I would hear giggling on the other end. It reached the point when friends would call just to hear her shout my name.

Being on the receiving end was an experience, too. I telephoned the house once to speak to my girlfriend and the conversation was just bizarre.

'Hello, it's Neil.'

'No,' replied Saudita.

'Hello?'

'Hello.'

'It's Neil here.'

'No house.'

'What?'

'Neeooh, no house.' The penny dropped.

'No, *I'm* Neil.'

'Neeooh, no house, no house,' she said impatiently.

'No, I'm Neil. It's me on the phone. I'm Neil.'

'Out. Neeoooh out. No house. Out.'

'I'm fucking Neil, you silly cow. Now will you please put my girlfriend on the line before I come home and kill you.' She hung up. I suppose I asked for it really but she was such hard work.

She once asked me to use the dimmer switch to turn down the lights in Indian. Understandably, I was fluffing her cushions, cleaning her windows, feeding the cat she never had and performing every possible household chore except the one she wanted. In the end, when she ran out of patience and I had run out of things to turn on and off, the woman moved from one side of the sofa to the other and turned down the lights herself. It would be generous of me to say that Saudita was somewhat lazy.

However, everything changed at the weekend. The apartment was cleaned, the shopping was done and Saudita changed her clothes. Yes, she changed them just once a week and how she did it was chilling. Standing at the kitchen sink, she would take off her shirt and bra and wash her hair and upper body without making any attempt to cover herself whatsoever. Now if there was one woman on the planet who had two gigantic reasons to conceal her chest, it was Saudita. Being a rather large woman in her sixties, her breasts came down like two sacks of potatoes. Without a care in the world, she would then take her newly washed shirt, lean out of the kitchen window and peg it to one of the washing poles that were outside, with her ample bosoms bouncing all over the place. That is not all. The apartment was on the eleventh floor and faced another block that could not have been more than 20 metres away. I used to imagine some little boy in the opposite block saying, 'Mummy, there's a woman over there hanging out her washing and she's got three heads.'

Like most apartment blocks in Singapore, Saudita's shower room faced onto the kitchen. After taking a shower one evening, I opened the door to be faced by my bare-breasted landlady making *roti prata*. Astonishingly, she made no attempt to cover herself and scolded me in Tamil for not being in the habit of walking around with my eyes closed. Not wishing to get a nipple in the eye, I made a sharp exit. It happened many times after that. She could be making a variety of sumptuous dishes, all of which would leave you salivating until you found yourself face to face with the bare-breasted woman and you would make an instant decision to never eat anything again. To this day, I cannot buy a bag of potatoes without thinking about Saudita's chest.

Despite her hard exterior, she was quite a caring woman. On a delightfully sunny Saturday afternoon, my partner hung some washing on the line and discovered two hours later that it had been saturated by some uncaring soul who had hung out a dripping wet duvet on the floor above. Of course, no one is saying that a duvet cannot be cleaned but there is an unofficial law of courtesy within the apartment blocks whereby you do not hang out something that is large and soaking wet if there is washing hanging below. Now, the woman above had broken that unwritten rule and Saudita did not stand for it. She stormed upstairs and convinced the guilty party, via some carefully selected Malay swear words, to bring in the duvet until our washing was dry. Consequently, the duvet was withdrawn to allow my sopping wet underwear to win the day.

However, it is important not to get carried away here. I do have a tendency to romanticise things that I am particularly fond of and the older generations would certainly fall into that category. Nobody is perfect and the older generation has faults like everyone else. For me, the worst one has to be dogma. Every individual is entitled to his or her opinions but not to the exclusion of everybody else's. Elderly Singaporeans remain doggedly loyal to their own culture, cuisines and customs but I sometimes wonder how appreciative they really are of those of other racial groups. Of course, the moral do-gooders will jump up at this point and cry 'racial harmony'. Well, a racially harmonious society is the ideal and the government is certainly bending over backwards with its recent Singapore-21 committee. Still, I am not convinced. Just scratch the surface and look beneath the rhetoric of government committees and grassroots banners to see that the elderly might tolerate other cultures and customs but they do not accept them. In a world of constant change, they are shackled stubbornly to the past.

In 1997, the infamous haze, caused by the forest fires in Indonesia, engulfed parts of Southeast Asia. Singapore was badly affected, with air pollution reaching unhealthy levels on several occasions. Without sounding overly dramatic, the haze was so thick that I recall the Sun being obscured for long periods. If you stayed out for too long, you stood the chance of getting a headache or feeling nauseous. Around November of that year, the haze seemed to peak with the daily Pollutant Standard Index (PSI) recording extremely hazardous levels of over 200. The sky looked like it stopped just above your head and resembled the pea soup days of London's smog in the fifties.

One day, I had no choice but to step out into the thick of the haze to go to the mini-mart. On the way, I saw an elderly Chinese guy performing a common Singaporean custom under his apartment block. He was burning paper money in a large dustbin in the belief that the money will reach deceased friends and family members. This is usually done during the hungry ghosts festival or after a funeral. Without getting into a pointless debate about the actual merits of such ancient customs (not to mention their appeal to greed with people actually burning paper houses and cars in the hope that they will be waiting for them in the afterlife), it was his timing that irritated me. There we were standing in smog that was so thick that it reduced visibility to around 25 metres and he was trying to recreate the 1933 Reichstag fire. Perhaps that explains why I turned into Adolf Hitler.

'Do you have to do that now?' I enquired, just a tad irritably.

'Huh?' he replied, looking puzzled because, I suspect, he had not understood a word I had just said.

'Look at the sky. It's dark and gloomy and it's only 3 o'clock. So why do you have to do that now? Can't you at least wait until the air is slightly less poisoned? I mean, is it that important that you burn all that paper now? Can't you see the thick black smoke you are causing?' I continued to bombard the old man with questions but to no avail. He merely cursed me under his breath and went about his business of trying to turn all his dead relatives into millionaires while children still living on this Earth could not play outside because of the poor air quality.

On these occasions, I do become somewhat miffed at the elderly's stubbornness. It is also one of the few times that the government is powerless to react. Apart from grassroots committees putting up posters in apartment blocks asking residents not to burn paper excessively, there is little else that can be done without ruffling too many feathers. It is almost as if traditionalists are saying, 'We're happy to have our arts and media censored but please, don't mess with our ancient customs or you'll really upset us.'

Medicine is another area where the aunties and uncles of Singapore still cling to old-fashioned remedies. Some, like acupuncture, have been proven to have positive effects upon the patient and have been implemented in the West but many of these remedies do not work. There is a poster on the wall at my doctor's surgery that urges people not to 'burn the snake' because it is extremely dangerous. It is a belief shared by the older generations that when someone, particularly a small child, has chickenpox, his or her head and tail should be burnt to rid the illness, hence 'burning the snake'. Of course, the ritual does nothing but leave the afflicted with burn marks on his or her stomach and lower back. Despite concerted efforts to improve awareness on the subject, my doctor says he still gets the odd case of someone suffering from both chickenpox and severe burns.

Now, do not get me wrong. There is absolutely nothing inappropriate about taking pride in beliefs and customs as long as they do not cause harm to others. Moreover, it should not be to the exclusion of others. I have had dinner with elderly Singaporeans who revel in telling me how they seldom eat Western food because it is so 'disgusting'. Then five minutes later, they shoot me a look more powerful than a Smith and Wesson just because I happen to mention that I am not too fond of shark's fin soup.

After returning from a holiday to England, an elderly colleague opened a conversation with me by saying, 'What do you *people* eat in England?'

'Why?' I asked, my pride more than just a little bruised.

'Well, there's not much choice is there? It's all chips and sandwiches. How can you live on that stuff all year round?'

I would love to say that I suffocated him with a chip sandwich but I just shrugged my shoulders. What else can you do or say to such a cantankerous old sod?

Despite these shortcomings, the aunties and uncles of Singapore are a warmhearted bunch who will gladly invite you into their home for food during Chinese New Year or Hari Raja celebrations.

If further confirmation of their warmheartedness is needed, I recall an incident that left me stunned. After shopping in Orchard Road with my girlfriend, we got on the MRT train to go to Bishan. The train was relatively packed and I was forced to stand, holding three or four shopping bags. Standing over my better half, we started talking about the usual trivial stuff. As the train pulled into the next station, an elderly Chinese gentleman who had been sitting next to my partner got up and offered me his seat before somebody else nabbed it. I thought this was a most considerate act and I thanked him as he left the train. However, the uncle did not alight.

As the train pulled out of the station, the uncle stood in front of me as large as life, occupying the space where I had previously stood. He had done this either to allow me to sit with my partner or get away from my brain-numbing chatter. In such a situation, you tend to get paranoid. There was a cute little baby sitting on her mother's lap next to me and I swear she would not stop staring at me. I am almost certain that I heard the baby say, 'In my considered opinion, mother, that tall ruffian should have politely refused the elderly gentleman's most generous offer. His ghastly behaviour is so quintessentially English.' To make matters worse, as we passed the next stop, the old man still did not alight. Instead he just stood there, grinning. By this stage, my left ear had begun to melt from all the verbal abuse my girlfriend was inflicting on it. All the stock phrases gushed forth, 'I've never been so embarrassed in all my life…', 'If only you had half a brain' and so on. By now, I wanted to publicly execute my elderly do-gooder just to give me some peace of mind. The man finally alighted at Toa Payoh, having towered over me for a grand total of two stops, during which time I had formulated at least a dozen ways to kill him using one of those flexible hand grips.

In many ways, the elderly are the most appreciative generation of Singaporeans, which, as far as I am concerned, has worrying implications. They still remember the Japanese occupation, the genuine threat of communism and the riots of the 1960s. They are also far more appreciative and respectful of the modern transport services, home ownership and improved medical and educational facilities. The younger generations, just like in England, have no such perspective. They have known only rapid change so it becomes difficult to impress or even pacify them. Tedium inevitably results. When I was at university, I decided to write a thesis on the birth and development of Dagenham, my home town. After interviewing pensioners, I was struck by the deep-rooted pride they still had in the town. They spoke excitedly about how it had taken them from the disease-ridden slums of central London and provided their families with a decent standing of living. For them, that was enough. They were prepared to overlook its shortcomings and the ineptitude of local government. Many have since died, taking their pride to the grave. I believe Singaporean aunties and uncles, by and large, will do the same.

In contrast, the younger generations have no sense of loyalty to their environment. In England, yobs on street corners perceive

Dagenham as both restrictive and boring. Many cannot wait to leave. Having taught at countless schools, I feel that Singaporean youngsters act in the same way. They are not interested in efficient transport services or in Singapore's struggle for economic success. Why should they be? They have known nothing else. I only hope they can learn a sense of perspective from their aunties and uncles before it is too late. There may well be more to life than a train that consistently runs on time but there is categorically more to life than soulless greed. As I sit on the train and watch faceless executives jabber endlessly into handphones, I often wonder how many of them would give up their seat to allow a strange-looking Caucasian to sit next to his partner. I do not kid myself though. I know the answer and so do you. That is the fundamental difference between the generations.

## *Chapter Three*

In Britain, we have curious phenomena that pop up occasionally to make strange sounds and shuffle around bizarrely. They are called grandparents. I often liken them to UFOs because you want to see them, you really do, but you are not sure why. When they are spotted, fear is the first reaction followed by a certain unease that never really leaves until the visit is over. You pretend to understand them but, in reality, you have very few shared interests and you often end up just staring at each other. To top it all off, your grandmother's forehead begins to grow, her face wrinkles quite rapidly and she starts to resemble E.T. In Britain, teenagers and young adults are constantly being reminded to visit their grandparents before they die.

This kind of emotional blackmail seems to be the only way that our dear deceitful mothers can get us to visit our elderly relatives. Well, that is what my mum used. I did love them but watching doddering relatives shuffle around a living room just could not compete with an episode of *Friends*.

My mother and I have acted out the same scenario so many times. She would storm into my bedroom and remind me first of my living arrangements because every conversation we had started this way. She would invariably open with, 'You treat this place like a bloody hotel. You leave your towels on the bathroom floor and you're still not making the bed. I might as well wear a bloody apron.'

At this point, I was always struck by what a boarding house owner would say to his son. 'Now look here, you're treating this place like a bloody hotel and I'm sick of it.'

'But it is a hotel, dad.'

'Don't be so bloody cheeky.' Whack! And so on. And so on for my mum, too.

'Take your feet off the bloody table. You're sitting there like a bloody tramp. And if you have to come in so late, do you have to make so much noise? When are you going to visit your grandparents? They haven't got long left, you know. They're not going to live forever. You're only sitting on your arse, you can go today.'

And that is it, you are sunk. As all teenagers in a similar position will testify, your answering technique, which has been thoroughly honed over the years, brings about your downfall. It usually works to your advantage. Listening for the appropriate pauses in your mother's speech, you deliver the correct expression of consent or disagreement. After a while, the technique has been perfected so it can be performed subconsciously. Complacency inevitably sets in and before you have a chance to retract the answer, the word 'yes' has left your lips and your mother has already pounced. Like a tornado ripping through the house, she has picked out your best clothes, informed her mother that you are coming and dropkicked you out of the house.

Therefore, I hope you see where I'm coming when I say that I had never heard of the term 'filial piety' until I came to Singapore. It means to be a devout or loyal son or daughter or, in broader terms, to respect and look after your family elders. I first came across the term when I was teaching a creative writing course and found it in a narrative written by a primary four pupil. After looking up the meaning of each word, I was stunned that a ten-year-old girl wielded such remarkable vocabulary and I recall giving her a ridiculously high mark. Talking to local colleagues later though, it became apparent that the term was common among Singaporeans, both young and old, because it is a fundamental family value. Filial piety runs right across the racial and cultural spectrum and is encouraged by teachers, religious leaders and politicians alike. In other words, aunties and uncles are protected and looked after, to some degree, by their children and grandchildren, which, in my book, is most praiseworthy.

There is more to it than that, though. Singapore, unlike Britain, is not a welfare state. State pensions and free medical and dental treatment for the elderly do not exist here. Indeed, Lee Kuan Yew, the country's Senior Minister and founder of the People's Action Party, the ruling party of government, does not believe in welfarism. In the book *Lee Kuan Yew: The Man and His Ideas*, he is quoted as saying he believed that the early intentions of welfarism to get Britain back on its feet after the war were honourable. However, he stated that by the 1980s, welfare had undermined the work ethic, creating societies in which people become dependent upon the state rather than upon the fruits of their own labour.

To counter this, Lee has argued many times that individuals work to improve their own lives and those of their families. Therefore, the Singaporean state has made a conscious effort to foster these traditional support systems that are inherent in the Chinese, Malay and Indian communities. Consequently, Singaporeans, in times of trouble, turn to their families and not to the state.

I can already hear my fellow Westerners feverishly picking holes with this argument, dismissing it as ultra right-wing and uncaring. However, without wishing to get bogged down in political arguments, I would like to pick out some of the benefits of such a system. Without fail, my friend David visits his aunties and uncles every Saturday night and he sees nothing irregular in this. For an Englishman like myself, distant aunties are usually only spotted sitting around tables at weddings, gossiping. They do this to keep away from their drunken husbands who are clumsily demonstrating that they can dance like John Travolta – a frequent event at English weddings that is only slightly less embarrassing than watching your aunties trying to dislodge the distant brain cell that contains your name. They usually end up saying, 'Ooh, haven't you grown?' To which you can only retort, 'Well no, I'm twenty-six years old and I haven't grown at all since the last wedding three months ago.'

In contrast, relatives are visited regularly in Singapore and are generally well looked after on birthdays, at festivals and on mahjong gambling days. They are respected members of the family. At the Chinese weddings that I have been to, I have always been introduced to parents, aunties and uncles and grandparents with a discernible sense of pride by my friends. And why shouldn't they be proud of them? In a society that does not support the values of welfarism, they have been clothed, fed and, most importantly, educated by their elders. In recent years, it has become a growing trend to send children overseas for their tertiary education and this does not come cheap. At a conservative estimate, my friend David reckons that his two-year stint at Manchester University would have cost around S$100,000 – not exactly chickenfeed, is it?

This, however, is where filial piety comes into play and it makes me feel just a little nauseous. You see, when parents get to a certain age, it becomes payback time. Their children must begin to look after them financially. Not just because it feels like the right thing to do but because it is a Singaporean custom. In fact, my friend swears that filial piety is a government law. I was sceptical about this. How could such a law be enforced? But I was quite stunned to discover that my friend was right.

In 1995, the Maintenance of Parents Act came into force and a tribunal was set up the following year by the Ministry of Community Development. The act helps parents who are over sixty and unable to support themselves claim maintenance from their children. In other words, elderly parents can sue their children, take them to court and demand that they look after them financially. I had hoped that very few people would need to take advantage of this ingenious piece of legislation but between June 1996 and December 1999, 541 applications were made to the tribunal, of which 404 were ordered to pay maintenance. This may not be a gigantic figure but am I alone in feeling saddened by the news that a court order was needed to remind over 400 citizens that they should be looking after their parents? I cannot help wondering how many more cases there would be if more ill-treated parents took their complaints up with the tribunal. In a society that is obsessed with 'saving face', I am certain that some families keep quiet.

Consequently, it is extremely common, especially when you consider property prices in Singapore, for parents to live with their children's family as they get older, which I believe shows remarkable tolerance on both sides. If my mother and I were to live together again we would, quite simply, kill each other.

I would get up to leave and I would hear her croaky voice ask, 'Where are you going now?'

'I'm going to visit friends. They've just bought a new car.'

'You treat this place like a bloody hotel.'

'Mum, it's my house.'

'You wander in whenever you feel like it. You don't tell me where you've been. I sit here night after night, worrying myself sick, not that you'd care though.'

'Mum, I'm 45 years old. When I go out, it's to collect my children from school.'

'Never mind all that, you're still leaving your towels on the bedroom floor.'

It would be a nightmare and I am sure my mother would agree. But the Singaporeans I know who are married and still live with their parents or parents-in-law bear their hardship with considerable goodwill.

In fact, it appears to be a very amicable relationship. While my friends are out at work, the mother will mop the floors and more often than not prepare meals for them when they return. Of course, I am sure the family picture of idyllic bliss that I have painted is not wholly accurate but I also know that a similar picture in England would have more colourful language.

'Mum,' I would begin tentatively, 'you seem to have more time on your hands since you've moved in with us. Could you help with the housework occasionally?'

'Fuck off.'

End of conversation. Generally speaking, though, this system works for the majority of Singaporeans so where does the nausea that I mentioned earlier come into it? Well, just humour me for a few moments. Can you recall clearly the last time you ate at a greasy burger establishment? Who served you?

Had I asked myself this question before I came to Singapore, the answer would have been a skinny teenage boy wearing a uniform that was made to measure for somebody else. Between serving customers, he would join his other teenage colleagues out back in a 'dipping your head into the deep fryer' contest to determine the greasiest head of hair. Incidentally, I always seemed to be served by the contest winner. Having purchased my food, I would then have to avoid 'greasy head's' twin brother knocking me flat on my face with his lethal combination of a big mop and a tiny brain. Lying on the floor covered in French fries and smelling of detergent, 'greasy head floor cleaner' would always say, 'I'm sorry, I didn't see you there.'

'Why? Because I'm only 6 foot 4 inches tall, you dopey prick,' I would respond. By which time he had already disappeared to take part in the deep fryer semi-finals.

After spending five years in Singapore, the imagery has changed. Instead of the young teenager, you are served by an elderly person, who shuffles slowly to get your order. It was a massive culture shock for me to be served by someone who was older than my grandparents when I first arrived here. I felt so sorry for them as they plodded over to get my order. It made me feel so guilty that I felt as though I should go around the counter and collect the meal myself.

On the plus side, they certainly exude less grease than their Western counterparts and that in itself is a reason to be grateful. But we know the sad reality. When you step into a packed burger bar in Orchard Road and spot three queues of roughly equal size, with two staffed by elderly employees, which line do you pick? In this hectic metropolis obsessed with speed and efficiency, it just would not be practical to be served by some doddering old lady, would it? Particularly when it is obvious that the slimy prick next to her with the artificial smile is just dying to take more orders to demonstrate his robotic speed and his multitasking skills. When I am not in a hurry, I find myself drawn to the elderly employees out of some sort of moral compunction. However, this is Singapore and how often are we not in a hurry?

It seems we are all so busy chasing that all-important dollar that we do not have the time to lift a used tray, walk ten paces to the nearest rubbish bin and empty it. What is the matter with us? I was with a friend once who got up to leave without taking the tray with him. I asked him why and he said, 'That's what they're paid for. Let them do it.' We were sitting three metres away from the nearest rubbish bin and I watched, dumbstruck and ashamed, as a tiny Chinese auntie walked from one end of the restaurant to the other to collect the tray. When she reached our table, she picked up the tray, wiped the table with a cloth and smiled at us. What the hell had we done to deserve such a warm smile? It crushed me. I waited on tables for ten years and hated every single minute of it. I certainly hope I do not have to do it in my sixties, spending my twilight years asking extremely obnoxious customers, 'Upsize for you, sir?' I have never left a tray on a table since.

Therein lies the greatest failing of a society that has no welfare. There is no safety net. I believe in the majority of the PAP's policies but they serve just that – the majority. Most Singaporeans live a safe, clean middle-class lifestyle that is, let's face it, the envy of Southeast Asia and, increasingly, other parts of the world, too. Yet without any form of welfare, there will always be a small number who, through no fault of their own, slip through the net. These people may have little or no family or they might not have the appropriate skills to work in a knowledge-based economy. Pride might also prevent them from dragging their own flesh and blood to the tribunal to demand maintenance.

The government, to its credit, is always coming up with laudable retraining schemes but the people who would benefit most from these schemes are usually preoccupied with the 'little things', like putting food on the table. Do not get me wrong, there is no perfect political system and no one can be completely happy with their lot. I agree with the English philosopher Jeremy Bentham and his famous notion of 'the greatest happiness of the greatest number'. I just do not think that filial piety alone, commendable though it might be, is enough to plug the gaps.

Besides, even if it was, there is still one final problem that I have with it that goes way beyond nausea. Having already mentioned that it becomes payback time for parents when they get old and need to be looked after by their children, the stage is then set for the gut-wrenching sequel 'Payback II – After Death'.

The plot is ever so simple. The main protagonist is the ageing head of the family, who is looked after by all her sons and daughters. During an intense emotional scene, which requires great method acting from the supporting cast, the old woman dies happily, knowing that she had a caring, loyal family. Then the flimsy twist comes. The old woman left behind a pot of money in the form of her apartment, which is now worth a small fortune. It is a flimsy twist because it is always the same. The old woman always dies and she always leaves her apartment behind because no matter how many paper houses she might have burned on this Earth, she cannot physically take her home with her. Then shock horror, all the affectionate relatives suddenly become green-eyed bastards who put up with her for all those years in the belief that she would leave the box of concrete to them.

So the audience, in other words the *Straits Times* readers, is introduced to a plethora of secondary characters who, until this point, had only been spotted buying the old lady the odd meal. Now they come to the fore and cry, 'She promised to leave me the apartment because she loved me the most and she wanted it to stay in the family. However, I really intend to sell the flat when the market peaks for an enormous fat profit. Then I can upgrade to those new condominiums being built on the coast and my shallow, unfulfilled life will finally be complete.' The plot thickens quicker than cold curry when not one but several characters come forward and recite similar well-rehearsed speeches.

At this point, the cynical members of the audience are already questioning the so-called moral values of filial piety. It now seems that the system works like this. You provide your child with the best education because that will improve his and, therefore, your standard of living later on. You then retire and live off your children if they have succeeded in life or, failing that, you take a part-time job mopping toilet floors. Finally, the children that you raised, whether they were successful or not, will all fight for your apartment when you die.

For those who think I am being overtly cynical, just read through the *Straits Times*. On any given day, you are bound to come across a financial or property wrangle between different generations of the same family. They are usually despicable affairs, with both sides washing each other's dirty linen in public in a pathetic bid to be awarded those shares or that luxurious condominium.

In 1998, for example, Janie Low took her father and her brother to the High Court and ordered them to buy over her shares in the family-owned food distribution company. She won the case when the judge discovered that as director, the father had, among other things, abused the company accounts for personal gain by charging holiday expenses to the company. Hence, the judge sided with

Madam Low and ordered her father to buy her shares at a non-discounted rate, which, I am sure, left her an extremely wealthy woman. By this stage, however, there was not much the public did not know about her personal life and her relationship with her father.

Then there was the famous Jumabhoy case, which was so ghastly and dragged on for so long that no one really wants the whole thing regurgitated here. Suffice to say, the Jumabhoys are a prominent Indian family in Singapore. The family's elderly patriarch, Rajabali Jumabhoy, who died two months short of his 101st birthday, sued his eldest son, Ameerali, and two grandsons for allegedly cutting out other family members in running property and hotel group Scotts Holdings. The case went on for years and the family name was dragged through the mud. It was eventually resolved in 1999 when the court ruled against Rajabali's claims. He died shortly after and certain prominent family members are still not talking to each other. Call me naive but I would rather plod along with my middle of the road income than put my family through such a farcical soap opera.

Such high-powered family struggles are by no means exclusive to Singapore. The United States is famous for them. Indeed, if the Jumabhoys had been American, they would have appeared on Oprah Winfrey at least twice and Jerry Springer would have told them to 'put aside their money troubles and bind together through the power of love'.

In Singapore, it is the little cases that sadden me, such as families going to the smaller courts to contest the will of their late father to try to get his old HDB apartment. These incidents occur all the time. When I was renting a room from Saudita, my Indian landlady, she had an Indian friend come and stay with her. She was pathetically frail, at least seventy-five years old and looked as though a strong wind might blow her over. For some strange reason, she was remarkably kind to us. Whenever she went shopping, she would always return with some bananas and insist that we took them. Now I would be lying if I said that I was close to the woman. To this day, I still do not know her name but one Sunday morning, she unfolded a tragic story that will haunt me forever.

Leaving to go over to the local shop, we asked her if she needed anything and she burst into tears. It was obvious that the poor woman desperately needed to confide in someone other than a woman who thought it was acceptable to publicly bare her breasts. So she chose us, which if nothing else, must give an indication of how desperate she was. Like most elderly Singaporeans, she was not well-educated but she and her late husband had worked hard through the years and scraped together enough money to buy a small three-roomed HDB flat. Now a widow, she told us that the flat was hers, lock, stock and barrel. That is when the vultures descended.

Her son and daughter-in-law moved into the flat and kicked her into the smallest bedroom. She did not object. Being a practical woman, she knew she was not going to live forever and the flat would be theirs eventually anyway. Then the problems started. Her daughter-in-law regarded her as no more than an irritant, an obstacle to her owning her own little castle. The arguments started when her daughter-in-law began to dictate the running of the house: when and what its occupants ate, who cleaned the house and so on. Initially, the husband acted as peacemaker. Eventually, he became incensed by his mother's so-called constant nagging. At this stage, the cynical side of me began to think that I had only heard one side of the story. Then she showed us the bruises and I started to get a prickling sensation that ran up and down my spine.

Her puny legs were blackened with dark purple bruises and her upper arms displayed similar marks. She started crying heavily and became almost incoherent. Things had come to a head and her daughter-in-law had beaten her up in her own living room while her husband, the victim's son and heir, watched. The daughter-in-law then threw the old woman out of her own house and onto the street shouting charming things like, 'If you come back here, we'll kill you.' The husband then decided to reveal, for the record, his true feelings on the subject when he got up to assist his wife in the task of kicking his mother out. This happened about a week before she told us the story and the bruises were still there. Since then, the old lady had made just one telephone call to the house, only to be told to 'fuck off' by her son, the person she had raised and clothed.

All of which begs the eternal question: why? Why did she not call the police and have the two greedy fuckers thrown out? Why did she not call the media and have the pair publicly disgraced? Why did she not allow Saudita to remove their limbs? In short, why did she allow them to live rent free in her property while she slept on a mangy old sofa every night, confiding her troubles to two virtual strangers? I asked her all these questions and more, to which she replied, 'He's my son.' What could we say to this? We just cuddled her and left.

That is the major problem I have with filial piety. It relies a little too much on people. Having no welfare means there will always be those who slip through the net and end up serving warm burgers or cleaning toilet floors for ungrateful customers. A chillingly relevant incident occurred outside the Tribunal for the Maintenance of Parents office in 2000. A 56-year-old woman, Chua Bian Neo, was stabbed to death in front of her 89-year-old wheelchair-bound father. She had just attended a hearing at the tribunal with her father to help the old man claim financial aid. The killer was her brother, the very person that she allegedly intended to take to court to get him to help pay a monthly sum for her father's maintenance. It seems that the brother was unhappy with this arrangement so he stabbed his older sister in the back as his disabled father looked on helplessly.

Such incidents are extremely rare in Singapore and I do not want to give the wrong impression of what really is one of the safest countries in the world, but it does highlight one of the fundamental weaknesses of filial piety. Although there is a parliamentary act in place, some people still do not feel obliged to look after their parents. Even the ones that do can sometimes leave you questioning their motives. In a country that is obsessed with property and financial status, there are those who fall victim to greedy, parasitic children. That is why I get just a tad pissed off when I hear the term filial piety. For most people, it conjures up positive images of children supporting their parents in times of need. For me, it reminds me of a frail, weeping old lady showing me the bruises on her legs. And it breaks my heart.

## *Chapter Four*

If there is one thing that I will always express the deepest gratitude for, it is the simple fact that Singaporeans who work in fast-food chains do not sell their own food. If they did, it would take them a lifetime to serve each customer. You see, Singaporeans of all ages, but particularly the elderly, love their grub and like nothing more than to give you the odd morsel of home-cooked food. I can just imagine it.

'Can I have a hamburger, please?' I would begin innocently.

'Certainly, and how about one or two of the curry puffs that I've just made.'

'No, I just want a hamburger, thanks.'

'But you'll love the way that these have been cooked.'

'Okay, I'll take one then, thank you.'

'I'll give you two anyway and some Chinese tea on the side.'

'But I'm not thirsty.'

'Never mind, I made this tea especially. My mother gave me the recipe. It'll stop you catching colds and improve sexual performance.'

'I'll take fifteen cups, please.'

'I'll put in some fried chicken for you, too, to go with the tea.'

'But I'll explode. I couldn't possibly...'

'Well, I've cooked it now. It's my great-grandmother's most famous recipe. Our entire family swears by it. Please take it. Otherwise, I won't be able to sleep tonight.'

You have no choice but to eat all the food, waddle out of the shop, proceed to a discreet corner and die. I know this to be an incontestable fact because I have expired several times after going to a friend's auntie's place to have a wee 'bite to eat'. It is always the same. Taking your place at the table, you are shocked to find that the table has, in fact, disappeared. No one told you that someone in the family was training to be the next David Copperfield. For the table has vanished under a multitude of bowls, plates and cups, all of which are full. Twenty-seven bowls of fifty-three different dishes later, you realise who the magician was. It was the lady of the house who kept whizzing past you to fill the table with various dishes at breakneck speed.

So let's not beat about the bush here. If there is one thing Singaporeans can be truly proud of, it is their dominant food culture that can be traced back to the origins of modern Singapore. When Sir Stamford Raffles was sent by the East India Company in 1819 to find trading outposts along the Straits of Malacca, he saw Singapore and said, 'That one looks fine, I'll take it. Do you take American Express?' Before long, Malays from all over the archipelago, Indians and mainly Chinese all flocked to Singapore to look for work or to trade. By 1841, the population had already passed 40,000 and continued to rise. What did they bring with them in abundance? Their local dishes, of course.

The Malays enriched their spicy dishes with coconut milk sauces. Their *nasi padang*, which is a choice of spicy meat, such as mutton or chicken curry, served with various vegetables on a banana leaf, is my favourite. Beef rendang is also delicious but even that pales in comparison to satay. Whether it be chicken, pork or beef, barbecued satay is one of those things that I could eat all day. Though I would like to point out a little fact to certain food court operators. If hawker centre stall owners can afford to sell satay sticks at 30 cents each, take a little profit and still make them taste divine, why, may I ask, do you have to sell them at 60 cents each? Please do not tell me that your overheads are so high that you must charge almost double for something that costs very little to produce. It is just a little observation that tends to make me say, 'Sixty cents for a stick of fucking satay,' when the mood takes me.

Then there is Indian cuisine. Ever since I was a young boy growing up in Dagenham, I have always had a penchant for Indian food after my mother declared it a Saturday night treat. It became a tradition. In parts of England, we tend to have food traditions.

For example, Friday night is usually fish and chips night. In truth, this was an occasion I dreaded more than I actually enjoyed as my mother would always make me run to the chip shop. She would not allow my younger sister to go to the shopping precinct after dark – an excuse my sister managed to get good mileage out of until she left home at twenty-two, I might add. So it was left to me to perform 'The Sprint' to collect the fish and chips. This involved a beanpole of a teenager, i.e., me, running for his life while holding a bag of piping hot fish and chip meals under his left armpit. Arriving home and breathing like a nymphomaniac, he would muster the strength to knock on the door. His mother would open it and, with a face like thunder, say, 'What took you so long? The chips are freezing cold. Look at them! I'm going to have to microwave them now and you know I hate microwaved chips. I'll go myself next time.'

That was our Friday night food tradition. Our Saturday night treat in later years was one I really did enjoy because it involved Indian food. There would be dishes of chicken briyani, various curries, mutton korma, Bombay potatoes, onion bharjis and piles of naan bread and yellow rice everywhere. After which, the family would sit, motionless and silent, on the sofa watching our stomachs swell and taking turns to either fart or burp. Happy times.

So when I came to Singapore, I was in cuisine heaven. Indians might only make up just over seven per cent of the population but they certainly make their presence felt in food terms. I am told that Northern Indian food is less spicy and uses more cream and ghee whereas Southern Indian dishes favour a greater use of curry leaves, mustard seeds and coconut milk. Ironically, Singapore's most famous Indian dish, fish head curry, is not an Indian dish but rather a regional creation. Still, it typifies local Indian cuisine and I have yet to come across a Singaporean who does not like it. Roti prata, my own favourite Indian dish, is as simple as it is tasty. Looking a little like flat pancakes and slightly bigger than a compact disc, these flour creations are delightful for supper when they are drenched in curry.

The best place to go for any of the above is, without a doubt, Little India in Serangoon Road. When I went to Little India for the first time, I went to Komala Vilas and had the South Indian plate. It was divine. For S$5, you get rice and a series of hot vegetable dishes. The best part is that it is free flowing. You go in, wash your hands, find a table, signal to the old Indian guy to put a banana leaf down and the eating begins. There is no time for any spoon and fork nonsense. I have participated in gluttonous competitions to see who could consume the most food. I must confess that I have never won but I have polished off two full plates of rice, curry and vegetables. Try to top that.

Now, let's talk Chinese. The Chinese are famous worldwide for their cuisines and I would regularly visit my local Chinese takeaway on the way home from the pub. Of course, food always tastes good when you are drunk and if you are really lucky, you get a chance to see it again in the morning. This was why I used to feel so sorry for Chinese restaurant owners in England. They often got to see their well-prepared dishes ten minutes later, usually sprayed up their windows or on the pavement outside their shop. Sometimes, I sit and watch the hawker stall operators and see how hard they work in sweaty conditions. Although they must have a hard life, I still believe that hawker stall workers are better off than those running takeaway restaurants in the inner cities of England.

Chinese restaurant owners in England undoubtedly enjoy a higher standard of living because Chinese food there is not exactly cheap. However, I imagine that around 11 o'clock, when the pubs close, their job becomes hellish. Drunks all over the world are renowned for their lack of charm and sophistication, and some in England would not feel out of place at a Ku Klux Klan meeting. In fact, the *Straits Times* published a report in April 2000 stating that violent attacks on Chinese restaurateurs in London were on the increase and appeared to be racially motivated. To be sure, the Chinese in England make a hell of a lot more money than they would if they ran a hawker stall in Singapore but hawker stall owners do not have to endure racist shit every other night.

This is just as well because it gives these hawker stall owners more time to concentrate on doing what they do best, producing good grub. There are far too many exquisite dishes to be able to list them all here so I will just mention my favourites. You cannot go far wrong if you ask for *char siew fun*, which is barbecued pork rice. I am also a bit of an expert on the old chicken curry, seeing as I eat it at least five times a week (I am not kidding), especially the Chinese version with its hot reddish curry and fat potatoes.

When I eat at a Chinese restaurant, I always get a plate of Chinese mixed vegetables regardless of what else I order. This dish includes carrots, broccoli, mushrooms, cauliflower and heaven knows what else and is cooked and served in an oyster sauce. I could eat it all day, along with ginger beef, which is strips of tender beef served with ginger and spring onion and cooked in a thick oyster sauce.

I suppose the best thing about Chinese food, and this is going to sound awfully obvious, is that it is so varied. With so many Chinese immigrants arriving in the 1820s to escape the poverty, famine and political unrest in China, Singapore soon became home to Hokkiens, Cantonese, Teochews and the many other Chinese provincials who joined the country's Straits Chinese. Yet if I had to highlight just one group of Chinese settlers for their dish, it would have to be the Hainanese for their chicken rice. For my money, if one dish were to symbolise and represent Singaporean cuisine, it would have to be this one. Its tender chicken is either boiled or roasted, cut into strips and placed across the best-tasting rice in, well, the universe. Cooked in chicken stock that is also served as soup, it is the fluffiest, juiciest rice in the business.

However, do not think that it is just the French who stuff their faces with frog's legs. There are several hawker centres and coffee shops that I have been to that keep dozens of live frogs in a tank for you to select from. I speak from experience here. After being in Singapore for about three days, David took Scott and me out for a late night supper and placed a mysterious dish in front of us that looked like undernourished chicken wings fried in batter. The titbits did not taste too badly. They tasted like greasy chicken but with very little meat around the bone. Of course, David then pointed out the tank containing the frogs and laughed – Singapore 1 England 0. Consequently, Scott and I made up some stories about the ingredients that went into some of the famous English dishes that we knew David had tried at Manchester. Let's just say that when he visits England again, I do not think that he will be eating shepherd's pie, toad in the hole or spotted Dick in a hurry.

There are two things to learn from this. First, the English do, to their credit, have some wonderfully eccentric names for their dishes. I believe this is to compensate for the fact that we do not have very many so we tend to go a bit overboard on our culinary creations.

Second and perhaps far more relevant, the extent and choice of dishes cannot be overstated in Singapore. I have barely scratched the surface with the few that I have mentioned. Despite its small size (it is only 641 square kilometres), Singapore has Thai stalls, Indonesian restaurants, Japanese sushi bars and places where you can get Vietnamese, Korean or even Mongolian food. Then around places like Holland Village, the so-called sophisticated area where all the expatriates hang out, there are Mexican, Mediterranean, Middle Eastern and even German restaurants. A food haven for the fussiest of Western tourists.

I feel, however, that I should point out a little observation about Western food served at hawker stalls. You see, it is not really Western food at all or it certainly is not English food. Whenever I walk past the food stalls in a coffee shop and I pass a Western stall, the owner will invariably say, 'Hello, sir. Chicken chop for you, sir?' This always makes me laugh. You see, call me uncultured but I had never even seen a chicken chop before I came to Singapore, let alone eaten one. I confess I am no English aristocrat but even this working-class urchin has eaten at cafés, restaurants and the odd hotel and yet I had never come across a chicken chop and nor had any of my friends. Pork chops, yes, and, of course, we had all eaten lamb chops but never a chicken one. Despite this fact, nearly every single Western stall in Singapore sells them. There is a stall in Toa Payoh Lorong 1 where the friendly owner actually calls me 'chicken chop'. At first, I thought he was asking me if I wanted a chicken chop but I realised he was, in fact, calling me one.

I would approach the stall and he would shout, 'Wah, chicken chop, what you want today?'

'Egg and bacon, can?'

'Can lah, chicken chop, no problem.'

Sure enough, eggs and bacon would arrive and that would be it. In fact, the eggs and bacon would arrive with cucumber and lettuce, a strange but refined addition to the traditional English breakfast. It is all delicious but I just cannot help wondering where the stall owners get their recipes from.

Eating out in Singapore is a social occasion whereas it is something that is done out of necessity in England. That is not to say that English people do not enjoy fine dining, we love our grub as much as the next overweight Western consumer. As a rule, however, the restaurant is not our major forum for social interaction, the pub is. Hence, Singapore has a food culture; England has a pub culture.

When I was eighteen, my step-dad was giving me a lift home one night when we passed the Robin Hood pub in Dagenham, which was notorious for its unruly clientele. As we pulled up at the traffic lights, we saw two guys fighting each other with snooker cues outside probably the world's shittiest pub. What I remember vividly about the incident was that it was only 10 o'clock in the evening and these two guys were openly brawling. Even more striking was the reaction of my stepfather, which was nothing. Having grown up in West London, he had seen it so many times before that he just made some passing comment about 'those silly bastards' and looked away. I was stunned. It was like a scene from Martin Scorsese's *Mean Streets*. The two guys were ripping lumps out of each other's backs while men and women just stood and watched. It really was nothing out of the ordinary.

That is certainly one advantage of having such a thriving food culture. You seldom hear of Singaporeans having a brawl outside a food court because they have both eaten too much nasi padang. The only violence I have encountered at a restaurant is me hitting companions with noodles as I fight a losing battle with a pair of chopsticks. I am hopeless with chopsticks. I have all the control of a baby holding a marker pen. I can just about manage the wooden ones but when it comes to those heavy silver ones you get in hotels, well, you might as well give me a pair of javelins.

Having such a dominant food culture does have its drawbacks though. An expatriate friend was on his way home from work one day when he decided to pop in on his Chinese girlfriend for a chat. Being polite, he called her first to let her know he was coming and told her that he had already eaten.

When he arrived, he discovered to his horror that her parents had kindly prepared him a meal. As you can imagine, there was plenty there. He sat down at the table and looked down at the food. He tried to muster the energy to eat it but he could not. His girlfriend urged him to make an effort because her parents had taken the time to cook it and he would offend them. A valid point. My friend then explained that he had just wolfed down a substantial meal and although he was extremely grateful to her parents and did not want to upset them, he had not asked them to prepare a meal in the first place. An equally fair point.

The girlfriend's mother then noticed that my friend was not eating his meal and had a discreet word with her daughter. The girlfriend then told my friend that her mother was a little upset because he was not making an effort. By this stage, the atmosphere was souring rapidly and what had seemed to be a rather trivial matter to him was on the verge of becoming serious. The parents told their daughter that although they understood that her boyfriend had already eaten, he was insulting them by not even trying the food and that he must at least attempt to eat it. When my friend heard this, he actually laughed at the incredulity of it all, which only served to piss off his peacekeeping girlfriend. Exasperated, my friend shovelled down forkfuls of what he later described as the most uncomfortable meal of his life. He spent most of a miserable evening at the girl's house avoiding her parents and then spent an even more miserable night on the toilet. Apparently, relations between all four protagonists cooled so drastically that it was several weeks before the matter was eventually resolved when my friend apologised.

Make of this incident what you will. Some would say it was a culture clash; that my friend was intolerant or the girl's parents too stubborn. Others would argue that the whole episode is stunningly trivial and overblown. I would side with this viewpoint if it had been an isolated incident. But it is not.

During our first week in Singapore, Scott and I were taken to an auntie's house for a meal and as always the dishes were delightful. All except one – peanut soup. Along with David's homemade shark's fin soup in Manchester, peanut soup is the worst thing that I have ever tasted. Perhaps it was our Western palates stubbornly refusing to acclimatise to a unique taste but the soup affected Scott particularly badly. No one else noticed but I saw him shudder as he swallowed it.

Now there should be nothing wrong with this. I have yet to meet a person who has liked absolutely everything that he has tasted. After all, we are only human. And I would wager that no one would actually enjoy my mother's baked potatoes with their razor-sharp, slit-your-throat edges. But as we sat at the dinner table, Scott and I were made to feel most uncomfortable. Our hostess insisted several times that we drank the soup so we grew to like it. Scott bore the brunt of it. He was hemmed in by over-eager aunties who watched him eat every mouthful. Luckily, I was sitting at the other end of the table where I had perfected the unoriginal technique of holding a glass of water in one hand and a spoonful of peanut soup in the other. When no one was looking, I would swallow the soup and then hose down my taste buds before they could cry 'What the fuck are you doing to us?' Scott had no chance. He drank at least half the soup before he was left alone. Back at home later that night, he spent over an hour redecorating the inside of our toilet bowl with the soup. Two years later, after he had returned to England, I met up with him and brought up the subject of peanut soup. With no hesitation, he said, 'I can still remember the taste of that stuff. I thought it was gonna fucking kill me.' Quite.

This is the fundamental problem with having such a proud, dominant culture of any kind: there will always be a fine line between pride and arrogance. Walk into any pub in England and tell the landlord that his beer is the worst you have ever tasted and you will not leave with a friendly pat on the back.

When my dad was drunk, he would champion the quality of British beer. 'Son,' he would say, 'I've said it before and I'll say it again. He might have played for Manchester United but George Best was the greatest.'

'Yes, dad. He could do it all, couldn't he, dad?'

'He could do it all, boy. He could shoot, head, dribble, cross, pass and he could get stuck in and tackle with the best of them.'

'Better than Pelé, dad?'

'Better than Pelé, boy. He could do it in all weathers: rain, sleet, snow, sun and gale force winds.'

'Strange weather in Manchester, dad?'

'That's right. And I'll tell you another thing. Never, ever, wear white towelling socks with trousers. That is bad dress sense. Never do it.'

'You're right, dad.' I would be fighting sleep by this stage. But when he paused to smile lovingly at his pint glass, I knew my night was over.

'But best of all, there's nothing in the world like a pint of beer. You could travel the world and never get a decent, cold pint like you can in Britain. British beer is something to be proud of. No one can make beer like we can.' He would then go and order a pint of Heineken beer, which is about as British as tulips and windmills.

Singaporeans, by and large, are the same with food. Food is considered to be superior so it must be eaten. This is in stark contrast to the British, largely because the British know, subconsciously, that they cannot cook. To get around this failing, they will beg you not to eat their food. My mother was brilliant at this. I would bring a friend to dinner and my mum would cook a meat pie and plenty of gravy to soothe our hard palates, which would be cut to ribbons by her potatoes with the razor-sharp edges. She would place the food on the table, which I knew had taken her an hour to prepare, and order my guest not to eat it.

She would say, 'There you go, Ross. Now if there's anything you don't like, just leave it on the side of your plate. Don't be shy.'

'Okay, thanks, Sue,' my friend Ross would reply, raising his cutlery eagerly, blissfully ignorant of the bloody massacre that awaited the roof of his mouth. Then my dear mother would start again.

'I mean it, Ross. If there's anything you don't want, just leave it on your plate. Don't think that I'll say anything, I won't mind. Please Ross, don't eat my dinner, I know you won't like it. Come on, I'll throw it away and we'll order a pizza.'

Of course, I would go over to Ross's house for dinner and his mother would similarly beg me to do the same. Mothers up and down the British Isles are right now ordering their guests not to eat their food. Meanwhile, your fathers and uncles are dragging you over to the local pub and forcing you to drink beer for the first time, even though it tastes like liquefied ashtrays. It is most ironic.

That is the price you pay for growing up in a country that has a thriving pub culture. Just as having an auntie zealously cajoling you into drinking peanut soup is the price you pay for living in a society where its people pride themselves on their cuisines. I know that there are Singaporeans who will only consider the Asian dishes on a restaurant menu, no matter where they are. And these are, inevitably, the same morons who will raise an eyebrow should I have the audacity to turn down a bowl of peanut soup.

Thankfully, though, this dogmatic attitude is evolving and giving way to a more cosmopolitan outlook. Younger Singaporeans now go to pubs to sample traditional Western fare such as bangers and mash or shepherd's pie. They are just as comfortable with a plate of spaghetti bolognaise as they are with a bowl of tom yam soup. This is the only way to go.

To be fair, not every Singaporean force-feeds you something you do not like and not every British drinker ends up fighting with a snooker cue. At this point in time, however, I know which culture I prefer. Where else in the world can you find such variety, such choice and at such low cost? Singaporeans should take pride in their food because, unlike Heineken 'British' beer, it really does belong to them. I am forever hearing about Singaporeans trying to build their own identity. Well, if their national cuisine is not a valid starting point, then frankly, I do not know what is. It does not matter where the dishes originated from, the likes of chicken rice, satay and fish head curry are now as Singaporean as the Merlion. And the best thing about local food is that whenever I sit down to eat in a hawker centre, I do not have to suffer my dad's drunken ramblings about George Best, white socks and the merits of British-Dutch beer. Now that is a cause for genuine gratitude, wouldn't you agree?

## *Chapter Five*

I will never understand what it is that draws me to chicken restaurants. The chicken, though undoubtedly tasty, is greasy and runs down the back of your hand and along your forearm, which is the most uncomfortable feeling in the world when you are wearing a long-sleeved shirt on a humid day. Instinctively, you reach for a napkin but, naturally, you have only been given two and they were both used on the first piece of chicken. You then have no choice but to turn to the mashed potato, which resembles baby food and is about as filling. Yet despite these irritants, we still find ourselves drawn to the smell of fried chicken. So there I stood one afternoon at the counter of such a restaurant in Toa Payoh, waiting to place my order. I remember vividly being served by an extremely attractive Malay teenager. 'She will break a few hearts one day,' I thought to myself. Five minutes later, I would have happily broken her neck.

'Can I have a two-piece baby food set, please?' I asked politely.

'One original set. Anything else?'

'No. But can I change my drink to Sprite, please?'

She started giggling at this apparently hilarious request. 'I'm sorry. What drink you want again?'

'Sprite, please.'

More giggles. 'Wah, your English so funny. You not English, is it?'

'Yes, I am. I am also an English teacher so could you tell me what is so wrong with the way I speak?'

Now this may seem a trifle aggressive but it is most irritating having someone laugh in your face. Besides, my accent has always been a cause for a little paranoia. Being a working-class lad, my cockney accent was certainly not the most common accent heard along the corridors of Manchester University so a little insecurity is inevitable. Having undergone phonetics training for my job, I knew that my pronunciation of the word 'sprite' was correct. I mean, as English words go, it is hardly supercalifragilisticexpialidocious, is it? But the counter girl had not finished.

'The way you say "splat" so funny, loh.'

'What? The way I say it correctly, you mean?'

'But you don't. You say "sprite" and I say "splat". It's really funny.'

'My chicken's getting cold and my baby food's melting. Do you think I could get my "splat" now?'

'Yes, of course.' With that, she went over to the drinks machine and filled my cup up with 'splat'. I thanked her for pointing out the gross imperfections of my English and soaked her with the 'splat'. That was as far as it went. To this day, it remains the most serious direct run-in I have had with a Singaporean youth. Just a little bit of playful cheek. No aggression, no bad language, no knives being held to my friend's throat, in fact, nothing more than innocent sauciness.

This contrasts sharply with the youngsters I grew up with in Dagenham. When I was fifteen, my good friend Ross was walking home from school when two young boys walked towards him and got his attention with the audacious shout of 'Oi!' Giggling, the small one piped up. 'Will you tell your mum to stop changing her lipstick?'

'Why?' Ross asked innocently.

'Because it's making my cock multicoloured.' They both laughed hysterically and walked on.

Ross merely laughed to himself and he told me all about the episode the next day at school. I laughed as well. Then he told me that both boys could not have been more than six years old so I laughed again. It made the story even funnier.

These were the kind of youngsters I grew up with. Sitting in a science class in secondary two, I was tapped on the shoulder by David, one of the class bullies. Turning slowly, I was greeted by the sight of an erect penis. David was having a sizing contest with Gary, another school bully, and they wanted an independent arbitrator to ... well, arbitrate. David gestured towards his exposed anatomy. He held a ruler in the other hand.

'Well, what do you think?' he asked excitedly.

'About what?'

'Look, Gary reckons his is bigger than mine. But have a look, mine is over six inches. His is nowhere near that size. He's got a tiny knob. Mine's definitely bigger, isn't it?'

'I don't know, do I? I haven't seen his, have I?'

'Oh yeah. Well, come to the back of the class, he's got his out. You can measure it. No problem.'

'No! I'm not measuring anybody's knob, all right?'

'But mine's definitely bigger than six inches, right?'

'If you say so. But don't expect me to put a ruler against it.'

'I knew it was bigger than six inches. Cheers, Neil. Oi Gary! I told you mine was bigger than yours. Your knob's tiny.'

I could fill a whole book with childhood stories like that. I have told a few to some Singaporean friends and it is interesting to watch their stunned expressions. Instinctively, they assume I am lying. They want me to tell them I am lying to reassure them. Partly because the London they know is the one that has the Queen, fish and chips, famous castles and quaint little bookshops in places like Notting Hill that are owned and run by gentlemen like Hugh Grant. They want to believe this so that they can cling to the ridiculous notion that Britain is a green and pleasant land, a positive place of democracy and free speech. In short, a society fit for the disillusioned Singaporean. Surely, they assume, such incidents do not occur in Britain? They are not allowed to. Surely, the teacher, the parent, the policeman or the politician would step in to check this anti-social behaviour as they do in Singapore?

The fact remains, though, that these incidents do occur among the youth in the West from time to time. Whereas I am fairly certain, having taught in Singapore for over two years, that they do not here. Call me old-fashioned but I have never seen a penis in a Singaporean classroom. Although I have been called a penis.

Teaching speech and drama to a nursery class a couple of years ago, I would line the children up at the end of every lesson and say goodbye. As each child went out, he or she would say, 'Bye Mr Bean' and giggle. I was a bit of a clown and it was a harmless nickname. One day, Malvin, a cheeky little chap, sprang a new term on me that left the rest of the class in stitches. He shouted, 'Bye-bye Mr Cuckoo Bird.'

Initially, I thought 'cuckoo bird' was a bizarre name to bestow upon a teacher but I did not give it much thought. However, when it reached the point where the whole class would cry 'Bye Mr Cuckoo Bird' in chorus and then leave the room with tears rolling down their cheeks, I knew something was seriously amiss. I found myself in one of those uncomfortable situations that are abhorred universally. I did not know something. How could I approach a colleague, a fellow teacher I might add, and ask him what a seemingly common noun meant? In my experience, teachers will remove their genitalia with a blunt instrument before admitting that they do not know something.

In the end, though, it bordered on the ridiculous. As the pupils left the class one by one, I started to notice that the parents were also giggling. I had no choice but to seek the truth and my attempts to do so can only be described as pathetic. Sidling up to the administrative staff after lessons one evening, I adopted my puzzled look.

'You know,' I started, 'you get a lot of birds in Singapore, don't you?'

'Yes, you do,' replied Chris, one of the admin girls, in a tone that suggested she had never heard such a dull question in her entire life.

'But you don't get cuckoos, right?'

'I don't think so.'

'Erm, cuckoo bird, cuckoo bird. It's strange.' I muttered aloud.

'Why are you saying those words?' Chris asked, giggling.

'Oh, for no reason. I saw this Singaporean documentary about wildlife last night and they kept referring to this "cuckoo bird" and it was a bit confusing.'

'Did they? Which programme was it?'

'Oh, it was that one on wildlife. I can't remember what time it was on.'

'Really? I didn't see it in the paper. What channel was it on?' She knew I was lying through my teeth.

'Okay, my children keep calling me Mr Cuckoo Bird and it makes them laugh hysterically. I have no idea what it means but it's got to the stage where I've caught their parents sniggering too. Quite frankly, it's beginning to irritate me. So if you know what it means, please put me out of my misery. If you don't, stop giggling.'

'It's a penis,' said Chris, like it was the most obvious answer in the world.

'It's a what?'

'It's a man's penis. You know?'

'Yes, I know what a man's penis is. Are you telling me that my nursery children have been calling me Mr Penis every week?'

'Well, yes. Cuckoo bird sounds like the word for "penis" in one of the dialects.' Inevitably, Chris found this a reason for much merriment and I became the penis man in the office for quite some time thanks to those adoring little bastards.

Penises aside, Singaporean youngsters were a pleasure to teach. I had only been in Singapore for a month when I was thrown in at the deep end and sent to teach at Victoria School. Victoria, or VS as it is more popularly known, is considered one of the best boy schools in Singapore. On my first day, I was standing outside my classroom and generally being nosy when a student passed.

'Good morning sir,' he said breezily.

'Hello,' I replied. 'Do you know me?'

'No, sir.'

'Am I teaching you this term?'

'I don't think so, sir.'

'Then why did you greet me just now?'

'Oh, we greet every teacher we meet, sir. See you.'

'Yes, see you.' I was stunned. With the exception of some of the better state and private schools in England, this kind of behaviour is not common. Such incidents were not exclusive to VS, though. Each school I have taught at, be it primary or secondary, neighbourhood or independent, I have always encountered extremely polite, conscientious pupils. There were, of course, one or two rare exceptions but they were never difficult to teach.

Without doubt, I sympathise with schoolchildren here because they are under such tremendous pressure to deliver the academic goods. From the day they can talk until the day they graduate from university, their parents are always just one step behind, prodding them forward. I think it is fair to say that when it comes to a child's education, the parents want the best that their money can buy. Not an unreasonable supposition, perhaps. However, there is a twist. The investor wants to see an academic return or someone, somewhere down the line, is going to get it.

When I was teaching, I often took calls from parents who were interested in enrolling their children for speech courses. A parent once asked if she could put her child, who had just won a public speaking competition at school, into one of our oral communication examination classes. These classes involved reciting poetry, drama passages and speeches from memory. I suggested that the child was too young. The classes were mixed in terms of age and ability so it was highly possible that the girl could be in a group with teenagers aged fifteen or sixteen. The mother was adamant that her child would manage because she was 'a very bright girl'.

After speaking to my boss, I came back to the phone and told the mother that her child really would not be able to cope with such group dynamics. She then scolded me over the phone, telling me that I had no right to pass judgement on her child without assessing her capabilities. I said that I did not have to. The girl was four years old. She was nearing the end of kindergarten one (K1) and her mother was demanding that she be put in a class with teenagers and entered for oral examinations. Words cannot aptly describe such imbecilic behaviour. The sad fact is that we had parents like that walk into our office almost every week. The neurotic mother eventually relented and the girl ended up in one of my classes. She was intelligent and her vocabulary was way ahead of her peers. She lived for the worksheets and the homework but when it came to interactive conversations about *Tellytubbies*, *Sesame Street* and *Star Wars*, she would withdraw and become distant.

That is the tragic compromise that many Singaporean children are subconsciously forced to make. When you are being shunted from one private lesson to another and from one textbook to another, how much socialising do you actually have time for? The sad fact is that textbook examination-oriented learning from such an early age rarely makes for riveting conversation and it is becoming increasingly difficult to see where these children's social skills are going to come from.

I have lost count of the number of times that I have stepped into a secondary school classroom in Singapore and been greeted by twenty academic shells. They are highly efficient robots who have been trained to reproduce information while travelling along the production line of examinations. It was soul destroying. I watched their expressionless faces and I could see that they could not compute the value of speech and drama. After all, it had no examination at the end of the course, no certificate and no promises of a highly paid job so the subject seemed illogical to them.

Gradually, the students would open up and they began to see the class as a welcome bonus in their timetable rather than a hindrance that stopped them from getting their maths homework done. I am not going to lie and say that I was Robin Williams and by the end of the course, the class resembled a scene from *Dead Poet's Society*, with them all vowing to be actors, singers and writers. The majority will still end up in the marketing or electronics sector because they have too many other influences to contend with. Despite watching academic shells blossom into more confident individuals in my class, I was resigned to the fact that they still had to produce results once they left. But at what cost?

In one drama lesson at VS, I caught a secondary two boy sleeping. He was not just dozing, he was in one of those 'I'm in such a deep sleep that I would barely notice if you ripped my vital organs out' types of sleep. In fact, it was his snoring that brought him to my attention. Without wishing to embarrass the boy further, I asked to see him at the end of the lesson.

After class, he apologised sincerely and promised that it would never happen again. After considerable prompting, the boy told me that he had been up until 2:30 a.m. that morning doing his homework. As he got up at 6 a.m. to come to school, the boy had only had three hours sleep. Moreover, he had been staying up late for most of that week to get all his homework completed. The poor boy was under intense pressure at home to lift his marks as one or two of his recent test performances had been deemed below par by his parents. He was thirteen. Bearing in mind it was around February and the school year was just two months old, I asked him what kind of academic work was so important that a thirteen-year-old boy had gone without sleep? After all, he was not doing his degree finals or writing a PhD thesis, he was just doing run-of-the-mill school homework. Yet the lad felt obligated to push himself to the limit to satisfy those around him, even if it meant snatching sleep during one of my lectures on Stanislavsky's method acting. The poor sod did not know what he was missing.

The worst part is, of course, that we all know he is not an exceptional case. I recently read a story in the *Straits Times* about the latest batch of O level results. Make no mistake, the majority of Singaporean students performed extremely well and ended up with a long list of As and A+s, which is undoubtedly impressive. However, my attention was drawn to the photographs, which accurately depicted the joy and despair of successful and slightly less successful (after all, there is no need to use the 'f' word here) students. In both pictures, the teenagers were crying. In the case of those who did not perform so well, the reasons were obvious. But tears were still shed by those who had achieved straight As. It was only after I had read one or two of the quotes that the penny dropped. The word 'relief' kept cropping up. On several occasions, students who passed with flying colours spoke of relief before they spoke of joy. The pressures must have been unbearable.

Of course, this is the case for students in any country. I remember the relief I felt when my GCSE results were satisfactory. However, there was one crucial difference. That relief was a result of pressure I had applied on myself. My parents trusted that I would perform to the best of my ability and left it to me. Not a single tear was shed over an exam result and my school had the dubious honour of churning out some of the worst GCSE and A level results in England.

That is how life was in Dagenham. Education did not and still does not have the prestige that it has in Singapore. Parents simply do not put such store in it. Their rationale is that there will always be enough jobs to go around as there was in their day. Such an easy-going, working-class upbringing does have one major advantage: social skills come in abundance.

If Singaporeans of all ages have one failing, it is that they are not streetwise enough. This rare type of intelligence is developed in most English children when they are very young. The sharp, fast-talking language of the living room is soon transferred to the school playground, the local park and then the street. English kids spend far too much time together messing around when they should be at home studying. That goes without saying. However, constantly being around their peers both in and out of school improves their communicative skills tremendously. Walk around any housing estate in Singapore at 8 p.m. and how many groups of kids do you see hanging out? Not too many because they are at home learning about the basics of supply and demand for an economics project.

I do not doubt for a second that if you pitted an average Dagenham classroom against an average Singaporean classroom in a general knowledge test, the results would be painful. The Singaporeans would win hands down. However, if the two groups were put together after the test and given the chance to chitchat, I am certain that the conversation would be extremely one-sided. I have lost count of the times that I have played 'Just a Minute' in class, a game where you speak spontaneously on a given subject for one minute, and been left wanting to scream. Singaporean youngsters are just not used to speaking freely. If given fun subjects like 'hairy armpits', 'bananas' or 'why I love *Baywatch*', they just freeze. If, however, I give them subjects like 'the Internet', 'computers' or 'Singapore', they simply regurgitate the relevant encyclopaedic entry for sixty seconds. In contrast, a typically brash Dagenham teenager will happily waffle away about bananas for hours. Yet I know that the former will end up earning US$10,000 a month working in property while the latter will probably end up in an office performing clerical duties.

This lack of social skills is about as worrying as it gets as far as Singaporean teenagers go, so allow me the odd chuckle when I hear friends talk about teenage gangsters here. My friend David is always reminding me to stay away from these dangerous gangsters who stalk the streets. These people are apparently so menacing that they have even been labelled with menacing names. The boys are called Ah Bengs and the girls Ah Lians. I have been warned by friends never to make eye contact with them, never to laugh at their ridiculous clothing combinations (white, skin-tight trousers and vest, black belt and a bright yellow handphone stuck to the hip) and never to get into an argument with them because they are usually armed with knives or, wait for it, parangs. Now this last statement floored me. A parang is like a huge sword and something similar to what we call a scythe in England. It is a truly lethal weapon. Think then about these Ah Bengs and their choice of clothing. Believe me, if it is not tight, they will not wear it, so could somebody please tell me where in the name of Al Capone are they going to hide a parang? Do they put it down their trousers and just pretend that they are pleased to see you?

At this point, Singaporeans may feel entitled to stand up and cry that I am addressing an extremely serious social issue in a flippant manner. There are a number of teenage crimes, often committed by these so-called Ah Bengs and Ah Lians. In January 2000, a lawyer was beaten up by a gang of teenagers outside a cinema in front of his wife. It was not a random attack. During the movie that he had just watched, the lawyer had asked one of the gang to stop talking on his handphone as it was disturbing and irritating the rest of the audience. The whole of Singapore, including me, applauded the lawyer for his actions. This anti-social handphone behaviour is driving the country crazy.

After the lawyer asked the teenager to stop informing the entire cinema how he had just spent Christmas, the gangly youth brooded in silence. Then, after carefully checking he had at least three to one odds, the anti-social phone guy cornered the lawyer outside. The lawyer's wife was held back while the rest of the gang gave him a good hiding before running off. The general public was outraged but, thanks to the extremely efficient law and order infrastructure here, the gang was soon rounded up and charged.

Such incidents occur occasionally and they jar the nation and remind its people that they are not invulnerable to crime, despite living in one of the safest countries in the world. These crimes also remind politicians, teachers and parents to reinforce positive social values into their children and to reiterate the dangers of going off the rails and the punishments that will result from a life dedicated to crime. Generally though, everyone tends to get a wee bit carried away as the majority of Singaporean youngsters are a decent lot.

To be reminded of the startling contrast, I need only read a copy of the *Dagenham Post*. My mother sends me a copy of my home town's local newspaper once a month so I can keep tabs on what is happening at home. You would assume that I could just click onto the paper's web site and read about the latest events in Dagenham from here but, alas, the *Post* is not yet online. No surprise there, I know of Dagenham residents who are still struggling with calculators.

The paper's content usually provides an unwelcome jolt back to reality and reminds me of what I have left behind. The lead story on page two of a recent copy was about a teenage mother who was once a heroin addict but had just succeeded in kicking the habit to look after her young son. She then died from an epileptic fit, hence the story. Now be honest, how many similar stories have appeared in either *The Straits Times* or *The New Paper*? The most alarming fact to remember is that this is just a small local paper that covers just one of the thirty-three Greater London boroughs.

In that same edition, the *Dagenham Post* reported a court story that involved grievous bodily harm. The incident was pretty gruesome. A couple in their mid-twenties had an argument in The Pipers, one of the most notorious pubs in Dagenham. The row was disturbing another group of people so one person from the group told the couple to shut up. Dean, the man who was arguing with his girlfriend, took offence to this interference and pushed a glass into the face of the man who had told them to be quiet. He, in turn, took offence to this, mysteriously produced a penknife and stabbed Dean. In fact, he stabbed him so many times that Dean could actually see his own intestines.

There were two things that immediately struck me upon finishing this story. First, the story was tucked away somewhere after page ten, indicating that the editor had realised that its news value, in a Dagenham context, was nothing extraordinary.

The second thing was that I actually knew Dean, the 'ooh, I think I can see one of my intestines' guy. I went to the same school as him. I only knew him because we both needed to take the train to get to school and his younger brother, Dennis, was in my year. Being reasonably close to his brother meant that I was usually spared from the bullying that would be routinely dished out to the other boys who took the train to and from school. His favourite pastime was to lift new students and plonk them onto the railway tracks as the train approached in the distance.

In stark contrast, his younger brother was quiet, placid and could not say words that began with 'sn' properly. For three years,

I would use his speech impediment to break the monotony of the train journey home. After which the poor sod moved with his dad and scumbag brother to an even rougher council estate because they could not maintain the rent payments. When the two boys were younger, their mother had died of a brain haemorrhage in front of them. Admittedly, it must have been an awful childhood but at least the younger brother proved that it did not have to end up with a knife in the guts. You do not come across many youngsters like these two in Singapore, yet when I grew up in England, I went to school with quite a few.

So I remain convinced that the way things stand currently, Singapore has little to fear from its younger generations. They respect family ties and values, are dedicated students (perhaps too dedicated) and cause few disciplinary problems. However, I cannot say that Singapore has nothing to fear.

Young Singaporeans are spoilt. No, let me rephrase that. The majority of Singaporean children rank among the most pampered children on the planet. Unlike their parents and grandparents, most young Singaporeans have experienced nothing but economic growth. Their childhood has been one of continual housing upgrading, decent education, modern shopping centres and fat *hong baos*, or red packets containing money that are given out at Chinese New Year. It does not take a sociologist to realise that such a comfortable lifestyle will have detrimental side effects.

In my classroom, I once had to pull a five-year-old boy away from his maid. He was kicking her because she had forgotten to bring his toys. On another occasion, my colleague Lawrence told me about a ten-year-old girl who submitted a composition about the family's maid. In the piece, she detailed the poor woman's incompetence and how she was so stupid because she did not always obey the instructions given by the girl. Lawrence consulted the girl's mother about the 'Why I hate maids' composition. She just sighed and said, 'But the maid is so damned lazy.'

If this is the attitude that is being instilled into Singaporean children, then the future is bleak. If they grow up believing that they must treat their family with respect but everybody else can be treated shabbily, then we have got a problem. If they also believe that the pursuit of money is the only pursuit in life, then I shudder at the consequences. I have come across enough brain-numbingly boring executives, with a fat wallet and a fast car, to last me a lifetime. These people are never satisfied. They buy a four-roomed flat, then they want a five-roomed one. They buy their first car, which has to be replaced by a Mercedes within five years. Their boss plays golf (squash is now so passé) so they buy a set of clubs and take lessons. It is unoriginal, predictable and depressing. As all of these pursuits take up so much time, they get the maid to wash the car because that is what she is paid for while they get an auntie to clear away their tray in a fast-food restaurant. Then, when they have children, they send them for extra tuition to keep them occupied. The children get everything they want because it appeases them and they shout at the maid because they have seen their parents do it. Suddenly, we have come full circle – Singaporean greed has reproduced itself in the next generation.

As today's teenagers become adults, they are understandably restless and ambitious. The prospect of having a modest flat, a maid and a small car does not pacify them because it is nothing new. So they either go out to chase the dollar at any cost or they emigrate.

I watched Prime Minister Goh Chok Tong give a speech to students a while back urging those who decided to study overseas to enjoy themselves but to make sure they came back to ply their skills here. He sounded like he was almost pleading with them and I cannot say I blame him. When I was teaching, students used to tell me how lucky I was to have grown up in England and how much more exciting it must have been. I used to tell them one or two not-so-good stories from my childhood, adding that the chances of similar incidents occurring here were almost negligible. In a nutshell, schoolchildren are better off here.

Of course, Singaporeans may not be the most socially adept youngsters in the world and children here are expected to work far too hard. Paradoxically, English pupils do not hit the books half as much as they should, yet they are never short of an answer or two in the street. It is a classic case of swings and roundabouts. If I had to choose between an environment in which the kids were a little shy but produced outstanding academic results or a place where youngsters were more outgoing but far less studious and were randomly flung onto railway tracks from time to time, I know which one I would pick, don't you? Quick! Make your mind up, a train is approaching.

# Chapter Six

I cannot stand shopping in Singapore. No, that is wrong. I cannot stand shopping with my girlfriend in Singapore. I spend so much time with her in Orchard Road and Bishan that I am considering taking a sleeping bag with me from now on. You see, like most women, she is a feeler. She simply cannot walk past an unfamiliar product without giving it a quick, discreet fondle. It does not matter what we are looking at, her hands impulsively shoot out to touch that unidentified sitting object. I would not mind but there are parts of my body that remain unidentified but she has never been overcome by an uncontrollable urge to touch them. I have seen her feel the most ridiculous of products ranging from baby clothes to tin openers. The most mystifying part of the process comes after she has given the unfamiliar product a squeeze, which, incidentally, she never has any intention of buying. Seemingly delighted that, for example, a roof rack for a BMW (we do not even have a car) feels exactly how she anticipated, her lips form a tiny, self-satisfied smile as she lets out a little 'hmm'. She can do this all bloody day.

So, after spending the whole day shopping one Sunday, it should come as no surprise that I was not in the best of moods as we queued up at a taxi stand outside Junction 8 shopping centre in Bishan. The sticky humidity that precedes a thunderstorm was not helping matters either. I was perspiring heavily, I had things to prepare for work the next day and the taxi queue did not seem to be going anywhere. There were about six taxis' worth of people in front of us when the most irritating thing happened. A Chinese lad, aged about twenty, swaggered towards the queue with his girlfriend. He was speaking Hokkien extremely loudly into a yellow handphone, throwing in plenty of swear words here and there just to remind his academically-challenged girlfriend how hard he was. As a taxi approached, the pair arrogantly walked to the front of the queue, flagged the taxi down and got in. As the unknowing driver pulled away, the Chinese guy dragged himself away from his phone momentarily to wave at the queue before disappearing into the night.

There were grumbles and disappointed sighs from a few weary shoppers waiting in the queue but I was livid. I had travelled to the other side of the planet to get some peace from these shitheads and I was furious with myself for letting the little prick get away with it. My home town was full of people like this.

I was still fuming when the Indian couple standing behind us walked away. I sympathised with them. They were just as pissed off as we were. When they left the queue, I assumed they had given up trying to get a taxi. Curiously, I watched them plod along Bishan Road. They had walked no more than fifteen metres when they stepped off the kerb and hailed a taxi that was making its way towards the stand. The couple quickly got in, probably hoping they had not been spotted, and the taxi then pulled away sharply. I could not believe it. I had been made to look a fool twice in two minutes. This time something had to be done.

As the taxi crawled up to the stand, I found myself inexplicably running towards it. 'You bastards!' I heard myself shout. 'You fucking little kiasu bastards. Don't pretend you can't see me. There are families waiting to get taxis here, you fucking bastards.'

So there I was in the middle of Bishan Road on a wet Sunday night screaming abuse at a taxi that was fast becoming a twinkling light in the distance. What was I doing? I still cannot explain it rationally. On completing my incoherent tirade of abuse, I turned, delighted with myself, towards the taxi stand. The sight of ten or so stunned shoppers greeted me, all of whom had no idea what to make of my uncontrolled outburst. Sometimes the Dagenham side of me comes racing to the surface because that is the side that stores all the swear words. There is little I can do about it.

Nothing in Singapore brings out that side of me quicker than kiasuism – a paranoid trait that made the Indian couple push in front of families with small children so they could be home ten minutes earlier than everybody else. It was kiasuism, I believe, that made the taxi driver pull over in the first place. He could see the long queue that he was barely fifteen metres from and I am sure he knew what the couple was doing, but he wanted to get his taxi meter running as quickly as possible and he could do it without the hassle of pulling into a taxi stand. Paranoid? I do not think so.

Had that incident occurred during my first week in Singapore, I am fairly certain that Scott and I would have called them 'cheeky bastards' and shrugged off the incident. Having now lived in Singapore for over five years, I experience some form of kiasuism every day. To me, it is the city-state's most negative (and most visible) feature.

In Hokkien, *kiasu* means 'to be scared to fail'. To a certain extent, it can be a positive characteristic in certain spheres of society.

For example, the fear of failing encourages parents to provide the best education possible for their children. But it never stops at this healthy level. Many Singaporeans like immediate, positive results. They cannot wait for things; they must have them now and they must be the first to have them. After all, what is the point of coming second? No one remembers the losers.

So what does all this lead to? Well, the 'Hello Kitty' 2000 phenomenon, of course. This phenomenon was not a national struggle to acquire the rights for a two-party system but rather the Singaporean population's desire to purchase the ugliest set of cat dolls humankind has ever seen.

The sad fact is that the Hello Kitty nightmare started calmly enough. These Japanese midgets had already been on sale in various guises and costumes in Singapore for some time when a fast-food chain announced that it would sell pairs of the dolls wearing different costumes with value meals. But if Hello Kitty products were already available elsewhere, why was there such a massive demand? Ladies and gentlemen, please allow the marketing gurus to step forward and take a well-deserved bow. They ingeniously tapped into the Singaporean psyche – the kiasu 'whatever you have, I must have' syndrome. It was one of the most successfully orchestrated marketing campaigns of recent times.

How did the burger chain pull off this marketing miracle and turn usually sane Singaporeans into cold-blooded, green-eyed Hello Kitty hunters? Simple. It slapped 'limited edition' all over the little felines. Thus creating a wonderfully unique situation for the kiasu consumer. That is, the 'whatever I have, you might not be able to have, ha' syndrome. Now if that is not waving a red rag to a kiasu bull, then I do not know what is. And boy, did many Singaporeans see red.

When the first pair of Hello Kitty dolls went on sale, the country went ballistic and the dolls were sold out within hours. Knowing this, people began to queue the night before the next pair of dolls were due to go on sale. Can you believe it? These people were even shown on the news camping outside various fast-food eateries. I was stunned. Until then, the only society of people I had ever come across that loved queuing was the British. It is one of our national pastimes. My fellow countrymen spend half their lives queuing and they are exceedingly good at it. Try to cut in a queue at the post office in Dagenham and you will be thrown looks that suggest you have just committed murder.

In Singapore, where the lifestyle is so hectic, I was given the impression that its citizens barely have enough time to breathe, let alone the patience to stand and queue. Even in my local bank, there is no need to queue. They employ a wonderful system, whereby you simply take a ticket, sit down in a comfortable chair, read a book and wait for your ticket number to be called. Increasingly, Singapore is becoming a queue-free zone.

So you can imagine how shocked I was when I read about the hordes of people eagerly queuing overnight for a pair of dolls. Many teenagers probably saw camping out as an adventure. And if these youngsters had been the only people involved, I suspect the whole episode would have been a comparatively light-hearted affair. But they were not. The kiasu brigade came in and took over. There were those who queued up to buy more than ten pairs of the dolls, which led to a limit on the number of sets each customer could buy. Then there were those who hired students to queue for them, thus creating the first professional queuers ever employed to purchase a pair of cuddly toys. People were arrested and fined for disorderly behaviour. At Bukit Panjang, stools were thrown at police officers. Others had fights in front of women and children over alleged queue cutting. Consequently, Cisco, a private security firm, was hired to place guards at some of the bigger stores. Finally, several people were injured when a shop window in Bedok shattered under the pressure of too many impatient fuckers leaning on it.

In the end, the fast-food chain placed a full-page advertisement in the national newspapers apologising for the chaos. The burger chain also guaranteed that the last pair of dolls would not be limited and supplies would match demand, thus ensuring the end of both overnight queuing and the Hello Kitty phenomenon in general. Of course, if this strategy had been employed in the first place, none of the above would have happened.

Once the farce had subsided, people were quick to step forward to analyse the incident and try to understand and even justify it. Some claimed impressionable adults and teenagers had simply fallen for a cunning marketing ploy. Others came up with the silly idea that Singaporeans had a penchant for queuing. Believe me, that is a complete falsehood. In a country where its citizens cannot wait three seconds for commuters to alight from a train before getting on, the very idea of standing in a queue for over eight hours would be anathema. No, it all comes down to greed. Pure greed. When those damned cats were stamped 'limited edition', it created a stampede of would-be entrepreneurs. Within days, these characterless toys were being auctioned on local web sites and they were being sold for S$50 or more at flea markets.

One of my closest friends, Victor, admitted that he had queued up for eight hours in Toa Payoh. I almost forgave him when he said he took turns with his fiancée to queue because they were getting married in a few weeks and he wanted a pair of the wedding dolls for good luck. I was none too pleased when he told me that he had managed to sell the other pairs for S$50 a go. This just floored me. The dolls cost about S$10 a pair so he had made S$40 profit on each pair that he had sold after queuing for almost a full working day. The most infuriating part was that Victor knew what he was doing. He said, 'I wanted a set for the wedding. But when I saw how much people were paying for the dolls, I thought "why not?" Everybody was doing it. I saw people being paid to queue. What to do? We love to have something free or be the first to have something.' That is the trouble with greed, it clouds all logic.

However, kiasuism goes way beyond greed. Undoubtedly, it ties in with avarice in the sense that you must be the first to have something whether it is a stuffed cat, a cinema ticket, a lottery ticket or a condominium. Ultimately though, it is a phobia. A terrifying dread of not winning, of coming second and possibly even, and I am going to have to use a rude word here, failing. Singaporeans would rather step into a boxing ring with a pissed off auntie before admitting that they might not have fully succeeded at something. So from the earliest age, they strive to be as efficient and as competent as they possibly can in the area of academic study because that is pretty much all they do in childhood. But then it progresses and becomes all encompassing. Kiasuism spreads rapidly though the brain (and in severe cases down to the anus because that is what badly afflicted victims talk out of) and eats away at you like Parkinson's disease.

My first direct experience of the kiasu syndrome came from listening to Melissa, a former colleague, complaining at work one day. We were all sitting at a table eating lunch when she just launched herself into a frenzy. 'Ooh, I was fuming at the MRT station this morning. I was waiting to get on the train when someone brushed past me and got straight on. The worst part was that there was a mother with her baby in a buggy waiting to get on the train as well but this guy just didn't care. He brushed past her as well. So kiasu.'

After that, I found out what kiasuism meant and began to hunt it down. It can be spotted every day on any transportation system. In a nutshell, people do not wait for you to get off the train before they get on. It is as simple as that. You are invisible. To the kiasu mind, you do not exist; he or she must get on the train as soon as possible. If it means brushing past ten people to do so, so be it.

I have only reacted to it once. Scott and I were alighting from a train at City Hall on our way to watch an S-League football match, when suddenly, thwack! My left shoulder was hit so hard that I bumped into Scott. 'You little prick. Couldn't you see me, you dopey bastard?' And the doors closed. I was angry because it was a young Malay lad who had arrogantly strutted onto the train with his girlfriend the split-second the doors had opened. He was showing off. Scott took no notice, of course; he was too busy giggling. 'You nearly got knocked out by a kid,' he said. So I pushed him down the escalator.

There is simply nothing you can do to stop the impending stampede as the doors of an MRT train open. In my more ludicrous moments, I have tried to devise a human dam, i.e., me, to hold back the tide. However, let me state for the record – I am no Moses. If you gave me a plastic bucket and spade, I reckon I would have a better chance of parting the Red Sea than holding back kiasu commuters. Even if I stand on the markings on the platform floor that show you where you should stand to get on the train and avoid alighting passengers, I can only block one side of queuing passengers so kiasu commuters simply walk around me and cut in from the other side. Believe me, if there is a gap, they will find it.

Then there are the Singaporean bus services.

When I was a kid growing up in the late seventies, there used to be a comedy show on television called *On the Buses*. It was quite funny and well written but it gave me nightmares thanks to Jack the bus conductor. Jack was supposed to be the Juan de Marco of London's bus service and the terror of all female passengers. Yet he must have been the ugliest man on the planet. Painfully thin, he consisted of a cluster of bones all held in place by the belt of his grey skin-tight bus uniform. His long, narrow face suggested he had spent his formative years trapped in a vice. Nevertheless, the scriptwriters seemed oblivious to all of his physical failings and gave him the sort of lines usually reserved for Brad Pitt. In some ways, the fact that the leering, dirty old man (he was in his late forties even then) did not look like Clark Gable made it funnier. However, as a four-year-old boy, he horrified me. When my mother took me shopping, I was afraid of travelling on buses in case Jack the bus conductor pounced. I knew that he would say some of the same lines to my mother and she would laugh and run away and leave me. I did not lose my phobia until *On the Buses* was taken off the air. By then, Jack was nearing retirement and chasing girls was leaving him visibly breathless. And Viagra was still a pipe dream.

My fear of buses returned with a vengeance when I arrived in Singapore. Jack the elderly sex bomb was replaced by 'Skippy the 238 Man', the crazed, hyperactive driver of the number 238 feeder bus service that covers the housing estates of Toa Payoh Lorong 8. I hear that the Singapore Bus Services (SBS) have cloned him countless times to take care of the other feeder services throughout the island. Rumour has it that he was cloned from the DNA of Skippy the kangaroo and mixed with a dollop of kiasuism to produce his unique driving style.

He pulls into the bus stop and you innocently board with your farecard in your left hand and a bag of shopping in the other. Just as you lift your card to slot it into the machine, he pulls away sharply. Suddenly, the bag of shopping has a pull stronger than the tide and you find yourself lying horizontally along the aisle still holding your farecard. It is a nightmare.

No matter who drives the number 238 bus, the methods for getting from A to B are identical. 'Skippy' will pull away from the bus stop as fast as he can and, not forgetting his intensive kiasu training, leaves it until the last possible second before braking. On a regular bus journey, such a technique would be mildly irritating. However, it is positively infuriating on a feeder service where stops can be as little as 200 metres apart. Many passengers refuse to sit down because if they do, they know there is a better than average chance that they will end up sitting on the lap of the person in front.

This erratic driving boils down to kiasuism. In fact, bus travel itself could be a case study. From bus drivers trying to cover small distances at recklessly high speeds to passengers rushing onto the bus to take the seats positioned near the exit door, it is all an upshot of trying to get things done quicker and getting to destinations faster to improve efficiency. By the way, if a picture ever painted a thousand words, it has to be the sight of twenty people sitting on the outside-edge of twenty double seats. Why do people do that? It means that the next poor sod that gets on the bus has to ask someone to move so that he can sit on the other half of the seat. When this happens, the person sitting on the edge of the seat shoots him a look that suggests she would like to kick him between the legs. Then, she sighs emphatically and merely moves her legs to one side, meaning he now has to squeeze past her to sit by the window. In this situation, I have perfected a technique in which I drop a shoulder, swing my rucksack around and deliver a deft blow to the side of the old bat's temple. I have asked many friends why Singaporeans do this as it does not happen in England. Some have suggested that passengers panic that they might miss their stop if the bus gets packed. I find this a dubious theory because, as I am sure you have noticed, kiasu types press the stop button 15 hours before the bus approaches the bus stop. Others believe that travellers want to sit away from the window to avoid the Sun or that they just want the whole damn seat to themselves. I suspect that it is an amalgam of all these theories, with kiasuism lurking in the shadows.

Kiasuism has even led to a bus crashing less than thirty seconds after I had boarded it. Travelling to work one Sunday afternoon after doing some shopping, I got on the number 16 bus opposite Dhoby Ghaut MRT station. Quite typically for a Sunday afternoon, there was heavy traffic and the bus was behind at least four other buses in the bus lane. It was real bumper-to-bumper stuff. The kiasu driver was impatiently revving his engine and edging forward. Looking further down the bus lane, he anticipated that the bus in front would start moving. Only it did not. Nevertheless, the bus I was in did move and we merrily smacked into the back of the bus in front, smashing our windscreen and its rear window. The incident was pathetic really. I had only just collected my farecard from the machine and was walking down the aisle when it happened. Having just left my partner at the bus stop, I could see her through the window laughing hysterically. The passengers all reacted with considerable good humour. Although the woman opposite me was clutching a Bible to her chest, which I thought was a little premature.

Without doubt, kiasuism is everywhere. I have seen, or rather I have heard, people taking handphone calls while sitting on a public toilet, doing bench presses in a gym, attending a wedding ceremony in a church and even teaching secondary school students in a classroom. The strive to be first and the desire not to miss out on anything has become overwhelming.

And in what I believe to be one of the most ironic chains of events in modern Singaporean history, kiasuism was cultivated by the very institution that is now trying in vain to quell it – the government. With legitimate intentions, I think the government unleashed within its people an uncontrollable human vice: greed. Think about it. When Singapore was kicked out of Malaysia in 1965, who could it turn to for help? The British had already screwed up once during World War II when, out of a mixture of ignorance and arrogance, they most kindly stepped aside for the invading Japanese forces. The British returned briefly after the war to top up their fading sun tans and then promptly buggered off again, this time for good. In 1965, Malaysia told Lee Kuan Yew to do the same. So Singaporeans were left with a fledgling government and an unstable economy, which needed to supply everything. With Britain and Malaysia out of the equation, no one was going to give Singaporeans anything. They were going to have to help themselves.

With incredible foresight, Lee Kuan Yew made a speech shortly after Singapore's independence in 1965 in which he predicted the country's transformation into a metropolis. The amazing thing is that against all expectations the government and its people achieved their goal and Singaporeans became one of the most productive labour forces on the planet.

Undoubtedly, such rapid progress is going to get the average man on the street thinking. Even in his wildest dreams, he probably did not expect to achieve so much so soon. Having secured a decent three-roomed flat for his family and a reasonable level of education for his children, he is entitled to assume, therefore, that if he raises his productivity further, the flat could increase to five rooms and his kids might be able to attend university. Inevitably, Singaporeans across the island make similar assumptions and push themselves and their families even harder to improve themselves socially and economically. This is wonderful news for the government as it is a clear popular mandate for its policies. So, in turn, the government makes an effort to increase productivity and efficiency within its spheres of influence, such as the civil service, housing, the national airport, the country's shipping ports and the nation's transportation services. Productivity targets are constantly being set and exceeded in all these areas, bank balances rise and shop tills keep on ringing.

However, when such a socioeconomic phenomenon peaks, two human weaknesses inevitably arise: greed and fear. Unlike the old days of struggle and shared hardship, Singapore has evolved into an individualistic rat race: a materialistic society in which anything is attainable if you work harder than everyone else. Years of being told by parents, teachers and politicians that you must provide for yourself, because no one else will, has moulded the average Singaporean into a kiasu king and transformed my generation into a bunch of greedy bastards. For the sake of economic prosperity, it forsook communal spirit for individual avarice. For laudable political reasons, the government unleashed a social disease that has no cure.

And to satisfy greed, you must maintain efficiency and that is where fear comes in. All over the country, employees live in fear of failing to reach their targets. I saw a sign at Toa Payoh MRT station guaranteeing that 94 per cent of all train services would be on time. This is an astonishingly high figure that helps explain MRT kiasuism on so many different levels. In a way, those annoying passengers who push and shove their way onto the train before others get off have valid reasons for doing so. It is quite simply because that annoying woman on the recorded message is already announcing that the doors are closing three bloody seconds after the doors have opened. It is an insane race against the clock to get on board. I can recall at least two occasions during rush hour when I have travelled with a large group of colleagues and one of the others did not make it onto the train. Both times, we ended up waving goodbye to the one left behind on the platform in the same way that soldiers waved to their loved ones in the old war movies. Why is it such a mad rush? Simple. The guy up front driving the train is shitting his pants that his train may not fall within the 94 per cent band, which would then affect his bonus and put back his flat upgrading by a year. Just like Skippy the 238 Man knows he must complete his designated route within very stringent time limits.

That, for me, is kiasuism. We are all guilty of it. I push past people to get on the train or the bus because I want to get on the damn thing. In those situations, it is a case of kill or be killed. Nevertheless, I really hate myself for doing it. I should know better and so should the Singaporeans who do it. The idea of self-help and pushing oneself to the limit was necessary for the republic to grow during its infancy but it is no longer necessary. The recent currency crisis, if nothing else, should have taught the shallow that there is more to life than greed. Living standards can still be improved without the need to eliminate all competition or to be first all of the time. So if you should find yourself at the end of a long taxi queue one day, waiting behind families and women with bags of shopping, do not be a prick and push in. There really will be another taxi along shortly.

# *Chapter Seven*

My home is surrounded by lunatics. Oh, I do not mean the likes of Hannibal Lecter or my mother but merely the harmless weirdos who seem to frequent my apartment block from time to time, with the explicit intention of affording me as many laughs as possible. It seems these people were placed on Earth for people to laugh at them. It is their mission in life.

And I am delighted to state for the record that living in Housing & Development Board (HDB) apartments in Singapore does provide the observant individual with more than enough nutcases to provide a few giggles. The best part is that they tend to zoom in on the quaint or the unusual, so being Caucasian and extremely tall, I get the lion's share of all the lunatics on my estate.

The first one latched onto me as I got off the number 143 bus at Jalan Toa Payoh one evening. He grunted the strangest greeting. 'Hey, big boy,' he shouted.

Distant memories of Scott and I being drunk in a Leeds gay bar during our university days came flooding back. 'Big boy.' There it was again.

I turned to find a large Chinese man walking just behind me, carrying shopping bags and wearing a huge grin.

'Sorry?' I said.

'Wah, you big boy, ah? So strong. Jim?'

'Who's Jim?'

'No, lah. You go gym to keep fit, is it?'

'Oh, I see. Yeah, a few times a week.' This was a blatant lie. You only need look at me to realise this but I was starting to like the guy. Then came the surreal interrogation.

'Where you stay?'

'Here. Toa Payoh.'

'You on holiday?'

'No, I live here.'

'Which country?'

'Singapore!'

'No, lah. Which country you from?'

'Oh! England.'

'But you so big, you know. How come so big?'

'Er, I play some sports.'

'Oh! I've just bought some fish for dinner. You eat fish?'

'A little.'

'How tall are you? Two metres?'

'No, about 1.92 metres.'

He looked me up and down, unconvinced. 'No lah, you two metres. Which block you stay?'

'Erm, that one over there.' I pointed to the block that faces mine to avoid the possibility of him knocking on my door in the dead of night, holding a measuring tape and ready to prove me wrong.

'Oh, I stay in that block.' Shit, he nodded towards the block that I really do live in.

'So, is your family tall?'

'Quite tall.'

'Yeah, I think so. I'm cooking fish tonight. Where are you going now?'

'Oh, I'm just going over to the shop to buy some groceries and a big gun. Bye.'

I still see the old sod now and again and he always calls out 'big boy', which has caused more than a few startled stares in my general direction. We usually talk about general stuff like my height, the weather, my height, food and my height. Whenever I have caught up with him, he is always on his own and I suspect he lives alone. Nevertheless, the jovial chap never stops smiling and likes nothing more than a brief chat, which is more than can be said for 'Vidal Sassoon'.

I first came across Vidal in a lift one morning, about three months after I had moved in. Wearing an old, faded samfoo, Vidal was already in the lift when I got in on the fifth floor. She then proceeded to stare up at me non-stop all the way down to the ground floor. That is only five floors, I hear you cry. Well, ask the person next to you to stare into your face for the next five seconds. It becomes just a trifle disconcerting, doesn't it? Stepping out of the lift, Vidal turned to stare a little longer, almost blocking my path. I had to step around the old woman to get past her or I suspect we would still be there.

The weirdest thing about Vidal is that she is everywhere. Wearing the same worn-out clothes and dirty flip-flops, I have seen her sitting at the void deck in the HDB estate, shuffling past the local coffee shop, strolling through Toa Payoh Central and even lurking at the end of Balestier Road, which is some two kilometres away. On each occasion, she always finds time to stop and stare at me with that same weary, expressionless face. It is quite chilling.

All of that is nothing compared to the most shocking encounter that I have had with Vidal, an incident that terrified me to my very soul. One evening, I was reading the paper at the table in my living room when my girlfriend screamed. Looking up, I was greeted by the sight of Vidal's little head peering through the door grille and into my living room.

Like most Singaporeans, I often leave the front door open and keep the door grille locked to improve air circulation and reduce stuffiness. People do pass along the common corridor outside but they usually mind their own business. I certainly did not plan for the door grille to become an observation post for loopy old women.

Momentarily, my girlfriend and I sat in stunned silence, as you do when a seventy-year-old woman stares at you sitting in your own living room. Luckily, she had only caught me performing the innocent act of reading the newspaper. I have the socially inept habit of scratching things that itch and it could have become quite a testing situation if I had been caught red-handed.

The problem was that Vidal did not say anything. She just stared and I knew for a fact that she either did not understand English or, at least, had problems interpreting it. Whatever sentence I threw at her, her brain would probably translate it to mean 'Hello, auntie. Please could you gawp at me for a little while longer because I'm really enjoying it.'

After about twenty seconds of suffering intense staring, I could see my girlfriend looking at me, motioning that it was time for me to do something.

'Hello, auntie. Ni hao ma?' My pathetic attempt to win her over by asking how she was in Mandarin caused absolutely no reaction.

'Okay, auntie. I think that's enough peeping for one day. Off you go. Bye.' I tried to shoo her away with my hand but that only titillated her. She then started to smirk at my partner.

'For fuck's sake, Neil. Get rid of her, will you? She's grinning at me now,' my girlfriend complained.

'Auntie, time to go. No more looking, understand? Go away.' More staring and more smirking. 'Enough now. Please go. Bye.'

Left with the distinct possibility of her standing there all night, I got up, smiled at her and closed the door. Walking back to the table, I was struck by the horrifying thought of my partner leaving for work the next morning and being greeted by a short, smirking auntie. The shock would probably have killed them both. I went back to the door and looked through the peephole to see if she was still there but the old bat had moved on to her next haunt. She still passes along the corridor occasionally but she merely turns her head and looks in briefly, she does not actually stop now.

But here is the remarkable thing. Although Vidal is always wearing the same tatty samfoo and the same old battered flip-flops, she has the smartest hairstyle. I have spotted her on my way to work in the morning and again late at night when I am returning home and she always looks as though she has just stepped out of a salon. I have pointed her out to Singaporean friends and they agree that Vidal (now you know why I call her this) is a bizarre phenomenon who defies all logical explanation. After all, how do you explain a woman who wears the same clothes every day, has the brains of a rocking horse, yet wears her hair like Cameron Diaz?

Nevertheless, even Vidal pales in comparison to 'bra lady', who, would you believe, also lives in my apartment block. Bra lady makes Vidal look like a professor in nuclear physics. She is so insane that I am convinced the asylum lets her out on day release just to provide the local community with a little comic relief.

Like me, bra lady's major hobby is travel, which she vigorously pursues in her spare time. However, like most people, I like to explore new countries and cultures whereas she likes to explore lifts. To be more specific, she likes to explore and travel in the lifts in my block throughout the whole bloody day. I think she believes that she performs the unofficial, unpaid duties of a lift attendant on behalf of the HDB.

I vividly recall the first time I caught her in action. After pressing the button on the fifth floor, my partner and I watched the lift descend from the twelfth floor, stopping at every floor along the way before reaching ours. Mildly irritated at the delay, we got into the lift to find that the only other person in the lift was bra lady. Why did I christen her bra lady? Because she was performing her lift attendant duties while wearing her bra *over* her clothes. As women are more observant in these situations, my partner was the first to spot the large pink bra over bra lady's shirt. My partner then elbowed me in the rib cage to get my attention. Trying to prevent myself from roaring with laughter, I distracted myself by approaching the lift panel to press the ground floor button. But, silly me, I had no need to fear because bra lady had already kindly pressed the button. In fact, she had courteously pressed every button on the panel, yet she did not alight at any of the floors and no one else got in.

When we reached the ground floor, my girlfriend got out but I paused briefly to watch bra lady as she meticulously performed her professional duties of pressing every button on the panel from one to twelve. Staring straight ahead at all times and never once looking in our general direction, bra lady closed the doors of the lift and she began yet another ascent.

I am fortunate enough to encounter cuckoos like bra lady, Vidal Sassoon and big boy on a fairly regular basis because I live in an HDB apartment block in Singapore. These government-built concrete, rectangular blocks, so often criticised by ignorant Western visitors, house all kinds of weird and wonderful people. In fact, by 1998, the HDB had built 833,814 units, housing 2,702,000 people – a figure that accounts for 86 per cent of the country's population. I have lived in various HDB apartments for over four years now and I would not live anywhere else. Condominiums might provide swimming pools, saunas, barbecue pits and tennis courts, and I would be lying if I said I would not like having such facilities at the bottom of my block, but they lack a certain vibrancy that comes with living in HDB flats.

Just a few weeks ago, a bunch of lower secondary schoolboys were kicking a ball around the void deck of my block. Now this is against the law and signs are plastered all around the void decks clearly stating that all ball games are prohibited. After all, these and other young lads could chip the paint, dirty the walls and cause considerable noise pollution for the residents living above. So being an upstanding young fellow of the HDB community, what did I do? I asked to join in, of course. We all had a great laugh. Then I received two major shocks. First, I found out that one of the Chinese lads was, like me, a West Ham United supporter and had been all his life. In a country where kiasuism prevails, Singaporeans have a tendency to follow winners like Manchester United, Liverpool or Arsenal. Therefore, I had never met a Singaporean who supported my East London team. The boy then floored me again by giving me a golden West Ham United sticker badge as a gift. The sticker badge now sits proudly on the side of my computer monitor. And as I stare at it now, it reminds me of the warmth, friendliness and safety that comes with living in an HDB flat. These feelings could not be extended back to England.

In my second year at Manchester University, Elizabeth, one of the girls I was sharing a house with, brought a guy she had met at a bar back home with her. If she had walked through the door with a so-called HDB heartlander, I would have relaxed but the guy was a violent local, who, when informed by my ever-so-subtle housemate that she did not want to sleep with him after all, promptly went mental. He took half a crate of beer (he had drunk the other half) and smashed it around the living room. He then proceeded towards the front door where he was met by a half-asleep Reza, our other housemate. Now Reza, who is half-Indian, half-Polish and born and raised in Lancashire, has this unshakable habit of being in the wrong place at the wrong time. That night was no exception. Taking a nap, he was woken up by the slightly odd sound of beer cans being smashed outside his bedroom. Rousing himself, he opened his bedroom door to find a psychopath redecorating our hallway with beer. Equally shocked by the presence of a half-Polish, half-Indian man dressed in pyjamas, the lunatic head-butted Reza before smashing his way out of the house. We later heard that the Mancunian lunatic lived nearby. Such neighbourly behaviour puts Vidal Sassoon's peeping Tom exploits into perspective.

It also helps illustrate some of the differences between the housing environment that I left behind and the one that I am a part of today. Here, Singaporean children play football below my HDB block and I join in. When I was living in Dagenham, children amused themselves by lighting fires outside the doctor's surgery located opposite my mother's house. Neighbours, including my mother, would tell them to pack it in or they would call the police. They were usually told to 'fuck off'. Quite a contrast.

Since its inception in 1960, the Housing & Development Board has, without doubt, done a remarkable job of building not only houses for its people but also creating a clean and safe environment for its residents. In 2000, Singapore had a population of 4.1 million, creating a population density of 5,900 per square kilometre. In the United States, the population density is just 29 per sq. km. In my country, it is 238 per sq. km. So we are talking about a lot of Singaporeans living in a very small space.

After writing a thesis on municipal housing at university, I find the HDB's accomplishments astounding. More so when you consider the state of Singapore in 1960. Then, wooden houses built on stilts formed *kampungs*, or villages. Although these kampungs fostered a sense of community, similar to the London slums at the end of the nineteenth century, the homes themselves could be hazardous. In May 1961, for instance, a fire at Bukit Ho Swee left around 16,000 people homeless. Remarkably though, the HDB had managed to build flats for all these people by February 1962. By the 1970s, the HDB had pretty much solved the nation's housing problems. They may not look pretty but, like my old housing estate in Dagenham, HDB apartments put a modern roof over the heads of its people.

A modern house, however, does not necessarily make for a home. When I studied my own housing estate, I discovered that its newcomers often returned to their London slums because they missed being part of a close-knit community. The Singaporean government is faced with that same problem today.

Residents often lament the loss of the kampung collective spirit that died when their wooden homes were bulldozed. My friends are forever telling me stories about how they shared cups of sugar with neighbours and how all the children in the kampung played together, went to school together and ate together. Nowadays, people tend to care only about family members living under the same roof. The grille to their HDB unit is locked and they close themselves off from their neighbours. They will exchange pleasantries in the hallway but that is about as far as it goes. If you walk along the void deck of any HDB block, the sight of old-timers sitting and chatting will invariably confront you. They still share that kampung bond. With the younger, more affluent generations now living in self-contained units, this bond no longer exists. The nature of one's improved environment has allowed individualism to supersede collectivism.

Of course, it is a social phenomenon that is not unique to Singapore. Even after my housing estate was built in the 1920s, its inhabitants valiantly tried to reestablish their old East London cockney communities. Back garden fences were kept low and neighbours would often chat across them. I once saw my mother hold a three-way conversation with two neighbours, each of whom lived five houses down from my mother's in opposite directions.

Moreover, our low back fence allowed my mother to show off her gymnastic abilities. Early one morning, she was hanging out some washing when she saw Charlie, our next-door neighbour, lying face down on the path in his back garden. Charlie was a lovely old man who dressed immaculately and never complained, even though I must have climbed over his fence more times than a cat burglar to retrieve my football.

On that terrible day, my mother sprang into action. She claims that she threw the washing down, hitched up her skirt and, with no concern for her own safety, jumped straight over the fence and went to Charlie's aid. After examining him, she pronounced him dead at the scene.

Charlie's death illustrates the sad social phenomenon that plagues England and, increasingly, Singapore. Had he died today, my mother would not have noticed. Our back garden now has a two-metre-high fence running all the way round it, as do most of the other houses in my street. Man has always been entitled to his castle but now he wants to build a moat around it.

Singapore is faced with the same problem. In 1964, the HDB launched the Home Ownership Scheme and thousands of Singaporeans bought their apartment units at affordable prices. Today, a staggeringly high 92 per cent of all public flats on the island are owner-occupied. Of course, the logic behind home ownership is politically sound. A resident will look after his home if it is his. However, when he closes the door to the outside world, he immediately severs those kampung bonds. The *Straits Times* often runs stories of elderly HDB residents lying dead at home for several days. In a non-welfare society that already encourages self-help in the workplace, such individualism cannot be helpful in the long run and the government knows this. Thus, it has employed various strategies, such as the ongoing upgrading programmes, to reignite that sense of togetherness within the HDB estates. These upgrading programmes aim to give older HDB estates, like Toa Payoh, a well-deserved face lift with an added room here and a lick of paint there.

My apartment block was recently upgraded and it proved to be an awful experience. Apart from being woken by the joyous sounds of pneumatic drills and sledge hammers every morning, I also enjoyed the added luxury of having the entire rat population of Toa Payoh pack its suitcases and move to the bottom of my block. I felt like I was sharing the apartment with the Stuart Little family. I would come home every night, look down at the building site below and play 'spot the rat'. My record, and I am not joking, was eleven. The average person would probably shrug off such a statistic but I happen to have a terrifying phobia of all things rodent. On many a dark night, Toa Payoh residents have been greeted by the sight of a blurred Caucasian sprinting past them screaming, 'It's a fucking *big* rat!' The building site is now a beautiful garden and the rodents have all moved off to the upgrading project across the road.

More seriously, the programmes have also made architectural attempts to bring the residents together again. Apartment blocks are now linked by sheltered walkways, more communal areas with tables and chairs have been built on the void decks and in the gardens while playgrounds have been built in the hope that more children and their parents will come together. Will these improvements work in the long run? Probably not. It is still largely the elderly who sit and chat on the void decks, although more kids play together in the playgrounds, which is encouraging news. The younger generations are, of course, at work chasing the dollar so the communal areas remain, by and large, deserted.

Apart from the upgrading programmes, in Toa Payoh alone there is a small public park, a modern library next to a new public amphitheatre, a swimming complex, a cinema and coffee shops all over the place. In fact, in every corner of Toa Payoh, there are discernible attempts by the local town council to bring its people together. Yet the town centre remains a brain-numbing blur of people scurrying to the bank, the post office or the supermarket before rushing back to their apartments.

Ironically, the only thing that does seem to bring HDB neighbours together is a good old-fashioned crime. As soon as a police siren is heard screaming outside your block, doors and front grilles are opened and before you can say '*kaypoh*', the corridor is brimming with eagle-eyed neighbours.

About a month after we moved into our flat, my girlfriend and I heard the sound of screeching brakes and shouting voices below so we went out to look. By the time I had opened the front grille, about twenty residents were already standing outside gossiping among themselves. Within five minutes, we had met and chatted with more of our neighbours than we had in the whole of the first month. I was convinced that they all had access to a police radio because they knew everything. They explained that a woman had stabbed her husband in an argument, then run out of the house and was now walking the streets, dazed and wielding a bloodstained knife. This all sounded a little melodramatic to me but who was I to argue with the people in the know? The incident lasted about an hour and by the end of it, we had given some clothes to one neighbour for her niece and a woman at the end of the corridor wondered if we had ever considered Buddhism.

The whole episode would not have happened in England. Fear would have kept everybody's doors firmly closed. I remember a police van pulling up outside my friend's house one night. Without pulling back the curtains, we peered through a tiny crack to see what was going on. Four policemen got out of the van and, after some running and lots of swearing, they arrested two brothers. The interesting thing to note is that not a single soul came out to witness what was quite a unique event. No one wanted to get involved for fear of recrimination. After all, what if the two brothers spotted you? They would assume that you had grassed them up to the police.

When I recall these incidents, I really do appreciate Singapore, its people and the benefits of living in an HDB block. In terms of architectural stature, the apartments may not be up there with New

York's Chrysler Building and, in an ideal world, I would prefer Singaporean children to have a garden to play in. However, when you have a population density of 5,900 per sq. km, what else can you do? The HDB makes the best of a difficult situation, even if it does weaken that wonderful kampung spirit.

And I am proud to live in Toa Payoh, Singapore's second satellite town, complete with educational, vocational and recreational facilities. To me, it is the Dagenham of Singapore and I have a strong attachment to both the place and its people. I love playing football with the young lads at the bottom of my block. It may be technically illegal but sod it. Build more football pitches and sports fields for the children and fewer condominiums and golf courses and we will stop playing on the void decks. I have fun watching the old-timers gamble, sorry, I mean play Chinese checkers on the void decks. I like feeding the turtles at Toa Payoh Park and eating homemade chicken and mushroom pies in the town centre on Sunday mornings. I could go on forever but I think you get the general idea. Besides I must dash – Vidal Sassoon is at the door.

# *Chapter Eight*

Every now and again, we find ourselves privy to some magnificent spectacle or event that serves to reaffirm our humble place in the great state of nature. It could be any kind of incident, such as an earthquake, a hurricane or even the ever-growing hole in the ozone layer, that reminds us that there is something bigger and greater than humankind at work. For me, there have been two spiritual awakenings in my life that have confirmed this.

The first came at the Singapore Zoological Gardens, where I was lucky enough to witness two giant tortoises mate. It took a whole five minutes for the male to muster the energy to climb on top of the female. Once there, let's just say, I hope for the female's sake the boat was of sufficient size because there was absolutely no motion in the ocean. If the subdued mating couple had died during intercourse, no one would have noticed. Nonetheless, they saw it through as do all tortoises around the world at some point. It then struck me how powerful nature is. Here is an animal that walks like it is treading water, carries its HDB flat on its back and makes love to a soldier's helmet, yet nature compels it to get the job done.

Thinking nature could not possibly astound me again, it presented me with the Grand Canyon one fine Summer morning.

Standing on the edge and peering down at Nature's craftsmanship, I realised conclusively that humankind would never be able to compete on equal terms. Nature constructed the Grand Canyon – I cannot even build things with Lego bricks. Without a doubt, I have never seen any landmark that surpassed the Canyon in its magnitude. It does nothing but impress you.

Unless, of course, you are one of the Singaporeans with whom my partner and I went on an American tour. They actually gave the impression that the whole Grand Canyon sightseeing trip was just one giant bore. They complained about the length of the journey from our hotel in Las Vegas to the Canyon. It appeared that due to their insular narrow-mindedness, they had assumed that the United States was like Singapore, where it is a case of turn left and there is Orchard Road or turn right and there is Raffles Place. They could not understand why the same geographical principles did not apply in the United States. You know, turn left and look, there is Disneyland or turn right and there is the Las Vegas strip.

As we were being thrown around the bus, I heard one guy say to our tour guide, 'Edward, how long will this take? I want to get back to the casino.'

My girlfriend and I looked at each other in disbelief. We had not even arrived at probably one of the most visually-arresting sites on the planet and one of our travelling companions was already saying that he wanted to go back to the casino.

I was convinced that once all the chattering Singaporeans stepped off the bus, the sheer magnitude of the Canyon would shut them up and the silent chasm would swallow any insipid kiasu comments. I was only half-right. The kids on the tour were mesmerised for about the first five minutes, which was to be expected. After a few genuine wide-eyed 'wows', there is only so much a primary school child can do with a view. Then I heard it. The gambling man, who inexplicably wore a blue mackintosh raincoat throughout the tour, even in Nevada, rushed over to his wife and said, 'Quick! Finish taking your photos and I'll ask Edward if we can go back to Las Vegas now.'

It had taken us three hours to get to the Canyon and this guy wanted to leave after fifteen minutes. As there was a general consensus from the rest of the group that they had seen enough, we left. Ever since I had seen the breathtaking, post-apocalyptic *Planet of the Apes*, I knew I would visit the Grand Canyon. And I did, for fifteen minutes.

Looking back, I should have known what kind of holiday it was going to be.

When I booked the West Coast package tour, the agent said, 'You do know that it is a Singaporean tour, don't you?'

Puzzled, I replied, 'You mean to say this isn't the Mongolian tour? Because I was told that it wouldn't be a problem getting two seats with the Mongolian tour.'

He stared at me blankly before reminding me that there was an orientation meeting on Friday.

When we arrived for the orientation fashionably late, my fears that this was not going to be an ordinary holiday were realised. As we entered the room, the guide stopped speaking and the whole tour party turned to stare at us. Had the late John F. Kennedy himself walked in, I do not think they could have conjured a more shocked reaction.

Breaking the deafening silence, the guide asked, 'Can we help you?'

'We've come for the meeting about the U.S. trip,' I replied.

'Are you with this group? Do you have your receipts with you?' After I showed the guide our receipts, he stopped asking questions and introduced himself as Edward. Then it dawned on me. We stood out like the white ball on a snooker table. Not only were we the only Caucasians in a group of about twenty-five but we were also the only non-Chinese. At the time, I put it down to coincidence and thought no more about it. That was a bad move.

Edward went through the basics, discussing things like departure times, the time differences and changing currency. I have to confess that I found the talk informative and I found myself asking one or two questions. I hoped they were rational and sensible because many of the other questions were not. The first came from one woman who seemed to be on a mission in life to redefine the word 'stupid'.

She was a rather petite lady, whom the late Barbara Cartland would have probably called buxom. She had a round face that she chose to accentuate by wearing too much rouge on her cheeks. From a distance, she looked like a strawberry. No, that is not true. She looked like a strawberry in tacky sunglasses. She wore those awful black ones that have gold sovereigns embedded along each of the arms. To the average person, these sunglasses say 'Here is a moron who wants you to know she's paid a lot of money for a pair of sunglasses that look about as attractive as the cheap ones in a night market.' However, to lamebrains like our 'strawberry' friend, these glasses represent the height of good taste. Consequently, she wore them everywhere. In the hotel lobby, on the shaded coach and even on the Terminator 3-D attraction in Universal Studios, which was pitch black! In fact, I think it was the combination of her silly sunglasses, her designer handbag with the awful gold chain handle and her round, red face that made a few American teenagers laugh at her. In these situations, I would have pitied 'strawberry' until she reminded me what a kiasu bitch she really was.

The first time she obliged was in the orientation meeting. Edward was explaining about our accommodation in each of the cities we were visiting when she piped up. 'Edward, why aren't we staying in five-star hotels all the way?'

The room fell quiet. The whole package with flights, hotels, transfers, theme parks and some meals was just over S$2,000. Return flights to the West Coast on Singapore Airlines (our airline for the tour) during peak season usually cost around S$1,400. Therefore, you do not need a calculator to work out that poor old Edward, who took care of hotel bookings, transfers and so forth, had to make S$600 go a very long way. He explained, rather patiently, that all the hotels had three stars and the Holiday Inn in San Francisco had four stars. As far as I am concerned, all the hotels were more than sufficient. But once strawberry had set the ball rolling, all the stupid questions came gushing forth as Edward struggled to hold back the kiasu tide. Blue mac, the gambling man, asked if we could extend our stay in Las Vegas. No, we could not because we were on a tight schedule came the courteous reply. No, we could not because this was a family tour so the selfish arsehole would have to play blackjack with himself would have been my reply.

However, if one topic dominated the tour, it would have to be food. From the orientation through Los Angeles, Las Vegas, Arizona and even San Francisco, the subject of cuisine was never far from my travelling gang's lips. It came up on our first night in Anaheim, Los Angeles. We went to what must have been the cheapest looking Chinese restaurant in Los Angeles. The food was tasty and plentiful, though it did seem somewhat surreal eating Chinese food on my first night in the United States. I felt, at the very least, that we should have been eating ribs or hot dogs and a big slab of mom's homemade blueberry pie. It seemed my companions did not agree.

We began chatting with a young couple who were on their honeymoon. They were pleasant company and we ended up spending a bit of time with them. Yet the guy said the strangest thing. I asked him what he thought of America so far, a crazy question I will readily admit because we had only been in the place for about four hours and they had all been spent in Anaheim, so they hardly counted. And he replied, 'I preferred Europe. It's got all the history, great buildings and everywhere is different.' He paused and then added, 'The food was better there, too.'

Now this startled me a little as he had only had one meal and that was Chinese so he had nothing to compare the European cuisines with. Somewhat stumped, I asked, 'Do you mean all the different Italian and French dishes?' Notice I did not mention English food. I did not want to destroy my credibility after one conversation.

'No, I mean the Chinese food was better.'

'The Chinese food? Where?' I asked incredulously.

'Well, all over really. But I remember a great restaurant in Italy.' And his wife nodded in agreement.

It was the first time that I had ever seen two Singaporeans fall into self-parody so easily. Italy is famous throughout the world for its spaghetti bolognaise, lasagne, cannelloni and its 101 different varieties of pizza. I do not profess to be a food expert. Having grown up on my mother's cooking I cannot be but even I wanted to laugh at this guy. I mean, he was excited about a place that was over 10,000 km away because it had restaurants that served the kind of dishes he could get at any hawker centre in Singapore for S$3.

Once we had broached the subject of food, the floodgates opened. Everyone on our table suddenly perked up, even strawberry, who, up until this point, had been stuffing her face with spoonfuls of sweet and sour pork. Her husband began to talk to the newlyweds about the best Chinese restaurants in Singapore. Eager to bring us into the conversation, he asked my partner and me if we had eaten Chinese food before. So I said, 'Funnily enough, no. Despite their exorbitant prices, we've eaten hamburgers every fucking day for the last three years. Hence the greasy skin, the huge waistline and my partner's habit of mooing when she's around grass. Quite honestly, we wouldn't be able to tell a stick of satay from a chopstick. Both of which I intend to insert up your rectum once I've managed to dislodge them from your wife's prodigious mouth.'

Indeed, this question always floors me. Not because people ask if I have had Chinese food before but because they do not ask me if I have had Chinese food in Singapore before? They cannot possibly assume that in twenty-odd years I have never eaten a Chinese meal in England. Singaporeans must know that London is generously sprinkled with hundreds of Chinese food outlets. Those who have visited England have probably dined at most of them as part of their effort to eat their way around all the Chinese restaurants in the world. It is sad really.

However, it is not as sad as how I felt on my first night in the United States after having listened to my companions discuss where to get the best *chendol* on a tiny island that was on the other side of the globe. This was America. We should have been talking about where we were going over the next few days and what were the best rides for the kids in Knott's Berry Farm Theme Park. Would there be time to stop in Beverly Hills to buy strawberry a more subtle pair of sunglasses? You know, holiday-type stuff.

Towards the end of the trip, as we made our way from Las Vegas to San Francisco, food reared its ugly head once again. Edward was describing our next hotel, the Holiday Inn, when strawberry decided to take a stand. 'Edward, no more Western-style breakfasts, eh?'

'No, it's okay,' Edward replied. 'I've managed to secure porridge for everybody. It will be brought to your room at 7 a.m. sharp.'

'Good, I can't take any more of that Western shit.'

And that was it. I refused to speak to the ignorant bitch for the rest of the holiday. It was only my sensible partner who prevented me from calling everybody on the bus a bunch of wankers. I mean, that comment really was a bridge too far. The selfish *tai tai* was so immeasurably stupid that she could not see that she might have seriously offended two Westerners sitting opposite her. Just humour me for a few seconds if you will. Imagine you are sitting at home with friends enjoying a meal. I walk in, point to your food and say, 'I can't take any more of your Asian shit.' Would you react? We are only human after all. And remember, it is not as if strawberry was in an Asian country. She was in a country where you cannot assume that Chinese porridge will be on the menu every morning, even though it had been for most of the tour thanks to Edward's efforts.

I had always believed that the whole point of travelling was to do the 'When in Rome' bit. With regard to the Singaporeans I went to the United States with, it was a case of 'When in Rome, do as the Singaporeans do'. The Singaporean deputy prime minister Lee Hsien Loong recently said, quite seriously, that Singaporeans can always be spotted overseas. I could not agree more with the chap.

Anyway, I was still seething over the 'Western shit' comment and the compulsory Chinese porridge so I had a quiet word with our beleaguered tour guide. 'Edward, I've got to say something about this porridge arrangement.'

'What's the problem?'

'Well, although I really like Chinese food proved by the fact that I've eaten nothing else all week, I don't really like porridge.'

'That could be a bit tricky, Neil.'

I could feel my anger rising. 'How can it be tricky, Edward? This is America, not Singapore or China or even Asia. All I want to do is to eat the food of the country I am visiting.' I was getting a little sarcastic, which I later regretted, but Edward was sympathetic and when he was one-on-one he was brutally honest, something I respected.

He said, 'Look, people want to eat Chinese food on these tours, which is good for them and good for me because it's cheap. I've been here many times and I know some great places to eat both Chinese and Western food but my guests are happy with Chinese food. Besides, we don't get ang mohs on the trip.'

This last part surprised me. 'Why not?'

'This is a Chinese tour.'

'It's a what?'

'A Chinese tour. We specialise in Chinese tours.'

That explained why there were no Malays or Indians on the trip. But I was still puzzled. 'But you advertised in the *Straits Times*. It's an English newspaper. There was nothing to say Chinese only. What if a Malay family came into the shop? Would you turn them away?'

'No, of course not. But they tend to have their own operators and the Chinese usually come with us. That's why I was surprised to see you at the orientation. But I'll try to organise a different breakfast for you.'

To be fair to the man, he did. He gave us the dollar equivalent in cash. So we slept in, had an early lunch at the famous Pier 39 and watched the sea lions sunbathe in the Bay before visiting the infamous Alcatraz prison. I was hoping to leave strawberry there but she did not go. Her family went with the rest of the tour group to San Francisco's famous Chinatown for, and I am not making this up, a meal at one of its fancy restaurants. It was such a shame because I knew that all the young lads on the trip really wanted to go to Alcatraz. When we met up with them later, they bombarded us with questions about 'The Rock' and all its famous inhabitants. I mean, if you were a fifteen-year-old Singaporean and you had a choice of windowshopping in Chinatown or seeing where Al Capone was incarcerated, which attraction would you choose?

I sympathised with the young lads because I have been in exactly the same predicament. When I was seventeen, my father took my sister and me to the Spanish island of Tenerife, which is the British equivalent of Bintan. It is cheap, sunny, full of beaches, and foreigners have overrun the place. Being young and inquisitive, I wanted to explore the island. Despite the fact that mass tourism has transformed the place into a tacky resort, Tenerife is dominated by a natural wonder – the volcanic mountain, Pico de Teide. Moreover, Franco met his officers on the island in 1936 to plan the nationalist rebellion that sparked the Spanish Civil War, so the island had some history. Did I get to explore any of this? Of course not. For two weeks, I spent my days by the swimming pool, doing my bit to help turn us all into the prune family, and I spent my nights in the bar, tediously watching my father work his way towards liver failure. In short, my father transported his England of beer, burgers and football and replanted it temporarily in Tenerife.

By the end of the holiday, he knew no more about Tenerife than he did when he first arrived on the island but he had swallowed a hell of a lot of beer. Similarly, the Singaporeans with whom I went to America consumed a great deal of Chinese food. In both cases, the bored children had no choice but to sit and watch.

The person in the middle of all this was poor old Edward, the tour guide. At the start of the trip, he looked immaculate. By the time we had reached San Francisco almost two weeks later, it was becoming increasingly difficult to distinguish him from the homeless guys dotted all over California.

Undoubtedly, the stresses of the job made the chap a character. Always fearful of losing one of the party, which I am sure must be any tour guide's nightmare, Edward always made sure he was easily identifiable. Apart from wearing bright pink shirts, he spent his time in the land of the free imitating the Statue of Liberty. No matter where I went, if I looked up at any given time of the day, I would invariably spot a pink Edward twenty metres in front, holding a map in his raised right arm. He always held a map and we always seemed to be chasing after him.

When we went to Universal Studios, we had from 9 a.m. to 4 p.m. to look around. Even though it was one of the busiest months of the year, we saw absolutely everything. From the Back to the Future ride to the studio tour, he somehow managed to squeeze it all in. At times, the group actually ran from one attraction to another. Just picture it. Twenty-five Chinese and two Caucasians all sprinting after a pink Chinese Statue of Liberty. I was pleased to go on the Jurassic Park water ride just to rest for three minutes. But like I say, by 4 p.m., we had seen and done everything. So I have to admit that kiasuism can really come in handy sometimes, especially if you are in an American theme park.

Sometimes, however, it does not. For months, my girlfriend had been driving me mad about Disneyland. Ever since she had watched *Mary Poppins* as a small girl, she has believed in flying umbrellas, talking penguins and nannies who break into song every time their charges misbehave. Consequently, I was fully prepared for the fact that she was going to be insufferable for the entire day. However, spending 12 hours with her inside the Magic Kingdom was nothing compared to spending just over 12 minutes with the kiasu gang outside its entrance. Poor Edward was bombarded with trivial questions.

Strawberry asked, 'Will my children be safe here?'

'No! The "double M" mouse family owns the place and runs a protection racket.'

'Will you be waiting for us when the theme park closes?'

'No, I've left you in the capable hands of a local triad gang.'

'Do we have to stay here all day?'

'No, blue mac, you can leave whenever you want but there are no casinos nearby so you'll just have to play with the traffic.'

Many other pointless questions were asked but the Pulitzer Prize went, rather surprisingly, to strawberry's husband. He said, 'Look at the long queues. Can't you do anything about the queues, Edward? We are part of a large tour.'

This insane request was then followed by a chorus of 'wah, so many people', 'must queue so long' and 'how to get on all the rides in one day?'

Edward promptly lost it. When we reached the counter, he steamed into the young American girl. He complained about having to wait in a long queue even though we already had tickets as we were a group party. Before the poor girl had a chance to respond, irate members of my tour suddenly surrounded the counter, all of whom were bitching to Edward or to the girl or scrambling for free maps. Naturally, blue mac was at the front rudely informing the girl that the theme park should implement a more efficient queuing system. His smugness suggested genuine self-satisfaction for 'educating' this girl, as he had probably done countless times to the waitress at his local country club. But this was America and the delightfully filthy look from the girl suggested that the prick could go fuck himself.

Meanwhile, the other Singaporeans in the group were greedily grabbing extra maps from the counter even though they had all been given a map with their ticket. The girl behind the counter had had enough. 'Look, can you just take one map each, please?' she said irritably but with remarkable self-restraint.

Edward came back to the counter and surpassed himself. 'I need some more maps. Some of my group say they don't have a map.'

'Yes they do, sir. I gave a map to each and every one of them.'

'Well, I need some more,' retorted Edward. I could hear people behind muttering disapprovingly.

'But I gave a map to everyone along with their ticket.'

'I need some more.'

'Oh, for Christ's sake. Take these.' She virtually threw three maps at Edward.

'That's not enough,' he said and then he leant over the counter, grabbed a handful and walked off.

'What are you doing?' the girl shouted but it was too late. Edward was already dishing them out.

When we caught up with the others, they were still bitching about the 'so rude' girl at the counter. Meanwhile, blue mac was telling Edward, who must have been to Disneyland at least twenty times, the best route around the theme park. I had already told Edward that we were more than happy to spend a long day completely lost in the Magic Kingdom so we went off to find the Indiana Jones ride.

As our monumental vacation reached its last leg in San Francisco, I was really pining for Singapore. I missed its safety. Having lived in Singapore for a couple of years now, even I had begun to take its security for granted. So there is nothing like a little bit of Californian poverty to bring you back to your senses. In Chinatown in Los Angeles, I saw an elderly black woman urinating in the street in the middle of the day. Obviously homeless, her clothes were ripped and torn and the poor woman was filthy. Being less than five metres away, we could see everything and she could see us. To calm my startled partner, I tried to revert to the old streetwise Neil of Dagenham, telling her that it was no big deal and that there was poverty in all the major cities of the world. I knew I sounded false and she knew it too. I had been conditioned by Singaporean safety and my words had a hollow ring to them. I was repulsed by the terrible hardship and I did not want to be there either.

Similarly in San Francisco, there were homeless people everywhere and it was tragic. They would beg openly for money and some even pursued us down the street. I hated myself for staying at a four-star hotel while these people slept on benches less than fifty metres away. I felt so ashamed for deliberately avoiding encounters with people who had a social background not a million miles away from mine. In fact, I probably had more in common with these people than I did with many of the group I was travelling with.

This was the other reason why I was homesick for Singapore. I was fed up with the Singaporeans with whom I was travelling. The whole rigmarole of taking photographs was driving me crazy by the time we had reached San Francisco. I seriously wondered if the whole point of them coming on this trip was to take as many photos as possible to prove that they had been there. I can think of no other rationale for my tour party's behaviour.

When Edward took us to a hilly peak that spoilt us with panoramic views of the San Fransisco Bay, it was unquestionably cold. However, I had a quick look around as I thought that I may never go back there, whereas my companions dashed off the heated coach simultaneously, clicked their cameras and then dived back on the bus again. It then occurred to me that they had performed the same ritual throughout the entire tour. At the Hollywood Bowl, where strawberry had famously wondered out loud why a lift had not been installed, the same thing happened. I wanted to explore it because the Beatles had recorded a live concert there but once the cameras had whirred, we hit the road. At the Grand Canyon, everybody posed and then asked to leave because it was too hot. In San Francisco, it was too cold. In fact, throughout the tour, the group always wanted to be somewhere else as soon as they had taken their photos.

That grievance, however, was nothing compared to the disgraceful homophobia that we experienced. I will admit that I was eager to visit the gay village of San Francisco to see how liberal it really was. Indeed, it was but it was also an absolute slum, which was depressing. What I did not expect, however, was for my companions to treat the village like a freak show.

As the coach drove through the streets of the village, they asked the driver to slow down so that they could get a better look. Some of the comments from so-called intelligent Singaporeans left me dumbfounded. At first, I wanted to scream at them, then I wanted to cry. By the end, I just felt numb. It remains the worst experience I have ever had with Singaporeans. The children were falling over themselves to get a better look at the 'freaks' while their parents whispered to them that such behaviour was wrong and evil.

I recall one particular boy who said, 'They're holding hands. Ugh, those men are holding hands, mum. It's horrible.' Then all the insane comments came gushing forth.

'It's sick, isn't it? They shouldn't be allowed to do it.'

'Slow down, slow down. That one's wearing make-up.'

'It's not right. It's disgusting. You're not allowed to be like that, okay? It's evil.'

'Why do they do it?'

'Because they're not well. Some can be cured but others can't.'

These comments gave me a knotted feeling in my stomach. I grew up in a very racist, sexist, homophobic environment, as many working-class children do in England, and I wanted to leave that world behind. Of course, I have gay friends in Singapore and I understand the problems they suffer but I had never directly encountered such large-scale Singaporean homophobia before. I am not saying that it does not exist in Britain because it does. However, homosexuality is not considered evil and the country accepts that gays exist. Singaporeans will not and I know that my travelling companions, both young and old, never will. I realised then; it was time to go home.

# *Chapter Nine*

There is nothing like a funeral to really ruin your day. Or to be precise, one tragic funeral that I had to cover as a reporter. A former national footballer had died and I was sent to the family home to interview the relatives. They say it comes with the territory but if I never have to interview grieving relatives again, I will be a happy man. After speaking to the family, I racked my brain in an attempt to conjure the words needed to write an obituary for a man I had never met. As I stood by the roadside, waiting for a taxi, it started to rain and I had no umbrella. What a day this was turning out to be.

I was then blessed with what probably has to go down as the greatest conversation of my life. Finally stepping into a taxi, I was initially startled when the middle-aged Chinese driver turned a full 180 degrees to say hello to me. This has never happened before. At best, the cab driver may nod through his rear-view mirror but usually he just stares straight ahead and says, 'Where you wanna go?' So there is nothing like a set of pearly whites beaming at you to make you want to slip back out of the taxi. Before I had even had the chance to contemplate such a drastic course of action, he spotted my notepad and away he went.

'Ah, you're a writer, is it?'

'Yeah, kind of. I'm a reporter.' I saw his eyes widen in the rear-view mirror and he sat up straight. 'What you write about?'

'Sports, but mainly soccer.'

'Ah, Fandi Ahmad?' he enquired brightly.

Fandi is Singapore's favourite footballing son, a fabulous striker who played for several European clubs. He is now the coach of the Singapore Armed Forces.

'Yeah, I sometimes have to speak to Fandi when his team plays,' I replied but the driver did not seem too interested in this. His fidgety body language suggested he was itching to get something off his chest.

'Listen, I have a story. But no name, eh? Like you say, off the record, okay?'

'Sure, Mr Ong, no problem.' I replied teasingly.

'Hey, how you know my name?' he cried out in despair.

'It's written on the name tag next to your picture, Mr Ong.' He began to look seriously distressed so I stopped teasing him.

'They'll know it's me if you say my name.'

'Who will know it's you?'

'The PAP.'

Now this was getting interesting. The taxi driver was referring, of course, to the People's Action Party, the ruling party of the Singaporean government. Generally speaking, the local men that I have interviewed here are more willing to talk publicly about their penis girth than they are about the negative aspects of the PAP. This guy clearly had something interesting to say. Unfortunately, he was insane.

Staring at me intensely as if he were Travis Bickle, Robert De Niro's character in *Taxi Driver*, he lowered his voice. 'If you get sick, don't go to government hospitals because they'll kill you.'

'What?'

'Never mind what illness you have, if you go government hospital, you will not come out alive.'

'Why?'

'I have a friend who is a doctor. I cannot tell you his name but he told me this so I know it's true. If you are healthy and go to hospital with a little illness, they will cut your organs in a private room and you will die.'

'But why?'

'The government sells the organs to rich people all over Asia.'

'But why?'

'For big money. How you think all big politicians have those large houses and rich cars.'

'Because they're big politicians?'

'No lah, because they make money from selling organs.'

'But Mr Ong...'

'No, no, no! You cannot say my name, okay? Hey! Why you writing? You cannot write, don't write my name down. I only tell you because maybe you can let public know. But you cannot say my name.' This guy was certifiable.

'I'm just writing down the facts for my own benefit. I'm not writing down your name. Believe me, I'll be telling your story to everybody for years. But tell me, how is it kept such a secret from the nation, but you know all about it?' I asked.

'I told you, I've got doctor friend who told me the story. He said that the government doctors who know about it cannot talk or sure get fired. And they earn big money too from the government for this.'

'They must do. What do they do with the organs?'

'They keep them in a freezer until someone buys them.'

I felt a vein near my brain explode with laughter. This was something else. I imagined a secret supermarket in the basement of Singapore General Hospital (SGH) called 'Fair-priced Organs' or 'Lungs R Us' – a place where wealthy big shots silently pushed a shopping trolley along aisles of open freezers that stocked everything from blood pumping hearts to two-for-one kidneys and the cashiers were all prominent politicians doing a spot of moonlighting. My mind wandered all over the place and it was marvellous. A quick change of traffic lights and screeching brakes brought me back to the real world of writing obituaries about dead sportsmen and I sadly realised my unforgettable journey was almost over. Nonetheless, I still had time to stoke the fire one last time.

'Hey! I went to SGH to have my tonsils removed. They gave me a general anaesthetic but when I woke up, all my organs were still there.'

'Ah, you were lucky. They don't really do it to the ang mohs. They prefer to use local parts.'

I was about to say that I was a human being and not a Volkswagen but he was off again.

'Also, easier to use locals, less problems. Easier to cover up. If they use ang mohs, your families and your countries will make checks, what.'

'Well, that's a relief,' I said. 'I want to keep my organs.'

He smiled at me through the rear-view mirror and we pulled over to the kerb.

As I got out, he said, 'Remember always use private hospitals, okay? Are you going to write the story?'

'But of course. It will be on page one on Sunday. It will be above the "Hitler is a trishaw driver" piece and next to the "Elvis was a Singaporean sailor" story. Rest assured, if I am feeling depressed, you will be the first person I call for a story. Take care and try not to dribble when you're driving.'

Of course, I made up the last part. Elvis was actually in the Armed Forces. However, the whole 'hand-over-your-organs' episode always serves as a reminder of how wonderful travel in and around Singapore actually is. The best part is that you get to do it via the wonderful local cabbies.

The island is positively crawling with such cabbies, over 15,000 to be exact, all ready and willing to take your money. They are also a permanent source of amusement for passengers like myself. Perhaps it is rare for them to pick up a Caucasian outside an HDB block in Toa Payoh because they always seem so pleased to see me. Without fail, they will do three things in a specific order. First, they will ask me where I want to go. Then, they will want to know where I am from and my entire life history. Finally, they will tell me about all the ang mohs they have picked up that week, month or year; depending on how talkative they are and how long the journey is. Over the years, I have honed a technique whereby I try to pace my answers because I have a habit of running out of things to say. With the really chatty drivers, I sometimes find myself recalling my favourite childhood memories before I have even left Toa Payoh.

What makes Singaporean cabbies unique is their reliance upon the passenger for navigation. This can be quite bewildering, especially if you have absolutely no idea where the place is, which is often the case for me. Nevertheless, drivers are insistent that you direct them.

'Where you go?' they ask.

'Bukit Batok West, please,' I reply breezily.

'Which way do you wanna go?'

'I'm sorry?'

'Which way you wanna go?'

'Shall we try the quickest?' This answer never seems to satisfy the chap in front and he then dazzles me with incomprehensible alternatives.

'We could go PIE, CTE, then BKE followed by a short stint on the KFC. But there's heavy traffic coming down Bukit Timah, so we could go Chua Chu Kang, then Phua Chu Kang and onto Liang Po Po, which is longer but less traffic. Which way you wanna go?'

'The quickest.'

'Hmm, the quickest. That could be tough unless we go through the CBD, pay extra ERP, turn left past McD and pay extra for the CHILLI. Go right into ABC and learn the rest of the alphabet so we can get to XYZ. Then we'll have to stop because I've run out of sad TLA's (three letter acronyms) that we are so fond of here. Which way you wanna go?'

'The fucking quickest, please!'

'Okay. We'll go down Bukit Batok Road and we should be there in five minutes. So you're from England? Let me tell you all about the ang mohs I've had in my taxi over the last fifteen years.'

And that's the great thing about Singapore – most places are only a few minutes away. For example, from my HDB flat in Toa Payoh, I am a five-minute walk away from shops, various bus stops, the MRT, two major highways, the national police academy, a country club and the Singapore Polo Club. My office is a fifteen-minute bus ride away. In a car, I am fifteen minutes from the beach and only twenty minutes from the causeway that joins Singapore to Malaysia. In short, everywhere is accessible, especially in a taxi, and it leaves me itching to explore.

The irony is that there are some truly wonderful places dotted all over the island and I know that many of my Singaporean friends have not visited half of them. Of course, it is not only Singaporeans who fall into this trap. I have met Americans who have seen the miniature Statue of Liberty overlooking the River Seine in Paris but they have not seen its big sister in New York. At university, I studied with an Egyptian guy who had never been to Luxor to see, among other things, the Valley of the Kings containing Tutankhamen's tomb. He had never seen the point. Yet I remember him getting excited when he told me he had just returned from seeing the historical sites of London.

However, the most ignorant guy I have ever met has to be me. It was only when I came to Singapore that I realised how disgracefully uninformed I am of my own country after speaking to Singaporeans who had seen more of England's treasures as a two-week tourist than I had in twenty years. Having studied and loved history for most of my academic life, I am ashamed to admit that I have never seen Stonehenge, a prehistoric megalithic monument dating from around 3,000 to 1,000 B.C., even though it is only a two-hour drive from my front door. Since moving to Singapore and becoming essentially an English tourist, I have developed a greater appreciation of the heritage of my homeland.

In time, I hope increasing numbers of Singaporeans become more enamoured with their own sights and sounds because there are some real crackers. Let's start with Sentosa Island. It is Singapore's most popular leisure resort, the home of the giant Merlion, which is the symbol of Singaporean tourism, and the place where I got my head smashed in.

Located 500 metres off the southern tip of Singapore, Sentosa was once a military base. Then, in 1972, some bright spark realised the island could bring in a dollar or two so the Sentosa Development Corporation was formed to transform the place into a haven for fun-seeking tourists and locals. Consequently, it has been filled with musical fountains, sound and laser shows, waxwork museums, golf courses and an impressive walk-through aquarium full of sharks and manta rays.

For an island that is just 4 sq. km, there is certainly not a shortage of things to do but my favourite place is undoubtedly Fantasy Island, the water slide park. I have visited similar parks in Spain and Greece but this one is by far the best.

Yet I have a fundamental problem with the logistics of water slides. I have never grasped the basic laws of physics, which dictate that tall, skinny people with legs longer than Cindy Crawford are not built for water slides whereas short, muscular types, i.e. the majority of Singaporeans, most certainly are. Consequently, I have had more kicks in the back of the head than I care to remember.

I am usually cruising down the slide when suddenly I hear the sound of flesh moving quickly through the water above me. More often than not, it is the discernible sound of a stocky teenager, with disproportionately large feet, bearing down upon me. I always try to accelerate but, without the necessary body mass, it is a bit like a paper aeroplane trying to outrun a nuclear missile. Anticipating the swimming pool ahead, a hairy big toe tickles the back of my ear before we fly off the slide as one long body, with the other person's feet clamped around my neck. When we emerge from our underwater embrace, I rub my eyes to find, as usual, that it is a teenage boy. Fate has never once allowed my ear to be tickled by Jamie Yeo or Cameron Diaz.

Fate, however, has conspired to make me stop altogether in the middle of a slide. On one occasion, I watched some teenagers push forcibly against the top of the slide to give themselves a better takeoff so I thought I would try the same thing. With all my feeble strength, I pushed off but I barely moved. It was stunningly pathetic. I stuttered down the slide with all the speed and grace of a dead snail. I realised trouble was brewing when the slide took a sharp vertical turn and my puny body defied all gravity and common sense by actually slowing down. At the same time, I could detect the foreboding sound of a sumo-sized Singaporean coming down the slide like a nuclear submarine. In a state of panic, I performed a kind of jerking motion through the water, which caused two things to happen. First, it produced hysterical laughter from some distant corner of the park. Second, and far more critical, my silly jerking caused me to come to a complete stop. As I lay there, I could hear the water slide world racing champion approaching.

After a prolonged bout of silly jerking, I began my slow descent once again. I could almost feel my pursuer's big toes brushing against the back of my neck. Then, I spotted the end of the slide. Although there were just a few more seconds to go, the guy was almost lying beside me. If I could just turn my body onto my left side, my speeding neighbour could pass on the right and we would both exit the slide together, I thought. Under the panic-stricken circumstances, this has to go down as a wonderfully quick piece of initiative. Waiting until the last second, I flipped my whole body to the left.

'Aah, fuck me!' I cannot apologise for the swearing. I nearly took my head off. As I was about to come off the end of the slide, I had inexplicably turned 90 degrees to the left, just in time to catch my head on the left-hand corner of the slide with such force that it almost knocked me out. Fortunately, a couple of my friends were waiting at the bottom and they later informed me of the semi-conscious behaviour that followed. I arose from the water like an intoxicated mermaid, rubbing a lump on the side of my head that was the size of the Merlion. Motioning to say something, I fell over again and swallowed far too much chlorine. Coughing and spluttering, I then informed everybody who cared to listen (and boy, did I have a big audience) that I intended to 'sue this shitty place for every dollar that I can get. I'll have this fucking place closed down in a fortnight. It made me smash my head in. Now, where's First Aid?'

That was not the only time that I have nearly killed myself at a Singaporean attraction. When my sister Jodie and her husband Kirk came to visit a couple of years back, one of the first places I took them to was Bukit Timah Nature Reserve. I was certain it would impress them. How could it not? Bukit Timah is one of only two rainforests in the world within city boundaries, the other being in Rio de Janeiro. At the top of the reserve is Singapore's highest peak, Bukit Timah Hill, which is 164 metres above sea level. In addition, the 164-hectare reserve contains more species of plants than the whole of North America and is home to the black spitting cobra and the Oriental whip snake.

Best of all, cute, but not quite so cuddly, long-tailed macaques also make their home in the reserve. Extremely intelligent, often vegetarian and quite happy to bare their arse to the world, these cheeky chappies are my kind of primate. The only threat they face comes, as ever, from man. Now, if Singaporeans are not throwing up condominiums on prime site land, they are feeding the macaques in Bukit Timah Nature Reserve. Despite signs being posted all the way up the hill reminding visitors why they must not feed the monkeys, they still do. Now you do not have to be an ecologist to realise that feeding the macaques will, to use a technical term, screw up the ecosystem. In time, they will stop finding their own food, thus breaking a link in the food chain. The constant feeding of macaques has already brought them into closer contact with human beings, which is a pressure cooker situation – either the human makes a sudden movement, scaring the monkey and forcing it to hiss through gritted teeth, or the monkey innocently approaches the smallest human in the group, forcing the concerned parent to react.

In these situations, there are two options available. Without alarming the monkeys, you can pick up the pace a little and walk on. Alternatively, you can protect your family of impressionable young children by waving a two-metre-long branch at anything that moves.

On the day that we were at the reserve, the latter option was adopted by a thirty-something Chinese chap who was walking towards us with his wife, the maid and his two young children. Whenever a 30-centimetre-high monkey approached the family, the guy stepped in front of his awe-struck family and, without a thought for his own safety, brought the branch crashing down. After watching the nimble primate easily evade the lumbering manoeuvre of its overweight attacker, it occurred to me that scientists might have made a mistake when calculating the stages of human evolution. How one had supposedly led to the other, I will never know.

It was an embarrassing situation for me. I could see Jodie and Kirk, both vegetarians, looking on with disgust. My sister had only been in the country a week and I was bending over backwards to give her a positive impression of the place. I wanted her to feel the way I did about the country and its people and this apeman was screwing everything up. I could not walk away so I reverted to my subtle, diplomatic disposition.

'Put the fucking stick down,' I found myself shouting.

'What?' the startled monkey-batterer replied.

'Put the stick down. What do you need it for? The monkeys won't hurt you.'

'But they are attacking my children.'

'Don't lie to me. You've got food in your hands. If you feed them, then of course they'll come near you, so put the bloody stick down.'

It was becoming quite tense. As I had confronted him in front of his wife and children, the guy was 'saving face' and refused to put the branch down. With my little sister and her husband watching, I was childishly doing the same. Edging towards the guy, I could see his wide-eyed young children staring at me. What could I do? Have a fight with the moron in the middle of a public park with his two pre-school kids looking on? Of course I could not so I improvised a compromise.

'Are you going to hit the monkeys with that stick?'

'No, I'm just keeping them away.'

'Well, you'd better not.'

With that, we continued walking up the hill. I regretted the use of bad language in the presence of small children but I was quite impressed with my self-restraint and I expected my due praise when we reached the summit. Yet the opposite proved to be the case. Over sandwiches, my girlfriend turned to me and said, 'You should have hit the bastard.' There is just no pleasing some people.

Trying to save a monkey's life was not the highlight of that day. Attempting to save our own necks proved to be the real high point. Looking back now, death seemed like a distinct possibility and I was the foolish one who had almost caused it to happen. I had arrogantly misconstrued the phrase 'big brother living overseas' to mean 'big shot who knows his way around dense rainforest without a guide'. Now you may snigger at this and, of course, I know that Bukit Timah Nature Reserve is hardly Brazil – but forest is forest. Furthermore, when you are covered in scratches and crawling on your hands and knees up a vertical slope amid greenery so thick that you cannot see the sky, I think you are entitled to panic a little. When I told my boss what had happened the next day, she looked at me and said, 'That wasn't very clever. Last year, an experienced trekker went missing in Bukit Timah and was later found dead by a helicopter.' It sent a shiver down my spine. I am not sure if her story is true but I do know that ours was a close call.

The ironic thing was that we were almost on our way home. We had been to the top of the hill and we were making our way down the public footpath when we were confronted by a couple of Indian guys who had just emerged from the forest. Curious, I asked them where they had been and they told us that they had been down to see the quarry. Genuinely intrigued, we followed the tiniest of footpaths into the forest for no more than a hundred metres and found the quarry, which was a magnificent site to behold. My brain started to whirr furiously, which is always a bad sign. On this occasion, it told me to tell the others 'if we found this quarry, a magnificent site to behold, without really trying, imagine what we could find if we explored further'. There was a chorus of 'good idea', 'come on, let's go' and 'Neil, why didn't you smack that guy with the stick?' so I knew that I had the group's committed support for my ill-conceived plan.

Without telling the others, I began to panic after about two hours. We had not really seen any kind of footpath since the quarry, the trees were tall and thorny plants were ripping our bare legs to shreds. None of us were equipped for this kind of trekking and it was almost 5:30 p.m. This meant that not only was the park due to close in half an hour but, far more worryingly, it would start to get dark after 7 p.m. We had no food or drink left, no mosquito repellent and we were positively melting. None of us were wearing hats and I lost count of the number of times that I was scratched on the head by thorns. I was then struck by the terrifying thought – no one knew that we were here. The reserve, sensibly assuming that no one would be foolish enough to leave the footpaths, had no monitoring system that I was aware of. We had not told anyone that we were visiting the nature reserve that day and I had no hand phone then. (Oddly enough, I bought one in Toa Payoh the following day, I cannot think why.) Put simply, we could scream and not be heard, we could jump around and not be seen and I was beginning to wonder if we could die and not be found. At about the same time, everyone in the group suddenly became upbeat and jovial. This artificial mood swing worried me. They, too, shared the same concerns as me.

With six o'clock rapidly approaching, we stopped for a while to think things through. We all agreed later that had we not conceived a viable solution then, we would have seriously started to panic. Something strange then happened. I am not a religious man but I am convinced that a touch of fate made me have one last look around an area that we had already covered with a fine-tooth comb several times. I vividly recall looking over my right shoulder and spotting a huge rock that protruded slightly through the trees. I was certain that we had walked past that rock on the way because I remembered seeing a squashed cola can, which had surprised me seeing as we were so far off the beaten track. Without saying anything to the others, I made my way over to the rock. The mashed-up coke can was by the side of the rock and just beyond it was a footprint made by one of Kirk's trainers. For a brief second, I shared the exhilaration of Howard Carter after he had discovered Tutankhamen's tomb. Then I felt like a man who had not eaten for three hours and I shouted at the others to get a bloody move on.

After reaching the footpath, I decided to use the video camera to record the episode for posterity. When I watch it with others now, I laugh at the craziness of it all. When I watch it by myself, I find myself quite shocked by it. While I recorded, the other three stood still in silence. None of them attempted to make any conversation and they only looked at the camera fleetingly. My girlfriend had a couple of awful gashes on her knee. Kirk was extremely red-faced and, like me, was covered in mud. Poor Jodie was wiping her tear-stained face and trying to regain a regular breathing pattern following a breathing fit she had had a couple of minutes earlier. We certainly learnt from the incident.

Despite the odd horror story, exploring Singapore can be a great laugh. The zoo, with its natural, open concept has to be one of the best in the world, while the first and only time I have stood transfixed was at the Night Safari, which is apparently the world's only night zoo, as a group of giraffes ran together across a field under the cover of darkness with the stars twinkling overhead. It may not be the Serengeti Plain and ultimately the animals are still not free but it is not a bad substitute.

At Sungei Buloh Nature Park, a great wetland reserve that is strangely ignored by many tourists, I encountered the fattest, longest monitor lizard that I have ever seen. It was relaxing by its swamp on a sun lounger, enjoying the midday Sun. For a working-class urchin from Dagenham, it was quite a wildlife experience. In the words of the great Sir David Attenborough, I shat myself. Obviously evicted from Jurassic Park, I was certain the miniature T-Rex was eyeing me up for dinner so I snapped a picture and ran off to change my trousers. Such creatures are rarely spotted down the high streets of suburban London.

Singaporeans complain that there is nothing to do here but, in the next breath, tell me that they have never been to the Night Safari or Sungei Buloh. However, they have been to London Zoo, which is quite simply crap in comparison to the one in Singapore, and Regent's Park. Just like I have never stepped inside St. Paul's Cathedral but I have marvelled at the architecture of Notre Dame in Paris. We are all hypocrites and I intend to make up for lost travels when I eventually return to England.

For a country that is only 42 km long and 23 km wide, the list of things to do, in my opinion at least, is mind-boggling. If Sir Stamford Raffles arrived with his family today, he would be flying down the water slides at Fantasy Island by day and getting sloshed with the other expatriates at Clarke Quay by night. Of course, travel is travel and I would never discourage Singaporeans from taking their families to experience foreign cultures but there is plenty to see here. So jump in a car, preferably your own, and head for the East Coast, Mount Faber, MacRitchie Reservoir or any place for that matter that you have not visited for a few years. I guarantee you will be pleasantly surprised.

## *Chapter Ten*

Sitting on an aircraft almost continuously for 16 hours does several things to the mind and body. First, it turns you into a battery hen with a backside so numb that if you fell out of the window at 30,000 feet and manoeuvred your body to land on it, your backside would save your life. Second, it becomes increasingly evident (Singaporean civil service departments and Singaporean bus companies, please take note here) that there are only so many times you can watch *Mr Bean* before it begins to seriously rankle with your senses.

Worst of all, air travel makes you Game Boy crazy. Or to be more specific, Tetris crazy. This is the game that transforms you not into a swashbuckling detective or a muscle-bound street fighter but into a bricklayer. Your mission, wait for it, is to build countless brick walls as fast as possible. Mark my words, there will always be one snotty-nosed kid, well within earshot, who will play the brick game at full volume while on an aeroplane. Within five minutes, you are left with no alternative but to approach the boy, grab the game out of his hands and whack him over the head with it. Anyone who feels my recommendation is a trifle brusque has obviously never heard the theme tune to Tetris. It is repetitive, childlike and seeps through your brain cells. Weeks later, you can be standing in a queue at the bank and find yourself singing at the top of your voice, 'Do dee do-do do do-dee do-do do do dee do-do do.' This irritating tune eats away at you for the rest of your life.

So imagine how Scott and I felt after 16 hours of all this as we made our way towards Singapore in late 1996. Mr Bean had just fallen off the diving board and lost his trunks again and the kid in front with the runny nose had just started his 485th game of Tetris. We were praying for something stimulating to happen. Having already formulated seventeen different ways to murder a small child with a Game Boy cartridge, I decided to leaf through my guidebook of Singapore.

In just one paragraph, we found our second wind and laughed so much that even snotty-nosed Game Boy paused his wall-building mission to turn around. The book noted that Singapore (i.e., the government) has tried so hard to reshape itself that it has fallen into self-parody. To support this claim, it quoted a Singaporean politician as saying the country had to pursue fun very seriously to stay competitive in the 21st century. What an inspired, unforgettable comment.

Once Scott and I had stopped laughing, we were struck by a worrying concern. What kind of people were we letting ourselves in for? Joking about it was one thing but if foreign observers were complaining that the country was dull and lacking in humour and politicians were responding with such a painfully-serious reply, were we heading towards an island of sombre, humourless Singaporeans?

Sitting open-mouthed and stunned in a cinema a week later, we were terrified that we might have been right. At the risk of being shot down in flames here, the locally produced movie *Army Daze* left us shell-shocked. David had suggested we watch a homegrown movie that would provide us with a slice of local life. It was a comedy that had been adapted from a highly successful stage play about the trials and tribulations of National Service (NS) and had been taking the country by storm. It did not turn the cast and crew into overnight millionaires by any means but at least it did not star Jean Claude van Damme or Sylvester Stallone so it was certainly a step in the right direction. The audience was made up prominently of young male Singaporeans in their twenties, i.e., people like David who had already done their NS and could relate to the story.

About twenty minutes into the movie, our worst fears were being realised. This really was an island of unfunny people. I genuinely believed I was watching the worst comedy since the terrible *Carry On Columbus*. Staring on in disbelief, Scott and I were stunned to find the auditorium roaring with laughter. No matter where we turned, we were faced with young, red-faced Singaporeans with tears streaming down their faces.

Initially, I went for the obvious conclusion that we were from a different culture and, therefore, could not possibly appreciate the localised jokes and the colloquial language. Having been so impressed with the country to that point, I desperately tried to enjoy the movie but the corny gags were relentless and only slightly less predictable than Scott constantly leaning over and shouting 'This film's fucking shit' every other minute. I remember one particular visual 'gag' that still makes me cringe. The limp-wristed, effeminate character, who was obsessed with his appearance, tried on his new army uniform and then walked up and down the corridor as if it were a catwalk. Even the camp *Carry On* movie series of the sixties, which I had watched as a child, had more originality than this. Nevertheless, bladders seemed to be leaking all around me.

Later that evening, I tried to console Scott who was deeply distraught by the whole affair.

'Look Scott, we've only been here a week. We haven't done national service and not all of the film was in English.'

'So? It had subtitles, didn't it?'

'Yeah, but you can't read.'

'Bollocks. I can't believe I had to pay S$7 to watch that shit. Chicken rice is only S$2 and I know which one I'd rather have. And what that fuck were they all laughing at?'

'It's just local humour, isn't it? We couldn't expect them to understand a film that was in a London cockney dialect.'

I was wrong on both counts and I knew it. Humour is universal as that bloody *Mr Bean* has proven over the years. I reminded myself of this just recently when *Army Daze* was repeated on television. Being a sucker for nostalgia, I settled down to watch it with my girlfriend who had never seen it. Guess what? It was still crap. Being more in tune with the local culture, there was only one joke that I had missed the first time. There was a fast-talking, Hokkien-speaking, gambling, streetwise teenager who behaved just like an Ah Beng and whose name happened to be Ah Beng. His character did make me laugh. As for the rest of the movie, well, it seemed dated when it was made and it now seemed prehistoric.

None of this, however, matters any more. I am no longer paranoid about a faceless mass of boring Singaporeans because they do not exist and I am not sure that they ever did. Since coming here, I have encountered more than a handful of funny Singaporeans, some of whom should be receiving psychiatric treatment.

Take crazy Chinese drummers, for example, or one huge Chinese drummer called Ah Heng to be precise. Ah Heng performed the drumming duties for the Tanjong Pagar United Fan Club.

Tanjong Pagar United is one of the professional football teams here and plays in the S-League, the national league. Do not ask me how but I somehow ended up becoming vice chairman of the fan club for a year or so and we managed to win the S-League Fan Club of the Year award in 1998, something that I am quite proud of.

I have always believed that a good testing ground for a community's sense of humour is on the terraces of its local football club. Needless to say, I was delighted to discover that Singaporean football fans also share the piss-taking wit of the terraces. Every time a referee makes a perceived error, one half of the stadium will instantly cry, 'Referee kayu, referee kayu.' After asking around, I learnt that *kayu* means 'wood' in Malay. In this context, then, the referee is 'dead wood' or a 'plank'. I have always loved the word 'plank' ever since I was endlessly called one at school. There are dozens of terms you can use to call someone a moron or an idiot but I love the word 'plank' because it sounds dopey too. Thus, whenever Singaporeans call a referee a plank, they do not hear any complaints from me.

Ah Heng, in particular, was very fond of the term and would scream it over the top of his incessant drumming in the terraces of Tanjong Pagar's football grounds. Now it must be said that he was no Phil Collins but he did have impeccable comic timing. Like football fans the world over, I despise professional footballers when they insult the average supporter's intelligence by performing their dying swan act. It fools no one except that plank with the whistle. We have all witnessed it. The winger breaks free on the left and hares towards the goal just as the chasing full-back accidentally sneezes some ten yards away. Right on cue, the winger goes down as if he has been shot by a cannon and before anyone has even had the chance to call the diver a wanker, the plank arrives to book the defender for the offending sneeze and to nominate the dying man for an Academy Award. To add insult to injury, the winger must now see his performance through and pretend he is really injured so the game is delayed while six fat guys pant and wheeze across the field with a stretcher. Enter Ah Heng, the perturbed percussionist with huge drumsticks. As the 'injured' winger groans theatrically, our drummer strikes up a sombre beat that causes hysterical laughter from the crowd. The first time Ah Heng played this beat, I asked the Chinese auntie next to me what he was playing and she told me it was played at Chinese funerals. Call me insensitive but I thought it was absolutely delightful. By this stage, other drummers had joined in, some of the kids were clapping along and just about everybody was laughing. It was marvellous. The world's worst actor was being carried off to the Chinese funeral march. West Ham fans performed a similar ritual when I was a kid. Whenever an opponent went down, be it genuine or feigned, the West Ham faithful would simultaneously cry 'Nee-naw, nee-naw, nee-naw, nee-naw', mimicking the sound of an ambulance. The Tanjong Pagar fans went a stage further and actually killed off the guy.

However, there is certainly more to life than football and there is certainly more to local humour than S-League football fans. Beginning to feel a little guilty for my savaging of *Army Daze*, I began to look out for other homegrown comedies and so started to watch *Under One Roof*. It is a sit-com based around a stereotypical Singaporean HDB-dwelling family. The wife is a caring but nagging, mahjong-playing housewife who loves to gossip with the neighbours, the daughter is a typical overachieving Singaporean student, one son is a lazy cad obsessed with get-rich-quick schemes and the other is a hypochondriac. These characters make the show watchable for many but, for me, it is the father who is the real scene stealer. His stinging rebukes to his children are razor sharp and he ends every episode with a story of extremely dubious origins.

I mention this character only because I have met Singaporeans who are really like this. My landlord, Uncle Kong, is a fine example. Larger than life, he loves spending time with what he calls his 'big family' and he kindly includes my girlfriend and me in this circle. He started laughing about five minutes after we first met him and I do not think that he has stopped since. No topic of conversation is beyond his amusement. We have discussed our apartment, starting a family, politics, moving back to England, the weather and even the soft drinks sold at a particular chicken restaurant and somehow he has always managed to make a joke out of whatever we have been talking about. The best part is that no one has ever found Uncle Kong's quips funnier than the man himself. We were once discussing the high crime rates in England as compared to Singapore and he immediately put it down to lifts.

'What's it got to do with lifts?' I foolishly asked.

'No good for burglars. Can only carry one thing at a time. Got to take the video, then go down. Come back up, take television, then go back down again. Have a rest, drink *kopi*. Come back up, take VCD player. It takes so long to rob HDB flats. English houses much better. No lifts so can take more much faster. Make more money, lah.'

However, it does not stop at Uncle Kong. At Tanjong Pagar United, we used to have regular fan club meetings and there were plenty of self-deprecating comments. There was a lovely guy called Sunny who, after being congratulated on the birth of his third child, said, 'We're going to call him Shafiq. So now we have Taufiq and Shafiq. Our next baby will be called traffic.' As in most cultures, names are taken quite seriously in the Malay community so for him to make such a joke in a room full of Chinese and Malays may not have been a laughing matter, but it was.

In fact, the younger generations are finding more comical outlets than ever before. In 1999, a small London-based gangster movie called *Lock, Stock and Two Smoking Barrels* sneaked into Singapore with little fanfare. Like most so-called artistic overseas movies, it was put on at the Picturehouse and should have realistically expected a run of around two weeks. If I recall correctly, it was playing to packed houses for at least six weeks and received rave reviews all over the island. I will admit that I had a vested interest because the actors in this film had the same accent as me, a rarity in most movies shown in Singapore. Nonetheless, Singaporeans found it hilarious, proving my theory that what is funny is funny no matter where you are. This was the London equivalent of *Army Daze* in that it was a homegrown movie about a certain London lifestyle. The film's dialogue was even sprinkled with cockney rhyming slang, which is not properly understood outside of London, so I sat in the Picturehouse with a warm glow as the laughter echoed around the auditorium.

If this sounds patronising, then I can only say that the facts do not lie. Singaporeans have traditionally chomped their popcorn while digesting the action fare of Jackie Chan and Sylvester Stallone in films where the humour is usually as subtle as a kick in the testicles. The majority of the *Lock Stock* audience were young Singaporeans. In fact, the audience had a similar demographic make-up to the one watching *Army Daze* back in 1996. Although cinema fans remain the same homogenous bunch in Singapore, their comic tastes are changing. It now takes a little more than just a limp-wristed teenager walking in an effeminate manner to evoke hilarity.

Even to this day, when talking to Western friends, I am still irritated by the negative perceptions of the Singaporean people. The stereotypical notion that the country is populated by passive, dull citizens remains a strong one and all the hip talk of transforming the island into a 'funky town' seems to have had little influence. I cannot think why. The very idea of calling somewhere a funky town smacks of self-parody and therein lies the problem for me. In Singapore, it is not the people who take themselves too seriously but the nation's government. And before anyone bursts a blood vessel, I am not being critical here.

When the PAP took control in 1959, it was hardly the time for fun and games. The fledgling government was left with a hungry population that was living in homes fit for demolition with the kind of sanitation fit for dysentery; not really the time to open a fine bottle of port, chomp on a cigar and crack a few funnies. Only Winston Churchill had that privilege, safe in the knowledge that Nazi troops were only 22 miles from his country's borders.

Naturally, the PAP spent its formative years getting its house in order. Its leaders went about providing modern education and medical facilities for its people and left the one-liners and the corny sound bites to the likes of Kennedy, Reagan, Thatcher and Major (okay, I put the last one in for a laugh). Call me naive but politicians are paid to formulate policy, not to be comedians, bent accountants or war mongers.

The trouble is that politicians are the front-line receptionists to the world. Singaporean politicians are the only Singaporeans that the rest of the planet usually gets to hear and see. My mates back in Dagenham are not going to get to laugh with the piss-taking Tanjong Pagar fans or chuckle at Uncle Kong's old stories but they will read on in disbelief when a high-ranking official makes comments about having to take fun seriously. To an outsider, it sounds like a nation completely devoid of a sense of humour. What other first impression could such a ridiculous comment possibly give?

Almost every day, some faceless bureaucrat gives some bog-standard response to a genuine enquiry in the Forum pages of the *Straits Times*. Whether the subject matter be road tax, crime rates or even the delayed start of a popular radio show, the official rejoinders are always given in an awfully patronising and robotic way. The only thing that surprises me is that the civil servant concerned is happy enough to sign his name to the drivel. Does he have no pride at all? Does his annual bonus mean that much to him? It saddens me because this is the Singapore that is read about all over the world, thanks to the Internet. Westerners cannot be blamed for forming the view that the country is mundane and humourless when these monotonous public replies are endlessly churned out.

The United States gave the world Coca-Cola, Oprah Winfrey and Jim Carrey. England gave football, most of the world's boy bands and *Mr Bean* while Singapore gave civil servants explaining, in a completely staid and restrained way, why lifts in HDB flats may have to be partly subsidised by the taxpayer. Not really funky, is it?

In fact, just the other day I was listening to Capital Gold, a London radio station, on the Internet and the D.J. was bemoaning the state of public services in England's capital, complaining, in particular, about the ambulance service. 'A recent survey,' he said, 'showed that the call-out time for an ambulance is now 18 minutes, yet your local pizza takeaway promises to deliver within three minutes. So I reckon the next time you have a heart attack, order a pizza and ask the delivery boy to drop you off at the hospital on his way back.' Now I thought this was funny. Could you imagine two local D.J.s making a similar wisecrack here? The civil servants would have an absolute field day.

There would be letters to the *Straits Times* from Mr Tan, the PR supervisor for the ambulance call-out timing department, stating something like 'We'd just like to point out that although we thought the D.J.'s comments were quite humorous in a comical sort of way, they were, in fact, quite incorrect. A survey shows that our ambulances arrive at the scene within 17.8 minutes, which would make them the most efficient in the Southeast Asian region and an improvement of some 15 per cent. This statistic is up on last year's figure by 6.8 per cent, which is part of an overall upward trend of 2.5 per cent over the last 4.8 years. By now, I should have confused you with all the statistics and you will have impatiently turned over to the Sports pages to check your 4-D results.' This letter would, of course, be printed next to a letter from Mr Tay, media consultant for the food, health, safety and pizza department, who would seriously rebuke the D.J. for his potentially dangerous misinformation by writing 'It's in the public interest to note that pizza delivery boys are not equipped to carry sick passengers to hospital. Even if there is a basket on the front of the moped, this basket is designed to carry no more than five pizza boxes. Research carried out suggests that the basket could not possibly hold a human being going through the advanced stages of an epileptic fit. According to pizza regulations, any delivery person caught carrying a sick passenger on their moped while on duty risks being transferred to a burger outlet.' Such letters appear almost every day and the rest of Singapore, including many of the politicians that these letter writers supposedly represent, is left with no choice but to cringe in embarrassment.

However, I am determined to show that the average man, woman or child on the street is not like that. Let's face it, civil servants are boring the world over, otherwise they would not be civil servants, would they? So we can throw them out of the equation and preferably into a bottomless pit. Singaporeans from all walks of life generally have a great sense of humour and they can laugh at others and, more importantly, at themselves. Being able to look in the mirror and laugh at yourself (I do every day – if you have seen me, you will understand why) is the only true test. Of course, there will always be a small group of people who take themselves a little too seriously and have the potential to screw everything up both in England and Singapore. And it is our duty to slap them into place.

Let me give you a very relevant example. When I was young, we used to have a caravan on a site in Clacton-on-Sea, a seaside town in Essex. It was an enclosed site that had a narrow gravel road snaking through and around it. Built only to serve caravan owners, the road was not wide enough to take two cars going in opposite directions so the site owner made it a one-way system. This was most convenient if your caravan happened to be near the entrance; ours was not so we had to take a tour of the site every time we wanted to get to it. Well, we would have done if my mother had wielded such admirable patience. Instead she decided to short fuse the circuit by going the wrong way round the one-way system. Considering the site was not exactly crawling with traffic, it was only a minor misdemeanour. She did not drive fast and, besides, driving into a ditch periodically to avoid an oncoming car was part of the holiday fun.

The only real obstacle we had to clear was a man who had his caravan parked at the junction between the right and wrong way.

A profoundly tedious man, he sat on a deckchair by the edge of the road and leapt into action whenever he detected a car (usually ours) driving in the wrong direction. Hands waving, he would run forward crying, 'Sorry, you'll have to turn back. It's a one-way road. Sorry, you'll have to turn back.' Being a lanky chap with long arms, he resembled a windmill. Initially, my mother would pacify him with the 'sorry, we're new here' routine and he would send us on our way with a warning.

After three years, my mother's defence began to wear a bit thin. On one memorable sunny afternoon, my mother took her regular shortcut. From nowhere came the boring, windmill man. With his hands gesticulating all over the place, he shouted, 'One way! One way! This is a one-way road.' Without missing a beat, my mother retorted, 'Well, that's okay then. We're only going one fucking way.' The windmill, who I am sure was a civil servant, never bothered us again. Sitting in his beloved deckchair, he would start to get up, spot my mother and force himself to smile and wave, making the conscious decision never to let his children play with me or my sister.

Dull people are universal and it is our duty to keep them in place. I read a letter in the *Straits Times* recently that was responding to an earlier piece about Singapore's income divide and how statistics can cloud the issue. The first letter stated, quite rightly, that a typical household's income could be calculated in many ways so we should treat figures with caution. The reply to this letter was something else. I think the guy was saying that the median income was a better yardstick for household income than the mean but I am not really sure. Take a dose of caffeine and read on.

The writer said things like 'The sample of households excluded those with no earned income and the typical household size was 3.6 persons. Thus, a household in the sample could have more than one income earner.' He went on in a similar vein for another seven riveting paragraphs before concluding 'The median is clearly a better gauge of average income. It mitigates any perception of income divide created by the mean.' As conclusions go, they do not come any punchier than that, do they? This mathematician could have teamed up with the windmill to form a double act. They could have sat in matching deckchairs, discussed Pythagoras and shouted 'one way' at moving vehicles all day.

That, however, is only if we let them. These dreary souls are still in the minority and we should be constantly on the lookout to keep it that way. If you are at work or at a party and someone makes a soporific comment involving statistics, money, property or the civil service, shoot the person. Plead to the judge that you did it on compassionate grounds to prevent the spread of what is commonly known as boringfuckeritis and the judge will throw the case out. Alternatively, send the afflicted to the terraces of Tanjong Pagar United for a season or refer him to Uncle Kong for a weekly consultation. Episodes of *Friends* and *Under One Roof* can also be administered. It is imperative that the symptoms are detected at the earliest possible stage to prevent them from spreading. In rare cases where the sense of humour has almost withered away, a literary injection of Spike Milligan, the legendary former goon, must be given immediately.

Should this extreme measure fail, then the victim is left with no other option than to pay up his life insurance and join the civil service. At least, the sick man will be in the company of other victims and he will get to spend the rest of his life pursuing this business of fun very seriously. Fortunately, most Singaporeans that I know have been spared this horrific disease but, for goodness sake, do not pursue every business you undertake too seriously. Look in the mirror each day, laugh at yourself and issue a dry slap to every boring person you encounter. Together, we can prevent this tragic social illness from spreading.

# *Chapter Eleven*

I have just got off the telephone from my mother and the call reminded me that, like most English mothers, she has two voices that are interchangeable. Mothers have an additional gene that can distort their vocal cords to produce their normal voice and a second, 'telephone' voice. The latter is triggered by an involuntary muscle spasm, which is the brain's defensive reaction to the sound of a ringing telephone bouncing off its neighbouring eardrums. Only mothers suffer from the telephone voice syndrome.

My own mother has had this syndrome for years. If it was a typical day, she would be screaming at us in her normal voice for not performing an exceedingly trivial task. 'If you don't put the bloody towels back on the rack properly, you're both gonna get it.'

'Sorry mum,' we would murmur in self-defence, hoping that our feeble apologies would pacify her. They did not.

'And Neil, I don't know why you bothered showering in the bath. You might as well have just stood on the carpet outside and showered yourself on it. Why do you keep spending so much time in the bathroom anyway? It's not normal behaviour.'

'I was just washing my hair, mum.'

'Washing your hair? You haven't got any hair and what you

did have is now sitting in the plughole. Is there any chance of you actually cleaning the bath when you're finished? I can't believe what a pair of lazy bastards I've brought up. Jodie, do you think you could tidy your bedroom? No, I suppose I'll have to do it as usual.'

That was the other thing about my mother, she always answered her own questions. So essentially, she was arguing with herself. Then the telephone would start ringing, which meant a temporary reprieve.

'There's the bloody phone now,' my mother would complain. 'Like I don't have enough to do already. I don't know why I'm even answering it. It's probably for you.'

Then as she lifted the receiver, the syndrome mysteriously kicked in and she went from being our mother to sounding like the Queen Mother.

'Hellooo, this is 2689. Can I help you...? Sylvie, how are you? Are you still working at the supermarket? Oh, that's wonderful because you wanted to work that shift, didn't you? I am pleased for you.'

She would then continue talking in this affected, BBC-styled voice that made her sound like the actress Judi Dench. The beauty of the syndrome for us was that she could not possibly use both voices at once so we would take our cue to have a fight on the living room floor. Having a smaller sister meant there would be the usual tears, headlocks and bruised dead legs but I would hang in there. By the time we were belly flopping off the top of the settee onto each other, we knew that the Queen Mother would need to make a royal pardon.

'Do excuse me, Sylvie. Could you please hold on for just a second? I have to take care of something.' My mother would then regally place the receiver against her chest, perform the royal wave and beckon her two scrapping children to pause momentarily.

'If you two don't stop right now, you're both gonna get it. Sit down and shut up or you'll be getting no fucking dinner... So sorry about that, Sylvie. Now, you were saying about your husband's vasectomy.'

When I grew taller, making it harder, but not impossible, for my mother to crack me across the head, I asked her why she put on a 'posh' voice whenever she answered the telephone.

She replied, 'You have to play the game. You never know who is going to be on the other end and you don't want to give the wrong impression, do you?'

Now I am not sure if my mother is in contact with the Singaporean prime minister but I feel her presence here, too. The way Singaporeans converse has become a national obsession over the last year or so. It began with Senior Minister Lee Kuan Yew who hinted that Singaporeans should polish their English. Before you could say government policy, Prime Minister Goh Chok Tong had introduced the 'Speak Good English' campaign. In other words, Singaporeans had to 'play the game' and adopt my mother's telephone voice to ensure that friends, colleagues and business acquaintances could understand them correctly, thus creating a favourable impression.

Being a former speech and drama teacher, my initial knee-jerk reaction was that the government had implemented a rational, logical policy to help improve business communications flow between East and West. I have met many expatriates working here who have experienced difficulty understanding locals on a day-to-day basis and vice versa. Quite surprising, perhaps, when you consider that the official working language of Singapore is English.

Every Singaporean student must learn English at school, irrespective of ethnic or cultural background.

Where then is the problem? Well, take the movie *Army Daze* for instance. Having been in the country for only a week, Scott and I could not understand some of the dialogue that was allegedly in English. This was mainly because it was not in English but rather Singlish, the local dialect of Singaporean English (some would say it is even a separate language) that is the result of the ethnic melting pot that exists on the island.

With Singlish, you often end up with the word 'can' at the end of sentences, rather than at the beginning, much like *ke yi* in Mandarin or *boleh* in Malay. Exclamations like *lah, aiyoh, meh* and *alamak* often find their way into Singlish, too. However, it is the vocabulary of localised English that I would like to emphasise because this is the most important aspect of Singlish.

In my last job, I enjoyed antagonising my Canadian friends by reminding them that, as a native-speaking Englishman, I had never encountered an English dialect that I could not understand. This fact is true but hardly a big deal, considering I cannot speak any other language. Canadians like my good friend Shawn, on the other hand, struggle with any accent that is not North American. When he saw the movie *Trainspotting,* he confessed that he needed the subtitles to understand the dialogue, as the cast spoke with strong Scottish accents.

As the British Isles is blessed with having so many different accents and dialects scattered over such a small area, I was confident, therefore, that Scott and I would have no problems coming to grips with the local tongue. English is English after all. However, some of what Singaporeans speak most certainly is not English and this is where we encountered some difficulty. What was even more worrying was that as I began to teach in Singaporean schools, it became apparent that students did not even realise that many of the words they spoke were not English. Even if they spoke slowly and adopted my mother's resonant telephone voice, words like *kiasu, kaypoh,* meaning 'nosy', and *gong-gong,* meaning 'silly' or 'stupid', were still being uttered. After discovering what these words meant, I went back to my classes and told disbelieving pupils that these words were not part of the English language. I recall one particular teenage boy who refused to accept that kiasu and kaypoh were not English words. He explained, quite rationally I thought, that these words were spoken by Singaporeans of all races and they could be heard and read in the national media. Although I agreed with him, I added that they were unique to the Singaporean vocabulary and would not be understood in other parts of Asia, let alone in places like England and the United States.

However, Scott and I were eager to fit in. Although we could understand most of a Singlish conversation, we still tried to learn some of its non-English words. The result was a most bizarre linguistic concoction. It must be explained that coming from strong working-class backgrounds, Scott and I had seemingly unshakeable Yorkshire and cockney accents, respectively. Now I hope you will appreciate that it is not easy to completely change the way you speak. But we had no choice. To get by in the coffee shops and mini-marts in Toa Payoh, a smattering of Singlish had to come into play for both of us.

At this point, you may wonder why we did not just learn Malay or Mandarin. I did learn conversational Malay to communicate with Saudita, my crazy old Indian landlady, but I never did discover the Malay for 'Can you please put some bloody clothes on?'

As for Mandarin, well, let's just say that some Singaporeans can be a wee bit obsessive about it. I think it is the four different tones of the language that does it. When I first arrived in Singapore, I was naturally wide-eyed and keen and would try to pick up a few words in Mandarin every day and then test them out on the secretaries or the Chinese teachers at work. For some reason, they would jump all over me. Apart from being laughed at, which I did not mind, there would always be the cry of 'Wrong tone! Wrong tone! It's in the wrong tone, ha ha. You're saying x not y.' Fair enough if this response had been now and then but it was relentless and rarely constructive. My attempts to learn Mandarin were gleefully ripped to shreds so I thought, 'Sod it, life's too short.'

Once we had decided to boycott the idea of actually learning a whole new language because we are lazy buggers, Scott and I decided to have a stab at Singlish. My God, did we sound awful. It was especially tough for Scott. In Britain, the demographic and sociological make-up is such that the further north you travel, the further away you go from Standard English and the more unintelligible the local tongue becomes. This linguistic phenomenon peaks at the top of the island in Scotland's John O'Groats, where its residents are only understood by relatives, neighbours and the local sheep population. Being from Leeds, I suppose Scott was somewhere in the middle of all this. He once told me that people from other parts of Yorkshire could not understand him, so try to picture how he must have sounded to a typical Singaporean once he had added a Singlish slant to his strong northern brogue. He would approach some poor auntie in a fast-food outlet and ask, 'Ellow, ken ye ge' meh eh tool piss cliss-beh chickin se', wi chips 'n eh cork, ken lah?' Although I sympathised with the clueless auntie, it was a priceless cultural encounter. It was made even funnier by Scott's attempt to localise his accent by throwing in 'can lah' at the end, almost as an afterthought. But if there was ever a monumental coming together of two great cultures, it had to be the first time Scott combined English and Singlish to pass a derogatory comment about someone pushing past him on the MRT. 'What a kiasu cunt,' he said simply.

However, as time passed, language became quite a sensitive issue for Scott. Despite his commendable efforts to take the rough edges off his Yorkshire accent, he was struggling to be understood.

'This is Singapore, not Leeds. You can't expect them to understand you when you go onto building sites or meet other architects,' I said to him.

'I know that but I'm bloody proud of the way I talk. I'm not ashamed of it.'

I had to agree with him. When we were at university, our accents, though completely different, were one of the things that bonded us. We were social lepers – no more than a tiny minority of working-class students who raised eyebrows every time we opened our mouths. Many in this situation reached a compromise and went for a more acceptable accent to fit in. Let's face it, we have all met Singaporeans who have studied in the United States and miraculously developed impressive American accents within a year or two. Be deeply suspicious of these people. Having worked with speech therapists, I have been told that it takes considerable effort to completely reshape your speaking voice so I often wonder what the motives of these pseudo-American Singaporeans really are.

As far as Scott and I were concerned, we were not going to change our voices for anybody at university. Instead we went to the opposite extreme and perfected the most common-as-muck style accents you could possibly imagine. I sounded like Michael Caine on speed and Scott spoke as if he had spent his entire life as a farmhand in rural Yorkshire. It was beautiful. We deliberately went out of the way to demonstrate that what we had to say was far more important than how we said it. And it worked.

I tried to explain to Scott that we could get away with the whole accent thing in England because our audience had been exposed to various dialects. The majority of Singaporeans, however, have only really been exposed to two types of English – Asian English and Hollywood English – and we spoke neither. We had no choice but to do the one thing that we would have ripped our tongues out before doing in England: compromise. Eventually, we got by but Scott was never allowed to order a chicken meal again.

Our predicament was a useful case study that I used to share with my secondary students. By all means speak Singlish at home and with friends, I would tell them, just as I would speak cockney in London, but, at the same time, they needed to have both the capability and the awareness to switch to Standard English when appropriate. Apply different codes of communication to different audiences, I said.

The trouble was that I did not believe in what I was saying. I have to confess that in the first six months or so my Western prejudices came to the fore. I thought Singlish was a joke – a complete mishmash of a dialect that was awful on the tongue and ugly on the ear. The sooner it was banished from Singapore completely, I thought, the better for all those with eardrums. I believed that I was on a mission to correct the horrendous speech faults of every student I came across. Working with youngsters who said 'one, two, tree' and believed that words like *siaow*, meaning 'crazy', were actually English, I failed to understand how they were going to be taken seriously in a so-called globalised economy.

Eventually though, I changed my mind for various reasons.

The most obvious being that I actually started to learn Singlish, thus eradicating my ignorance. I had noticed that good friends like David and Victor tried to standardise their English around me, assuming that I would understand them more easily. The only way around this artificial, uncomfortable situation was for me to speak Singlish back to them as and when I could.

Then, I came across one or two middle-class, well-to-do Caucasians who spoke impeccable English and revelled in mocking Singlish at every opportunity when Singaporeans were not around. They would say things like 'Shall we go to the cinema, lah?' or 'May I have a cup of coffee, lah?', placing heavy emphasis on the 'lah' and sometimes even punctuating the word in the air, using their fingers to mime quote marks. For me, the annoying punctuating alone ranks right up there with incest and warrants a lethal injection.

At first, I would smile politely but it soon became apparent that it just was not funny. Largely because I knew that these same arrogant arseholes would have been ridiculing cockney or some other localised accent had they been in England. These wealthy wankers were the same people I had rebelled against at university and I was buggered if I was now going to sit with them in Orchard Road and take the piss out of the average Singaporean on the street.

Therefore, I did a complete 360 degree turn and began to champion the use of Singlish in everyday situations. I still reiterated the importance of speaking Standard English to my students and banned the use of Singlish in class but the trick is knowing when to switch from one to the other. Even my old boss, Juliet McCully, who set up the Speech Therapy Unit at Singapore General Hospital and one of the first speech and drama centres in Singapore, spoke positively of Singlish, explaining that communication was, in essence, all about transmitting your message successfully. How you did it depended entirely on your audience. Even now when I visit England, I revert back to cockney when I am speaking to friends, partly because it is my natural accent and mainly because I do not want them to assume that Singapore has transformed me into a rollneck wearing, Volvo-driving, suburban-living twat. When I go shopping or eat at a coffee shop, I throw in a bit of Singlish and when I am at work, I spontaneously use this bizarre Singlish/English concoction that is neither one thing nor the other.

Then along came the government's Speak Good English campaign, which has the potential to wreck everything. If it was called the 'Speak Good English When Necessary' campaign, you would not hear a peep out of me but it is not. Being a former teacher, I initially thought that the campaign could not do any harm. Although I admire Singlish, I still come across countless Singaporeans who cannot speak anything else. Thus, I thought the campaign could be a success if it could raise the awareness of Standard English in conjunction with its many varieties. The campaign, however, used a sledgehammer to swat the tiniest of flies.

Before you could say 'kiasu reaction', Singaporeans across the nation were encouraged to speak Standard English as often as possible. Television and radio presenters were asked not to slip into their local tongue. Local English-speaking actors were redubbed to remove any traces of a Singlish accent, which served only to make them sound bloody awful. Finally, and most ridiculously, Phua Chu Kang was sent for English lessons – a course of action that raised, for me at least, memories of taking fun seriously.

Phua Chu Kang is the name of the lead character in one of the local comedies. A money-grabbing building contractor, he is an over-aged Ah Beng who plays the fool and speaks nothing but

Singlish. He often reflects the attitudes of the man in the street, albeit in a farcical way. The powers that be were concerned that, among other things, impressionable (and supposedly stupid) Singaporeans would be duped into thinking that his awful English would be interpreted as the standard version and adopted around the island. Thus, it was advised that the character be sent for English lessons in the show. Although the show remained quite funny, I found the storyline depressing. It missed the point of Phua Chu Kang's humour. To understand many of the show's jokes, you must know the correct pronunciation for unusual words. For instance, Phua Chu Kang always gets a laugh when he says 'façade' because he pronounces it 'fer-car-day'. Now if Singaporeans did not know how to say this word correctly, how on earth would they find it funny?

The infuriating thing is that the English campaign came about at a time when Singaporeans, I feel, were beginning to take a real pride in their version of English. Like Changi Airport or the Merlion, Singlish is something that is quintessentially Singaporean. It is a dialect that everybody speaks and understands and is something that could provide the cornerstone for a unifying cultural identity. For the first time, movies like *Money No Enough* and *12 Storeys* were not only being shown on the big screen but, more importantly, their characters spoke the language of the Singaporean on the street. Their mix of Hokkien and Singlish made the jokes and situations seem funnier to Singaporeans because they were more identifiable and realistic. Other local movies like *Liang Po Po* soon followed. Although they were not as successful as *Money No Enough*, it became evident that Singlish and the average man on the street was becoming hip. Forget Tom Cruise, actors like Jack Neo and Gurmit Singh were speaking the language of their audience. It was cool to be like Phua Chu Kang. The cynical side of me suggests this trend shift was one of the factors that prompted the government to act. Speaking like Jim Carrey was one thing but speaking like Liang Po Po, well, that was a different mouthful of words altogether.

The question is: Is Singapore trying to build a cultural identity or not? With so many races and cultures all living under one roof, it is extremely difficult to draw out unifying features but Singlish is certainly one of them. It is the language of Singapore and something to be proud of, just like cockney is for Londoners. As long as Singaporeans are aware that they must switch into Standard English when conversing with foreigners, as Scott and I had to, then frankly I do not see what the problem is.

## *Chapter Twelve*

One Saturday morning, Scott and I decided to play football. We purchased one of those cheap, plastic balls at the mini-mart and set off to find a football pitch. After an hour, we had found only two pitches and they were both private school pitches. Out of sheer desperation, I did something that I am still embarrassed by to this day. I went into the school looking for a teacher, which was quite difficult as it was a Saturday, to ask if we could use one of the pitches. As bold as could be, I strolled into the gymnasium and, I am blushing now just thinking about it, approached the PE teacher who was working with a group of teenage students.

In the middle of their gymnastics lesson, I said, 'Hi there. I'm sorry to bother you but I work here as an English teacher and my colleague and I were wondering if we could use your football pitch for a while, just to get some practice, you know.'

'Er, yes, I suppose so,' the stunned man replied. And as calm as you like, I went back out to tell my 'colleague' the good news.

Since becoming familiar with the local education scene, I realise how bizarre I must have looked that day. In a small neighbourhood school in Toa Payoh on a quiet Saturday afternoon, a 1.92 m Caucasian wearing Bermuda shorts and holding a plastic ball that only nursery kids play with walked into the middle of a Co-Curricula Activity (CCA) and asked if he could have a kick about on their pitch. If you had been that young teacher, what would you have said? Whenever I pass that school now on the bus, I always recount the story to whoever I am with and they cannot believe what a prat I was.

Playing football that day brought it home to both Scott and me that you can take the man out of England but you cannot take England out of the man. We both grew up in an environment that had a dominant football culture and we are both extremely passionate about sports in general. Thus, we were delighted to discover that Singapore has a professional football league known as the S-League, which meant that we would be able to attend football matches here. Like most things in Singapore, our local team, Balestier Central, was virtually on our doorstep. The team's first match was away to Geylang United over in Bedok and we decided, quite impulsively, to go. Just as we used to do in England, we found out where the stadium was, plotted our route and decided where we would eat before the game. We subconsciously re-enacted all our prematch rituals. Strangely, I had no expectations whatsoever and I ended up being impressed despite the match being an anticlimactic 0-0 draw.

Aside from the football, we were both struck by the same negative observation. There were non-Singaporean football shirts everywhere. To be more specific, there were Manchester United and Liverpool shirts everywhere and hardly anyone was wearing Geylang or Balestier shirts. On entering the stadium, Scott and I had been given Geylang United polo shirts as free door gifts. We went straight to the toilet to put them on even though we were there to watch Balestier. Yet as we proudly stepped onto the terraces in our new Singaporean football shirts, we were greeted by the sight of more United jerseys than we had seen in Manchester's city centre.

To our astonishment, the Geylang-Balestier match was not a fluke gathering of English football fans. Take a walk down Orchard Road on any given day and look out for the English Premiership jerseys. They are everywhere, both on people's backs and in shop windows. Many shops even stock West Ham United shirts, which amazes me, although I have noticed that they are usually quite dusty and covered in mothballs.

Being an Englishman, I have to put my hands up and admit that my knowledge of the English Premiership certainly did me no harm when I began to teach in Singaporean secondary schools. In the beginning, it was comforting to know that I had something in common with many of the students. Furthermore, it was most convenient, initially at least, for both Scott and me to be able to pick up a newspaper or switch on the television and find out how Leeds and West Ham had performed the day before.

After a while, the apathy towards local soccer began to irritate us a little. We watched Balestier on a semi-regular basis and took quite an interest in the S-League. We bought a couple of S-League shirts and began to look forward to our Saturday night football match ritual. However, we were in the minority. We asked many of our Singaporean friends to join us but no one was interested. Furthermore, many of my students could name the girlfriends or wives of the Manchester United players as well as recall the date of Ryan Giggs's birthday but they could not name more than half a dozen S-League players. The ones that they could name were always the usual suspects such as Fandi Ahmad, V. Sundramoorthy and Nazri Nasir; in other words, seasoned national players who had been around for years.

The reasons for such a lack of interest in local football and sports in general are painfully obvious. Singaporeans want winners. For many years, football gave them just that courtesy of the Malaysia Cup (formerly the Malaya Cup). Started in 1921, it was a Malaya tournament involving Singaporean and Malaysian football teams. Just like the old home internationals between England and Scotland, there is nothing like a contest between two rival neighbours to set the blood racing. The best part was that Singapore won the Cup several times and tens of thousands of Singaporeans turned out on both sides of the Causeway to see it happen. At the end of 1994, however, both the Malaysian and the Singaporean soccer bodies decided that they should go their separate ways and focus on building their own leagues.

The S-League was born in 1996 and Singaporean teams started playing each other instead. With the island being so small, the talent pool is obviously limited and the fan base of each club is even smaller. Consequently, the playing standards and the numbers on the terraces have dipped tremendously from those glorious Malaysia Cup days. There is also nothing like the added incentive of national pride to make you play and cheer that little bit harder, but that too died, to a certain extent, in 1994.

Moreover, no self-respecting kiasu parent is going to allow his or her child to pursue football, or any other sport for that matter, as a long-term career when the chances of success are very slim. Sports can be played at school, and possibly at the weekends when all the homework is finished, but that is about it. I mean, how could you let your son pursue his dream of being the next Fandi Ahmad and earn up to S$5,000 a month when he could probably earn that in a week working for a dot.com company? I have to say that when I was involved with the Tanjong Pagar United Fan Club,

I noticed that the Malays tended to have a slightly different perspective. Many were more philosophical in the sense that if football was an opportunity for an improved standard of living, then so be it. After all, Fandi Ahmad had a tough, kampung upbringing and now he is a millionaire and a role model for the Malay community and Singapore in general. In contrast, Chinese Singaporeans tend to play the odds carefully. They believe that a child who hits the textbooks more often than he hits the back of a net has a greater chance of financial success.

Unfortunately, such an attitude can only have one result. In February 2001, the Singaporean national team competed in some pre-World Cup qualifying matches at the National Stadium. Not a single player in the starting XI was Chinese. They were either Malay or Indian. Knowing that this country has over four million people from which to choose its sportsmen and women, 77 per cent of whom are Chinese, the implications are obvious. Unless rare exceptions like discus thrower James Wong or the swimmer Joscelin Yeo come along on a regular basis, sporting glory will remain the stranglehold of countries that regard sports as more than just something to watch on television or, worse yet, to place a bet on.

Just listen to this. I was sitting at my desk eagerly waiting for the first English FA Cup final of the new millennium to start. I had a vested interest. Turning to a colleague, I said, 'I hope Chelsea wins today.'

'But you're not a Chelsea fan, are you?' she asked curiously.

'Oh, it's not for me. It's for my brother.'

Then she said something that I thought was outrageously funny. 'Why? Did he "take" Chelsea to win?'

'"Take" Chelsea to win? He's only nine years old. He doesn't "take" teams. He supports them. How many nine-year-olds do you know that hang out in betting shops?'

But wait, there is more. During the Euro 2000 tournament, another colleague was upset because her beloved Italy had lost in the final. I consoled her by saying, 'At least your team made it to the final, my team didn't get past the qualifiers.'

A friend walking past at the time heard this and enquired, 'Who was your team then?'

'England, who else?' I replied, somewhat perplexed.

'Yeah well, I'm Singaporean but I don't always "take" Singapore. Sometimes I take Thailand.'

We were on different wavelengths. I was talking about supporting a team; he was talking about 'backing' a team. Do not get me wrong. When Scott and I were studying in Manchester, we would pop over to Ladbrokes every Saturday morning for a little flutter on the Premiership. We were serious punters and sometimes we would go all the way and bet £1 but never against our own team.

However, this is where gambling takes on a whole new meaning. My very first assignment as a sports reporter here was to interview an English football player who had been called up by the Corrupt Practices Investigation Bureau (CPIB) for questioning. He played in defence for a team that was competing in the S-League and his team had been throwing in some crazy goals at the time. He was found not guilty of match fixing but the impression I get from some players is that match fixing, so prevalent in this part of the world, still goes on in the S-League. Simply because gambling is everywhere.

When Singapore Pools legalised football betting in 1999, S-League attendances mushroomed overnight and matches took on a certain edge for some people. When I was helping out with the fan club for Tanjong Pagar United, I vividly recall one Chinese chap sitting a few seats away who was positively beside himself with anxiety. He was off his seat every few seconds, screaming the most awful abuse at the referee. Unless he usually sat in another part of the stadium, which I seriously doubt, I suspect that it was the first time that he had been to the ground; just a week after the betting system had been introduced. Call me a cynic but you can spot a genuine fan from a fake one just by reading a person's body language and this guy was definitely a phoney.

Of course, local sports gambling must be put into perspective. I know for a fact that the majority of fans are not there for financial reasons. Nor are they there to beat the living daylights out of their opponents' supporters. I have yet to find a grunting ape with tattooed forearms and cropped hair sitting on an S-League terrace and singing 'You're gonna get your fucking 'ead kicked in.' I have, however, encountered quite a few of these gentlemen at West Ham matches in England. I have even had the pleasure of being punched on the jaw by one of them. This happened at a reserve match when a drunken cripple on crutches (I am not making this up) mistook me for a Millwall supporter. In contrast, I have witnessed nothing serious in the stands of the S-League. Although there was one particularly heated conversation that almost become serious. A lovely auntie and a dedicated Tanjong Pagar fan once gave Scott two fingers of a Kit-Kat while I only got one. This left me quite antagonistic but I retained my composure and let the woman off with a stern warning.

Chocolate bars aside, I enjoy watching S-league matches as and when I can. Each club now has a small base of dedicated supporters who bring some atmosphere to the games and there is little risk of me being clumped by a drunk old man. I just feel that the local football scene and Singaporean sports in general could be much bigger and more lucrative if they were not hindered by kiasuism and their lack of social status.

Tragically, this mindset applies to the arts too. Singaporeans are more than happy to drag themselves to the cinema every week to marvel at Western talents like Tom Hanks – it is the national pastime. However, if a Singaporean child told his parents that he wanted to be a singer or an actor, I think we both know what the response would be. After all, where is the financial security in that? Prancing around on stage every night is not going to pay for the maid, let alone the condominium to put her in.

Of course, the situation is not helped by the likes of James Lye. For those who are not familiar with his work, Lye was a handsome, hardworking Singaporean actor. In fact, I will have to be honest and say that he is extremely good-looking as my other half constantly reminded me every time he stepped into frame. In Singaporean terms, he was at the peak of his professional powers. He came across as a pleasant guy and he delivered the goods on both English and Chinese shows. He had even crossed over to Hong Kong-financed movies, which were distributed across the region. He was, undoubtedly, a decent role model for budding local actors.

What did he go and do? He quit working in television to become a product manager with one of the largest banks in the region. Far be it from me to question his motives as I am sure the guy had valid reasons for making such a radical career shift. When I heard the news, however, two things struck me. First, and perhaps predictably, the media and the general public by and large saw the move as a positive one as he faced greater financial prospects in the long term, better chances of promotion and all that other materialistic bullshit. The more worrying concern for me, and I know I am being idealistic here but I do not care, was what kind of message was being sent out regarding the local arts industry? Something like 'For heaven's sake, do not consider a career in the arts, the exposure is good but the pay is terrible' or 'Give up your dreams, put on your best smile and sell your bank's lucrative interest rates to wealthy investors.' Call me naive but I did not think that was what the arts was supposed to be about.

Two of my big screen heroes, Robert De Niro and Al Pacino, lived hand to mouth in their early acting days but they did not quit. Somehow, I could not imagine De Niro going up to Martin Scorsese and saying, 'Yeah, I know *Taxi Driver* will be great exposure but I'm in a bit of a pickle. You see, First National Bank has offered me this great desk job and the hours are fixed. There's even a subsidised canteen and, wait for this, I get a travel allowance to boot. I've got my long-term security to think about, you know.' It just would not happen, would it? And before the obvious retort comes in, these guys were not always earning millions of dollars per film but they still took the gamble.

Like I say, only James Lye will know why he really quit the acting profession. It was the public reaction that was so depressing. My cynical friends said that he was probably commanding the sort of high salary in his new job that would tempt the devil himself. Please do not tell me that it just comes down to the filthy lucre again. It is bad enough that we now have to watch uncomfortable Singaporean actors try to deliver their lines in Anglicised accents. Do we want to eradicate them completely by encouraging them to take up secure positions in the corporate world? There is enough American rubbish on television as it is and I, for one, would like to see this junk continue to be diluted a little with more local productions. Singapore is not the biggest of islands and if it discourages the very few talented young performers that it has from pursuing a career in the arts, then this country will never be able to take the business of fun very seriously.

The infuriating irony for me is that I know that talent is out there. I am no scout but I can certainly tell a good actor from a bad one. When I worked as a speech and drama teacher, I was convinced that there were a couple of rough diamonds that had the potential to be polished. After lessons, I discreetly informed these students that I believed they had potential in the dramatic arts. In return, they shot me looks that suggested I had just told them that each of them had the makings of a fine pimp.

Undeterred, I pursued the issue and offered to pass them telephone numbers of some television casting agents but to no avail. They told me that they intended to be engineers or lawyers because that was what they and their parents supposedly wanted. Both are fine careers with rewarding futures but I just wanted them to consider all the options available to them. Nevertheless, I sympathised with the pressure they were under and I appreciated the fact that parents insisted that their children should choose careers in engineering or law. I grew up around kids whose parents did not give a toss about academic pursuits. My own father was none too impressed when I told him that I was going to university but, in the next breath, admitted that he had almost cried when my younger brother scored a great volley in a Sunday league match. Now, if that is not a cultural irony, then I do not know what is.

In fact, my own upbringing helps to explain why I was so insistent that my drama students considered other career options. When I left primary school, my report book read 'Neil has a gift for drama'. If I recall correctly, I had co-written two plays, directed one of them and performed in both by the age of eleven. We also did a reworking of *The Wizard of Oz*. I played the part of Scarecrow and the sizeable audience was treated to the sight of an anorexic beanpole with an uneven haircut performing a song and dance routine. Not bad for a young lad brought up in one of the worst boroughs in the country, academically speaking. However, the next time I did anything remotely dramatic was when I read for a part for some ridiculously pretentious play at university.

My secondary schooldays went by without so much as a dramatic whimper. You see, in my working-class world, the only people who did any sort of acting or singing were homosexuals. Wearing make-up and pretending to be someone else on stage meant that you were gay and you risked social castration. I hate to say it but many of my peers and their families were so prehistoric back then that you could be a bricklayer when you left school and command serious respect but you could not dress up and deliver a few lines.

Consequently, I have been a part of two cultures in which many people just do not get the point of the arts. In England, for example, I only went to the cinema for two reasons. When I was young, it was to ogle beautiful young girls. When I was older, it was so I had a place to kiss average-looking girls.

In Singapore, as we all know, people like to go to the cinema so they have a quiet place to answer their telephone calls. Just as the on-screen killer is about to pounce, you hear 'Hallo, what you want, ah? No lah, cannot. I'm watching movie one. No, cannot what. Show damn good. Yeah, after show, can. We go for makan. Can, no problem.' Before you get a chance to think, you have already turned around and said, 'Look you little prat, if the movie's that good, why don't you just turn your fucking bright yellow handphone off? Second, a "show" is something like a circus that has elephants and live performers jumping around. We, however, are watching a series of moving pictures projected onto that large screen, hence the word "movie".' Well, honestly.

When handphones are not beeping all over the place in the cinema, you can be sure that those stupid red laser pointers are being flashed all over the screen. A couple of years back, my friends and I went to see *The Crucible*, a film I had been waiting to see for some time as I like the work of both Arthur Miller and Daniel Day Lewis. The opening titles had barely gone up when the red laser appeared. Before you knew it, the red spot was tickling Lewis's ear, going up actresses' noses and generally being really boring. No one in the auditorium seemed to find the prank even mildly amusing and I was really losing my temper when I heard 'For fuck's sake, turn it off.' I turned to my friends, who were all staring at me with horrified expressions on their faces. That was when the penny dropped and I realised that the voice must have belonged to me. Momentarily humiliated, a round of applause at the back of the cinema lifted my spirits and I am delighted to say that the red laser was not seen again.

The bottom line is that the arts have not yet acquired the kind of social status that they have in other parts of the world. As long as local universities continue to plug their technological and scientific (money making) degrees, sports and the arts will continue to take a back seat. Watch any play at Victoria Theatre and you will invariably meet young actors and directors outside the building trying to hand you flyers and desperately encouraging you to come down and support their next production. These are the Singaporeans that I truly admire. They appreciate that the buzz that comes from audience applause cannot be matched on a balance sheet. Along the way, they have probably had arguments with relatives over their career choices but these guys have persevered and they are

Singapore's only chance of creating a so-called funky town.

Until that day happens, Singaporeans are going to have to continue to live with certain things. They will still have to rely on the West or Japan for their entertainment, be it on the stage, in the cinema or on the Walkman. There will always be a dearth of artistic talent as long as Singaporeans are encouraged to be stockbrokers or personal bankers. Artists in Singapore should not have to beg you to come and watch their performances nor should they have to tell you to switch off all irritating electronic devices once you are inside the theatre or cinema. But they do. And I cannot see this changing until there is a mindset shift and Singaporeans begin to see a career in the arts as something that can be emotionally rewarding.

The same can be said for sports. No parent can guarantee that their son will grow up to be the next Fandi Ahmad so it is much safer to play the percentages and send him into the corporate world of large salaries and fixed bonuses. When these 'safe' corporate citizens return home, they can switch on their televisions and watch real winners like Manchester United, the Los Angeles Lakers or Pete Sampras, or perhaps they will watch a Hollywood movie and add a few dollars to one of Tom Cruise's bank accounts.

In fact, most Singaporeans were probably doing one of the above on a glorious night back in 1998 when, against all odds, Singapore won its first national soccer trophy, beating Vietnam 1-0 in the Tiger Cup final. I sat on the edge of my seat for 90 minutes. When the final whistle was blown, I ran around the room cheering. I felt privileged that I had somehow been a part of Singaporean sporting history. I was the only one cheering, though. When England scored against Germany in the 1996 European championship semi-final, you could hear the whole street celebrating in Dagenham. However, here, I was in an HDB block with common corridors and I did not hear a thing. I went out into the corridor to overhear the television sets and the majority were switched to one of those period dramas, with lots of kung fu fighting and crying. Hardly anyone was watching the final. It must have been assumed that Singapore had forgotten how to win a football match. Now that they had, no one was really interested. To me it was a really deflating, anticlimactic realisation, a bit like being smacked on the jaw by a man who supports the same team as you. It became obvious that sports, like the arts, are considered something that you do at school or play occasionally to keep fit but neither are considered viable career options. All the Tiger Cup wins in the world will not change that. Depressing? It is enough to turn you into a personal banker but, please God, don't.

# *Chapter Thirteen*

Scott was given seven days to leave Singapore. Just a day after he had opened his first bank account and a month after he had moved into his own room with a lovely Indian family, he was ordered to clear off back to England. We were both devastated. When I returned from work that Saturday night, I was shocked to find Scott and our friend Victor sitting on Saudita's sofa. Scott broke the silence saying, 'Immigration has told me to fuck off. I've got until the end of the week. The bastards.'

I could not begin to imagine how he felt. To plant firm roots in a country, only to have them mercilessly ripped out by an anonymous bureaucrat must be soul-destroying. The poor sod told me he stepped out of the immigration building and started to cry. What else could he do? All his plans and ambitions for the next couple of years had been crushed by one man's 'no'. On top of this, Immigration is not obliged to give a reason for rejecting work permit applications so it did not. I know that Scott is just a number to them, a name on a piece of paper, but a 'sorry' would have been nice rather than something along the lines of 'Sod off. We do not want you here. We accept that you've just moved into a new apartment with a lovely Indian family and have paid out over

S$1,000 in rent and deposits but tough shit. As for the reasons for rejecting you, even though your work record is exemplary, we do not have to give them so we will not. Goodbye.'

That is water under the bridge now and Scott has not looked back. The silly sod is now working for an up-and-coming architect's practice in Central London. He has also married a beautiful girl from Wales. Make no mistake; he has come back with a vengeance. However, he is still prone to the odd cock-up from time to time.

There is a London gangster movie called *Villain* that I absolutely love. Set in 1970, the movie stars the great Richard Burton as a sadistic gang boss. When I heard it had been re-released in England, I asked Scott to send me a copy and he kindly obliged. Then came the cock-up.

One morning, I received a card from the Singapore Board of Film Censors informing me that a package had arrived for me and requesting that I go down to their offices for a little chat. It turned out that Scott, the dopey but honest soul, had carelessly noted that the contents of the package contained a video. Therefore, the parcel had been re-routed to the Board.

I have always abhorred censorship so I knew that I might say something that my employment pass would later regret. As a precaution, I took Greg, my old boss and good friend, with me. Now Greg is as cool as they come and I suspected I might need to exercise his calm diplomatic skills and possibly his knowledge of other local languages. When we arrived at the offices of the Board of Film Censors, the guy at the counter produced my package and explained that he could open it only in my presence. Reluctantly, I agreed and surprise, surprise it was my movie from Scott. The guy then highlighted my 'options'. I had the right to return the parcel to its sender, settling the issue on the spot. Alternatively, I could *pay* the Board to kindly view the film for me. The Board would then decide what was suitable viewing for *me* and I would have to pay them again if any cuts were made.

True to form, I completely lost it. 'Are you telling me that guys in this building, who have never met me, are going to decide what I can watch?'

'Yes.'

'Wait a minute. This is a gift from a close friend. How would you feel if one of your close friends sent you a gift, only for me to intercept it? I then open it and inform you that a stranger is going to examine it to decide which parts you can have. A service for which you have to pay. How would you feel?'

'You can just send it back if you like.'

'But it's a gift. My friend has taken the trouble to send it. Why the hell would I want to send it back?'

'In that case, you can have it viewed by the Board. Here are the charges.' He then gave me a leaflet containing all the charges. It was so many dollars per 30 minutes and then a couple of dollars per cut. It was insane.

'I've never heard of this policy. I know films are censored but I didn't know you had a policy like this,' I argued back.

'Would you like to send the film back?'

'No, it's my bloody film. I don't see why I have to pay you to cut it for me.'

'Those are your options.'

'I didn't know about them, though. It's not as if these leaflets are available in supermarkets or in MRT stations, is it?'

We were going around in circles so Greg intervened, 'I think there's a lack of awareness here. My friend hasn't been in Singapore for very long so perhaps it would be worth considering the idea that such material be made more readily available for foreign workers at airports and at immigration. This would be in the best interests of both parties and episodes like this could then be avoided.' He was not saying anything radical but it deflated the situation a little.

'I'll pass on your feedback,' came the quick, diplomatic reply.

'That's still not going to help me, is it?' came the even speedier retort.

I knew I was fighting a losing battle so I took a calculated gamble and lost. 'Okay, I'll pay you to watch my gift. I've watched the film dozens of times and I've seen more violence on a Channel 8 kung fu "family" drama. I'm convinced there's absolutely nothing you'll find worth cutting,' I said confidently.

When I collected my film a week later, it had two cuts and I received a bill for around S$10. It was impossible to fathom what scenes in the movie could be deemed cut-worthy. However, I was presented with a cute little censor information card, detailing the cuts and why they had been administered. Only a thoroughbred civil servant could have written the card. I have still got it somewhere and it says something like 'Cut number 1, 58th minute, lady exposing both breasts.' I burst out laughing. They are certainly taking the business of fun seriously down at the Censors Board.

The lady in question was exposing not one but, shock horror, both breasts. If she had only exposed one of her breasts, perhaps the cut would have been half as long. The Board was right, of course, but it was such a trivial breast showing incident that I had forgotten all about it. Prior to beating a guy senseless in a men's toilet (which is, of course, acceptable), Burton chats with the victim in a strip bar while a topless belly dancer is doing her thing in the background. Thus, I will put my hands up here and admit that I had missed that one. I had completely forgotten that you are permitted to watch a man be savagely beaten on the silver screen, a gruesome scene that I have been lucky enough never to witness in my life, but you cannot watch a woman baring something as natural as her breasts, a quite wonderful scene that I have been lucky enough to witness twice in my life.

The second cut just knocked my socks off. Part of the scene in which Burton chats to his victim in the strip bar was cut. Why? Well, as the card says: 'Poster on wall in background has pictures of women exposing breasts.' The card did not go so far as to say whether the women were exposing both of their breasts but I suppose it is serious enough when more than one woman is involved. Now excuse my uncensored language but these people need to get a fucking life. Despite the number of times I had previously watched the film in England, I had never noticed the poster. Who on earth is censoring and cutting our movies? Have they ever been with a woman before? If they have not, I have a shocking revelation to make – women have breasts. Admittedly, they come in all shapes and sizes but women nonetheless have them. Why Singaporean film censors are hell-bent on denying their existence is a mystery to me. And let's be brutally honest here. I know for a fact that you can see the real thing for almost the price of a movie ticket at any of the brothels in Geylang so what is the bloody point?

Calming down a little, my foray into immigration and censorship is my long-winded way of coming round to the subject of politics and government. The reason being, as I hope I have made clear, you can feel the hand of the Singaporean government everywhere. An inevitable reality perhaps when you consider that we are living in what is essentially a one-party state. However, before anyone panics, namely civil servants and my publisher, I am not about to turn this book into a political treatise. I have no intention of writing an academic text on the nature of Singapore's government largely because so many other writers (i.e., Singaporeans) could do a far better job. Besides, I have more positive things to say about this government than I do negative, which may surprise many people.

My formative years of studying history had taught me that Singapore was a trading post for the British, founded by that fella whose name is now shared with the hotel where you get the famous cocktail. Interestingly enough, the British prime minister at that time was one Lord Liverpool. Now wouldn't it be marvellous if hotels, streets, airport lounges, MRT stations and goodness knows what else here were named after him? That would really make my day if the thousands of local Manchester United fans had to go into the Liverpool bar in Liverpool Street next to Liverpool Place station to watch their Devils play.

I soon realised that knowledge of the East India Company, British imperialism and nineteenth-century trading routes was not heavily sought after in Singaporean coffee shop conversations. I also accepted that I could only take the Lord Liverpool joke so far, although he did have a foreign secretary called Lord Castlereagh who engineered the settlement after the Napoleonic Wars and then went and slit his own throat in front of a mirror. This, of course, has no relevance except for the fact that I use any excuse to tell that story. Consequently, I knew that I needed to brush up on my knowledge of this modern metropolis.

Reading through travel books, I kept stumbling across the term 'soft authoritarianism'. Western writers wrote of 'subservient', even 'cowed', Singaporeans who always did what they were told.

Democratic elections were a formality as the People's Action Party had been returned to power with huge majorities on every occasion since June 1959. Lee Kuan Yew was the youngest prime minister in the world at that time and when he chose to step down in 1990, he had become one of the longest-serving party leaders in modern leadership. I then discovered that one of his sons, Lee Hsien Loong, was deputy prime minister. Well, this sounded like a fun, Orwellian place to be with an all-powerful nepotistic government.

Consequently, I was completely opposed to the Singaporean government for about two months after my arrival. I was totally appalled by the seemingly infinite number of fines that the government had introduced for what appeared to be such minor misdemeanours. For example, there are penalties for not flushing toilets, littering, eating or drinking on any form of public transport and jaywalking. Both Scott and I could not believe that such draconian measures were still being implemented and, more importantly, enforced in this day and age. I was becoming quite depressed by it all so I asked Justyn, an expatriate friend who had lived in Singapore for a number of years, if he believed that Singapore was an authoritarian state.

He said, 'Well, look at it this way. What is there that you can't do? You can earn a decent living but you are not allowed to commit crimes. Really, there's not a great deal that you can't do except for the things you shouldn't want to do.'

I slowly began to agree with him. I have learnt to accept and agree with the majority of Singapore's harsh laws. The obvious retort to this is that I have lived in the country too long and have fallen for the rhetoric. On the contrary, it was living on a working-class council estate for almost twenty years that changed my mind. It became an absolute joy to walk down streets that were not strewn with litter, dog shit and chewing gum that sticks to your shoes and requires the services of a welder to remove.

When I first returned to England for a holiday over the Christmas period, I found myself complaining like a grumpy old man. There was litter everywhere and teenagers were still hanging out on street corners, only their language had become cruder. The local newspaper could print nothing other than murders, muggings, burglaries and demands for increased welfare benefits for Dagenham's high population of teenage mothers. Sure, I could step into any store and buy an uncensored movie but why would I bother? There was plenty of sex and violence in my former home town to keep me entertained. Ironically, the setting up of closed circuit television (CCTV) cameras just about everywhere confirmed that there was a 'Big Brother' world after all. Fortunately, I had left it to live in Singapore.

So what are some of the so-called draconian laws enforced by the Singaporean government? Western travel writers constantly bemoan the fact that Singapore is a 'fine' city and tourists even buy the 'Singapore's a "fine" city' T-shirts that mock all the things that cannot be done here. To me, this is such a naive perception. At the end of the day, if you think that the fines are ridiculously steep (for example, around S$1,000 for littering), then the simple solution is not to break the laws in the first place. I will not apologise if I sound like an eighteenth-century Tory here. Singapore is spotless and it has some of the cleanest public amenities I have ever seen; a fact that is all the more impressive when you consider its high population density.

When I was growing up, I had the misfortune of needing to visit the little boy's room urgently on several occasions and had no choice but to use the ones found in London Underground train stations. The foul stench numbed the sinuses on entry. Graffiti was everywhere and, in some instances, it seemed marker pens were not readily available so the artist had managed to 'produce' a different kind of writing material. Unsurprisingly, there was hardly ever any soap in the dispensers and as for finding any toilet paper, well, you had more chance of bumping into George Michael. In Singapore, of course, all of the above offences would carry fines, but most public facilities are rarely abused or mistreated. Funny, that, when you think about it.

Please do not think for a second that England is a lawless society, far from it. The home secretary has got laws coming out of every orifice. These laws, however, are not enforced in the same way. That is the crucial difference. Being caught on the train or the tube without a valid ticket in England makes you liable for an on-the-spot £10 fine (about S$25). In Singapore, on the other hand, if the ticket inspector finds you without a valid ticket, he will usually take your farecard and charge S$1 to it (just 40 pence).

When I was a teenager, I needed to get a train to and from school. I always had my train fare but I would more often than not spend the money on something else and sneak through the station without paying. Looking back, this was, sad to say, probably as easy as it sounds. All you had to do was evade the eyes of one guy. That was it. One guy, who was usually overweight, would sit in his little glass cubicle and you would flash your school pass or your daily ticket at him and walk past. It was such an easy, low-paid job and most of the time the guy only gave a token glance up at the hundreds of blurred tickets that whizzed past him. Still, when I was thirteen years old, it seemed like Mission Impossible.

Of course, it was wrong to evade paying my fare and thus break the law, but it was so easy. If I was caught, I would just tell the man that I had made the shortest journey possible and give him 30 pence to pacify him. Officially, he was supposed to hand all monies in but when he walked home, he could play the tune of 'Jingle Bells' without moving his lips. That was how it was in England, just about everyone broke the law on British Rail.

Now, there are ticket barriers at the entrance and exit of each train station, while London Underground has gone one step further and installed CCTV cameras and alarm barriers that can only be opened with a valid ticket inside every tube station. Have these improved the system? What do you think? Little laws have been broken for so long that there is now no turning back.

Coming home on the tube a couple of years ago, I watched dumbstruck as two kids jumped over the barriers and walked off without showing their tickets. They did this under the watchful eye of the CCTV cameras and in front of commuters and the on-duty station officer. The boys made no attempt to run and no one, including me, dared to stop them. Life is just too short. I would have lacked the balls to carry out such an act of bravado at their age. Then it occurred to me. They were roughly the age I was when I used to carry out my Mission Impossible routine. The obstacles might have changed but the crime remains the same. Both they and I have been conditioned by an environment in which laws are rarely enforced. And as for that seemingly draconian on-the-spot £10 fine? Flummoxed Metropolitan police officers are continually being given false names and have to spend thousands of pounds of taxpayers' money to track down the offenders to retrieve the fines.

Singapore, on the other hand, enforces its laws and is not afraid to mete out punishment. Admittedly, the size of the island certainly aids law enforcement as criminals are not exactly overwhelmed with a choice of safe houses. If you rob a petrol station, expect imprisonment. If you commit rape, expect imprisonment and the cane. If you commit a murder or bring heroin into the country, expect the rope. To middle-class Western academics, who tend to live in little suburbs with white picket fences and are very quick to criticise Singapore's stance on crime without actually living here, my retort is simple: do not break the law. I know what to expect, Singaporeans know what to expect and Michael Fay knew what to expect.

In 1994, the American teenager achieved global fame when he was given four months imprisonment and four strokes of the cane for vandalising cars. Like many expatriates here, he obviously had too much time on his hands and was soon bored with the kind of luxuries that the Singaporean kids living in my HDB block can only dream of. The spoilt brat deserved everything he got. After all, I do not like everything about Singapore but if I am content to take home its dollars every month, then I have to accept certain things like having my video censored for me. Similarly, Fay's family had to accept that 'when in Rome', they cannot behave how they please, safe in the knowledge that Uncle Sam will come in and save the day.

After doing a search on the Internet for Michael Fay-related sites, I was quite surprised to find that he did not have too many sympathisers. In fact, one or two Americans even applauded the no-nonsense and no-exception policy of the Singaporean government. After all, if its lawmakers chose, quite correctly, not to spare the life of Filipina maid Flor Contemplacion after she was found guilty of two murders in 1991, why the hell should they spare some irritating American adolescent from a few strokes of the cane?

Of course, the Singaporean government is not perfect and sometimes its leading ministers make pronouncements that send me reeling in disbelief. There are just two areas that really rankle with me: censorship and homosexuality.

I have absolutely no problem with being hanged if I import heroin or being fined S$1,000 for dropping an ATM receipt. However, I do have a major problem with being told what I can and cannot watch at the cinema, on stage or even in the privacy of my own home. In our so-called New Economy, any form of censorship is going to be pretty much redundant. It was no secret that when the movie *Titanic* was released, Singaporeans were watching it over the Net to see the uncensored scenes of the actress lying naked on a couch.

The technological age is progressing so rapidly that the laws on censorship seem like an anachronism of the previous century when, perhaps, they had more validity. I can understand how ultra left-wing movies might have caused problems in the 1960s or films criticising neighbouring countries and trading partners might not have gone down well in the 1980s but what is there to fear now? If I am missing the point somewhere, it really does not matter because Singaporeans can access those 'fearful' things on the Net anyway.

Now do not assume that I escaped censorship just because I grew up in a Western society. I was raised during the Thatcher years; a time when former British agents had their books about spycatching banned in their own country and the national tabloid, the *Sun*, selected our government for us. Therefore, I am no stranger to a little censorship and manipulation but that does not mean that I will condone it.

Ironically, the funniest part about censorship is that as soon as something is banned, everybody wants it. It is basic human nature. Watching Singaporean friends distribute chewing gum excitedly after a trip to Malaysia is painfully embarrassing to watch. In my last job, colleagues would leave messages on the staff noticeboard informing us that they had a box of chewing gum. Before you could say 'It's just a stick of gum that cannot be swallowed and looks like a small brain when you've finished chewing it', everyone was diving into the box.

Just recently, I watched the movie *Me, Myself and Irene,* which was a gross bodily-function affair. What was really irritating about the film was that the local censors allowed all of the gross scenes to stay but omitted some of the funniest dialogues in the movie. That is, the fast-talking jive between three young black actors because, I assume, of the word 'motherfucker'. I am not saying that it is not an unpleasant word but is it any worse than watching a man (and a dog) defecating on a lawn?

This highlights the fundamental problem I have with any form of censorship. It is determined by the opinions of a small group of strangers. Just because they are upstanding and usually wealthy and successful members of the community, what right do they have to tell me what I can watch and hear? Whether it is Frankie Goes To Hollywood's 'Relax', which was not allowed radio play in Britain at one time, or Oliver Stone's *Natural Born Killers,* which was banned in Singapore, if I am not allowed to hear or see either of them, then I am left with one radical course of action – to switch on my computer and click my mouse. The ability to disseminate information has progressed so rapidly that continuing to censor artistic performances seems about as ridiculous as me paying a man to open up and cut a gift that was addressed to me. Therefore, I suspect that the laws on censorship will change over the next decade or so before they become redundant.

But I do not suspect that views on homosexuality will change. I have a close friend, a Singaporean accountant, who is gay. He shares a wonderful relationship with his mother but he can never tell her that he is gay. He fears it would break her heart and she would never speak to him again. He suspects the same reaction from his father. When he told me, I was disgusted and shocked because he bore no resentment to either parent. 'That is just the way it is,' he said. Due to these deep-rooted values, my friend has to spend the rest of his life living a lie not only to his society but also to his own parents. What does that have to do with the PAP?

Well, it is true that conservatism breeds conservatism. But which came first? A politically-apathetic, traditional society of Singaporeans or a repressive government? I do not know the answer and I do not care. All I know is that I do not see people on the streets demanding freedom of expression or equality for gays. Can a people be that easily afraid or, more depressingly, that easily bought off? Whatever the reason, many Singaporeans give the impression of being conservative. As I write this, a number of letters appeared in the *Straits Times* Forum pages demanding the *Harry Potter* series of children's books be banned on the grounds that they dabble with the occult. If any of those letter writers read this, highly unlikely as they are probably attending a neo-Nazi book burning rally, can I please say 'Get a life'. As one sensible Singaporean retorted, *The Wizard of Oz* deals with witches and wizards as does *The Chronicles of Narnia* so should we ban them as well? While we are at it, Enid Blyton wrote about elves and shoemakers while Roald Dahl wrote a book about some witches and it was a comedy. How dare he, the bastard. Now with Singaporeans like these, who needs soft authoritarianism?

It does not stop there. In a quite tragic incident, a girl was killed in 2000 when a plant pot fell from an HDB block and hit her on the head as she walked beneath the block. It was a sad, million-to-one tragedy. Nevertheless, it happened and the government was right to take action. Residents in my block do leave objects, such as pots and prayer objects, hanging precariously over the edges of window sills and ledges and these objects are undoubtedly dangerous. After the incident, the HDB and Town Councils stipulated that a written warning would be issued to any resident storing 'killer litter' and if the resident did not take heed of the warning, further steps would be taken. That seemed the rational approach to take. For some, however, it was not enough. There were public demands for residents to be evicted or to have their flats confiscated if found guilty. I found myself laughing at the insanity of it all. By all means, fine residents but to take away their S$400,000 property and leave them homeless for hanging a plant pot on a window ledge seems a trifle excessive. Once again, the demand had come from below and not from above.

Almost every Singaporean over thirty that I know, in some cases younger, has no great desire to see censorship abolished or homosexuality legalised. If they do, they are certainly not going to risk their status and financial security to bring it about. I know of gay doctors who are not happy with the status quo but do not want to risk their standard of living to change it. Maybe Singaporeans have been bought after all and Lee Kuan Yew, after looking at the political and economic turmoil in the region over the last couple of years, really does understand his voters. If you had grown up in a kampung but now had a home, a car, a steady income, an annual holiday and could provide a decent education for your children, what is a little censorship and homophobia?

Of course, not every Singaporean in the twenty-first century grew up in a kampung. Younger Singaporeans are becoming more aware of societies that have greater artistic and sexual freedom. This, I feel, is the greatest threat to the future of the Singaporean government. Cleanliness, safety, efficiency and strong moral values may be able to retain the likes of me, simply because I have already had a bellyful of the alternative, but these guys have experienced nothing else. And it is going to take more than a Speaker's Corner, which could end up just attracting tourists like the one in London's Hyde Park, to keep them here. An increasingly intelligent, knowledge-based population, which is what the government wants, may feel restricted and somewhat insulted if they can make big bucks during the day but cannot cuddle up with the partner of their choice and watch uncensored films by night. It is a compromising situation that will be enough to retain the greedy, kiasu brigade but it will not be enough to keep those few talents who view life as something more than just accumulating dollars.

So let's remove the shackles on the arts scene and have a few laughs. Allow actors to speak Singlish, crack a few jokes, be homosexual, play football or do whatever they like if it is all in the name of realistic performance. If a young couple is madly in love, let them walk down the street hand in hand, whether they be two men, two women or even a pair of American tourists. None of these changes can be considered particularly radical today and I am positive that it will not lead to the government being toppled.

Aside from my old secondary school's sixth form committee, over which I happened to be the chairman, there is no such thing as a perfect government. However, for my money, the PAP does okay. It guarantees a standard of living that few countries in the world can match. It has no welfare, which keeps taxes low, yet its educational and medical facilities are heavily subsidised and affordable to almost everyone. And unlike many British governments, its members do not have the habit of being found in uncompromising positions with hookers and independent auditors. No government can ever be completely secure in its position but the PAP comes fairly close. So if it could just open up on issues pertaining to sex, freedom of speech and artistic expression, something that the Net is doing anyway, then it might plug that brain drain.

While it is at it, perhaps the government could introduce a law that stipulates all public servants must smile and answer their telephones or risk imprisonment. And if the government could also deport on sight any tourist found wearing white, knee-high socks with sandals, then Singaporeans could truly say that they have never had it so good.

# *Chapter Fourteen*

I suppose it was a Caucasian dressed as a banana and giving away cocktails that drew us to the place. We needed a bar to celebrate one of our colleagues leaving and this particular one looked ideal. Tucked away in a little side street off Orchard Road, it was directly opposite where we worked. The majority of its clientele were Caucasians, or ang mohs. This is hardly surprising as the banana at the door was giving away delicious banana cocktails to anyone who entered. Most of the ang mohs I know (myself included) will walk barefoot over broken glass to get at cheap drinks. Our party that night all agreed with banana man that this was the place to be.

It was almost a classic night. Scott and I drank so many banana cocktails that we could have been peeled by the end of the evening. Everything was going along swimmingly and we all promised to be the best of friends until the end of time. Then everything went pear-shaped. There was a group of obnoxious blokes in their forties who began to make some lewd comments to some of the ladies in our group. It culminated with one guy leaning over to my missus and saying he liked her so much he intended to 'put his hand up her skirt'. Things became a little hysterical after that and an excellent evening was thoroughly spoilt.

So allow me to ask you a question. Bearing in mind that both Singaporeans and Caucasians were in the bar, who were the cavemen that night? I must have been in dozens of Singaporean bars and nightclubs and things have only ever got heated twice. On both occasions, they involved ang mohs. On that particular night, the trouble was caused by a group of Australian tourists who were determined to intimidate as many people as possible. When informed that my partner was not only seeing someone but that he was standing opposite her in the bar, the Aussie Neanderthal replied, 'Good.' It just warms the heart, doesn't it?

Apart from skin colour, I have nothing in common with these Caucasians. To be honest, I have very little in common with the expatriates who live in Singapore either. For a start, most of the ang mohs that live here, particularly the ones from Britain, tend to come from the upper-middle classes. Singaporean employers are not going to search the far reaches of London, New York and Paris to find road sweepers and table attendants when there are plenty of poor souls from India and the Philippines that they can offer crap wages to instead. Second, ang mohs here are highly-skilled in line with Singapore's 'foreign talent' policy. Sorry, I mean 'global talent' policy.

Highly trained for nothing when I first arrived, the global talent policy was about as useful to me as a pair of sunglasses to a man with one ear. With large broking firms unimpressed by my ability to highlight the differences between Stalinism and Nazism, I began to seriously resent those ang mohs strutting around the business district with their briefcases, handphones and Brylcreamed hair. As I sat on a bench overlooking the Singapore River in a pair of Bermuda shorts and flip-flops and eating Scott's cheese slice sandwiches, it became obvious that I had more in common with the local guys who drank Tiger beer in my Toa Payoh coffee shop. The snotty-nosed guys called Arthur and Charles, whom I had so despised at university, had arrived in Singapore in their thousands to earn big bucks and live in condos with swimming pools. Call it jealousy or envy, call it whatever you bloody like, but I could not bring myself to like them. Almost immediately, Scott and I began to distinguish 'us' from 'them'. If I was asked to accurately define 'them', I probably could not. All I can say is, just hang out at, say, Holland Village, Clarke Quay or any coffee bar around Orchard Road and you will see them and their tourist brothers and sisters everywhere.

The funniest part is that if you happen to be in a lift or a train carriage with one of them, they treat you like a long-lost colonial cousin; a fellow son of Mother England, keeping a stiff upper lip in the face of unknown Asian adversities. They seem to believe that there is a shared British bond, or a subconscious connection, that is somehow going to turn us into instant friends. Now there would be nothing wrong with this if it was not for the fact that these very same people used to walk past me in their thousands as I travelled to work each day in London. When I was a lowly temp working at Britain's top stockbroking firm, there were colleagues sitting opposite my desk who did not even know my name. Put these people on a train in Singapore and suddenly they want to share their life history with me.

My girlfriend and I were coming home from work together once when we were collared. Both being teachers at that time, we were discussing our classes when a guy resembling Charles Manson came over.

Straight to the point, he asked, 'So you're both teachers here then?'

'Erm, that's right,' I replied cautiously, acutely aware that half of the carriage was listening to us as ang mohs, particularly Americans, have a tendency to converse loudly in public places.

'Oh, I thought so. I overheard you taking about it.'

'Really? Are you a teacher as well?' I asked politely. At this point, my partner shot me a filthy look. She has barely enough patience to sustain a conversation with me, let alone one with a complete stranger.

'I was. Weren't we all? Ha ha. I taught English as a foreign language in Spain and I did it here for a while too. What else can "we" do here? Ha ha.'

Well, 'we' could keep our voices down a little, I thought. But he had no intention of letting up.

'Then I travelled the world a bit. Well, you've got to, haven't you? While you've the chance, that is. How long have you been here then?'

'On this train? About ten minutes.'

This puzzled Charles. 'No, I meant how long have you been in Singapore?'

'Oh, I see. About six months now. Oh, Toa Payoh. This is our stop. It was nice talking to you.'

'Yes, you too. So you live here do you?'

'No, we live in an apartment just around the corner.'

'What? Oh I see. Well, take care. Maybe I'll see you around. Bye.' The doors closed and Charles disappeared into the night.

I was twenty-two when I had that conversation and it was the longest I had ever had with a British stranger. Yet I had to come all the way to Singapore for it to happen.

Of course, the conversations are not always as long as that. We were having a barbecue at a friend's condominium once and I got into the lift to get some charcoal from his flat. An ang moh also got in the lift, spotted the S-League football shirt that I was wearing and got quite excited about it.

'So you're a professional footballer over here, are you? That must be exciting. Which team do you play for? I expect the money's good, isn't it?'

'Sorry, I'm not a footballer. I'm a teacher. I just wear this for fun, mate,' I replied.

'Oh, sorry. I thought you were a footballer out here.' He was visibly crestfallen.

'Are you a footballer?' I asked cheerily.

'No, I'm not,' he replied miserably.

'Oh well, that's settled then. I'm off to get some charcoal. Bye.'

It is not only strangers who act in this manner. Even my mother somehow expects the Brits abroad to stick together. When Nick Leeson, the rogue trader who almost destroyed Barings Bank, was imprisoned here at Changi Prison, my mother telephoned me.

'Hello mate,' she began innocently, 'have you heard the news?'

'Did Gary get that promotion?'

'No, have you heard about poor old Nick Leeson.'

'Nick Leeson? No, what's happening? Are they releasing him?'

'No. They say he's dying from cancer. He's been moved to the prison hospital.'

'Really? That's a shame, isn't it?'

There was a slight pause on the other end of the line before she asked, 'Well?'

'Well, what?'

'Well, can't you visit him or something? He is British and he probably hasn't got many friends out there. If you visit him, it might cheer him up a bit.'

Now this sounded ridiculous. I might respect the guy and sympathise with his predicament. After all, any working-class bloke who almost single-handedly brings down an archaic, nepotistic crappy old institution is all right by me. As for me strolling into a prison hospital with a bunch of flowers to chat with him, just because he happened to be born on the same island as me, is taking things a little too far.

I tried to explain this to my mum. 'But I don't even know him, do I? I have more in common with my next-door neighbours. They keep an eye on our apartment when we're on holiday and we give them clothes for their nieces and nephews. What have I got in common with Nick Leeson?'

'He's a Brit.'

'So are thousands of people in the hospitals around London and they don't all have people to look after them but we don't worry about them.'

'All right, all right... Oh, by the way, Gary got the promotion. He's in charge now.' She did not mention Leeson ever again.

Shortly after that conversation, the former trader was released from prison and returned to Britain. I sincerely hope he recovers and makes as much money as he possibly can out of the wonderful Barings Bank incident. I can safely say, though, that I do not expect us to be on each other's Christmas card list this year.

I suppose it is because I fall under the Hon school of thought. Hon is a Cantonese guy who lived on our corridor in the halls of residence at university. Unlike many of his friends, he refused to join the Hong Kong Society. When Scott asked him why, he replied, 'If I wanted to hang around with people from Hong Kong, I might as well have stayed in Hong Kong.' We liked him immediately.

I have to say that I agree with Hon's profoundly simple outlook on travel and cultural exploration. It is no coincidence that I have more local friends in Singapore than I do Caucasian. With over four million of the former, and only a few hundred thousand of the latter, how could it be any other way? In fact, I would have to actually go out of my way to seek ang mohs to hang out with. Surely no one is going to do that, are they? But of course they are. That is why I cannot blame local friends when they introduce me to expats thinking that I will be grateful because that is what all the others seem to be doing. Have a look for yourself. Go to any Western-style bar and you will see white people drinking with more white people. Alternatively, take a tetanus injection and have a cultural encounter at the legendary Papa Jo's nightspot in Orchard Road. Like vampires, the ang moh crowd comes out at night, dressed in their best shirts and armed with plenty of tax-free Singapore dollars to woo those local darlings tragically struck down by the Pinkerton syndrome. Like the character in Madame Butterfly, they are somehow lured by the attraction of drunken voices and the possibility of a fat wallet.

Many of the expats I come across merely uproot their Western lifestyle and replant it here. Go to any hawker centre in the HDB heartlands and play a game of 'spot the white man'. To be honest, you would have better odds if you went over to Pulau Ubin and played 'spot the tiger'. However, your chances of success would skyrocket if you played the same game at any French-style sandwich outlet. And what is it about these places anyway? Am I alone in thinking that the food is dry, bland and far too expensive? My mother makes more exciting sandwiches and rolls and she does not have to wear those sad, unrealistic French maid aprons while she is doing it.

I went into one of these Western hellholes in International Plaza once in a bid to tackle a raging thirst. As it was lunchtime, the place was heaving with city-slickers. Saying hello to the Chinese auntie behind the counter, I was greeted with the kind of facial expression that suggested I had just vomited on her counter. I picked up a can of warm diet coke and asked her the price.

'S$1.70,' she replied, without even looking up. Momentarily stunned, I thought she had said S$1.70 so I asked her the price again. My ears were not deceiving me.

'Excuse me, do you inject bacardi into it or something? Only it's not even cold and I'm taking it away so it won't even come with ice.'

'It's S$1.70.'

I threw the can at her silly apron and walked out. Approximately five metres away was a little hawker stall. The cheerful Chinese uncle sold me a cold can of coke for S$1, asked if I wanted a straw and said goodbye. His stall, though doing a thriving trade, did not have a single ang moh around it.

It does not stop there. I have ang moh friends who refuse to set foot in a hawker centre, who drink in Western-style pubs and only eat Western food. Their wives stay at home and perform the dutiful role of housewife. They sit by the swimming pool or watch videos of English soap operas or dramas that they have either rented from the British Council or had sent out to them by relatives. Their children go to international schools and mix predominantly with other rich white children. After work, they drink in coffee shops in Western-style areas like Holland Village. In other words, there is little attempt to acclimatise to the local way of life. They live in a cocoon, a Western bubble of condos, cars, maids, cable television, bars and restaurants, thus ensuring they have only minimal contact with the average Singaporean and his way of life. Such a self-centred lifestyle can only further exacerbate the idea of 'them' and 'us' and make Singaporeans less susceptible to the notion of foreign talent, even if it is euphemistically called global talent.

It infuriates me because I know exactly how Singaporeans must feel. When I was at university, I have to concede that our good friend Hon was very much a minority. The Asians who lived on our corridor brought their little bit of Asia with them. Before you could say haute cuisine, our kitchen was stocked with rice cookers, chopsticks and those huge chicken rice choppers. With the exception of David, I never saw an Asian cook anything mildly resembling a Western meal in three years. Whether they were from Malaysia, Hong Kong, Brunei or Singapore, they always cooked rice and noodles. On top of that, they always cooked together. In fact, they did most things together, such as eating out and going to the cinema. They never came out to the pub or played football with us, no matter how many times we asked them. Such a relationship raises cultural barriers and, after a while, it became a 'them' and 'us' situation, which makes for fraught living conditions.

Ironically, Scott and I were more willing to hang around with the Asians on our corridor than we were with our fellow Caucasians because we were in the middle of our (admittedly childish) class war. In truth, we really did have far more in common with Dave from Toa Payoh than we did with spoilt, rich arseholes from London or York. We would chat about global issues such as Manchester United, Singaporean snakes and pornography. However, we always went our separate ways when it came to going out in the evenings and that inevitably bred a little resentment. They would go off to the Chinese food wholesaler to stock up on rice while we went to the pub to stock up on cider.

Like Hon, though, there are always exceptions. I have many good friends here who have made every effort to assimilate themselves into the culture. In fact, one of my friends, Fran, tried so hard he ended up marrying a Singaporean. Lawrence refused to eat anything Western because it was too expensive and there was too much local food to choose from. Shawn, another friend, who went a little further north and married a Korean girl, enjoyed the company of Singaporeans so much that he would bare his buttocks to them at every opportunity. Why he could not just shake their hand is a mystery to me.

We were having a few drinks at Fran's HDB apartment one night when trousers started being dropped with mind-numbing predictability around midnight. On this particular occasion, Shawn got his wires crossed. After half a bottle of Fran's Chivas Regal, he assumed that Lawrence, who had just mooned him, was in the kitchen. Consequently, Shawn went down on all fours and dropped his trousers to reveal his backside and a little of what can only be called the world's scrawniest chicken. For what seemed like an eternity, he stayed in that position saying things like 'Get a load of that, you bastard.' Only Lawrence was not in the kitchen. He was sitting at the bar with Fran and me, watching this bizarre episode unfold. Fran's wife was in the kitchen preparing some snacks and she saw a side of Ontario that night that I hope she never gets to witness again.

Such drunken buffoonery is uncommon among most Singaporeans. This is because they substitute beer with good food, something that I begrudgingly admire. Eating a delicious plate of *hor fun* may not stimulate the kind of excitable behaviour required to bare your bottom to friends but it will not inspire you to try to put your hand up a complete stranger's skirt either.

Of course, the differences between locals and ang mohs are endless but it is the peculiar ones that intrigue me. In England, for instance, hairdressers like to talk profusely. I knew a gay hairdresser in Manchester who used to cut hair at the local old folks' home and recalled in minute detail all the old ladies who had died in the chair while he was still cutting their hair. He even expressed regret that he had not been paid for the cut. Then, there was the girl in Dagenham who kindly informed me that I had the kind of hair that was impossible to cut and that she could do absolutely nothing with it. At my old Singaporean hairdressers in Toa Payoh, however, they said nothing. Partly because their command of the English language was not the best but mainly because they just could not be bothered. I would walk in, the hairdresser would ask, 'Wha you want...short?' and that would be it. No pleasantries, no chitchat, nothing. If I am in an HDB lift with Singaporeans, they want to know my life story; when I am in a Singaporean hairdresser's chair, he or she wants me to shut up.

The one thing Singaporeans most certainly do not do is scratch their testicles in public. This is in complete contrast to the Western male. I had assumed that it was a British phenomenon connected to the seasonal weather. Then I realised that Canadians, if Fran, Shawn and Lawrence are any yardstick, were also guilty of it. Singaporeans, on the other hand, keep well away from their nether regions. This, to me, demonstrates remarkable self-restraint. In a country that sits on the equator and is humid all year round, I have to ask: how *do* you do it? It is impossible for me *not* to resemble Captain Hook with chickenpox when I am sitting on a non air-conditioned bus in the midday Sun and feel the sweat trickle down my inner thigh.

Somehow though, Singaporeans can resist the temptation to

rip open the underside of their scrotum. Yet strangely, some, particularly the older ones, cannot resist emptying their throat of phlegm whenever the need arises. My next-door neighbour has a spitting session in his bathroom every morning at the same time. His James Brown impressions almost serve as a wake-up call. He saves his best performance for Sunday mornings when he sounds as if he is trying to raise the *Titanic*. I know that spitting is a sensitive issue in Singapore and Caucasians tend to zoom in on it when they pick out negative traits, but I have to confess that it was quite a startling observation the first few times I saw it happen.

When my missus arrived in Singapore, Dave and I took her to the best roti prata place. We called over one of the women at the stall to take our order. As she stood beside our table, she turned her face to one side, spat into the gutter and continued to write down our order as if nothing had happened. Now, this was not the first impression I wanted my better half to get of the place. Ironically, though, it is the only time that someone has spat while taking our food order in all the time that we have been in Singapore. However, it is not an incident easily forgotten.

As I say, it is a cultural thing among the older generations and it will eventually die out. What is funny though, in a sick way, is how hip these people would be on the streets of Dagenham. Growing up in my home town, everyone seems to go through a compulsory phase of thinking that it is cool to spit. Thus, that little spitting gang of Singaporeans could fit in well with London's teenagers. They would just fall down in the ball-scratching department.

Yet despite our testicle touching, our teenage spitting, our chatty hairdressers and, more importantly, our tendency not to embrace the Singaporean lifestyle, there is still a discernible emulation of the West here. And it is the quirky Western obsessions that amaze me. I am proud to say that in my entire life, I have only ever stepped in one Hard Rock Cafe. It was in Sydney and I was there, ironically enough, because my partner had been asked to get a few shirts for her Singaporean friends. Singaporeans just cannot get enough of this kind of American merchandise. What is it all about? By all means, wear a product from a country that you have actually visited but I know of many Singaporeans who have never been to any of the Hard Rock or Planet Hollywood outlets but wear their T-shirts. In fact, night markets all over the island sell imitation shirts by the dozen. I could go to Bishan and buy a phoney Hard Rock Bangkok shirt, but why would I? Does the younger generation here have no pride in its culture at all? I see youngsters wearing branded shirts that have come from everywhere but Asia while an Asian-themed restaurant called Celebrities Asia closed down because the long-term interest just was not there.

However, it is Singapore's attachment to its colonial past that really baffles me. The average citizen takes pride in his independent nation and believes that the role of the British should now be consigned to the history books. I could not agree more. Nevertheless, the invisible touch of the former colonial power can still be felt everywhere.

Just take a perfunctory glance at the city's major place names. Walk around the business district; street and building names like Raffles, Cavenagh, Victoria, Stamford and Canning will pop up. All of these places have been named after pompous English imperialists. Taking this even further, Fort Canning Hill was known as Bukit Larangan, which means 'Forbidden Hill' in Malay, before Raffles arrived in 1819. The hill was a sacred site to the Malays, who buried one of their kings there. Then Singapore's first British

Resident William Farquhar arrived and said, 'Malays, we're in charge here so piss off. This place is not of any practical use to anyone so I'm going to stick a nice bungalow at the summit. That way, I'm near to the bus stops, the MRT and P-Mart department store. If you don't like it, I'll have you shot. Now fetch me a drink.' A fort subsequently replaced the bungalow in 1859 and had to be named. Some bright spark must have pointed out that Farquhar was such a funny sounding name that it could lead to American tourists pronouncing it Fort 'fucker' Park. Although, in truth, that might have been more appropriate. Instead, the fort was named after Viscount George Canning, govenor-general of India at the time. That is fair enough. However, unless I am very much mistaken, Singapore has been an independent nation since 1965 and these days Britain is struggling to retain the Falklands Islands' sheep population, so I am convinced that there would be little uproar in Westminster if Fort Canning Hill was renamed Bukit Larangan. It would not affect the tourist dollar and besides, Singapore is trying to build its own identity.

Building its own identity, however, will not come about if the country keeps naming everything after bloody Raffles. I mean, how many public sites, roads and buildings can be named after one man? And I would also like to state for the record that Raffles did not build Singapore at all. The migrants who flocked to Singapore in the nineteenth century built this country, not a man who spent less time on the island than my mate Scott.

Nevertheless, Singapore persists with maintaining links with its colonial past. If you are not convinced, go to either the Phoenix or Westin Stamford Hotels and order a taxi. There will be a porter on hand to hail the taxi on your behalf. Only this is no ordinary porter. This is an old Chinese guy dressed up to look like Phileas

Fogg on safari. He is togged out in the most embarrassing colonial costume. His polished brown shoes neatly complement his knee-high socks, which are invaluable leg protectors from all the reptiles and poisonous insects that hide in the vast undergrowth that is Somerset Road. His matching khaki shirt and shorts set ensures he does not get separated from his party of jungle explorers while his pith helmet not only keeps the spears of those tribal natives at bay but also guarantees that the poor man spends his entire working day looking a complete prat. I used to see the porter outside Phoenix Hotel every day on my way home from work and say hello. Of course, what I really wanted to say was 'Dr Livingstone, I presume?'

I have only picked on these two hotels because I have actually seen the extras from *Dad's Army* in action. I have been told that porters at some other major hotels have to wear similar uniforms. In fact, for all we know, there could be a string of uncles up and down the country standing outside a hotel right now, dressed like one of the country's old colonial masters. A rational explanation is quite beyond me. Surely it cannot possibly be in the money-driven name of tourism. When I stayed in Luxor, I was not greeted by porters dressed like Augustus, the Roman Emperor who conquered Cleopatra's Egypt. Having said this, I did spot people wearing silly costumes when I visited the Luxor Hotel in Las Vegas but this is a country that bought the wrong London Bridge.

If hotel management is so hell-bent on dressing up its staff, then it should at least allow them to wear their own period costumes. Why not, for example, allow the staff here to wear the *kebaya* or a sarong? At the very least, the uncles should be allowed to wear the shirt and blazer that the rest of the hotel staff wears to achieve consistency. Given the choice, I would rather wear a giant condom than a khaki suit once worn by a British aristocrat. I have got more in common with the condom.

As far as I am concerned, leave the West to the Westerners. After all, and I hope the MTV generation is paying attention here, they are so much better at being Western. So those Singaporeans who put ang mohs on such a bloody pedestal, stop it right now. Nothing would make me happier than to see Singaporeans dressing, talking, eating and drinking like Singaporeans. At this point, someone will say 'But there is no particular Singaporean identity for us to hang our coat on.' My response is: What the hell do you think I have been trying to say? Forget the colonial past, sidestep those bars full of pissed Australian tourists and turn away from the stars and stripes. Singapore only has an interesting future if it is a unique one and this will never come about as long as there are old Chinese porters dressed like Stamford Raffles on safari.

## *Chapter Fifteen*

The only problem I have with Singapore's wonderful climate is that it makes me pee. Well, the humidity gives me an unquenchable thirst, which I try in vain to satisfy by drinking half of the country's Malaysian water supply. Recently, I needed to urinate so badly that I became cross-eyed and developed a walk that suggested I had one leg shorter than the other. Making my way to the public toilet, I noticed that an infuriating yellow 'do not enter' sign was blocking the doorway. I have a strong suspicion that these signs actually begin their life brilliant white but turn yellow over time as frustrated toilet-goers urinate over them.

Not easily deterred, I noticed that the cleaner had almost finished mopping the floor so I asked her if I could go in. She nodded and stepped outside to let me pass. Letting out one of those healthy 'aahs', I was in the middle of my private call of nature when I heard a swooshing sound. Taking a discreet look over my shoulder, I realised that the auntie was standing right behind me, mopping the floor without a care in the world. Thinking I was imagining things, I rubbed my eyes (with one hand, of course) and took a second look. To my horror, she was most certainly there, cleaning the floor just millimetres from my feet. It suddenly dawned on me that if I turned anything other than my head around, I could be arrested for gross public indecency. I was half tempted to whip around and cry 'What do you think of that then, auntie? You don't get many of those to a pound, do you?' But I strongly suspected that she might have giggled and mentioned something about already having *bee hoon* for breakfast.

This is not the first time that this has happened. Off the top of my head, I can recall three separate occasions when an auntie has been cleaning a public toilet while I have had the old willy out and none of them displayed the slightest hint of embarrassment. Yet I have never had such a strange encounter in a public toilet in England before. The closest I have ever come was when I went home for Scott's wedding last year. I was in the toilets in a club in Dagenham when I found myself in a conversation with a young bloke who inexplicably began and ended every sentence with the word 'fuck'.

It was most bizarre. I was washing my hands and chatting to a friend about my new job in Singapore. When I mentioned the word 'journalist', a voice said, 'Fucking hell, mate. You're a journalist, fuck. For which paper?'

Looking up, I saw a guy in his early twenties walking towards me, doing up his zip. He joined me at the sink.

'It's called *The Straits Times*, mate. It's the national paper in Singapore, mate.'

If it sounds like I was using the word 'mate' quite frequently, all I can say is strike up a conversation with a loud, drunk chap in an empty public toilet (my friend had disappeared pretty sharpish) and see what approach you would adopt.

'Fuck,' he continued, 'that's great, mate. Nice one. What do you write about then, like?'

'I cover local sports over there.'

'Fucking hell, mate. That's blinding that is, mate. So what the fuck are you doing in Dagenham?'

'I'm from Dagenham. I'm visiting my family.' I hoped that a shared socioeconomic background might impress the bloke, who seemed to have no intention of leaving or washing his hands for that matter.

'Ah, you're from Dagenham, fuck. Yeah, I live in Dagenham as well, mate. Fucking hell, small world, innit? So Singapore, lot of thieving over there like there is over here?' This was a loaded question and I had no idea what kind of answer would pacify him.

I said, 'Well, there's good and bad everywhere. I've got respect for both places. Anyway, I've got to go.' And I left him to his swearing.

In among all that nonsense, there was an obvious truth. I do sincerely respect both places. I love Singapore. For a country that is considered, again by Westerners who rarely come here, to be static and uniform, I still find it wonderfully varied. Where else in the world could you empty your bladder while an endearing old auntie, whom you have never seen before, stands over your shoulder?

This is the country where I can be sitting on my settee in my boxer shorts watching television, when Mr Eggy knocks on my door. He is a lovely old Chinese guy who walks along the corridors of my HDB block selling trays of eggs from a trolley. No matter how many eggs I already have, I make a habit of always buying a tray from him. Because as far as I am concerned, computers, the Internet and all those other geeky things will never replace the warmth of the personal touch. The same goes for the owners of the local mini-mart who always try to have a conversation with me using their smattering of English. Not only is it humbling because my knowledge of local languages is so inadequate but it unfailingly serves to remind me why I enjoy the company of the average Singaporean so much.

This was further brought home to me after a trip to the wonderful Sungei Buloh Nature Park. I went with Lawrence, who was returning to Canada shortly after and wanted to take in as many sights as possible. The park is set way back on Neo Tiew Crescent, which is in the middle of nowhere and dotted with just the odd industrial site and a few farms. I would thoroughly recommend the park to any Singaporean or tourist but would advise a couple of precautions. If you have a car, take the car. Alternatively, order a taxi or ensure that you leave the reserve by 7 p.m. to catch the last public bus of the day. Lawrence and I failed to do any of the above so we found ourselves stranded outside the closed park at 7:30 p.m., facing the prospect of an extremely long walk just to get to the main road because we had no loose change to call a taxi.

Having foolishly walked for most of the day on an empty stomach, we were left with only one rational alternative. We decided to hitchhike. It sounds crazy but at least it gives an indication of how utterly desperate we both were. A lorry approached and we both waved to the driver who, understandably, pulled over to the roadside with extreme caution. A Chinese guy in his mid-thirties warily leaned over and asked what we wanted. I put on my most sincere face and said, 'We're really sorry to bother you but we've just missed the last bus and the only way out of here now is to walk. We were just wondering if you wouldn't mind dropping us off at the main road.'

He thought about it for a few seconds, his mind obviously entertaining a number of doubts, before he finally agreed. We could not believe it. Lawrence sat in the front with the guy and I sat in the back. Coming out onto the main road, I realised that the guy was going even further and intended to drop us off right outside Kranji MRT station. Now he was going way beyond the call of duty. There was a dusky cool breeze blowing and as we travelled along one of the more rural parts of the island, I vividly recall watching Lawrence through the window having an animated conversation with our Singaporean Samaritan and I remember feeling lucky to be here.

The guy said he ran a guppy breeding farm. Well, if a guppy breeder who once gave a lift to two ang mohs ever reads this, can I just say that you are a thoroughly decent human being. But then so are the majority of Singaporeans that I have come to know. Whether they be the eccentric characters in my HDB block, the fans of S-League football or the hundreds of schoolchildren that I have been fortunate enough to teach, they have all been honest, hardworking people.

But I wonder how things will be for Singapore in future. All the things I love about Singapore are evolving in the name of efficiency and productivity. Just like in England, the little man is mercilessly being crushed.

Take hawker centres. My uncle's café in London eventually succumbed to the larger supermarket chains with their everything-under-one-roof concept. And there is nothing to suggest that hawker centres will not go the same way. Sanitised, expensive food courts are already in the process of replacing their grimy predecessors but at what cost? These food courts are ripping the soul out of what is a fundamental component of Singapore's food culture. Step into any food court and you will detect the lack of atmosphere. The whole place is subdued, conservative and, dare I say it, boring. For me, at least, a meal in a hawker centre is an adventure. It is land of a thousand faces. Loud, rumbustious stall owners try to entice you to their particular delicacy while groups of diners at a hundred tables talk animatedly. Old timers sit and watch the world go by while nursing a Tiger beer as dozens of school kids rush in to grab their lunch. That is an eating experience. But going to a food court, with its fluorescent lighting, is about as exciting as a trip to the dentist.

To me, that is just one of the signs of the kiasu times. The money-driven people have no time for the hawker centre. They eat on the run and get back to the office to add a few more cents to their annual bonus. That is what the nation's government wants its people to do. A good citizen is a productive citizen. Whether it is the auntie mopping the floor while I am in the toilet or the stock trader in Shenton Way, they must all contribute to the country's primary goal of bringing in the green. A non-productive Singaporean is a bad Singaporean. Retraining is the order of the day. We must keep learning, whether we are five or sixty-five, so we can continue to raise productivity and the nation's coffers. Then, and only then, can the majority afford the car, the condo, the maid and the country club and be just like everybody else.

But wait a minute. This twenty-first-century 'Brave New World' concept has one major flaw. This production line could well run out of producers. With young executives hell-bent in turning their three months bonus into a 3.5 months bonus, where is the sex? There may be just enough time for a quick shag with one's fellow executive colleague (clever people cannot sleep with stupid people) before collapsing into bed. But as for having babies, well, one or two is all the maid can realistically cope with. A third baby might put the condo back a couple of years and we cannot have that now, can we?

This unquestionably leads to falling birth rates and Singaporeans are now failing in their civic duties to bolster the nation's labour forces. Hence, the government has introduced financial incentives to encourage couples to have that third child. Many Singaporeans, thankfully, have been appalled by this course of action. Producing a life should not be decided by one or two token subsidies but one or two letter writers to *The Straits Times* have expressed gratitude to the government for reducing the financial load of having a third child and they now consider it a viable option.

Since when did a human life evolve into a consumer durable? I remember watching the annual budgets when I was a kid and my mother being concerned by the tax increases levied on cigarettes. If they had not been raised too much, she would send me out to buy a packet. She kicked the habit a couple of years ago, I am proud to say. Well, in Singapore, there are village idiots acting in a similar fashion with babies. I can imagine them at home watching the prime minister's speech and saying 'Ooh, that latest discount on a third child is a good deal. We should get one now before the special offer ends.' It will end if and when the birth rate begins to rise again and there will then be a special offer introduced for those who stop at having one or two children. It is ironic really because pessimists once painted a miserable Orwellian future for Singapore. I believe Huxley's *Brave New World* is now much closer to the mark – a place where everyone aspires to be the same thing: a greedy, selfish arsehole.

And if this world is to become a reality, what will happen to the locals that I really do admire? There will be no place in a condo for the likes of Mr Eggy, the aunties in my mini-mart or Saudita, my legendary old landlady. The very people who helped build this country will be left by the wayside and all the spiel in the world about 'retraining' will not change that. Wonderful but crazy characters around my HDB block like Vidal Sassoon and bra lady will have no role to play in the New Economy. And when that tragic day finally comes and the geeks and the greedy take over completely, I like to think that I will be sitting in a coffee shop with Mr Kong, laughing at one of his eccentric reminiscences.

This, however, is all in the future. It might yet be avoided if the government declares kiasuism to be a disease of the mind, which requires a spell in a mental institute.

Right now, though, Singapore remains a great place to be. Despite spending most of my life on the outskirts of a sprawling, unpredictable city like London, Singapore is still a colourful, vibrant metropolis that is full of variety if you go looking for it.

Where else in the world would you encounter a landlady who has a penchant for preparing food with her bared breasts bouncing all over the kitchen? Or adorable kids not only refer to a penis as a cuckoo bird but also call you one for good measure? This is a country where its cab drivers are either demanding your life story or warning you of the perils of organ stealing government hospitals. The island's most feared group of people are the hordes of aunties who can carry half a supermarket in two plastic bags, knock out an entire bus queue with one shoulder, barge and be on call to drown any unwanted rats with their bare hands. Believe me, no two days are the same in Singapore.

My partner teaches at a pre-school that is tucked away in a little rural haven. After a stressful morning of chasing rich kids around a classroom, my girlfriend retired to the lavatory to be alone with her thoughts, plan her afternoon's activities and, most importantly, empty her bladder. Sitting on the throne, she heard a gentle splashing sound, which was somewhat startling because she had not actually started doing anything yet. Slowly, she got up and turned around to find Singapore's biggest frog gamely attempting the breaststroke. Her initial scream terrified the entire school and almost broke Freddie the Frog's concentration. However, the shock was short-lived. She quickly regained her senses, washed her hands and gently picked up the frog and released it into the garden. She said he looked grateful but muttered something about having his 'bloody training schedule messed up for the amphibian Olympics'.

Her bravery left me speechless. Had the same incident occurred to me then, I guarantee that Tanglin Road would have been greeted by the sight of a lanky Caucasian, waddling like a penguin with his underpants round his ankles, waving his tackle about and shouting, 'There's a fucking frog up my arse!'

I cannot deny it. My urban working-class upbringing has left me totally unprepared for the trials and tribulations of living in a tropical Asian country and it is wonderful. Every incident in Singapore is a brand new experience that I am wholly unequipped for. And the best part is, I know another one will come along tomorrow.

Of course, the time will come when I will return to England to the faint strains of my mother's voice crying 'Where the hell are my grandchildren?' And eventually, in the dim and distant future, I will find myself in an English pub having yet another futile argument over the quality of life. Only this time, I will lean across the table, wink knowingly and whisper, 'You know, you ain't never lived until you've had a huge frog swimming laps in your toilet bowl.' My friends will fall silent and I will sit back contentedly, with a boyish grin slapped across my face. That, in a nutshell, is why I would rather be here now.

SINGAPORE'S NATIONAL BEST-SELLER

# NEIL HUMPHREYS

# Scribbles From the Same Island

# *ACKNOWLEDGEMENTS*

THERE are many kind people I'd like to blame for forcing me to write a second book. P N Balji, my big boss at *TODAY*, was convinced that the newspaper's readers would be interested in my meandering drivel. I must thank him and everyone at *TODAY* who said: "Produce a witty column every Saturday or you're sacked."

The persistence of Times Media, my publisher, should also be acknowledged. After the unexpected success of my first book, there was a polite enquiry about a sequel. Within six months, this had given way to: "Give us another book, you lazy bastard."

I'm grateful, too, for my family's generosity. I've nicked just about every funny story they've ever told me and I've yet to be sued by either my inspirational mother, my sister, Jodie, or any of the Garys that I know.

As always, the missus is on hand to say: "I don't know why you bother, your writing's still crap." Thanks, Tracy, for tolerating all that late-night typing.

But the nights were spent in the incomparable world of Toa Payoh, where the residents are funny, warm, honest and occasionally insane. It's the greatest community I've ever known. Thank you, Toa Payoh, for putting up with this *ang moh*.

## *Introduction*

I CAN'T stand expatriate columns in Asian newspapers. They are, invariably, full of condescending crap. You either get the '10 Best Pubs in Singapore' rubbish or the paternalistic CEO who is down with local culture because he eats chicken rice and has visited a hawker centre twice.

So when my bosses at *TODAY* toyed with the idea of me writing a weekly 'expat column', I lied and said I was keen. But I really wasn't interested. Who would I be writing for? What would I say? I don't know many of the white community in Singapore. We have little in common. So I kept stalling.

Of course, I could see P N Balji's frustration. My big boss was launching *WEEKEND TODAY*, a new edition of the paper for weekend readers, and wanted the content to be a little off the beaten track. At the same time, my first book on Singapore — *Notes from an even Smaller Island* — had sold remarkably well and was still on the best-seller list when *WEEKEND TODAY* was launched.

But I sincerely believed that I'd said all I had to say about Singapore in my first book. As much as I'd like to, I can't forever stress the need for landladies to walk around with their boobs out. Being the eternal pessimist, I wasn't even sure my style was suitable for a national newspaper.

Then, a magazine asked me to write a one-off piece and it all went a bit bloody crazy. The deal was, the book would get a plug in return for an article on Sarong Party Girls. You know, those Singaporean women who supposedly go for white men with big wallets. Here we go again, I thought. There's me fighting to avoid writing a weekly column full of Western stereotypes and they're asking me to comment upon possibly the biggest. So I reached a compromise. I would only do it, if I could move away from the SPG thing and talk more about inter-racial relationships in Singapore. They agreed.

And my bosses at *TODAY* hit the roof. I wasn't in the meetings, but I think the gist of the discussion was: "This *ang moh* prima donna won't write for us, but the bastard does for everybody else! Get this article in *WEEKEND TODAY*."

When I explained that this wasn't an expat column, just me rambling on about both the British and Singaporean cultures, S Murali, the *WEEKEND TODAY* editor, replied: "That's all we want. Just write in the same way you wrote your book, whenever you have an issue. And make sure it's bloody funny."

Two weeks later, the article was being discussed everywhere. In offices, coffee shops and on national radio. I was being praised by around 80 per cent of the emails I received and threatened by social, and literal, castration by the other 20. I even received email requests from troubled readers who wanted 'agony aunt' advice about their inter-racial relationships. It was an astonishing public reaction. Subsequently, "whenever you have an issue" became "Every bloody week and we don't care if you're trapped in freezing conditions in the Arctic and have lost the use of your hands." So when the publisher asked me to get off my arse and write a second book on Singapore, I thought of the columns in *WEEKEND TODAY*.

Wait, don't put this book back on the shelf. I haven't just lazily thrown together a dozen columns and said 'buy this'. There are completely new topics in here that just couldn't be discussed in a family newspaper. Moreover, I often spend more time cutting my columns than I actually do writing them. So I liked the possibility of expanding and updating them and, of course, using more colourful language. It's not me, you understand, but I must be accurate when putting words in my mother's mouth. She criticised the first book for it's lack of authenticity. She never swore enough.

So here is the second book on Singapore that I never intended to write. If you bought the first book and/or read my columns in *WEEKEND TODAY*, then it's all your bloody fault.

Neil Humphreys
May 2003

## *THE SPG*

FOR some reason, I am an endless source of fascination for taxi drivers in Singapore. After being told I'm from London, they always ask: "So, your wife Singaporean?"

"No, I'm not married. Sorry." (First shock)

"Oh, you stay here? Trellis Towers?"

"No, the HDB block opposite, in Toa Payoh." (Second shock)

"Oh, your girlfriend Singaporean?"

"No, she's British too." (Third shock).

Yes, I'm sorry to disappoint, but my long-time girlfriend, Tracy, is of the English working-class variety and I was with her before I came to Singapura, that sunny island in the sea.

"What, girlfriend *ang moh* ah? Then why you come to Singapore, ah?"

Let's face it, you can hardly blame the average taxi driver. We all know what he's talking about. I come from London — that fab and groovy place with democracy, a two-party political system and pornography. Why else would a single white male leave all that for Singapore, if not for the chance to pocket a fat enough paycheck so he can live in a nice condo, invite tanned, bikini-clad Singaporean girls over for pool parties, and sample the local flavours, so to speak?

To quote my eloquent Singaporean colleague on the Sports Desk: "Don't bluff ah. You bastards come over here, take our money, bang our women, and then leave."

He's only joking of course, but the sad truth is: If there weren't expats over here doing that, then his joke would have no meaning and it wouldn't be funny.

It hasn't happened to me though God knows I've tried. I haven't really. I'm quite happy with my missus — besides she'd cut the old balls off if I did, and deservedly so. I've heard of stories where Westerners have come over with their wives but have still felt compelled to have a taste of the local cuisine.

Though the *ang mohs* are wankers for cheating on their wives, they shouldn't be apportioned all the blame. Despite the recession, the predators are certainly out there, sniffing for good looks, fat wallets and condos (I have none of them so I'm pretty safe).

In fact, living in an HDB flat, I've certainly caught the attention of the ladies around Toa Payoh. But they've caught me first thing in the morning, unshaved and wearing unwashed clothes, sleepily buying bread at the mini-mart. Hardly Brad Pitt, more like a gravel pit.

But I have seen the *ang moh* hunters in action, with my very own eyes, dozens of times in my seven years here. I've seen so many Singaporean women approaching white guys at a bar to start a conversation. It's even happened to me once at Zouk.

Because I'm an ugly bugger and it was dark, the two young ladies said they found me funny. Unfortunately, I wasn't cracking any jokes at that time, but merely trying to dance to garage music.

In my first job here as a teacher, I had a Canadian colleague who deliberately went looking for young, Caucasian-favouring Singaporean ladies mostly at Papa Joe's — that old *ang moh* haven along Orchard Road — a place he described as having "an impressive strike rate".

I remember one of his Chinese girlfriends, in her mid-20s, who told me she had only ever dated white men. Slightly stunned, I asked her why, and she said that Singaporean men were "so boring, childish and predictable" (her words, not mine).

Personally, I feel that her judgement is a little unfair — tedious arseholes are a universal phenomenon. Men who really find a new handphone and all its ringtones exciting, think it's super cool to work 14 hours a day, and find talk of property prices, stocks and shares and Tiger Woods riveting, exist from here to Zaire. Though I must confess I've stumbled into more than my fair share of these boring sods in Singapore. But if I'm being honest here, you only have to look beyond their wallets and their company cars and there are plenty of *ang mohs* in the boring category too.

Yet, despite that, I have noticed what I'll call the "Western-educated Asian" phenomenon. Singaporean women who went to universities in the West, particularly Britain, tend to gravitate more to Western men when they return.

After all, they now "get" Ali G's jokes, follow the trials and tribulations of Cherie Blair and know what Damon Albarn in Blur is singing about in his ditties about suburban life in Britain.

You don't see it the other way round very often, do you? A gang of Chinese blokes, educated in, say, Manchester or Sheffield, hanging out at Boat Quay with a group of blonde bombshells who have big fat purses is a sight I've yet to see.

To be honest, I'd happily give up a week's salary to watch that. But, I'm deeply disappointed to admit that I've often been a major letdown to the Western wannabe. While some of them think they've got lots in common with me, I must admit, the feeling isn't that mutual.

Firstly, Westerners are just so much better at being Western — and that's one of the reasons I left in the first place. If I wanted to get pissed in pubs, fall over and then vomit on the road, I could have stayed in London. The beer is cheaper, more plentiful and tastes better. I didn't come halfway round the world to do that down at Emerald Hill. Secondly, my England, if you like, is vastly different from the England of the average Singaporean overseas student.

On a couple of occasions, I've nodded politely when a beautiful young Singaporean girl waxes lyrical about Yorkminster or the Roman relics of Bath. And she has usually dragged me to a Delifrance or some other overpriced Eurocentric café to do it, too.

Ms. Delifrance often feels she cannot find the same "intellectual" or "soulful" connection with some poor sod who grew up in the HDB heartlands. This is a double irony, of course, because not only is there a statistically high chance that she actually grew up in an HDB block herself, but I also grew up in the London equivalent of a three-room flat.

So what I really want to say is: "Look, I grew up in a working-class council housing estate in Dagenham, which is just outside of East London. I never had the money to go to Yorkminster or Bath, and I had never even been in a pretentious Delifrance until 20 minutes ago, when you invited me. Now, are you going to eat the rest of that overpriced curry puff, or not?"

But a Sarong Party Girl, who supposedly favours all things white and rich, is different. I usually meet them through that aforementioned Canadian colleague of mine, and for those girls (at least, the ones I managed to have conversations with; some were one-night stands I never got to meet), it was a case of money, casual sex, a brief fling or, occasionally, a bit of all three.

The best part was, the Canadian cad never actually had any money and often relied on his British credit card (me). But I believe — and I know I'm going to get a custard pie in my face for this one — money is the ultimate goal. Can we just be honest here for a minute? Whenever we've walked down Orchard Road and observed inter-racial relationships where one of the partners is Caucasian, how many toilet cleaners or garbage collectors make up the numbers?

Do you ever hear a beautiful young Singaporean say: "Have you met Graham? He's from England. We first met when he was flushing out the u-bend of the toilets at my apartment. He just has a wonderful smell about him, don't you think?"

It just doesn't happen like that. Aside from money, there is undoubtedly an element of social climbing involved. Having watched a couple of Singaporean girl-Western man relationships, I've noticed that the girls from the HDB heartlands often begin to act like they were educated at Eton. And where the hell did that accent come from?

A former colleague of my girlfriend was an avowed SPG. She was pleasant company until she met up with Mr. Prat (not his real name). He is one of those upper middle-class Brits, who's always very pleased with himself and is convinced that every utterance he makes is jaw-droppingly funny (a complete prick, in other words.) For some reason, Singapore has had to endure more than its fair share of these boring Brits, especially around the Padang area at City Hall.

Yet, our friend hung on Prat's every word and even attempted to ape his plummy Hugh Grant accent, which was hilarious, because she would flit from Emma Thompson to Liang Po Po in a single sentence. For example, one day over lunch, she told me that Prat's hair was ginger, only she pronounced it with two 'Gs' (as in got or go). I nearly choked on my sesame chicken.

She now wears clothes where the labels are actually genuine and not pasted on by the uncle at the *pasar malam* (night market) — and Prat has a stunningly attractive woman on his arm who pretends to find his jokes funny. Do they love each other and is there a future in the relationship? I have no idea. It is never easy to mesh cross-cultural values together anywhere in the world.

I know the traditional Asian value of filial piety will be a stumbling block eventually, because Ms. Papa Joe's has elderly parents here and yet both she and Prat want to live in the English countryside (naturally) — so something has got to give.

Prat also finds it extremely difficult to have sex with his partner when he knows her parents are asleep in the next room. After all, they are not 18 anymore. But he always seems to get the job done, nonetheless.

As for me, I personally hope that genuine Singaporean girls want more out of a relationship than just regular sex, an affected, artificial accent and Prada bags.

If they don't and they're really that empty, then they might as well rip up the Women's Charter and follow Prat back to the caves, where they can sit around and laugh at "oh-so-Western-aren't-we-intellectual" type jokes.

To be honest, I'd rather have a meaningful relationship with a taxi driver than an SPG. It'd be more stimulating and my girlfriend wouldn't cut my testicles off for it.

**NEIL'S NOTE:** I was actually asked to write this article by a women's magazine. Initially, I was most reluctant to touch on the subject of SPGs because it was such a cliché. My first book avoided the topic, quite deliberately, almost completely. So I agreed to write the piece, only on condition that I could go beyond the tanned legs and the sarong jokes to talk about this discernible obsession in some quarters with all things Western, which, quite frankly, gets on my bloody nerves. But the magazine article caused quite a stir, so my editor reproduced it in *TODAY* and it all got a little bit surreal after that. For a couple of weeks, I became one of Singapore's most loathed/loved men all at once. Despite the ongoing water disputes with Malaysia at that time, it became one of the most popular discussion topics in the country. Unsurprisingly, Singaporean men praised it and those in inter-racial relationships, er, didn't! But over 80 per cent of the responses were complimentary, rather than critical.

And somehow, it gave birth to a weekly column. But some of the replies I received, well!

# *THE REPLIES*

WELL, I have ruffled a few feathers, haven't I? My relatively harmless topic of superficial, inter-racial relationships has generated the sort of response usually reserved for greedy bus operators who extort an extra five cents from their customers.

The newspaper that I work for, *TODAY*, received more letters about SPGs, Western wannabes and Caucasians living in Singapore than it did on the government's Newater recycling scheme and on transport operators' plans to increase fares on buses.

What does this suggest? That we will tolerate drinking water that has been urinated in but don't mess with us when it comes to white men and Singaporean women or you will really piss us off (pun intended)?

The SPG piece has been lauded for its honesty, despised for its "stereotypical comments"' and applauded for addressing a taboo subject in Singapore.

I have been warned by one irate writer that I should remember that "generalisations are dangerous" in Singapore. More dangerous, it would seem, than drinking recycled water.

She added that I am an expat who does not have a "housing allowance, much less a company car and definitely no fat wallet".

No arguments there but she hinted that this was because I was an "ugly bugger". A tad harsh, but it's true that I avoid job applications that state: "Ugly buggers need not apply".

The most perceptive criticism came from a Singaporean girl who had just returned from her studies in Britain. Understandably, she was critical of my claim that some Singaporeans return from the West with a touch of Western wannabe-itis. She wrote: "Mr. Humphreys, obviously male, is writing about female culture in Singapore — SPGs and what have you."

Well, I hold my hands up on that one. It is true that I am male; and in some aspects, "obviously so", though not in others, which is most unfortunate. So I suppose being male — that terrible, genetic failing of mine — must have had a subjective bearing upon my writing. Though the criticisms were most welcome, they were surprisingly few. The article certainly touched a nerve with so many Singaporeans.

One writer, obviously female, wrote: "I must say that your observation is something that most of us are embarrassed to talk about. It has become a norm to see a Singaporean girl-Western male couple. I've seen middle-aged Western guys with young Singaporean girls along Orchard Road, buying them branded stuff."

Well, who hasn't? And, according to some readers, it isn't just about money. One writer, who was also educated in Britain, wrote: "I guess some of them do it for the money. Many of them do it for what they imagine to be glamour. Little do these sad creatures know that back home, many *ang mohs* here are working-class individuals."

Another reader added: "Most local women don't realise that these *ang mohs* are your average Joe in England. They are only somebody in Singland, primarily because they are 'white' (no racist remark intended)."

None taken because, as I mentioned last week, I could name a handful of Caucasians who fall into that category, as could many other Singaporeans, it would seem.

It was interesting to see the situation from the other side of the fence. A Singaporean wrote: "My ex-girlfriend clearly suffers from the 'Western' syndrome, the details of which are too painful to put down in writing."

Of course, there were those who saw such "bitching" as a case of sour grapes. Letters arrived from people who are in happy inter-racial relationships, complaining that the article was too harsh. But even one of the sternest critics, on the subject of SPGs and Western wannabes, admitted: "That's not to say there aren't any. I know a few."

Don't we all? Judging by the overwhelming response from readers, many Singaporeans certainly do. That's the point. And, thankfully, it's hardly a taboo subject now. The can of worms has been spilt all over Emerald Hill. But then, would you rather talk about drinking water?

**NOTE:** Six months after the article and the subsequent reply came out — and I'm not making this up — my old friend Fran called me up and asked: "Did you say in the press that you wouldn't date a Singaporean woman?" Now this was a delicate issue, to say the least, because I've known Fran for years. And he's Canadian. And he's married to a Singaporean. But when I explained that I never said that at all, but merely commented on those who are only in it for the money and the social status, he was pacified. It transpired, though, that he'd been in Canada on vacation and when he'd returned, he heard a couple of colleagues refer to the article. Six months after it came out! It's bizarre. Nothing I have ever written before or since has touched a Singaporean nerve like the subject of inter-racial relationships. Funny, that.

## *THE DOCTOR*

I DON'T like doctors. I didn't like them in England and, until recently, I didn't like them in Singapore. From the first time I heard the words, "You'll just feel a little prick in your bottom", I've viewed all forms of medical practice with a respectful distrust.

This uneasy relationship began when I was four years old. Sitting in the back of a delivery van with no seat belt on, my father hit the brakes sharply and I attempted, quite spontaneously, a Superman impression from a sitting position. The subsequent head injury required six stitches and my first ever tetanus injection.

Having been forced to expose my tender bottom to a rather buxom nurse (weren't they all, back then?), she whispered that immortal sentence involving "pricks" and "bottoms" for the first time. There was a slight pause, which allowed a builder to come in and insert a pneumatic drill up my arse.

Laying face down on the bed, my legs kicked out like a bucking horse, striking the terrified nurse in the chest. Though in truth, this was a difficult target to miss.

She jumped back clutching her breasts, I waddled off the bed with my trousers around my ankles like a petrified penguin and my mother slapped me for embarrassing her in a public place.

Since then, I have treated every successive visit to the doctor's surgery with mild apprehension, though my phobias of needles and breasts have subsided in recent years. But last week, the fear of all things clinical returned with a vengeance in the surreal waiting room of a doctor's surgery in Toa Payoh. My regular doctor, over in Lorong 8, was closed and I required urgent treatment for a brain tumour. What this hypochondriac really needed, of course, was a stronger pair of contact lenses and a deft blow to the head for wasting the doctor's time.

Luckily, I stumbled upon a doctor's surgery in Toa Payoh Central, which was still open. Two things should have struck me at this point. Firstly, how many private surgeries do you know that stay open after 8pm on a Saturday? Secondly, there was not a single patient in the waiting room, just two young receptionists watching a Chinese drama.

After registering at the counter, I started to read the posters in the waiting room. I was struck dumb with terror. My regular surgery had the usual warnings about vaccines for polio and hepatitis, but these were something else. For a start, they were handmade with marker pens and a stencil, which gave them a personal, homely touch. But the lines were jagged and shaky and I swore to myself that whoever the artist was, he would never be granted the opportunity to insert a needle in my bottom unless there was either an anaesthetic or copious amounts of vodka involved. Not that I was ever going to let myself be treated by a man who offered such a diverse, bizarre range of services.

On a single poster, he offered medical check-ups for work permits, hair replacement programmes, treatment for "sexual problems", medicine to improve the passage of stools and ear piercing! I pictured patients walking into the surgery, with some difficulty of course, and saying: "I've come to speed up my stool movement, not to mention my sex drive, and while I'm here, do you think you could put in these lovely diamond earrings because I'm going to a swanky dinner and dance." I'm sure she would look beautiful at the dinner, just make sure you're not caught sitting next to her when the stool potion kicks in.

If that wasn't enough, though, there was a printed poster next to the homemade efforts, which tackled the issue of herpes around the genitalia. Little was left to the imagination, but I'm afraid I'm going to leave it to yours. Let's just say there were enough graphic images of both men and women to put you off having sex — for the rest of your life.

Perhaps if the doctor offered a "set treatment", like a "set meal" at an economy rice stall, his waiting room would have more patients. Something like, one Viagra, a clear back passage, two earrings and free-flowing hair for 100 dollars.

The Chinese doctor was a most affable chap, who admitted that he specialised in cosmetic surgery, hence the unusual treatments and services on offer. But his surgery struck me as somewhat ironic. According to stereotype, Singaporeans are supposed to be the boring, ultra-conservative Asians and the British are supposed to be the gregarious, liberal Westerners. Yet every male member of my family, back in England, would cut his penis off before discussing his sex problems with a National Health Service doctor. In Toa Payoh, no discussion is even needed; one can point at poster A, B or C and say: "I've got that one there. The one with lots of weeping fluids."

I was so impressed by the openness of the surgery. After all, what is there to be ashamed of?

With National Day fast approaching, there is the usual talk of what it means to be a Singaporean, what makes a Singaporean a Singaporean and so on. Well, I propose that this Aug 9, we celebrate the unique and wonderful diversity of the average doctor's surgery in Singapore.

I'm no globetrotter, but I've visited enough countries to know that any medical establishment that can cure constipation and fix a receding hairline in one sitting is pretty special and a cause for celebration, surely. You don't think it will take off? Well, that's what cynics said about Viagra.

**NOTE:** The doctor's surgery is still there in Toa Payoh. Funnily enough, I've never been back since.

# *THE CROCODILE*

CALL me a geek, but I visited the excellent Raffles Museum of Biodiversity Research recently. I went because I had read somewhere that old Stamford Raffles, Singapore's founder and British imperialist, was a bit of a naturalist. Rather excited by this, I went to the Museum at the National University of Singapore hoping to find lots of old oil paintings of Raffles in the buff and baring both cheeks for the artist.

Imagine the postcards one could send from Singapore. The two statues of the old Imperialist would have to be knocked down and two new *erections* would be in order. But, alas, Raffles the naturalist had a love for all things living and enjoyed cataloguing various plants and animals in his spare time. Apparently, he was fascinated by zoology and founded the famous London Zoo in Regents Park.

I'm sure all this nature talk is riveting, so allow me to reveal what I discovered at the Raffles Museum — there are still WILD CROCODILES IN SINGAPORE! Not baby ankle-biters that could give a nasty nip on your big toe, you understand, but two-metre-long buggers that can split you in two with a mere peck on the torso.

I bet that's got your attention, because it certainly got mine in the Raffles Museum. Noticing that estuarine crocodiles are indigenous to Southeast Asia, I said, as a joke, to one of the curators: "I saw one mauling a durian seller outside my block in Toa Payoh last week."

And he replied, almost casually: "Oh, we still find crocodiles in Singapore from time to time. An estuarine crocodile usually gets spotted once every few months in the wild."

I shit myself. It must be remembered that the housing estate I grew up on was not renowned for its wildlife. Two stray dogs mating beside a zebra crossing was about as exotic as it ever got.

Consequently, I still get excited when I see a gecko in the kitchen, but a crocodile is something else altogether. Estuarine crocodiles, would you believe, can grow up to 40 feet in length and favour mangrove-lined estuaries in this part of the world. Singapore's northern shore seems to be the preferred habitat for crocodiles. The Sungei Buloh Nature Park, with its wet, swampy environment, is a popular holiday destination for the bloody-thirsty reptile.

"Yes, we sometimes find crocodiles in Sungei Buloh," the curator told me casually, as if he was talking about crows being found at a hawker centre.

"In fact, one was photographed there in May 2002. It was only about two metres long. But it probably wasn't wild, it probably just escaped from a local crocodile farm."

This statement is most disconcerting for two reasons. Firstly, if it wasn't wild, how do you lose a two-metre long crocodile? When the crocodile farmer locks up for the night, surely he must say something like: "Right, final check: wallet, car keys, handphone and crocodiles. Hang on, where's Dorothy gone?"

But, more worryingly, were you convinced by the curator's reassurance that the crocodile "probably wasn't wild"? Does it really matter? It's not as if one is going to go paddling in a little stream near Kranji, spot the snout of a partially submerged Dorothy and say calmly: "It's okay dear. Don't panic, this crocodile's not wild. It's come from the farm. In fact, bring the kids and the camera down and we'll take a family photograph. Oh fuck, have you seen my leg?"

This is, of course, absolute nonsense. Should you spot a peckish Dorothy while out on a family picnic, run like hell and then change your underwear at the first opportunity. But seriously, the Singapore Tourism Board should be singing my praises for this wild discovery. Forget the Merlion spouting water, Singapore has crocodiles again. If it's good enough for tourists in the Australian outback, it's good enough for tourists here.

To substantiate my point, have you heard of Steve Irwin? He's that endearing, though clearly insane, crocodile hunter on the Discovery Channel. He might have more scars than Freddie Krueger, but he's an international celebrity now and a movie star to boot. More importantly, he has become a symbol for Australian tourism, just like Paul Hogan's Crocodile Dundee before him.

Now, Singaporeans can do the same. Let's have a Singapore Dundee. Prominent personalities and leading politicians could dress up in khaki safari suits and wear hats lined with crocodile teeth to promote this exotic metropolis. Overnight, it would transform the tourism trade into a billion-dollar industry.

In truth, nature lovers have about as much chance of

seeing a wild crocodile in Singapore as they have of spotting a tiger on Pulau Ubin. But Western tourists with fat, gullible wallets don't need to know that, do they?

Singapore already has monkeys and primary rainforest to rival Rio de Janeiro; now it can also boast two-metre crocodiles sneaking up its riverbanks. Forget the Northern Territory in Australia; the fierce creatures are here. Modern Singapore remains a wild island. After all, it was founded by a man who liked to run around baring his arse to the world. And life doesn't get any wilder than that.

**NOTE:** Shortly after this article came out, another crocodile was spotted doing a spot of breaststroke down at Sungei Buloh. I told you. The buggers are coming.

## *THE GRADUATION*

WHEN I graduated from Manchester University, the degree ceremony resembled one of those prehistoric scenes in the BBC series *Walking with Beasts*. Like the primitive Neanderthals, those in attendance grunted, whooped and cheered every time a student went up to doth their mortarboards for the university's chancellor. By the time the occasion got into full swing, the grand hall witnessed chest-thumping, cartwheeling and chants of "you da man" — and that was just my mother.

The BBC's stunning depiction of early man is nothing compared to the ape-like behaviour of British parents celebrating their offspring's academic achievements. I was reminded of this recently, when I attended my first university graduation in Singapore.

As my girlfriend was one of the graduates, I felt obliged to attend and, besides, there was no football on TV that night.

Crammed into the ballroom at the Ritz-Carlton Hotel with 200 graduates and their families was, truly, an unforgettable experience. But then, so is an enema up the rectum.

A graduation ceremony, remember, is like a wedding — it's repetitive and poke-me-in-the-eye-with-a-chopstick boring. At a church wedding, we all "ooh" and "aah" in the right places and say "doesn't the groom look lovely in that white dress" (I've been to some liberal weddings), but what we're really doing is thinking about the food and alcohol back at the hotel reception.

Similarly, at a graduation, we clap politely as walking student gown No. 253 shakes hands with the chancellor and we wait — until our next of kin goes up on stage. Then, we stand up, take more photographs than the paparazzi and, then, we sit down again. That's how it's supposed to work — but no one told the irritating, impatient *kiasu* (literally meaning afraid to lose, in Hokkien) brigade this at the Ritz-Carlton.

As the chancellor called up the first batch of graduates, there was nothing. No cheering, no clapping, nothing. Apart from some stifled applauding, obviously from the graduates' families, there was virtual silence. There must have been 500 people in the room, yet the volume of applause was generated from no more than a handful of well-mannered folk.

Feeling the need to compensate, I began to resemble a performing sea lion. This caused the Chinese auntie next to me to stare at me. Her puzzled expression suggested she didn't know whether to laugh or throw me a fish. When it became apparent that I was merely clapping for strangers, she opted to laugh. So I hit her with my camcorder.

Before the ceremony started, a rather naive MC asked the audience: "Please stay seated, please do not block the middle aisle and please turn off your handphones."

The audience surpassed itself. Not only did it fail to comply with any of these polite requests, some of its more excited members managed to do all three at once. Before you could say "itchy backside", the audience was up and down more times than a convention for diarrhoea sufferers. The more adventurous *kiasus* actually left the ballroom, only to return, several minutes later, with plates of food that were supposed to be served only after the event had finished.

*Kiasuism* is an exhausting business, remember, which requires plenty of sustenance. The middle aisle, for instance, was meant to allow graduates to return to their seats. The organisers had even employed two Australians, with shoulders wider than the Singapore River, to keep the aisle pest-free.

They were the sort of muscle machines that could single-handedly keep 10,000 Melbourne maniacs away from Kylie Minogue. But the poor souls didn't stand a chance with the *kiasu* brigade. The area was soon besieged by hordes of enthusiastic, though very amateur, photographers. Graduates suffered the indignity of using their scrolls as *parangs* to cut a path through the crowd. And those who remained in their seats had their view obscured by countless, fidgety bottoms.

With my girlfriend's turn on stage fast approaching, I could see little more than one man's behind. So, like his damn camera, I snapped.

"Excuse me," I enquired. "Is this a lap dance club?"

"Huh?"

"Well, do you think I've paid 150 dollars to see the ceremony or your arse wiggling? And may I point out, you are no Kylie Minogue, so please sit down."

"Oh, sorry ah."

To his credit, he moved — a massive four centimetres to the left. In these tribal situations, of course, there must be leaders and there must be followers. Fortunately, there was a leader in the shape of a very prominent Singaporean politician, who had been invited to give the occasional address.

In my humble opinion, he had already completely cocked up his public performance by spilling water all over his speech notes. To compensate, he ad-libbed in a muffled voice for over half an hour. I've had wisdom tooth surgery that took less time.

During the on-going ceremony, however, the politician surpassed himself. He spent his time most productively — sending SMS text messages on his handphone, while sitting on the stage. What a role model for the proud graduates who walked past him unnoticed. Bring on the next courtesy campaign!

I tried to find the MP after the ceremony to discuss the importance of politicians practising what they preach, but he had gone. And, disastrously, so had all the *makan*. The *kiasu* brigade had eaten much of the food *during* the ceremony. In future, these occasions should come with a public health warning: "Eat before you go in and those who stick their buttocks into other people's faces risk a discreet elbow in the kidneys".

A celebration of academic achievement? Frankly, I'd rather sit through a convention for diarrhoea sufferers.

**NOTE:** Just to jog my memory, I watched my camcorder video of the graduation ceremony the other night. It's like sitting through a bad pornographic movie. The sound is really poor and every few minutes an arse pops into frame. Then it disappears; then it reappears. This goes on throughout the ceremony. And I was right about the guy's backside, too — a wide-screen TV wouldn't do it justice.

## *THE BREAK-DANCING*

THE United Nations is clearly wasting its time. A workable solution to the Iraq crisis won't be found in peacekeeping soldiers wearing blue helmets in the Middle East. Instead, the answer has been found in Singaporean break-dancers wearing bandanas at Far East Plaza.

One Saturday afternoon, I inadvertently found myself in the basement of the shopping mall, which now poses as the labyrinth of cool. It has become a mini-funky town of hip clothes, music and pop culture, generally. Teenagers with model looks who personify sophistication stand outside the shops looking devastatingly handsome.

Yes, fair enough, I found it by accident and was about to leave when the PA system announced a dancing exhibition to promote some trendy camera the size of a thumbnail. You hang the camera around your neck like a pendant. The idea being, I suppose, that you never know when you are going to get caught stranded on a desert island. This way you can take photographs of your environment so that, when your body is found, your relatives will have some souvenirs from your final days.

Several elderly aunties, who had either bought one of the cameras or, like me, were clearly in the wrong place, were heading for the escalator when they started cooing excitedly.

"Wait *lah,*" said the apparent leader of the group. "Watch dancing first. Come we go near the front. Can see better from there."

Quite obviously, they were expecting a ballroom dancing display or a line dancing routine perhaps with a group of well-rehearsed senior citizens wearing cowboy costumes. And then seven youngsters came out, wearing jeans that would have been too baggy for Coco the Clown, and started spinning on their heads. It was truly priceless. The aunties' faces transformed from a kind of eager expectation to a kind of "what the fuck is this?" expression. The music was so loud that the baselines made the floors vibrate — in Toa Payoh. There was robotic body-popping, head and body spinning, back flips and cartwheels and the occasional shout of "Let's go, you mothers!" And that was just the aunties.

But I thought I'd been transported back to my childhood. When it was 1982 and lots of electric boogaloo. Break-dancing was the thing to do. And I couldn't do it. Attempts to do the caterpillar across the living room floor often culminated in my lanky legs flipping up and kicking me in the back of the head. My mother would then slap me for blocking the television and I would promptly pass out.

Yet, here we were in Far East Plaza in 2003 and break-dancing was back and it was happening. One of the younger aunties had even started to clap along with the frantic hyper base throbbing. Initially, she appeared to be waiting for Engelbert Humperdinck to come out and start crooning, "Please Release Me". But now, I half expected her to turn her cap around, somersault across the floor, high-five the other funky dancers and join in. When the rather impressive exhibition had finished, there was generous applause from a 200-strong crowd while the eager auntie pumped her fist and shouted, "woo, woo, woo," as the performers left the stage.

After the show, I had a chat with the dancers and they spoke to me like I was mentally ill. They told me break-dancing had been dead since the '80s, but now it was making a comeback as part of the hip-hop culture. And who's part of the hip-hop culture, I asked 17-year-old Gianna. These guys were strictly one-name people.

"Oh, it's guys like Eminem and Missy Elliot."

"Miss C who?" She looked at me with benign pity, as if I needed help to cross the road. Or my incontinence knickers needed changing perhaps.

"Missy Elliot? The singer? You know who she is right?"

"What? Me and Miss C? Are you kidding? I've got so many of her albums, we're almost friends. She is up there, man. Miss C is up there with M C Hammer and Vanilla Ice."

I felt 128 years old.

The break-dancers called themselves Radikal Forze, with a 'K' and a 'Z' no less. There were seven of them — five Malays, one Chinese and one Caucasian and their ages ranged from 14 to 36. Being the minority, I asked National Serviceman Felix if he felt like an outsider.

"No way, man," the Chinese teenager told this 'man'. "We come from different races and different backgrounds. But we just work and practise together because we love what we do. There are no barriers, man."

And that's when I realised that Felix is right and the United Nations is wrong. In the '80s, conflicts and disputes between rival gangs on the streets of New York were often settled through break-dancing. There were movies and documentaries about it. A body-popping contest, or 'burn', to use its street name, would be held and two enemies would attempt to out-dance the other into submission.

When I was 11 years old, the school bully summoned me to 'burn' with him in the playground. It was spectacularly awful. Neither of us could perform any dance moves, except the 'arm caterpillar'. Do you remember that one? You just flicked your left arm like a caterpillar and moved through to the right arm in one fluid motion. Well, we stood chest-to-chest and did the 'arm caterpillar'. For an hour. Until the bell went. In the afternoon, neither of us could lift our arms, except when they involuntarily flicked into the 'arm caterpillar'. The spasms were most inconvenient. The history teacher kept assuming we were putting our hands up, in rather extravagant fashion, to answer questions on Stalinist Russia.

And that brings me back to current dictators with moustaches. That 'burn' between the bully and myself was a success in the sense that we left each other alone after that. So if it worked for schoolboys, it'd certainly work for George Bush and Saddam Hussein, wouldn't it?

Get them both down to the United Nations' headquarters (Bush will cry and tell his daddy if he doesn't have home advantage) and send out Radikal Forze with both their 'K' and 'Z' to train the two leaders.

Then, before the world's news cameras, Missy Elliot could bang out a few tunes and Bush and Saddam could stick out their chests in that belligerent pose popular with world leaders and totalitarian pretenders and get to work on the 'arm caterpillar'. Once the 'burn' has reached a satisfactory conclusion, the schoolboy-cum-national leaders must thrash out their differences. Incidentally, has anyone else noticed that if you say Saddam backwards, it comes out as 'mad ass'?

Now, you may think I'm naive and out-of-touch (the break-dancers certainly did), but wouldn't it be rather wonderful if we could solve global disputes with body-popping, rather than gun-popping?

# *THE GEEK*

MY missus has seriously contemplated leaving me recently. And I know precisely where and why it happened. We were at the Kranji Reservoir, a beautiful green spot that overlooks Malaysia in the north of Singapore, when I heard a distinct rustling in the long reeds hanging over the edge of the bank. A bird had landed. Not just any bird, you understand, but a grey heron. With no time to lose and absolutely no thought for my own safety, I dashed off in pursuit. Stopping some 10 metres from the long-legged bird to compose myself (and I haven't done that since I last frequented the tacky nightclubs of my youth in Essex), I crouched down to allow the long grass to provide some natural cover.

And then, the bird looked up at me. Quickly but calmly, I reached for my trusty pocket book, entitled *A Guide To The Common Birds Of Singapore*, and sought out my tasty bird. Well, I just could not contain myself.

"It's not a common heron, mate," I shouted to the missus. "The beak is black. It could well be a little egret. Hang on, I'll get a bit closer and compare the photographs."

"Neil!" came the rather urgent reply.

"Yes, mate?"

"You look a complete fucking wanker."

"Yes, mate." Her comments threw me off kilter slightly. She rarely called me names, well, not in public at least. Luckily, at a largely deserted Kranji Reservoir on a Sunday afternoon, there are usually only teenaged courting couples eating each other on the benches. Their only concern is whether or not they can get away with a quick shag in the park without being spotted by a passer-by, an *ang moh* amateur ornithologist or, worse still, their parents. So I knew I hadn't suffered public humiliation. But the unnecessary swearing rankled a little. I mean, I'd been called a wanker by various members of my girlfriend's family more times than I care to remember. But the f-word meant she was somewhat perturbed. This was hardly a trifling matter.

"What was all that about?" I asked, adopting my best hangdog face. It never works, though; I always come off more like a rabid dog.

"What the fuck are you doing getting on your hands and knees and making a tit of yourself for?" God, I love her. You don't get brutal honesty like that from the snotty-nosed types in the wealthy suburbs of England.

"I was looking for wild birds, weren't I? You knew that. That's why we came here in the first place, didn't we?"

"No, you said we were going to look for some wildlife. That's fine. I didn't expect you to roll around in the mud, looking at pigeons."

"It's an egret."

"I couldn't give a shit what it was. You look bloody stupid."

And then I saw another exotic bird swoop down and land beside the egret/heron and I lost my senses. My missus, on the other hand, lost the will to live.

"Shit. There's another one," I shouted and ran off again. But my excitement superceded my concentration and the sound of a red-faced Caucasian stumbling through the reeds terrified my birds and they flew off into the trees. Now, it was the wanker's chance to retaliate.

"Are you happy now, you stupid woman? They've gone. That's it. I'm buying a pair of binoculars and not some cheap kiddy's pair neither. I'm getting a decent pair like ornithologists use."

She looked at me, throughly horrified. Initially, my little rant had rendered her speechless before she managed to compose herself.

"Wait a minute," she said. "You want to buy a pair of binoculars so you can sit under a tree for hours looking for birds?"

"That's right. I don't sound too silly now, do I?"

"Look, mate," she replied calmly. "If you buy those binoculars, you will never be the father of my children."

She was only joking. At least, I hope she was because I really fancy a pair of binoculars. But seriously, she was right. What have I become? What has Singapore done to me? I'd become a wildlife geek — one of those weedy, bookworm types that parents would make their children avoid on buses when I was growing up in England. Living on the working-class council estate of Dagenham, the only animals I ever saw came in batter next to my chips. That was the perfect symbiotic relationship as far as I was concerned.

But Singapore has irrevocably changed that ignorant perception towards my fellow earthly species forever. During that weekend when I went heron hunting, we encountered monkeys at Bukit Timah Nature Reserve and Pierce Reservoir, a couple of sizable monitor lizards at Lower Seletar Reservoir and then came the icing on the geek's cake.

Having a well-deserved break at Lower Seletar, we were sitting in front of the catchment area admiring the view when we witnessed something straight out of a documentary for the Discovery Channel. I noticed a bird (I feel like such a sad twat when I know that you now know, instinctively, that I am referring to the feathered variety) circling above the water. It was certainly a bird of prey and, on closer inspection, I realised it was a kite.

Now, before you laugh, I went to Australia last year and they were all over the Northern Territory there so they're easy to spot. Then, suddenly, just as I was about to divulge the feeding habits of the kite to the missus, the brown beast stretched out its talons and swooped towards the surface of the water. The huge claws went below the surface and came out swiftly bearing a rather stunned fish. Despite the fish being over half the size of the kite and wriggling like a lunatic, the kite gamely held on and took its supper back to the trees. Not 10 metres away, incidentally, stood a rather nonplussed fisherman, who boasted rather expensive fishing equipment, but had caught nothing other than a decent suntan. At times, nature has a wonderful way of reminding man of his real place in the world.

Moments like that have not only given me a greater appreciation of living in Southeast Asia, but have also fueled my rather geeky obsession with wildlife and ecosystems. Singaporeans, particularly those who've completed their national service in the few remaining jungles and rainforests around the Republic, are probably wondering what the big deal is. A bird catching his dinner? That sounds riveting. Do you remember what time it was so we can choose our 4-D lottery numbers?

But you must put it into context. I grew up in Dagenham. A tiny London borough full of endless, monotonous rows of red-bricked council houses. The only exotic wildlife I ever saw was on the BBC, which showed documentaries often made in South-east Asia. That could have been 10 miles from Jupiter for all I cared. The only wild animal that I ever saw was my mother when I was 17. My girlfriend's extremely forgiving parents brought my drunk body home to my mother one night and she turned into some sort of chimera and proceeded to batter me for the next two hours for embarrassing her in front of strangers.

In Dagenham, a stray dog could stop the traffic. Drivers would stare at the beast in the same way that village idiots of medieval times used to come out of their huts and take their dunce caps off to point at the moon. But my apathy towards animals came about after living with two of the stupidest animals since the dinosaurs looked up at the meteors, nudged each other and said: "It's all right, John. It's just a passing shower." My first dog, Duke, enjoyed pissing on the legs of fellow dog owners at my local park. On one occasion, a burly man with a urine-soaked trouser leg chased me in retaliation. It's probably the only time a 12-year-old boy has outrun a Doberman.

My second dog, Bruno, went blind at a very young age, which was tragic. What is far more tragic, however, is the perverse sense of fun the family still has from watching my mad mother throw sticks for the poor dog, who then spends the next 15 minutes not finding any of them.

So, before I came to Singapore, my appreciation and recognition of my fellow species never went beyond the odd nature programme and tying Duke to the garden fence and forcing him to play goalkeeper. The bastard dog still won most of the penalty shootouts.

Therefore, my transformation has been nothing short of remarkable. I now think I'm Southeast Asia's answer to David Attenborough. And yet, of course, there is a certain irony to all of this. Outsiders, and insiders for that matter, perceive this tiny city-state to be the archetypal concrete jungle. Like Dagenham, Singapore's skyline is punctuated with unremarkable municipal housing blocks. There is little variety in terms of shape, design and colour and they have largely swallowed up the greenery that once covered the land. The town planners of the London County Council dug up the peaceful farmlands of Dagenham in the '20s. Forty years later, the HDB planners were cutting down the Asian rainforests here. The only difference was, once the bulldozing had finished, Dagenham didn't continue to breed lizards, monkeys, lemurs, pythons, cobras, the odd wild boar, the occasional crocodile and, last but not least, kites, herons, eagles and egrets.

Unfortunately, my first encounter with a wild mammal was an underwhelming experience, to say the least. Having been in Singapore for about a week, I went to the bottom of the HDB block to make a call. Not only did I arrive in the country without the customary expatriate package (condo, car, maid, Singapore Cricket Club membership), I didn't even have a phone. It was around midnight and I was chatting to my girlfriend when I abruptly interrupted her with the gentle cry of: "FUCK ME! IT'S A RAT."

Believe it or not, it was the first rat I'd ever seen. Despite growing up near the London Underground tube lines (a popular holiday destination for the little bastards), we had never had a formal introduction. But my phobia of rodents is primal. It goes right to my soul, or arsehole if you will. It's hereditary and the fear comes from my mother, reinforced by a couple of incidents that will have you screaming in your sleep tonight. Just listen to this. When I was 11, I returned from the cub scouts, starving as usual, and my mother informed me that there was some soup in a saucepan on the cooker. As I touched the handle, a gluttonous mouse jumped out of the saucepan, having consumed its weight in soup first, ran along the sideboard and disappeared. That was terrifying enough. But the soup was tomato. The rodent, which was more Fat Bastard than Stuart Little, jumped out of the pan drenched in soup and staggered away like a hairy tomato, leaving little blood-red footprints along the way.

But there's more. And this one will put you off your dinner. About a year later, my mother cooked us roast potatoes one night and kept cooking oil, or lard, in the baking tray and left it to solidify overnight. This was a common way of recycling the oil and saving a few pennies. However, the next day my mother opened the oven, lifted out the baking tray, screamed and, then, promptly dropped it. You see, an adventurous young mouse allowed greed to supercede his common sense. Nipping through the back of the oven for a little tipple of lard, the obese bugger didn't take the hint when the temperature started to cool. Consequently, the oil solidified and he inadvertently got trapped. And my mother found him the next day: suffocated, extremely stiff and trying to perfect the spreadeagled pose in death.

Unsurprisingly, I seriously contemplated leaving Singapore that night. Living among mice in London was horrifying enough, living with their Asian big brother was a different gang of rodents altogether. I actually made enquiries about the extent of the rat population here. Such as which parts of the country they favoured, what their dietary habits were and whether or not I could be arrested for firebombing every sewer in Toa Payoh. However, they actually bother me far less now and I seldom see them. When I first moved here, there was upgrading work everywhere and now that's finished, many have had to relocate to some of the condos being constructed out in the East Coast.

But my run-in with king rat was, admittedly, an inauspicious start to my wildlife expeditions in Southeast Asia. Fortunately, I stumbled upon the Bukit Timah Nature Reserve after about three months and watched, transfixed, for hours as a long-tailed macaque skillfully cleaned its offspring of fleas, in a tender, maternal fashion. And I was hooked. Sublime incidents like that had a profound effect on me and the missus, who actually became a vegetarian as a result.

At the risk of sounding like an anally retentive presenter from the Discovery Channel, I have to admit that living here has forced me to develop a greater respect for the various ecosystems and all of their components, having seen many of them in action.

At Bukit Timah, I sat for 15 minutes and watched intensely as a monitor lizard burrowed its snout deep into the soil in a rhythmic fashion, not quite sure whether it was searching for food or merely picking his nose using an obscure prehistoric method. But then, the reptile snapped its head back sharply, pulling a worm from the ground and throwing it into the air in one fluid motion. Within milliseconds, it had caught its dinner and was chewing away quite happily. I waited patiently for another few minutes, but crocodile hunter Steve Irwin never jumped out and shouted: "Did you see that? What a beauty. Woo!"

At Sungei Buloh, I saw a monitor lizard swim for the first time. This was a rather hair-raising incident for three reasons. Firstly, I didn't know monitor lizards could swim. Yes, I know I'm ignorant. Didn't you hear where I grew up? Secondly, I assumed it must have been a crocodile because I know they can swim. Thirdly, crocodiles eat people. When I was a kid, I used to watch the James Bond movie *Live And Let Die* endlessly. There's a famous scene in the film where Roger Moore has to run across the backs of several crocodiles to escape. I thought I was going to have to do the same at Sungei Buloh. That's no way to die. Can you imagine the headlines? "ANG MOH WRITER DIES AFTER USING MIDGET CROCODILE AS A SURFBOARD" — there's no disgrace in dying at the jaws of a beast that has been around since the age of dinosaurs, but it can be a trifle embarrassing to go down to a crocodile that suffered from stunted growth.

But the real wildlife highlight was catching two lizards shagging. The young reptiles couldn't have been more than 25 centimetres long, but length isn't everything. They didn't need any patronising government campaign on love and romance, I can assure you. Playing tennis at the time, I went to the back of the court to collect some balls and found a couple more than I expected. Right on the doubles line were two little love-makers going through the lizard *Kama Sutra*.

It was spectacular. I dropped my racket and sat beside them and watched, fascinated. My only regret was I didn't have popcorn for the matinee performance. I called my tennis partner over to have a look, but he muttered something like "Fuck me, it'll be farmyard animals next, the filthy bastard," and then said he had to stop by the local police post to report some pervert.

I don't know what he was going on about. But I was mesmerised. I'd seen plenty of stray dogs having sex on the way home from school. And I caught a few bare arses going up and down in the back seats of Ford Cortinas over my local park after late football matches. But the only fucking reptiles I'd ever seen in England sat in Parliament in Westminster. So I hope you can appreciate how truly happy I was sitting on the floor of a sun-baked tennis court observing two lizards performing an act that often requires a night out, copious amounts of alcohol and three hours of begging before two humans have a bash at it.

After that life-altering experience, I've become an eco-tourism addict. I won't go anywhere now unless there is wildlife involved. Trekking in Langkawi's rainforests in Malaysia, we witnessed a full-scale monkey brawl as two sides fought viciously before retreating to opposite sides of the path to check their injuries. It was like a monkey audition for *West Side Story*.

In Western Australia, we got up close to southern right whales who were heading up the coast of the country towards their annual breeding grounds. In an isolated spot in Indonesia's Bintan Island, I spotted a family of wild boars out for a pint at a deserted stream.

On another occasion, in Bintan, I was sitting on a bus when an elephant walked past the window. Admittedly, it wasn't wild. But think about it. How often does Dumbo go past your window when you're sitting in a traffic jam?

In England, the only mammals that approach your windows at traffic lights are the human kind, who wash your windscreen, whether it needs cleaning or not, and demand payment when they are finished. Give me a cumbersome elephant every time. I wouldn't have been impersonating Daft Attenborough in any of these places had it not been for the tiny, so-called concrete jungle that I'm now living in.

And then, the little-known village of Chek Jawa made the headlines and I wanted to punch every *kiasu*, small-minded, short-sighted politician and prick in Singapore. Tucked away in the far-eastern corner of Pulau Ubin were the rich sand and mud flats of Chek Jawa. It was hidden behind an old British bungalow and was largely ignored by nature lovers and tourists because of high tides. Then, in late 2000, old homes of the island's villagers were destroyed in preparation for land reclamation. And the path was open for intrepid wildlife explorers to find, well, everything. This mini-coastal forest had mangroves, a lagoon, coral rubble and hitherto rarely discovered marine and wildlife. The Nodular Sea Star, flower crabs, hornbills, the hairy Heavy Jumper spider (it looks a bit like a tarantula and I just love the name), the dog-toothed cat snake (again, what a name), the Banded Bullfrog and the good old wild boar are just some of the residents of Chek Jawa. Believe me, there are dozens more.

The discoveries of so many wonderfully varied ecosystems (six, in fact) seemed almost too good to be true. Singapore had found a new Eden within its narrow borders. But they were to lose it again. The bulldozers were ready to go in and rip it up. The government, via the Urban Redevelopment Authority, had decided in the revised Concept Plan of 2001 that the eastern coastline could be spared for land reclamation. Do you know what the land was going to be used for? New HDB flats? Schools? Hospitals perhaps? Of course not. The plan was to create land for military training. That's right. Either experienced soldiers would run around the place shooting things and blowing other things up. Or inexperienced teenagers, performing their National Service duties, would miss targets and such things initially, before blowing things up at the second attempt. And then the government has the audacity to brand people "quitters" for seeking, in many cases, to give their children a more wholesome, varied upbringing in another country.

Can you imagine taking your grandchild to Chek Jawa in 20 years and the young boy saying: "Granddad, what are all those explosions banging over there? And why are there huge fences and 'KEEP OUT OR WE'LL BLOW YOUR FUCKING HEAD OFF' signs everywhere?" What could you say to that? Perhaps you could sit the innocent boy on your knee and say: "Well, this was once a paradise, son, full of the kind of wildlife you now only see in zoos. Animals, fish, trees and seagrasses everywhere. It was stunning. Now, there are teenagers dressed in green camouflage, running around with machine guns shooting, er, things."

"I think I prefer it the way before, Granddad." We should fill parliaments with children. They don't bullshit each other. They haven't been engulfed by cynicism and, in their simplicity, they speak, at times, with a profound wisdom. But we don't. So we're stuck with the middle-aged cynics. However with the Chek Jawa issue, they came unstuck. This one couldn't be swept under the mud flats, as it were. There was considerable protest.

In England, this would involve 100,000 nature lovers marching around the streets of Westminster with placards. Here, that is not allowed, so there were several strongly worded letters to the Forum pages instead. Sometimes, politicians here forget who elects whom. Fortunately, on this occasion, there was not a shortage of wonderful Singaporeans eager to remind them. The researchers and volunteers from the outstanding Raffles Museum of Biodiversity Research and the Nature Society of Singapore just refused to go away. They undertook surveys and, despite limited resources, recorded an impressive list of species that could be lost forever. It was a death list.

In the wake of such vehement protest, the government relented, albeit temporarily. In late December 2001, just days before the bulldozers were about to go in, the official reprieve came. The Chek Jawa beach would be left intact — for 10 years. But the fact remains that if the government then decides that land is needed, then that will take priority, of course, over some daft multi-coloured fish and some crabs with silly names that would look much better on a plate with a bit of chilli anyway, right?

Forgive me if I don't shit myself with excitement at the news that Chek Jawa has been spared. You see, when the news broke that the rural haven was about to be destroyed, Singaporeans were encouraged to see for themselves just what they would be taking away from their children. Many turned up, in their thousands, in fact, which was truly amazing for a so-called apathetic nation.

But some brought carrier bags. This wasn't a nature expedition. It was a treasure hunt. Seriously distressed guides tried in vain to stop many taking sea urchins, sea cucumbers, starfish, seagrasses and even fish as souvenirs. Ridiculous trinkets from Chek Jawa. Marine life was actually taken out of the sea and suffocated just so it could pose for a family snapshot. When the carrier-bag brigade left, the beach was strewn with dead species. Ironically, these fuckwits were killing the very ecosystems that more sensible people were fighting to save. In the current age of environmental awareness and appreciation, this ignorance is not just exasperating; it's bloody terrifying.

And you know, you just know, that these are the same *kiasus* who sit around and whine that "Singapore is so boring" and they have to pay thousands to take their children to Sea World to watch a dolphin jump through a hoop. And they tell me to visit Malaysia and Indonesia if I want wildlife. Why? It's here in abundance. For a country so small and urbanised, it is remarkable how much wildlife the Republic still has. But how much more needs to be wiped out, before Singaporeans say: "Shit, maybe this country really will be soulless and boring if all we have left are people, handphones, golf courses and concrete." The tiger has already gone, which is probably just as well because some *kiasu* cab driver would knock him down in Orchard Road. The beast's testicles would be removed before you could say: "You know, there is Viagra for that medical condition now. Those bloody testicles you are holding would work much better on the tiger, don't you think? You prick."

Of course, Singapore isn't Brazil. It's not Yellowstone Park, the Serengeti or even Sarawak or Borneo, but it's the wildest city I've ever known and not just because of the availability of hookers. Just recently, for instance, I was at the Lower Pierce Reservoir at dusk, my favourite time of the day in Singapore. Walking along the water's edge, we came across members of the nature society. There were around 20 of them, all pointing and gesturing frantically towards a tree opposite them. It was a barn owl. A huge bugger, in fact. I almost wet myself with excitement. One of the society's members lent me his binoculars so I could see right into the owl's eyes. I started jumping around like a big kid. That's when the missus decided to pipe up: "You really are a wanker, aren't you?"

And she's right. In Dagenham-speak, I am a sad wanker and proud of it. You should be too. So put this book down, grab a pair of binoculars and explore the island for yourself. There's plenty to see in Singapore, more than enough to go around. It's bloody marvellous.

## *THE TOILET*

USUALLY, I would not resort to toilet humour, but on this occasion I believe I have found the answer to one of Mr. Goh Chok Tong's problems. The Singapore Prime Minister knows that his residents are migrating in droves to Australia — that financial oasis with cut-price suburban houses, cheap cars and kangaroo poo everywhere. He is trying to convince the "quitters" to remain with the loyal "stayers", but this is no easy task.

The brain drain is a real headache for the Prime Minister. But, fear not, because I have found the answer — Australian public toilets. These "amenities" are the most irritating, most expensive and most bewildering on the planet. Collectively, they should provide a deterrent to all Singaporeans who are considering settling Down Under.

Having just returned from Australia, I speak from bitter experience on this one. The reason why properties there are so cheap is because you have to take out a second mortgage to use a public toilet. Every trip costs a whopping 50 cents. Only 50 cents, you say? This is the middle of the Alice Springs desert, where large quantities of water are essential to stay alive.

I was using the little boys' room more often than George Michael. It was costing me three dollars a day and that didn't even include those cute packets of tissues given out in Singapore. When it reached the stage where my wallet had to make a choice between urinating and eating, I headed for the local K-Mart supermarket. Surely the facilities would be free there? Indeed they were, but they were locked — deliberately. Frantic and cross-legged, I asked a girl at the checkout if they were being cleaned.

"No," she replied. "You can get the key from me."

"What key?"

"The key to the toilet. And could you please bring it back when you're finished."

Bring it back? What the hell did she think I was going to do with a key to a K-Mart public toilet? Pretend it was an Aussie souvenir and send it to my mother? Though, in truth, if I stuck a magnet on the back of it, she'd happily stick it on the fridge.

In the end, the thought of carrying a large toilet key around a supermarket was just too embarrassing. I hadn't even bought anything. So I headed back to the "we-rip-off-bladder-bursting-men" establishment.

Slightly perturbed that the 50 cents didn't include piped music, light refreshments and a full massage from a Swedish sex siren, I asked the chain-smoking attendant why: a) most public amenities were locked and b) why the rest cost a small fortune.

"Aborigines," she replied. "If we don't charge or lock up, they defecate on the floor and vomit up the walls. Some even go in to sleep. I wouldn't like to think about the amount of diseases that must be in that toilet." And then the ignorant woman took my 50 cents and blew smoke in my face. Now, has that put you off emigrating yet?

The only negative experiences I have had in a Singaporean urinal involved being watched by a disturbingly zealous cleaner. Many times I have asked the female toilet cleaner at my office if I might relieve myself, only to find her still cleaning the floor behind me. I had expected her to wait outside. But no, she decides that the spot right by my feet, which is shockingly close to my exposed testicles, must be cleaned at that exact moment.

I have also cut a path to several toilets at hawker centres — an expedition which required side-stepping the unwashed plates of *mee goreng*, hopping over the cigarette cartons and sliding along various liquids of an unknown origin. It was only the absence of a giant, concrete ball that prevented me from resembling an incontinent Indiana Jones.

But these public antiquities are in rapid decline and will soon be replaced completely by those state-of-the-art amenities in most shopping centres. Yet, be careful; these could become a dangerous social menace. PM Goh suggested recently that if Singaporeans are to succeed, they must become more self-reliant. These modern toilets encourage anything but self-reliance. Recently, I went to a toilet that flushed the urinal for me, dried my hands automatically and, wait for it, released water from the tap without touching it.

Just putting my hands under the tap's censor did the trick. Now, I know we need to conserve water, but this is ridiculous. I appreciate the "Keep toilets clean" campaigns and their importance, but, surely, Singaporeans can turn a tap on for themselves. I've met some loonies in Toa Payoh, but not even they would go up to a tap and say: "Now, this must be the dimmer switch for the lights."

Whatever next? Perhaps plumbers will install a magnetic contraption above the urinal, which automatically undoes the zip on your trousers? That might be worth 50 cents.

Until then, let's demonstrate remarkable self-reliance and stupendous multi-tasking skills by flushing our own toilets and washing our own hands.

Believe me, it's a better alternative than going up to a supermarket cashier and asking for an oversized toilet key like a guilty schoolboy. But if we really want to curb Singaporean migrations to Australia, then I would seriously urge the government to consider that magnetic zip idea.

**NOTE:** I received an irate email concerning this article, from a man who thought I was trivialising the stayer-quitter emigration debate in Singapore. He reminded me, quite forcefully, that the state of a country's public toilets is not high on the list of priorities for potential emigrants. This wasn't an issue, he claimed, that would affect 'normal' people. I tried to picture these 'normal' people, but I quickly stopped. They were starting to scare me. Nevertheless, I thanked him for his email and for pointing out that the majority of Singaporeans don't have public urinals on their minds when they are choosing what country to spend the rest of their lives in. Of course, what I really wanted to say was: "Please, please let me pay your airfare to Australia and don't ever return to Singapore again, you sad bastard." But I didn't.

## *THE GAMES*

SINGAPOREAN killjoys ruined the Asian Games 2002 celebrations. Despite the five gold medals won by the Republic, there were still pessimists on hand to cheapen the achievements of its bowlers and bodybuilders. And that's tragic.

It's not easy to knock down 10 milk bottles with a plastic cannonball, you know. It's no small feat to slip on a pair of skimpy Speedos and strike a pose without slipping in all that cooking oil that has been smeared all over their bodies either. Bodybuilders are under intense pressure to ensure that they bulge in all the right places — especially as they are only wearing a pair of skimpy Speedos. There are no extra points awarded for that muscle. And we shouldn't even consider what sort of training programme it would require.

But no one should downplay these sporting accomplishments, particularly when they bring the medals in at such a prestigious continental competition. In fact, why stop there? Let's exercise cool calculation rather than sporting snobbery and petition the Olympic Council Asia (OCA) to include other widely practised "sports".

According to the OCA, a sport must have a high participation rate to be considered for inclusion in the Asian Games. That being the case, I humbly nominate the sport of queuing. By definition, it requires mass participation and Singaporeans have turned it into an art form.

Queuing encourages Sports-For-All and collectivism, which will keep the government happy. It is also cheap. Unlike elitist sports such as horseracing and sailing, queuing equipment can be afforded by just about everybody. A singlet, loose-fitting shorts and a pair of flip-flops should guarantee maximum performance.

Like a melodrama made for the Hallmark Channel, children would sit on their mother's knee, look up in admiration and say: "Mummy, when I grow up, I wanna be like you. I want to queue, too. But I don't want to do it just for a cheap quilt with matching pillow and bolster cases; I want to do it for my country. Mummy, I want to queue for Singapore!"

Regional queuers could congregate at the National Stadium for the referee to announce: "On your marks, get set, HDB flats for sale!" The last, sleep-starved person who remains upright wins the race. It might not measure up as a spectator sport, but consider the medal potential for Singapore.

The same could be said for the sport of queens. And when I say queens, I mean talking aunties. Put any Singaporean woman over the age of 60 on a bus. Tell her to talk, incessantly, on any subject she likes and I guarantee she will shut out all competition, quite literally. Foreign aunties would be screaming for an oxygen tank before any Singaporean woman finally stops talking. Though the English old lady would run her a close second, I must admit.

The referee could stand between them and shout: "On your marks, get set, gossip!" to begin the inane conversation. Incorporating the three-strikes-and-you're-out rule, the jabbering aunties should be supplied with three prompts if the chatter starts to flag. At intervals, the referee could shout subjects like: "food", "noisy neighbours" and "grandchildren" to keep the contest going.

Be warned, though. Singaporean aunties have a tendency to disagree, whereas their English counterparts love to agree with everything. So the final talk-out could well consist of: "Grandchildren? Cannot tahan. No, no, no, no, no."

"Ooh, I know."

"Very naughty one."

"Ooh, I know."

"Kids today; no discipline."

"Ooh, I know."

"No, cannot. No, no, no, no, no."

"Ooh, I know." It would be riveting stuff.

However, if you're looking for a testosterone-charged, pumped-up, adrenaline-filled extravaganza, then you might consider the 4 x 100-metre bookie runners' relay. Using their handphones as a baton, four illegal bookies would settle in the starting blocks, wearing the appropriate sporting attire — a singlet, loose-fitting shorts and flip-flops. The race referee would then cry: "On your marks, get set, Manchester United half ball!"

To make it a fair contest, the illegal runners must all natter continuously into their handphones to take bets, check the form-guide and discuss their upcoming court cases. Even if they didn't win the race (they'd face strong opposition from the gambling Thais), they'd make a few dollars by the time they crossed the finish line. Indeed, money and sport are intrinsically linked in the modern era so there's every reason to include illegal VCD sellers at the next Asian Games.

Weightlifting already has the 'clean and jerk' and 'snatch' categories, which are pretty vague to most sports fans. Initially, I thought they involved pornography. I'm almost certain you need to do one before the other anyway. But Singaporeans should petition for slight variations — the 'jerks, clean and pack' swiftly followed by the 'snatch the cash'.

Training funds would not be required from the Singapore Sports Council — experienced *ah bengs* are fully trained. The sport's set up is simple enough. Two competitors (from Woodlands and Johor Baru, respectively) would warm up behind two old wooden tables full of illegal VCDs. Their strict training regime usually involves furtive glances along the street and continuous smoking.

The athletes could perform in whatever they feel comfortable in — though a singlet, loose-fitting shorts and flip-flops appear to be remarkably popular. Then, the referee could mutter: "On your marks, get set, *aiyoh*, CID!"

In such situations, *ah bengs* demonstrate quicker reflexes than any martial arts exponent. The jerks can clean the table and pack away the VCDs before you can say: "Was that the Pamela Anderson-Tommy Lee home video?" The first athlete to then grab the box, snatch the cash and sprint away wins the gold. The defeated opponent, however, must settle for silver and six months in Changi prison.

Nevertheless, with these new sports added to the Asian Games' schedule, Singapore could easily become the most bemedalled country in the region. If nothing else, imagine what these additions could do for the local flip-flop industry.

**NOTE:** A friend of mine, who works at the Singapore Sports Council, said this column was well received around the office. I expect to be made SSC chairman any day now.

# *THE DANCE*

UNLIKE those Coyote Ugly beauties down at Mohammed Sultan Road, I can't dance. On a good night, I look like a break-dancing C3PO with rusty joints. Such talents are hereditary. My father was famous (in his house) for his Michael Jackson moonwalk. After his seventh beer, I would hear: "Come and see this, son. I taught Michael Jackson everything he knows. Watch this moonwalk."

"Dad," I would reply. "You're just walking backwards."

"No, son, look and learn from the white man who taught the black man. Now, watch the Jackson spin. Ready? Here, that's no place to put a basement."

He has emptied dance floors from England to Spain. But as long as you granted my dad some floor space (by dancing in another club), he was essentially harmless. Rather like bar-top dancing in Singapore. Well, at least I think so and I have the support of Prime Minister Goh Chok Tong on this one.

Speaking on National Day 2002, the PM suggested that Singapore might allow bar-top dancing. It doesn't at the moment.

According to the Public Entertainment Act, dancing has to be confined to a dance floor that is "demarcated by permanent fixtures at least one metre high."

Er, *what?*

Never mind the Dutch coverage needed to get up and bar-dance, I'd need a few beers to understand the law preventing it. What I want to know is, who are the people who waste trees to write this rubbish on paper? Have they been to a club before? Have they conversed with women before?

I'd love to see them chat up women with a line like: "Excuse me, madam, but you have a lovely pair of 'permanent fixtures'." But it seems that bar-top dancing, as seen in the American movie *Coyote Ugly*, is a really, really serious issue for some Singaporeans. The subject was a topic for discussion on a Mediacorp TV talk show I watched one evening and I noticed that two phrases kept popping up — "Asian values" and "good monitoring".

I respect and admire genuine Asian values, with their emphasis upon the family unit and filial piety, but on this occasion they are being used as an excuse, not a reason. It reminds me of newspaper headlines like: "Maid Abused For Not Giving Wealthy *Tai Tai* Face" ('It was Asian values, Your Honour').

On the talk show, I heard someone say: "We grow up with Asian values, which means we are not prepared for those evil Westerners who corrupt us with pretty, scantily clad girls dancing on bars. These dancers will poison the young, insult the aunties, arouse the uncles, bring down the parliamentary system, cause anarchy in the streets, intensify the haze and global warming and force a passing meteorite to hit Mohammed Sultan Road in 2010."

Or words to that effect anyway. Besides, anyone who uses the term 'scantily clad' deserves our attention at all times — preferably through the window of a padded cell.

Then there was the idea of 'good monitoring'. There must be 'good monitoring' to protect the perilous dancers as they perform their death-defying routines. Some suggested protective clothing and iron bars. But that's not going to guarantee the young ladies' safety, is it? So, I'm offering a solution — The Mummy Bar-Top Dance. Realising that some Singaporeans like fads (Hello Kitty, bubble tea, sushi bars and Manchester United), I came up with a new one.

Bar owners should swathe their dancers from head to toe in protective bandages. Wellington boots should also be thrown in to prevent slipping, while sunglasses can reduce the glare from strobe lights. The dancers can then get into a glass cage, which is assembled at a safe distance from the crowd — 50 metres should be sufficient. Bouncers who would make Mike Tyson look like Mini-Me from *Austin Powers* will protect the cage.

Cushions can then be placed around the bar. Remember, these bars can reach astonishing heights — some are even rumoured to be one metre high. And as a final, safety measure, an ambulance, a doctor, two stretcher-bearers and a full medical crew will be on standby.

There is still a fear, however, that such erotic mummy dancing could arouse male drinkers. So, they can be hosed down with ice-cold water at 30-minute intervals, thus ensuring that the only things in the bar that remain erect are those 'permanent fixtures'. This is, of course, ridiculous. Yet, the rest of the world is watching this on-going farce.

Remember, foreigners are not interested in tedious facts about low crime rates and high living standards, they are interested in stereotypes, which are much more fun. And this bar-top nonsense has added another bullet to the gun.

Having just returned from Australia, I had to endure all the usual jokes. In Alice Springs, I was asked: "You're from Singapore? Don't they cut your hands off for chewing gum?"

"No," I replied, giving my stock answer. "That's for littering. Chewing gum warrants decapitation. After which, your head is stuck on a spike in Orchard Road to deter future gum-chewers."

It's most annoying and this dancing debate is adding fuel to the fire. So if bars like Coyote Ugly want to introduce the American dance craze to boost revenue, then why not? In this recession, I'd rather watch beautiful girls performing well-rehearsed routines, than sit in an empty bar with all the atmosphere of a mortuary.

God knows I've been to enough Singaporean bars where I've had to suffer deeply boring men screaming into handphones. On one or two occasions, I've even been to nightclubs and watched executives tapping away at their laptops. Other than using a hammer and a chisel to knock their computers up their back passage, I really don't know what you're supposed to do with these people. Give me a sexy, well-paid dancer over a *kiasu* ugly man every time.

So let's make it happen, preferably without the mummy costumes, but hey, whatever brings in the customers. If it doesn't, then I'm tempted to unleash a far more dangerous dance routine upon Singapore — my drunken father doing the moonwalk.

**NOTE:** I've since been to Coyote Ugly, for purely research purposes, of course, and I was delighted to see the dancers up on the bars and having a few laughs. Unsurprisingly, the heavens didn't fall, the seas haven't risen and the bar hasn't been struck by an evil plague of locusts. But the place is doing tremendous business. I can't think why.

## *THE TRIP*

HAVING just returned from a weekend in the Indonesian island of Batam, I was reminded of two absolute certainties in life.

First, I always live up to my *ang moh* billing and bring back a face redder than a blushing lobster. I only have to poke my head out of the shade momentarily and the Indonesian sun will insist on giving me a souvenir. For the rest of the weekend, the hotel chef fries his eggs on my forehead.

Secondly, and more importantly, the *kiasu* brigade always decides to spend a loud weekend with me. It's got to the point where the travel agent asks "When would you like to travel?" and I reply, "I'll go with the *kiasus* because I'm emotionally imbalanced and my psychiatrist needs the income."

These Batam trips have already put me in a psychological conundrum as a result of the recent national stayer-quitter emigration debate. Within 24 hours of returning, I was on the psychiatrist's couch asking: "Does it really make me a bad person? I mean, I think I'm a stayer. But when I go to Batam for the weekend, I rarely, if ever, have nostalgic pangs for Singapore. I don't think about chicken rice, Orchard Road, one-party governments or anything. Does this make me a quitter? Because when I'm here, and no one is around, I do have guilty, longing thoughts for Batam. What do you think?"

"I think... Oh dear, time's up. That'll be 50 dollars. And, I must say, have you seen the state of your sunburn?"

Incidentally, if I ever mention the riveting stayer-quitter debate again, you may take a red-hot poker and thrust it repeatedly in my groin. Such a course of action is also useful when dealing with the *kiasu* brigade.

Unlike secret societies, *kiasu* members reveal themselves early, usually at Batam's ferry terminal. It's only been 45 minutes since we left Singapore, but they just couldn't wait to spring into action. Indonesian Immigration officers who, rather mischievously, open only two counters are partially to blame. When the queues are long enough, they open a third counter and announce: "On your marks, get set... *kiasu*."

One chap, carrying a bag full of golf clubs, *sprinted* from one queue to another — covering a distance of 10 metres in 1.5 seconds. His wife, who had been holding the hands of her two unsuspecting children, followed just behind. For several seconds, the children were airborne. By the time the breathless mother had caught up, her two offspring had completed two cartwheels, a double-back somersault and had contemplated a career in acrobatics.

My vision blurred after that. There were vague images of aunties running, luggage trolleys trundling over my toes, shopping bags scratching my legs and someone losing their patience and poking a runner in the eye. Though, on reflection, that could have been me. Then, miraculously, the dust settled and a third queue had formed.

And then it occurred to me. The *kiasus* should be head-hunted by the Singapore Sports Council. The Olympic 100 metres final would be a formality, if certain apparatus were permitted. Line up the *kiasus* against the finest American sprinters and set them off. After 50 metres or so, wheel out an immigration counter and place it at the end of their track lane. It wouldn't even be a contest.

For eager *kiasu*-watchers, though, ferry terminals certainly have a high strike rate. At the Singapore arrival hall, there was a delay at the security checkpoint thanks to — potato chips. A traveller had brought back enough bags to feed Toa Payoh. The snacks only cost 20 cents in Singapore, so after spending 40 dollars on his ferry ticket, how much money is he saving? Does he know something we don't? Are we on the threshold of a global potato-chip famine? If so, then this man stands to make, well, 20 cents a packet.

The Batam tourism board must be informed. It should come up with a new slogan — forget the golf, come for the potato chips. Currently, the island is sold as a rural haven — 45 minutes from Singapore, with rainforests, a warm climate and a fine cultural heritage. In Singlish, this is translated as: "Cheap *makan*, seafood also can. Cheap golf, cheap hotels, cheap shopping, fake branded goods also can. Cheap VCDs, illegal one also can. Pay Singapore dollars? Also can."

In fact, at my hotel, a Singaporean couple complained because they only had Singaporean dollars and they had calculated that the item they wanted cost less in Indonesian rupiah. Now, where's that red-hot poker when you need it?

As for me, I visit the island periodically because I'd heard Batam is a popular place for Singaporeans to keep a mistress.

And when you're a foreigner, you must try to fit in and adopt the local customs.

I caught a rather beautiful Indonesian waitress looking at me so I flashed my Toa Payoh library card (it looks like a credit card if you do it quickly) to win her over. It worked. She came over, looked into my eyes and said: "Have you seen the state of your sunburn?"

**NOTE:** I still go to Batam regularly. I still get sunburnt.

## *THE DRIVE*

I CAN'T drive. No, that's not quite true. I can drive, I just can't pass the test. For some reason, driving instructors and examiners have always lost faith in me for minor lapses of concentration, which have resulted in knocking off another car's bumper during a three-point turn, mounting a kerb and narrowly missing a parked car and almost causing a 15-car pile-up at a gargantuan roundabout known as Gallows Corner in Essex. I'm not making any of that up. My sublime driving prowess is hereditary. My mother never passed her test either because she has a penchant for driving into ditches. It's a rare skill. I've spent many a childhood summer climbing out of a vertically parked car to enjoy the sunshine.

For some reason, my mother favoured country lanes because they were low on traffic. Unfortunately, they were high on roadside ditches. As we approached a bend, cries of "Mind that ditch" were always followed with "What ditch?"

"That fucking ditch! The one we are now sitting in. Sideways."

Until recently, I believed it was a curse against my family.

But finally, my sister broke the spell by passing her driving test. She's up there with Michael Schumacher as far as I'm concerned. After demonstrating remarkable reflexes to avoid that roundabout pile-up, my driving instructor turned to me and said: "I just don't know what to do with you anymore. You've reached the stage where you've actually become a danger to yourself and the other drivers around you. What happened at the roundabout... Well, I'm still shaking. It was just luck that stopped us from crashing. I've never seen anything like that."

In my defence, though, he'd never driven in Singapore. In England, when you drive as recklessly as I did, you fail every time. In Singapore, such behaviour appears to be rewarded with a Mercedes Benz and a free handphone. Now I know that criticism of Singaporean drivers has almost become a cliché in itself. I had never commented upon it before because we'd never had any direct experiences to draw upon.

Then, a week before Chinese New Year, we decided to hire a car. Despite having the mental age of a slightly backward four-year-old, my girlfriend is remarkably competent behind the wheel. We were toying with the idea of having a mini-driving holiday over the New Year period, with a drive up to Mount Ophir in Johor, Malaysia, which I'm told is a peach of a place with wild environments and animals aplenty. But the missus had never driven in Singapore before so we decided to spend the weekend burning rubber along the expressways. I mean tyre rubber, not the rubber they burn in parked cars up Mount Faber. She'd driven all over the south of England, Western Australia and along dirt roads in the Northern Territory's Outback. Singapore should be a breeze — like a drive in the country (with no ditches), right?

We witnessed two accidents in two days. My girlfriend has driven for over 10 years now and had never seen a crash while driving before. And in two days in Singapore, we saw two. What does that tell you? Admittedly, we were on the roads for at least eight hours each day but still the odds must be outlandish. The first incident was comparatively minor. At the busy junction off Bugis, a taxi clipped another car as they both turned right. Aside from a little broken glass and a crumpled wing, there was little to see. But that didn't stop the traffic crawling along so *kaypoh* drivers could gawk at the taxi driver and the woman who was in the other car. It also gave me a chance to criticise women drivers. Yes, I will take every opportunity to bolster my suspect masculinity.

The second crash, though, was more serious. Sitting at the traffic lights beside Lower Seletar Reservoir, my missus shouted: "Neil, he's going to fall off." There was a motorcycle turning right into the other side of the road, but he took the corner too sharply. Carrying a heavy load on the back of the bike didn't help and he toppled off, sliding along the fast lane for a couple of seconds. He actually stopped only a few feet from our car. But we were separated by the central reservation divider. The guy was obviously in some distress. Then, we saw the sort of thing that only fuels my misanthropic tendencies. The kind of incident which makes you think that an apocalypse might not be the end of the world.

The traffic lights changed so cars from the other side of the road moved across the junction and towards the stricken motorcyclist. They slowed, I assumed, to enable someone to get out and help him. But they didn't. They slowed to overtake him. That's right. As the injured man lay on the floor clutching his bleeding leg, cars pulled out and around him. They paused briefly, of course, to stare at the poor chap, and then they drove off. At least half a dozen cars did this. It's highly unlikely that such people will ever read this book. They're usually devoid of a sense of humour and spend their free time either boring listeners about property prices or battering maids. When they're not overtaking crash victims, of course. But should one or two of them pick up this book, having incorrectly assumed they can grow rich with it, then may I humbly say: You are a disgrace to humanity. If you could drive to the top of Mount Faber and then kindly jump off it, then there'd be one less *kiasu* prick for Singaporean society to worry about. Consider it your civic duty.

I'm sure you're not surprised that such parasites still live among us. A few years ago, I was on my way back to the office when my colleague and I saw a motorcyclist slam into a taxi. We quickly stopped and ran across to help. It was one of the worst injuries I have ever seen. The screaming motorist's foot was hanging off at the ankle. Moreover, the bones around his foot and ankle had been broken and twisted so severely that his foot pointed inwards, effectively in the opposite direction. I phoned the office to let the guys know I was going to be a bit late because we were going to wait for the ambulance and I was reprimanded. I was ordered to get back to the office immediately. When I returned, I suggested the decision was a bit harsh so I suffered the standard lecture about "my priorities and how the company should always be at the top of the list".

In Singapore's corporate world, you hear this hackneyed bullshit quite often in the office environment, don't you? Whenever I hear the sentence, "Well Neil, you must question your priorities," I stifle a yawn and head for the classified section.

I no longer work for that company. My general rule of thumb has always been: 'Unless you're a hooker, avoid working under too many arseholes.'

At the junction off Lower Seletar Reservoir, I was beginning to think the drivers on the other side of the road were all heading for a 'We're All Arseholes And We Love It!' convention. Eventually, and I'm really not making this up, a Mercedes attempted to drive around the victim's motorbike, but the car was too wide, jutting out dangerously into the next lane. So the driver pulled back and got out of the car to help him. Then others joined her. They had no choice, did they? Her Mercedes was blocking their path completely now. I went across the divider to help just as the lights changed, which meant my missus had no option but to pull away, do a U-turn into the side of the road where the bike crash was and drive off into the opposite direction because there was nowhere to stop. When she tried to slow down, she was beeped by other cars behind. I tried to beep back at them, but they couldn't hear me and I was busy trying to get the bike off the road with the help of a couple of taxi drivers. In the end, the missus got lost, drove a couple of kilometres in the wrong direction before completing one giant loop to come back and get me. By then, the motorcyclist was sitting on the grass verge speaking to his boss on his handphone, his bike had been moved and most of the debris had been cleared and I was roasting in the midday sun. By the time Mrs. Schumacher returned from her jaunty tour of Lower Seletar, I was ready to throw the daft cow into the reservoir.

We never drove to Malaysia for Chinese New Year in the end. There was no guarantee that I wouldn't end up in a police cell, charged with extreme road rage. On three separate occasions, the missus pulled me back into the car as I attempted to play 'Hide the Gearstick up the Rectum' with other drivers. I'm not sure what the offending drivers must have thought when they saw a lanky *ang moh* jump out of the car shouting: "Right, that's it, you *kiasu* fucker. That's one overtaking too many, you impatient bastard. Hang on, my minuscule missus is pulling me back into the car. But if she wasn't here..."

There are two prerequisites required to being accepted in the Singaporean driving community. Firstly, you must overtake continuously. In any lane. At any time. A bird's eye view of any major road in Singapore would just be a blur of zigzagging vehicles, gliding past each other like some well-choreographed dance routine. I'm sure it's necessary because the Republic is such a vast country, isn't it? If you were travelling from, say, Toa Payoh to Junction 8 at Bishan, the zigzagging manouevre must shave whole seconds off your driving time.

And don't forget to horn! Many drivers, particularly cabbies, seem to grab their horn and show it off to the world more frequently than a porn star. My particular favourite is when you are sitting in a mini-traffic jam waiting for the lights to change. Even though you could be six or seven cars down the line, the second the lights turn green up ahead, if you haven't revved your engine, you will get another man's horn. Now, you may call me old-fashioned in the modern age of sexual liberalism, but I've never wanted to receive another man's horn. You should savour it, gentlemen, only using it on special occasions. Otherwise it will become predictable and ordinary and it will lose its rarity value. Besides, if you waste your horn on me in a traffic jam, I will inevitably retort: "There are six cars in front of me. Where the fuck would you like me to go? You prick."

But that's just me. Or so I thought. In early 2003, there was a high-profile case of road rage in Singapore. A prominent expatriate businessman, from England, lost his temper with a taxi driver and punched him. Well, that's what the judge eventually concluded, based upon the cabbie's facial injuries. According to the expat twat, he merely "brushed the cabbie aside" during their little skirmish. The bruises on the cab driver's face suggested he'd been brushed aside with a hammer. As I'm sure you've discovered by now, there are expatriates in Singapore who are masterful bullshitters, borderline con men, really. They are capable of some absolute whoppers if it helps them get a highly paid job, keep a highly paid job or get a reduced jail sentence.

It reminds me of another mini-court case that involved a car crime. At my university hall of residence, a guy on my corridor got drunk one night and stole a radio from an unlocked car. The hall held an impromptu kangaroo court to determine whether or not the idiot should be kicked out. When asked how he came to be in the possession of another man's radio, the idiot replied: "Well sir, I'd had a few drinks and things were a bit hazy. It was foggy that night so visibility was a bit poor. Then, I looked down, and suddenly I was holding a car radio. To this day, I have no idea how it got there." He was booted out of the hall and screwed up his university degree. It wouldn't surprise me if he was a CEO in a Singaporean company now — still lying his arse off.

But for the guy who can smash in people's faces with a mere brush-off, bullshit would not save him in Singapore this time. The driving savage was sentenced to four months — a ridiculously small sentence. I can't see a Singaporean being treated so leniently, can you?

But his case both alarmed and shamed me. On three occasions, I was only one step away from losing my rationality. Perhaps all aggressive drivers or passengers should drive with my missus. For many years now, Singapore has spoilt many Caucasians by providing them with lucrative salary packages, condominiums and, quite often, an undeserved cultural pedestal to stand on. It would be disgraceful if expatriates, particularly British, reciprocated by promoting two of their biggest social successes — a drinking culture and road rage.

But, ironically, Singaporean drivers have gone to the opposite extreme. There is a kind of laissez faire apathy on the roads. Other drivers overtake on the inside line, narrowly missing your vehicle, so you have no choice but to do likewise, right? Other idiots like to sound their horn at traffic lights, so the sheep follow the shepherd and the intolerance and impatience endures.

I asked my old mate Dave, a Singaporean and a bloody good driver, how this selfish, reckless driving culture evolved. He told me: "In Singapore, it's just the way it is now. If you don't do it, you won't get to work on time. You will be late. So if you don't cut in and pull out on another car, you'll be stuck there waiting to turn left all day. Because no one else will let you out. That's how it is. Everybody does it."

That's how it is. The apathy endures. Everybody does it, so what choice does the average Singaporean driver have? I disagreed with Dave. There are one or two Singaporeans who batter their maids and leave their so-called children in 24-hour daycare centres, but that doesn't mean I must follow suit. Though I am more than willing to employ these bastards as road obstacles the next time I take my driving test.

But this nationwide apathy is like a disease permeating through society and it threatens to rip out the soul and break the backbone of one of the greatest countries I've ever known. To me, it seems top-down. In a one-party state, you have no alternative in the political sphere. You have no alternative in the economic sphere, with this never-ending recession. You have no alternative in the social sphere, because if you emigrate you will be labelled a "quitter" so don't even think about trying to come back. And now, it seems, you don't even have an alternative behind a bloody steering wheel. This mindset has taken Darwinism to its most extreme and boring form.

However, that is nothing compared to the 'Mercedes culture'. Where in the name of social snobbery did that come from? I was out with a friend once and a Mercedes cut right across our car, missing the left wing by a few inches. Pulling down the window, I was about to offer my compliments for an outstanding manouevre which almost maimed me when my friend pulled me back.

"Don't say anything to him," he warned.

"Why not?"

"That's an expensive car he's got there. Probably a big-shot CEO or something. Better not say anything." Do the words 'bull', 'red' and 'rag' mean anything to you? They did to me and I was even more determined to shout at somebody.

"You're telling me I've got to allow this prick to drive recklessly because he has a bigger bank account than us?"

"It's not that," my friend explained carefully. "Singapore is a tiny place, especially in business. The chances of you running into this guy at a meeting or in the office are quite high. If you don't give him face, he could remember it and screw your career."

"Yeah? I'd never thought of it. Well, in that case, fuck him."

This Singaporean symbiotic relationship between material wealth and social status has got to be broken up. Money does not equate to courtesy. It might be just me here, but have you noticed that some of the biggest arseholes — the most self-centred, selfish, tedious, dogmatic individuals — that Singapore can offer are often *towkays*? Rich, miserable old bastards who assume they can bypass you at the queue in the garage and force you to brake sharply on the expressway so their luxury vehicle can smoothly dominate whichever lane it chooses.

Just a few weeks ago, I was standing in the middle of a junction at Toa Payoh Central, waiting for the lights to change, when I watched some moronic *tai tai* attempt a U-turn in her Mercedes. There's nothing illegal or inconsiderate about that. However, she tried to turn the wheel of her huge car with her right hand, while she held her handphone with her left. In the middle of her earpiece-free conversation, it was painfully obvious that her minuscule powers of concentration were being stretched to their limit. She turned so slowly that oncoming cars were forced to slow down as she straddled two lanes, forcing other cars to swerve away from a huge insurance bill. But she was oblivious to all of this, of course. Without so much as a casual glance in her rear-view mirror, the silly bitch continued her conversation and pulled away.

These buggers do not own the road. And I'm going to be brutally honest here. I've been in a car with my face-giving friend on several occasions and listened to him savage other drivers. He says things like: "You see that bastard there overtake me? Look at his number plate. He's a Malaysian, what do you expect?

Buggers can't even drive properly." Or "Look at that shitty car there. A cheap Nissan and he thinks he can drive around like a big shot." He is the same person who says things like: "Never mind *lah*. Did you see his BMW? That's the new model, *shiok* right? Costs about 150k, that model."

By the time he's finished arse-kissing the vehicle's owner, he's forgotten that it was only his quick reflexes that prevented the '*shiok* new model' from knocking his wing mirror off.

So it's time for the Singaporean government to step in and ban inconsiderate *towkays* and *tai tais* from ever driving a car in this city-state again. Should one or two of the more liberal members of this society consider such a stipulation a tad harsh, then I recommend employing chauffeurs. Such distinguished citizens should have no problem paying for a personal driver. Now, I've spoken to my mother and she's more than willing to do the job. We've just got to find the deepest ditch in Singapore.

## *THE SNIP*

LIKE many movie distributors in Singapore, I've also been punished for trying to show uncensored films.

When I was a child, my younger sister and I would raid the video cabinet as soon as our mother left for work in a bid to find the juiciest material. We succeeded but, unfortunately, our movie selections were always discovered. Our mother would return and notice that two videotapes — *The Violent Return of the Sick, Sordid, Sadistic Serial Killer* and *The Sound of Music* — had not been rewound.

"How many times have I told you? You must stop your little sister from watching violent films," our mother would shout.

"Sorry, mum. I was too busy watching Julie Andrews in my bedroom. I'm sorry."

"Sorry?!" she would scream. "That's not good enough. Sorry? I'll give you 'sorry'."

She did not give me a 'sorry', whatever that was. Instead, she gave me a forceful slap on the face that sent me over the sofa like an Olympic hurdler. I've been opposed to all forms of artistic censorship ever since.

Over the years, though, I've managed to block out my mother's random acts of violence. But the memories came flooding back when video censorship sneaked into the news again.

A report in *TODAY* said that those guys down at the Films and Publications Department (FPD) had cut the outstanding *Gosford Park* DVD before it was sent out to the stores. Apparently, the British social satire showed a man's buttocks during its cinematic release, which was R(A)-rated, earlier in the year.

Now, call me old-fashioned, but I don't go to cinemas to ogle men's bums. If I wanted to look at a hairy, greasy and slightly flabby backside, I could stand on a mirror. So I can't even recall the two-second scene, but nothing gets past those eager beavers on the Films Advisory Panel who help to decide a movie's classification in Singapore.

They cut the scene for the DVD release, which has, in turn, thoroughly ruined the director's audio commentary. Nevertheless, we can all sleep safely in our beds now because there is one less bare bum out there. If that monu-mental decision doesn't single-handedly revive Singapore's flagging economy, then, frankly, nothing will.

And don't underestimate the workload of the FPD. After visiting its fascinating website, I learned that of the 39 movies reviewed from August 10 to September 9 in 2002, seven were passed only after cuts were made.

Some, of course, do not make it to the Republic's cinema screens at all. In February 2002, Ben Stiller's satire on the modelling industry, *Zoolander*, was denied a cinematic release. The silly, comical plot involved assassinating a mythical Malaysian president and was deemed insensitive.

Taking this issue into serious consideration, it might be an opportune time to reexamine the *James Bond* series. After all, there are several plots involving megalomaniacs seeking world domination, often at the expense of global superpowers. They might only be the work of fiction, but does the rest of the world know that? Downing Street and the White House must be informed.

But seriously, the *Gosford Park* farce hardly comes as a surprise. I've been a victim of the excitable, but clumsy, cutters at the FPD. A friend sent a British gangster movie to me, as a gift, and it was rerouted to those wonderful FPD employees.

Confident the film would escape the censors scissors, I paid for it to be viewed by those wonderful FPD employees, who decide, on my behalf, what parts of my gift I'm allowed to take home. However, I was staggered to learn that the movie was awarded two cuts, which I also had to pay for. One of the cuts involved a pair of exposed breasts *on a poster, in the background and out of focus*. Now, I'm quite partial to that area of a woman's body, but I must confess that I'd never even noticed the poster. But, thankfully, those wonderful FPD employees certainly did.

Are we supposed to deny the existence of breasts? Because, with the exception of Pamela Anderson's, they're real, you know. And there isn't a man (or woman, for that matter) who should not give thanks to their respective gods every single day. A slightly different chink in the evolutionary chain and breasts could have been shaped like cows' udders, which would've been a genuine reason to cut them completely from the movie-making process.

But interestingly, certain productions fall under the FPD's exempted categories. Examples include sports programmes, training videos, karaoke tapes and ballet recordings.

Has anyone at the FPD ever watched ballet on television? Those lycra numbers leave absolutely nothing to the imagination. It only takes a close-up, frontal shot of a male dancer pirouetting and I can't look at a chicken rice stall for a week. There are all sorts of things wiggling about in that costume. A performance of *Swan Lake* has more perfectly toned torsos than 20 viewings of an uncensored *Gosford Park*. For the sake of social cohesion and chicken rice stall owners everywhere, it is time for the FPD to take its scissors along to the ballet.

Certainly, some of these neurotic censors need to get out more and get a life. If that doesn't work, they can always get a gentle slap from my ever-willing mother.

**NOTE:** Within three days, I received a wonderful page-long letter from the FPD, which was subsequently published in the letters page of *TODAY*. The government body never took me to task for any of the content. It couldn't. It was all based on facts or actual incidents. But the censorship body felt the need to explain why the scissors came out for movies like *Gosford Park* — so it could receive a general certificate. In other words, making the cut means more copies of the DVD can be sold to a wider audience. I must admit I was quite impressed with FPD's reply, because it showed that the guys there just had a job to do and they all took the column in the right spirit. But it remains disappointing that in the interests of making a few extra dollars, art continues to come off second best to greed in Singapore.

## *THE PHANTOM*

MY senile grandmother doesn't understand the concept of recycling. Environmental issues mean nothing to her. She can't even spell 'environment'. She endured London's pea-soup smog of the '50s, when levels of sulphur reached lethal concentrations with no fuss and typical working-class resilience. Indeed, if she visited Singapore, she would consider the haze a 'slightly overcast' day.

I asked her once what she thought about recycling and she said: "If your granddad was still alive, you could've asked him. He was never off that bloody bike."

Like many of the aunties and uncles in Singapore, she has little time for recycling. But for a country that could easily fit into several Canadian lakes, wastage is like a foul odour that won't go away. Recently, a number of environmentally conscious Singaporeans have complained about the lack of awareness regarding the various laudable recycling programmes that have existed for some time.

The Ministry of Environment, which has, in truth, made commendable efforts to minimise the waste of some four million people, should send a team down to Toa Payoh. Tucked away in an HDB block is the phantom recycler, a potential environmental envoy for the country who could keep the country green for your grandchildren. I discovered him when I moved house. Yes, it was time to call it a day on Toa Payoh Lorong 1. We had some good times, but we decided to part ways to maintain an amicable relationship.

I moved from Lorong 1 all the way to... Lorong 2. You didn't seriously think I was going to turn my back on Toa Payoh, did you? If I go any further north than Bishan, I start to get a nosebleed.

It was a rather bizarre moving day anyway because the moving lady possessed the unique skill of conjuring rabbits. Apparently, someone on my old corridor had to get rid of a pair of rabbits because they were mating like, well, rabbits. They were producing the kind of numbers that Romancing Singapore campaigners can only dream of and all that 'producing', scratching and cries of "oh yeah, bunny boy" were keeping the old timer awake at night. So, he gave the rabbits to my removal lady. But she never told me.

Can you possibly imagine what your reaction would be if you unloaded your belongings off a lorry and discovered two randy rabbits that you know you didn't have 20 minutes ago? You would probably say: "Excuse me, auntie. Sorry to trouble you, but where the fuck did you get these shagging rabbits from?" Or something like that.

But that was only the first illusion during a weekend that quickly became a David Copperfield special. Like most people, we'd accumulated too much junk for a three-room flat. I'm still not sure why I have a life-sized Darth Vader mask, for instance, but there you go. First, we called in the Salvation Army. I wasn't aware that they'd moved into recycling. When I was a child, they just blew out a few Christmas carols on their trumpets and disappeared again until the following December. But they collected six bags of 'why-in-the-name-of-impulse-buying-did-you-buy-THAT-you-stupid-woman' stuff and promised to pass it on to the needy.

Then, we called in the collectors at SembCorp Waste Management to take the rest, that is, the sort of knick-knacks that the Salvation Army turned down, giving you an idea of the crap my girlfriend had accumulated. But no disrespect to either recycling programme; nothing compares to the resourcefulness of the phantom recycler of Toa Payoh.

In a rare moment of recklessness, I'd bought a junior snooker table once, swearing that it would have to be prised from my dead hands before I'd get rid of it. The missus threatened to leave me if she bumped into the green beast one more time on her way to the toilet in the dead of night. So I took it down to the HDB lift lobby to get rid of it. But, before that, I took a box down containing the snooker cues, the balls and so forth. When I returned less than five minutes later with the table, the box had vanished. There was no trace of it. Now, I suffer from a rancid imagination, but, without the table, what the hell does a person want with a pair of snooker cues and another man's balls? Frankly, I was genuinely stumped on that one.

I considered David Copperfield but quickly dismissed him. I know he made the Statue of Liberty disappear, but could he make his balls disappear outside an HDB lift in Toa Payoh? I was intrigued, so I staked out a nearby void deck and watched my snooker table for 10 minutes. Nothing happened. Bored and hungry, I went back upstairs to lock up and when I returned, the table had disappeared! Who the hell was doing this?

Growing alarmed, I grabbed a passer-by and said: "Hi, I've just moved into this block. I wonder if you can help me?" By his concerned reaction, I'm sure he visualised all-night parties, too much beer, English Premiership matches blaring out at 4am and drunken brawls between rival supporters. But he shouldn't feel compelled to invite me over. So I hurriedly continued: "Have you seen a snooker table outside the lift?"

"What's it look like?"

"A washing machine."

"Really?"

"No. It's big, green, rectangular, with pockets in every corner."

"No, I haven't. But I know someone who can get the new Incredible Hulk movie on DVD if you're interested?"

I wasn't. But I am keen for the environment ministry to employ the phantom to improve its recycling statistics. In 2000, Singapore generated 4.6 million tonnes of waste and recycled 1.8 million tonnes of them, giving a recycling rate of 40 per cent. In 2001, that level increased to 2.2 million tonnes from 5 million tonnes of waste. Thus, the recycling rate increased to a commendable 44 per cent. And it's trying to raise residential awareness with the National Recycling Programme (NRP), which was launched in April 2001. If you're interested, household participation began at around 15 per cent. It reached 30 per cent by October last year. The NRP is aiming for a 50 per cent participation rate by the end of 2003, and I sincerely hope it succeeds. I don't want to leave a

Singaporean rubbish dump for your grandchildren, do you?

But I'm convinced that even the optimistic target of 50 per cent would be a conservative estimate if the environment ministry recruited the phantom recycler of Toa Payoh. Get the Internal Security Department to hold stakeouts at the HDB blocks in Toa Payoh Lorong 2. The agents must scour the void decks to find this man immediately. He will clean up this country before you can say: "Have you seen my bloody snooker table?"

## *THE FARECARD*

THE peaceful tranquillity of Malaysia's Tioman Island was shattered, when my partner grabbed my arm and exclaimed: "We need to get an ez-link card!"

I had no idea what the stupid woman was talking about either. Sitting at the jetty waiting for a ferry, this was hardly the place to be discussing the Singaporean public transport system. We had spent a rustic weekend at a simple village, where the locals were so laidback they were almost horizontal. When the ferry was 10 minutes late, I asked the operator: "What time is the ferry due?"

"When it gets here," came the humbling reply. "Don't worry, sit back, relax and feed the fish."

Great advice, but I didn't have any bread and, besides, we had to rush back to Singapore, apparently, to embark on our ez-link card mission. An eager bus driver had informed me the previous week that the prehistoric farecard was to be bumped off on October 1, 2002, and that we risked social castration if we didn't have an ez-link card by then. So, from the serene silence of Tioman, we joined the shuffling feet at Toa Payoh's MRT station. The queue for the ticket booth was longer than the Great Wall of China. What were they all queuing for? I'm convinced that some had no idea.

"Look at that!" Passers-by must say to their friends. "Now that's what I call a queue. Sure must be a free gift at the end. Come *lah*."

In the end, though, I was granted a temporary reprieve. After calling a charming woman on the TransitLink hotline, I discovered that the death of the farecard would be a long, drawn out process. She said it could be "November or even December" before the ez-link card usurps its predecessor and takes complete control. That being the case, I will doggedly persevere with the old farecard until Dec 31.

And I know this will irritate fellow commuters. On buses, when I slow down boarding time with my farecard fumbling, the perverse side of me quite enjoys the accompanied critical mutterings. If they persist, I turn the card upside down, look aghast when the machine spits it back and say: "Excuse me, there seems to be something wrong with the machine and I'm really in a hurry here." God, where do they get these people from?

But I struggle with relentless change. My generation has grown up in a society where Blitzkrieg technological development is the norm. There is no time to stand still. I admire those who stand up for some continuity in their lives.

In England, there were cases of shopkeepers being forced, by law, to adopt the metric system of weights and measures in line with European Union stipulations. Despite the threat of a fine, and in extreme cases a prison sentence, they still stuck by their pounds and ounces. They were my heroes.

These grocery guys would rather take on the European Union than risk the wrath of little old ladies coming in and asking: "What the bloody hell is a gram, you silly young man? Now, give me two pounds of sugar before I box your ears."

In some ways, this was a wise move because the only people that measured in grams when I last lived in England were drug dealers. And they're most welcome to them. So, I will continue on my crusade to preserve some traditions and hold back the technological tide for as long as possible. But it's difficult not to get trampled under the march towards greater efficiency.

According to the various transport operators in Singapore, the new ez-link card relies on the Global Positioning System (GPS) of satellites to track the location of the bus. So if you're reading this on a bus while picking your nose, then let me assure you that the GPS has you in its sights. Think about that. Now, go and wash your finger.

But when the ez-link card was first introduced, there were some glitches in the system with cards being misread or overcharged on buses and trains. So, in April 2002, a Bus Task Force was established to remove the kinks and increase ez-link's efficiency.

Yes, that's a Bus Task Force — in proud capital letters, no less. I assume this means that muscle-bound men in ski masks, abseil from helicopters onto the roofs of buses and shoot, on sight, anyone whose ez-link card is rejected by the reader. Machine-gunning their way through the bus, the fearsome task forcers will cry: "Right, you dithering bastards, the next person to slow down this bus by pissing about with their ez-link card will get a bullet in the balls. Oh, sorry, I didn't realise this was a school bus."

If that doesn't speed up boarding time, nothing will. No, wait, perhaps they should introduce those moving floors that they have at airports. You could just step on and have your ez-link card scanned as you glide past. If the machine fails to read the card, rather than emit that repetitive beep, it should administer an electric shock. Watch how fast the commuters move down the aisle then.

Don't laugh; there's probably a civil servant involved with public transport reading this and thinking: "Actually, an electric shock device could speed up boarding time by 0.3 seconds. That would make each bus route 4.7 seconds faster. And that, most importantly of all, could add 0.8 per cent to my increment at the end of the year."

It could happen. And when the Bus Task Force starts landing on my bus in Thomson Road, I'll head for Tioman. You'll find me lying in a hammock, fanning myself with my old farecard.

**NOTE**: True to form, I continued with my trusty farecard until December 2002, when I returned to England for a working holiday. When I came back in the new year, I went straight on the bus and tried to use my farecard. My fellow passengers looked at me as if I had just shit on the floor. I had to use cash in the end. But to this day, I still forget to swipe the ez-link card as I leave the bus. So, if you spot a sweaty *ang moh* running back towards the bus eloquently shouting, "Wait, you bastard, I forgot to beep this fucking stupid card", please refrain from calling the police again.

## *THE SKIN*

EVEN though it was my friend's birthday, I didn't want to go to a nightclub. I no longer drink and when I try to dance soberly, the crowd parts frantically and someone usually makes a desperate call to the Singapore Zoo to discuss my recapture.

"But it's your boss' birthday," my colleagues pleaded.

"I've never even heard of the club," I retorted.

"It's off Orchard Road. The area's also known affectionately as 'the four floors of whores'."

"I see. What time are we leaving?"

Once I'd handed over a month's salary in exchange for an entry stamp and a tepid Coke, it became immediately obvious that something was amiss. The clientele's diversity was staggering. There were over 50 white, expat males, which made up around 80 per cent of all the men in the club — and just two white women. Many of the men were older than my father. Some even danced like him, which was most disconcerting. I thought he was a one-off.

Just where do these people go during the day? If you stopped reading this book right now and walked 50 metres in any direction, I'll wager that you'll encounter very few *ang mohs*.

Step into any nightclub along Orchard Road at the weekend and you can't miss them. Like vampires, they prowl the dance floor looking for female victims and, my god, there was no shortage of eager sacrifices that night. I thought all this SPG nonsense was going the way of the expat CEO.

Have these young ladies not read the news? In recent months, *ang mohs* with fat wallets have been dropping like flies. Many are fleeing back to the West quicker than you can say: "You know, perhaps we should have hired that Nanyang guy after all. The New York guy nearly ruined us."

But no one, it seems, has relayed this information to the beguiling beauties currently doing the nightclub circuit. I've never encountered so many women harbouring obsessions with ageing 'foreign talents'.

There was only Ulrika Jonsson in England. The stunning TV presenter had a fling with the talented, though slightly unusual looking, Sven-Goran Eriksson. But Jonsson has had affairs with several sporting personalities, so it's difficult to deduce whether she actually had feelings for the England coach or just loved the smell of men's dressing rooms. Yet, even she would be out of her league in Orchard Road.

One gorgeous Malay girl, wearing a dress the size of a handkerchief, spent several hours flirting with no less than four different white men before settling for a plump, American chap. He couldn't believe his luck. She couldn't believe his wallet.

Clearly, there were just not enough *ang mohs* to go around. And this fact became painfully obvious when a tipsy 30-something made a beeline for me. Now, I'm not going to kid myself here. In England, women have remarked that, in a certain light, I resemble James Dean — albeit after his fatal car crash. I attract women like an Opposition candidate attracts votes in Toa Payoh. Yet this did not deter my new, distinctly exotic companion.

"Wha' your name?" she slurred.

"Stamford Raffles."

"Ha. Would you like me to dance with you?"

"Er, no. Thanks."

"Come lah, let me dance for you."

"With me or for me?"

"I dance for you."

"No, really. Thanks." Like the leaflet distributors, she just wouldn't bugger off.

"Don't be shy lah. Come, I sit on your lap."

"What?!" But it was too late. Before I could move, her backside came at me like a Tomahawk missile. My first reaction was to scream, my second to call for security and my third would've involved several sharp toothpicks. A quick shift to the left allowed me to narrowly escape her weighty plunge.

Yet, my physical rejection merely encouraged her. She stood up again, eager to launch herself a second time, so I dashed off to join my friend in the toilet. This desperate measure suggested that I was gay and she backed off, finally.

My poor friend at the urinal was besieged by questions. Who is that woman? Why does she want to gyrate on my groin? Where the hell did that long-stemmed red rose come from? And, most worryingly of all, where the bloody hell did she intend to put it? But that's it, as far as I'm concerned. The next time I go to a club, I'm wearing a sign — a huge placard across my chest that will say: "I NOT RICH, I NO CONDO, I LIVE IN HDB."

It's ironic, really, because in every other facet of Singaporean society, there is an increasing realisation that white skin does not automatically equate to a greater talent or bank balance. Except, of course, in the nightclubs — a situation that *ang mohs*, fat wallet or no fat wallet, are always keen to exploit.

But do not fear, because what goes around comes around. On the way home, I spotted a pair of middle-aged *ang mohs* chatting with two lanky ladies, while brandishing their wallets. As I approached, I noticed that the two women were, in fact, heavily made-up men — a biological fact that had gone unnoticed by the two drunks.

Now that's a truly novel way of introducing expats to the concept of value-added services. I just hope the two 'ladies' offered to show the *ang mohs* their long-stemmed red roses. But seriously ladies, it's time to stop putting *ang mohs* on a pedestal — or your lap.

**NOTE:** Unsurprisingly, quite a few letters came in over this controversial issue. But this time, interestingly, every one of them agreed with my rather critical views of exploitative Caucasians and naive Singaporeans. Many were just getting tired of the predictability of it all. So am I.

# *THE BAN*

WHEN I was 18, I was banned from my local pub. Considering I grew up in a part of London where chicken molesting barely raised an eyebrow, this was quite an achievement. The public house was so dilapidated that when I first asked the barmaid where the toilet was, she replied: "You're in it."

On one hazy occasion, I found myself looking for the men's urinal in the ladies room. For some reason, the sight of women applying lipstick in the mirror didn't warrant concern. Probably because I was being strangled at the time by an irate landlord, who kept shouting obscenities like "pervert" and "dirty little bugger". Apparently, he was not impressed when I said I was looking for the jukebox. So, I was banned from one of the worst pubs in London.

Among friends, there was a certain cachet to being booted out of a notorious drinking den. The incident awarded me some priceless street-cred. It allowed me to concentrate on my A-Levels and gave me the opportunity to use the word 'cachet'.

But in Singapore, however, it is ridiculously easy to earn yourself a ban of any kind. Last year, a journalist was not allowed to attend functions of the Comfort Group, the taxicab company, after penning a critical commentary about its CEO and his supposedly generous salary package. This is grossly unfair.

I mean, where's the slap from incensed ladies whom you've embarrassed outside the toilet cubicle or the kick up the backside from bouncers? At the very least, a credible ban must be followed with a severe battering from your mother, preferably with a broom handle. It always did for me anyway. I mean, if bans are given out so cheaply, then why can't I have one and all the kudos that comes with it?

Attempting to answer this question, I met covertly with one of those 'disgruntled staff members' of the Comfort Group. There are plenty of them — they're called Singaporean taxi drivers. On the condition of anonymity, one cabbie told me everything. "Though must be careful, *ah*?" He cautioned. "Must protect my rice bowl. Unlike my bosses, my rice bowl very small. It's like my taxi — cannot smash."

He then proceeded to discuss the hypocrisy of big bosses at Comfort, the high rental of his vehicle and his astronomical insurance and petrol costs. It seemed too good to be true — this guy was revealing the complete inside story, a scoop no less, which would guarantee a ban and subsequent notoriety in media circles. It was too good to be true, however, because the driver was a raving lunatic. An utter fruitcake — his hands spent more time gesticulating than they did on the wheel. In fact, he treated the steering contraption like an electric fence and the more animated he became, the less he touched the wheel.

"Comfort threatened to sack me twice. You know why or not?" he bellowed.

"For not keeping your hands on the wheel, you bloody madman?" I offered.

"No, because I've had two accidents. They said I was a bad driver. Ridiculous right?" And then, he turned round to ascertain my reaction. That's right. We were careering along Thomson Road and the old loony turns around so I can reassure him that he is a competent driver. I wouldn't have trusted him with a shopping trolley.

"But what about your big boss?" I asked, pointing towards the windscreen, something he didn't acknowledge very often. "Was it fair of him to ban that journalist?"

The cabbie shrugged and said, "Singapore's like that. Even before your time, it's been like that."

Now, call me naive, but I thought those hip, swinging Singaporeans of wealth and power were dancing out of the shackles of stereotype. In a desperate bid to keep the younger ones from living with koala bears, kangaroos and crocodile hunter Steve Irwin, the Republic's elite is supposed to be more open and more tolerant of criticism. We're allowed to know the incomes of CEOs of public-listed companies, I'm told, because of something called 'corporate transparency'. But not everyone in the corporate world is ready to embrace this freewheeling, radical notion of transparency.

The Comfort Group proudly announced that the 'disgruntled staff member' who leaked news of the journalist's ban to the media has faced 'severe disciplinary action'. The employee was to be hanged, drawn and quartered, but the rack was still rusty after all that exertion during the Spanish Inquisition. So the guilty party settled for castration, followed by a quick, lethal injection.

This is just the kind of carefree, trusting environment that will convince the quitters to flood back to Changi Airport, isn't it?

Incidentally, if the bigwigs at Comfort ever feel like relocating to Australia, then my cabbie friend and I will gladly pay your airfare. I'll even get Mr. Look-No-Hands to drive you to the airport. Is that enough to earn me a ban now?

**NOTE:** Apparently, it was not enough to earn me a ban, which I was devastated about. I couldn't sleep for a fortnight afterwards. In media circles, I had to stand on the periphery and watch big-shot writers discuss their various establishment bans. It was so humiliating. However, having the article published in this book will certainly not do my chances any harm. So if you've bought this book, you have possibly contributed to a major transport operator banning me from ever being allowed to step into one of its taxicabs again. Nice one.

## *THE SEX*

WELL, what a miserable month October, 2002, turned out to be for me and many other Singaporeans. Despite interviewing Oasis songwriter Noel Gallagher just the week before, the bad boys from Manchester proved to be no more than choirboys in the end. After the tragic Bali bombings, they decided that Singapore was not an oasis and returned to England with their guitars between their legs.

They had been due to play their first ever Singaporean gig at the Singapore Indoor Stadium, but the belligerent brothers shit themselves after a terrorist attack thousands of kilometres away. If there were similar nightclub bombings in Spain's Costa del Sol, would they cancel a gig in Britain? Besides, is Southeast Asia really that dangerous for Westerners? Surely the average British celebrity has more to fear from being cornered by British TV star and man-hunter Ulrika Jonsson at a showbiz party.

I'm a white man living in Singapore and the only bodily harm I fear is from being tapped to death by my mini-mart owner. Her palms pummel my forearms with every word she utters. And she does enjoy a sentence or two.

"Ah *ang moh,*" she begins brightly, tapping my hand and arms. "More toilet rolls, is it? Too much curry again, is it?" Tap, tap, tap.

"You must watch your diet, eh?" Tap, tap, tap.

"Stop tapping me! I need all this tissue to wrap around my sore arms, you daft old bat."

I have left the shop with more bruises than a sadomasochist, which, incidentally, is my subtle way of introducing my next topic — sex. To be honest, it salvaged a miserable month as far as I was concerned. Rather depressed with the regional news, I was delighted to learn that, in some quarters, I'm considered to be obsessed with the physical act of lovemaking.

I received an email from a reader who said something like: "We've read your newspaper columns and come to the conclusion that you must be a pervert. Therefore we are promoting a number of board games designed to improve sexual relationships, and we thought of you."

Well, I was appalled, at first. And then I asked them to send me one of the games. Two days later, *FOREPLAY — A Game For Lovers* arrived on my desk.

It's like *Trivial Pursuit* for nymphomaniacs. You play the game with your wife or lover (or wife and lover, if you're feeling really bold) and, through a series of questions, you learn more about your partner's sexual desires, preferences and ambitions. The game finishes, hopefully, with you and your partner moving onto something a little more physically stimulating. No, not *Scrabble*. But you do get extra points for length.

The game is proving quite popular, I'm told, and can be bought by Singaporeans at *www.sensualfire.com.sg*.

But I remain skeptical. This is Singapore. In this country, you cannot even have SEX on a number plate — for several reasons. Firstly, the number plates aren't wide enough and you'd fall off and scratch your bare arse on the tarmac. Secondly, 'sex on a number plate' sounds like a song by Eminem. Thirdly, and perhaps most importantly, the Land Transport Authority recently decided against using vowels as the middle letter of three-letter prefixes in vehicle licence plates. Thus, sensitive words like SEX, SIN and SUX are avoided.

One *TODAY* letter writer applauded the decision, saying that her young son should not see his mother driving around in a car with the word SEX on it. How times have changed. When I grew up in Dagenham, which is on the outskirts of east London, children hoped to avoid seeing their mothers having sex *in* the car.

Considering that startling thought, is it fair to say that we are dealing with a more conservative society here? This is a country where a sex scene in Eminem's movie, *8 Mile*, has been cut even though both Eminem and his screen partner are *fully clothed* throughout their lovemaking session. The game's distributor, Passions Of Life, disagrees though, claiming that Asians invented the *Kama Sutra*, while Bangkok is the sex capital of the world, with Geylang, I believe, coming a close second.

This was the line I took with my girlfriend when I asked her to play *Foreplay* with me — all in the name of investigative journalism, of course. But the game didn't last long. One of the cards instructed her to sprinkle talcum powder on my neck. The dust irritated my sinuses, and I ended up looking and sounding like a pig with respiratory problems.

This irritated my girlfriend. I know because when I asked her, "Under what circumstances do you think the most enjoyable lovemaking sessions occur?" she replied, "When you're at work."

Rather miffed by her sarcasm, I asked two girls in the office to play the game together instead. This was a somewhat pitiful attempt on my part to realise a long-harboured fantasy involving two young ladies, preferably with bisexual tendencies and a steamy shower. Nothing of the sort happened. Though I was engrossed by the constant giggling and playful slapping, which was a trifle disturbing. In truth, though, it's just a bit of saucy fun and, God knows, we've needed some of that recently.

Without wishing to trivialise major global issues, I'd rather play *Foreplay* on a Saturday night than watch news of the latest gig cancellation, shooting or bombing. In fact, I fancy a game right now. Do you know Ulrika Jonsson's handphone number?

To be honest, though, I've got a better chance with the mini-mart auntie. No slap and tickle, just lots of bloody tapping.

**NOTE:** I was really pissed off when Oasis and a couple of other acts cancelled their Singaporean gigs after the Bali attacks last year. It demonstrated, once again, many Westerners' short-sighted and blinkered views of the region. If you read the British tabloids you could be forgiven for thinking: "All Muslims bad, all Asia Muslims, so all Asia bad."

On a personal level, Oasis has been my favourite band for years. I even managed to somehow mention the group in the introduction of my previous book, *Notes from an even Smaller Island*. So, as you can imagine, I was well chuffed when I got to interview Noel Gallagher, the creative force behind the band. Two days after the article was published, however, Oasis cancelled its gigs in both Singapore and the Philippines. I felt a right prick. Luckily for me, I had a new board game to cheer me up.

## *THE WHEEL*

THE screaming was deafening. As the train pulled into the Canary Wharf station in east London, the pitiful high-pitched whine drew the attention of everyone on the carriage. It was most embarrassing because the panic-stricken voice was mine. We were going to crash! Demonstrating my characteristic strengths of Jonah, this was my first time on the state-of-the-art Docklands Light Railway and I end up with a driver who thinks he's Houdini. The bastard had disappeared.

"Look mum," I bellowed. "There's no driver. He's jumped out. We're going to smash into the station. We're all going to die."

My humiliated mother, as always, muttered something about "her stupid son showing her up in a public place" and silenced me with a subtle, but effective, slap across the face.

I should have maintained my cool. I should've known that the new transport system was automated and required no driver. I mean, I was 16 at the time. But I've always been extremely backward when it comes to transport and technology. When I first ventured onto the archaic London Underground as a boy, I was left deeply traumatised when I discovered that the trains did not have jovial, red faces on the front with names like Thomas the Tank Engine or Percy the Pink Pervert. The surreal prospect of travelling on a driverless train could only be the work of Jules Verne as far as I was concerned. So I thoroughly empathise with the Singaporean commuters who, in October 2002, suffered at the mechanical hands of the automated LRT trains, which service the HDB heartlands.

Before you could say, "Wheel, you are the weakest link, goodbye", the LRT industry almost came off the rails — for six or seven minutes. That was how long a driverless LRT train travelled along the Bukit Panjang line after a guide wheel fell off, damaging the track and causing a power trip. Stranded and seriously delayed, the shocked passengers were understandably furious.

Pragmatic officials of the SMRT system have already formulated a proposal to channel that fury. Should a train breakdown again, commuters will be able to lift individual flaps under their feet and run along the track, based on the Flintstones' model of kinetic energy. Watch how many executives will be late for work when their destiny lies in their own feet.

But to give the LRT network its due, services resumed within a couple of days. The repairs would have been quicker, but SMRT failed to agree terms with a certain Malcolm Higgins. In some circles, Higgins is revered as a technological genius. In other words, he's a sad geek who should've got out more when he was a teenager. In April 2002, he promised to rescue the British rail industry with, wait for it, a laser gun. The inventor claimed to have developed a laser beam, which could be fitted under trains to vaporise the leaves on the tracks.

Allegedly, he was sane when he made this bold claim. Though he whooped a lot and concluded by saying, "If lasers were good enough for Han Solo, then they are good enough for British Rail. Now, get your fucking hands off my gun!"

But that is the fundamental difference between Singaporean and British train services. Falling leaves can bring the entire rail network of southeast England to a standstill. In October 2000, for instance, wet leaves were blamed for a train derailment in Surrey, where the train went through a red light and just missed a commuter train. Fortunately, no one was injured, but the passengers now refuse to walk under trees during the autumnal months.

I wouldn't wish to downplay or trivialise the genuine grievances of LRT commuters of late, but if the driverless system has had just 50 problems since it began running in 1999, then it should be lauded, not lambasted.

The London Underground encounters more difficulties and breakdowns every day. According to a 2001 survey, one in 20 peak trains don't run, escalators remain broken for months and some stations have been neglected since they were built. The decaying, Victorian tube system is estimated to need 1.2 billion pounds worth of immediate investment and a further 400 million pounds annually just to keep it going. And then you have the additional problems that really are beyond the company's control.

When I was 18, I found myself virtually alone on a deserted platform at London's East Ham station. Considering it was only a couple of days before Christmas and the high street was packed with shoppers, the empty station was slightly unnerving. The station controller asked me to leave and when I asked why, he pointed to a sports bag, just two metres away and said: "Because we think that's an IRA bomb, mate."

The bag had been left under the same bloody bench that I was sitting on. It wasn't a bomb, it rarely is, but it was the fastest working laxative I've ever known.

So it is a little premature to suggest the wheels have fallen off the LRT industry. Yes, I know there was another one. But if you've survived bomb scares and the odd public battering from your mother, you're entitled to the occasional pun in your book.

Having depended on the crumbling, rat-infested London Underground to get me to school every day, I can safely say that SMRT manages the greatest public transport network I have ever known. It just needs to make its trains less impersonal. Painting smiling faces on the front and naming them Thomas or Percy has proved extremely popular. And if another wheel falls off, 'Han Solo' Higgins says he's ready with his laser gun.

**NOTE:** I received some criticism over this one from a Singaporean chap who thought that I was being somewhat harsh on the London Underground and that I was making an unfair comparison between the two transport models — one being modern and the other prehistoric. It's certainly true that the London Underground, built during the Victorian era, was a revolutionary, technological breakthrough in its day. And I genuinely believe that Britain is unfairly criticised for being a pioneer in many of its social policies — for instance, the London Underground, municipal housing, the welfare state and organised football. At the time, they were all sound ideas that immeasurably improved the living standards of the working classes. The said services put a roof over my head, gave me free school milk and took me to work and school every day. Indeed, the last one gave me a hobby where I could swear at 11 grown men and not get told off by my dad. Having said that, you still have to take your hat off to the Singaporean government on this one. They retained the best qualities of all of these policies and discarded the rest (the S-League being the possible exception). Being a rather late arrival into the world of nation-states, it's difficult to say whether this was by chance or design. (Singapore lacked the infrastructure to support a 'from-the-cradle-to-the-grave' system of welfare in 1965, even if it had wanted to.) Nevertheless, Britain's welfare state, like its public transport services, needs a ridiculous cash injection just to prevent its collapse in the new millennium. Why should Singaporeans care if the London Underground came first and SMRT had the benefit of hindsight garnered from another country's mistakes? Despite huge government subsidies, the London Underground loses thousands of pounds every day, while the MRT and bus services in Singapore actually turn a profit at the end of each financial year. Even if the odd wheel does fall off from time to time. But that's the reality, so be damn proud of it.

## *THE FREAK*

ONE of the most difficult aspects about living 10,000 kilometres away from England is that my annual whirlwind visit is an exhausting trek to each of the relative outposts. I'm not complaining. I'm the selfish one who chose to live in Singapore. But it does mean, of course, the incomparable visit to my grandmother. Born just after the First World War and married by the Second, she proudly boasts that American servicemen ensured that she never needed to buy her own drinks for the full six years of conflict. A remarkable woman.

But she is a trifle off-balance. Every year, she assumes Singapore is the Asian equivalent of Hell's Island and I'm England's answer to Papillon, always seeking to escape.

"Are you still out in that place?" she begins cheerily.

"Singapore?"

"Yeah."

"Yeah."

"Shame, really. When do you think they will let you come home?"

"Nan, I love it there. I have a great job. We have lots of mates and it's a great place to live."

"Yeah, you write books and newspapers, don't you?"

"Well, sort of. But we're having a good time."

"Still, if they are pleased with all that work you are doing, they might let you come back early, right?"

"Nan, for the last time. It's a country, not a prison."

But I know she's stopped listening. That's assuming she ever paid attention in the first place. By then, she's already moved on to her mission in life — to feed her guests until they die. In this respect, she is similar to her endearing Singaporean 'auntie' counterparts. She asks the same question every year and always gets the same response.

"Would you like a sandwich, Jodie?"

"Her name's Tracy, nan."

"Sorry, Tracy. I've got ham, cornbeef, cheese. Which one would you like, Jodie?"

"She's vegetarian, nan. Remember, I told you before, right? She can't eat meat."

"Did you? Oh that's right. I forget everything now, silly old bastard I am... What about turkey?"

"She can't eat meat, nan."

"Oh yeah. Shame, really. When do you think you can start eating proper food again?"

"She does eat proper food, nan. She just chooses not to eat meat."

"Does she? Shame really."

We've endured the same interrogation for seven years now, so we can usually answer the questions on autopilot. But my nan's forgetfulness and harmless ignorance still left my poor girlfriend completely unprepared for the stunned reactions she gets in Singapore. Here, she is a freak. Informing friends, dinner guests and strangers generally that she is a vegetarian generates, at best, looks of puzzlement or, at worst, withering looks of contempt followed by an unpleasant grilling that wouldn't be out of place at the Internal Security Department. I've told her before that she might as well say: "I'm a cannibal. It's hereditary. I used to have seven brothers and sisters, but we ate them. So, please, eat everything up, so there's more for me later." Believe me, the horrified expressions couldn't be much worse than those she suffers now.

The negative reactions from aunties and uncles, like my grandmother, are understandable. As Singapore struggled in its formative years, putting food on the table was difficult enough. Asking for a soya burger with low-fat mayonnaise during the '60s would have been rewarded with a slap from your mother, and deservedly so. It was no different for my grandmother. During the austere post-war years, which came with ration books and coupons, housewives queued for free horsemeat because it didn't require coupons. Feeding screaming babies took precedence over saving a few well-fed hogs.

But the response to my missus' vegetarianism from the 30-somethings was more of a surprise. Singaporeans around my age often feel the need to challenge my girlfriend's moral choice. And, just like a visit to my grandmother, the same, tedious questions always come thick and fast.

"You're a vegetarian? But why?"

"Oh, it's just a personal thing. No big deal," my patient girlfriend replies.

"Are you allergic to the taste of meat?"

"No, it's not that."

"Oh, it must be religion, right. I thought so. You're part of a religion where you can't eat certain animals, right?"

"No, I'm not religious."

"Then why don't you eat meat?"

"Oh, just for the animals, you know. I don't like eating other animals."

"That's it? That's why you're a vegetarian? You want to save the animals. Ha." For some reason, this always gets a big laugh and my girlfriend always gets embarrassed. Only on one occasion have I retaliated. The 'vegetarians-are-weirdos' jokes were getting really predictable and tiresome. One of the jokers didn't eat certain meats on religious grounds and as the so-called quips developed an undercurrent of nastiness, the hypocrisy became nauseous.

"So let me get this straight," I asked. "Not eating meat on the grounds of a faith for a god we never see is tolerated. But not eating meat on the grounds of protecting actual, living creatures that we see around us every day is a subject worthy of ridicule? This hypocrisy really pisses me off."

The embarrassed silence that followed my little outburst told me I shouldn't take that subject any further and I won't here. But for many, my missus is a social freak, often treated like an invalid.

Yet she never complains. I've lost count of the times when a friend has sighed melodramatically and said: "There's great food here. Let's eat here. Oh shit, we can't, can we? We can't because I know they don't have any vegetarian dinners. Hang on, you can eat french fries, right?" Unlike a born-again Christian, she doesn't act like a born-again vegetarian, preaching to other

Singaporeans by saying: "Come follow me, people. I've found the path to enlightenment. A meatless diet will provide the key to the afterlife."

But she is a sneaky one, burrowing away quietly and laying the foundations for the future. The five-year-old kids she teaches in Singapore must be the most environmentally aware pre-school students in the world. A parent once came in and told my girlfriend that her child had lectured her for killing some cockroaches. Another student reprimanded a friend for killing a make-believe spider. A little extreme perhaps, but these little guys might just save the world that we've fucked up.

According to the academics, my girlfriend is an ovo-lacto vegetarian, which is generally the most commonly practiced dietary regime. The ovo-lacto mob won't eat any meat or fish, sticking to vegetables, eggs and dairy. That is, food products that don't involve anything with a face being killed.

Don't get me wrong, the missus doesn't want to eat anything that's a product of factory farming either. But drinking soya milk made her vomit, literally, and she lost weight at an alarming rate. Finding free-range products is possible here, but it's about as likely as telling the average Singaporean that you're a vegetarian and not getting the piss taken out of you.

That's why I admire her. It's so difficult to be a vegetarian here, especially if you're not a big fan of vegetables in the first place, which she isn't. I couldn't do it. In the West and Australia, a vegetarian culture has mushroomed over the last 10 years or so. In supermarkets, whole aisles are devoted to mock meats and various meals for vegetarians. Even vegans, who avoid all dairy products and won't wear anything that is derived from an animal, are well catered for in the West.

Indeed, it has become hip for younger Westerners to denounce meat-eating. According to a *TIME* survey in July 2002, some 10 million Americans consider themselves to be practising vegetarians and another 20 million have flirted with a meat-free diet. And this is a country where babies are born in hotdog buns and thrown onto the barbeque at a very young age. If it ain't got a pulse, they ain't gonna eat it. Indeed, the country certainly has the best damn steak that I've ever tasted. Yet 25 per cent of adolescents polled by Teenage Research Unlimited in America said vegetarianism was "sensible" and "cool", according to *TIME* magazine.

There are also health reasons. Aside from the usual additives, there is that fun stuff in meat like the E. Coli bacteria and Britain's contribution to fine dining — Mad Cow Disease. Do you remember reading about that? Britain's mooing population started staggering around with their underpants on their head and barking at their farmers, who were feeding them the remains of just about every other animal species on the planet. The poor cows were deranged. I remember one being interviewed on TV about the disease and he replied: "Mad cows? Never heard of it, mate. I'm an octopus. Do you want to see my tentacles?"

To be fair, my grandmother continued to eat meat during the Mad Cows furore and there was no discernible difference in her behaviour. But then, this is a woman who would perform her Hawaiian dance without invitation and flash her knickers to anyone who was foolish enough to watch. Had she contracted the virus, it might have been nigh on impossible to spot the symptoms. Despite piles of dead cows all over the English countryside, it still took some time for the missus' family to come to terms with her vegetarianism. But eventually they did, albeit reluctantly.

But in Singapore she remains a social outcast. The nation has an entrenched food culture that it is fiercely proud and protective of, and rightly so. The plethora of choice at any decent hawker centre or food court puts Singapore in the food Premiership. In England, you can have fish with chips, meat with chips and chips with chips at most food courts. And when the hungry pay a visit to their local Indian or Chinese takeaway in England — they order chips. I cannot think of any English environment, where there can be at least 15 to 20 completely different dishes all under one roof. I have seen it in the United States, but not, I'm afraid, in the southeast of England.

There is a tendency, however, to become too protective of one's culture. Some Singaporeans can be very elitist when it comes to their dishes. Fish is my Singaporean failing. I simply don't like it. I never have and I never will. End of story. But it isn't. It's never allowed to be in Singapore. Lengthy explanations are required to pacify your host and dinner guests; occasionally, it gets offensive. I have been told so many times: "You know, it's actually quite rude not to eat a dish that's been prepared for you." I should reply: "You know, in England, it's actually quite rude to humiliate someone in front of friends and strangers at a dinner table. You know, in England, it's actually customary for me to smack you in your mouth about now." But, of course, I refrain. I bite my tongue instead. That way, it becomes numb and I can no longer taste the fish.

So I have a confession to make. For seven years now, I've been living a lie. It's time for me to come clean, publicly, in this book. I'm not really allergic to fish. It doesn't liquify my bodily waste and leave me sitting on the toilet for four hours. Nor does it make my eyes weep a yellow pus. Nor does it render me impotent. I've used all of these stories and more to pacify my dinner company, when they enquire about my non-fish eating. It's a last-ditch attempt to thwart the oncoming sales pitch. But it rarely works.

You see, if I don't like the fish, my eating companions often try to 'sell' it to me. When informed that I don't like fish, they look as if I've just stepped off a spaceship and reply: "But it's been cooked steamboat style, you know. It's really good."

"I believe you, but I just don't really like fish. I never have."

"I know. But this tastes different. It's cooked in a steamboat."

"I understand. But it wouldn't matter if it was cooked in a canoe."

"But it's been steamed. It's been fried. It's been grilled. It's been boiled. It's been baked, barbequed and roasted. It's been firebombed and it's one of Singapore's most famous dishes, you know."

"I'm really sorry." And then comes my favourite.

"This fish is very expensive, you know."

"Look, it doesn't matter if the fish has the brains of Free Willy, the figure of the Little Mermaid, has been boiled in liquid gold for 15 years and you had to sell your HDB flat to buy two kilograms, I really don't like fish."

That's when the comments usually come in about offending the cook, the custom, or the festival and how this *ang moh* doesn't understand local culture. I do. I really do. I just don't eat fish. That's about as complicated as it gets. But that food protectorate is ever present. I rarely eat Western food, unless the girls at the office bring some back, because it's too expensive. Yet the second a french fry touches my lips, someone from the Food Force seems to be on hand to say, "Why don't you try fish ball noodles, *roti john, nasi padang,* chicken rice, *rojak* or *satay*? There's so much more to eat than just burgers." You don't say.

Yet I've got Chinese friends who won't go near an Indian or a Muslim stall. I had a late night supper of chicken curry at an Indian stall, while a Chinese friend tactlessly informed me that he'd never order from a stall like that. I know Indians who have never eaten fish ball noodles in their life. And I once asked a Malay friend to pick up some *char siew fun* from the coffee shop and he didn't know what barbecued pork rice was, even after I'd explained it to him. Yet, because my girlfriend is a vegetarian and I don't take fish, we're the ones who get criticised for not assimilating into another man's culture? The hypocrisy is astounding. But we can't even go there, can we? Religious and racial harmony and all that. Let's not rock the steamboat. Point the finger at the *ang moh* instead. There will be less repercussions and, ultimately, it's safer.

That's why my girlfriend's vegetarianism is a testament to her patience. Having endured disparaging comments for over four years, she's coped remarkably well. I would join her, but I know I would end up punching someone. Besides, as I'm always cruelly reminding the missus, mutton *korma, nasi briyani* and beef *kway teow* all taste so bloody good, don't they?

But the mood is changing. Most Singaporean teenagers wouldn't consider vegetarians as freaks. The younger generations are increasingly spurning sharks fin soup, refusing to serve it at their wedding dinners. Singapore will evolve quite nicely in the hands of these brave, politically aware heroes of mine.

They've watched the documentaries. They've witnessed what a despicable, bloody process removing the shark's fin is. It's hardly clinical. The sharks are often baited with fish and smashed over the head by the fishermen to keep them from struggling. The fins are hacked off in a pretty haphazard fashion and the shark is thrown back into the sea. Like mammals who have lost a limb, the shark will soldier on for a day or two in excruciating pain before succumbing to its fatal injuries.

Without its fin, the imbalanced shark struggles to swim properly and he either drowns or bleeds to death. It is an agonisingly slow and painful death. The old *Jaws* argument that sharks fin soup ensures that mankind has one less man-eating predator to worry about is utter nonsense. Shark attacks usually account for around 50 human deaths a year. They are usually accidental, with the shark often mistaking a surfboard for an injured seal. To avenge this statistic, man is responsible for around 100 million shark deaths a year, according to Wild Aid. That sounds fair.

Yet, for these wonderful Singaporeans, it's not just about saving the sharks. These guys face tremendous parental and peer pressure to maintain 'face' and follow Chinese tradition. Sharks fin soup, once served up by the Chinese aristocracy, represents affluence and wealth. In extreme cases of parental dogma, they risk alienation. To the older generations, not serving the traditional 10-course meal with all the usual dishes would be about as popular as not serving alcohol at a British wedding. But the couples are valiantly sticking to their guns and sharks fin soup is no longer the status symbol it perhaps once was. Just as it's 'cool' among teenagers in America not to eat meat, it's becoming 'cool' in Singapore not to serve Jaws' broth at wedding dinners. I'm probably biased because you already know my stance on fish. But sharks fin soup tastes like cat's piss to me so I'm all for keeping it off the menu.

Moreover, public awareness, again among younger Singaporeans, concerning issues such as the environment, animal rights and the crumbling ecosystems is spreading rapidly. I know the government would like to take credit for this with their countless campaigns and community slogans, but the answer is far simpler — cable television. When I was a child, Ronald McDonald was an icon on television. Today, Singaporean children watch crocodile hunter Steve Irwin remind them that the ugliest lizard they've even seen, which is usually green, has three horns, five eyes and a protruding sphincter, is still a "beauty" that must be respected and protected.

It was cable television that converted the missus. At times, I don't know whether to celebrate or curse the day the Animal Planet Channel arrived in our living room. Normally, the soppy woman cries when Forrest Gump loses his mother or when ET leaves Earth, which actually makes the alien a 'quitter' in the eyes of the Singaporean government. But she cried me a river when *Animal Hospital* failed to save an iguana called Colin. And she is not alone. In HDB flats across Singapore, children are learning about the ecosystems of the South American rainforests on the Discovery Channel, the emotional intelligence of elephants on the National Geographic Channel and the lack of emotional intelligence of Steve Irwin on Animal Planet.

Ironically, the Singaporean government resisted satellite television for years, fearing uncensored filth, pornography and sleazy behaviour would be beamed into our homes. But no one wants to watch the daily session of Britain's House of Lords anyway. Instead, the government can hope that it might just end up with a generation of global citizens aware of issues beyond the economic sphere, who respect the moral choices of others. Not because the government tells them to, in the interests of religious and racial harmony, but simply because their understanding tells them it's the right thing to do.

I'm not saying that they should, or will, become vegetarians. That would be grossly hypocritical because, at the moment, I'm not one. But the new kids on Singapore's block will be more informed and less inclined to say: "You don't eat meat or fish? Never mind *lah,* you can eat this. It's chilli crab."

## *THE TOURIST*

THE Bangkok weather was surprisingly cool; the riverboat was cruising along the Chao Phraya River and my view was obscured by an arse that could have covered Mount Everest.

Prior to booking the Bangkok boat trip a couple of years back, I hadn't realised that the Pentax pair were also coming. You've met them, right? They're those red-faced *ang moh* tourists, usually American, with a penchant for floral shirts and knee-high white socks with sandals. They speak only one language — touristese — and they speak it loudly.

On that Bangkok trip, they bellowed comments like: "Gee, Mary Jane, I got me a real Thai pauper here. He ain't wearing nothing but a pair of ripped shorts and a toothless grin. He's doing his laundry in the river. You see him, Mary Jane? Come on, honey, get your glasses on and get yourself some culture here. You see him? Right there, in front of his wooden stick house. Be quick now, Mary Jane, I got me the long lens on my Pentax ready, so you just wave and get that peasant to wave right back."

The Thai economy depends on the Pentax pair and their tourist brothers and sisters worldwide to bring in foreign currencies, by selling the more intimate aspects of its culture. And now, Singapore wants to do the same.

In March 2003, the Singapore Tourism Board announced that it was contemplating taking over two vacant HDB blocks in Tiong Bahru Road so it could transform them into budget hotels. The idea is that tourists will scratch beneath Singapore's superficial veneer to gain a greater understanding of real, heartland life. The scheme is aimed primarily at an increasingly affluent and jet-setting middle class in China, because they're big spenders here. They are only in Singapore for a couple of days, but, apparently, they whip out the credit card more frequently than most other tourists, including the Americans and the British.

Well, the average Chinese teenager must be beside himself with excitement after hearing of the Singapore Tourism Board's plans here. "So let me get this straight, mum," he will say, in Mandarin. "You want us to get on a plane, fly to Singapore... to look at people... living in tower blocks. No wait, that's not quite correct, is it? You want us to look at predominately Chinese people living in tower blocks. Now that's something I've never done before. Do you think I could rebook that appointment to have my irritable bowel removed?"

Don't get me wrong. I'm all for tourists moving away from the colonial track and the spectre of Stamford Raffles. It takes a week just to visit every statue, street, monument, school and so forth with the man's bloody name on it. I don't know about you, but I have better things to do with my time than listen to Singaporean tour guides say: "And on my left is a statue of a fat British imperialist with silly sideburns. And on my right is a street named after a fat British imperialist with silly sideburns.

Indeed, in the days of the British Empire, Charles Dickens and public floggings, it was considered necessary for imperialists to be fat and have silly sideburns. They were prerequisites for the job. Public servants were required to resemble the Empire's ruler — Queen Victoria."

And while we're on the subject of Singaporean sightseeing, the city-state certainly has more to offer than the Merlion, which is the nation's tourism symbol. Once the initial, disturbing image of a cross-dressing lion wears off, there is little to be excited about other than its basic plumbing.

"Look at the Merlion spewing water. Isn't it fabulous, kids?" Desperate tourists ask their distinctly unimpressed children as they glide along the Singapore River.

"Yeah, mum. But our shower does that every day and we don't all stand under that to take pictures, do we? If we did, mum, you'd be arrested. And another thing, mum, does this mean that Singapore was created when a randy Lion shagged a hormonal mermaid on the banks of the Singapore River?"

Undoubtedly, providing the coach parties with more sightseeing options is certainly an admirable plan. But are the HDB heartlands of housing blocks the place to go? I can imagine the poor guide travelling past my block in Toa Payoh.

"And on my left, ladies and gentlemen, we have the large troughs for leaflets and flyers. There has been a misconception, judging by the pungent smell, among those who believe them to be urinals. They are, in fact, a place to throw junk mail for lazy bastards who cannot walk two metres to the nearest dustbin."

But, to be honest, the notion of affluent tourists snapping away at HDB dwellers is both intrusive and patronising and I speak from experience on this one.

Last year, some bright spark decided that my old hometown — that east London borough called Dagenham — was a suitable tourist destination. Having lived there for 20 years, I have no idea what the attraction is, but guided tours now snake around the streets. Coaches actually travel past the countless, two-storey terraced houses, which once formed the world's largest municipal housing estate. There were rumours that some coach drivers actually got lost because every house looks the bloody same. The biggest mistake, though, was playing Groundhog Day on the coach's video. Three Japanese tourists had a nervous breakdown that day.

Aside from town planners and die-hard fans of Dudley Moore and Terry Venables (who were both born in Dagenham), it's difficult to know what attracts sightseers to the place. You must understand that when the eyesore was designed in the 1920s, the London County Council's architect obviously built the original model from Lego. Unfortunately, he only had red bricks left. Singaporeans might deride the monotony of HDB estates, but at least your blocks differ in shape and size.

Apparently, Dagenham tour guides say things like: "On your left is Parsloes Park, a popular place for drunken teenagers to have sex and catch frostbite on their arses. Contraception is optional, ladies and gentlemen, and you might be interested to know that the London Borough of Barking and Dagenham has one of the highest rates of teenage pregnancy in Britain, which, in turn, has one of the highest teenage pregnancy rates in Europe. So you're actually witnessing a social phenomenon here, you lucky devils."

"And on your right is the Robin Hood Pub, a popular place for drug dealers, drunken brawls and police raids. Though, in fairness, the pub does serve a bloody good pint of lager and a decent sausage sandwich."

I'm all for a greater understanding of another man's culture, but when you intrude upon the working man's abode, whether it be in Bangkok, Tiong Bahru Road or Dagenham, it's not tourism; it's just bloody *kaypoh*. We already have burglar alarms and grills on our windows to prevent unwelcome intruders from stopping by in the dead of night. Now, if you take the Singapore Tourism Board's grand scheme to its logical conclusion, we've got to contend with chattering tourists in floral shirts shuffling along our corridors and poking their sunburnt noses through our windows.

Would you want patronising coach parties turning up at your HDB block? Should the Pentax pair pay a visit to my home asking to take a cultural photograph of "the working-class *ang moh* hanging out the washing", I will allow them to take just one, of a certain part of my anatomy, which I will then invite them to kiss. And you just know where that bamboo pole is going to end up...

## *THE CASINO*

THE disturbed auntie was clearly unwell. Attempting to look through a crack in the door no more than 5 mm wide, the elderly Singaporean shouted: "*Oi*, what time you open, *ah*? Can come in or not?"

Unsurprisingly, the crack in the door failed to reply. The auntie's daughter, obviously embarrassed by a mother who likes bending over to talk to inanimate objects in public places, made an attempt to shoo the elderly woman away. It failed. So she made a last-ditch appeal to the auntie's dwindling common sense.

"Mama," she started. "The casino will not open until we reach international waters."

"International Waters," came the reply. "Where's that, ah?"

I had only just been welcomed aboard a luxurious, five-star cruise ship when I stumbled upon this family cabaret.

A fortnight earlier, my company said that it wouldn't mind paying for its staff to enjoy an all-inclusive weekend cruise along the coast of Malaysia. What could I say? If *TODAY* newspaper wanted to celebrate its second birthday by feeding me six times a day in opulent luxury, then I would just have to grin and bear it.

But I love cruise ships and all their inimitable quirks. Where else in the world can you be fined for throwing "foreign objects" down the toilet? Sitting on the 'throne', I read a warning that stipulated that "foreign objects" could cause a blockage and my room would be charged $200 to pay for the plumber.

Terrified, I almost ran out into the corridor to check with a chambermaid. But I reasoned that the sight of a semi-naked Caucasian running at you with his trousers around his ankles, waving his tackle about while holding a toilet roll and screaming: "Was this made in Singapore? Is it a Singaporean toilet roll?" might be a tad disconcerting.

The ship's telephone operator was also in a league of her own. Eager to speak to a couple of mates, I called and said: "Can I have the room number of Kenneth Goh please?"

"I'm sorry, he's not on our guest list," the breezy operator replied quickly. "Do you know his Chinese name?"

I didn't, so I tried another mate.

"No, I can't find a Mr. Leonard Thomas on the list either," said the cheery operator. "Do you happen to know his Chinese name?"

Cruise tickets may not always be inexpensive, but comments like that are priceless. Playing in the ship's casino, however, does come at a price. Forget the swimming pools and the lounge singers; for many passengers, the wonderful vessel is just a floating Singaporean casino. It's tragic, but that's the reality, and that's not good for the industry's family-oriented image. So according to the ship's flyer, there really wasn't a casino covering half of one of its decks. There was an entertainment area that provided "games of chance" instead. So I turned up ready to play a quiet game of Monopoly.

What are "games of chance" anyway? It's rather like saying Geylang's brothels provide "activities of pleasure". The only difference being you are likely to spend a hell of lot more money on the former, than you would on the latter — unless you have the sexual voracity of a well-hung stallion, of course. But these "games of chance" do not exactly appeal to the most positive traits of the average Singaporean gambler.

"I know I shouldn't say this, but the Singaporeans are very *kiasu* when it comes to gambling," said the ship's food and beverage director, a rather harried Malaysian chap.

"We aim to open our restaurants half an hour before the designated times to reduce queueing. Then we avoid pushing and shouting matches. Many want to get into the casino as soon as possible, you see."

"Couldn't you install a turnstile that connected the casino to the restaurant?" I offered, unhelpfully.

"No," he replied. "They'd break it getting in."

And that's when I discovered it's all a question of timing. The discerning punter knows that the casino cannot operate until the ship reaches international waters, so he eats quickly before the doors are opened.

Many passengers are unconcerned, or even unaware, of the ship's course or eventual destination. Under the cloak of darkness, the captain should spend the twilight hours circling Sentosa endlessly. Gamblers wouldn't notice the difference. Passengers who notice the Merlion in their porthole for the seventeenth time will just put it down to either seasickness or alcohol. I'm not kidding. When I was checking out at 11.15am, a passenger asked what time the ship would arrive back in Singapore.

"At 11am, madam," came the stunned reply. "We docked 15 minutes ago."

I acknowledged the woman's acute observational powers by poking her in the eye with my cardkey as she left.

When I visited the casino at 1am and again at 9am, it was never less than packed. And on both occasions, I saw the mad, gambling auntie telling everyone "what a great holiday resort this International Waters" was. That's the reality. So why on earth is the government stalling on the proposal to legitimise casinos in Singapore?

In the latter part of 2002, the Tourism Working Group, a government-appointed task force said it was time for one or two "games of chance" to be set up on Sentosa.

Calls to build a casino came about during the last recession in 1985-6. It's a guaranteed money-spinner. Local betting revenues generated $500 million during the soccer World Cup.

I don't gamble, but I don't begrudge people who do. So I say to the chaps in government: Build a casino on an exclusive Sentosa resort, tax it and if my insane auntie friend wants to fritter away her life savings on the roulette wheel, then so be it. And if it offends your personal or religious beliefs, then don't go. The cruise proved that Singaporeans will never stop gambling, so the government might as well cash in on it. But most importantly of all, I discovered that foreign objects should never come into contact with one's bottom.

**NOTE:** I've been to casinos in Las Vegas, Perth, Malaysia's Genting Highlands and on a cruise liner and I've always met Singaporeans. And my mother has just told me that she visited a casino near her home in Ramsgate, Kent, which is a seaside resort tucked away in the south corner of England and she ended up chatting with some Singaporeans there! When it comes to the English Premiership, the millions of dollars that are generated by illegal football betting in this tiny island is nothing short of obscene. And that will never change. I know there are religious sensitivities to consider. But I can't believe that the Singaporean government, which has to be the most fiscally minded on the planet, is still content to allow these vast revenues to be lost on someone else's blackjack tables.

## *THE WAR*

I HATE Saddam Hussein. Given the opportunity, I would gladly pull out his moustache hairs with a pair of rusty pliers. I have nothing against men (or women) with moustaches, you understand, just men with moustaches who also happen to be murderous tyrants. Using the examples of Josef Stalin, Adolf Hitler and Omar Sharif, my mother sat me down when I was five years old and said: "Neil, never trust a man with a moustache."

With the benefit of hindsight, I suspect her jaundiced view was due to the fact that my parents had just divorced and my father had fashioned a trendy hairstyle on his upper lip during the marriage. He went for Tom Selleck in *Magnum*, but bore a closer resemblance to George Harrison in *Sgt. Pepper*.

I know Hitler was responsible for the Holocaust and Stalin engineered the Great Terror, but my father often came home pissed on a Friday night, so you can see where my mother was coming from. But "Mad-ass" Hussein is a different kettle of moustaches altogether. On Friday, March 21st, 2003, that evil bastard made me walk down 28 flights of stairs.

Since the world was plunged into yet another war, security

measures have become even more stringent in Singapore. Yes, I know, the conflict really only involves Iraq, the United States, Britain and a few stragglers, but Americans have a habit of singing songs like "We Are The World". Say no more.

But with the disobedient Hussein refusing to die, as instructed by the Texan in the White House, Singapore has been forced to tighten its belt and keep its citizens on its toes. So on that fateful Friday, at 2pm, there was a fire drill in the office. Over the PA system, a robotic, but strangely sexy, female voice said: "This is a fire drill. Imagine the place is being ravaged by flames and you are choking on the smoke and everyone around you is screaming: 'Get out of the fucking way, you dopey prick, there's a fire'. Well, ignore all that and make your way slowly to the staircases."

I finished my sandwich and read the paper. There was hardly a mad stampede for the door. I expected John Cleese's hotel manager, Basil Fawlty, to storm in and shout: "I don't know why we bother, we should let you all burn."

I don't wish to sound flippant, but it's difficult to take fire drills seriously. We all know that in the event of a real fire, we'd all be running around like headless chickens and thinking: "Now, if I boot that dithering auntie out of the way, push over that meandering woman who's carrying four children and knock out that uncle with the fire extinguisher, I should be the first one down the stairs."

And, may I ask, have you ever attempted a brisk walk down 28 flights of non-air-conditioned stairs at 2pm in the humid afternoon? If the government posted Newater officials at the exit at the bottom of the stairs, the water dispute with Malaysia would be settled immediately. They could just wring us out.

Indeed, there should have been water stations on the way down, like those in the Singapore Marathon. Every 10 floors, volunteers should hand out isotonic drinks and shout words of encouragement, such as: "Come on, you sweaty, red-faced *ang moh* prick. Stop ogling equally sweaty secretaries and get a bloody move on."

I wouldn't mind, but my fellow evacuees and I were not even awarded certificates or rosettes when we made it out into the dazzling sunshine. At the very least, the soundtrack to *Chariots of Fire* could have been played over the PA system. And security guards could have held up a silk ribbon so we could "breast the tape" as we crossed the finish line.

Why is the Singapore government wasting its time with the National Healthy Lifestyle Campaign and investing in sports stadiums, running tracks and subsidised gymnasiums for national servicemen? Organise two fire drills a week and Singapore will become the fittest country on the planet. It is certainly the most attractive, at least during the time of war. Since the Iraqi conflict began, Singaporeans have been flocking to the hairdressers, according to an informed source of mine. The day after the fire drill, I was taken off the glucose drip and released from hospital, so I thought I'd treat myself to a haircut. I waited two hours. Two bloody hours. When I asked Alvin, my hairdresser, why he was so busy, he replied: "Don't know man, it's been like that since the war started."

And it wasn't even self-conscious men lining up to have their moustaches shaved off. The room was full of women, predominately aunties, all sitting there having trims, washes and perms. Some were even sitting under those huge helmet-like radio headsets, listening, I presume, to the latest news on

Iraq. But how did this come to pass?

Did concerned aunties watch the outbreak of hostilities on TV, call their friends and say: "*Ah Soh*, it's started. It looks like Baghdad won't fall for another month. We better go get our hair coloured. Yep, it's that serious."

Perhaps they meet friends and say: "Love your tight perm. You had that done after allied forces entered Basra, didn't you? Yeah, me too. No choice, right?"

Discussing haircuts and fire drills might appear insensitive during a time of war, but life must go on. I know, because Nicole Kidman told me so on TV, during the recent Oscar ceremony.

Besides, I'd rather talk about moustaches than money, which seems to be the most popular topic of discussion in Singapore since the allied forces started bombing Baghdad. I swear if one more dull Singaporean tells me that people dying in Iraq is going to weaken the strength of the dollar in the pocket, I will gag them with a two-dollar bill.

Singaporeans, who have been polled on the streets by the various media for their views during the war, have come out with some real crackers, such as: "We must be prudent with our spending", "Our recession is going to get worse", "This war is bound to affect our pockets" and "I'm a boring bastard obsessed with economics".

While the world is hitting the streets to protest against an unjust war, what are these people doing? To be fair, six Singaporeans attempted to stage a peace protest outside the American Embassy on the eve of the war, but were stopped by plain-clothes policemen. Apparently, two of the protesters were checked by police before they had even taken their peace placards out of their bags. These are wonderfully courageous

Singaporeans. It's impossible to feel anything other than admiration for such global citizens.

But what about these fiscal fuckers fretting over their bank accounts? What did they do during the Iraqi conflict — sit at home and count their money on a calculator? Perhaps I'm missing the point because when I was at school, I only used calculators to write the word "boobs" on the screen. That always impressed the girls.

I'm not seeking to tempt fate here, but should an invading army ever make its way through Malaysia and across the Causeway, I often wonder how the money-minded will react. Perhaps then, those mass protests for peace that were held all over the planet, except in Singapore, of course, won't appear so futile. Perhaps then, the greedy gang will accept that, in most cases, one's savings book is not a bullet-proof vest.

Aside from moustaches, my mother always told me it was uncouth to discuss money matters publicly. But to selfishly lament the weakness of your country's dollar because citizens elsewhere have the impudence to die is so staggeringly inhumane, it is beyond comprehension.

After the terrorist attack on the twin towers in New York in 2001, I remember a Singaporean friend expressing his concern. He worked for an American corporation and knew that September 11th would damage the American economy. We were discussing the tragedy when he said: "Never mind the attack; I didn't know the people who died. All I know is, this is going to really fuck up the American dollar. Our company is really going to struggle because of this fucking thing."

You can't talk to these wankers. You can't rationalise with them. How do they sleep at night? I just cannot understand, let alone tolerate their logic.

To keep your sanity, I would advise you to steer well clear of these people. Personally, at a time of war, I'd rather get my hair coloured at Alvin's hairdressers with the mad aunties. Their actions make more sense to me.

## *THE AMERICANS*

I'M NOT sure whether it was the blustery winds, the lack of warm clothes or a combination of both because I wasn't my usual, tolerant self. For some reason, I wanted to rip out the American lady's vocal cords and strangle her with them. A little harsh, perhaps, but she never stopped bloody talking.

I was in the United States to interview an actor because his upcoming movie was about to be released in Singapore. I'd never been to New York before, but to me it was the movie capital of the world. Like many Singaporeans, I'd seen its famous landmarks in so many films and TV programmes, I felt like I'd lived there.

Naturally, I wanted to see as many of its famous sites as I could during my whirlwind 48-hour trip. As soon as it was daylight on a brisk November morning, I headed for the Statue of Liberty. The old lady had terrorised me as a child when I saw her sticking out of the sand in the post-apocalyptic world of the Planet of the Apes. I still expected to find a distraught Charlton Heston banging the ground in bitter frustration, wearing nothing but a loincloth. Instead, I found a daft old bat from Kansas who rattled my eardrums.

From the moment we left Manhattan, I suffered her mindless chatter across the choppy Hudson River all the way to Liberty Island. Initially, she seemed almost normal.

"Gee, doesn't the Statue of Liberty look fantastic?" she asked.

"Yes, she looks good," I muttered.

"Gee, you're not from round here are ya?"

When I concurred that I came from England, she spewed the kind of verbal diarrhoea usually reserved for parliamentarians.

"Gee, England?" she began. "I love your train stations. They're just great. Gee, I thought Harry Potter was fictitious. I never knew that all the stations really were like that. They're the same. Where is Hogwarts Station? Is there a real one?"

"Oh yes, of course," I replied. "It's in Kent."

"Gee, really? I guessed as much. Gee, that's real cool."

"Excuse me, if you say 'gee' one more time, would you be awfully offended if I smacked you with my souvenir Statue of Liberty figurine?"

I didn't really say the last part. The figurine was a gift for someone and it was quite expensive. But Americans do say the daftest things. They certainly help to put Singlish into perspective.

Fearful of the social stigma attached to a 'street' dialect, Singaporeans are often worried about being pigeonholed with the lower classes if their sentences are littered with the odd *lah, aiyoh* and *referee kayu.*

Well, stop fretting over it because the Americans, particularly New Yorkers, really don't care what they say or how they say it. They, too, have their own dialect and, unlike some Singaporeans, they are most proud of it. It's called shouting. If human beings came with built-in remote controls, then God would hit the mute button on New Yorkers. They love to say what they think — though not always in that order.

Having lived in both England and Singapore, two conservative societies by comparison, it is both intimidating and invigorating. New Yorkers want to share their opinions with the world. Stunned to learn the Statue of Liberty was closed, I asked a gum-chewing park ranger why. Without hesitation, he replied: "Because of those bastard terrorists."

Well, quite. Fortunately, his colleague, a rather buxom woman, who never stopped eating, had a readymade solution. "Find a field," she said. "And stick George Bush and Saddam Hussein in it. Then let them punch each other out. They obviously have issues, right? So let them beat the crap out of each other and leave us out of it. If that don't work, stick 'em on Jerry Springer."

Being a contentious issue, I kept quiet. Fortunately, her geopolitical views had been shared with just 500 other tourists of all nationalities. We were waiting in line for a full body search, which involved being patted down by a young man, who seemed to pat far more zealously around the groin area.

Understandably, since September 11 the heavy hand of security can be felt everywhere. It's a constant reminder of the tragedy. Eager to pay my respects, I tried to locate Ground Zero, but it was hidden among Manhattan's labyrinth of streets and avenues. When I thought I'd spotted it, I asked a Wall Street trader if I was right.

He said: "What you mean is that big hole in the middle of the street with cranes and construction guys everywhere? I'm thinking — yes, you've found it."

He wasn't being flippant or insensitive. Tourists posing for holiday snaps in front of the devastated site — that's insensitive. Street vendors selling framed photographs and t-shirts of the disaster right beside Ground Zero — that's insensitive. This guy, like most New Yorkers, just wants to return to some semblance of normalcy.

There is a discernable citywide effort to become bolder and brasher than ever before. This is positively terrifying: New Yorkers were bold and brash in the first place. If you don't believe me, just ask one of them for directions. I did — and I'm suing the bastard for causing deafness in one ear.

"Waddaya wanna go to the Chrysler Building for?" He bellowed. "The Empire State Building's got a viewing platform. No? Okay, you gotta make a left on 59th, then a right on 38th, a zigzag on 5th, followed by a hot shoe shuffle on 42nd. Then cross to 9th and make over to 63rd."

"Now, take away the number you first started with and waddaya got?"

It was like doing one of those silly mental arithmetic games when I was in school. And it's exhausting work — enough to make you say 'gee', in fact. But that's not advisable.

There are enough Singaporeans with phoney American accents as it is. In the United States, it's their mother tongue and they still say the daftest things. So don't tell the government, but you're better off with Singlish, don't you think? Anyway, I'd better stop there. I'm meeting my family at Hogwarts Station.

**NOTE:** An irate American reader said I had no right to pigeonhole New Yorkers, or worse yet, over 250 million Americans as being 'daft' after spending just one weekend in Manhattan. He's absolutely right, of course. Powerful, intelligent Americans have contributed so much to the world — hot-dogs, hula-hoops, American football, the list is just endless. Take the most powerful man in America, the president. He's not a daft man, is he? He never says funny or peculiar things. I mean, as the leader of the people, he can't. Though I still think there is a 'u' missing in that last word. Incidentally, I had a Singaporean friend who spent a year studying in the United States and returned sounding like Jennifer Aniston. She hasn't spoken to me since this article came out. That's strange. Perhaps she's been busy.

## *THE SPY*

I WAS walking past New York's Bloomingdales department store when it hit me. There is one man who can resurrect Singapore's economy.

The Ministry of Trade and Industry has been churning out depressing figures of late regarding the Gross Dyslexic Peacock and all those other exciting economic statistics. So allow me to add a positive figure of my own — 007. Don't worry. The suave super-spy will stir up the Singaporean economy and shake it to its very foundations no less.

To celebrate the 40th anniversary of Ian Fleming's creation on the silver screen, Bloomingdales had a mini-Bond exhibition on display in its store windows during the 2002 Christmas period. After 20 official movies, it's no less than the British naval commander deserves.

But then it occurred to me. When was the last time you saw the dapper gentleman in Singapore? You haven't. In over 40 hours of screen time, his polished brogues have never set foot on the Changi Airport runway.

The Republic has been mentioned though, twice in fact. In Sean Connery's *You Only Live Twice* and Pierce Brosnan's *Tomorrow Never Dies*, spy chief M refers to "our satellite in Singapore".

Now, where is this top-secret satellite and who the hell is operating it on behalf of Britain's Secret Service? It's probably an illegal bookie living in Toa Payoh, trying to receive the English Premiership on ESPN without paying for it. But seriously, I'm going to impart classified information and reveal the satellite's location. It's at the summit of Bukit Timah Hill. Have you noticed that fenced off "military" area at the top? There are those graphic signs, depicting a matchstick man being shot for trespassing.

Should you pass that deterrent, there is another sign, showing a trespassing matchstick man having his testicles removed with an MRT farecard. (You might as well do something with them now that the ez-link card has mercilessly replaced them.)

That's where MI6 is hiding its communicative hardware for Southeast Asia! But who's operating the satellite — the monkeys? Surely they can't be running the intelligence agencies of both London and Singapore? Luckily, this isn't the case. Sources at the Internal Security Department intercepted a recent transmission sent out from Bukit Timah.

The male voice said: "M? It's Beng in Singapore. Getting interference *lah*, cannot *lah*. Trying to watch Man Yoo. Big game *lah*, half ball some more. Get that *'ham-sum' ang moh* called Bond James Bond can? Let him fix problem, so can watch match in peace."

That's right. Get Bond out here. Let's have the franchise's producers, the Broccoli family, bring their US$100 million budget to Singapore and allow the Republic to be the exotic Asian location for the 21st instalment.

Japan (*You Only Live Twice*), Hong Kong, Thailand (*The Man with the Golden Gun*), Vietnam (*Tomorrow Never Dies*) and now Korea (*Die Another Day*) have all been featured in the Bond series. Thailand actually renamed the island used in Roger Moore's *The Man with the Golden Gun*, calling it the James Bond Island. Its near Phuket and tourists flock to it every week.

And what does Singapore have after 20 high-tech Bond movies? A satellite. But all that's going to change. In the next movie, the world's favourite spy will be met, in the customary fashion, by the local operative at Changi Airport. Pierce Brosnan will step into the Singaporean sunshine and mutter the immortal words: "My name's Bond. James Bond. Licensed to kill."

"My name's Beng. *Ah Beng,*" his opposite number will reply. "Licensed to squat on MRT trains."

They can compare drinks — Bond has his martini "shaken, not stirred", Beng has his Tiger Beer "bottled, no cup". And consider their wardrobes. Bond's handmade suits are bought from a tailor in upmarket Chelsea. Beng gets his matching white singlet and trousers from a night market in Choa Chu Kang.

Moreover, setting the movie in an unfamiliar Asian location will inject fresh impetus into an ageing franchise. We've all seen the ski chases, the car crashes and the jump from Paris' Eiffel Tower in *A View To A Kill*. We can all do that.

Get Bond to jump off an HDB block and see if he can open his parachute in time. Now that's a stunt sequence. Should he fail, at least Singapore can boast that it was the country that finally killed 007. And *Ah Beng* can pick his 4-D lottery numbers based upon the floor his dead colleague jumped from.

Then there's the diabolical megalomaniac. Thirsting for totalitarian control, the Bond villain must be contemptuous of his underlings and dismissive of his opponents.

Oh dear. Do you think Singapore could fit all its "villains" into one movie? But I'm opting for the durian seller. *In Live and Let Die,* Tee Hee had his hook, while Oddjob had his bowler hat in *Goldfinger.* In the Singapore movie, the durian seller will have his *parang.*

The dastardly cad would allow Bond, who is so enamoured with the double entendre, to deliver throwaway lines like: "Well, Durian. I like your aftershave. And is that a *parang* in your trousers or are you just pleased to see me?"

And if the director needs beautiful, but one-dimensional, women to fawn over Bond, then he should head for Orchard Towers. Two hours and a large wallet should do the trick.

Whatever way you look at it, all the essential ingredients for a formulaic 007 movie are here in plentiful abundance. It's time for the Singapore Tourism Industry to bring Bond to Bras Basah. And "Bra Bizarre", incidentally, makes a great name for a Bond girl.

Should you get a chance to watch the latest Bond offering again, watch the end titles closely because I understand the next movie will have a poignant plot twist. The final credits will read: "The end of *Die Another Day*. But James Bond will return in *Ah Beng Die Die Ah.*"

# *THE ENGLISH*

IT TOOK me seven years to master the rudiments of Singlish. It would take me seven lifetimes to understand Mancunian English. In hawker centres, Singaporeans converse in a relaxed fashion. But on the streets of Manchester, locals speak with a relaxed brain. It's very time-consuming. Casual greetings with strangers took so long that I often nipped away and grabbed a bite to eat, before returning to hear the rest of the sentence.

"Helloo, luuurrrvvvveeee," they would begin. "Ahhh yaaa, all-riiiiiight?" It was three days before: a) I realised I was being asked, "Hello love, are you all right?" And b) I shoved four Duracell batteries in their mouths to speed up vocal delivery. Officially, of course, I was in Manchester, in the freezing north-west of England in December 2002 to cover entertaining Premiership matches and, if I was free, to also watch Manchester United.

Unofficially, I was in Manchester to track down every loony, nutcase and space cadet that Lancashire had to offer. I've been working on this mission in Toa Payoh for several years now, but I never realised that my duties extended to northern England.

My first basket case found me while I waited at a bus stop in a Lancashire village called Worsley. The place is so quiet that the local council has been discussing shooting its duck population because residents have complained that the occasional quack has increased noise pollution by 45 per cent.

As you can see, the deranged elderly have a lot of time on their hands in Worsley. So, they like to while away the hours with the odd, impromptu mime class.

When I was at the bus stop, a bus pulled in, so I tilted my head to read its destination on the side. An old woman, who was sitting on the bus above the sign, smiled at me and then tilted her head. Slightly disturbed, I rolled my head towards my other shoulder and she did the same.

Safe in the knowledge that a bus separated me from the lunatic, I began moving my head backwards and forwards and she copied my every move. We looked like a pair of those cheap, nodding dogs people have on their shelves in Singapore. Then, demonstrating the first signs of spontaneity, the daft old bat started to wave at me vigorously and gave me a toothless grin. I've got more fingers than she had teeth.

Unfortunately, just as I contemplated asking the old dear to come and live with me, the bus pulled away. I was devastated. Priceless nutters like them can be so hard to find. Luckily, they find me. I went into a newsagent for directions to the nearest post office and regretted it instantly because only one of us was fluent in northern English.

"Helloo, luuurrrvvvveeee,"' said the shop owner. "Where? Aye. You wanna ge' a boose. It's tool fah t'wark."

"No, I don't mind walking." That was a mistake. Manchester only has two seasons — June and winter.

"Riiiiiight, aye. Tech the furs' riiiiiight. Goal pass the red paws box and yule see paws office next t'it."

After I'd gone through my English/northern English dictionary and translated her directions, she added: "Boot it worn be open now, luuurrrvvvveeee." I took one of the quacking ducks from the nearby canal and threw it at her.

Compared to Mancunian, Singlish really is a walk in the park. I'd forgotten, incidentally, that during those walks in the park, loonies do enjoy a heated argument with themselves.

Strolling through Manchester's Piccadilly Gardens in the city centre, I saw a rather intoxicated chap screaming abuse at his alter ego about that "fucking waste of space, Tony Blair".

Then in the next breath, Dr Jekyll replied: "But look how the Prime Minister's cleaned up this place."

This infuriated Mr Hyde, who retorted: "Nope, Tony Blair is a fucking Tory in a cheap Labour suit."

It was positively wonderful. My only regret was the old tramp didn't start fighting with himself. I would have brought in popcorn and charged admission for that.

The Singapore Tourism Board (STB) should pay his salary (a cheap bottle of cider and a urine-stained overcoat seems to make him extremely happy) and bring this man to Hong Lim's Speakers' Corner. Give him any issue you like — foreign talent, Medisave, ez-link cards, prescription chewing gum — and let him go to work. He doesn't need to read up on the subjects because from what I understand, facts merely cloud his judgement. Just give him plenty of room and a discreetly placed bucket. Both Jekyll and Hyde, unsurprisingly, have an acute bladder problem.

Indeed, if the STB is serious about providing quality street entertainment, then I suggest they secure his services now.

Because I've heard he shares a room in the asylum with a really good mime artist.

**NOTE:** I received a letter from an expat who had actually worked in the Manchester village of Worsley. Well, someone's got to I suppose.

# *THE CAMPAIGN*

AFTER leaving my family behind in England, having spent Christmas and the New Year with them, I was rather depressed and needed cheering up. I'd just infuriated a Singaporean busload of impatient commuters by waving my old farecard at the ez-link card reader. Surprisingly, the machine wouldn't beep. Unsurprisingly, my uncensored language produced a few beeps of its own as I struggled to come to terms with the latest technological miracle of efficiency.

I'd only been away for five weeks, but it might as well have been five years. In the end, a teenager rather patronisingly explained that the farecard was now defunct and I had to use an ez-link card instead.

The embarrassing scene was reminiscent of the time I showed my grandmother how to use a VCR. "So you put the tape in like this, Nan," I told her, while performing the task in slow motion. "This slot is only for videotapes, okay? It's not a mailbox. This is the last time I'm getting the letters out, all right? Now, stop dribbling."

Back on the bus, I thanked the teenager with a discreet farecard paper-cut to his forearm and sulked all the way to the MRT station at Toa Payoh. And then, the dark clouds dissipated and sunlight filtered through my black mood.

The blinding light came in the form of an SMRT poster, which proudly announced the all-new Courtesy Awareness Campaign for 2003. The acronym is CAP, though I'm sure there should be an 'R' in there somewhere. Perceptively aware that commuters might, at this stage, gouge out their eyeballs to avoid reading the poster in its entirety, this campaign vowed to be "more fun and exciting".

Now, there is a quiz. That's right, there is an online quiz to determine whether you are a selfless angel or a *kiasu* bastard when travelling on Singaporean public transport. I couldn't wait to get home to participate.

In entertainment terms, the quiz might fall short of, say, *Who Wants To Be A Millionaire* or an irritable bowel, but it's an enlightening exercise nonetheless. I won't spoil the content for you, but let's just say the quiz writers are fond of pregnant women questions along the lines of: "If a pregnant lady goes into labour on a train, would you cut the umbilical cord and give up your seat for the newborn baby?"

If foreigners participate, they could be forgiven for thinking the MRT is full of nothing other than heavily pregnant women. As a precaution, SMRT should look into this and ensure that its drivers are all fully trained midwives. I'm only bitching because I scored a pitiful nine out of 16 and my scorecard read: "Kind, but could be kinder."

That's a rather cruel character assassination. I've secured seats for pregnant women on countless occasions by bundling little old ladies to the floor.

But Singapore loves a condescending campaign or two doesn't it? There have been campaigns for, among other things, courtesy on public transport, killer litter, cleaner toilets, feeding stray cats and picking your nose at family gatherings.

No, hang on, that last one came from my mother, not the Singapore government. There aren't any posters for that one and Gurmit Singh hasn't made any commercials for it. But my mother's campaign does come with a slap across the head, which has enjoyed considerable success over the years. Perhaps SMRT should adopt a similar approach.

The network's efforts to cultivate a more gracious and courteous commuter should be applauded, but will a poster and a quiz really transform the *kiasu* elements of this society? To be fair, having spent Christmas travelling on the crumbling, litter-strewn London Underground, one shouldn't be too hard on SMRT.

Besides, the airline industry is still 30,000 feet ahead when it comes to patronising its fellow passengers. Whether it was Changi or Heathrow, I still had to go through that pathetic 'terrorist' interrogation. A Changi Airport employee asked the same tired, old question: "Did anyone approach you to carry something through for them?"

Does she seriously expect me to reply: "Well, do you see that man over there; the one wearing the balaclava? He asked me to take through two souvenir M16s for him. I put them in my suitcase because they were too heavy for my hand luggage. Do I get extra air miles for that?"

Within six months, don't be surprised if Changi Airport unveils the "fun and exciting" Say No To Terrorists quiz, with questions like: "If someone asked you to carry a teddy bear in your luggage and it started ticking, what would you do?"

No one is disputing the threat of global terrorism since Sept 11. But airport officials asking such banal questions will not bring about the collapse of Al Qaeda. Hold that thought, while I pick my nose in peace. That's about the only public campaign that hasn't been launched in Singapore — yet.

**NOTE:** I remain deeply impressed with how many campaigns this country nurtures in a year. The originality really is quite staggering. They'll be campaigns on love and romance next...

# *THE ROMANCE*

WHEN I was a teenager, I'd like to think young ladies were drawn to me at social gatherings. I made other men feel insecure in my presence. I was a bit of a sex magnet in fact. To visualise this scenario, however, I have to imagine that the only other males in the room were Mr. Bean, George Michael and Barney the dinosaur, but it's my imagination damn it and I'll go wherever it takes me.

But the dream never lasts long anyway. The bubble always bursts when the Michelle Pfeiffer-lookalike rips through my banter by declaring that she's seen *Jurassic Park* 12 times and she has an inexplicable fetish for the colour purple.

To be honest, I attracted about as many women as Singapore attracts opposition candidates at general elections. If only women could've been encouraged to like me. If there had been, say, a group of geeks who went around Dagenham, my hometown, ordering single people to get together, my chances would've improved tenfold. But who the hell would go to all that trouble to create a taskforce to promote romance and social couplings?

Stand up, Singapore, and proudly take one matchmaking step forward. In a bid to get more Singapore citizens to have sex (and, I presume, conceive babies to bolster the workforce in 20 years time), February 2003 was designated the month to be one of love, life and relationships. The lovemaking campaign — Romancing Singapore — was launched by the bigwigs. Sorry, I'm wrong. It isn't a campaign — of course it isn't, the Republic doesn't have campaigns — but a festival and celebration of love.

Don't reach for the sick bucket just yet; this celebration shouldn't involve hippies, peace symbols or Beatles songs. There will be no mimicking of Woodstock, with mass gatherings of sex-starved youths at Sentosa. But there is, however, a Task Force. The organisers, Family Matters! (with an exclamation no less), have spared no expense to ensure that Singaporeans celebrate their love for one another. So you'd better be bloody romantic in February or they'll send the Task Force troops in.

Some of Singapore's finest military men have been trained by social workers and are going into the combat zone armed with candles, flowers and copies of the international bestseller, *Save Your Marriage! Forget Barney, He's Not As Well Endowed As He Looks.*

If you're sitting in a cinema with a young dating couple beside you and they start bickering, resist the temptation to drown them in popcorn. Just wait five minutes for the Romancing Singapore Task Force to arrive and they'll do it for you. Armed with guns, knives and heart-shaped pillows, the sensitive soldiers will have the little domestic fracas resolved in no time.

Covering all the angles, naturally, the Task Force even has a website, www.romancingsingapore.com, which gives invaluable tips on how to be a romantic. Whether you are married, dating or single, there is something for everyone here.

Married couples, for instance, are encouraged to watch a midnight show, which I'm sure is a foolproof way of shoring up a drooping love life. After all, camcorders are relatively inexpensive these days so you just need to find space in the bedroom for the tripod.

Dating couples are encouraged to spend a night at a museum. Another inspired idea. Some of those displays are older than the fossils. A young couple could spend hours up there before they're discovered by the wheezing security guard.

Of course, there are liberal-minded cynics who'd claim this Task Force is yet another Orwellian example of third-party interference: A rather desperate, transparent attempt to get more people to have more sex, more of the time.

Well, all I can say is; where the hell was this Task Force when I was 16? I grew up on a council housing estate in Dagenham where there were only two residents NOT having sex — the church vicar and me. Where was my Greater London campaign to generate a fine romance or two?

I could make girls laugh at times. Sexy classmates often said: "Do you know, for an ugly beanpole, you're occasionally funny."

To which I replied: "That's bloody marvellous. But how many times does a girl have to laugh before she contemplates removing some underwear — preferably mine?"

I was usually slapped and deservedly so. But if there had been a romance Task Force at my side, things would've been different. My tormentor would've been severely reprimanded for disrupting our love vibes and punished for hindering any chances of a relationship. She'd feel humiliated, I'd bask in my minor triumph and the romance taskforce would march off to deal with the next crime of passion.

And then, the humbled girl would kick me in the testicles and walk off into the sunset — with the guy who had a nose like Barney.

**NOTE:** I received several emails from Singaporeans who were irritated by what they saw as yet another attempt by certain people to interfere in their private lives. If a woman is happily single, for instance, does she really need some ridiculous festival full of do-gooders making themselves busy and encouraging her to pair off with some soppy sod?

Can you imagine if it was sex-related? If any of these festival planners ever approached me and said: "Good afternoon, sir. We're from Romancing Singapore and we hear you're having problems getting it up?" I'd take his clipboard and shove it up his arse. That said, the festival continued unabashed across the country. For almost a month, advertisements were placed in newspapers and magazines giving patronising and largely useless tips on how to improve one's love life. It was stunningly pathetic and trivial. In the middle of a never-ending recession, you'd think the governing powers would have more pressing issues such as rising unemployment, political apathy, Islamic extremism and migrations to Australia. They shouldn't waste their time by telling single Singaporeans whether chocolates or flowers are more suitable on a first date. It's up to the individual. The busybodies should mind their own bloody business.

# *THE PYJAMAS*

IT'S finally over. For a while there, it seemed like it would never end. No, I'm not referring to the recent budget speech, but the recent Romancing Singapore campaign/celebration/festival. From what I understand, prostate examinations are quicker and less painful.

If you recall, indeed I'm sure you'll never forget, the month of February 2003 will go down in Singapore history as the month of love, romance and a rather large helping of Singapore's all-girl band, *Cherry Chocolate Candy*. All of which was organised by the Singapore Task Force on behalf of Family Matters! And don't you dare forget that exclamation mark damn it!

There are website rumours that George Lucas is rewriting a key love scene in Episode III of *Star Wars*. Anakin Skywalker and Senator Amidala will exchange heart-shaped pillows and Obi-Wan Kenobi will utter the immortal line: "Remember, the Singapore Task Force will be with you, always."

But you certainly can't fault the Task Force for effort, can you? They spread out across the island like a battalion of love-makers organising everything from gentle river cruises under a starry, starry night to nostalgic drive-in movies.

The latter was a bit of a tragedy for me. I can't drive and, with hindsight, turning up on a BMX bicycle was probably a bad idea. It was a big turn-off for the ladies and I ended up with a sore groin. Moreover, the wicker basket at the front was, I suspect, a touch too feminine, hindering my chances of impressing all the pretty girls. But that particular activity was inspired compared to the late night pyjama party for singles, which was an unmitigated disaster.

Have you seen a grown man in nothing but a pair of stripy pyjamas? He looks about as sexually desirable as, well, a grown man in a pair of stripy pyjamas. Slumber parties are for teenaged girls to eat popcorn and gossip wistfully about handsome teenaged boys. Or in Dagenham, where I grew up, all night parties were for teenaged boys to discover pornography and recognise the importance of being well endowed.

A skinny adult, however, in stripy pyjamas looks like a giant blob of toothpaste. Would you invite Mr. Aquafresh into your bedroom? According to media reports, only one man turned up appropriately attired at the campaign's pyjama party. He is my hero. He should be the next Singaporean president. In fact, he should be the next Singaporean president in stripy pyjamas. If Mr. Aquafresh doesn't impress foreign dignitaries then no one will. By all accounts, my hero wasn't inhibited at the party, but he took the precaution of sewing up his frontal flap first. He was a little disturbed, perhaps, but he didn't want to come across as dangerous.

But the post-puberty pyjama party was not as baffling as the festival's obsession with the beach. First, there was the kissing competition at the Pasir Ris beach. Now I'm not bitching because the organisers turned down my request to be both judge and demonstrator, but why pick the beach for a snogging contest? If I threw 50kg of salt onto a damp floor, would you lay down with your partner and start eating each other?

But it didn't end there. On the Romancing Singapore website, (there is always, always a website) there were several polls, loosely related to shagging. There was one question that asked: Which was the romantic beach in Singapore: East Coast, Pasir Ris, Changi Point or Sentosa? The actual answer should be of course, none of the above. Has the Singapore Task Force of love-makers never stepped on a beach? We smother ourselves in tanning creams, get sun burnt, then the wind blows, the sand gets stuck to our skin and we spend the rest of the day looking like a jam doughnut. Would you invite Mr. Jam Doughnut into your bedroom?

The one glaring omission from the website's plethora of romantic questions was: Who would you rather date Mr. Aquafresh or Mr. Jam Doughnut? But the Task Force was relentless. Even commuters on the No. 65 bus were not spared the message of love and sex. In the middle of February, *Cherry Chocolate Candy* jumped aboard and gave away free CDs of love songs. Bewildered aunties were heard to ask: "You Cherry Chocolate wha'? Got free ice cream is it? Got sample or not?"

This wasn't such a big deal to me. Where I grew up, many of the old drunks in east London wouldn't have been too impressed with *Cherry Chocolate Candy*. Having staggered onto the last night bus after the pubs had closed, they think they see beautiful women bearing gifts every night. Of course, what they actually see is a woman in blue, bearing a breathalyser.

But now that the hilarity has subsided and the rip-roaring activities have concluded, the campaign/festival/celebration/

baby-making exercise has come to a sad end.

A colleague in the office said it was a noble plan that was poorly executed. No, it wasn't. That's grossly unfair on the volunteers and organisers who genuinely worked hard throughout February to make the festival a success for many people across Singapore.

On the contrary, Romancing Singapore was a poor plan that was nobly executed. The campaign's intentions were hardly honourable. This was top-down cynicism at its worst.

What sort of festival or campaign can we expect next? A free savings account with every pregnancy? A $1,000 discount, per baby, off the latest Space Wagon? A nationwide ban on contraception? Perhaps Aquafresh and Jam Doughnut could form a singing duo and re-release that Guns And Roses classic, *Sweet child of mine. Let's make babies all the time.*

But that would be ludicrous, wouldn't it? And yet, an anal civil servant desperate to reach the next rung on the bureaucratic ladder, could be reading this right now and thinking: "That song has a catchy lyric. It might just work. I mean, if we can get grown men to wear pyjamas..."

# *THE HOOKERS*

"WE'RE coming to Singapore," she said. "I've been on the Internet and I've found some hotels and they're really cheap. You told me Singaporean hotels were expensive, but these are much cheaper than anything in London. With a bit of saving, we could easily afford these prices." My mother was so excited. It had been five years since I moved to Singapore and she hadn't yet visited. But, according to her, that was about to change.

"These hotels are budget hotels, but that's all right. We're not snobs, are we? They're near to buses and trains apparently and not that far from that place, Orchard Road, where the shops and restaurants are."

"That sounds great, mum," I replied, rather enthusiastically, over the phone. "Where are they?"

"In some place called 'Gay-lang'. There's a chain of them called Hotel 81. They say it's a lively area."

"It certainly is a lively place."

"Yeah? Will there be things for your step-dad to do there? To keep him busy?"

"Oh, absolutely."

"What about your little brother?"

"I bloody hope not mum, it's the red light district."

"What? You mean prostitutes?... Fucking hell... We won't bloody stay there then."

"Fair enough, mum."

"What sort of place is this Singapore? You said it was clean and safe and you can't eat chewing gum. Now you're telling me the place is full of old tarts with all their bits hanging out on street corners?"

"Yes, mum."

"What about little Gary then, eh? You think I can let your little brother walk about when there's all these tarts all over the place?"

"No, mum."

"No, mum is bloody right. We'll spend a fortnight down in Ramsgate instead. I mean, I know we have to put up with the smell of horse shit from the stables next door, but at least your little brother can go out on his bike in peace. And I won't have to worry about him bumping into some old tart's tits."

"Fair enough, mum."

Sometimes I wish I hadn't told her. I can imagine my mother, who's not one to keep her opinions to herself, expressing concern at the number of women standing in line along the streets.

"This is terrible. Singaporeans aren't too bloody bright are they? I've only been here for five minutes and I know that the bus stop is further down the road. I'd better go and sort them out... Excuse me... the bus stop is up there. The buses won't stop here... I'm sorry?... Fifty dollars for what?... Here, there's no need to be so bloody rude. I should wash your mouth out with soap and water if I were you."

But the world's oldest profession continues to thrive in Singapore. I've been down to Geylang's red-light district several times because there are some decent coffee shops in the area. Well, that's my story and I'm sticking to it. My old friend David, who was the first Singaporean I met, took me to the various houses of ill repute during my first week on the island. It was a novelty, at first, because women wanted me. Usually, they don't. But in Geylang, a tall Caucasian seems to suggest a rather large wallet. So the compliments came thick and fast. I was frequently asked "Hey handsome (pronounced 'ham-sum'), you want a good time?" Or "Hey, big boy, come inside." Curiously, I've been called 'big boy' on numerous occasions in Singapore, sometimes by old uncles. It's most flattering, but also, a trifle disturbing.

I know the ladies of the night only wanted the money they assumed I had, but I lapped up the attention nonetheless. Call me fickle and shallow, but in 28 years I've perfected the art of repulsing women. To be sure, many men say this, usually in a transparent attempt to appear sensitive in an 'aw-shucks' kind of way. But I can honestly say it's the truth. Indeed, I actually achieved the impossible with the opposite sex — British prostitutes turned me down and it was their job to say yes.

When I was studying in Manchester, part of our post-pub drunken routine was to tease hookers by asking for the price list. "How much will a shag cost?" we'd ask, before roaring with laughter.

"Fuck off, you student wankers. You ain't got no fucking money," came the humbling, but truthful reply.

Along the streets of Geylang, however, I was treated like a white god. Like respectful tourists, we walked along the seedier streets, peering into the dimly lit living rooms that served as brothels and then we left and had a *prata* supper.

But that wasn't the end of it. Years later, some colleagues and I went back to Geylang's mean streets out of curiosity. This trip wasn't fun, however, it was horrifying. Watching young girls sell their bodies at 3am was deeply disturbing for me. My parents divorced when I was four years old, so I grew up in a house with two wonderful, hard-working women. In 20 years, both my mother and sister taught me more about feminism than any pretentious textbook or patronising, middle-class sociologist ever could. Consequently, I never had the inclination to discuss prostitution in Singapore. It's been done before and has become a tedious cliché in itself. Besides, I've always argued that, despite the assumptions of other western writers, there is so much more to Singapore than Sarong Party Girls chasing rich white men and hookers chasing any men. That belief still holds. Yet I can't deny that prostitution eats away at this society like a stubborn tumour that simply refuses to go away.

A little research discovered that there are around 400 brothels in Singapore. Yes, that's 400. To be fair, I'm sure that figure wasn't arrived at via a comprehensive survey. If anything, the statistic could be higher. If you are the proprietor of a number of illicit brothels, you're probably not in a great hurry to register your business, are you? But still, for a country smaller than greater London, that's a lot of hookers. Apparently, there are something like 10 to 20 prostitutes in each brothel, which means dirty old men have approximately 6,000 women to choose from.

You won't find photographs of these ladies in the Singapore Tourism Board's *Things To Do In Singapore* guide, of course. But everybody knows where they are. What I didn't realise was that these places are not just ad hoc meat racks established in various nooks and crannies. These brothels operate in geographically, and legally, defined districts of Singapore. They are termed designated red-light areas (DRA's). Only a Singaporean civil servant could come up with the term 'designated red-light areas' and not laugh.

In England, hookers operated in areas known as NFPA, which stood for No Fucking Policemen Around. But prostitution was never as organised, much less legalised, as it is in Singapore. It's so systematic it's terrifying. Hookers must carry a yellow health card at all times, which can only be earned through regular hospital check ups. In London, a quick post-pub nightcap with a Soho 'working girl' and you risked catching 'the clap', which is a wonderfully romantic colloquialism for a sexually transmitted disease. No chance of that in Singapore.

The commonly known DRA's, and I'm sure there are others, are Desker Road, Orchard Road's Orchard Towers, which is tastefully known as the four floors of whores and, of course, Geylang. Home to some great hawker centres, thousands of foreign workers and countless brothels, Geylang serves Singaporeans in the same way that Soho serves Londoners. It's a haven for the sex-starved. I've been there several times with friends and we laugh, ogle and make predictable, juvenile comments, male banter and all that bullshit. But honestly, the place is a public sewer. You end up feeling like Robert De Niro's deranged *Taxi Driver*, praying that torrential rain will wash away the sleazy clientele and blow the nocturnal nightmare from the memory.

I've encountered prostitution before, of course. I'm not going to pretend I was Dagenham's answer to The Artful Dodger, but I did come across one or two stone-faced ladies selling their wares in Manchester's city centre late at night, when I was there as a student. But I never felt sympathy for them in the same way that I do for the young girls in Geylang. In Manchester, and this will sound grossly stereotypical I know, the women were so typically fierce and resilient. Hard as nails, they could humiliate you in front of your peers with one savage tongue lashing. Metaphorically, of course, not literally. Undoubtedly, that may have been a facade. No one wants to be standing on Manchester's Oxford Road at 1am, trying to somehow make a frozen body look sexually desirable. Nevertheless, if their ferocious independence was an act, it was pretty damn convincing.

In Geylang, the poor girls look so young and fragile, you want to rescue them like some patronising Victorian liberal. You certainly don't want to sleep with them. Many of the girls are from China, of course, and I'm aware of the scheming Chinese "Crows" who arrive here to work these Singaporean streets paved with gold. Perhaps the girls I've seen, standing outside seedy hotels at 3am, are merely keeping up appearances too. Perhaps, their demure, innocent, slightly startled look is all an act too. But if they really are heartless, ruthless money grabbers then they, too, are pretty damn convincing.

I've watched Geylang girls, still in their teens, smile weakly as disgusting middle-aged uncles, wearing sweaty vests and dirty flip-flops, haggle over the price. Small groups of men gather round to discuss the merits of each prostitute, providing heartwarming critiques of each girl such as: "That one not bad, ah? She look so young one. Like schoolgirl. But her chest so lousy, she got nothing what. Forget it lah, that one not worth 50 bucks."

The Dickensian scene reminded me of a British movie called *Mona Lisa*, where actor Bob Hoskins trawls London's underworld of crime and prostitution. Ironically, you cannot buy this classic movie in Singapore, uncensored at least, because it contains one or two tame sex scenes. But not to worry, you can get the real deal for less than the price of a DVD down at Geylang anyway. The hypocrisy is stunning.

Singapore sells itself, if you'll pardon the pun, to its citizens, to foreign talent and to tourists as one of the safest, cleanest and most wholesome countries on the planet. And in many respects, it is. But if you cut through the government's rhetoric and slice open the society's underbelly, you'll find 18-year-old girls wearing too much make up telling 50-year-old men that oral sex and full intercourse can be arranged, as long as the price is right. Or perhaps you'll discover the skeletal, chain-smoking, pockmarked pimps hovering around the hookers at a safe distance. Supposedly, there are no pimps, like there are no street walkers. But a nod and a wink to the greasy man with tattoos standing in the background and you've got yourself a cheap, but not free, date for a couple of hours.

But we can't go down that road because, apparently, it doesn't exist. At election rallies or during National Day speeches, when was the last time you heard a politician say: "We must continue to tighten our belts. I know we said that last year and the year before, and the year before. But you all must be losing weight, from all those extra, unpaid hours, not to mention the lunch breaks you keep missing, so there's still one more notch left on your belt. So we can squeeze a little more, before you either burst or emigrate to Australia. We have no choice. Banking and finance is down 4 per cent, thanks to China. The electronics sector is down 13 per cent, thanks to China. And manufacturing is down 28 per cent, thanks to China. Fortunately, the hooker industry experienced a 4 per cent growth in 2003, thanks to

China. Those desperate girls are so much cheaper than those in Southeast Asia. Keep up the good work, girls!"

You haven't, because society chooses to close an eye to the various DRA's. Besides, according to a popular stereotype, these brothels are there to service the thousands of sex-starved foreign, construction workers living on the island. That's certainly true. But they have to wait their turn, along with the Chinese, Malay, Indian and Eurasian Singaporeans that I've seen hovering around the prostitutes. And did I mention the *ang mohs*? Both the so-called foreign talents and the western tourists. Without their wallets, Orchard Road's four floors of whores would have been downsized years ago.

And Desker Road, which appeared to be the seediest and cheapest DRA, enjoys the company of a Caucasian or two in the twilight hours. Of course, Desker Road is unlikely to be referred to on the news, in current affairs programmes or on welcoming posters at Changi Airport. The next time you arrive at Terminal One, don't expect a poster that says: "Welcome to Singapore. Get a tan at Sentosa. Get laid at Desker Road." It should, therefore, come as no surprise that I actually discovered Desker Road after a visiting friend from London told me about it. I'd vaguely heard of local friends joke about the place, of course. But my travelling Londoner knew that the street was popular with transvestites, 'lady-boys' and hookers who've had sex change operations. He was aware that this particular DRA boasted some of the lowest prices in Singapore, but the services were not as reputable or as clinical perhaps as Orchard Towers or Geylang.

How did he know all of this? From a British-made travel documentary, hosted by Lily Savage, a popular drag queen in Britain. Taking an off-beat, underground route, Savage pokes fun at the seedier side of Singaporean life. I'm told the documentary is very funny. But would it be shown here? Would a similar travel show be made by a Singaporean production team here? What do you think? Outsiders, some 10,000 km away, are allowed to know what really goes on in this tiny city-state in the small hours, but don't expect Singaporeans to be allowed to watch such a show. They only live here. I'm sure most Singaporeans are not interested in the more sordid aspects of their culture. But they should at least have the choice.

If nothing else, paying a visit to Desker Road, gave me the chance to see the finest pair of breasts I'd ever seen. Listening to my guest explain, in disturbing detail, every aspect of Desker Road's services, curiosity got the better of me so we persuaded my old Singaporean friend, David, to be our chauffeur for the evening. Driving along the street at 4am while it was raining was probably not the most astute decision we'd ever made. Desker Road looked about as exciting as an HDB void deck at 4am. Short on customers, the few call girls who had braved the monsoon conditions were undoubtedly aware of the situation and sought to liven up proceedings. Driving past slowly in the car, a young woman walked over and flashed her breasts at us. There's no need for gory details. But, suffice it to say, my friend grabbed my arm and shouted: "Fucking hell, did you see that? That was, without doubt, the greatest pair of tits I've ever seen. Did you see 'em, Neil? Fucking hell. They were perfect. Just perfect. Dave, Dave, turn around so we can see them again. You got to see them. What a fucking pair."

We did turn around. The breasts were once again exposed and, this time, David and I saw what all the fuss was about. The chest was indeed flawless. The only drawback was the boobs belonged to a man. A minor detail that David and I felt necessary to point out to our travelling friend.

"What? That can't be right. They were the greatest pair of knockers I've ever seen," he replied.

"Well, of course," I explained. "If you're going to have cosmetic surgery, you might as well get the most for your money right? It's very common around Orchard Towers too. I've seen quite a few around there. They're easy to spot after a while. Your documentary didn't teach you that, did it?"

"Fuck the documentary. I'm just glad you two are here. I might have shagged him otherwise. What a waste of a great pair of tits."

No arguments there. But at least my tourist friend knew where to find them. I didn't. And I'd been in Singapore for over four years before I went on my first, and only, excursion to Desker Road. I've got better things to do with my time than watch 50-year-old *ang mohs* discussing terms with a group of 'ladyboys' at 3am. I'm sure you do too. But that doesn't mean we should gloss over prostitution in Singapore and pretend it isn't there, in the same way many people ignore blind tissue-paper sellers or abused maids.

Think about it. There are more teenaged hookers in Geylang than there are Stamford Raffles statues in Singapore, but you won't see any 'ladyboys' on the cover of tourist brochures. Perhaps the Singapore Tourism Board should look into this. It is keen to provide visitors with a more enriching, cultural experience, which is more realistic and less superficial than the usual tours of famous colonial sites. And I'm sure more HDB dwellers have been to a Geylang hotel than Raffles Hotel.

In some ways, it would have been entertaining had my

family opted for that cheap hotel in Geylang's red-light district. My step-dad would've had women all over him like a rash. He'll claim this is nothing new to him, though he'd be secretly tickled by all the attention. But I'm sure the novelty would wear off. It did for me. When a Chinese hooker, who should still be in school, comes up and says: "Hey, you want blow job? Only 50 dollars. Or 80 dollars for you and your friend together," you feel like a US Marine in a bad Vietnam movie. And you feel sick. Because there's nothing funny about the situation at all, is there?

# *THE ACRONYMS*

SINGAPORE'S hip-swingers have renamed Holland Village. I spoke to a 'trendy' friend who suggested a trip to the recently renovated haven of coffee shops, bars and bistros. What he actually said was: "Hey, let's check out Holland V."

To which I replied: "What the hell is Holland V, you stupid man?"

The only *V* I knew was a cult, science fiction TV show that I watched as a child in the '80s. If I recall correctly, the *V* stood for visitors — the unwanted extraterrestrial kind, not the Inland Revenue variety.

I therefore assumed that 'Holland V' was the sequel, where Dutch aliens turned up in clogs, handing out tulips and hookers from Amsterdam. But seriously, many Singaporeans are certainly fond of the odd acronym or six aren't they?

When I first arrived, a receptionist in my office would ask cheekily: "Are you an SPG fan or an S-N-A-G?"

My reply that I was, in fact, a Sagittarian never pacified her. Indeed, it merely aroused her curiosity further. "So which is it?" she would continue, "An SPG fan or an S-N-A-G?"

"Look, stop throwing letters at me. This isn't bloody Sesame Street."

But that was the overbearing first impression for me. The Republic must have been instructed to speak in acronyms, a doublespeak-like code from the novel *1984*. The powers that be must have declared in 1965: "We hereby proclaim Singapore an independent state and from this day on you will speak only in short forms, abbreviations and initials, preferably TLA's (three letter acronyms), so we can confuse our regional neighbours and antagonise the British, who pissed off during World War II and returned 50 years later wearing knee-high white socks with sandals."

When I was living in England, the only TLA I heard in my house was 'HRT', which was usually uttered by my mother through gritted teeth. I had no idea what HRT meant, but its mention was often preceeded by frequent swearing and complaints about those "fucking doctors".

In Singapore, however, acronym-ese is another language altogether. If you can't converse like a dyslexic rapper, you'll soon get left behind. For example, last weekend, I went with a friend, who's a CEO, in his car to the SIR to get my EP to take to the HDB, via the MRT, using the card they call E-Z, then on to JB, along the BKE, for a cheap DVD.

Doesn't it all sound a little punch-me-in-the-face-and-cut-out-my-windpipe annoying? Forget Eminem and his gangsta rhymes. If Americans can produce the rapper's movie, *8 Mile,* then Singaporean filmmakers should get a camera crew down to the hawker centres and shoot *Lorong 8,* with fast-talking uncles spouting acronyms.

Even national newspapers resort to countless short forms

in their stories. Take the recent 24-hour child-care scandal, for instance. Rather than write out, in full, that the infamous child-care centre operates around the clock, newspapers settled for "24/7" instead. That's almost as lazy as the parents who sentenced their innocent children to the pre-school prison in the first place. Besides, the short form is incorrect. It should read "24/7 4 U BASTARDS."

Of course, the quirky aspects of any language can be titillating. My eccentric grandmother, whose vocabulary was complete before World War II and hasn't been expanded since, has a fondness for questioning my sexuality. When I visit, she looks concerned and says: "You know, you're looking ever so queer."

My nan, bless her, thinks she is expressing concern for my welfare. But in modern parlance, she is suggesting I have the physical characteristics of a fine homosexual.

But these short forms and abbreviations, on the other hand, are not amusing; they're irritating and often overused in a desperate attempt to sound cool.

Teenagers in my block tell me that they've hung out at "Macs" or "BK", as if they lack the breathing apparatus required to finish the sentence using gigantic, exhausting words such as McDonald's and Burger King.

Is the pace of the Singaporean ratrace now so fast that we lack the time to speak in full sentences? Instead, we have to converse in nonsensical gobbledegook that wouldn't look out of place in a Lewis Carroll novel.

Be careful, though. In a desperate attempt to prove they are *au fait* with Singaporean culture, bewildered expats will adopt the acronym jargon to show they have truly assimilated.

A Canadian friend once told me he'd had a great night down at "BQ". The idiot, of course, meant Boat Quay. This tickled me because in England, "B and Q" is a hardware store. You'd struggle to find an SPG there, but Caucasians with a screw loose are most welcome at both places. So let's tighten those screws before it's too late.

The next time a loony asks you to check out 'Holland V', 'Orchard R' or even 'Raffles P', give them a gentle slap and say: "URA ****". Oh, just use your imagination.

**NOTE:** Writing about the seemingly harmless topic of acronyms and short forms triggered an unexpected response. A rather self-satisfied, smug expat (and Singapore's not short on those, is it?) wrote to criticise my description of acronyms and abbreviations and proceeded to highlight in remarkable detail what constitutes an acronym, a short form and so on, all of which spectacularly missed the point. She seemed determined to put this working-class ruffian in his place and I'm sure it gave her something to boast about to her pals around the swimming pool at the condo. From more rational Singaporeans, however, I received some great responses. A frustrated father complained that he had just attended a parents' evening at his child's school and the teachers had spoken in confusing, unexplained acronyms and abbreviations all night long. He wanted to know what kind of message that was sending to the pupils. The bloody wrong one, we both agreed. *TODAY* published his letter and then the school replied the following day. It was hilarious. Not only was the letter appallingly written, which served only to further undermine the school, but it, too, missed the point. Instead, the principal droned on about how it was important to allow pupils to express themselves freely in class, ignoring the fact that they sound like spoon-fed robots when they just lazily regurgitate initials and short forms. Where's the originality in that? All I can say is there will be those in society who will miss the point from time to time and I do sympathise. So allow me to explain, "URA twat."

## *THE THIEF*

WITHOUT wishing to sound flippant, Singaporean detectives have had the easiest policing job since Sergeant Jim Bergerac. Good old Bergerac, you see, was a fictional detective on a popular BBC drama, called *Bergerac,* which ran for 12 years from 1981. Within 60 minutes, the copper always got his man. Not through deduction, forensic science or even bribery (which is quite popular in Southeast Asia), but through geography.

The sleuth plied his trade in Jersey, one of the Channel Islands off the southern coast of England. Now, this island is a gigantic nine miles wide and five miles deep. If I recall correctly, Jim Bergerac would tick off the local sheep population from his list of suspects, thus leaving 14 people, three dogs and a couple of stray cats that swam over from Guernsey. Having deduced who the bad guy is, there would be a 30-second car chase just to get the ball rolling and prevent viewers from switching over to watch *The A-Team*. Then, Bergerac would get out of his car, have a croissant and wait for the villain to complete one round of the tiny island, before arresting him on the way back. Variations of this plot were repeated for 12 torturous years, which says more about the average British TV viewer than it does about the charismatic qualities of Jim Bergerac.

But the efficiency of Jersey's Colombo came back to me when I read a heartwarming report over the Chinese New Year holidays. On the first day of the Lunar New Year, four scumbags snatched around $1,300 in *hongbao* money from a mother in Yishun. The poor woman was with her daughter and the pair was on their way to visit relatives, but still she wasn't spared.

Within the hour, however, the four thieves had been caught at a nearby HDB block. Yes, that's within the hour. Now, I'm not sure if Bergerac serves as an adviser to the Singaporean police force, but I'd love to think his technique was at work. Apparently, one or two officers questioned the staff sergeant in charge of the very short case.

"But sir, if they've made off on foot, they could be halfway to Woodlands by now," said the youngest and most eager police officer.

"Relax, I've got more experience than you. I've been working in the heartlands for 20 years and I've got every episode of Bergerac on video. The blur buggers will just run around the block. You see, here they come now, all sweaty and out of breath. Be a good chap, will you? Stretch out your arm and grab the little bastards."

The four culprits were swiftly apprehended and, would you believe it, charged in court the following day. Now that's what I call justice. Like Jersey, Singapore has certainly benefitted from being small when it comes to policing the island. There can't be too many criminal safe houses in Yishun.

Having said that, success can't altogether be attributed to the Bergerac School for Small-Town Law Enforcers. When I was

17, I was mugged in a McDonald's in east London at knifepoint as two police officers sat in a patrol car OUTSIDE the restaurant. While I handed over the cash, I prayed that the two coppers would look up, ascertain the situation and beat the shit out of the young offenders. Instead, they did nothing except expand their waistlines with a Big Mac. Had the muggers run out to the patrol car brandishing their knives and their ill-gotten gains while singing *I Shot the Sheriff*, the bloody boys in blue would have done nothing. Except move on to their French fries perhaps.

Can you imagine those two at the scene of the crime in Yishun? The distraught woman would run up and scream: "Those four guys have stolen my *hongbao* money!"

"Your hong what?"

"Never mind. Never mind. Quick, it's those big guys there."

"Those Big Macs where? Hey, that's near the McDonald's. Come on, I haven't eaten for four minutes."

"But what about my money? I don't have any money."

"Now look, don't worry about that, madam. As it's Chinese New Year, we'll treat you this time. But you're only getting a Happy Meal. Is that alright?"

They would be utterly useless. In stark contrast, Singapore's public services have been in fine form over the festive period. Aside from police officers catching thieves in record time, the Singapore Civil Defence Force had a raging fire at the Thomson Road flower nurseries under control within 20 minutes on the second day of Chinese New Year. They had to fight through not only leaping flames, but also *kaypoh* drivers who stopped their cars to watch the blaze. I know many Singaporeans enjoy the odd firecracker or two to bring in the Lunar New Year, but this was ridiculous. And yet, despite these hazards, the SCDF tamed Thomson's towering inferno without suffering a single casualty or injury. Having lived with a younger sister who enjoyed setting fire to our kitchen periodically, I can only salute the Force's achievement. To be fair, they were never greeted by the sight of a seven-year-old girl standing in the middle of a sizeable fire and saying: "Well, what do you think? It's much bigger than the last one, isn't it?"

But their effort was impressive nonetheless. While most of the country has spent the weekend counting *hongbaos* and *mahjong* tiles, those guys have been out there salvaging *hongbaos* and half of Thomson Road. It's been a stirring start to the Year of the Goat so remember this ancient Chinese proverb: "When a thief steals your money in an HDB estate, let him run around the block first — and then kick the little shit in the balls when he comes back."

## *THE CYCLISTS*

THE Singapore Police Force has publicly put its foot down. In response to a number of shocking stories and letters in national newspapers recently, the Force has boldly declared that selfish cyclists found cycling on pavements can be fined $20. Now the governing powers of Singapore have often been criticised for their rather eccentric laws, but this really is a Draconian bridge too far. A $20 fine just for riding on the pavement? What kind of law is that? Cyclists who harass law-abiding pedestrians should be strung up by their dangly bits, preferably with piano wire, and summarily executed. That's the only way Singapore is going to rid itself of the scourge of humanity. As far as I'm concerned, pavement-riding cyclists rank just below serial killers, but just above Romancing Singapore campaigners.

Incidentally, if one more TV commercial tells me I must find a partner, buy her flowers, kiss her passionately and produce lots of Singaporean babies then I will end up in court charged with 'killer TV litter'. But it's these *kiasu* riders that are currently proving to be the bigger menace.

There was a story recently that a poor woman was flagging down a bus at a bus stop and was knocked down by a speeding cyclist. She ended up with a cracked leg bone, a year-long limp and $10,000 in medical bills.

In Bukit Batok, a heavily pregnant woman tripped and fell after making a desperate attempt to avoid a cyclist who was riding like a deranged maniac behind her, according to an eyewitness.

I have the deepest sympathy for these victims. The lift doors have often opened at my HDB block and I've had to jump back to allow Evel Knievel to whiz past. There's never a plank of wood, or a blunderbuss, around when you want one is there?

The lazy cyclist, and motorcyclist for that matter, exemplifies the *kiasu* traveller in every sense, cutting corners both literally and metaphorically.

Behind my block in Toa Payoh is a narrow pedestrian crossing beneath the Pan Island Expressway that allows people to get to the bus stops in Thomson Road. Concrete bollards have been erected to deter cyclists. But that's not enough to deter these gormless erections, is it? Consequently, *kiasu* cyclists and motor-cyclists, eager to bypass the pillars, have created four paths on the adjacent grass patch, so they now have a ready shortcut instead of having to go all the way around Lorong 1 to reach Thomson Road.

Morons on magnificent motorbikes have tooted the horn at me several times to get out of the way. But I've usually relied on my horn to remind the bugger who has the right of way. In extreme cases of persistent overtaking, I've tried to pursue the rider to kick him in his horn but alas, I've yet to hit the target.

Now, my girlfriend and I have created a little dance that we do as we walk along the footpath. Whenever a motorcyclist revs up behind us, we continually move in the same direction as the bike to prevent any overtaking, singing: "To the left. And to the right. Keep it going, keep it going. It's all right."

I've warned my girlfriend not to do this when she is alone for fear of antagonising the impatient cyclist. The joke could turn quite nasty. And, alas, it did — for the motorcyclist.

One morning, an annoying little bastard kept his hand on his horn, one that emitted high-pitched sounds, all the way down the path, forcing irritated pedestrians to throw themselves against the fence to allow the bugger to pass. Reluctantly, my girlfriend also let him pass, otherwise, knowing her, he could still be there with her jumping in the same direction as the bike and refusing to let him pass.

Just a couple of seconds after riding around my missus, though, the prick attempted to overtake two schoolgirls, but his handlebars clipped the fence and he fell over the top of his motorbike. According to biased reports from my girlfriend, it was marvellous.

Clearly unruffled by the incident, she approached the fallen rider, stepped over him and continued to the bus stop as if nothing had happened. Priceless. But where did these people come from? What kind of sphincter is so impatient that he must overtake two schoolchildren on a motorbike on a public footpath?

When I was a kid all we had to worry about as junior pedestrians was being knocked over by shortsighted old ladies driving motorised vehicles. Without their mini cars, these people were passive, adorable old aged pensioners. Behind the wheel, they became geriatric Michael Schumachers shouting things like: "Take that, you little bastard. That's the last time you kick your ball into my front garden."

At a supermarket one Saturday morning, I swear I heard one pensioner saying to another: "I only got two this morning, Rose. I got that little bastard at number 21 who keeps stealing my pints of milk. And I got that Humphreys boy at number 15 who giggles at my blue-rinse hairdo."

Generally speaking, though, we tolerated the elderly's motorised deathtraps because they suffered a World War and Cliff Richard records for us. But I would watch *Summer Holiday* endlessly before I'd move aside for some impatient, tooting motorcyclist behind me. So the only solution is this — shoot the bastards. And I'm sure those crow killers would dutifully oblige. I once saw them gleefully massacre a family of crows in Toa Payoh Central, so they seem the trigger-happy type. They could hide under the tree to shoot crows and then they could hide in the tree to take aim at reckless cyclists. Proudly wearing those luminous, government-issued sashes, they could be Singapore's first official crow/cyclist shooters — licensed to kill parasites.

Any crow found stealing a chicken wing from a table at a hawker centre: the death penalty. Any motorcyclist found overtaking schoolgirls on a pedestrian footpath: the death penalty. Alternatively, the Singapore Police Force could pay me $20 and I will gladly hide at the Thomson Road pedestrian crossing and shove a branch into the spokes of every passing motorcycle.

**NOTE:** It is nigh on impossible to predict which topic or subject will evoke public reaction. But I can honestly say that the seemingly harmless topic of selfish, impatient cyclists would not have been at the top of my list. Not for the first time, I was proved to be utterly incorrect. Dedicated cyclists were rather miffed by my criticisms. One particular writer said I should experience the sufferings of the leisure cyclist over at the East Coast Park, before I make such accusations. I have, many times, and he is right. Roads designated for cyclists are constantly being swamped by joggers, dog-walkers and skateboarders. And, when you think about it, in the interest of fairness, there's only one solution to that problem, isn't there? They should be shot, too. In Singapore, god knows it's difficult enough for anyone to find a bit of space to themselves. In an island so desperately scarce in land, anyone who invades the personal space of another, whatever the circumstances or vehicle, is a bit of a selfish bastard when you think about it. Now, where's my bloody gun?

## *THE FAMILY*

MY mother just called to tell me she's back safely from the hospital. She was there for a pre-op checkup. She's having a trapped nerve in her hand fixed. As always, there was a story to tell. When she went into the nurse's room, she was shocked to learn that she had to strip for a number of routine tests. This caused a bit of apprehension. Firstly, my mother is rather self-conscious. Like most people, she's not one for prancing around in a nurse's room with exposed genitalia. Secondly, she hadn't shaved her legs that day and had, in her words, "legs like a fucking Italian footballer." To top it off, she wore a pair of my stepdad's white, toweling sports socks. According to her, she looked "fucking awful".

Understandably, she got a little worked up, which forced her blood pressure to go through the roof, which in turn made her more worked up and so on. As a result, the wonderfully patient nurse couldn't get an accurate reading from her stressed patient. So the nurse said: "I know what's wrong here, Sue, you're a bit nervous aren't you love?"

"Well, yeah, I am a bit," replied my poor mother. "I don't do this sort of thing very often."

"Is it the nakedness that's making you nervous, dear?"

"Well, yeah, it is a bit uncomfortable."

"Don't worry, love, we'll soon fix that." And with that, she whipped off the top half of her nurses' uniform. Please, allow me to say that again. She whipped off the top half of her bloody nurses' uniform. The middle-aged woman stood there in a bra that could have housed a small family in each cup. Don't think sexy soft pornography here. Think Carry On Middle-Aged Matron Who Should Know Better. Suddenly, the Italian footballer's legs and Andre Agassi socks didn't seem to concern my poleaxed mother. Headlines like "Teaching Assistant Suffers Deranged Lesbian Attack In Hospital" occupied her thoughts instead.

"Does that make you feel a bit better now, Sue? A little less awkward perhaps?" The kind, but semi-naked, nurse asked.

"Oh, yeah. Thanks." My mother lied. Speaking on the phone shortly after the visit, my mother told me: "The next time I go back, I'm going to make sure my pulse and blood pressure are so low, they'll think I'm dead. I can't have that bloody nurse getting her tits out again."

I really miss my mother. That was my way of telling you that. I came off the phone with tears in my eyes and a stomach-ache. No one can make me laugh like my loopy family. Telephone calls like that always give me a slight pang of homesickness. Not for the country, you understand. I don't get homesick for any country. Flag-waving patriotism is best left behind in Hitler's bunker. But I miss my family terribly. And despite what anybody living overseas may tell you, it never gets easier.

In late 1996, when I was 21, my mother kicked me up the arse, threw my suitcase at me and said: "Right, now fuck off. And don't come back until you've seen a bit of the world." One of her regrets when she was younger was that her poor, working-class upbringing had denied her the chance to travel, so she was delighted when I informed her that I was off to Singapore for a long working holiday.

She gave me three months, which was the usual stay for social visit pass holders. I gave myself three weeks. The eternal optimist. Seven years later, I'm still here and my dear old nan living in east London is still asking her neighbours: "Is it common for people to have seven-year holidays? It never was in my day. We either got a day out at the seaside or we went to the countryside to do a bit of scrumping at the local orchard. Do they have seaside places in Singapore? I still don't know why he wanted to go to China in the first place."

But that's my batty grandmother. Let me give you an idea, if I may, of what a truly unique woman my mother is. Though she rarely says anything positive about me (until I was 15, I thought there was a linguistic rule which stipulated that the words "Neil", "fuck" and "off" always had to go in the same sentence), I know living 10,000 km away is difficult for her. Yet she doesn't want me to leave Singapore, despite never having visited the city-state.

She knows I have economic and personal security and live in a completely safe environment that is now only guaranteed in small pockets of England. Just recently she said on the phone: "I know you could get a decent job here and earn better money, but did I tell you about the bloke who was stabbed down at the harbour last week?... No?... Well, he died on Tuesday." She's full of chirpy vignettes like that.

But I have to concede that my time away from England has given me a greater respect for Singapore's emphasis on filial piety. When I discovered what it meant, I was initially skeptical. Teachers, parents and politicians are constantly being urged to inculcate positive family values in the nation's children. I thought it was a governmental cop-out. We don't have a welfare state or pensions for the citizens who gave us fifty years of their working lives so you'll just have to take care of your own parents or they will starve, seemed to be the government's line of thought. Moreover I still read about greedy children fighting over the estate of their dead parents like incorrigible vultures squabbling over carrion.

Nevertheless, I have Singaporean friends who look after their ageing parents and relatives simply because it is the right thing to do. There's no ulterior motive. And with every act of filial piety I come across, the more aware I become of the distance between my family and myself. My youngest brother was three years old when I left for university and six when I settled in Singapore. Aside from missing most of his childhood, I'm also completely out of sync with his interests and understanding of popular culture. First, it was *Thomas the Tank Engine*, and then it was *Star Wars*. When I last visited, I asked: "So what do you think of Darth Maul then?"

"Shut up you sad twat," he replied, kicking me in the balls and flipping me onto my back like a rag doll. "I'm The Rock."

"You're a rock?"

"No, stupid. I'm The Rock."

"Oh, are you?"

"Yeah. Can you smell what The Rock's cooking?"

"You've learnt how to cook? That's great."

"No, stupid. God, don't you know anything? That's what the wrestler, The Rock, says."

"Does he? That's marvellous, Gary. Do you think you could stop sitting on my head now?"

I missed almost 10 years of that brotherly banter. I also wasn't around when my grandparents died. They passed away within two months of each other. Now, this may sound cold and heartless, but when you live abroad, a certain detachment inevitably results. Distant relatives pass away and you're sad, but the sense of loss can never be the same because they are names spoken over the telephone. You didn't visit them in the hospital. You didn't watch them deteriorate. And you didn't attend their funerals.

To some degree, it was the same with my grandparents. They were in tremendous pain for several months before they died. And of course the illness of one only further exacerbated the suffering of the other. But I never saw any of that. The last time I saw them was at their house, when my grandmother told me I had a deformed neck and looked like the giraffe on the cover of my previous book. I wasn't there for my own mother as she watched her stepfather and then her mother slowly waste away in a hospital bed. I didn't even go to my grandparents' funerals. I offered to come back, but my mother said there really was no point. Remember them how they were, before they got sick, she said. She's right, of course, but her pragmatism did nothing for the guilt I felt when I returned at Christmas and my grandparents were not there anymore. Then it hits you just how detached you've become. Then you realise that not being able to do anything was not an excuse for not coming back. I should've been there with my family.

Fortunately, I had an emotional crutch to lean on, didn't I? Because in Singapore, I am part of a much larger 'family', aren't I? A 'family' that could have appreciated my confused state of detachment and loss, because these guys are all in the same boat as me. There are always my *ang moh* brothers and sisters ready and willing to embrace me in a foreign land, aren't there? Those Singaporean expatriates all ready to muck in together, get pissed together, console each other, recreate their western ways of life together and generally overlook the fact that they are no longer in a western country. Being so far away from their loved ones, it's understandable that they should seek to be part of a bigger 'family' in Singapore. It just shouldn't be predominately white.

When my grandparents were ailing, my mood in the office was, naturally, not the best so a Singaporean colleague tried to cheer me up. "What you worried about?" he said. "Go to that British pub in Boat Quay. Find a few *ang moh*s. Can talk, reminisce about English weather and then go out and bang a few local women. What's the problem?"

Call me naive, but I've never done that in my life. I was never good-looking enough for a start. But in Singapore, there are plenty who have. They really are one big happy family in an Asian land. You've met them, right? In the various jobs that I've had here, I've had the pleasure of meeting dozens of my so-called fellow family members. Some have a resume that's so shady, you'll need a torchlight to read its 15 pages. They've either been a principal at some obscure language school in Made-up Street, Swansea, Wales, where the register contained four students, two sheep and a shepherd called Taffy Williams, who'd only ever conversed with four-legged mammals. Or you get the journalist who was night editor at the *Liechtenstein Times* and has written award-winning columns, apparently, for the *Cockroach Collectors Journal* and the *Sheep Dip Recipe Guide* (old Taffy Williams was a subscriber).

One of my favourite Singaporean *ang mohs*, though, is the 'foreign, talented' footballer. In my line of work, I've met quite a few. This guy has played for every English club you've never heard of and claims to be better than David Beckham was when they played in the England Under-Fives together. He could "have been a contender, Charlie", but Beckham stole his apple juice after the match, so they had a fight, he lost and the psychological scar has blighted his playing career ever since. Will Singapore reach the World Cup finals in 2010 by bringing in such stars to enhance the local football scene? Singapore couldn't reach a community cup final in Woodlands with these con artists. I've watched local footballers listen politely while these English professionals (oh, they're pros alright) discuss their knowledge and all the time I know the Malay lads are thinking: "If you're that good, why the fuck would you come to Singapore to play for $5,000 a month and deprive one of us of a first-team place?" The answer is, of course, so that the overweight beer barrel can join up with his happy *ang moh* gang here and live like a 19th century colonial.

In all fairness, Singaporeans could think the same of me. It's a natural assumption to make. But unlike other *ang mohs* I've encountered, I didn't come here because I couldn't find work anywhere else. Being 21, I'd never worked anywhere else. Aside from six months in a London stockbrokers' office, I came here seven years ago with nothing but some decent qualifications, a Game Boy, bags of enthusiasm and a rather dwarfish, but brilliant architect called Scott. I've worked my balls off ever since. It's always been an honest, two-way relationship and I sleep soundly at night. Some of these 'talented', 'experienced' *ang moh*s must require huge condos to fit all their skeletons into their closets. If I meet one more suspect teacher, footballer or businessman, who thinks he's Mr. Chips, Michael Owen or Richard Branson, I'm calling Singapore Immigration. You should too.

In some ways, though, you can't blame these deceivers. Utilising their capacity for extreme bullshit, they're capitalising on the white-man bias to enjoy the kind of respectable living their mediocre skills really don't deserve. It's up to those Singaporean bananas, and we all know a banana or two, to wheedle out these buggers and drive them from the country. 'Foreign' really isn't a guarantee of 'talent'. Sometimes, it can mean 'a complete fucking waste of space'. Well, it does in my dictionary.

Ironically, these *ang moh*s will force me to leave this country quicker than any Singaporean. Their hypocrisy is nauseating. I don't want to be tarred with the same brush. Keep me well away from that 'family', please. At times, I've found myself cornered by one or two at a pub or some social function. Not often, but it happens. The bullshit goes into overdrive. I hear about this 'deal' and that 'deal', this 'contact' and that 'contact' and how cheap it is to have a maid in this country. And I laugh. Their cover would be blown in seconds in a place like Dagenham and they know it. With all that verbal diarrhoea, the residents of my old hometown would smell them coming a mile off. That's why these wankers will never leave Singapore, not while they can still smooth talk their way into a luxurious lifestyle. They will never return to their actual family in the west. They're having too much fun with their adopted family in the east.

But I will. Undoubtedly, Singapore's been nothing but good to me. However, those family ties, both in England and Australia, have been stretched to the limit. Sooner rather than later, I will be surrounded with predominantly white people again. The major difference being my parents don't live in condos they don't deserve, nor do they profess to having enough skills and working experience to justify a five-page resume. Instead, we'll sit around and laugh as my mother tells stories about half-naked nurses. Surreal, perhaps, but honest. And that suits me fine. After seven years in Singapore, I've heard enough *ang moh* bullshit to last a lifetime.

## *THE LOVERS*

WATCHING your grandparents going through the preliminary stages of sexual foreplay is something you tend not to forget. When she was barely five years old, my mother decided to hide under the kitchen table while her 70-year-old grandmother did the washing up. For reasons she never did divulge, the old matriarch often favoured a baggy string vest with no bra on while she did the dishes.

On this particular occasion, her husband came in and sneaked up behind her, grabbing a part of her body that had long since given up the fight against gravity. Then, he kindly said: "Ooh, You've still got a fine pair of knockers there, haven't you, love?" The elderly pair both giggled. He went back and read the paper, she finished the washing up and my stunned mother vowed never to play hide-and-seek on her own again.

Outraged members of the moral brigade, who tend not to get out enough, would denounce such a vulgar incident. But, it's a wonderful story.

My great-grandparents endured tremendous hardship in a post-war London. They lived in the east London borough of Bethnal Green, which was ravaged by the Blitz and largely ignored by Westminster policymakers. Yet they loved each other dearly. And they went at it like rabbits until my great-granddad died. A heart attack killed him. I'm not bloody surprised. My great-grandmother lived on for another 20 years and died a week before her 90th birthday. But she never did the washing up with the same vigour after her husband died.

But I was truly delighted to discover that my great-grandparents were not alone. In late March 2002, some 300 Singaporeans, many of them elderly, picked up and passed on love tips at a public forum. That's right. A load of oldies voluntarily came together to discuss their relationships. From keeping the partner happy in the bedroom to learning to duck when the wife attempts decapitation with a kitchen plate, many aspects of maintaining a harmonious marriage were discussed.

This forum, which was organised by the Singapore Action Group of Elders and *Lianhe Zaobao*, has unearthed 300 Singaporean superheroes. There were men in their 80s asking, quite sincerely, how they could sustain their sex lives. Aware of my 'energy levels', I'll be lucky if I can raise a smile when I'm 80, never mind anything else. I'm fairly sure that the word "erection" will not be part of my vocabulary by then. Words like "adult", "diapers" and "incontinence" almost certainly, but not "erection".

My favourite hero at the forum was a hip 86-year-old, clad in jeans and sunglasses, who wanted to know how he could be more loving to his wife. How he could be more loving? What a truly humbling thought. Apparently, there was another elderly chap suffering from a failing sex drive and seeking views on how it could be rectified. He asked: "My wife is demanding and I'm not getting any younger, you know. I'm worried I can no longer satisfy her. We used to make love every day but now, it's dropped to six times a week. What should I do?"

The virility of some of these old-timers is terrifying. I'm only 28 and, increasingly, my idea of a night of hedonistic pleasure is a DVD and a bowl of instant noodles. Yet, there are couples who were making babies long before the People's Action Party was born and they're still doing the business in the bedroom.

At the time of the forum, Singapore was enveloped in a gloomy depression, thanks to the war in the Middle East and the deadly virus at its doorstep. But the trusty elderly led the way once more, by coming together to discuss the importance of a loving marriage. I just wish the nation's pioneers could hang around for another 50 years to sort out the younger generations. Though, I've heard rumours that if anything does go wrong, one or two of the more prominent senior citizens will rise from their graves to correct any problems. I certainly hope so. They speak about love and relationships, while their dour children fret over the economy, incompetent maids and the latest ringtones. Where did it all go wrong?

We needed these fun-loving pensioners at the recent Rolling Stones' gig. Some friends of mine managed to secure a couple of tickets by forfeiting most of their CPF savings and were rewarded with some good seats, which they found once they'd fought past the middle-aged Caucasian men with young Singaporean women that made up much of the audience, of course.

During the concert, my friends received a public dressing down — for having the audacity to sing along to the Stones' classic *Angie*. Fancy that! Singing at a rock concert! What a gaggle of selfish, inconsiderate bastards! Quick, grab the cane and bring back public flogging before this self-destructive nation descends into anarchy.

In fairness, I've heard my friends sing before. Collectively, they sound like a goose farting in the fog. But, that's hardly a cause for complaint, is it? It was for a group of women, in their early 30s, who were sitting in front. One of them turned and said: "We must thank you, gentlemen, for ruining a beautiful song." To which my friend replied: "You're most welcome. I usually charge for our performances, but seeing as you are devoid of a sense of fun, a personality and, quite possibly, a life, you may continue to listen to us geese — free of charge. You miserable fuckers."

My Singaporean superheroes wouldn't have tolerated such sullen behaviour. "Now listen here, young lady," one of the 80-year-olds would've retorted. "You think you've got problems. You youngsters moan about the economy, the price of cars and HDB flats. Well, listen to me missy. I'm 82 years old and now, I can only get it up six times a week. So, get some perspective and get down to *Jumping Jack Flash*."

Let's hire these virulent, vivacious aunties and uncles to track down boring buggers islandwide. They've been around long enough to know what it's all about. After all, they talk 'love' while everyone else talks 'war'. Sounds bloody good to me.

# *THE HUNCHBACK*

SHORT of chopping my head off and handing it to the bus driver, I don't know what else to do on single-deck buses. For the umpteenth time, I suffered a right bloody whack against the roof of the bus as the excitable driver treated his handbrake like a bicycle pump. Fellow commuters were treated to an *ang moh* beanpole rubbing his head furiously and shouting: "I've hit my fucking head... again."

In some respects, my lack of courtesy to my fellow passengers can be attributed to the Singapore Science Centre. Don't get me wrong, I love the place and I believe every child should visit it at least once a year. When I was in primary school in England, we took annual coach trips to London's Science Museum. The excursions were so tedious that the highlight was the peanut butter sandwiches on the bus, largely because they weren't mine to start with. I had cheese. But my old mate, Ross, used to decorate the windows with his cornflakes just as we pulled out of Dagenham. So the tear-stained teacher got her handkerchief ruined, and I got Ross' peanut butter sandwiches. There was very little educational advancement involved during these museum trips.

I suspect that's why I get a tad irritated at the impressive Singapore Science Centre. Its hands-on exhibits merely serve to remind me that I have the scientific understanding of plankton. My mathematical knowledge barely gets me through a *Barney* VCD with my Singaporean goddaughter. Now Nicole's moved on to *Sesame Street,* I struggle to keep up with Bert and Ernie's number counting. Incidentally, are those two gay? Only I've never seen them in the company of women, have you? And they're always bloody smiling.

Back in the Science Centre, I was attempting, unsuccessfully, to take a number of wooden bricks of various shapes and sizes and fit them into a cohesive cube. A 10-year-old boy, patiently waiting for his turn behind me, whispered words of encouragement like: "*ang moh* so stupid" and "so slow, blur like *sotong* (squid)" just to spur me along.

Finally, his patience snapped: "*Aiyoh* can I show you how? ... Okay, this rectangle goes there, you see? ... That square one fits in there and you turn that round ... *aiyoh* ... you had that one upside down ... *wah lau* ... and then you slot that one inside the hole and you're finished, can?"

"Look, I went to university, you know?" I hissed, in a rather pathetic effort to resurrect my self-esteem. The brat's brief, but vocal, demonstration, had drawn a crowd.

"University ... Really ah? ... *Wah lau* ... Can I take it apart and build it for myself now?"

"Of course. Tell me, have you ever put the cube together after being poked in the eye?"

"No."

"Well, now's your chance. You little bastard."

We left the Science Centre soon after. Apart from the cube

incident, the security guard caught me going down the slide in the pre-school playground. Shouting "whoopee" was probably not a good idea.

An hour later, I was performing my excruciating, cabaret routine for a captive audience on my local SBS Transit bus. The No. 232 is a single-deck feeder bus that serves the residents of Toa Payoh Lorong 2. And when I board, young children actually cry: "Mummy, here comes the *Homo erectus* man. He's so funny. He can clean the roof with his neck and sweep the floor of the bus with his knuckles ... all at the same time!"

You see, I am 1.92 metres tall. And single-deck buses in Singapore aren't. Scraping my neck and shoulders along the roof of the miniature buses, I have collected everything from bus tickets to stunned mosquitoes saying to each other, "what the fuck was that?" in my collar.

On that brief journey following my sojourn to the Science Centre, I suffered multiple neck lesions and stumbled around the packed No. 232 bus like Frankenstein's monster. By the end of the trip, I had perfected the posture of Quasimodo and staggered off the bus a full two inches shorter than when I had boarded, shouting: 'The bells! The bells! They make me deaf, you know?"

Unsurprisingly, I wholeheartedly concur with a couple of Singaporeans, who recently asked SBS Transit for more double-deck bus services. The transport authority replied that on certain bus routes that just isn't feasible, due to a number of tree-lined avenues and low flyovers.

What kind of excuse is that? Has no one at SBS Transit seen James Bond's *Live and Let Die*? In one scene, the fleeing Roger Moore steals a bus and coolly drives it through a tunnel, slicing it in half, without raising even one of his trademark eyebrows.

Now that could work. It would certainly reduce stuffiness on the upper deck and create more headroom for those who remembered to duck. But I doubt the transport authorities would approve. An SBS Transit spokesman would soon be informing the general public: "We'd like to reassure passengers and remind drivers that removing the top half of their buses is not permitted, even on humid days. Whether it is via a tunnel, a bridge or any low-lying apparatus for that matter, unapproved bus separations would litter the roads, disrupt traffic flow and scratch the buses' expensive paintwork. And we've only just changed the logos on most buses, so that could prove rather troublesome.

"But we thank Quasimodo for his feedback and suggest a weekly massage to reduce the hump."

So, in desperation, I'm turning to the guillotine. That's the only solution for lanky buggers like me on single-deck buses. Place a sensor-triggered guillotine above the ez-link card reader. Anyone who registers above 1.9 metres in height gets his head lopped off. That'll speed up commuter flow and increase headroom, so I'm sure the transport authorities will commission a guillotine feasibility study.

Apparently, Joseph Ignace Guillotin, who championed the cause of painless executions during the French Revolution, was most unhappy at having his name attached to such a murderous device. He only advocated more humane killings, not the actual machine that had been around for centuries. Until his death, he sought to distance himself from the old head-chopper. Both in literature and literally I would have thought. But then, old Guillotin never travelled around Toa Payoh in single-deck buses, did he? I do, every hump-inducing day. So get that bloody blade sharpened.

## *THE PROTECTORS*

UNDERSTANDABLY, many concerned Singaporean parents have been obsessed with their children's personal protection and cleanliness of late. My mother was no different. She, too, was preoccupied with my personal hygiene, or complete lack of, when I was growing up in England. She would challenge my powers of contortion by making impossible requests, such as: "Just look at the dirt behind your ear, you dirty bastard."

Invariably, I would cut my head in half and examine the aforementioned area. Her frequent threats of death were most unnerving. On hearing that I'd crossed the road without checking both sides first, she'd bellow: "How many times do I have to tell you? I mean it, Neil. If you get run over by a bus, I'll bloody kill you!"

My personal favourite, though, was when she spotted a smudge on my face on the way home from school. Employing a technique popular with many British mothers, she'd take out a tissue, spit on it, or in some cases lick it, and then, scrub my face with it. Having rubbed a hole into my cheek, she would stand back, admire her handiwork and say: "There, that's better."

"What do you mean, 'that's better'? I've got a face full of your saliva and a smidgeon of lipstick and I've lost all feeling in my cheek." I usually got a slap on the other cheek for that. It helped to balance the redness on both sides.

With the spread of a deadly virus, Singaporeans have been concerned with the hygiene standards of their children and their families recently and it's a legitimate concern. There have been rational requests to don face masks in crowded areas, wear gloves when handling food or rubbish and use tissues when sneezing. But the need for greater personal protection becomes a tad irritating when it descends into moralising, not to mention patronising, condemnation.

I've lost count of the number of letters written to the media that have said: "Please don't spit, ladies and gentlemen, in the street, at each other, or on your own clothes, because spitting is ... wait for it ... bad."

At this point, I assume four million Singaporeans are supposed to jump up simultaneously and cry: "That's it! My god, she's bloody right, you know? Spitting is bad. Give that woman a hankie."

Perhaps we should rename Singapore 'Asia's Animal Farm' and we can all wear woolly jumpers, crawl around on all fours and bleat: "Spitting bad, hankies good. Spitting bad, hankies good".

This condescending fluff reminds me of a letter I received recently from an irate reader who criticised me for making fun of that poor, much maligned dictator Saddam Hussein. She challenged me on this and felt the need to point out that — now get ready for this — "War costs lives".

Do you ever wonder who these Singaporeans are? I do. They must pore over the newspapers every day, shouting: "Filth!

Outrageous! Smut! How dare he try to be funny in this deadly serious world we live in? Filth! He's left me with no choice. I must point out that war costs lives. He can't possibly know that. And then, when I'm through with that insensitive cretin, I'm going to remind all Singaporeans that spitting is just, well, bad. Filth! Baa."

Of course, I can't deny that there are still some pockets of resistance among the saliva gang in Singapore. There are some spitting gold medal contenders in my Toa Payoh estate, but then there are Dagenham teenagers who smash beer bottles in the High Street of my own hometown when they're pissed. These parasites do exist. It doesn't mean we should waste oxygen or ink advising others not to follow suit.

Yet, the National Environment Agency obviously disagrees. As I write this, I'm looking at a marvellous advisory that the Agency published in a newspaper recently. The letter reminded Singaporeans that it is an offence to "spit or expel mucous". I didn't even know what "expel mucous" meant. I thought it was the stage name of a nightclub DJ, as in "Fat Boy Slim and Expel Mucous". That could work.

My own regret was that the letter wasn't longer, otherwise I would have framed it and hung it in the living room. But at least, it saved the best for last. The last sentence included the suggestion that "those who find that they have to spit or blow their nose should do so with a piece of tissue paper". Because you weren't sure, were you? But if the Agency is capable of giving out such sound advice, it shouldn't stop there. The advisory could have continued: "We'd also like to remind Singaporeans that walking can be achieved by putting one foot in front of the other. Where possible, try to perform the act in a straight line to avoid bumping into your fellow walkers. Thus considerably reducing the chances of you spitting in their faces."

The theme of self-protection is everywhere. Fortunately, not all of it is gloomy. My news editor recently handed me a press release and said: "This one's for you, pervert."

Indeed it was. The press release was proud to announce that a reputable condom manufacturer had introduced a bigger condom to cater to the well-endowed man.

At a time when cynical, ruthless companies are exploiting the nation's fears by promoting everything from hand cream to anti-bacterial toilet paper, the big condom campaign stands out as the work of a marketing genius. The new, enlarged product is supposed to be 2 mm thicker than existing condoms. But whether or not you actually need the extra space is utterly irrelevant, isn't it? Men will be queuing up in supermarkets and convenience stores to ask, in very loud voices: "Excuse me. Do you happen to have the new condom that caters for the well-endowed? You know, the one for men who are hung like horses?"

Apparently, the condom company held in-house tests and 97% of users preferred the bigger product. How were these tests conducted? More importantly, how does one participate?

The National Environment Agency has emphasised the importance of improving one's personal protection in Singapore. So I am more than willing to take part in the next in-house condom test. In times of trouble, I must be prepared to go the extra 2 mm for the nation.

## *THE CHARACTERS*

AMONG my family and friends, I was fortunate enough to be surrounded by a number of imbalanced individuals while I was growing up in England. Spending time with some serious cuckoos builds character, according to my mother. But then, I think she just used that as an excuse. When she was sweeping the kitchen floor once, she suddenly had a schizophrenic seizure and thought she was legendary batter Babe Ruth. At least, I think that's why she chased me around the living room, trying to hit my head with the broom handle for a home run. But, rather deftly, I deflected the blow with my right ear and she only made first base.

But dealing with slightly left-of-centre characters became a regular occurrence during my childhood. On the corner of my street was Maltese Tony. A wonderfully considerate and kind bloke who had emigrated from Malta to Dagenham when he was a young man. If you've ever seen both the stunning landscapes of Malta and the council housing estates of Dagenham, you would immediately gain a basic understanding of Maltese Tony. He had screws loose.

On arriving, it seems that the first English expression he heard was "mind you", but he never fully grasped its meaning, so he never said it in context. He said things like, "I have to go to the mind you shop to buy some cigarettes." The fact that he also had an incurable stutter never helped matters. I'm not making this up. When he stuttered, he became the only human being to experience rapid eye movement while he was awake. Blinking furiously, he would say: "I was stuck in a bastard m-m-m-mind you traffic jam for 20 m-m-m-mind you minutes yesterday." To make matters worse, he was a taxi driver. And taxi drivers were expected to engage in a little small talk. The only problem was his small talk could take an hour.

But his *piéce de résistance* was his complete lack of awareness behind a steering wheel. The world never existed when he was driving the car. The fact that he was a taxi driver only made it all the more fun, or terrifying if you were the passenger. His favourite trick was the 'homemade cigarette'. Stopping at a traffic light, he would pull out his tobacco tin, take out a pinch of tobacco, spread it out across a small, square piece of cigarette paper and then carefully roll it into a cigarette. Making these nicotine-filled burritos used to be quite popular in Britain. But the process was time-consuming. It could take up to five minutes. He would do it at a busy road junction, where the traffic lights changed every 30 seconds. And, frankly speaking, he didn't give a shit. Frustrated car drivers would scream abuse, bang on their horns and screech around him and he'd be completely oblivious. Eventually he would get annoyed and shout: "Why are you making all this bastard mind you n-n-n-noise? You bastards."

He was fond of the word 'bastard'. If he still hadn't finished and the complaints around him intensified, he would really lose it. "I can't even make a m-m-m mind you bastard cigarette in peace, without you making all this n-n-n-noise. You mind you bastards!"

"Er, excuse me," his startled passenger would finally pipe up. "I think they are shouting at you. The traffic lights keep changing and you still haven't moved."

"Who was mind you talking to you? This is none of your business. Get out of my taxi, you mind you bastard!" He would throw so-called mind you dangerous passengers out of his vehicle every week and then complain that the job paid meagre wages.

To be honest, I thought I'd never be fortunate enough to meet anyone as quirky as Maltese Tony again. In England, he's one in a million. But in Toa Payoh, he'd just be one of the residents living in my estate. There was a fine collection of entertainers in my old block in Lorong 1 and, having moved in recent months to Lorong 2, I miss them dearly. My favourite was Rock DJ Auntie. In truth, she was once the infamous 'bra lady', whom I've mentioned before. But in the last year or so, the mad old bat went through a stunning metamorphosis that would've made Kafka proud.

'Bra lady' was famous, in my old HDB block at least, for travelling up and down in lifts all day, stopping at every floor. She performed this civic duty while wearing a pink bra on the OUTSIDE of her clothes. The cups were so large, they wouldn't have looked out of place on an ageing elephant. But, alas, that's all in the past. Now, she's Rock DJ auntie. My girlfriend reported the transformation one evening. Out of breath, she ran into the flat and said: "I've just seen bra lady coming back from the shops!"

"So what? We see her nearly every day. Pink bloody bra and everything."

"No, but she's not wearing the bra today."

"Well, you don't expect her to wear it every day, do you? I'm sure even she must take it off occasionally, otherwise the stench would knock her out."

"Shut up and come and see. She's wearing something else."

And she most certainly was. When I was growing up in the late '70s, my parents had a pair of those, enormous leather-padded headphones to plug into the hi-fi. Do you remember them? They had a plug the size of a screwdriver and when you put them on you looked like Princess Leia in *Star Wars*. Well, old 'bra lady' was wearing the biggest pair of those old leather-padded headphones that I'd ever seen. Think Princess Leia some 30 years after menopause and you'll get a rough picture of what I saw across the void deck. 'Bra lady' was dead. Long live Rock DJ Auntie.

Transfixed, we sat at one of those concrete tables that really make your bum itch and watched her approach. Then came the revelation. The giant headphones were plugged in — to nothing. The coiled lead was hanging loosely by the side of her body. Quite clearly, I could see the screwdriver plug brushing against her knee. What the hell was the purpose of those headphones? Earmuffs? In Singapore? This woman was utterly insane.

Or perhaps she is a genius. Just two days before writing this, I saw her again. Whenever I smile at her, she never reciprocates, her vacant, slightly puzzled expression never changes. Rock DJ Auntie looks right through me as if I'm transparent. Then it occurred to me, perhaps I am. She is on another dimension to the rest of us, mentally speaking. She has reached another level and is communicating on a higher spiritual plane. The signs were always there, weren't they? Of course, she doesn't need to plug her headphones into any electrical source because her power source is looking down at us and not the other way around. That's what the pink bra was – a signal no less. A polyester satellite communicating earthly messages to an outerworldly paymaster. Yes, that's the answer. Everything is clear now.

On the other hand, of course, she could be a complete fucking lunatic.

It would be grossly unfair, however, to categorise Madam Bed Linen as a lunatic. Slightly off kilter perhaps, but she's so endearing, she's almost edible. Short and rather plump, she doesn't quite reach to my chest which makes our brief liaisons all the more memorable. About six months ago, we were in Toa Payoh Central hunting for a new quilt, bedsheets, pillowcases and so on. As a rule, I find this kind of shopping about as entertaining as plugging into headphones without a Walkman. But as I tend to emit the odd comical sound while I'm in bed, I was forced to concede that I was partially responsible for the demise of the old quilt.

Luckily, Madam Bed Linen introduced herself and I've since bought three quilt cover sets. We were in a small department store, one of those that always sticks an employee in the bed linen section, assuming perhaps that if we have a blue-and-yellow bedroom, we would need those colours pointed out to us by a conscientious shop assistant. We can't take the bedroom with us, right? So it's better to be safe than sorry. Normally, I have little patience with these shop assistants. I know they are only doing their job, but I get irritated when you tell them your bedroom is indeed blue and yellow and they show you the remains of an explosion in a paint factory and tell you that it will match.

But Madam Bed Linen in Toa Payoh was different. Firstly, she never stopped giggling and mumbling to herself, which was a little disconcerting initially. She also spoke in a high-pitched voice and agreed with everything you said. We'd say: "We actually want a blue-and-yellow set."

"Ha! Blue and yellow. This one okay?"

"It's pink."

"Yeah, very nice."

"We want blue-and-yellow."

"Ha! You want blue-and-yellow... How about this one?"

"It's a plain, white quilt."

"Yeah, it's a plain quilt. But it's cheap, got offer one."

"But we want a blue-and-yellow one."

"Ha ha! You want a blue-and-yellow one?"

It began to feel like a Jedi mind trick after a while. But the best thing about Madame Bed Linen was actually two-fold. Firstly, she had a slight lisp. And secondly, she pronounced sheet as 'seat'. After we'd selected a quilt, she asked: "Beth-seat for you, sir?"

"I'm sorry?"

"Ha ha, would you like some beth-seats?" She pointed at the bedsheets and I had to walk away, complaining of a throat irritation. I know this is terrible, and I'm going straight to hell, but I bit my tongue, returned to this lovely lady and formulated as many ways as possible to make her say "bed-sheets". Picking up a quilt cover, I would say: "Would these fit on a queen-sized bed?"

"Ha ha! That's a quilt cover, not beth-seats."

"What are these blue ones?"

"Ah, they are okay. They're beth-seats."

Now, whenever she spots me in the store, she shouts cheerfully: "Hello, ha ha! Beth-seats, I got beth-seats. You wanna see my beth-seats? Ha ha!" Her inexhaustible chirpiness whenever we meet attracts some concerned stares.

Every time she invites me to see her bedsheets, she sounds like a middle-aged hooker with a speech impediment. But she's wonderful company and I always have a chat with her when I'm in the shop, no matter what I'm doing. She never says she's too busy and will make time to talk, like the majority of the Singaporeans I meet in and around Toa Payoh. When I was promoting my previous book, a journalist said he'd lived in Singapore all his life and had never encountered half the characters that I claim to have met in a small corner of Toa Payoh. He suggested it was due to the novelty factor. A white man in Toa Payoh evokes reaction and curiosity. People are generally nosy by nature and will seek to find out what the *ang moh* is doing in their lift, void deck or coffee shop. It's a possibility, though a touch patronising. Neighbours and strangers are naturally inquisitive, it's hardly a crime. And call me self-indulgent, but I will actively go out of my way to meet people in my estate and chat with them. That was the reason I decided to travel in the first place.

Life is so fast-paced now, apparently, that there is no time for small talk. You know, a little bit of harmless nonsense that helps break up the mundane and makes a predictable working day more fun. When interested Singaporeans take a *kaypoh* interest in my life, I respond. It's not exactly profound. I don't give a two-word answer and disappear into a lift, like many of the younger executive types do in my block. These hardworking chaps may not be unhinged, quirky or colourful. They're just boring.

Observe the HDB void decks. Invariably, they are filled with old-timers doing nothing except gossip and chat. Occasionally, they have the odd beer to lubricate the old vocal cords. Among the younger generation, conversation (at least conversation that doesn't involve the economy, gambling or golf) is a dying art in Singapore. It's no coincidence that most of my favourite eccentrics are amomng the elderly. They like to talk and I like to listen. It's not a complex relationship.

Similarly, Singaporean children can't seem to keep their mouths shut either. It's fabulous. Not yet tainted by race, religion or politics, they rarely hold back. There's a gang of primary school kids from my old block who are a sublime mix of innocence, honesty and insanity. Indeed, the cheeky bastards are so open and gregarious that they could have had me arrested.

For a couple of years now, they've been playing football on the void deck. That's how I met them. A mixture of Chinese and Malay boys aged from six to around 12, they're more streetwise than Jack Dawkins and audaciously insist the "tall *ang moh* come play" every time I pass. Our ad hoc five-a-side matches had attracted some curious glances. But that was nothing compared to the reactions I get from strangers now, whenever the boys shout their greetings.

Almost two years ago, a journalist came to my flat with a photographer to interview me about my first book, *Notes from an even Smaller Island*. We took some photos in front of the block while my football posse playfully mocked me in the background. The interviewer suggested taking some pictures with my 'gang', but they refused. Normally, you can't get the boys to shut up. On this occasion, though, they were struck dumb by stage fright. Fair enough.

However, once the journalist and the photographer had left, the gang's cockiness quickly returned. About a week after the interview, I was walking home with the missus when the gang waved at me from the children's playground. One of them shouted: "Hello, *ang moh*. You remember us, you wanted to take our photograph last time? Do you remember? You wanted to take our photograph!" At that moment, if I'd produced an axe and screamed "Here's Johnny!", I don't think my girlfriend could have expressed greater horror. I tried to explain the boy's claim.

"No, it wasn't me who wanted to take your photograph was it, boys?"

"Yeah lah, it was you what," replied the cheeky one. "You wanted to take photographs of all of us, with you also in the photograph, right?" I could have strangled the little bastard.

But it never stopped. To this day, if I bump into any of the young void deck footballers, they bellow: "Hello, remember us? You wanted to take photographs of us? You want to take now?" And they always say it just as a respectable, middle-aged couple is crossing my path. Their timing is impeccable. My girlfriend is constantly on hand to remind me that I have the unsmiling face of a serial killer, so the kids' banter is just enough to have people crossing the road to avoid me.

They surpassed themselves, however, when my girlfriend's parents came to Singapore for her graduation ceremony. Arriving back at the block after a day of sightseeing, we were discussing our evening plans when the void deck boys spotted me.

"Hello *ang moh*. Remember me?"

"Yes, I remember you. How can I forget you? You're here every day."

"Yeah lah. You remember you wanted to take our photograph last time. You want to take it now?" The boys giggled. My future parents-in-law questioned their daughter's judgment.

"Look, for the last time. I never asked to take your picture."

"Don't bluff ah. You always ask to take our photograph what?" More giggling.

"No I don't."

"Okay lah, never mind. Next time can ... You want to play with our balls instead?"

Well, the dropping pin was deafening. And before you say anything, they were referring to their bloody footballs! They always took more than one because the surplus balls were used as goal posts opposite the void deck pillars. Both my girlfriend and I spent half the night explaining this to her parents, while retelling the journalist/photographer story. Though I've been forced to concede since that the possibility of carrying a camera with me, on the off chance that I should meet the void deck posse, is looking increasingly likely. I could whack the little bastards with it.

They just can't keep their mouths shut, which is unlike my old mini-mart owner who rarely said anything. Except on weekends, when we held the same conversation on every occasion. Handing over my change at the counter, he would smirk and say: "I read your funny column in the newspaper today."

"Yeah?"

"Yeah ... hmm."

And that's all he ever said. He would grin at me, all-knowingly, and hum. It's happened dozens of times. He never comments on the column, never refers to it or makes any further conversation whatsoever. I ask my girlfriend to go in on weekends now, because I know I lack self-restraint.

Recently, he said: "I read your column again ... hmm." And I could feel myself saying: "Hmm fucking what?"

If that wasn't enough, I have a similar chat with a real Toa Payoh lunatic every Saturday. Without fail, she will approach me, usually around lunchtime, and say: "I read your humour column today mate."

"Yeah?"

"Yeah ... it was shit."

But I have no choice but to exercise self-restraint with that fruitcake. I live with her.

Having switched apartments, I no longer come across the living legends of Lorong 1. Aside from 'bra lady'/Rock DJ Auntie, there was Vidal Sassoon, whom I've referred to before. An elderly lady who lost her marbles in 1962, she used to wander around my block and peer into my apartment whenever the mood took her. The poor woman dressed in dirty, ripped clothes, but had the most immaculate hairdo I've ever seen this side of the Oscar's ceremony. But, sadly, I haven't seen her in a year now. She might have died, but I suspect it's more likely that staff at the local mental hospital got fed up with chasing her around Toa Payoh with a big net. Wherever Vidal is right now, I'm sure there isn't a hair out of place.

Now I'm in Lorong 2, I've yet to meet my fellow funny farmers. But I'm not unduly concerned. They usually find me. But there is a postscript to my humming mini-mart owner. Two months after I moved, he sent an email to my office. I'd never even given him the email address. In the email, he said: "I've noticed that you no longer come to my shop so I assume you moved to a new flat. Consequently, our sale of fizzy drinks, particularly the raspberry flavoured one, has dropped significantly. Would you therefore like me to arrange a case of raspberry drink to be delivered to your new apartment? Your shopkeeper." It was a wonderful, piss-taking letter. Though I was disappointed that it didn't contain a single hum.

I love these people. Despite the persistent stereotyping, they're willing to laugh at themselves and God knows, they have absolutely no problem laughing at me. That's why I've never lived anywhere else, but Toa Payoh. Why should I leave? Where would I go? To a condo? I can't see myself spending weekends by a swimming pool, listening to Caucasian con artists spout bullshit all day. Those places are more suited to the clientele at the Cricket and Polo Clubs, where I suspect I'd be about as welcome as a fart on an MRT train.

For the most part, Toa Payoh's residents have been nothing but warm and generous to me. To dismiss such kindness by attributing it to the 'white man factor' is insulting. I've lived in this estate for seven years now. Where's the novelty value in that? It's nonsense.

On top of all that benevolence, of course, are the fringe benefits. Here, I get a giggling old woman offering to show me her 'beth-seats', a geriatric Princess Leia impersonator and cheeky school kids waving their balls at me. True, we had the stuttering Maltese Tony in Dagenham, but nothing compares to the characters in my Singaporean neighbourhood.

With family ties to consider, I have no idea where I will be living five years from now. But wherever it is, the place will have a hell of a lot to live up to. Because Toa Payoh, in my humble opinion, is a bloody great place to live in.

SINGAPORE'S NATIONAL BEST-SELLER

# NEIL HUMPHREYS

Neil's Farewell Tour
MALAYSIA
Johor Bahru
Fish Crisps
FLOSS
Kranji
Woodlands
Marsiling
Sembawang shipyard
Sembawang Park
Sungei Tengah
Lim Chu Kang farms
Choa Chu Kang cemeteries
Seletar estate
Jalan Kayu
Punggol
Sengkang
Buangkok
Pulau Ubin
Pasir Ris
Changi Point
Peirce Reservoir
MacRitchie Reservoir
Toa Payoh (end of tour)
Jurong
Chinese Garden
Bukit Timah
Botanic Gardens
Pandan Reservoir
Holland Village
NUS
West Coast Park
Clementi Woods
Haw Par Villa
Kent Ridge Park
Mt Faber Park
Queenstown
Orchard
Arab Street
Fort Canning Park
Marina Bay
Geylang
Joo Chiat
Katong
East Coast Park
Sentosa (start of tour)
Kusu Island
St John's Island

# ACKNOWLEDGEMENTS

I must thank all at Marshall Cavendish for enquiring about the possibility of a third book every seven minutes. Joo Sin and Leslie championed that cause for a couple of years before I finally caved in. My indefatigable editor Katharine was then on hand to point out my various shortcomings. Usually every seven minutes.

This kind of book could not have been written without the dedicated support of staff at the National Heritage Board, the National Archives of Singapore, the National Museum of Singapore, the People's Association, the National Library Board, the Raffles Museum of Biodiversity Research and the magnificent National Parks Board. The great team at Sungei Buloh Wetland Reserve tracked down "Mr Bob" for me and NParks' Benjamin Lee went to commendable lengths to ensure that I did not die in the jungle.

Everyone at *TODAY* deserves praise for not laughing when I announced my grand plan to drop everything and embark upon a tour of Singapore. Mano, Margie, Clement and Zul offered content suggestions, many of which I dutifully pinched, and Puay Koon even agreed to illustrate my tour with a superb map. I should also apologise to my fellow columnist Siva Choy for stealing his story on the Dagenham Girl Pipers.

A decade ago, my mother ordered me to "see a bit of the world". Scott accompanied me and David guided us to Toa Payoh for a short holiday. The incomparable people of Singapore did the rest and I am indebted to all of you.

But I dedicate this book to the wonderful woman who shared my Singapore story. Thanks, Tracy, for making it such an entertaining journey.

# PROLOGUE

On 1 January 2006, my wife and I thought we were going to be arrested for loitering. We certainly looked like burglars. We were standing beside the rubbish chute on the 40th floor of the biggest Housing and Development Board (HDB) apartment block in Singapore when the shocked owner of the nearby flat appeared.

"Er, good evening and Happy New Year," I mumbled to the middle-aged Chinese woman. "We're hoping to see the fireworks."

The startled woman digested this information slowly, clearly unsure whether to call the police or hit me with her full bag of soiled nappies.

"Oh, I see. The fireworks have already finished," she replied warily. "About five minutes ago."

"That's a shame. We really wanted to see them. Okay then, we'll go back home."

"Yah. The view was great from up here. Could see everything. The fireworks were so bright and colourful. Went on for a long time, you know."

Now she was just rubbing our noses in it. We stepped aside so she could throw the bag down the chute and then headed sheepishly towards the lift.

"Happy New Year," the woman shouted after us, now reassured that we were not casing her property. "Have a good 2006."

Her sincere words were most appreciated and timely. We needed all the good fortune we could get. We had welcomed in the New Year from the woman's apartment block knowing that it would be our last in Singapore. The travel bug that brought us to Southeast Asia had gripped us again and we were now ready to head down under because we were convinced that we really needed to spend some time in a country that offered "roo poo", several of the world's most venomous snakes and Steve Irwin. The year 2006 marked our tenth here and it seemed appropriate to move on after enjoying an unforgettable decade in Singapore. That in itself was a remarkable achievement considering I only came to this sunny island for a Christmas holiday.

On 20 November 1996, I set foot on Singaporean soil for the first time. My reasons for visiting were extremely honourable: I wanted to see an exotic world beyond the red-bricked, monotonous council houses of Dagenham, England, and, more pertinently, my dear Singaporean friend David had offered free accommodation. I arrived with my old mate Scott, an architecture graduate from Yorkshire, ready to conquer the country. He planned to contribute to the soaring skyline around Raffles Place and I would ... Well, I would think of something.

Unfortunately, I did not. Scott received two tentative job offers within a fortnight. I, on the other hand, received lots of curt advice.

"I see you've got a good degree," one stockbroker said during a very brief interview at her swanky Robinson Road office. "But what can you offer *us*? What can you actually *do* in Singapore?"

And the truth was, not a lot. A six-month stint at a London stockbroking firm got me that interview, but my degree was in history. That proved to be about as useful as a Singaporean concert pianist living in London. My chances of succeeding in this country were only marginally better than the political opposition. As we sat in the flat that belonged to David's family in Lorong 8 Toa Payoh, Scott tried to be upbeat.

"You'll get a job here, Neil. The economy's booming," he said encouragingly, while trying to batter a feisty gecko with a packet of curry noodles.

"Yeah, in bloody electronics, engineering and construction. What do they need me for? My degree is in modern history. The job market isn't looking for someone to tell them who won the Crimean War."

I found the irony deeply depressing. The Singaporean economy reached its ceiling in late 1996 as Toa Payoh residents waited greedily for their five-roomed flats to hit the half a million mark. Teenagers had never experienced a recession, no one had heard of SARS and the phrase "Asian Currency Crisis" sounded like a bizarre oxymoron. Newspapers even reported the phenomenon of negative unemployment. In some sectors of the economy, there were more jobs than people.

Imagine that.

And I still could not get a bloody job.

Imagine that.

But Singapore was a different country then, in every sense. The pound cost only S$2.20, which meant a 50p bag of chips in England set me back just over a dollar. Today, every pound is almost 80 cents more expensive. And that bag of chips now costs Londoners £1. When I used to say I was from London, Singaporeans occasionally replied, "Ah, Nick Leeson." Now, they say, "Wah, so expensive."

In 1996, Singaporeans bought pirated VHS tapes from the Malaysian town of Johor Bahru on the other side of the Causeway for $10 and hid them in their golf bags and glove compartments on the drive back. Today, Singaporeans buy DVDs for $5 each and have them delivered to their homes. Failing that, a Chinese auntie turns up once a month to sell them from a rucksack, in an office broom cupboard. On the big screen in 1996, cinemas were showing some awful, low-budget film called *Army Daze,* which had grown men wetting themselves with laughter in auditoriums across the country. Not familiar with Singlish or local culture, I thought it was a terrible film. Now familiar with Singlish and local culture, I still think it is a terrible film.

On our first weekend here, Scott and I tried to find out the latest English Premiership scores, but there were no live matches. Indeed, English-language television appeared to be preoccupied with showing reruns of *Mr Bean.* Thank God that does not happen anymore. In the end, we found the BBC World Service on a crackling old radio in the apartment and sat on the floor in our sweaty boxer shorts waiting for intermittent sports updates. Today, you cannot flick through Singapore's cable channels without finding a washed-up English footballer spouting meaningless clichés to bored Asian audiences.

On the other hand, locally produced English programmes were at the peak of their popularity then, with *Under One Roof* and *Growing Up* regarded as must-see TV, even for foreigners like myself. The first was a comedy about a local family who spent most of their time arguing in a living room. The latter was a period drama about a local family who spent most of their time arguing in a living room. Both programmes are no longer on the air and Singaporeans now gather to watch a comedy about a building contractor named Phua Chu Kang, who wears yellow wellington boots, shouts at everybody in Singlish and picks his nose with a long fingernail. Oh, he is such a hoot.

Singlish was a bit of a mystery then, too. My initial inability to understand the nuances of the local dialect painted a terrifying picture of how children were disciplined here. In England, naughty children were "told off" by their parents. In Singapore, they were "scalded" by their parents. The Asian emphasis upon the hierarchical extended family is well-known, but chasing little Harry around the living room with a hot iron because he admonished the maid seemed a tad excessive. I soon discovered, of course, that Singaporeans were not saying "scalded", but "scolded", a quaint verb, last uttered in Britain by Queen Victoria in 1847 when she "scolded" Prince Albert for admonishing the maid.

The intricacies of Singlish were as confusing as they were entertaining. I was alarmed by how comfortable local men were discussing their reproductive organ. I can vividly recall David saying, "That guy likes to talk cock." Does he now? The dirty old bastard. And I thought Singapore was a conservative society. Growing up in England, friends would discuss their erratic bowel movements before they would ever tackle the subject of their tackle.

But everyone "talks cock" in Singapore now. There is a website devoted to that very pastime. There was even a movie, unoriginally called *Talking Cock, The Movie,* which I shamelessly mention only because I played Singapore's founder Sir Stamford Raffles in the opening scene.

Other than its residents' desire to still talk cock, little else remains from the Toa Payoh of 1996. My adopted hometown, one of Singapore's oldest and proudest estates, was transformed in the ensuing decade. The hawker centre where I had ginger beef in oyster sauce on my first night was knocked down, along with the old bus interchange. Apartment blocks were upgraded and painted several times, new parks and gardens were landscaped and new public facilities were opened. The shops where I bought my first mobile phone, CD, VCD, DVD, badminton racquet, tennis racquet, polo shirt and some ill-fitting underpants all came and went. In Dagenham, my former hometown in England, a new shop could stop the traffic.

Even the swanky, 40-storey apartment block where my wife and I missed the firework display did not exist in 1996. Toa Payoh, like Singapore, is a different world now.

And I planned to explore that world one more time before I left. I did not want to say goodbye to a country standing beside a rubbish chute filled with dirty Pampers, staring up at an empty sky. Where is the fun in that? No, Australia could wait. I wanted to see Singapore as I had first seen the country 10 years ago: on foot and unaware. I would venture to places I knew well, places I was vaguely familiar with and places I had never heard of. I would embark upon a farewell tour of an island I fell in love with a decade ago when I called my mother and said, "Singapore's all right, I suppose. But I'll probably be back in England within three months."

# CHAPTER 1

Singapore was laid out on the map before me. The north offered Woodlands, the gateway to Malaysia and beyond, and Kranji, home to the only wild crocodiles left on the island. The west promised the Chinese Garden, where I make an annual pilgrimage on my birthday. The south boasted a vomiting lion-fish and the east had Fairy Point. Fairy Point? That caused a double take. I had never heard of the place and certainly did not know that there was a designated area for fairies tucked away in the northeastern corner of Changi. That was definitely on the must-see list.

So I closed the door behind me, took a deep breath and spent a few days walking around Toa Payoh. You do not want to overexert yourself on these things. My trip needed the royal stamp of approval as I intended to follow in the footsteps of my queen. In 1972, Queen Elizabeth II, her hubby Big Phil and daughter Anne visited Toa Payoh and toured the blocks of 53 and 54 in Lorong 5 and I thought that exact location would make an appropriate starting point. Not because I am a royalist, but because it is only a 10-minute walk from my apartment.

On the way, however, I was sidetracked by the biggest pair of pink knickers I had seen since my grandmother used to perform the cancan in her living room. I ambled past Block 99A and there they were in all their hypnotic glory. They caught my eye because they were one of three equally roomy, and equally pink, pairs, and they were not pegged to a bamboo pole, the traditional platform for breezy knickers, but hanging beneath a window. It was a cunning method because that side of the apartment block enjoyed direct sunlight. Every time the clouds parted, the pink frillies glowed, like a scene from the old TV programme *Highway to Heaven.* God obviously likes pink knickers.

Those glowing knickers brought my attention back to Queen Elizabeth II and her visit to the Big Swamp. In Chinese, *Toa* means "big" and *Payoh* is the Malay word for "swamp". So the royal family popped by the Big Swamp. Marvellous. Apparently, there had been a number of letters to *The Straits Times* in the 1960s and 1970s demanding that such an uncouth name be changed to something more tasteful (and snobbish) like Orchid Avenue. Fortunately, common sense prevailed.

Toa Payoh was built on swampy ground and it was the largest housing estate in Singapore (rather like my native hometown of Dagenham curiously enough, which was once the biggest municipal housing estate on the planet and was built on Essex marshland beside the River Thames to the east of London), hence the name. The Big Swamp is both relevant and unique. Orchid Avenue belongs on a Monopoly board.

As I stood in front of Block 53, it was obvious why those wily government chaps of the People's Action Party (PAP) had picked this particular block for the queen's inspection. It provided a microcosm not only of Toa Payoh, but of Singapore's public housing in general, encapsulating the success of the Housing and Development Board (HDB) in sweeping away the decaying kampongs and creating a modern, urban metropolis in their place. Attempts to re-ignite the kampong spirit of community were evident at every turn. The block boasted an amphitheatre for grassroots events, a street soccer pitch, a basketball court, a decent playground, three barbecue pits (all numbered, naturally) and a fitness corner with pull-up bars, parallel bars and monkey bars.

The fitness corners are reasonably popular with the elderly across the country, but I have always viewed them as a touch Orwellian: a healthy nation is a fit nation is a happy nation and all that nonsense. But my cynicism probably was not helped by my attempt to try one pull-up. The blood rushed to my head, I felt faint and someone in a flat above giggled.

Block 53 had also been painted since I had last seen it. More aesthetically pleasing shades of peach, orange and white replaced the dark greens, blues and purples I recall of Toa Payoh when I first arrived. Indeed, gentler, more soothing pastel colours appear to have covered the harsh primary-coloured blocks that were once eyesores around the country and HDB deserves credit for that. There are also fewer blocks with their number painted down the side. I apologise if you happen to live in one of those apartment blocks, but they remind me of kindergarten drawings when a child paints "No. 15, Mummy and Daddy's House, Singapore, Asia, the Earth, the Universe" in the middle of it.

What were the town planners thinking? I think they were pissed. Sitting around the plans after a hearty lunch and a few Tigers in the midday sun, someone probably slurred, "We should paint the block numbers 50 feet high, in bright red paint, down the side of each block."

"Er, why?"

"Because red's a lucky colour."

"Yeah, but won't it be a bit dazzling for residents and passers-by, like the pilots of a commercial flight for instance?"

"Nah, it's perfect. Think about when you're pissed and you can't remember exactly where you live. You'll be able to tell the taxi driver to look out for a 50-foot-high block number ... Don't spill your beer on the plans."

Block 53 had a viewing gallery at the top when it was first opened to enable residents and visitors to watch Toa Payoh (and the other HDB estates in nearby Ang Mo Kio and Bishan) slowly rise up around them. There was no cable television in those days.

I was heading for the lift of Block 53 when a voice beckoned.

"Hey, you okay? You look lost?" A middle-aged Chinese chap, holding a bag of shopping, stood beside me, eyeing my notepad with a benign mixture of curiosity and concern.

"No, no. I'm an author. I mean, a writer. You know, a journalist."

My hang-ups have always made it ridiculously difficult for me to explain what I pretend to do for a living. An author is something well-spoken children from English counties like Berkshire or Hampshire say they want to be when they grow up and no one in their family laughs. A writer is what teenagers assume they are when they have written four angst-ridden poems as a woefully inadequate substitute for sex. And a journalist is someone who stands bravely in front of a toppling statue of a murderous tyrant in Baghdad, explaining how much the locals appreciate a good, strong Bush. I, on the other hand, stood in Toa Payoh with a lovely man who was holding a bag full of Maggi noodles.

"So what are you doing here?" he asked warily.

"Well, I heard that the British queen once visited here back in 1972."

"Yah, yah, the queen come here. She come to my block," he said excitedly.

"And did you get to meet her?"

"No, I was out."

I thought that was marvellous. Britain's monarch, the queen of the Commonwealth and the former figurehead of the old empire, popped by for a glass of 7-Up and Mr Maggi Mee was out.

"No, no. I mean, I was out of Toa Payoh," he corrected me. "I moved here later but my friends still remember her coming here."

Like many of the town's residents, Mr Maggi Mee was proud to live in Toa Payoh. He had lived in the block for many years, worked hard, put his son through a decent education and spoke with tremendous pride when detailing the academic record of his son, who taught at one of the country's finest schools. It is a familiar story in Toa Payoh. The once working-class town (many of the residents now fall into the lower middle-class bracket) bears many similarities with Dagenham, with one major difference. A child's education takes precedence over everything else, as Mr Maggi Mee pointed out: "You got children? ... No? ... When you do, make them study hard. When your son makes you proud, it's the best. When your son is an idiot, it's the worst. Don't have a 'half-past-six' son."

I adore that expression. A popular, and unique, Singlish turn of phrase, it loosely means "incompetent" or "screwed up", but "half-past-six" is much more creative. Its origin is supposedly sexual and refers to the angle of the penis. Naturally, half-past-six is droopy, while midnight is impressive. Quarter-past-three needs urgent medical attention.

"No, lah," Mr Maggi Mee continued. "Half-past-six son no good. Don't want one who smokes, drinks or takes the ganja and that white powder. What's it called?"

"Cocaine?"

"No, not that one. The other white powder. Heroin! That's it. Don't take that white powder heroin."

He sounded like a government health campaign. I only asked if he had met the queen. But I shook his hand and said goodbye, promising not to have a half-past-six son, before heading up to the 19th and top floor. Those Singaporean urban planners of the 1960s were rather clever chaps, weren't they? Toa Payoh lies pretty much in the middle of the diamond-shaped country, the municipal jewel in the centre. And Block 53 finds itself at the heart of the Big Swamp and provided both the perfect location for a royal visit and a viewing gallery.

The queen is still going strong, but the same cannot be said about the viewing gallery. I sneakily climbed a stairwell that was clearly off-limits on the 19th floor, only to find a door locked with the biggest padlock this side of Changi Prison. This happens a lot here. The government builds something, then does not fully trust its populace to use it properly.

Even from the 19th floor, however, the view was spectacular. Providing almost complete and unblocked 360-degree panoramic views of the entire country, this was not an arresting vista. It was an IMAX experience. Seu Teck Sean Tong, the bright, exotic Buddhist temple of Toa Payoh, was below me, a building that has long provided an imperious entrance to Toa Payoh for those travelling in from the north, via Braddell Road. And spotting the housing estates of Ang Mo Kio and Bishan a little further north was easy enough.

Walking around the corridor, I picked out the skyline of Raffles Place in the south, two of the floodlights of the National Stadium in the east and the green summit of Bukit Timah in the west before returning to my original vantage point, which was wedged between two plant pots that belonged to a resident whom I hoped would not pick that particular moment to water her miniature botanic garden. The clouds cleared a little and I spotted what could only be the Malaysian coastline of Johor. Hazy, a little blurred but clearly too distant, and too green, to be Singapore, Malaysian land was clearly ahoy beyond Selat Johor (the Johor Straits).

Pleased with my powers of observation, I left a happy man, albeit a slightly hurried one because one or two heads had begun to pop through the grilles of their front doors. Nevertheless, it was well worth the uneasy stares. While the coach parties and the backpackers hand over a small fortune for their minimum-charge drinks at plush rooftop bars and restaurants around Orchard Road and City Hall, similar views are free in Toa Payoh. But then, more tourists should come here anyway.

Although Queenstown came first, Toa Payoh was the first complete estate in Singapore. It is the HDB's crowning glory with polished gems on every corner. With the kampongs being bulldozed by the day, town planners built Singapore's "Dagenham" on the Big Swamp, throwing up homes for 200,000 people, one tenth of the entire country's population at that time. Missing the communal collectivism of the kampongs, not everyone was pleased to be moving to a concrete block, so developers moved quickly. Toa Payoh soon had everything: shopping centres, schools, clinics, a fine public swimming pool, sports halls and community centres, a cinema, gardens, playgrounds, a town park, hawker centres and a sports stadium. All of which were valiant attempts to foster a sense of community and belonging in a new, alien environment.

Over 90 years after the London County Council first conceived the housing estate where I would eventually be raised, Dagenham is still suffering from the short-sightedness of its architects. Social amenities and facilities never kept apace with the bricklayers throwing up the houses and my old estate increasingly resembles a ghost town, with boarded-up shops covered in graffiti and "to let" signs dotted around an estate that is in desperate need of some regeneration.

Toa Payoh has not made that mistake. As a social experiment, it was nigh on flawless. Singapore's public housing policy is undoubtedly one of its greatest success stories, epitomised by my adopted home. The oldest satellite town now looks like one of the newest, having had an extreme makeover in recent years. Boasting a new shopping hub and the country's only entirely air-conditioned bus interchange, Toa Payoh has upgraded just about everything since I first arrived, namely the apartment blocks, the swimming pool, the cinema, the central community centre, the schools, the public library, the food courts and the town garden. Everything. Like many other housing estates across Singapore, nothing is permitted to stand still in Toa Payoh. There are even two private condominiums in the area now, which means other *ang mohs* are encroaching upon my Toa Payoh turf. Apparently, they kept coming across books and newspaper columns that told them what a great place it was.

Even the queen thinks so. In 2006, she returned to Toa Payoh to revisit the same family she enjoyed a 7-Up with all those years ago. The family still lived in Toa Payoh but had moved to a newer block. I hear that the queen still lives in the same house and that it is getting on a bit. But Her Majesty cannot seem to get enough of this place and who can blame her?

As I wandered along Toa Payoh's Lorong 5, I was reminded, yet again, how grateful I am that my dear friend David was not only Singaporean, but also lived in Toa Payoh. I recalled his kind invitation to visit his homeland as we sat in our room in Grosvenor Place, one of the better halls of residence for Manchester University students, while it inevitably pissed down outside. Scott and I were initially apprehensive. Scott was not sure if he would get work as an architect in such a competitive industry. I was undecided if I wanted to live in China.

If our Singapore story had begun in Yishun or Bedok it might have been equally exotic, but Toa Payoh became our first home. And the Big Swamp proved to be my only home for a decade. If it was good enough for the queen—twice—it was good enough for me. Extremely pleased with that thought, I headed over to the Lorong 8 hawker centre. I was hungry and it was getting late. It was almost half past six.

# CHAPTER 2

It is not often that you are greeted by the sight of six arseholes. But there they were. Six photographs each depicting a pair of buttocks being pulled apart by a pair of hands.

Of course, these bottoms were no ordinary bottoms. Oh no. These bottoms suffered from acute piles. I am not a doctor, or any kind of anal specialist for that matter, but when the hands are pulling the cheeks so far apart that an MRT train could pass through, it is fairly obvious what is wrong. The photographs were mounted proudly on a sizeable piece of bright yellow card, which rested on an easel. On the off chance that the passer-by somehow missed the sore sphincters on display, a couple of colourful arrows had been drawn on the card with a disturbingly energetic marker pen to capture your attention. It was surreal. I had not seen so many arseholes in one place since a gang of drug addicts mugged me in a Dagenham park in 1996.

But this home-made board of bums was not pinned up on a wall of a doctor's surgery, but at a *pasar malam*, a night market, where I usually enjoyed a cup of sweetcorn. I threw the sweetcorn straight into the dustbin and cut out the middleman. The stall full of bottoms sold some ridiculous cream that promised to cure all of the terrifying ailments depicted in the gory photographs. Surprisingly, the remedy for piles sat proudly beside a stall selling pineapple tarts, the sausage-shaped ones, which looked remarkably similar to some of the symptoms displayed in the photographs. Not surprisingly, sales appeared slower than usual at the pineapple tart stall.

I had two queries regarding the piles cream. First, how brave do you have to be to approach the stall owner? Surely, pointing to one of the bottoms on the menu and saying "I've got that one there. How?" was not an option. Second, and more important, who were the lunatics who agreed to pose as the models? That is surely not a photo shoot to put on your résumé.

Obese people are often willing to pose for "before" and "after" shots for slimming campaigns, but would you get your arse out for a "before" and "after" piles campaign? The photographer must have barked out some bizarre requests at the shoot. "A little more to the left, that's it ... More cheek darling, more cheek ... Push them together, now pull them apart ... Beautiful, baby, beautiful. That's a wrap ... Fancy a cup of sweetcorn?" I can only hope the hands that pulled the cheeks apart in each photograph belonged to the owner of the bottom.

*Pasar malams* are fabulous though, aren't they? The night markets are one of the highlights of living in Singapore and I cannot comprehend why the Singapore Tourism Board does not do more to woo tourists away from Chinatown and Little India and send them into the unique world of *pasar malams* around the HDB estates. Whenever I am preparing for a trip back to England, the following text message goes out to everyone I know: "Is a *pasar malam* in your town? Need fake branded purses and bags for mum and sister." At *pasar malams,* I have seen handbags manufactured by "Pradha", "Pada" and occasionally even "Prada", which only adds to the fun.

Street markets have fascinated me ever since my mother dragged me around the Dagenham Sunday Market every, well, Sunday. I only went along because she always promised to buy me a "Dagenham Dog", which was an enormous hotdog with greasy onions. When I got older, a "Dagenham Dog" ended up meaning something else entirely. But they were still just as greasy. On this occasion, the *pasar malam* was one of the larger ones that visit Toa Payoh Central just before Chinese New Year and occupied the space around the amphitheatre.

Selling everything from mobile phone covers and screwdrivers to pyjamas and cream for piles, *pasar malams* exude a warmth and cosiness rarely surpassed anywhere else on the island. My wife has followed the travelling markets all over the country, always checking with the stall owners where their next port of call will be. The byword of any *pasar malam* is cheap and their appeal is universal. Children look at the toys (including the first fake Monopoly board game I had ever seen), teenagers buy the latest CDs and jeans (both inexpensive and of dubious origin), women go for the purses and handbags (Gucci and his brothers "Guci" and "Gucii"), men hover around the DIY stalls and I buy Malaysia's finest Ramly burgers.

The *pasar malam* was beside the Toa Payoh Community Library, which I popped into because it has the coolest air-conditioning and I needed to use the toilet after the Ramly burger. During my first year in Singapore, the library (which opened in 1974, the same year I was born) became something of a second home. Just before Christmas in 1996, my future wife joined me in Singapore and we rented a room from a tyrannical Indian landlady, who had a penchant for removing her clothes and baring her boobs to the world on laundry day. Her massive breasts could plug a sink. And as she leant over to do her washing, they almost did. So we were desperate to get out of the flat of the world's oldest glamour model as often as possible.

My wife has always loved public libraries while a lovely lady called Juliet McCully had decided to give me a job at her speech and drama school on the proviso that I hit the textbooks and attained the relevant teaching diploma. So we spent many happy evenings together in the Toa Payoh Community Library.

Singapore really does boast one of the greatest public library systems in the world and, more impressively, the library is still considered a viable place to hang out by children and teenagers here. In contrast, libraries in Dagenham are frequented by senior citizens who borrow books about steam engines and Tupperware. At the age of four, I was thrown into the nearest library by my mother and ordered to read more. I subsequently spent many happy years at that library, looking up rude words in all the dictionaries and finding illicit passages detailing hot steamy sex in the romance novels. When I returned to Dagenham a couple of years ago, my old library resembled a prison. It was surrounded by high perimeter fencing topped off with ferocious-looking spikes to prevent climbing. The library itself had shrunk; there were fewer books available to take out thanks to a reduction in local government funding. Working-class children need well-stocked municipal libraries and parents must force them, at gunpoint if necessary, to use them regularly. The public library is more than a source of entertainment; it is an escape route. Singaporeans should never take their magnificent library service for granted.

After rearranging my books in the Singapore section, I left the library and walked back through the first L-shaped shopping centre built here in the 1960s. With Chinese New Year approaching, the festive lights were coming on and the streets of Toa Payoh were packed with families. The relaxed mood is always convivial for shopping in the evenings. At dusk, the humidity relents a little and I often sit on one of the many benches the town council kindly provides as my wife dashes from one shoe shop to another. She is no Imelda Marcos; she just gets rather excited when she spots shoes going for less than $5, something that seems to happen quite a lot in Toa Payoh. Why are tourists not flocking to this place?

The atmosphere is quite wonderful. Apart from an overriding sense of safety and security, there is always a communal feel to shopping in Toa Payoh. Customers and shop owners know each other and chat. Uncles sell ice cream or hot chestnuts from their bicycles. Aunties read palms for a few bucks and tell strangers their fortunes. Mothers stop in the packed street to gossip while their children play or browse around the toy shops. The mothers never have to worry where their children are. It is Pleasantville, Singapore-style, and it still exists in the 21st century. I see it every night in Toa Payoh.

This scene was repeated at Heathway, the nearest shopping parade to my Dagenham home, when I was young. I knew the butcher, the baker, the greengrocer and the fish and chip shop owner because my mother sent me on regular errands to all four. Alas, there was not a candlestick maker. Today, however, Dagenham children are thrown into the car, buckled to the backseat and driven to a nondescript, all-under-one-roof shopping monstrosity on the outskirts of town. It is a dull, retail behemoth where greasy teenagers earn £5 an hour to tell you that the product you want does not fall within their area of expertise so could you kindly get lost because a senior citizen has fallen into the cornflakes' display. Britain's concrete car parks and shopping blocks are uniform, impersonal and repetitive, but they are cheaper than neighbourhood shops and an inevitable consequence of globalisation, apparently.

If you want to sample that future of shopping in Toa Payoh, step away from the family-run businesses around the older parade and head for the ultra-modern HDB Hub. Opened in June 2002 at the costing of over $380 million, the Hub has a shopping centre and a 33-storey office tower that now overshadows, literally and metaphorically, the neighbouring older mall.

It did bring about 5,000 office workers to the town centre, but they work mostly at the bland HDB headquarters, a skyscraping eyesore that towers above Toa Payoh. And yet its image is wiped from your memory as soon as you have passed it. It may have cost over $380 million but it is instantly forgettable. Whichever way you look at it, that is quite an achievement. Of course, you will find everything you could possibly need for a healthy, balanced lifestyle there: a McDonald's, a Burger King, a Coffee Bean, a Mos Burger and a Kodak photo-developing shop. The trouble is, they are everywhere else too. Eventually, a shopping trip in Toa Payoh will be about as gripping as a shopping trip in Dagenham because the shops will be exactly the same.

Before it got too dark, I bought some *ikan bilis* (dried anchovies) and gladly left the Hub hordes to have a quick peek around Toa Payoh Town Park. Although small and across the road from the choking fumes of the bus interchange, this green spot has always been a pleasant diversion with its stone bridges that surround its centrepiece—a 0.8-hectare carp pond that is also filled with turtles. When Scott and I first arrived, we often spent weekends at the park feeding the turtles after a Chinese uncle showed us how it was done. Okay, it was hardly a trip to Disneyland but we had not been in the country long and needed an afternoon attraction that cost less than $2.

It started to drizzle as I peered into the pond but several plump turtles popped their heads out of the murky water and, in my eagerness to feed them, I inadvertently almost knocked their heads back into their shells with a handful of dead anchovies. At that moment, two urchins appeared from nowhere, looking like they had stepped out of a Charles Dickens novel and into Toa Payoh. The older Malay boy, about 11 years old and clearly the brains of the operation, pushed a bicycle along the edge of the pond while his younger brother, a tubby lad of about 7, leant over the water's edge and dropped in a toy boat. Then he began slapping the boat on the surface of the pond. All that frenzied thrashing caused the turtles to disappear.

"What are you doing, boys?" I asked, a tad annoyed.

"Fishing, lah," said the tubby one, flashing a cheeky grin.

"Why are you banging that boat against the water?"

"So the fish will come over and see what I'm doing." The logic was flawed but he was serious about the job at hand.

"If the fish do come, how will you catch them?" I enquired.

"With my hands, loh." His contemptuous look suggested I had just asked the stupidest question he had ever heard.

"Do you think you'll need a fishing rod?"

"No need, lah. Aiyoh, just grab them."

And he continued to thrash the boat around in the water like a deranged munchkin while his older brother shouted words of encouragement. Bidding a fond farewell to my fisherboy friends, I had a quick look at one of the strangest buildings in Singapore. Okay, one of the ugliest.

The Toa Payoh Viewing Tower stands at the end of the town garden and looks down upon the town centre. Built in the 1970s to complement the garden, the vertical tower stands at a height of 27 metres. It has a light green exterior with a dark green spiral staircase running through the middle. The top of the cylindrical building juts out on one side, something architects usually call a feature. This means, of course, that the "iconic" tower resembles a giant penis, complete with bulbous foreskin at its summit. Being green merely underscores its aesthetic shortcomings, suggesting that the penis has recently caught a venereal disease of some unsavoury description.

As part of the town park's recent upgrading, the tower was repainted and given a little moat with cute fountains spouting muddy water. There was even a small path leading up to the entrance of the tower, which was blocked by a green grille. Naturally. When are the authorities going to learn to trust their own people? For whatever reason, the viewing gallery over at Block 53 was locked, the empty shell of what used to be a restaurant overlooking the carp pond was locked (even though the second storey provides pleasant views of the park) and the Toa Payoh Tower was locked. The message was clear: Look but do not touch because you cannot be trusted. That is how you speak to highly-strung grandchildren.

When I came to Singapore, the tower was still open and I climbed to the top to get a bird's eye view of Toa Payoh. There were used condoms all over the floor. Many couples once took their wedding photographs in Toa Payoh Town Garden. Even more couples used to have sex at the top of its tower. Combining two significant erections at least gave the tower a purpose. It is no coincidence that the government's preoccupation with falling birth rates has intensified since the town council closed the Toa Payoh Viewing Tower. To the people in power, might I make a humble suggestion: Reopen the green penis and the townsfolk will gladly shag for Singapore once again.

# CHAPTER 3

I decided to return to my first home in Singapore, only to find it was a mess. I moved into the HDB flat of David's late grandparents in Block 230, Lorong 8, Toa Payoh, in November 1996. We lived on the 13th floor. That was not unlucky, but sharing a bedroom with my then girlfriend (now wife) and my best friend Scott was a touch horrific. Allowing us to stay at the apartment, rent-free, for a couple of months was an extremely touching gesture on the part of David's family but our living conditions were becoming a Freudian nightmare. So Scott rented a room from a lovely Indian family while my girlfriend and I rented a room from a mad Indian woman who made *roti prata* with her enormous boobs exposed. We all remained in Lorong 8, though. Returning there now, the place was in a terrible state.

The government's Main Upgrading Programme (MUP) was in full swing, which meant new car parks, gardens, a basketball court and renovated apartment blocks were on the way. I visited in the interim period and found myself surrounded by scaffolding, tins of paint, bags of cement, water-filled ditches and yellow boots. The incessant drilling was intolerable. But I was here now and decided to have one last peek at our first home on the 13th floor. As the lift doors opened, I heard a voice mutter "*chee bye*". The block was haunted by a foul-mouthed ghost. I immediately wanted to move back in.

Disappointingly, the Hokkien vulgarity came from a plasterer beneath my feet, who was busy laying new tiles outside the lift.

I had unknowingly stepped on his work, knocking a couple of tiles out of place. He had a right to be cross.

But isn't *chee bye* a wonderful vulgarity? It is truly delightful and easily my favourite Singaporean expletive, precisely because it does not sound like one. It is Hokkien for "vagina", but it is so much jauntier than its British four-letter equivalent, which sounds so guttural, particularly when it is said sneeringly through the side of a Londoner's mouth. Like my mother's. That always got my attention when she called me in from the street.

*Chee bye,* on the other hand, comes across as a formal farewell to the unfamiliar ear. You can almost imagine Jeeves and Wooster crying "Cheerio! Bye!" Such a breezy exclamation, it appears to crop up at the most inappropriate junctures. Two drunks argue in a Toa Payoh coffee shop and, no matter how personal and objectionable the bickering gets, they conclude by shouting "Cheerio! Bye!" Well, that is jolly decent of them, isn't it?

Having apologised profusely to the plasterer, I found myself in a scene from a science fiction movie. The door to each unit was covered in plastic sheets. It was like *E.T.* At any moment, I expected a scientist to step out from one of the units in a radiation suit and take away my BMX. I got nowhere near my old flat. Even the lift was boarded up, which at least provided some priceless examples of Singaporean graffiti.

In a society where respect for law and order is a given, examples of anarchic behaviour often seem so pitiful, they are almost endearing. Rather like those American teenagers who occasionally loiter around Orchard Road with their skateboards, baggy pants and baseball caps, imitating white trash from a Detroit trailer park. In reality, of course, they invariably attend an international school here, their fathers are high-salaried executives and their real home is a leafy suburb in Middle America.

Singaporean graffiti is equally as lame. On one side of the lift, someone had scribbled "Your backside!". Perhaps he manufactured cream for piles. Underneath that hard-hitting attack, someone had retorted with "NO NEED TO SHOUT! Don't grumble like old lady!". On the other side of the lift, a vandal had changed tack by writing "Merry Xmas, may peace with you". The scribbler was so sincere, he obviously felt correct grammar was not required. Indeed, when Singaporean graffiti does bear similarity to the more explicit stuff often spotted inside London's telephone boxes, the grammatical deficiencies weaken its impact. In a public toilet in the Specialists' Shopping Centre, I once read "Miss X will hard suck you". Now, that would make your eyes water. And it would make you grumble like an old lady, too.

Speaking of grumbling old ladies, I felt compelled to return to the home of one of the most famous in Singapore. I wanted to revisit my second home in Lorong 8 to see if my infamous bare-breasted landlady still ruled the apartment block with an iron fist and her enormous boobs. So I left the dusty, discordant upgrading work of the government and headed over to the ageing, largely neglected world of the political opposition.

Toa Payoh is truly a fascinating place to begin a valedictory tour of Singapore, and not just because it happens to be my home. The town encapsulates the general landscape of the country and Lorong 8 illustrates its political make-up. It is a street where two distinct political worlds collide. My first block, 230, falls under the jurisdiction of the Bishan-Toa Payoh Town Council, a Group Representation Constituency (GRC), which was formed in January 1997 and covers three main estates: Toa Payoh, Bishan and Thomson. It is controlled by the PAP, the party of government led by Prime Minister Lee Hsien Loong.

A five-minute walk led me to my second home in Singapore, Block 220, which is also in Lorong 8. But this small corner of Toa Payoh falls under the Potong Pasir Town Council, a single member constituency currently under the control of the Singapore People's Party's secretary-general, Chiam See Tong, who has gamely been the constituency's MP since 1984. I say gamely because he is up against an incumbent party that has been returned to power with massive electoral majorities since Lee Kuan Yew took control in 1959. Chiam and the residents of Potong Pasir are well-respected by politicians on all sides of the spectrum, and they damn well should be.

The contrast between the two sides of the same street was obvious. The area around Block 230 was being transformed with an amphitheatre, new sports facilities, car parks, gardens and upgraded homes. But the area around Block 220 desperately lacked such swanky social amenities. There was no multi-storey car park, the units had no additional rooms, the children's playground was basic, there were no landscaped gardens and the void deck where I sat a decade ago was still filled with odd, battered chairs that had been donated, I presumed, by the residents. Everything about the estate still felt rudimentary.

Moreover, in recent general election campaigns, the PAP has often played hardball, telling voters that the estate will only be upgraded after those under PAP control have been spruced up. In other words, if you do not vote PAP, you do not get an extensive makeover. Yet the admirable Potong Pasir residents, young and old, still believe the glass is half full in their estate. Ignoring the enviable building work across the street, they proudly focus on the upgraded "speaking" lifts and the freshly painted blocks and, most important of all, the fact that their MP offers an alternative voice in Parliament. He still does. Three months after I visited my old home, the admirable people of Potong Pasir returned Chiam to Parliament with a slightly increased majority in May 2006. Political pride had triumphed over material incentives once again.

Quickly stepping down from my soapbox, I headed over to the lift lobby of Block 220 to visit my formidable old landlady. I was certainly apprehensive. The woman was now in her late seventies and I had written about her tendencies to flash her boobs and her penchant for verbally battering the neighbours before. In fact, her antics had become well-known in certain circles and I owed her quite a lot. When I knocked on the door, I half expected her to laugh and knock me out with a swift left hook. Instead, a Filipino girl answered. She told me that the flat had been sold several years ago to an old Chinese couple. "That big-sized Indian lady" had moved somewhere else, but had left no forwarding address. For some inexplicable reason, I was deeply saddened by the news. One of the most entertaining, and most memorable, chapters of my life had finally closed. I had told stories about the old woman for years and was eager to say "cheerio" (the appropriate one) to her before I left Singapore.

But I knew that wherever my old landlady was, some other poor soul was now enduring the odd nipple in the eye. Strangely comforted by that surreal image, I meandered over to Lorong 7 to see Victor, one of my oldest Singaporean friends. Just a few days before Christmas in 1996, he allowed me to use the fax machine in his photo-developing shop—for free—so that I could send off my résumé to an English speech and drama school. Victor and I became friends, I got the job and, a decade later, I found myself asking him to take me on an unusual, and slightly macabre, tour of his neighbourhood.

Adrian Lim was one of the most infamous people Toa Payoh has ever known. On the morning of 25 November 1988, he was hanged for his role in the ritual child killings that had taken place seven years earlier. In 1981, the bodies of a 9-year-old girl and a 10-year-old boy were found outside an HDB block in Toa Payoh. Lim was soon arrested at his home in Lorong 7 and the subsequent High Court trial of 1983 became one of the most sensational in Singapore's history.

Singaporeans were stunned to learn that Lim was a self-styled spirit medium, who lured women of all ages to his flat. Using cheap tricks and simple gimmicks, Lim claimed he possessed supernatural powers. The charlatan said he could cure young women of their various ailments through the guidance of the sex gods, which invariably enabled him to commit unmentionable sexual acts on women who usually consented. Lim, a thoroughly despicable and evil man, preyed on the weak and the mentally disadvantaged, who flocked to his home in Toa Payoh, willingly offering money or sex in exchange for a little attention from the gods.

Rituals included covering crucifixes and Hindu and Taoist idols in blood, dispensing tranquillizers and applying electric shock treatment. At the trial, it was revealed that one of Lim's mistresses had allowed her husband to suffer the electric shock treatment to get rid of evil spirits. It killed him.

From his "altar" in his flat, Lim told his mistresses that he needed to offer human sacrifices to the gods. They obliged. The heinous crimes committed against the young girl and boy before they died do not bear repeating here.

Victor was around the same age as the victims, when the bodies were found around Block 11 in Lorong 7. Victor lived in Block 9. He was terrified. "It was really bad. Couldn't go out and play," he recalled. "I used to play at the playground where they say the women looked for children to take back to Lim. And the church. They went to my church, too. I always used to say I was a potential victim. I lived in the flat next door and I was the same age as those kids who died. I was a potential victim. Ask anyone in Toa Payoh, they'll remember Adrian Lim."

That is why we stood outside the apartment block where the killer had once lived. Almost every Singaporean knows Lim's name. The dead man has become an omnipresent monster, the country's pantomime bogeyman, the ghost who can be called upon to scare children to sleep. Singapore's Jack the Ripper. Throughout the 1980s, parents could order their children indoors at the mere mention of his name. Yet he was arrested in 1981 and hanged seven years later. Why is the name still so familiar in Singapore? Because he is the only one. There has only been one Adrian Lim. There have been other murderers of course, but none so reprehensible.

In Britain, there can be two different murders involving children in a single week. It happened shortly after I met up with Victor. Over seven days, I read about two teenage girls being stabbed and shot. Only one survived. That was followed by a story highlighting the "happy-slapping" phenomenon, whereby teenagers pay warped homage to Stanley Kubrick's *A Clockwork Orange* by assaulting innocent strangers and recording the beatings on mobile phones, which are subsequently posted online. In one attack, a young barman was kicked to death. Although the details of both cases were published in the national newspapers, I can no longer recall any of the individuals involved. In Britain, there have been countless Adrian Lims, to the extent that their identities are now indistinguishable. And monsters are only forgotten when there are too many to remember.

# CHAPTER 4

Singapore's Mass Rapid Transit (MRT) train system is the finest in the world. It is cheap, efficient and inexpensive and never suffers from the union problems that dogged the London Underground when I was growing up. The MRT is a public transport network that Singaporeans are rightfully proud of. It has only one minor fault. What happens if the curry you consumed the night before suddenly decides to bid your bowels a fond farewell while you are waiting on the station platform? Has that thought ever crossed your mind? It certainly crossed mine as I dashed off the train at HarbourFront Station, making more noise than the brass section of the Singapore Symphony Orchestra. When there is too much broccoli and cauliflower in my vegetable curry, I can usually mimic the trumpet on "All You Need Is Love" the following morning.

But there were no toilets on the platform. Opened in June 2003, HarbourFront is part of the ultra-modern, $5-billion North-East Line (NEL) operated by SBS Transit. NEL takes Singaporeans from the new towns of Sengkang and Punggol into the business district and transports tourists to Little India, Chinatown and Sentosa (via HarbourFront). The trains are futuristic, fully automated and driverless contraptions with TV screens and bright bucket seats in every carriage. But if you need to pee, you are buggered.

Of course, most MRT stations have toilets above ground and I only made the HarbourFront's public amenities with seconds to spare. Any longer and I might have left a trail. Like most of the MRT toilets, this particular one had just been cleaned. The floors were still wet (I had been in the country for months before I finally realised that most public toilets are cleaned every few hours. I thought Singaporeans were peeing all over the floor). The cleaners were busying themselves around the sink. I closed the door and ruined all their hard work in an instant. Then I listened in on the conversation. There is nothing like eavesdropping while you are sitting on the throne.

"Cannot *tahan* already, the *chee bye,*" one of the cleaners said. Do not hold back, mate. Say what you really think.

"Yah, I know. What to do?"

"He take any small thing and make it into a big thing. I tell you, any small thing, he want to make it into a big thing. So I fuck him, lah."

They were criticising their supervisor, I believe, but the dialogue could equally have detailed a gay romp they had enjoyed the previous night. I opened the cubicle door cautiously, hoping not to find them both smiling and pulling up their trousers. But they were still cleaning their taps so I left them cursing and headed for the tourist attraction I have visited more times than any other in Singapore.

The prevailing attitude towards Sentosa in this country has always intrigued me. Say to most Singaporeans that you are off to the island at the weekend and it is usually greeted with a hollow laugh followed by a litany of reasons why the place is "so boring". Some are almost embarrassed by the fact that next to one of the world's busiest and most famous ports is a resort that is not Disneyland, or Universal Studios, or Dream World or Genting Highlands. It is not even close.

But therein lies its charm. The island won me over when we first met in 1997, precisely because it was so schizophrenic and difficult to categorise. Sentosa had beaches, but it was not a beach resort and Bali certainly had nothing to worry about. There was rainforest and nature trails, but it was hardly a walk on the wild side of Borneo. There was a water slide park and the odd simulator, but it was not a theme park. There was Images of Singapore, but the place was not a metropolis of museums to rival New York. There were golf courses, but these only appealed to a minority. And there were food courts and restaurants, but both were more expensive and less plentiful than on the mainland. In essence, many Singaporeans felt it was everything to nobody.

For a few bucks, however, the island provided a bit of nature, some greenery, decent beaches, a couple of football pitches, an escape from the millions swarming around Orchard Road and a half decent light-and-laser show to round off the evening; that is all I am really looking for from these kinds of places. But it was not enough. Unlike the Singapore Zoo, many of Sentosa's visitors were tourists and attracting locals back to the place was proving difficult. So a theme-park specialist who had worked on setting up Tokyo Disneyland was hired. Shortly afterwards in 2002, an ambitious $8-billion revamp was unveiled to drag Sentosa into the 21st century before destinations such as Hong Kong Disneyland swallowed it up altogether. By 2010, the island aims to attract eight million visitors a year. Take a moment to process that extraordinary figure. It is double the population of the entire country, and Sentosa is only a 500-hectare resort.

That explains why my wife's parents found the quaint island rather enchanting in 1998 and why my mother was none too impressed when she visited it in 2004. By that stage, Sentosa was nothing more than a glorified building site, with the Merlion offering panoramic views of half-naked Indian construction workers hanging out their washing. Indeed, my favourite attraction, the water-based theme park Fantasy Island, had been transformed into a car park. So many attractions were being closed and new ones opened that it was difficult to keep up. But Singapore can rebuild an entire island quicker than Londoners can rebuild Wembley Stadium and I was eager to see Sentosa's progress and find out why over five million people were still flocking to the incomplete resort every year.

I returned to the island the same way I had first visited it in 1997. On foot. This proved to be an infuriating experience. Turning right out of HarbourFront (which was not even there in

1997, we had taken the No. 143 bus from Toa Payoh), I headed down Gateway Avenue to walk across the bridge. The area was a mess. The spectacular VivoCity project, which will be the country's largest shopping centre (because Singapore really needs another one) with over 350 retailers when it opens at the end of 2006, was not finished and I was beginning to think I was being pursued across the country by a team of deep sea drillers. Overhead, the Sentosa Express, a $140-million light rail system, was also being hammered into shape. When it is completed, the Express will run along the top of the bridge above the cars and coaches. But I could not even get onto the bridge. A security guard checked my path.

"Where you going?" he asked, none too pleasantly.

"I'll hazard a guess and say Sentosa."

"Cannot."

"I cannot go to Sentosa?"

"No, you cannot walk across the bridge. It's closed to the public. They're doing upgrading work. Take the bus."

I muttered my consent, but I had no intention of taking the bus. A Singaporean cyclist had just whizzed past, taking the very bridge that was supposedly closed, followed by a Singaporean jogger. And the security guard had stopped neither. The bridge to Sentosa was not closed. It just was not open to those fresh-faced tourists from Changi Airport. Taking them from the HarbourFront Bus Interchange directly to the island's arrival centre meant they could bypass the dusty building site and all those scary construction workers and head for the sanitised world of Sentosa.

But I sneaked over the bridge and immediately regretted it. I saw at the counter that there was only a combined bus and entrance ticket. But I had not taken the bus. Indignant, I approached a member of staff at the turnstile.

"Excuse me, how much should I pay because I didn't take the bus. I walked over."

"You walked over. Are you sure?" He spoke to me like I was dribbling and wearing a bib.

"Yeah, I think so. I was there."

"But how did that happen? Who allowed you to cross the bridge? Who allowed you to get through?"

I felt like Papillon on Devil's Island. The corrugated iron fences dotted around the ferry terminal reinforced the feeling. A quick makan at the Sentosa Food Centre would have cheered me up but that was boarded up, too. Oh, this trip was turning into a barrel of laughs. There were a few construction workers hanging around outside the place and I asked what had happened to the food court.

"Must close. Gonna build casino here. Make more money than a food court," one of them said, laughing.

It was true. After months of deliberating over what the entire country already knew to be a foregone conclusion, the government gave the green light to an "integrated resort" (the government avoids using the word "casino" for fear of offending religious sensibilities). The family-oriented integrated resort will be sold to the highest bidder and then coach parties will come from across the continent for a bit of blackjack. I had only been on the island 15 minutes and I already wanted to leave.

So I got on my bike, a rented one, that is, from the northern corner of the island and made a valiant attempt to circumnavigate Sentosa by pedal power. After speeding past the rather artificial and rather lame Lost Civilisation and Ruined City, I savoured some splendid scenery as the trail ran along the edge of the island with the sea immediately beneath me. Labrador Park stuck out in the far corner of the mainland and passenger ferries bound for Indonesia's Batam Island sped up and down Keppel Harbour. I praised the island's planners for building such a picturesque bicycle trail. Then I cursed them when the trail ended abruptly behind Underwater World and I nearly went over the handlebars and headlong into a bloody fence.

As I got off the bike, there was a rustling in the undergrowth. Not the rustling of a skink or a gecko, but the rustling of something that eats cyclists' feet for breakfast. Taking three tentative steps, backwards, I spotted the head of a monitor lizard sticking up above the grass. As reptiles go, it was a big old brute. From forked tongue to tail, it was around 1.3 metres in length. Indeed, it was only a couple of metres from my feet, and stumbling upon it so abruptly had clearly made us both nervous. Then something extraordinary happened. Something I will tell my grandchildren in a pitiful attempt to sound like an intrepid explorer. The beast edged cautiously down the rocks and then slipped into the sea. The sea! Not some pond, lake or reservoir at a nature park but the open sea. A day trip to Sentosa had turned into a National Geographic documentary. The water was quite choppy, but the lizard swam beautifully, keeping its bobbing head above the waves. It drifted out about 20 metres and, as it turned left, it dawned on me what the clever little bugger was doing. There was a tiny beach to my left, no more than 10 metres across, which was adequate for a fleeing lizard. After swimming an arc of about 50 metres, the cunning reptile stopped about 2 metres from the shore to check that the coast was clear. Satisfied, it effortlessly paddled the rest of the way before slinking off up the beach and back into the undergrowth.

It was a beautiful moment, more so for its irony. The wild encounter occurred behind the entrance of Underwater World, an adequate, if expensive, attraction with an 83-metre-long tunnel for visitors to stroll along while sharks and stingrays swim overhead. I had visited Underwater World three times, but not one of those occasions compared to my close encounter with Godzilla. No artificial environment, no matter how realistic, can ever compete with observing wild animals in their natural habitat.

I headed into the optimistically titled Jungle Trail. Sentosa is no jungle, but the secondary rainforest has proven to be remarkably resilient, considering the British military and then Japan's occupying forces cleared most of it, using the wood for fuel in the 1940s. According to an information board, Sentosa is part of a regional archipelago that is home to one of the richest plant communities on Earth, with over 2,300 species. I had no time to count them all, so I took their word for it. Snakes with fancy names like the oriental whip snake and the paradise tree snake also hang out along the nature trail, but it is those buzzed winged beasts you have got to look out for in the equatorial rainforest. A sign warned: "Watch out for the giant black bees and the orange hornets, they may hurt you, but only if offended." How do you offend an orange hornet? Do you go up to it and say, "I'm not being funny, but orange really isn't your colour. When it rains, and my God it never stops in this place, you look rusty."

I passed a rain shelter and noticed a young Indian chap and a Malay woman engaging in a little jungle boogie. Their hands were all over each other and their tongues were more active than the monitor lizard's. They thought they were alone until an infantile *ang moh* went racing past singing Marvin Gaye's "Let's Get It On". About 15 minutes later, I paused for a drink and allowed the mosquitoes around my thighs to do likewise. As I sat under a rain shelter, the young couple sauntered past holding hands. They were both smiling and he was smoking a cigarette. It was good to know Sentosa still offers some attractions not found on the island map.

From young lovers to married couples, the island catered for all. At Siloso Beach, a bride and groom posed for their wedding photographer at the water's edge. They were not the only newly-weds having their pictures taken at Sentosa that day and I have often found their choice of venue slightly surprising. No matter how skilled the photographer, certain photos will inevitably feature some 50 container ships queuing up on the horizon. Unless your husband is Popeye, it is difficult to understand why a bride might favour such a cluttered backdrop.

Siloso Beach provided a clear indication of Sentosa's future direction. There were more eateries and the introduction of "surfer, dude"-type beach bars, something I do not recall the island having 10 years ago. There was the obligatory 7-Eleven, naturally, which is housed under the new Beach Station, one of the stops on the Sentosa Express. As much as I miss the quaint, discontinued monorail, the new station was impressive. Stopping just metres away from the beach means pampered travellers will step into their air-conditioned bubble at the bridge leading to Sentosa, trundle across Keppel Harbour, cut through the island and alight at the water's edge. I suppose that is a good thing.

The beach had been transformed. It still had that animal show, the one in which the domesticated monkey cleans up all the rubbish (a tad annoying as long-tailed macaques are native to the island and belong in the trees behind the amphitheatre, not picking up Coke cans for applauding tourists), but the beach and lagoon had clearly been spruced up. They were packed with teenagers of all ages playing various sports. Of all races too. Watching a beach volleyball match, it suddenly dawned on me that there were Chinese, Malay, Indian and Caucasian teenagers playing together. It is rare to see such natural integration (rather than integration gently enforced by schools, the church or the workplace or even the product of some patronising racial harmony campaign). After a while, though, I was not sure if I was watching the match to celebrate its racial harmony or to ogle at the thongs that some of the young women had opted to wear. A trifle concerned, I got back on the bike and pedalled off to Tanjong Beach.

I wanted to see Tanjong Beach simply because I had never been there. Hidden in the southern corner of Sentosa, Tanjong Beach comes after Siloso and Palawan beaches and is therefore the least crowded. If Tanjong and Siloso represented the "before" and "after" stages of redevelopment, then Palawan was the "during" stage. Portaloos and piles of sand greeted me as I hurried through. Other than that, there was nothing to see.

Tanjong Beach provided the perfect getaway, not only from bustling Singapore, but from the Palawan Beach building site. Being further off the beaten track, the beach hosted just a handful of Singaporean teenagers playing football. Otherwise the beach was deserted. Currently a peaceful, beautiful retreat, Tanjong Beach awaits redevelopment with baited breath. Until then, enjoy the soft sand, the clearish lagoon and the gentle sea breeze before the coach parties that currently stop at Dolphin Lagoon move a little further along the coastline.

# CHAPTER 5

After biking around Sentosa, I wanted to explore Pulau Blakang Mati. I came across the obscure island when I met the inimitable Cliff. It was mid-November 2004 and I was standing outside the Smithsonian National Museum of Natural History in Washington, DC, waiting for it to open. I was there on a writing assignment and had some time to kill. Cliff was there because he needed to pee. A jovial, ruddy-cheeked elderly chap, he ambled up and asked, "Are you English? Because I really need to pee."

"Are the two related?"

"No, I asked another chap where the nearest toilet was and he didn't speak any English and I really do need to pee."

"Well, I think there's one in the museum, which opens in a couple of minutes."

Not a moment too soon for poor old Cliff. With the cold wind exacerbating matters, he appeared to be turning blue. To take his mind off his sprinkler, I enquired why an elderly Englishman was travelling alone around Washington. His story was both amazing and humbling. After his wife died, he signed up for the Heroes Return programme, a noble travel package financed by British lottery money that allowed World War II veterans to revisit the countries where they had once served, some 60 years after VE Day. Cliff had never served in Washington, but he had family there and was recharging his batteries before heading for Australia, New Zealand, South Africa and Asia. The brave, resolute man was 81 years old and still eager to conquer the world. I praised his fortitude and wished him bon voyage. Six months later, the phone rang in my Toa Payoh apartment. The voice was initially hesitant. Then it boomed down the line.

"Hello? That you, Neil? I'm standing in some place called Clifford Centre and I really need to pee."

It was Cliff. In the flesh, in Singapore and still in urgent need of a urinal. I had given him my business card in Washington and thought no more about it. From the American capital to a food court beneath Raffles Place, Cliff had tracked down one man but could not locate a public toilet.

"Hey Cliff, how are you, mate?"

"I'm fine, fine. Wondered if you wanted to get that Tiger Beer we talked about. Still tastes the same after all these years, you know. I've borrowed this phone from a lovely woman, who's standing next to me ... You really are nice to let me borrow your phone, love. You don't mind me talking to my friend, do you? Thanks, love. We met when I was looking for a toilet in Washington."

We spent an unforgettable day together in Singapore. Cliff served in the British Royal Navy during World War II as a signals yeoman and was stationed near Penang. He joined the navy at 15 because he assumed it was an easy way to meet women.

"But you ended up worrying about the men," he said, sipping a Tiger Beer at Boat Quay. "When we were in the Malacca Straits, the bloke in the bunk above me kept reaching into my hammock. And he wasn't after my bloody boot polish, I can tell you."

In September 1945, Allied forces left Cliff's ship off the Penang coast and set foot on Malayan soil for the first time since the Japanese Occupation. On 12 September, Admiral Lord Mountbatten accepted the Japanese surrender in Singapore, thanks to Cliff and his brave band of brothers. This man was not just entertaining company, he was living history.

After the war, Cliff stayed on in Singapore for a few months, working in naval communications. Over 60 years later, my wife and I took him back to the Padang to pick out all the places he remembered: the Fullerton Hotel (then a post office), the Victoria

Theatre clock, St Andrew's Cathedral and the Supreme Court. But one place eluded us.

"I'm trying to get over to Blakang Mati," he told me and I nodded. But I nodded in that slightly patronising way. Like you do when your grandmother points at the television and you say, "Yeah, nan. That's right. It's called a t-e-l-e-v-i-s-i-o-n. You can press this thing here. It's called a remote control. It changes the channels so you watch different programmes."

"Fuck off, funny boy, I want to watch *Desperate Housewives*."

The name sounded familiar and I knew I had heard it before. Perhaps he meant Bukit Merah.

"Ah, you mean Bukit Merah? Little estate in the south, not too far from Queensway?"

"Were the Allied forces stationed there after World War II?"

"Don't know. But I think IKEA is there if that helps."

Of course, he was right and I was wrong. A few months later, dear old Cliff wrote to me and said that he had visited Pulau Blakang Mati, although he had barely recognised the place. Because Blakang Mati no longer exists—it is now called Sentosa. I had not put the two together at the time, but as I stood in front of a machine gun post overlooking Siloso Beach, I thought about dear old Cliff.

The post was called a machine gun pillbox and its location was ideal. Hidden within the dense foliage, the lookout had an unblocked view of the sea. Built between 1936 and 1940 in anticipation of rising Japanese militarism, the pillbox once housed two Vickers machine guns and most probably two extremely bored soldiers. Because, as we all know, while they played pocket billiards with each other, the Japanese came through the Malayan jungle and across the Causeway, invading Singapore from the north. Some of them came over on bicycle. By the time the poor bastards in the south around Labrador Point and Blakang Mati knew what had hit them, it was too late.

All of which makes Sentosa's relaxed setting today rather ironic. Even its name (Sentosa is Malay for "tranquillity") is at odds with its history. With pillboxes every 550 metres along the coastline, the island once formed a strategic part of the overall beach defence plan. The island had been a peaceful fishing village before it became a military fortress, first for British forces and then for the occupying Japanese. After World War II, the British used the island as a military base once again, which was when Cliff stopped by. Some of the troops, including my late Uncle Johnny, knew the place as the "Island of Death from Behind".

My Uncle Johnny was desperate to return to Blakang Mati before he died but he never made the trip. In 2004, my mother paid pilgrimage on his behalf and was left deeply disappointed. She expected sombre, touching tributes to the members of the Allied forces who had defended and protected the country from here. Instead she found a poor man's Disneyland—an island dotted with half-finished attractions, piles of rubble, fenced-off building sites, incessant drilling and crowded beaches with inadequate facilities.

Fortunately, that is changing. The superb Fort Siloso has been upgraded considerably since my previous visit. Not only does the tour take visitors around Singapore's only preserved coastal fort, but it has been thoroughly updated with life-sized replicas and interactive exhibits to give a taste of what life was like here for men like Cliff and Uncle Johnny. And rightly so. The history of Blakang Mati, both botanical and political, is there but it needs to be hunted down. The nature trail provided information boards detailing the role the dense forest played for the military and a surprising number of machine gun posts have been preserved along the coastline. Hidden among the 7-Eleven stores, the surf shops and the bistros, they were subtle reminders that even though Sentosa is evolving by the week, Blakang Mati will never be forgotten.

After a glimpse of the past, I had a quick peek at Sentosa's future. It is called Imbiah Lookout and offers several new attractions. There is the Sentosa 4D Magix, which is one of those cinemas that involves all your senses by spraying water in your face and tickling your feet, while the Carlsberg Sky Tower is Singapore's tallest observation tower (131 metres), from which you can see the surrounding Indonesian islands on a clear day. No doubt the tower will be followed by the Coca-Cola Roller Coaster and the Maggi Mee Merlion.

The Imbiah Lookout provided some splendid views of the mainland and the port, which is one of the world's busiest (a fact you are constantly reminded of in Singapore), but it also had its Coffee Bean, Subway and a pizza place, making it a little too anywheresville. But the place was crammed with tourists and locals who seemed happy enough to gorge on mediocre pasta in the midday sun.

But I was here to try the new Sentosa luge, which operators proudly claim is the first in Southeast Asia. Now, might I be so bold as to suggest that that is a rather strange boast to make. You can imagine an elderly couple from Middle America discussing where to stop off on their luxury world cruise:

"So, which is it gonna be, Ella May? Singapore or Sarawak?"

"Well, you know how much I been wanting to meet an orang-utan, don't cha?"

"I sure do, hon'. But wait, says here, this place called Sentosa has got the only luge in Southeast Asia. It's one-half go-kart, one-half toboggan and one whole lotta fun."

"Really, dear? Well, then, screw it. Put me down for the luge."

I sat down for no more than two minutes to determine where I was going when a bird left its mark on my Sentosa map. It had the entire stretch of pavement on the Imbiah Lookout to choose from but, no, it chose my island guide. Birds should focus their efforts on more deserving targets. Like anyone wearing a Hawaiian shirt.

Fortunately, the luge was only a short distance away so I threw my map away and grabbed a crash helmet. I did not get very far.

"Have you driven a luge before?" the young luge assistant asked me as I struggled to squeeze my gangly frame into a vehicle that was clearly designed for ewoks.

"No, this is my first time. Do I need to pass a driving test first?"

"Of course not, it's very simple."

And he proceeded to reel off a list of instructions that must have been lifted from a NASA flight manual. The luge was like a small plastic bike, with no visible wheels or pedals. To start the luge rolling, I had to lift the handlebars and push them forward slightly. If I did not push them hard enough, the luge refused to budge. If I pushed them too hard, the brakes came on. It was incredibly complicated. As I sat there, motionless, jerking backwards and forwards like a hormonal teenage boy, children barely out of nappies whizzed past me, shrieking at the fact that they had managed to get the hang of the luge faster than the dopey *ang moh.* I was ready to burst into tears. Eventually, after further intervention from the giggling assistant, I managed to push the handlebars forward to the correct millimetre, and I was off down the slope.

Right, I thought, I will soon wipe those grins off their grubby little faces. Using my additional weight, I gained momentum and found myself hot on the heels of the Evel Knievels from kindergarten. One more bend and I would zoom past them with a wave of the hand and a deep, theatrical laugh. But these contraptions were not built for me. Probably for Mini-Me, but not me. Scrunched up in my luge, I turned the bend too sharply, the vehicle veered dangerously to the left and my right knee came up and whacked me in the cheek. Dazed, I had no choice but to concede defeat to the nappy gang.

Undeterred, I vowed to take my revenge. I had three more goes, but those pesky, little brats caught me every time. I felt like the villain in *Scooby Doo.* If I am honest, though, I used the children as an excuse to keep going back on the luge. I loved it. But caution is advised if, like me, you have the inside leg measurements of a giraffe.

Before leaving Sentosa, I felt duty-bound to visit the old Merlion. The tourism symbol of Singapore, it is a strange creature whose origins are dubious to say the least. Surely, it can only be the offspring of an escaped African lion that had sex with a mermaid at the edge of the Singapore River. Perhaps that is what Sang Nila Utama really saw back in 1299. According to the *Malay Annals,* the Sumatran prince spotted a strange animal, possibly a large cat, running into the forest. As tigers had lived across Southeast Asia for thousands of years, he naturally assumed the animal was a lion. No one said he was a smart prince. So he called the island Singapura, which is Sanskrit for "Lion City". I prefer my interpretation of events but I have no idea what the Sanskrit is for "Lion Caught Shagging Mermaid City".

But their love child was in a dreadful state. On its left, sweaty construction workers were busily finishing off the Merlion Station, part of the new Sentosa Express. The station platform was practically in the beast's mouth. Can visitors really not walk anywhere anymore?

The dust from the building site had clearly taken its toll on the concrete hybrid. There was a sizeable brown stain down one side of the Merlion's chin, suggesting it had been eating fish head curry. But I am sure someone will have wiped its chin with a handkerchief and it will be accompanied by a gleaming train station by the time you read this chapter. And when you do visit, behave like a child and go and play in the Merlion's tail. I always do; the water pools and mini-fountains are much more fun than the Merlion itself.

I thought I had better have a polite look around a gift shop before I left. My God, I hope Sentosa's upgrading programme incorporates its gift shops. I have never seen so many things I did not want or need (except my books of course, well done Sentosa!). A souvenir shop inside the ferry terminal sold a toy poodle money bank, for what I believe was $22.90! Are they expecting Paris Hilton to pop in?

My favourite Singapore souvenir was a computer monitor cleaner that was shaped like a Scottie dog. Why are they selling such a household product? Surely every home on the planet already has one? Get one of those little beauties wrapped up and you could solve your shopping woes at a stroke. Return home from Sentosa and say, "I couldn't decide on the 'Singapore is a fine city T-shirt' or the cheongsam. In the end, I realised they don't really sum up what Singapore is all about. They don't encapsulate the mood of the people or the city's modernity. Fortunately, this computer monitor cleaner shaped like a Scottish terrier does."

Realising I was a credit card swipe away from buying every Scottie dog in the shop, I headed for Mount Faber.

# CHAPTER 6

I knew I had forgotten something. How could I leave Sentosa without watching its light-and-laser show, with musical fountains, dancing fountains and a fiery Merlion shooting green beams out into the night? And best of all, the show was free.

The attraction has certainly come a long way since 1997, when I recall it was nothing more than a few fountains swaying to classical music, with a few green laser beams thrown around. In the realm of entertaining technology, it was about as futuristic as an Atari—that enthralling tennis game in which each player was represented by a stick and every time the ball struck the stick, it made realistic beep and boop sounds. That was how hi-tech the old musical fountain show was at Sentosa.

The new version was clearly geared towards the Playstation generation. On a wall of water, images of balletic dolphins were projected dancing into the air before splashing back into the ocean. Robots shuffled along the water and beautiful women did some weird, supposedly exotic, wooing at the audience. The older spectators "oohed" in all the right places and the children appeared sufficiently entertained. Although it was not exactly a ride on a roller coaster.

But the show's storyline must have been written by someone high on LSD. The MC, who served as a conductor for the musical fountains, was energetic to an alarming degree and possibly in need of psychiatric help. To spice the show up a bit, Kiki, an animated green monkey, turned up and invited the MC into his "world".

Appearing on a video projected onto the wall of water, the two of them explored the deep seas surrounding Sentosa. Then a beautiful princess rose above the surface and Kiki, the monkey boy, declared his love for Princess Pearl, who, I think, was supposed to have pearls in her hair. On closer inspection though, they looked like inflated condoms. The infatuated pair blew kisses at each other, the Merlion shot his green laser beams all over the island and, suddenly, the lights came on and the show was over. It was like an acid trip. If I understood the story arc correctly, a hyperactive MC chased a green monkey into a dark tunnel, but the primate was not interested because he had the hots for Miss Condom 2006. Try telling that bedtime story to your five-year-old. Distracted by the images of a randy, animated monkey, I left for Mount Faber.

When Scott and I first arrived in Singapore, David selflessly accepted tour-guide duties. He drove us around the city in the early hours of the morning: three young men looking for some action. This was before hubs and all-inclusive societies were the order of the day. Singaporeans still went to New Zealand for their bungee jumping, 24-hour party people belonged in Bangkok and bar top dancing remained a wet dream. So we drove to Mount Faber to watch young couples have sex. Not literally, of course. We did not intend to peer into car windows and give marks out of 10 for length and longevity; we merely drove past rocking cars pretending to be undercover CID officers.

I thought Mount Faber was fabulous. As it rises to around 117 metres, it provided an arresting vista, with Sentosa and the old World Trade Centre on one side and the skyscrapers of Raffles Place and the Orchard Road hotels on the other. For the first time, Dagenham seemed like a long way away. From the top of Dagenham Heathway, a man-made hill built to allow the District Line Tube service to run underneath, the only visible landmarks were hundreds of red-tiled rooftops and the Ford Motor Company's car plant. At Mount Faber, the twinkling lights of an Asian metropolis sparkled in every direction. It looked like Manhattan. If you squinted. But there was no one there. On foot at least. There were a lot of cars rocking to the Kama Sutra on the way up, but Faber Point at the summit was deserted. I had always believed that the 56-hectare site had been underutilised by a government famous for developing and cultivating its land to the nearest square inch. But apart from providing a quiet place to have sex, Mount Faber offered little else other than a cable car station to take dissatisfied tourists back to Sentosa. Something had to be done.

It was. And my sitting on a No. 409 bus bound for Mount Faber proved that. The bus service leaves the bus interchange beside HarbourFront MRT Station every half an hour after 6pm on weekdays and only recently came into existence. The loop route around Mount Faber Road was established to serve The Jewel Box (a spiffy new restaurant and bar for the more discerning diner), part of the $8-million makeover the old hill has enjoyed. There was also a bistro, which offered a panoramic eating experience that would cost at least twice as much around City Hall.

I got off at Faber Point and was pleased to see that I was not alone, even though it was almost 9pm. But I was the only single person there. Countless couples huddled together on benches holding hands, with bulges in all the right places. They had only one thought on their minds: I wish that leering *ang moh* would get lost. Trying to avoid stepping on a saliva-sharing couple was difficult. Faber Point was a minefield of randy men and women. There was a signboard with a labelled photograph highlighting all the visible landmarks from Faber Point, but I could not get near it because a pair of young lovers were leaning on it and eating each other. At one point, the girl almost had his head in her mouth. It was like one of those crocodile shows in Bangkok. Pornography might be illegal but, at Mount Faber, you get a great view and a free live show.

I lingered around the signboard because I really did want to pin down the Marriott Hotel at the corner of Orchard and Scotts roads. From there, I would be able to make out Toa Payoh. But I was crossing the line from being an interested tourist to becoming a dirty *ah pek*, so I went downstairs, where there were some fine sculptures by an artist called Sim Lian Huat that depicted Singapore's history. They kicked off with the country's humble beginnings as a 14th-century trading settlement and progressed to the arrival of Stamford Raffles in 1819. Now, I have a question about old Raffles: Why is he so often portrayed in the same pose? You know, the one where he is folding his arms and tilting his head slightly to his left. The other sculptures displayed all the usual suspects: the arrival of cheap immigrant labour from China and India in the early 1900s, the Japanese Occupation, the PAP's quest for self-governance and the racial harmony bit, which, to be honest, gets a bit wearing after a decade or so.

With another 20 minutes before the No. 409 returned, I took a slow walk down Mount Faber Road. Dozens of bats flew overhead and I instinctively ducked every time one came near me. My wife always laughs at this. Behind our old block in Lorong 1 Toa Payoh was an underpass that provided a welcome short cut to the bus stop on Thomson Road. But the underpass was also a popular hang-out for bats and I was convinced that one of them would eventually fly into my face.

"Why do you keep ducking? The bats won't come anywhere near you," my giggling wife would say.

"That's easy for you to say, midget. But some of them are swooping to within 2 metres of the ground. They could take my head clean off."

"God, you really are stupid, aren't you? Bats have got echolocation. They send out sound waves, which hit an object and bounce back. The bats know where you are long before you even see them."

"All right, David Attenborough. I'm telling you, they get complacent in Singapore as everything bounces off shorter people like you. No one's almost 2 metres tall like me. The bats don't expect to encounter someone as tall as me here. When their sound waves bounce off me, they think I'm a tree."

And I swear that is true. Asian buses are not ready for me. The buttons inside lifts never expect me to be so tall and MRT trains misjudge my height. A flying mammal will eventually do the same and I will end up with a bat in my belfry. So I will continue to duck, thank you very much.

I came across another old bat at Mount Faber. She was a Caucasian woman (a number of expats live in the Telok Blangah area around the hill). Wearing ill-fitting Lycra leggings that Caucasian women of a certain age tend to favour when they are exercising, she marched towards me. She was one of those power-walkers who are taking over the planet. Have you seen them? They storm across nature parks and town gardens like demented gamekeepers and you feel compelled to shout, "Either walk like a normal person or run because you look bloody ridiculous."

This woman looked particularly menacing because she wielded ski poles. I am sure they have a technical term among the power-walking fraternity, but they were essentially ski poles, which she used to plough her way through the difficult terrain that is the smooth tarmac of Mount Faber Road. She looked really, really cool. When she passed me, she breathed that heavy, theatrical sigh popular among overtaking power-walkers. It was a real effort not to kick away one of her ski poles.

With time to kill, I wandered down to the Marina Deck Restaurant, which was shaped like an old, timber-built sailing vessel. It looked nice and nautical but was largely empty and strangely eerie. The upper platform had no lighting and I heard whispering voices moving around behind me. This is it, I thought. I have been here before. I know the signs. Whispers in the shadows inevitably lead to me being left out of pocket. I moved to Singapore after being mugged twice in England and, after spending 10 crime-free years in the country, I was about to complete an unwanted hat-trick.

Then I heard a female voice giggling. I turned reluctantly to discover yet another courting couple fumbling around in the dark. For heaven's sake, Mount Faber was developing into a retreat for the matchmaking Social Development Unit. Don't these people have homes to go to? Of course, they do, but they are invariably packed with parents and siblings. Space is at a premium in Singapore.

So is sex. The government is obsessed with the country's ageing population, the falling birth rates and its future labour force. Ministers claim Singaporeans are not reproducing fast enough. Well, all I know is, it is not for the want of trying.

# CHAPTER 7

When I was young, I wanted to be Samuel Pepys. You must have heard of him. He is quite a significant figure in British history. He was an English diarist who wrote for the *Dagenham Post* every Wednesday. Hidden among the teen pregnancies and the drug busts was a weekly column that talked about, well, not a lot. Old Pepys chronicled his shopping trips with his wife and other such intrepid adventures such as buying a new car or visiting his relatives around Dagenham. A columnist who wrote about his mother every other week? That will never catch on, I thought. But his inane musings about life in Dagenham proved strangely addictive and the elderly readers of the newspaper could not get enough of him.

Then I visited the Monument one afternoon in the City of London. Designed by Sir Christopher Wren, the Monument stands as a tribute to the rebuilding of England's capital following the Great Fire of London in 1666. The historic site notes that the Great Fire, along with the terrible Plague that had preceded it a year earlier, was recorded in the detailed private diary of one Samuel Pepys. Not only was Pepys a key administrator under King James II and a Member of Parliament, he also played a pivotal role in establishing the British Civil Service. And yet he still found time to write a weekly column for the *Dagenham Post.* What a humble guy.

Imagine my devastation, then, when I discovered that old Pepys had died in 1703, which would have made it almost impossible for him to write about getting the spark plugs in his Ford Cortina changed at a Dagenham garage in the 20th century. The *Post* writer was using a pseudonym. Borrowing the name of the most famous diarist in English history. How dare he? I never quite recovered from the shock.

So when the street sign Pepys Road leapt out at me as I trundled along Pasir Panjang Road on the No. 143 bus, I knew that it was the very stop for me. My plan for the day was to take a gentle amble through Kent Ridge Park, cut through the National University of Singapore (NUS), take a break in Clementi Woods because it sounded like a location from *The Blair Witch Project* and finish off with a sunset over West Coast Park.

But I got sidetracked. Heading down Pepys Road, I glimpsed a sign for a national heritage site called Reflections at Bukit Chandu, a World War II Interpretative Centre. It was at the edge of Kent Ridge Park, which I had visited before, but I had never noticed the museum. Oh well, I could always spare 15 minutes for a national heritage site. I stayed for over two hours.

This exhibit was truly one of the National Heritage Board's hidden gems and a compulsory visit must be included on the curriculum of every Singaporean student. With the exclusive address of 31K Pepys Road, the old colonial house was the only one left around Bukit Chandu, an area that forms part of Pasir Panjang on the west coast. Bukit Chandu, by the way, means "Opium Hill" in Malay and possibly refers to a British-owned packing plant that was located there in 1910. Yet another proud legacy of the old empire. The house had been charmingly restored and served as a deeply poignant tribute to one of the most heroic acts of bravery recorded in Singapore's military history. Notice I say Singapore's, and not British, because most of the men came from the 1st and 2nd Battalion Malay Regiment. The soldiers were mostly Malay Singaporeans, not British, or even Australian. They fought not for a Union Jack, but for a land that was their birthright.

As most Singaporean students will tell you, the invading forces of Japan took just 55 days to overrun Peninsular Malaya and had reached Johor Bahru by 31 January 1942. The Japanese eyed Malaya, known as the "Dollar Arsenal" of the British Empire, because it had produced half of the world's supply of rubber and tin since the beginning of the 20th century. Expecting an attack from the south, the British forces were pushed back quickly as the Japanese poured in from the Causeway and Pulau Ubin. In desperation, the guns that faced out from Labrador Point, along with the ones that I had visited at Siloso Beach, were dramatically turned inwards to fire on their own country.

But it was all in vain, of course. Local forces retreated to Bukit Chandu and prepared for their last stand. The battle should have been a formality. As most of the soldiers at Bukit Chandu were from the Malay Regiment, they were considered to be less experienced and battle-hardened than their Western officers. They were outnumbered and running out of ammunition but they simply refused to yield. The bloody battle at Bukit Chandu on 14 February 1942 was essentially a battle for Singapore and the odds were insurmountable. When the Malay soldiers ran out of ammunition, they resorted to hand-to-hand combat, displaying immeasurable valour in a battle they knew they could not win.

The British surrendered the next day, but the Japanese were reportedly so outraged by the indomitable spirit of the Malay Regiment that they took revenge in the most savage and cowardly fashion. They stormed the nearby Alexandra Hospital. Being used as a British military hospital, there were around 200 injured soldiers and civilian medical staff there. An unarmed British lieutenant rushed out to meet the Japanese soldiers, waving a tragically pathetic ad hoc surrender flag—a hospital bed sheet. He was mercilessly bayoneted to death.

In the hospital, doctors, nurses and civilians were stabbed. According to one survivor, the Japanese entered an operating theatre and murdered all the medical staff in the room, before bayoneting the patient lying on the operating table. This went beyond collateral damage. This was mass murder. A handful of survivors were herded into a small room and locked in with no food or water. Some were taken out later and executed, others died in the night through medical neglect (most were injured in the first place). Of the 200 who were attacked in Alexandra Hospital, no more than five survived to ensure that this monstrous act would never be forgotten. There is now a memorial to commemorate the tragedy at the hospital.

Singapore's government, particularly its old guard, is forever reiterating the importance of remembering and respecting the country's past. I could not agree more. Singaporeans are spoilt today. Children of the "maid generation" barely know how to make instant noodles by the time they go to university. They have never ironed a shirt, washed their school uniform or mopped their bedroom floor. There is little, if any, appreciation of the suffering that paved the way for their pampered existence. I am not sure they even care. While I wandered around the fascinating Bukit Chandu museum, a group of students, all around 15 or 16, were ushered in to watch an informative video about the Malay Regiment's courageous final stand and the massacre at Alexandra Hospital. Some looked bored. There was fidgeting and the occasional glance at a branded watch. I find that infuriating, particularly in a country that barely has a recorded history. The "maid generation" does not need to regurgitate every relevant fact about the island since the 14th century, but it must recognise that Singapore's history does not begin in 1959.

After lunch, I headed up the steepish slope outside Reflections at Bukit Chandu and into Kent Ridge Park. It was only 47 hectares, but its ponds and natural vegetation, including rubber wood, wild cinnamon and those sturdy *tembusu* trees, made it an unusual park stuck in the middle of the concrete labyrinths of the National University of Singapore and the Singapore Science Park.

There was also the superb Kent Ridge Canopy Walk, which was not here when I last visited. Built at a cost of $1.3 million, the 280-metre-long boardwalk opened in November 2003 to link the Reflections at Bukit Chandu museum with the park. And what a graceful combination of nature and history it was. The walk was a breezy stroll among trees that were helpfully labelled until

I reached its centrepiece—the site of the actual battle between the Japanese and the Malay Regiment. A blown-up photograph allowed me to pick out Alexandra Hospital between the trees and it seemed almost incredulous that such a serene setting marked Singapore's plucky last stand in 1942. Plant nurseries now occupied the old battleground. Somehow that seemed appropriate.

As it was a Monday afternoon in the middle of February (coincidentally, the same week that Singapore had fallen to the Japanese 64 years earlier), I had the Canopy Walk all to myself until a teenager swaggered towards me, singing aloud to whatever he was playing on his iPod. His headphones were bigger than a couple of Belgian buns and he favoured those massive aviator sunglasses that I thought had gone out of fashion with *Magnum, P.I.* When he got closer, I realised he was not only singing to himself, he was also talking to himself, which is a rare feat for those of us not living in a padded cell.

"Excuse me, mate," I asked tentatively. "Is NUS this way?"

"Yeah, man," he replied, still bouncing along to his iPod. "Keep going straight, man."

"Thanks. Are you a student there?"

"What? Hey, no way, man. No way."

He looked disgusted. I had apparently insulted his intelligence. A university education was clearly beneath him. But then if he spent all day talking to himself, he would always be first among equals.

Kent Ridge Park had one of those signs that the conscientious guys at the National Parks Board diligently provide at their green havens across the garden city. It simply read: "Lookout Point". Because if the sign was not there, you would not know, would you? The sign smacked of a fledgling garden city trying too hard. I think I speak for all park visitors when I point out that if I am standing at the top of a hill that provides unblocked vistas of the southern islands, I can deduce for myself that it is a lookout point. What is more, signs such as this one are meaningless because they offer no information. A lookout point for what? Pink dolphins? A sinking Chinese junk boat? Crazy Horse dancers jiggling their boobs?

The phenomenon of pointless signs is not isolated to national parks either. Take a walk around any shopping centre in Singapore and follow the signs. The first one will say "shops". And the second? "More shops". Well, that is informative, isn't it? And here I am thinking that I will turn a corner in Suntec City Mall and find myself confronted by an escaped rhinoceros.

In Britain, shopping centre signs sensibly inform the shopper that Woolworths and Boots are on the left and Marks & Spencer and The Disney Store are on the right. It is not a complicated system. I remember Scott, an architecture graduate, being fascinated by the lack of information when we first toured Orchard Road. He would stand under a sign in Takashimaya Shopping Centre and shout, "Here Neil, you'll never guess what they've got down there on the left?"

"What?"

"More shops! And on the right, they've got, now this may come as something of a surprise, more bloody shops! How the hell did they build such a modern mall and then fail to provide the most basic information to the shopper?"

Perhaps the fad culture is to blame. With fashions and crazes coming and going faster than you can make a cup of bubble tea, shop turnover rate is high. Retail units at Far East Plaza, for example, appear to change every week. Signs that indicate the location of Hello Kitty, cinnamon bun, 10-minute haircut and *luohan* fish shops would need updating frequently. Maybe it really is easier to simply say "more shops".

After spending a few minutes at what was indeed a splendid lookout point, I jogged down the steps that led to the two ponds in the park. Unfortunately, the native wildlife was conspicuous by its absence. The team of drillers digging up the path around the pond did not help matters. By now, I was convinced they were tracking me around the country. Reluctantly, I trudged back up the steps. It was about to rain; the humid air was oppressive and my damp clothes were stuck to my skin. And I had climbed the wrong steps. A gentle ramble around a park had somehow turned into a never-ending trek up a troublesome hillock. Then I spotted a turnstile at the top of the steps. Rather fortuitously, I had stumbled upon a side entrance to NUS, where an air-conditioned food court waited for me. Or so I thought.

"Woah, woah, woah, woah! Where you going, ah?" shouted a sprightly Chinese chap in his sixties, striding up the steps behind me. How the hell had he caught up with me so quickly?

"You got a pass? Must have a pass. If you don't have a pass, cannot go in. No, cannot go in without a pass. Must have a pass." I had not uttered a word. The man was having a heated argument with himself.

"I'm going out on a limb here, but am I right in saying that I must have a pass? I need a pass just to walk through the university campus grounds?"

"No, no, no. This not the university. No, no, no. This is private property. University not here."

"Then where is the university?"

"Don't know. Not here. See the sign. This private property."

"I've just walked up a thousand steps to get here. Why wasn't the sign at the bottom of the steps instead of at the top? Is there any way I can get back into Kent Ridge Park without going all the way back down the steps?"

"Kent Ridge Park? Where's that, ah?"

"Where's Kent Ridge Park? It's there! Right beside you! You see that huge forest right next to you, full of trees, bushes and plants? That." I wanted to kill him.

"Oh, follow *longkang*, go by *longkang*, *longkang*. You want *longkang*, *longkang*."

And he was gone, through the turnstile and into his private property. And I was left wondering whether he was repeating himself or calling me a *longkang*, or drain.

On the way down, I was accompanied by a younger Chinese man who left the mysterious building as the uncle went in. Wearing an expensive shirt and a sharp tie, he obviously did not clean the *longkangs*.

"If it's not NUS, what is it?" I asked, as I wrung out my sweaty, soaked shorts.

"We're called DSO," he replied, rather hesitantly. "It's a research company, defence and stuff."

"Wow! You work for the government. Singapore's answer to James Bond. What are you working on at the moment?"

He laughed politely as we continued to walk down the steps together. But he did not reply and the penny eventually dropped. I was dumbfounded.

"You're really not going to tell me, are you?"

"Better not, lah."

So he did not and we parted ways at the car park. I later discovered that I had chanced upon DSO National Laboratories in Science Park Drive. DSO is Singapore's leading defence research and development organisation. According to its website, it essentially strives to improve national security, working to increase the operational effectiveness of the Singapore Armed Forces and create cutting-edge defence technology. I was lucky I had not been shot.

But some perspective is also desperately needed here. The last time I watched one of his films, James Bond was not a lanky, red-faced *ang moh,* wearing sweaty shorts and moaning about "these bloody steps". But that is life in Singapore. Self-censorship has become a reflex action from the bottom up. How many times have you opened a newspaper and read about an interviewee who has refused to give his full name, even though his comments are usually inane? Indeed, it is quite common to read paragraphs such as: "An eyewitness, who only wanted to be known as Mr X, said, 'I stood on my balcony every evening, watching the dramatic events unfold. I eventually realised that when the sun goes down, the moon always comes up.'"

Some Singaporeans are so conditioned to regulate their own thoughts that, in some instances, it has become detrimental. In 2005, the country was shocked by a series of revelations concerning the National Kidney Foundation. One of the most respected and wealthiest charities in Singapore, the NKF has benefitted countless dialysis patients over the years with its vigorous fund-raising programmes. Truly commendable stuff. Until it became apparent that its top executives had helped themselves to first-class travel and luxurious business trips while staff members had received numerous increments in a single year and run up inflated expense accounts. The final straw came when an independent audit revealed that only 10 cents of every donated dollar actually went to the people that mattered—the kidney patients.

But it was what came out afterwards that really struck a chord. Subsequent stories hinted that one or two NKF employees had been concerned for some time that extravagant spending was going on, unchecked, in high places, but had opted to say nothing for fear of the repercussions their allegations might have had on their "rice bowl". One extremely courageous soul within the NKF had questioned the wasteful spending via an e-mail but was soon slapped into place by a lawsuit in 1999. There is too much deference given to figures of authority here, particularly in the corporate world. It is such a shame. Look through the country's short history and it is exceedingly difficult to find an Erin Brockovich, the woman who successfully waged war against a national American gas and electric company, or a Dr Jeffrey Wigand, the insider who took on the American tobacco industry.

Always wise after the event, there were repeated calls at every level after the NKF scandal for more Singaporeans to speak up when they suspect any wrongdoing along the corridors of power. Now the island is expected to become a nation of four million whistle blowers. But it is not as simple as that. For over 40 years, most Singaporeans did not even know they had a whistle.

# CHAPTER 8

Scott and I had never experienced such domestic bliss. Our dear friend David had moved us into his late grandparents' five-roomed flat in Toa Payoh just in time for Christmas in 1996. I thought the tiled floors in every room added a touch of opulence. We had never lived in a climate warm enough to accommodate living without carpets. If you sat on a tiled floor in a Manchester flat in the middle of February, you would require the services of a welder to prise your frozen backside off the floor. Our new Toa Payoh abode was palatial in comparison. With its marble tiles and whitewashed walls, the HDB flat resembled a Mediterranean holiday villa. A couple of Grecian urns, a six-pack of San Miguel and Sky Sports playing on cable in the background and it could have been a family jaunt to Tenerife.

Just 12 months earlier, Scott and I had been living in the most decrepit terraced house in the north of England. On the positive side, our Victorian hovel was close to the University of Manchester. But then, so was the local park. And on most nights, its benches were warmer than our living room. Rising damp was a perennial problem. In the bathroom, the wall turned black every month. The landlord solved the health hazard by painting over it. By the end of the year, the paint on the wall was an inch thick. The box bedroom beside the bathroom was even worse, with a bubble the size of a pillow emerging in the centre of the ceiling after three months. But our penny-pinching Fagin followed strict health and safety regulations. He burst the bubble and painted over it.

Walking up Kent Ridge Road now reminded me of those hard times. We were not destitute by any means in Manchester, but we rarely had any money and lived in a crumbling dump fit for demolition. Singaporean students, on the hand, are a pampered lot. They should be. Studying for one's future takes precedence over everything else here. They should not be preoccupied with fiscal concerns, inadequate housing or a Fagin-like landlord, such as ours who sincerely believed that a washing machine was a superfluous consumer durable (sad, but true). I spent most of my second year in Manchester's fine John Rylands University Library. Not because I was the university's most conscientious student, but because the library was much cosier than that hovel.

In comparison, the accommodation at the National University of Singapore looked more like jaunty seaside chalets. I felt the slightest pang of envy when I strode past King Edward VII Hall. With the sea as their backdrop, the students' rooms were modern, uncluttered blocks, similar to the holiday retreats at Pasir Ris. As I followed the winding, precipitous road, a sulphur-crested cockatoo let out a distinctive loud screech as it flew over my head and landed in the tree above. Lucky bastards, I thought. Those students attend a first-class university (NUS was ranked 22nd in the world's best universities, according to the *Times Higher Education Supplement* World University Rankings in 2005. That figure attracts just as many raised eyebrows here as it does plaudits), the accommodation is top-notch, the institution is surrounded by the greenery of Kent Ridge Park, Clementi Woods and West Coast Park and they are visited by confused wildlife mistaking the place for Darwin.

But they do not have a bar. I still find that incredible. Sitting in a food court at Yusof Ishak House, I was surprised to see a sushi restaurant and a bakery on campus, but no pubs. Some of the guys have already carried a gun through the Pulau Tekong jungle during their National Service, but they cannot wield a pint at university. As I had been struggling up Kent Ridge Road earlier, a pizza delivery boy whizzed past me on his scooter and it now occurred to me: Why did anyone on campus need a pizza? No one was drunk.

Singapore boasts more gamblers than serious drinkers, yet NUS undergraduates cannot have a beer together at a student bar on Friday night but gambling addicts will soon have two gleaming casinos to choose from, at Sentosa and Marina Bay. The irony is bewildering. But then, if student bars provided over 30,000 jobs, attracted coachloads of tourists and contributed billions to the economy, then I am sure they would be springing up all over the country, too.

At the food court, I took out my trusty street directory to determine whether or not Clementi Woods was within walking distance. As usual, I found myself distracted by the street names. Just a little further north was Dover Road, with Folkestone Road, Maidstone Road, Sandwich Road and Deal Road branching off. I could not believe it. They are all towns in the English county of Kent, where my mother now lives. Deal is one of the family's favourite seaside towns and my brother goes to Sandwich Technology School (where they told my mother during induction week that the curriculum was based on the "Singaporean model"). I had been here 10 years and had no idea that there were such poignant reminders of my family back in England. To Singaporeans, this small enclave was tucked away behind the Transview Golf and Country Club and had little significance. But to me, almost every street name represented a memory.

I took a bus down Clementi Road, missed my stop and ended up walking back down Commonwealth Avenue West, passing some schoolchildren messing around at the fitness corner of their HDB estate. Then I crossed over into Clementi Road, passed some Singapore Polytechnic buildings, turned into Dover Road and overtook some giggling teenagers from New Town Secondary School before finally reaching Folkestone Road.

And I stepped back into the 1920s. The tiny street had a charming, rural setting. Trees sheltered the houses, which were almost identical. Detached, spacious whitewashed colonial residences with black window frames were complemented with lovely gardens, swimming pools and space for two cars, which were typically Lexus, Mercedes-Benzes and BMWs. Why are rich people so shockingly unoriginal when it comes to their choice of car here? Why do they never say, "Screw it, I'll have a 1959 pink Cadillac?"

The palatial homes were aesthetically pleasing, but strangely incongruous beside the HDB estates that I had only just left in Commonwealth Avenue West. Perhaps it was not the houses, it was the people. There were no Asians. A young British girl came out of one house riding a scooter, overtook me and then knocked on the door of a house further down the same street, where other British children played on a trampoline that was bigger than my living room. At another mansion, a female British voice shouted instructions to her children and I saw another small group of my fellow countrymen playing in the back garden.

I am sure there were Asians living in "Little Kent" but, on this particular day, I only saw three—an old Chinese uncle cutting a front lawn, a young Filipina who was walking her employer's dogs and another, older Filipina who gave me a warm smile as she closed the gates of one of the houses. Everyone else was white.

It was a shock to see my culture in such an unusual environment. Every race has its favoured enclaves in Singapore, whether the government chooses to admit it or not. And everyone knows that Caucasians frequent Holland Village, River Valley Road and Cairnhill but I had never realised that bastions of Little Britain remained within HDB estates. It was extraordinary, as if several streets had been airlifted from the real Kent in England and replanted here. I could not have been more surprised, even if Somerset Maugham had wandered across in a white silk suit and enquired if I fancied joining him for a pink gin and a chinwag on the wonders of Raffles Hotel while the ladies showed off their charleston steps on the veranda. I later discovered that "Little Kent" was once a housing estate called Medway Park for British officers, who named the streets after the English Channel ports in the county. Singapore has been independent for over 40 years, but little has changed at Medway Park. When they are stationed in Singapore, naval officers still occupy some of the black-and-white mansions and the area remains a thriving expatriate community. Now, I do not begrudge the expatriates who occupy these houses. I am sure the head of every household contributes to global security or oversees a multinational corporation that generates zillions towards Singapore's GDP and generously patronises an arts scene desperate for every cent. But as I walked briskly along Commonwealth Avenue West trying to escape a cheerless shower, I noticed those schoolchildren again. They were still playing on a cycling machine at their fitness corner. Many of the gardens around the colonial residences in "Little Kent" were bigger than the fitness corner that served an entire HDB estate. Somehow, it just did not feel right.

Clementi Woods was a bit of a disappointment. There was actually nothing wrong with the park. Indeed, it was a pleasant little town garden, with the usual fitness corners, acacia and *tembusu* trees, a children's playground and a closed-down seafood restaurant. But its name had suggested I needed a miner's helmet with a torchlight. I had expected country bumpkins to stroll over from the village pub, look up at the sky and mumble, "Stay on the path, yah? It's a full moon." Or, at the very least, three disparate bears moaning that someone had eaten their porridge. But no, the atmosphere was all too convivial and laidback so I made the short walk over to one of Singapore's finest parks.

West Coast Park is easily one of the country's best-kept secrets. Residents who live in the area use it frequently and smile knowingly when they pass each other, as if they are masons walking across sacred ground, the keepers of a natural treasure. The rest of Singapore, of course, goes to East Coast Park. I have got nothing against the East Coast, even if it is a mite overrated. Indeed, when I first arrived in Singapore, I followed the expatriate dictum: You are an expat. You will go to the East Coast. You will eat its seafood and pretend you understand why everyone makes such a fuss over it. You will cycle up and down its congested paths. You will hire Rollerblades and make a complete tit of yourself. Okay, I did everything except the last part. You must draw the line somewhere.

But it was eight years before I visited West Coast Park, and even then it was not intentional. Part of the reason it is overlooked is its size. The park is only 50 hectares, a fraction of the East Coast's 185 hectares that stretch over 20 kilometres. But therein lies the attraction. With the exception of its filthy beach (which was in the process of being cleaned up by the town council), West Coast Park offers everything the East Coast offers: green spaces for sports, sea views, a bird sanctuary, more wildlife, barbecue pits and, most important of course, a huge McDonald's. And to think it all stands on the sea. The park was built on reclaimed land back in 1979 and redeveloped in 2000.

When I got there, a football match occupied the sizeable fields. Nineteen men who clearly could not count made up two teams of plump, have-a-go footballers. It was marvellous. I stood on the sidelines for 5 minutes and never witnessed a tackle. The game was played at a walking pace, which contrasted sharply with the social football at Dagenham's Parsloes Park when I was a kid. Crop-headed types with massive sovereign rings kicked the hell out of each other for 90 minutes. As the old joke goes, 10 minutes before the end, a game of football broke out. Indeed, I once observed a full-scale brawl. There was screaming and shouting and the fists finally flew when someone shouted, "Why don't you mind your own business, you fucking nosy cow?" And they were the footballers' wives and girlfriends watching from the sidelines! It was unforgettable. As the tackles flew on the pitch, the peroxide partners abused each other on the touchline. When the women began pushing each other, and this really is true, I debated whether I should intervene and play the noble peacemaker. But I shaped up the situation by examining their brawny partners. Then I looked down at my partner. I was a 13-year-old walking skeleton and my partner was a poodle puppy called Bruno. Well, it was none of my business really.

No chance of a brawl with these guys at West Coast Park. They lacked the energy. I left them to their gentlemen's game and crossed the Marsh Garden Boardwalk, which led to a pond popular with ornithologists. I was delighted to spot a purple heron, a bird more commonly found around Kranji. I knew it was a purple heron because it looked dead. This bird stands still for so long that it begins to blend into the reeds around it and you begin to think it is a model. Then just as you are about to complain to the National Parks Board for pulling such a cheap trick, the heron suddenly stabs its beak into the water and comes up with a fish stupid enough to mistake the heron's legs for reeds. And that is exactly what happened here.

I was having trouble savouring the experience though because mosquitoes were chomping through my calf muscles. Irritated by their persistence, I took out my insect repellent, bent over my legs and engaged in a petulant spraying frenzy. Then I heard a cough and the distinct phrase "*kan ni na*". That was an extremely unpleasant Hokkien vulgarity, I thought. Still bent over, I glanced through a gap under my armpit just in time to see the last of a substantial cloud of insect repellent float into a seething teenager's face. That was most unexpected. I had not realised she was there. Standing on the other side of the viewing platform, she rubbed her eyes repeatedly while her boyfriend comforted her and contemplated throwing me into the pond. With my chin sheepishly tucked into my chest, I had little choice but to exit stage left. I was eager to avoid causing a scene at the Marsh Garden Boardwalk. And I had run out of insect repellent.

# CHAPTER 9

There is an unwritten rule that owners of landed properties in this country must own a dog. Not a cuddly canine that hangs off Paris Hilton's cleavage, but a drooling, snarling, brutish creature that spends most of its days locked in a dungeon with its testicles tied up with barbed wire. The dog has only one purpose—to sniff out the poorer classes and bite off any swinging appendages. And should an unknowing stranger inadvertently stray past the capacious cavern owned by its master, the beast's testicles are unleashed and it flies at the gates, sensing proletarian blood.

I know. It happened to me. I was wandering down Pasir Panjang Road, admiring the private houses, when I walked past the garage gates of one particularly lavish property. In a split second, I glimpsed the dog. Suspended in mid-air. Going for my jugular. Although I did not catch its name tag, it looked like an Alsatian, but could have been a lion for all I cared. This startling image sent me reeling backwards. His bark almost threw me under a bus. Only divine intervention prevented me from a vicious mauling. That and the garage gates.

In Singapore, the bigger the house, the bigger the dog. It is a rather transparent status symbol. HDB flats only permit small dogs. When I amble across the garden beneath my Toa Payoh block, I always check my shoes to make sure there is not a squashed sausage dog underneath. Some of them are no bigger than a toilet roll and have that scrunched-up face that suggests they have chased one parked car too many.

But no such regulations are in place to deny the landed property folk. They want the world to know where they live and a slathering, farting savage apparently does the trick. Walk around some of the wealthiest private estates off Sunset Way and you will discern dogs bigger than their owners. Honestly. When they take Digby for a walk, it is like a scene from *Honey, I Shrunk the Kids.* You can almost hear the owner saying, "Yeah, I know. It's an Afghan hound. Big, isn't it? Wouldn't get that in an HDB flat, would you? No way. I've got three of them and they've all got their own maid. Yep, I know what you're thinking, my house is *that* big. Now, as the notice on my driveway clearly states, members of the working class will be exterminated, so piss off."

I actually had no plans to even be in Pasir Panjang Road. I had been on a Clementi-bound bus when I saw the entrance to Haw Par Villa, with a banner advertising the attraction's free admission. That surprised me. I thought Haw Par Villa had closed down years ago, and so did some of its neighbours. When I got off the bus, I double-checked with a teenager to see if that really was the old villa up ahead.

"Yeah, that's Haw Par Villa, but you sure you wanna go there?" He appeared to find me amusing.

"Well, I was hoping to. Otherwise, I'm just a weirdo asking strangers to point out national landmarks for me."

"Well, cannot visit this one. Haw Par Villa shut down already. Been closed for years."

I was not amused. Having narrowly avoided losing my reproductive organs to a flying Alsatian, my fractious mood might not have tolerated a No Entry sign. But, to my pleasant surprise, Haw Par Villa was open and admission was free. Yet a teenager who lived no more than 400 metres from its entrance was adamant that it had been closed for years.

That is not as strange as it seems. Haw Par Villa enjoys a bizarre love-hate relationship with Singaporeans and even though I had lived here for a decade, I had never had an overwhelming desire to visit. No one has ever approached me and said, "Oh, you must visit Haw Par Villa." East Coast, yes. Sentosa, yes. The four floors of whores at Orchard Towers, yes. But never Haw Par Villa, even though its history is full of eccentricity, spontaneity, egotism and philanthropy; colourful quirks that are rarely encountered in this country.

In the mid-1930s, Aw Boon Haw was one of Asia's wealthiest businessmen. An entrepreneur ahead of his time, he had a flair for marketing, ensuring that his Tiger Balm ointment was the ointment of choice all over the Malayan peninsula. It still is among the aunties and uncles. Whether you have got a mosquito bite, a sprained ankle or gonorrhoea, they will slap some Tiger Balm on the affected area before you can cry out, "Ow! That stings. Shouldn't we be using live yoghurt instead?"

With his fortune secured, the charismatic Aw woke up one morning and decided to purchase a site to build his brother Boon Par (hence the name) a house. But not just any house. Oh no, this had to be a dome-shaped mansion on the top of a hill, with six rooms, sea views in every direction and sprawling gardens containing hundreds of statues and tableaux depicting traditional Chinese myths, customs and virtues. I was impressed. I only got my brother an iPod for Christmas.

With no expense spared, the lavish villa was finally completed in 1937. Visitors flocked to the place and the surrounding Tiger Balm Gardens became one of the most photographed sites in Singapore. Although there was hardly any competition back then. Sentosa was a British military base and there is only so many times that you can take a picture of Raffles Hotel.

Of course, time waits for no tableau and Haw Par Villa began to lose its lustre. Tourists were being drawn to the Singapore River, Sentosa was slowly taking shape and Singaporean children were having more fun in Genting. The appeal of standing in front of a statue of a laughing Buddha had worn thin. The park fell into disrepair, forcing the government to intervene. The macabre and the horrific became the order of the day. Some $80 million was reportedly spent remodelling the place, with lots of electronic gadgets to jazz up the fading statues. The operators employed budding actors to work as ghosts and ghouls. There was even a boat ride and fancy indoor theatres to rehash Chinese folklore. All that was missing was an ice show.

But it came at a cost. When Haw Par Villa reopened in October 1990, the admission ticket set adults back $16. And it was another 10 bucks for the kids. Now that is a lot to fork out for the privilege of standing in the baking sun to look at a few statues. After an initial upswing, attendance eventually took a tumble, the park haemorrhaged money and it closed in 2001.

I did not even know it had reopened. But here it was in front of me, clearly desperate for any kind of patronage. It was Saturday morning, but the park appeared to be empty. This did not seem like a good idea. I was already castigating myself for my impudent behaviour when a souvenir stall owner beckoned me into the park. He practically pleaded. Oh well, I was here now. I would buy an ice cream I did not want from him and take a respectful, but hasty, walk around Haw Par Villa.

Well, it exceeded all my expectations. True, I never had any. And I will not pretend that a trip to Haw Par Villa equates to a week in Las Vegas. But the place was so damn bizarre, so eclectic and so disorganised in a country that is renowned for being none of those things that it felt like I had temporarily left Singapore and jumped into a Lewis Carroll novel.

Like every other visitor to Haw Par Villa, I headed towards the 10 courts of hell. I passed quite a large gift emporium, one of those period costume shops where you can dress up like a member of the Tang Dynasty and have your photograph taken and a coffee shop. All three were empty and the employees of each were sitting together at a table reading the Chinese newspapers. They virtually begged me to "come inside, take a look", so I compromised. I patronised their toilet.

Patronise is the right word because outside the toilet, someone had left a money box with the handwritten message "Toilet paper, 10 cents" scrawled on the side. That is not uncommon in Singapore.

But we were not talking a sealed packet of tissues here. These were individual sheets of paper torn from a roll and folded into pretty little patterns. If the guy's days as a toilet paper crook are numbered, he will always have a future in origami. I know Haw Par Villa needs every dollar it can get, but 10 cents for a couple of sheets of ripped toilet paper seemed a touch cheeky. Exorbitant, really, and it was not even absorbent.

The toilets themselves were surprisingly trendy, with smartly tiled floors and a few potted plants around the sink. Everything said modern, except the empty toilet-roll holders. Someone is making a mint here. There is probably a toilet-roll baron living off his ill-gotten gains in a colonial bungalow over in "Little Kent".

After drying my hands, picking my ears and blowing my nose to make sure I used up every last sheet, I handed over a token $1 admission fee and headed into the 10 courts of hell. The signs proudly stated that terrified children once ran out of this exhibit screaming. Which just goes to show that children were stupid in those days.

The 10 courts of hell depict what will happen to us after we die, according to Chinese mythology. The courts are controlled by Hu Fu Shi Zhe, who manages the ghosts and devils in an executive capacity, and guarded by Ox Head and Horse Face. Their grotesque 2-metre-tall statues reminded me of the bouncers who once stood outside Hollywood's Nightclub in Essex, the nocturnal dive of choice when I was a teenager. I felt most at home.

The first court of hell is judgement day, where a dead person's deeds are reviewed. The good guys are sent over the golden bridge to paradise, where there is no poverty or famine and West Ham United win the Champions League every season. The bad guys are told to stand before the mirror of retribution. With heads bowed and bottom lips sticking out, they are sent to the nine torturous courts to atone for their sins. And the exhibit has created a freakish tableau for each of the courts.

Do not go looking for subtlety in the 10 courts of hell. There is red paint splattered all over the place. Evildoers are thrown head first into volcanoes, drowned in filthy bloody ponds, tied to a tree of knives and crushed by a large stone. The lucky ones, who probably stole half a slice of stale bread or something, merely get their hearts removed. Rumour-mongers have their tongues pulled out, a fact I gleefully passed on to my wife and mother-in-law later.

Each court seemed to be progressively more violent than the last and it did get a bit repetitive. There are only so many times Chinese children can be told to be good otherwise they will get their heads cut off with a sharp implement before it gets tiresome. When I was little, I was informed that if I misbehaved, Father Christmas would not drop off a VHS copy of *The Karate Kid.* Here, they tie you down, rip your tongue out, cut out all your vital organs, stamp on your heart and throw you into a volcano. It did not seem fair really.

At the 10th court, the sinners are taken to the pavilion of forgetfulness, presumably with their head, limbs and organs all in a basket, to determine whether they will be reincarnated as a human or an animal. Just for the record, I would like to come back as a sloth.

After the blood and gore of the 10 courts of hell, I stepped back into the daylight and studied the bare breasts of the virtues and vices tableaux. Essentially a list of dos and don'ts, each scene depicted a vice or a virtue and its repercussions. The most controversial tableau championed the importance of filial piety. It was more gruesome, and certainly more distasteful, than anything offered in the courts of hell. I suppose there are many ways to demonstrate filial piety: by carrying grandmother's shopping perhaps, or cleaning her windows, cooking her food and sweeping her floor. I am sure you could come up with your own example but I bet it would not top Haw Par Villa's. They had a young woman feeding her elderly mother-in-law, from her own breast! I have never seen anything like it and I have visited Desker Road in the twilight hours.

Rather than being shy about having a boob thrust into her face, old mother-in-law apparently could not get enough of the good stuff. The milk actually dribbled down her chin as she suckled on the nipple. It was a real Freudian nightmare: a pornographic horror movie.

The other tableaux were a bit of an anticlimax after that and I have not had a glass of milk since. But the sheer eclectic range of statues made the park intriguing. There were crabs with human heads, a human band with animal heads, a miniature Statue of Liberty and, my own particular favourite, a family of oversized gorillas eating fruit under some trees. Anyone mad enough to put a statue of King Kong in his brother's front garden is all right by me.

I liked Haw Par Villa because it was essentially pointless. It is highly unlikely that such a daft project would ever get commissioned in Singapore today, when almost every landmark, green space, heritage site and tourist attraction must have a purpose, a function and a revenue target. The old villa and the surrounding Tiger Balm Gardens owe their existence to the eccentricities of one flamboyant Chinese philanthropist. In 1937, that was reason enough. There was no tourism task force required to set visitor attendance and profit targets. Just one guy who woke up one morning and said, "Yes, I see it now. A tableau of a brass band, where each band member is a human being but has the head of a cat, duck or monkey, and statues of beautiful young women with exposed breasts. Have someone build that in our garden immediately."

I left Haw Par Villa a happy man. After spending a third of my life here, it was reassuring to know that Singapore could still surprise me.

# CHAPTER 10

I do not like technology. Or rather, I am not overly keen on people who do like technology. Usually because they are indescribably dull individuals who naturally assume that everyone around them is equally tedious. If buying the latest gizmo and gadget simply because they have not got it is not irritating enough, they feel an irrepressible urge to share their contraptions with the world. Unfortunately, there are a lot of these people in Singapore. Far too many really. You cannot move in the office without someone saying, "Have you seen my new handphone?"

"Well, I have now, seeing as you've just thrust it under my nose."

"Yah. It can take pictures of 50 pixies and store them at the bottom of your garden with the fairies. Because it's hands-free, I can call someone, play Europe's "The Final Countdown" from the MP3 and take a huge dump without getting up from the toilet."

"You are a deeply boring man."

"Yah, but I'm gonna trade it in next week. They've got an upgraded model. It's purple and has Swahili ringtones."

"That's just marvellous. Tell me something, have you ever kissed a girl?"

And they are all such experts, aren't they? In a rare moment of weakness, do not ever reveal you have succumbed and invested in an incomprehensible piece of technology. It will always, always, be the wrong model, bought at the wrong price.

"You've bought a phone made by *knock-off?*" they will say, in a voice that is so loud and so theatrical that you will find yourself ripping out their trachea. "No, you should've bought a phone made by *semen.* That'll never go down on you. Why didn't you come to me first?"

"Because you're extremely sad and annoying."

"Yah, that may well be the case but I could've got you one for half of the price. Where did you get it?"

"Far East Plaza."

"Should've gone to Sim Lim Square."

"I was joking. Of course I got it at Sim Lim Square."

"Should've gone to Far East Plaza."

"Fuck off."

I encountered a tech lover on the platform at Clementi Station. He caught my attention because he was holding his child in one of those rucksack baby carriers and sitting beside his wife on a bench. The couple, in their early thirties, were both showering their child with attention, lots of cooing and giggling. It was a heartwarming sight. There was no maid. It is becoming increasingly difficult in Singapore to spot a middle-income family without one.

The father took out his mobile phone from the rucksack to entertain the child. He switched on the MP3 player and treated the entire platform to a burst of that '80s pop classic "Forever Young" by German band Alphaville. If you are of a certain age or, better yet, of a certain taste, you might have been spared this ghastly song with lyrics that demonstrate English clearly was a second language for the band. "The Final Countdown" sounds like the work of Philip Larkin in comparison. But it is an *ah beng* anthem here, played a couple of times a week on mainstream radio. I had never even heard of the song until I came to this country. But then, I had never heard of the Danish band Michael Learns To Rock either. There are no push factors related to my decision to leave Singapore. But Michael Learns To Rock comes close.

The country's fascination with, dare I say it, '80s music has long fascinated me. In that particular decade, some fine bands, including Madness and The Police, came to the fore in the music world. But they seldom get airplay here. No, Johnny Hates Jazz,

Rick Astley and Sheena Easton are the order of the day. It has taken me 10 years but, thanks to Singapore's radio stations, I now know every word to that James Bond classic "For Your Eyes Only".

There is nothing wrong with nostalgia. One of the most popular radio stations in Britain is Capital Gold, which plays hits predominantly from the 1960s and 1970s. But its popularity generally derives from the sheer quality of its selections, from The Beatles to Motown. Gold FM plays similar music here. But Singapore must be the only country left in the civilised world where a mainstream, contemporary radio station still plays Kajagoogoo's "Too Shy, Shy" with a straight face. The music is safe and conservative and the lyrics repetitive and simplistic. It is pre-Beatles bubblegum pop set to synthesizers. This particular brand of '80s music is benign and non-threatening, which could explain its longevity despite its overwhelming blandness. Either way, Singapore finds itself stuck in a musical Groundhog Day, where the nation wakes up every morning to the tune of "Brother Louie, Louie, Louie/Oh, she's only looking to me". The band behind "Brother Louie", Modern Talking, is no longer modern and no longer talking. But those German musicians, like their compatriots Alphaville, will always be forever young in Singapore.

I got off the train at Queenstown. The western town is famous for being the oldest housing estate in Singapore, predating even the birth of the Housing and Development Board in 1960. Indeed, the first blocks in Queenstown were initiated by the same chaps who built Dagenham—the British! The Singapore Improvement Trust was established in 1927, after the British colonial government finally recognised that the kampongs were crumbling and citizens deserved decent, affordable housing. The Trust drew up the initial plans that finally came to fruition, thanks to the more efficient HDB, in the 1960s. Toa Payoh proudly took the prize for being the first complete estate constructed by HDB planners, but Queenstown did, in fact, come first.

For a while, you could tell. When I began visiting the area around Tanglin Halt Road and Stirling Road on a regular basis in the late 1990s, some of the blocks were in a dreadful state. The climate had taken its toll; the paint was peeling and the apartments had taken on a dirty, greyish colour. Pavements were cracked and pockmarked, window frames were rusty and gardens were virtually non-existent. Many of Singapore's poorer families, and I have to be honest here, a high proportion of whom appeared to come from the country's minority races, lived in the Queenstown area and it was difficult not to conclude that these residents were getting a pretty raw deal.

That has all changed. The town council must be commended for breathing new life into Singapore's oldest municipal estate. Almost every block has been upgraded, with the additional room at the back, and most of the paths, void decks and corridors freshly paved. The estates, particularly around Tanglin Halt Road, now enjoy landscaped gardens that are actually being used. In Toa Payoh, it is rare to spot children around town after 6pm. They are mostly at home drowning under a sea of textbooks, tuition timetables and the *kiasu* demands of their parents. And that is just the pre-schoolers. But as I meandered around Queenstown, children were doing something quite unusual; they were playing. Dashing in and out of corridors, void decks and each other's ground floor units, some eight or nine children played hide-and-seek. Perhaps it was a coincidence, but they were all Indian and Malay. They certainly looked very happy.

And I was in Queenstown to return to a place that once made me very happy. Well, two places actually, but we will come to the Commonwealth Avenue coffee shop later. I was here to revisit Queenstown Stadium. In 1998, my wife and I decided to take the plunge and rent an entire apartment. We were craving space. Our Indian landlady already had us packed into one small bedroom and two Filipinos in another when she decided to sleep on the sofa and rent out her third and final bedroom. The prospect of seven adults, four languages and a woman lying on the sofa with her enormous boobs hanging out was a bridge too far. So we rented our first home, a three-roomed flat in Lorong 1 Toa Payoh from the affable

Uncle Kong. After signing the contract, he asked, "You're English, ah? You like football?"

"Of course. I support West Ham United."

"Never heard of them. Anyway, if you like football, go meet my daughter, Christine, at Queenstown Stadium. You can help her, tell her you know all about Manchester United."

"It's West Ham United."

"Never heard of them. Go see Christine at Queenstown."

And that is how I got involved with Tanjong Pagar United Football Club, which was then one of the best S-League sides in the country. I met the overworked and underpaid Christine (a familiar tale for Singaporeans working in sports administration) and she asked if I would help out with the fan club and write the odd piece for the club's newsletter. It was enormous fun, even if Christine had a habit of talking up her new *ang moh* assistant. I remember at one of Tanjong Pagar's matches, she took me to a half-time reception and introduced me to the S-League CEO by saying, "This is Neil Humphreys. He's joined us from West Ham United."

The closest I ever got to becoming part of the administration at West Ham came at the age of 12 when I joined the fan club and was taken on a stadium tour. We went onto the pitch, visited the dressing rooms and had a look at their trophy collection. The last did not take long.

Coincidentally, and I cannot take any of the credit for this, the year 1998 proved to be the most successful in Tanjong Pagar's history. They won a cup double, lifting the Singapore and FA cups, finished second in the S-League on goal difference and picked up the S-League Fan Club of the Year title at the end of the season. And there were some genuinely memorable matches that season watched by up to 5,000 fans. English clubs in the lower leagues cannot guarantee such attendances on a regular basis. Tanjong Pagar played to packed stadiums almost every week and was clearly destined for bigger things.

Today, the club no longer exists. At least in a footballing sense. After several years of walking a financial tightrope, the club's management eventually threw in the towel after the 2004 season. They dropped out of the S-League, citing debts reported to be around $600,000. They vowed to return but they played no part in the 2006 league season and the silence coming from the club's management remains deafening. A club that once had strong roots in Singaporean football, beginning life as Tiong Bahru United in the 1970s and producing several national players along the way, has gone.

I saw the banner sign above Queenstown Stadium's entrance. "Home of the Jaguars" it proudly boasted. Tanjong Pagar's nickname was the Jaguars. Like a Jaguar's coat, the sign was once striking with its red, black and white stripes. Now, it was faded and pathetic. After two years, no one had even thought to take down the "next fixture" window box that provided details of the upcoming match and it remained stuck to the wall beside the turnstile. A ghost town would be the obvious analogy, but for the fact that there were three guys sitting on the kerb outside the stadium. Red-eyed and surrounded by empty Tiger Beer cans, they were gently swaying from side to side in that harmless, intoxicated state, while trying to hold and read a newspaper. What the hell were they doing here?

But, of course. Inside the stadium stood the S-League's greatest legacy—a Singapore Pools betting outlet full of punters boning up on the evening's Premiership fixtures. The football club may have gone, but the gambling will always endure. Legalised football betting on the S-League and the Premiership was introduced to provide additional revenue for the likes of Tanjong Pagar. But the S-League was nothing more than national service. The English Premiership was the real cash cow and still is.

I drifted along the running track and up the concrete terrace to see the old Tanjong Pagar fan club and admin office. It was still there, but only just. The Portakabin (the management could not accommodate a permanent office inside the clubhouse; the space was reserved for the jackpot machines) was covered in rust and moss stains, suggesting its days were numbered. If anyone can actually be bothered to knock it down, that is.

With nostalgia getting the better of me, I sat in what was once my favourite spot in the empty stand. It was Saturday evening and there used to be over 3,000 people crammed in this stadium. Now there were just two joggers; one an elderly chap, the other a disturbingly tanned fitness freak, pounding the track around the pitch. HDB flats still look down on the stadium. On match nights, neighbours watched from their windows. I loved that. It reminded me of the tower blocks that overlooked West Ham's Upton Park. When we were young, my friends and I each promised to buy one of the East London flats so we could watch Tony Cottee and Frank McAvennie for free every week.

Then I sat in the press box, the name of which always was a bit of a stretch. It was nothing more than a row of plastic seats with a wooden work top laid across the top and a crackling phone line that had probably been installed by Alexander Graham Bell himself in 1876. From that seat, I once composed scintillating prose for those *Straits Times* readers dying to know what had happened between Tanjong Pagar and Balestier Khalsa. There were only about 3,000 of them, I suspect, and they were already sitting with me in the stadium. I am sure sports readers would have been preoccupied with far more important news that day, such as David Beckham getting his head shaved.

But in some respects, the perilous state of Tanjong Pagar United sums up the state of professional football in Singapore today. It is a dead S-League football club with a packed betting outlet. And no one really seems to care.

After visiting the ghostly Queenstown Stadium, I needed cheering up a bit. So I strode purposefully over to a Commonwealth Avenue coffee shop to find arse man. In keeping with time-honoured traditions nurtured at West Ham United, Tanjong Pagar matches were often complemented with supper at this particular coffee shop, which was popular with both fans and players. I always found that aspect of the S-League fascinating. You would have to go back to the days of the maximum wage in English football to see West

Ham fans and players sharing a table at a pie and mash shop in Green Street. But I was not here to spot Jaguars, I had come to ogle another man's buttocks.

Arse man worked, I seem to recall, at a Western food stall, although I could be wrong. He had two visible distractions that rendered all other memories hazy. In a certain light, the stall assistant could have been Singapore's answer to Cliff Richard. He wore large aviator glasses and had the same big hairstyle once popular with the Bay City Rollers, the one that middle-aged Chinese men inexplicably favour. But it was his shorts that made him a minor celebrity and earned him a photograph on the front page of *The New Paper.* They were once jeans, I assume, that had been cut down to shorts. But these things had been massacred. They made the famous Daisy Duke hot pants in the *Dukes of Hazzard* look like flared trousers. When this guy turned the other cheek, everyone in the coffee shop saw it. The shorts were cut at least one inch above the groove between bum and thigh, showing off the pale white fleshy parts. When he bent over, the little hairy brain was almost visible. No one ever ordered his chicken frankfurter.

His bizarre ensemble was rounded off with a pair of wellington boots, which, in my mind's eye, are yellow but that could be attributed to Phua Chu Kang. He was certainly a sight to behold. With the aviator glasses, the wellies and the exposed crack, I had always hoped he would suddenly throw down the plates and give us a quick verse of "YMCA".

I checked every stall, but he obviously was not there. He is not a man who is difficult to pick out in a crowd. The Western stall where I thought he worked was closed, so I asked the neighbouring stall holder about him. Now, this was a difficult conversation.

"I'm looking for a guy who worked at this coffee shop. I think he worked at the stall next door to you."

"Sure thing, man. What he look like?"

Now, how was I supposed to answer this question? He was a Chinese man in his 30s who looked like Cliff Richard and mooned all his customers.

"Er, well, he's Chinese, wears big spectacles and likes to wear, er, shorts, you know? Short shorts."

I demonstrated their cropped length and the old uncle smiled. He knew who I meant.

"He's not working today. Doesn't work weekends," he laughed. "But don't worry, he still works here."

That was good to know. Singapore's oldest housing estate needs a little continuity. Its S-League football club may have gone, but there are compensations. Arse man is still around. May he bare his chiselled buttocks to all and sundry for many years to come. Feeling strangely uplifted by that thought, I ambled back to Queenstown Station humming "Forever young! I wanna be forever young!"

# CHAPTER 11

At this point of my farewell tour, I decided to take a detour. I planned to visit Singapore's sprawling empire. Like neighbouring Indonesia, Singapore has a number of islands under its flag. Indonesia has over 13,500; Singapore has Kusu Island and St John's Island. Yes, all right, I am being flippant. Singapore has tens of islands it can proudly call its own but they are not serviced by a ferry on Sundays. Kusu Island and St John's Island are. These two islands form part of the Southern Islands, which are located about 6 kilometres off the coast of Singapore. Until the Sentosa Leisure Group started providing regular ferries to both islands, visitors had to rely on old sampans and bumboats. But we are spoilt now; all I had to do was be at Sentosa Ferry Terminal by 11am.

Inevitably, I was 2 minutes late. Still stuck in the stubborn mindset that I can reach anywhere within half an hour, I left Toa Payoh at 10.20am and fully expected to be 10 minutes early. I took the train from Braddell Station, changed at Dhoby Ghaut, alighted at HarbourFront, ran like a madman who never exercises to the bus interchange to catch the Sentosa feeder bus, then grabbed a poor teenage member of staff wearing the bright orange Sentosa shirt and ordered him to send a message to the ferry terminal. But I was so out of breath I could barely speak.

"Tell ... them ... wait. Don't shoot off ... I coming ... over ... John ... right now." The boy looked scared.

The bus got caught at some traffic lights as the clock on board read 10.59am. At the Sentosa arrival counter, I made the same plea before dragging my shaking legs and nauseous stomach off to the ferry terminal. I looked at the clock on the wall. It was 11.02am. There was no ferry. At the counter, the sign read "Next ferry: 1pm". I suddenly felt faint.

"Next please," said a far too chirpy girl working behind the counter. She got a shock when she saw a sweaty, blotchy-faced *ang moh* desperately trying not to vomit over her counter.

"Has the 11am ferry gone already?"

"Yes, sir, it left right on time." I looked up and down Keppel Harbour but could not see it.

"Excuse me, is it a ferry or a rocket-propelled speedboat? It's completely disappeared?"

"Ooh, it's very fast. Always leaves on time."

No, it does not. After spending the next two hours in an oxygen tent, I returned to the ferry terminal promptly at 12.50pm and was the first person on the bright orange ferry, which boasted agreeable air conditioning and comfy plush seats. We did not move for what seemed like an eternity.

"What's the time, mate?" I asked a Malay chap next to me.

It was 1.05pm. I was not pleased. And I really should start wearing a watch. The ferry's captain sounded the horn for departure then stopped to allow three extremely handsome and giggling young German couples to board. It was 1.07pm. Cheeky bastards. I have nothing against Germans, you understand, I am just deeply suspicious of any nation that sends David Hasselhoff to the top of its music charts.

Finally, after I had visualised several ways to drown six young Germans at Kusu Island without being caught, the ferry zoomed away. The counter girl was right. It was a fast vessel.

Like many Singaporeans, I first visited Kusu Island during the ninth lunar month (which falls between September and November, according to the Lunar Calendar). Cheap ferries take across thousands of devotees for their annual Kusu Pilgrimage to pray for health, peace, happiness and the winning 4D numbers. I go to stock up on cheap Buddha statues for my mother. You cannot move in her house for laughing Buddhas with fat bellies. They giggle at you from the living room, the dining room and even the back garden. It is certainly an interesting blend of cultures. My mother lives in a semi-detached house in Kent. She loves to tell the story that her son braved the elements in an old sampan to visit a remote, cloud-topped island in the South China Sea. There, the indigenous people spend many months mining for precious stones before handcrafting beautiful delicate Buddha statues, a tradition that has been passed down from generation to generation. In reality, of course, I boarded a packed ferry during the ninth lunar month and bought three statues for $10 on Kusu Island.

I do like Kusu Island (Kusu means "tortoise" in Chinese). Tortoises loom large in the island's legends because there is a similarity in shape, hence the island's name. According to one legend, a magical tortoise transformed into an island to save two shipwrecked sailors, a Malay and a Chinese, which sounds plausible enough. Just 5.6 kilometres from Singapore, Kusu is only 8.5 hectares in size, giving it a cosy, intimate feel. At its centre are the turtle lagoon and a Chinese temple called Da Bo Gong (God of Prosperity). The temple was built by a wealthy businessman in 1923 and is where the Chinese come in droves during the ninth lunar month. I had a polite look around. Unless you have a penchant for looking at pythons locked up in a cage with a donation box stuck on one of the bars, there really is not much to see. But I was desperate to escape from the insufferable midday heat.

The tortoise sanctuary outside the temple has always intrigued me because it is usually full of turtles. On this particular day, there were dozens of turtles splashing around in the concrete bay and just a couple of tortoises thrown in to ensure that Sentosa Leisure Group does not fall foul of the Trade Descriptions Act. I spent several minutes watching an elderly tortoise do nothing. Is there a more boring animal on the planet than the tortoise? A gathering of tortoises is not an exhibit; it is a tableau. A couple of Chinese teenagers took several photographs with the tortoise sanctuary behind them. Why? The backdrop is not going to change. You will never hear a tourist say, "Quick, Alfie, stand still. I want to get you and the tortoise in the same shot ... Damn it, the tortoise just ran off."

The tortoise sanctuary was certainly a more pleasant experience out of season. The coming of the ninth lunar month is the death knell for most of the defenceless animals. I visited one evening a couple of years ago and watched a cleaner sweep up half a dozen dead turtles. He said it was a daily feature of his work, but not a surprising one. Idiots grabbed the turtles to pose with them for photographs, turned them over and poked them to satisfy their morbid curiosity or, worse yet, handed them to their small children to play with. Of course, pick up any creature and it will react. Admittedly, a turtle hardly has the reflexes of a cheetah, but the reptile's head suddenly withdraws and its stumpy feet stretch out. This reaction invariably leads to some ditzy teenager screaming and throwing it across the sanctuary. When this happens, the food chain's hierarchy has to be seriously questioned.

I ambled round the back of Kusu to my favourite part of the island. It is nothing more than a beach really. But it is an undisturbed, pristine one. The sand is soft and always clean, the blue lagoon is generally pellucid and a decent spot for some rare snorkelling and the splendid scenery includes Singapore's Lazarus Island on the right and Indonesia's Batam Island way off on the left. And I usually get it all to myself.

I sat down under one of the many beach shelters to remove my sweaty socks and allow the red ants to eat my toes when I spotted my German friends again. With the entire lagoon to themselves, they were picnicking, sunbathing and snorkelling. Behind them was a rugged hillock with a Malay shrine of three *keramats* (holy shrines of Malay saints) at the top, which added a touch of Asian exotica to the setting. There was even a lifeguard on duty to ensure the German tourists did not drown. The beach setting was so tranquil, so perfect, I am surprised Alex Garland has not written a novel about it. Rock stars are always bitching about travelling to the far ends of the Earth to find an exclusive beach in the Caribbean to escape the paparazzi. Nonsense. Come to Kusu Island. Privacy is always guaranteed. No one will ever find you.

And what about Singaporeans? In contrast to the golden sands at Kusu, East Coast Park and the Sentosa beaches are crowded at the weekend, even though they offer dirtier beaches and certainly fewer snorkelling opportunities. And cleanliness is a given here. I noticed three cleaners sweeping the paths and beaches and there could not have been more than 50 people on the entire island. Kusu's beaches may be few, but they are immaculate compared to those at both Bali and Phuket and you will not be bothered every five minutes by locals asking to braid your hair or massage your back.

The cost of an $11-ferry ticket provides Singaporeans with a secluded location for a few beers with poly mates, safe beach shelters and a lagoon where you can ogle your girlfriend's white bits and perhaps even squeeze one or two of them. Suggest a weekend trip to Kusu Island to most Singaporeans, however, and they will laugh. But they will never have the last laugh. That is reserved for the German tourists who had a stunning blue lagoon to themselves on a glorious Sunday afternoon.

I had high expectations for St John's Island as I had never been there before. The island is 6.5 kilometres south of Singapore, making it the southernmost point of my valedictory tour. And I was fascinated by its modern history. It is generally agreed that in his search for a post to protect British trade in the region, old Raffles came to Singapore in 1819 and anchored his fleet of eight ships off St John's Island. You would think there would be a plaque to commemorate this event on the island, but if there is one, it is well hidden.

The island's history then gets juicy. In 1874, the island became a quarantine area for cholera-stricken Chinese immigrants. By the 1930s, St John's had achieved the proud status of being the world's largest quarantine centre, screening both Asian immigrants and pilgrims returning from Mecca. Now, why isn't that little-known fact included in the Singapore Tourism Board's guidebooks? The country is always looking for opportunities to be the world's biggest or best. Best airline, best airport, best container port and best cholera quarantine centre. Why not? The day after I visited Cholera Cove, I mean St John's Island, there was a coordinated attempt at all the golf clubs in the country to set a new world record for the biggest simultaneous golf tee off. And the story made the prime pages of all the national newspapers. That is, unfortunately, one of the drawbacks of living in a comparatively crime-free, corruption-free country. You have to endure unbelievably humdrum news stories from time to time.

But a former cholera colony sounded so exciting. I half expected the ghosts of the victims, with sunken eyes and wrinkled skin, to float between *tembusu* trees and throw coconuts at unsuspecting visitors. But alas, all I encountered was a sun-burnt German tourist. Clearly agitated, he paced up and down the jetty three times before re-boarding the ferry. Perhaps he knew something I did not.

It is not just Raffles and cholera though. In the 1950s, St John's Island also hosted political detainees, including the late Devan Nair, who went on to become Singapore's third president (1981–1985). The island then enjoyed a spell as a rehabilitation centre for opium addicts before some bright spark decided to turn St John's into a resort for holidaymakers in 1975.

The fruits of that labour were self-evident as soon as I stepped off the ferry. Construction workers were putting the finishing touches to a bridge that connected St John's with Lazarus Island. The Sentosa Leisure Group now controls the Southern Islands of Kusu, Lazarus, Seringat, Sisters and St John's and plans to join them all together by ferry or walkway.

Even without that connection, St John's is a 39-hectare hilly island that has long been touted as a premier nature haven. So I followed a path past the Holiday Bungalow, which was basic and rustic but in dire need of a lick of paint, and into the little forest that remained. There was a distant, spooky hum. Paranoia might be to blame but I was convinced that it sounded exactly like hundreds of cholera victims groaning all at once. I was also aware that I was completely alone. I continued along a path that led to the Tropical

Marine Science Institute, where one of those threatening signs that are so common in Singapore warned that all trespassers would be hung, drawn and quartered.

Not wishing to retread the same path, I stumbled around in the forest for a bit only to encounter broken, concrete staircases that suddenly stopped halfway up the slope or paths that ended abruptly at a fence. I appeared to be going round in circles. Wherever I looked, there were crumbling staircases or remnants of brick walls lying in the undergrowth. Thick tree roots dramatically protruded through cracked paths at regular intervals. Naturally, my foot found the biggest root and I managed to execute a near perfect forward roll while wearing a rucksack. Like the film tag line once said: "In the forest, no one hears you scream, 'Bloody bastard of a tree!'"

This is it, I thought, as I pulled the spiders' webs out of my hair and examined the scratches on my leg. This is where I am going to die. I had no idea where I was and I had drunk the last of my water hours ago on Kusu. I was hungry, increasingly sunburnt and had just ruined the home of an irate black-and-yellow spider the size of my hand. Although St John's Island had a certain ring to it, as John is my middle name and the name of my father, it just was not glamorous enough. If I had to die prematurely in Singapore, I hoped to be knocked down by a hot *mamasan* in Chinatown's Neil Road. That is almost poetic.

This, on the other hand, was a shambles. Eventually, I completed one big circle of nothing in terms of places of interest and ended up back at the ferry terminal. Kusu Island was a weekend on *Temptation Island* in comparison. I headed off down another path and walked past a tired-looking basketball court that was fenced in and surrounded by rolls of rusty barbed wire. In obsessing over finding something of interest in the forest, I had been oblivious to an obvious feature of the place. The island was surrounded by high fences and barbed wire. In every direction. There were even watchtowers. It felt like a childhood holiday to an old Butlins Holiday Camp in England, where once you had paid your admission fee, the barbed wire was employed to keep you from escaping.

I had another look at the map of St John's and noticed, to my surprise, that the island did at least have a cafeteria. And it most certainly did ... but it was closed. Being on a hillock, however, it did offer me sweeping views of the nearby fences and watchtowers. If you substituted the Raffles Place skyline for that of San Francisco Bay, this could have been Alcatraz. When I returned home, I discovered that, in 1999, a part of St John's Island had been sectioned off to detain illegal immigrants. Now, doesn't that sound just the ideal destination to take the kiddies for a game of beach volleyball?

On its website, Sentosa Leisure Group says its redevelopment plans for the Southern Islands will eventually include "residential, resort, and entertainment facilities", but is rather short on details. Whatever the plans are, execute them quickly. St John's Island offers little attraction because it has no focal point. There is no real reason to come here. Kusu Island has its temples and beaches, Bukit Timah has its summit and nature trails, East Coast has its seafood and water sports and Pulau Ubin has its nostalgic kampong lifestyle. St John's has barbed wire and watchtowers.

Dehydrated and exhausted, I sat at the jetty and waited for the last ferry back to Sentosa. I was early, but there really was nowhere else to go. Apart from a handful of Malay fishermen, I was the only person there. Low, dark clouds accompanied by thunderclaps suggested a downpour was imminent and the whole island now looked gloomy. In the distance, I spotted about 10 birds of prey hovering somewhere behind Lazarus Island. Through my "geeky" binoculars (so christened by my wife), I realised they were white-bellied sea eagles. Common off the coast of Singapore, it was still unusual to see them in such numbers. Considered to be the biggest bird of prey found here, they glided effortlessly across the sky using the warm air currents to float upwards. It was an impressive sight. But as the drizzle started, St John's Island looked increasingly eerie behind me as the huge eagles continued to soar ominously overhead. For some strange reason, the ferry could not come quick enough.

# CHAPTER 12

There are certain things I have never understood about Singapore. I have never figured out why the elderly slap an empty seat on a bus before they sit down. It is most bizarre. They shuffle along the bus looking every inch the benign auntie or uncle, spot an empty seat and promptly go ballistic. Acting as if the seat offended them on a previous trip, they lean over and give it a damn good thrashing. Innocent bystanders are generally confused by the violent and unprovoked attack because it achieves nothing. No dust ever flies up and there is no physical altering of the seat. But still, they slap away like a demented sadomasochist before finally deeming the seat acceptable for their ageing buttocks.

Second, I have yet to be given a satisfactory explanation as to why two parents sitting at a dinner table require the services of a maid to feed their own child. Is it too much for them to feed themselves and their child at the same time? Will their arms fall off if they shovel spoonfuls of rice from two plates instead of one? Or maybe it is the complexity of the procedure. After all, it is a complicated task, cutting up fish balls and rolling them into the screaming brat's mouth.

And finally, I have never fathomed why Westerners and Western wannabes are so enamoured by Holland Village. Apparently named after Hugh Holland, an architect and early resident of the area, Holland Village is touted as Singapore's Bohemia, a little enclave of eateries, bars and art galleries. That may be the case, but Manhattan's Greenwich Village has nothing to worry about. In

10 years, I have not visited the area more than a dozen times and just cannot recognise its attraction. Believe me, it is not through want of trying.

When I arrived, Singaporean and foreign colleagues said, "Oh, if you want a good place to hang out, you must go to Holland V. It's a great place for chilling." Be deeply suspicious of anyone who feels compelled to use the word "chilling" in everyday conversation.

"It's called Holland V? What's the V stand for?"

"Oh, it means 'village'. But I always call it Holland V."

"Why? Is there something wrong with you?"

Whenever the modern marketing weapons of short forms, abbreviations or acronyms are deployed in a desperate attempt to sound hip and clued in, I reach for the snooze button.

But I was an eager tourist back then, dutifully following any direction offered so I took a leisurely stroll around Holland Village one afternoon. Yes, I set aside an entire afternoon. The tour was completed in 10 minutes. I spent more time in my Dagenham minimart when I was young, sneaking peeks at the big and bouncy magazines on the top shelf. I seem to recall a handful of restaurants, some banks and, by Singaporean standards, a tiny, colourless shopping centre.

The only memorable evening spent at the bustling Bohemia (it makes me laugh just typing it) came after a last-minute victory for Tanjong Pagar United when I celebrated with one of the players at Wala Wala Bar. We were watching a 1998 World Cup match when I felt something tickle my feet. I looked down and saw a confused, baby rat trying unsuccessfully to find its way back to its burrow. My suriphobia made it exceedingly difficult for me to return after that. But the rat encounter was eight years ago and nothing stands still in Singapore.

Holland Village had changed, quite dramatically in fact. It was an orderly shambles. In other words, the shopping enclave was marked by yet another building site, complete with cranes and those industrial, deafening drills that apparently need to bore their way through to the Earth's core to allow the new MRT Circle Line to trundle underneath Holland Village in 2010. In the stifling midday heat, I stepped off the bus and the dust in the still, humid air was everywhere. How the poor shop owners put up with these noisy, irritable conditions I will never know. The construction site was surrounded by a 2-metre-high corrugated iron fence right in the heart of Holland Village. Visitors had to negotiate a narrow walkway with the obstreperous drilling on the left and dusty shopfronts on the right. I am sure in the evenings, when dust hopefully gives way to dusk, shopping here is a more agreeable experience, but it is bloody awful in the early afternoon.

The shops in Holland Village were the usual haunts frequented by expatriates and younger Singaporeans: one or two European restaurants, the odd grille, The Coffee Bean and a Burger King. The two-storey shophouses offered fake branded goods, some Singaporean souvenirs and the odd dentist. Intriguingly, there were also a number of motorbikes parked in Lorong Mambong, behind Holland Road. It felt like a dislocated Bali. In effect, Holland Village was Bali without the beach. More so when I visited, with all that bloody dust providing an uncomfortable substitute for sand. Picture a few tanned Scandinavians in sarongs, a group of elderly locals massaging the feet of fat *ang mohs* and some grungy old German hippy running a bar along Lorong Mambong and Holland Village really could be Bali.

Perhaps that is why the buzzing Bohemia does not quite work here. It is out of place. If the entire village could be lifted and transported wholesale to the East Coast, I suspect it would be a massive hit with backpacker types from all over the world. The setting would certainly match the clientele. Holland Village has everything Bali or Koh Samui offers: bars showing Premiership football, restaurants offering decent international cuisine, fast food outlets, cheap clothes, postal services, banks, bakeries and reasonable parking for scooters and motorbikes. On a much smaller scale, Holland Village does offer the young Singaporean, the tourist, the backpacker and the expatriate all of the basic essentials of a bohemian lifestyle, except sand, sea and sex, that is, which tend to be the most important ingredients. Concrete is no substitute for sand and sex on a building site just does not have the same ring to it.

But the little shopping parade is not without its plus points. The long-established newspaper and magazine stall offers publications from just about every major country in the world. Although it comes at a price. I do not doubt for a second that the *Mail on Sunday* is not a quality weekend read, but I am not sure it is worth $12.50. The windmill on the top of Holland V Shopping Mall is quaint and you cannot complain about the breadth of cuisine offered here. German, Lebanese and Mexican restaurants are all close to each other and there was even an eatery offering "Brazilian". I was not even sure what constituted Brazilian fare and the restaurant's façade did not give much away. There were no photographs of dishes in the window so I had a closer look. There were several shots of women's legs and the word "WAX" featured prominently on the walls. There was a "male menu" but its offerings should only appeal to Olympic swimmers, Tour de France cyclists and those who frequent Orchard Towers on Friday nights. An employee in the shop glanced up at me and smiled. I almost fell over my hairy legs to get away. That was all I needed. I could have popped in there for a little plate of Brazilian and come away with a giant walnut between my legs.

But I was neither hungry nor in need of a German newspaper, so there was little else to keep me in Holland Village. I took a bus to Buona Vista and then a train to a spiritual haven that has made me far too superstitious for my own good.

Scott and I were in a really good mood. And not because we were lying on a bed together in our boxer shorts. It was 4 December 1996 and I had just signed a two-year contract as a speech and drama teacher. Scott already had a job as an architect in the bag and the next day was my birthday. After three weeks of job hunting and almost no sightseeing, we could finally drop the former and do a little of the latter. Besides, we had to get out of the apartment. We were sleeping in the same bed, cooking for each other and generally turning into Toa Payoh's version of *The Odd Couple.* In a certain light, Scott was beginning to resemble Jack Lemmon and I found him rather fetching in his tight, cotton boxer shorts. We desperately needed fresh air, a temporary escape from instant curry noodles and a chance to mix with fully clothed people again. After much deliberation, we settled on visiting the Chinese Garden. Not because we were particularly fond of pagodas and stone lions, but because it was cheap and beside the MRT station of the same name.

The Chinese and Japanese Gardens afforded us our first glance of the country that existed behind the housing estates. Ironically, the green spot was cultivated in the mid-1970s to serve those very housing estate workers and residents, but it was our first glimpse of the garden city. Until then, we had only seen the city. The 14-hectare Chinese Garden and the 13-hectare Japanese Garden were beautifully landscaped and, like most Western visitors, we were impressed with the traditional features of Chinese gardening art, particularly the seven-storey pagoda modelled on the Ling Ku Temple Pagoda in Nanjing, China. The only viewing tower we had encountered so far was in the Toa Payoh Town Garden and that really was a limp erection in comparison.

We stopped for lunch at the Bonsai Garden because the cheese slices in our sandwiches were melting. In a conversation I will never forget, we sat there for at least an hour, plotting our spectacular ambitions for the following year in Singapore. Some we achieved, some we did not. Scott could not fulfil the easiest and most important ambition—to stay in the country. Thanks to those incomprehensible civil servants at Immigration (although there is another, more adequate description of their profession beginning with "c"), Scott had his employment pass application rejected three months later. There was no explanation given. Treated like a criminal, he was ordered to leave the country within seven days. I have never forgiven the immigration authorities for their inexplicably draconian, heavy-handed behaviour. For the record, Scott is now an accomplished architect living in Hertfordshire with his wife and son and is reaching most of the targets he laid out while eating sweaty cheese sandwiches in the Chinese Garden a decade ago. Well done, Singapore Immigration. You really made the right decision there.

On my birthday the following year, I took my partner back to the same spot at the Bonsai Garden for lunch, told her about the conversation with Scott and we inevitably ended up discussing our plans for the next year. Being a creature of habit, I have returned to the same spot on the same day almost every year since. At the risk of sounding like a pretentious wanker, the annual trips feel quite spiritual. If I go alone, I analyse the year that has passed and lay down what is realistically achievable in the next 12 months. When I am alone, I find myself muttering aloud although I am not sure why, or to whom. On one occasion, I failed to notice that a cleaner had wandered in to sweep the footpath. He spotted a lanky lunatic eating a cheese sandwich and giving a sermon on the mount at Bonsai Garden and nearly fell into the pond. I may not be able to turn water into wine, but I can almost always make cleaners fall into the water.

There was one birthday, somewhere in my late twenties, when I had to travel to England for an extended writing assignment and missed my annual pilgrimage to Jurong. The following year did not go quite according to plan. It was probably a coincidence and I may well be talking rubbish, but I have not missed a year since.

One of the advantages of visiting the Chinese Garden today is that it is free. Like Haw Par Villa, Sentosa, Holland Village and countless other tourist attractions around the country, the Chinese Garden was currently in the midst of redevelopment and most of the Japanese Garden had been fenced off. The operator rightly assumed that it would be presumptuous to charge visitors for the privilege of admiring piles of sand, No Entry barriers and the exposed backsides of foreign workers.

Do you think there will ever come a time when the upgrading ceases in Singapore? Can you ever envisage a day when the hammering in your neighbourhood stops? Let's dream of a day when some bright spark at the Urban Redevelopment Authority eventually stands up in front of his colleagues and cries, "Let us put down our drills, step down from the cranes and tear down the fences. Let's stop digging holes in the country today!"

"But what would we do with all that corrugated iron fencing?"

"Bury it on Pulau Semakau for all I care. I've had enough."

"But you know the economic threat Singapore faces. What about China and India?"

"All right, bury it there then. Along with the drills, cranes and concrete mixers. Let's just allow the country and its people a five-minute respite to breathe a little."

"Sure, Chu Kang. Whatever you say, mate ... Can we get a straitjacket, please? Now, lie back and close your eyes. You'll just feel a little prick."

The seven-storey pagoda was closed. I was quietly pleased. Had it been open, I would have been compelled to climb it in the oppressive heat. Instead I popped into one of the most noticeable beneficiaries of the ongoing upgrading—the public toilets. Clearly modelled on the Night Safari's original and highly successful concept, the toilets had a rural, open-air feel, with no wall to separate the trees and plants from the sinks. This was rather startling. From the urinal, I noticed a middle-aged Caucasian couple strolling along the footpath towards the toilet. If I could see them, they could almost certainly see me. And no one is getting a glimpse of my pagoda. How did the planners overlook the obvious fact that male visitors can be peeped on while peeing? Admittedly I am taller than most Asians, but the sinks are low enough to affect just about everybody. Unless Snow White's pals fancy a day trip here, every other man will feel embarrassingly exposed.

The site of my spiritual home in the Bonsai Garden was also closed. I was bloody apoplectic. The main gates to the Japanese Garden were also locked. This was getting ridiculous. As appealing as it may sound, I did not fancy dissecting my year at the nearby "live" turtle and tortoise museum that was now housed within the Chinese Garden. I might mutter to the occasional cleaner, but I draw the line at talking to a turtle.

At least the smaller twin pagodas were open. I climbed the spiral staircase to the third storey and surveyed Jurong Lake. From one vantage point, it was easy to pick out all of the basic ingredients of Singaporean living: a reservoir with an accompanying town park, HDB estates and condominiums fighting for the best view of the lake, MRT trains trundling over a canal, a golf and country club, a stadium, a community centre, a shopping centre and the faint outline of an industrial estate. If a foreign visitor wanted a visual microcosm of life on this island, a trip to the top of the twin pagodas would suffice.

I strode through the magnificent main archway of the Chinese Garden, crossed the white stone bridge and thought about the delectable Cleopatra Wong. In 1978, not long after the Chinese Garden had opened, the superbly cheesy martial arts flick *They Call Her ... Cleopatra Wong* was released throughout Southeast Asia. A sexy, deadly secret agent, Wong was Singapore's answer to James Bond who, through wit, ingenuity, lots of sex and a crossbow, took out currency counterfeiters from Hong Kong to the Philippines. It was exploitation film-making at its most surreal, cashing in on an industry that had been kickstarted by Bruce Lee. But the film turned Wong into Singapore's first and only international movie star to date. The actress now lives a quiet life in Katong but, in 1978, half of Southeast Asia wanted to sleep with her.

I watched a grainy print of the movie a couple of years ago at a film festival and was genuinely surprised by its cinematic legacy and its impact on contemporary pop culture. Wong's striped leather costume and matching crash helmet, her motorbike, her martial arts and her sassy persona were all thrown into Quentin Tarantino's melting pot to create Uma Thurman's assassin in *Kill Bill.* The debt Tarantino owes Singapore's only international superstar is considerable, but sadly the link between *They Call Her ... Cleopatra Wong* and *Kill Bill* is seldom made by anyone outside of Tarantino's circle of friends, so I am more than happy to do it here.

I thought of the sexy siren now because there is a wonderful scene in the film that is so daft that it could only come from a film dating to the 1970s. Never one to miss a trick, the Singapore Tourism Board must have had a hand in the film's production because every attraction the country had to offer back then features in the movie at some point. And there clearly were not too many. Fleeing from the bad guys on what I believe is Sentosa, Wong jumps into a cable car. There are several shots of her looking behind nervously at the villains in the cable car behind. This goes on for quite a while. Looking terrified, she glances over her shoulder as the snarling scoundrels close in, smiling as their prey appears to draw closer. Now, how is this possible? They are both in bloody cable cars. They are travelling at the same speed and the cars are equidistant on the same cable line.

Refusing to let science get in the way of a good cops-and-robbers chase, Cleopatra Wong flees the cable car and dashes to her Mercedes at what looks like Mount Faber. And not a moment too soon because the pursuing villains are, well, just as far away as they were when they were in the cable car. Wong floors the accelerator at Mount Faber, turns left and crosses the stone bridge that leads to the main archway at the Chinese Garden! From the southern tip of the country to the west with just one turn of the wheel. Cleopatra Wong was one classy act. Of course, the Chinese Garden was not the Chinese Garden but the secret, reclusive home of Asia's most dangerous criminal. It took Interpol's finest secret agents half the film to track down the hideaway because an extravagant Chinese mansion that size would be nigh on impossible to find in Singapore. Scott and I found it in less than an hour.

Delighted with our impressive sense of direction, I now strode purposefully down Chinese Garden Road trying to picture Cleopatra Wong astride her motorbike in her skintight leather suit. But it was an exercise in futility. I could only see Scott astride an armchair in his boxer shorts.

# CHAPTER 13

My mother loves to walk. Some of my earliest memories are of my little sister and me being dragged out of the house to "go for a walk". We strolled to markets on Sunday, shopping centres on Saturday and distant beaches on our Clacton-on-Sea holidays. Clacton, by the way, was once the popular destination of choice for the working classes of Essex and East London. Think Batam with fewer palm trees and more "kiss-me-quick" hats. My mother always led the way, guiding us past A-roads, speeding juggernauts bound for Dover, salivating dogs and the occasional motorway so we could find a distant Essex beach away from the sunburnt hordes. We would walk for hours to locate the beach, sit down for 15 minutes before she would say, "Come on, we can't waste a day sitting here, can we? Let's go for a walk." And we would be off to another mystery destination that was after Clacton, but before Land's End.

My mother still does it now. We barely have the chance to drop our suitcases in the hallway before she cries, "Come on, you haven't come all the way from Singapore to spend your time in the hallway, let's go to Deal! Then on to Sandwich, Broadstairs, Cliftonville and back to Ramsgate. Then we can have some breakfast. Right you lot, follow me!"

I have spent entire holidays in England when I have only ever seen the back of my mother's head. It usually disappears over a grassy hillock and reappears at the next seaside town. It stops occasionally to reprimand us for "walking too bloody slow" and to berate Bruno for "pissing up the side of that baby's buggy". Bruno is the family's pet poodle. He is not an incontinent uncle.

My mother's fondness for long ambles through the city streets and country lanes of England is matched only by her impatience at bus stops. Now that is a sight to behold. When I was young, many a sunny afternoon was spent walking 5 miles home from a distant shopping centre because my mother's fidgety feet had taken charge.

"Come on," she would say to my exhausted sister and me. "We can't stand here all day waiting for a bus that's never going to come. Let's walk to the next bus stop."

"Mum, we've only been here for 37 seconds."

"Yeah, but by the time it does get here, we could be home."

"But this is Romford. Dagenham is 5 miles away. My feet ache and Jodie's managed to fall asleep standing up."

"Oh, stop moaning. Jodie, wake up! We're walking home. Come on, follow me!"

Of course, we would walk 50 metres and the No. 174 bus would go racing past. My mum would pretend not to see it while I would mutter some half-baked complaint under my breath and then duck really quickly. My oblivious sister never saw the red double decker, having perfected the art of sleepwalking years earlier.

"That's the trouble with buses here," my mother would say an hour later as we stumbled through the front door. "You wait for ages and they don't come. Then when you start to walk home, what happens? Fifteen come at once. And they never stop where you want them to stop. Might as well bloody walk home ... Neil, what kind of brother are you? Go and carry your sister up to bed. Can't you see she's tired?"

I planned to follow in my mother's footsteps and take a heroic saunter from the Chinese Garden, along Yuan Ching Road, past the former Tang Dynasty City, turn into Jalan Ahmad Ibrahim, amble over to West Coast Road and then push on to Pandan Reservoir. I got as far as a food court opposite Tang Dynasty City. It was rather pitiful, but the scorching sun was relentless. You could have fried an egg on my forehead. Both starving and parched, I ordered mushroom noodles and received what can only be charitably described as spaghetti and shiitake mushrooms drowned in Campbell's mushroom soup.

After my mediocre makan, I found a bus stop outside the former Tang Dynasty City on Jalan Ahmad Ibrahim. The bus services in Singapore are truly outstanding. I was standing in the middle of a highway, the street was deserted and the area was more industrial than residential, yet the No. 30 bus picked me up and dropped me beside Pandan Reservoir. Commuters are so well served here and I think their occasional gripes in the newspapers lack perspective at times. Buses in Singapore are generally frequent and inexpensive and there really is no need to walk 5 miles to your destination, unless you really want to. Of course, that did not stop my mother when she visited Singapore for the first time in 2004. She was a visitor whereas I lived here and yet I spent most of the fortnight following the back of her head. It was most peculiar.

But at Pandan Reservoir, however, I turned into my mother for several draining hours. Have you ever been to Pandan Reservoir? It is bloody huge. According to an officer at the Public Utilities Board, the reservoir was completed in 1975 and boasts a track that is 6.2 kilometres in length. Cyclists and joggers adore this place and speak lovingly about the sun rising above the reservoir as they fly around the gravel track every morning. The lake is also available now to canoeists and rowers for the odd tournament. But they all have one advantage; they are fit. I, on the other hand, had turned up at 7pm already exhausted from my trip to the Chinese Garden. But the cooler, dusky air made a walk around the reservoir deceptively inviting so I thought, "Since I'm here ... "

I trotted briskly along the gravel path that separated the narrow Sungei Pandan from the main Pandan Reservoir. Surrounded by water, I savoured the gentle breeze and quietly cursed every fit bugger who dashed past me without having broken into a sweat. Then, as I turned a bend and found I had the entire reservoir to myself, night happened. There was no warning. It just happened.

The sun dropped behind the housing estates of Jurong and Bukit Batok and it was suddenly pitch black. There was no dalliance with greys or dark blues. The sky simply said, "That's it, I've had enough. Make it night. Now! Let's scare the shit out of that *ang moh* below who has decided to walk around an entire reservoir after 7pm. Idiot. Right, here we go then ... let it be night!"

No one had thought to light the path around the reservoir because no one had thought that anyone would be daft enough to go for a stroll after dinner. I quickened my pace by imagining my mum was ahead of me shouting, "For goodness sake, Neil, hurry up, it's almost dinner time. And you've got to go to the fish and chip shop."

Then I was attacked. It was my own fault really. No one should head off on an impromptu trek into an unlit area after dark, even if it was on property controlled by the Public Utilities Board. I felt a minor blow to the back of the neck, then another to the side of the face. The aggressors were unmistakable—midges. They pounced from every angle until there was a sizeable cloud of them permanently above my head. From a distance, I must have looked like Roger Moore in *The Saint.* The tiny flies flew into my ears, my eyes and my mouth, often all at once. One kamikaze midge even flew up my nostril, where he was quickly drowned in a reservoir of snot.

In a fit of temper, I threw my rucksack down onto the ground, grabbed the insect repellent and sprayed like a madman in every direction for a good 30 seconds. My random, uncontrolled spraying stung my eyes and I petulantly screamed, "Bloody midges!" An action I immediately regretted. There was no need for such uncouth, uncivilised behaviour. I am sure David Attenborough does not scream "Bloody midges" when he is in the Amazon. He would know the exact breed of insect he was cursing.

I sprayed my hair, my neck, my cap, my rucksack and all my clothes but the swarm pursued me right around the rim of Pandan. I could have surrendered. I could have waved a white flag and stepped down from the path and onto Jalan Buroh, a main road that ran alongside the reservoir. However, I stubbornly persevered, determined to complete the circuit. If I could walk from Romford to Dagenham at the height of summer when I was 11, I could perambulate the boundaries of Pandan Reservoir. Besides, the view from the other side of the lake was quite spectacular. The lights of the housing estates reflected off the water and, from where I stood, it all looked rather serene. Of course, I hardly saw any of this because I had a street directory stuck to the right side of my face. With the wind blowing towards me, the swarms of midges were splattering into my cheek. The street directory provided a temporary respite from the persistent little bastards.

But I completed Pandan Reservoir and, feeling that momentum was now on my side, decided to push on further west. So I shook the dead midges out of my hair, wiped them off my street directory and strode off into the darkness of Jalan Buroh.

I thought I had made a mistake at first. I walked for hours. Wandering through the deserted Jurong Industrial Estate at 10pm felt like a cross between *The Hills Have Eyes* and *Wolf Creek.* Although the area was not unsafe, there was still a perceptible sense of uneasiness. I know that Singapore is one of the safest countries in the world, but the dark, eerie atmosphere still lent itself to the remote possibility that drunk fishermen could jump onto Jalan Buroh Bridge, rip my eyeballs out with a fishhook, garrotte me with a filament line and leave my carcass to the packs of stray dogs that patrolled the area.

Jalan Buroh was an endless line of factories, dotted with the occasional piece of vacant land, the long grass of which provided an unkempt shelter for the strays. I rarely saw the dogs, but they were there. I could hear them running through the grass and occasionally howling at the moon. Almost every factory was labelled in the street directory. Except one. No. 51. It was just marked as a sizeable pink square, indicating it was a public or commercial building. This told me nothing. It could have manufactured anything from condoms to concrete. The property was certainly spooky. The security post was empty and its windows were broken. Grass and weeds grew through the fence, around the gates and up the security post. In the distance was a lone lorry parked in front of a dark warehouse that had its shutters raised high enough for employees to go in, but not high enough for casual observers like myself to see what was going on inside. But the strangest part was that there were no signs anywhere. Not one. This is Singapore for heaven's sake, a country that indicates lookout points at the top of a nature reserve. Nevertheless, here was a property sitting on quite a chunk of prime industrial land and it was not labelled. And it was deserted. I did not spot a single employee and I stood there for several minutes. In the distance, I could hear a faint, rhythmic pounding. Someone was clearly banging an object repeatedly, slapping it down on a table, turning it around and hitting it again.

Of course. No wonder the guys inside wanted to maintain a low profile. They must have been playing mahjong. It was an illegal gambling den. I expected the police to arrive on the scene and drag out a mahjong table, hundreds of packets of instant noodles and a dozen middle-aged aunties. Then I made out the tiniest of road signs that said "Jurong Abattoir". Ah. That made more sense than an illegal gambling den run by triads, even if it was far less glamorous.

A couple of days later, I called the Agri-Food and Veterinary Authority (AVA) and asked for the exact address of Jurong Abattoir to satisfy my curiosity. The conversation would have been less conspiratorial had I called the Internal Security Department instead.

"Ah, hello. I'm just calling to check if 51 Jalan Buroh is the address of Jurong Abattoir," I asked an AVA officer in my best telephone voice.

"Why do you want to know where Jurong Abattoir is?" That was indeed a very good question. Other than being a nosy bugger, I did not really have a reason. So I made one up.

"Well, because I'm standing outside it right now," I replied from the sofa of my Toa Payoh apartment. "And there are no signs outside. I'm looking for a factory in Jurong and I don't want to walk into an abattoir by mistake because I'm having pizza later."

"Oh I see, then yes, No. 51 is Jurong Abattoir. That's where we slaughter pigs."

Ah, touchy subject. Hence the secrecy. Checking the map again, however, I noticed that the property next door at No. 53 was marked down as a pet hotel. A bloody pet hotel! Imagine getting those two buildings mixed up. It was not as difficult as you might think; one of them was not even signposted. I hope no one ever uses No. 51 as a short cut to get to No. 53. That would be one short hotel stay for poor Lassie. A bellboy would not be much help, but a taxidermist might be of some assistance. The street directory calls No. 53 a pet hotel, but the AVA prefers the term "Jurong Animal Quarantine Station". Naturally.

The closer I got to Jurong Pier Flyover, which is the turn-off for Jurong Island, the quieter the street became. By the time I had reached an SPC garage, I was venturing into the land that time had forgotten. Indeed, the garage could have been a saloon from an old western. It just needed a pair of louvre doors for me to push open. There were no customers, only a couple of elderly employees sitting on a wall stroking a dog. The snarling canine was golden in colour, but its breed was difficult to ascertain. Its perpetual drooling suggested it was born in a test tube in South Korea. As I headed towards the petrol pumps, the eyes of the two men and their salivating pet followed me across the garage forecourt. I fully expected one of them to spit out a toothpick, kick over a spittoon and, in a slow, Texan drawl, say, "Where might you be goin' stranger? You better git goin' real soon or little Clint here will bite yer bawls off. And if that don' work none, I'll set the dog on ya."

But instead they kindly pointed out the toilet to me. The dog, however, was far less welcoming. It barked at me incessantly and I was forced to walk in a big arc to avoid it and get to my temporary refuge. I locked the toilet door but it had those slats at the bottom for ventilation and I could clearly see the dog sitting just a couple of metres away. It was waiting for me. That much was obvious. I had no idea what its plans were, but I had no problem relieving myself, I can assure you. The two uncles made half-hearted attempts to calm their mad dog but were far more enthusiastic discussing their supper plans. I had already spent five minutes locked inside the cubicle and it is generally not a good idea to hang out in a men's toilet in an empty garage in a deserted industrial estate at 11pm. The loneliness of the long-distance lorry driver is well-known. But the prospect of being dragged past the petrol pumps by a mongrel of dubious origin did not really appeal either.

In the end, the compassionate uncles came to my rescue. They whistled and Frankenstein's monster returned to its masters and sat by their feet. When I saw through the door slats that they had grabbed its collar, I took my cue. Red faced and perspiring heavily, I flung the toilet door open, dashed across the forecourt and hared off down Jalan Buroh.

Almost five hours after arriving at Pandan Reservoir, I reached my final destination for the day—the lookout tower at the top of Jurong Hill Park. Just 100 metres from Jurong BirdPark, the observation tower and its accompanying restaurant provided cracking views of the private Jurong Island nearby. Opened in 1970 for residents living in the increasingly cluttered industrial area, the tower was built at the top of a 60-metre hill and resembled one of those circular car park ramps, with extremely wide walkways. Having struggled along from one end of Jalan Buroh to the other, it was a bit of an effort to get to the top, but I could hardly quibble with its wheelchair-friendly design. Despite its size and prominence, I actually had trouble finding the damned thing initially and walked aimlessly down Bird Park Drive for several minutes. Then I realised a few cars and vans with young couples inside were driving up a hill on my left. They were either going to the tower or heading to a mass orgy. Either way, their destination was well worth a peek.

Sure enough, the summit presented me with a view of a dozen canoodling couples. There was a middle-aged Chinese chap beside me pecking at the neck of an extremely young, attractive Chinese woman. They took a breather, probably to allow his pacemaker to recover, and had an animated discussion that lasted quite a while. Although they may have been ruminating about the hypnotic lights of the oil refineries twinkling under the starry sky, I suspect they were haggling over the price.

I took off my steaming shoes and sat on the concrete floor, staring out at the bright lights of the big city. Midnight was approaching, but the entire west corner of Singapore appeared to be lit up and blinking back at me. It really was beautiful and I no longer cared that my entire body ached. The walk through Jurong had been interminable at times, but one that was thoroughly rewarding in the end.

My old mum had been right after all.

# CHAPTER 14

She will probably never speak to me again, but I must tell you this story. My mother visited Singapore for the first time in 2004 and, as a 50th birthday present, we also took her to Perth to look up some old friends and relatives. Knowing that mobs of kangaroos had overrun most of Australia, I was eager to see the marsupials in their natural habitat. We were told to visit Pinnaroo Valley Memorial Park, a cemetery famous for its kangaroo population. The place was big, grassy and secluded; the only visitors being those who came to pay their respects or to watch the kangaroos grazing. For a week, I had stubbornly insisted that we were not flying back to Singapore until I had been to "kangaroo cemetery", as it is known locally. My wife and younger brother were also keen, but my mum was a little uncertain.

"So you really want to go to this kangaroo cemetery, then?" she asked.

"Yeah, it'll be great. It must be amazing to see."

"I suppose so," she said, clearly not convinced. "I'm not sure they'll be that much to see and it sounds a bit morbid to me."

"It's only a cemetery, mum. Think of all those kangaroos we'll see running around."

"Running around? What are you going on about? They'll all be dead."

"No they won't. Who told you that?"

"You did. You said it was a kangaroo cemetery." Apparently, she had thought it was a pet cemetery for kangaroos! She insisted that "kangaroo cemetery" must be a place where Aussies gathered to bury their beloved, bounding friends. Fifty thousand graves, all filled with dead kangaroos. The headstones would certainly make for interesting reading: Here lies Joey. Son of Joey. He leaves behind a wife and a dozen children. All called Joey.

My mother's kangaroo cemetery came back to me as I respectfully observed a stray dog enjoying some shade. It was sleeping beside a grave near the back of Choa Chu Kang Chinese Cemetery. I had no plans to visit the cemetery. I was heading to Old Lim Chu Kang Road but the startling image of hundreds of graves, spread out in almost identical rows across the grassy hillside, had caught me off guard. It is not a common sight in Singapore, but it is if you grow up in Dagenham. Churches all over the parishes of Dagenham and Barking have gravestones going back hundreds of years. Dogs pee on them, vandals desecrate them and drug addicts leave their needles among the flowers. Even in death, peace is not always guaranteed.

But cemeteries are difficult to find in Singapore—they are not a popular place with the many superstitious folk. Coffee shop cynics will whisper that the *gahmen*, the affectionate colloquial term for the government, does not advocate burials and insists that the dead are cremated. This is not quite an urban myth but it is not entirely untrue either. In 2001, it was announced that the 26-hectare Bidadari Cemetery had to go to make way for housing projects. Well, naturally. The graves (around 58,000 Christian and 68,000 Muslim) were to be exhumed so 12,000 new high-rise homes could house 40,000 residents at the junction of Upper Serangoon Road and Upper Aljunied Road in central Singapore, not too far from my home in Toa Payoh. Most of the remains were eventually relocated here at the Choa Chu Kang cemeteries. But their descendants were not amused. The cemetery, one of the oldest in Singapore, opened in 1907 and 5,000 graves belonged to foreigners, including Australian and British servicemen who had died during World War II. Furious relatives from all over the world sent letters to the media, asking for the men who had once defended the country to be left in peace.

But obstacles to economic progress are easily sidestepped, so a few silent corpses did not pose too many problems. The exhumation project went ahead and was completed in 2006. Even in death, peace is not always guaranteed.

I know that land is scarce in Singapore. It is a mantra that is drummed into Singaporeans from their first history lesson at primary school. But again, I do wonder, and I always will wonder, how many apartments and shopping centres does a country actually need?

Contrary to popular belief, however, Singaporeans can still be buried in Choa Chu Kang Cemetery if they are willing to pay the price ($940 per adult, according to staff at the Chinese Cemetery). Behind the rows and rows of circular gravestones, often adorned with stone lions and pagodas, new plots had been freshly dug. Like the graves, most of the plots were dug in rows that sloped slightly along the hillsides off Lim Chu Kang Road. I was told this was to accommodate drainage during heavy downpours. Even in death, the authorities are stunningly practical.

The smell of incense was everywhere and charred paper money blew all over the place. Several graves were covered in burnt litter. They looked dreadful. Making sure dead relatives have cars, houses and money in the afterlife is most commendable, but some visitors neglect to consider the impact it has on the living.

I reached the end of Path 19 of the Chinese Cemetery. Had I ventured any further, I could have been shot. The reservoirs of both Poyan and Murai in the northwestern corner of the country are live firing areas for the Singapore Armed Forces. I noticed a couple of young Chinese guys digging plots while an older chap, possibly their boss, sat on the back of his van calculating sums on a notepad.

"Excuse me, do you work here?" I asked cautiously. He viewed me with the kind of suspicion reserved for tall, strange Caucasians carrying notepads around graveyards in the middle of the day.

"Yah, what you want?" Time for another story. And I am going straight to hell for this one.

"Er, a distant relative is sick and she wants to be buried here."

"Can, can. Still got plots. Look, can see. But not cheap. Each plot costs $940."

"But someone told me it's better to go for a cremation."

"You know why or not? The *gahmen* don't want burial. Cremation better. Where got space for so many burials? But if you know where to go, can still bury. No problem."

I thanked him for the advice and left but he called me back. He smelt a sale.

"Hey, you need burial or not? You got a contractor? Need a contractor to make the stone?"

He was the Phua Chu Kang of the graveyard industry.

"No, it's okay. But rest assured if anyone dies, I'll certainly come to you first."

He smiled broadly at the prospect of a death in my family. I had clearly made his day.

I had a quick stroll around the Muslim Cemetery which, if truth be told, did not suffer from the littering problems of the Chinese Cemetery. The graves were more pristine and far less cluttered. Then I crossed the near-deserted Lim Chu Kang Road, took a side turning called Lorong Rusuk and headed into the rustic solitude of Old Lim Chu Kang Road.

When I decided to embark upon a farewell tour of Singapore, I was keen to examine its underbelly and its darkest corners: I wanted to see the *ulu* bits. *Ulu* means "remote" in Malay. In Singlish, *ulu* refers to the distant four corners of the country where taxi drivers will not respond to calls and will not take a passenger there without moaning for the entire journey about how he will never pick up a fare on the way back.

Old Lim Chu Kang Road was lovely. Full of vegetable farms and undisturbed forest, the street had a timeless, old world feel to it. Singapore has evolved from a kampong community to a global city, but this rural estate has stood firm against rampant redevelopment. Wearing those wide-brimmed straw hats, workers still picked the vegetables by hand, just as they did 50 years ago. This was not just another time; it was almost another country, bearing closer similarity to the neighbouring Malaysian state of Johor than to the nearby HDB estates in Choa Chu Kang. Backpackers who still insist that Singapore is all stylish shopping centres and has no substance should come here. Now I know I do not want to sound overly whimsical and naive. It is backbreaking work in harsh, humid conditions for the farmers, whose efforts are largely overlooked in a city-state focused on rapid urban growth. But it is an alternative lifestyle and that is a rarity here. If you are lucky enough to come across anything that might be deemed alternative in Singapore, cherish it.

The right side of Old Lim Chu Kang Road was largely devoted to Singapore's military forces. Nothing particularly alternative about that. I ambled past Lim Chu Kang Camp I and noticed a Coke machine just inside the entrance. I asked the guard on duty if I could buy one.

"Sure, man," he replied. "That's what it's there for." Bless his little camouflaged cotton socks. I hurried out of the army camp as soon as possible though. The guard was politeness personified, but five pairs of eyes still followed my every move.

As I crossed Lorong Serambi, a middle-aged Chinese farmhand walked towards me. He worked at the sizeable vegetable farm I had just passed. It looked impressive, but they could have been growing marijuana for all I knew. He stopped for what my mother's generation calls a "crafty fag".

"What do you grow here?" I asked curiously as he blew smoke in my face.

"Everything really. Lettuce, spinach, *kailan* and *cai xin.* Got most kinds of local vegetable here."

But the kindly uncle was more interested in my welfare. It was getting dark and Old Lim Chu Kang Road was hardly a kaleidoscope of bright lights.

"Hey, where you going, ah?" he asked, genuinely concerned. "Getting dark, no taxis here. Only one bus. Nothing else to see, just got army camp."

"Yeah, I'm gonna have to get that bus before the ghosts come and get me."

I laughed. He did not. He just looked up at the moon and nodded thoughtfully. They still look up at the moon in Old Lim Chu Kang Road.

But the stargazer was right about one thing. Time was getting on and I was hungry. According to my street directory, there was a bus terminus at the end of Lim Chu Kang Road, with a jetty overlooking the Johor Straits. That sounded most inviting. I was just a short bus journey from a food court, maybe a respectable cluster of shops and some lookout points (signposted, of course) around the jetty.

Do you know what the Lim Chu Kang Bus Terminus consisted of? A lay-by. That was it. The buses pulled in, dropped you off, turned around and went on their merry way. There was more life at the cemeteries. I barely had time to step off the bus before the manic driver swung the steering wheel around and floored the accelerator. Until another bus pulled into the "terminus", I was stranded. And the place stank of rotting fish. I had a perfunctory peek at the so-called jetty. It was nothing more than a dozen wonky planks nailed together. They were also rotting away. I stood on them and they creaked loudly, threatening to give way at any moment. There was a locked gate at the end of the jetty. A sign ordered me not to proceed any further. It was hardly surprising as it was the end of the jetty. The government does like to state the bloody obvious at times. Had I proceeded any further, I would have fallen arse over tit into the sea. What next? A sign at the edge of the Bukit Timah summit ordering me not to take another step?

I did not linger on the jetty. There was nothing to see and I was under surveillance the entire time. The Lim Chu Kang Base of the Police Coast Guard was on my left and a policeman in a watchtower was observing my uncertain movements. I understood why. No one comes this way. Unless you are a fisherman, there is no reason to be here, particularly after dark. Then a beep went off and I almost dived onto the jetty with my hands behind my head. It was not a police sniper's rifle, but my phone welcoming me to Malaysia.

"I'm still bloody here," I screamed at the stupid contraption as it cheerfully informed me of the various cheap rates I could enjoy if I called friends and loved ones back in Singapore. My moaning caught the attention of the policeman on guard outside the Coast Guard Base.

"Is everything okay, sir?" he asked warily. There really was no reason for me to be in such a remote coastal area so late at night. And my fractious mood did me no favours.

"Not really, mate. No. I got off at the bus terminus for some makan and there's nothing here. Bloody nothing," I groaned. "I'm stuck in the middle of nowhere waiting for a bus and my crap phone is using a Malaysian network. I might as well be an illegal immigrant from over there."

I pointed over at Johor Bahru. He laughed nervously.

"And another thing," I continued crankily. "What the hell is that rancid smell?"

"It comes from the fish farms near by. We can't stand it either. Luckily for us, we eat all our meals inside."

The policeman was a lovely guy really. He kindly showed me how to switch my phone back to a Singaporean network manually (I already knew how to do it, but he had a gun). Then he suggested some eateries back in Choa Chu Kang and we talked Premiership football. When all other forms of communication fail in Southeast Asia, you can always fall back on the universal language of the English Premiership. Then things took a surreal turn. There was a concrete slab in front of the police post for visitors to stand on. While building up Liverpool's Champions League chances (the man with the gun was a Reds fan), I stepped onto the slab. A stray dog had been sleeping there. It did not appreciate being woken up. And it really did not like a white-skinned stranger intruding upon its territory.

As I flew off down the country lane like a firecracker, I reached the conclusion that Singaporean dogs do not like me. Every dog

I had when I grew up in England treated me benignly. They wrestled on the floor with me and occasionally farted in my face when the chance presented itself. But they were generally harmless. Around the quiet coastal towns of Singapore, however, myopic stray dogs appear to confuse me with a 6-foot bone. It is a tribute to the bravery of the Liverpool-supporting police officer that I did not end up in hospital. I sincerely mean that. He shielded my canine assailant from my tender calves for a good 10 minutes. But the dog refused to heel. It barked at me continuously and forced me to hide behind a policeman half my size. I only had to poke a little toe around either side of my human shield and the dog pounced.

We settled on a temporary uneasy truce. The black brute paced up and down in front of us. It never took its eyes off me and it never stopped barking. Between us stood the copper, about 5 metres from both of us. If the dog tried to sneak around him, the boy in blue raised a boot to cut it off. On one or two occasions, he had to physically push the snapping stray back and could have lost a couple of fingers in the process. Yes, it was that serious.

Then the bus arrived. The driver pulled into the lay-by and swung the vehicle around 90 degrees so it stretched across the road. Its inviting, open doors faced us in the distance. I screamed at the driver to wait. It was going to come down to a sprint—man against monster. With the bus on our right side, the copper shooed the dog away to our left. That was my cue. But the dog was not easily fooled. It moved before I did. There was no policeman between us now. The pursuing beast, and this is absolutely true, started snapping its jaws at my ankles. My justifiable terror got the better of my social etiquette.

"Get your gun out and shoot the fucker," I screamed. "It's gonna kill me."

"Cannot, cannot. Just keep running," the composed copper shouted back, still giving chase to the uncontrollable feral fiend.

"It's gonna catch me! Just shoot the bastard in the leg. Don't worry about negative publicity. I'm a journalist. I'll make you a hero. Shoot the bastard!"

Fortunately, the bus was just a couple of strides away and I heard the indefatigable policeman calling Blacky back. The mad mongrel never gave up the chase, but the copper's commands were enough to distract it. My leap onto the bus was so dramatic that the horrified driver raised his arms to break my fall. We almost ended up cuddling in the driver's seat. I slumped into the nearest seat and dropped everything on the floor: my bag, my phone, my notepad, my wallet. Everything. I struggled to pick up the slim notepad from under the seat. My hands and legs were shaking. Then my phone beeped. It was a message from my newfound friend and saviour. I had passed the policeman my name card just before the Asian werewolf in Lim Chu Kang had woken from its slumber. The message read "Glad you made bus okay. Sorry about the dog."

Can I just take a moment to declare my unfettered love and admiration for the Singapore Police Force? They go way beyond the call of duty to assist citizens and employment pass holders in their moment of need. My anonymous copper was courageous, selfless and utterly unflappable. But I still think he should have shot that bloody dog.

# CHAPTER 15

The following morning I took the military express back to the farming estates of northwest Singapore. It was actually the No. 975 bus from Choa Chu Kang, but it served several army bases, a police academy and that bloody Coast Guard Base popular with murderous dogs. I was the only person on the bus not wearing a uniform. I wanted a gun just so I could fit in.

The No. 975 bus route has to be one of the most splendid public transport journeys in Singapore. It proceeds past the plant nurseries of Sungei Tengah, trundles alongside the cemeteries of Lim Chu Kang and turns into Old Lim Chu Kang Road (a silent country lane surrounded by vegetable farms and overhanging trees) before heading back down the near-empty Lim Chu Kang Road with its dense, forested areas and reservoirs along the coastline. Those who favour the sounds of silence over the city's cacophony really should venture out this way. Even those who collect gun magazines and have posters of tanks on their bedroom wall would like it here. You cannot move without seeing a tanned man in uniform. It was like a holiday camp for The Village People.

When I stepped off the bus beside Neo Tiew Road, I was confronted by a prominent red sign bearing a skull and crossbones. It was yet another live firing area for Singapore's military. But for one terrifying moment, I thought they were filming the sequel to *The Pirates of the Caribbean* here.

I strode purposefully up Neo Tiew Road. This part of Singapore was once home to much of the country's farming industries and rubber estates and I wanted to explore how much of it actually remained. When you think of rubber plantations and vegetable farms, you tend to think of Malaysia. Like rainforests and orang-utans, anything tilled, cultivated or ploughed is usually associated with Singapore's cousin across the Causeway.

But that is not quite the case. According to a recent newspaper report, there are 114 fruit, vegetable, plant, dairy and fish farms in the Kranji area. To its credit, the Singapore Tourism Board has finally recognised that there is more to a country's soul than retail outlets and Sentosa and now actively encourages tourists (and local schoolchildren) to visit the *ulu* farms and nurseries here.

It is not an artificial experience. Many are long-standing, family-run working farms that predate high-rise housing and, dare I say it, the PAP. They are that old. And they are a damn sight more Singaporean than the Merlion. It is most ironic. Singaporeans lap up those short farm stays in Perth, complimenting the back-to-basics, rustic bliss of the simple life. Surrounded by haystacks, animals and Aussies, they welcome the escape from the grey drudgery of life in a sprawling metropolis, and rightfully so. But there is still a place here where they can amble around for hours, spot more wild animals than people, pick a ripe banana off a tree, walk in the forest, fish in a stream, eat an organic meal, drink the freshest milk and feed a goat. All within 30 minutes of their front door.

Neo Tiew Road was a slower, more congenial world than urban Singapore. Here, drivers in passing cars waved at me. Vegetable and fruit pickers shouted greetings in just about every Southeast Asian language. A fellow walker told me to have a nice day while several farmhands, and I know this resembles a scene from *The Waltons,* sang tunelessly in the sunshine. I passed cherry trees, African tulip trees and durian trees while the unkempt elephant grass towered above me in some places. I loved that. The grass outside my HDB block is not allowed to reach a height of over 5 centimetres before an alarm goes off at the Bishan-Toa Payoh Town Council and the legions of gardeners are deployed with their trimming weapons to take down the offending blades. Today, it is just a blade of grass. But tomorrow, it is a lawn.

I noticed a sign outside the Green Circle Eco-Farm encouraging visitors to pop in. With the merciless sun beating down, it certainly looked inviting. If nothing else, it had a roof. Calling itself Singapore's first biodynamic organic farm, Green Circle grows over 60 food crops on its premises, using no artificial pesticides or fertilisers. This is about as natural as organic food is ever going to get in Singapore. There was a middle-aged Chinese couple frantically completing orders, packing lettuces and other green vegetables into various boxes to be delivered. When they are not growing their own, as it were, the couple gives environmental talks to schoolchildren and conducts tours of the farm. I was suitably impressed.

"How do you guys do it?" I asked, awed by their dedication.

"It's hard work, must keep growing and selling to survive," replied the woman. She never stopped juggling lettuces. I was clearly in the way.

"But it's a 2-hectare plot of land. Why hasn't it been redeveloped by the government?"

Right on cue, the screeching sound of something airborne and armed flew overhead. It was an SAF fighter jet of some kind with luminous felt-tipped missiles and heat-seeking odour-eaters hanging beneath its wings. I am sure some boring bugger, who quotes lines from *Top Gun* and sleeps with an Action Man every night, will point out that the Singapore Armed Forces has recently received an order of a dozen condom-coated rockets to be attached to a pair of Blue-Tit Fat Fighters. But I really could not care less. Discussions on military hardware are right up there with the yardage of a golf course and the price of new cars.

When the man in his magnificent phallic symbol disappeared, taking his noise pollution with him, the lettuce lady glanced up at the sky and said, "That's why we're safe. We're surrounded by army bases so they can't build houses. Would you live here?"

There is irony for you. As long as excitable young pilots are tearing through the sky in their latest technological toys while soldiers dash through the forest shooting inanimate objects, the remnants of Singapore's farming culture can quietly go about its business of nurturing its peaceful sanctuary next door.

I had planned to find a shady bench somewhere to eat a rather austere packed lunch consisting of a bottle of water and a packet of crisps when I chanced upon a little dining delight. I had a vague recollection of there being a vegetable farm owned by Ivy Singh Lim in the area, but I had never expected this. A handcrafted sign shouted at me from across the road: "Bollywood Veggies: chicken curry, local delights, cold drinks and beer". Then I noticed a car park, an air-conditioned restaurant with a fruit and vegetable farm behind it and a decent-sized bungalow, all within one estate. The anomalous view was extraordinary. After ambling for several hours along a deserted lane surrounded by empty forest save for the odd farm, it was most bizarre to find a bustling restaurant with waitresses dashing around taking orders. The peculiar discovery was akin to floundering around in the sand of the Nevada Desert for days on end before finally stumbling upon Bugsy Siegel's Flamingo Hotel.

But Bollywood Veggies was not out of place. In fact, its location was ideal—a country restaurant in the country, with its homegrown food providing the ingredients for many of the dishes at its Poison Ivy Bistro. Half a dozen expat housewives and about 10 Singaporeans were eating inside. I was surprised. I had expected the eatery to be empty. Behind the bistro, a coach party from a special needs school was being given a guided tour of the Bollywood farm, which grows everything from papaya to avocados. Watching the enthusiastic guide stressing the need to protect the Singaporean countryside, I felt obligated to stay for a curry.

Then Ivy Singh Lim appeared. Married to a successful businessman, the indomitable, outspoken woman is a well-known socialite in Singapore. But you will never find her sitting by the pool berating the maid. A dogged campaigner for the Singaporean countryside and a staunch supporter of the local sports scene, she became president of Netball Singapore and turned the game into the most popular sport in the country for girls. In 2005, Singapore won the Asian Netball Championship. A media darling, she takes every opportunity to smack down the laborious, pen-pushing civil servants who have long dominated sports associations and government bodies in Singapore. I had met her only once before when I was a rookie reporter at *The Straits Times.* As she was being introduced to all the gathered journalists, she singled me out and said, "This *ang moh* doesn't know what to make of me, does he? He's been watching me the whole time with those piercing, cynical blue eyes of his."

And here she was, walking towards me wearing an army-style camouflage vest, khaki shorts and a pair of hobnailed boots. There was also a leather knife sheaf on her hip. Kranji's answer to G.I. Jane then noticed my Green Circle Farm leaflet on the table.

"Ah, are you part of the Kranji Association?" she asked. The Kranji Countryside Association was established by 10 farmers in 2005 to encourage more Singaporeans to visit and learn about the countryside. There are no prizes for guessing who the Association's president was. With an almost military bearing, she towered over my table.

"No, I just wanted to see some of Singapore's more *ulu* spots," I replied coyly. "I wanted to get away from the city for a couple of days. I'm, er, very impressed with what you're doing here."

"Well, just remember this," she said, with her hands on her hips for greater impact. "The baby gods may run the global city but Ivy Singh Lim runs the country."

I did not disagree. She had a knife.

I had intended to visit Hay Dairies Goat Farm, a few kilometres north of Bollywood Veggies, but the BBC came calling. Further along Neo Tiew Road was a sign that read "BBC World Service: Far Eastern Relay Station". Here I was in *ulu* land and all I had to do was take a lane called Turut Track and be confronted by the regional home of the greatest news service on the planet. I knew it was only a transmitting centre full of satellites and enormous aerials, but this was the BBC—the grandaddy of broadcasting. There were bound to be plaques, exhibits and blown-up photographs of Spike Milligan and Peter Sellers in *The Goon Show* and The Beatles performing at the BBC. Without hesitation, I made an impulsive, patriotic decision to savour a slice of my homeland in the middle of the Asian jungle. Delighted with my spontaneity, I marched off down the deserted country lane singing the only patriotic song I knew off by heart:

"Rule Britannia,
Marmalade and jam,
Five Chinese crackers up your arsehole,
Bang, bang, bang, bang, bang!"

I trudged along for a couple of kilometres, leaving a snail-like trail of perspiration behind me. And do you know what I encountered when I stopped outside the hallowed grounds of the BBC? Nothing. Bugger all. Just a dreary, boxy white building with narrow windows, the kind that was popular in Britain in the 1960s. The drab office block was surrounded by red-and-white pylons, all of which was fenced off. That was fair enough. But there was not even a plaque or an information panel to provide visitors with a brief overview of the BBC's role in Singapore, from the colonial days through to independence. They had even neglected to provide another human being, preferring one of those intercom speakers at the gate instead of a security guard. Feeling more than a tad fractious, I was tempted to push the button and ask for a double cheeseburger with no gherkins.

An hour later, I waved the white flag and threw myself at the mercy of benevolent truck drivers. I hitchhiked. There is no safer country in the world to do so and my legs refused to go any further. Besides, I did not fancy fainting in some ditch in *ulu* land and being left at the mercy of the stray dogs that wandered in and out of the forest. Somewhere along Lim Chu Kang Lane 3, I stuck my thumb out and, this really was true, the very first driver pulled over and picked me up. I scrambled up into his truck and slumped into the passenger seat. I almost dozed off.

"Aiyoh, look at you," said the shocked middle-aged Chinese driver. "Cannot walk in the sun for so long. Radio say it is 34 degrees now. Got no cloud and no rain today. You mad to walk in this heat. Where you going?"

"Hay Dairies Goat Farm. It's in Lane 4."

"Wah, with your face like that, you could scare the goats."

Hay Dairies Goat Farm is the only goat farm in Singapore. The Hay family built up a small fortune in pig farming, but the government decided in the early 1980s that pig farming was out, so the Hays invested in some alpine goats from Minnesota instead. Now they have got over a thousand and serve a niche market for Singaporeans allergic to cow's milk. I arrived at 3.50pm. As the farm was closing at 4pm, I rushed over to the lady at the counter and said, "Hello, Mrs Hay, can I buy a bag of your hay please, Mrs Hay?" She did not laugh either.

After a lightning dash around the goat pens, feeding as many goats as I could, I retired to a table for a drink. I felt a tap on the shoulder. A beaming Chinese chap in his mid-forties looked down at me while his pal collected a case of goat's milk from the counter.

"Where you from?" he asked.

"Toa Payoh."

"No, where are you *really* from? You don't look like you're from Toa Payoh."

This insensitive, anachronistic observation drives me mad, as I am sure it does the thousands of fair-skinned Eurasians whose families have lived in Singapore for generations.

"Really? What do people from Toa Payoh look like then?"

"No, no, sorry. What I mean is ... "

"I used to live in London." I let him off the hook. He was a decent guy really.

"Ah, I went to London in 1982 for business. I got an orchid farm. Used to sell one type of orchid to a big store. Called Mark and something. Mark and Son?"

"Marks & Spencer?"

"Yah, that was it. Mark and Stencil. We sold orchids to Mark and Stencil for three years, but then the contract suddenly stopped. Dunno why."

Probably because he kept referring to the store as "Mark and Stencil".

Shortly before sunset, I found myself stranded at the end of Sungei Tengah Road. On the map, the northern tip of the road was bordered by forest and surrounded by the streams of Sungei Tengah and Sungei Peng Siang. It certainly looked *ulu* on the map. It was. Too bloody *ulu*. On foot, the dense foliage was inaccessible to the most ardent of explorers, let alone someone who should have called it a day after Hay Dairies. Outside Seng Choon Farm, half a dozen foreign workers piled into the back of a truck. Rather melodramatically, I stepped hastily in front of the vehicle and pretty much demanded a free ride back to civilisation. It was presumptuous, but I was desperate. The Chinese driver found me so amusing he offered me a seat in the back. My fellow foreign workers, who were all Indian, gladly made space for one more sweaty body. Conversation was difficult as their English was about as proficient as my Tamil. But through a combination of hand gestures and guffawing, they managed to express their firm belief that despite coming from a country of over one billion people, they had never seen such big feet. I was outraged. India has elephants.

The guy beside me then took out a knife. That was an alarming, unexpected development and I was a trifle concerned. Then he produced a papaya, cut a slice and handed it to me. I was humbled by his generosity. We were all foreign workers on that truck, but I did not kid myself. Our Singapore stories contrasted sharply. Their wages are often appalling and their living conditions even worse. These poor guys are the country's invisible people—seen, but rarely acknowledged. They build Singapore's homes, offices and expressways and clean and paint the HDB blocks and hawker centres, but spend most of their time here in the shadows. We had almost nothing in common, not even a language. But for

15 minutes, we huddled together and enjoyed a breezy ride through the countryside, a glorious sunset and some papaya. The journey was bumpy, my entire body ached and I had to sit cross-legged all the way to Choa Chu Kang's town centre. And yet I had never felt more comfortable.

# CHAPTER 16

Unlike almost every other male over 18 in Singapore, I have never fired a gun. Nor have I ever shared a bunk with another man. And I have never joined other young men in the jungle to paint helmets. National Service in Britain was abolished back in 1960, which means I am at a disadvantage in Singapore for several reasons.

First, I never get time off from work for reservist training. Singaporean male colleagues disappear from the office for the odd weekend jaunt claiming they are off to serve their country. I have no idea where they go, but they invariably return slimmer and tanned. I think they all go to health spas.

Second, National Servicemen are all fluent in bizarre Hokkien and Singlish phrases that mean nothing to anyone else. Approach a Singaporean woman and say "fuck spider" and she almost certainly will not clean your rifle. In the army, however, the spider refers to the dirt in a rifle during an inspection. Then there is the bizarrely sexual Hokkien rebuke often used by a superior officer to berate an idle subordinate. He might say something like, "Recruit, I told you to make your bed, but you just *kiao kah yo lum par.*"

For non-National Servicemen, *kiao kah yo lum par* roughly translates into "raise your legs and wiggle your balls". Now, I find it a mite peculiar that an officer orders a soldier to jiggle his genitals, but there you go. Like the masons, Singaporean men possess the ability to converse in an exclusive, members-only language. It is not Malay, it is not Singlish, it is not even Hokkien. It is Army Speak. If you do not know the language, you can go "fuck spider".

Finally, there is the big fish phenomenon. When three anglers discuss their respective catches together, the fish always get progressively larger. National Servicemen are the same. They have seen and caught everything in the jungle. They are *Buaya* Dundee. At times, you wonder whether Singaporean men carried out their Basic Military Training on Pulau Tekong or in Serengeti National Park. If you mention casually to a male colleague that you spotted a small monitor lizard in a canal at the weekend, he will nod slowly and then ask in a piteous voice, "How long was the lizard?"

"Well, it was about this long," you demonstrate proudly with your hands. "That, with the tail."

"Aiyah, when I was on night duty on Tekong, I saw a lizard so big I thought they were filming *Godzilla.* We needed a helicopter to get a leash around its neck. Couldn't send this one to the Singapore Zoo. Sent it to Universal Studios instead."

If you see a monkey, NS men have spent three months on Planet of the Apes. If you come across a wild boar on Indonesia's Bintan Island, they have lassoed a herd of buffalo with their own belt. If you spot a snake, they have wrestled an anaconda (and then probably wiggled its balls). In fact, they wrestled it, speared it, killed it, skinned it and ate it, using nothing more than twigs from a *tembusu* tree.

But one elusive beast remained. One rare creature that I knew guaranteed a certain cachet in masculine circles if I could find it. The deadliest predator in its environment, this guy's ancestors did not walk with dinosaurs, they ate them, to paraphrase the National Geographic Channel. This particular species is the largest reptile on the planet, found in northern Australia and across Southeast Asia. And at least one has been photographed roaming freely along the banks of Singapore's coast. I had spent five years trying to track it down, but to no avail. In desperation, I had asked the staff at Sungei Buloh Wetland Reserve to phone me if the reclusive reptile ever made a cameo appearance.

Then the call came. It lasted 10 seconds. "Hi, Neil, it's Andrew from Sungei Buloh ... Crocodile!"

"Right, I'll be there in 25 minutes."

I was there in 20. But the traffic along Kranji Road still suggested my desperate dash had been in vain. The estuarine, or salt-water, crocodile, the biggest reptile on the Earth, had submerged again. At low tide, the beast tended to appear on the banks of Sungei Buloh Besar, a stretch of fresh water, bordered by mangroves, that flow into the Johor Straits. But it came up only to allow the sun to roast its back. When it was overcast, the *buaya* (Malay for "crocodile") buggered off.

"You must be patient," said Andrew. "The crocodile bobs up and down every day. That's why we call him Mr Bob. When the sun comes out, so will he."

And in one sublime, unforgettable moment, Mr Bob's snout appeared above the murky water. To borrow a relevant phrase here, he was a beauty. His snout was long and brown, but he looked surprisingly benign. Crocodiles have been known to kill lions, bring down ungulates and attack sharks so I had expected to be exhilarated and petrified in equal measure, but I was just quietly respectful. Mr Bob glided effortlessly over to the water's edge to lie on the rocks, providing a stunning view of his entire body in the shallow water. His body was a muddy brown, with black, scaly squares down his back. This particular estuarine crocodile was not going to shatter any records, but he was still a respectable 2 metres in length. Toe to claw, he was longer than any human being on the island. But he was slenderer than most crocodiles, about 25 centimetres at his broadest point, and only a little wider than the fatter monitor lizards at Sungei Buloh. That could explain why he did not look fearful. (I must stress to Singaporeans and tourists here that there is nothing to be fearful of. You have got more chance of winning the Singapore Sweep first prize and then being struck by lightning on your way to the betting outlet to collect your fortune than you have of being killed by a crocodile in this country.) Instead, Mr Bob was a picture of serenity. Oblivious to the handful of gaping nature lovers who stood just metres above him on the overhead bridge, he was content to bask in the sunshine.

Then a suicidal fish brushed across his teeth, so he nonchalantly opened his mouth and ate it. That was a sight. His open jaws protruded out of the water like a jagged letter V as the witless fish wriggled around before they were quickly snapped shut. Clearly, Mr Bob had thought, "Look, I'm not hungry but don't take the piss. I'm one of the world's oldest predators and you're swimming in and out of my teeth. You wouldn't wiggle your arse in front of a heron's beak, would you?"

A little overcome with excitement, I became an impromptu, unpaid guide for the day. Whenever visitors passed, I pointed out Mr Bob (even though he was 2 metres long, he was still well camouflaged among the rocks) and stressed, rather manically, how lucky they were to catch a glimpse of him. A young Chinese couple peered down for five seconds, clearly unimpressed that they stood over Singapore's only known wild representative of a group of reptiles that can be traced back to the Triassic Period, roughly 230 million years ago.

"Oh, yah, it's a crocodile," said the bored 20-something woman. She could have hosted her own nature programme. "Not very big, is it?"

"How big would you like it to be?" I shouted after her. But the child of the American blockbuster movie had gone.

A couple of German tourists expressed their understandable shock at encountering such a prehistoric creature in a city-state. Lucky bastards. I spent a fortnight in Australia's Northern Territory and the closest I got to a wild crocodile was seeing a photograph of Paul Hogan in a glossy magazine.

Only an elderly Chinese couple matched my enthusiasm. Indeed, I am surprised that their excitable exclamations and constant jiggling did not trigger a bout of incontinence, particularly when I insisted that they check out Mr Bob. I was quite blasé about it by now. In fact, I had turned into a National Serviceman.

"Yah, there's a wild crocodile over there," I said, while casually flicking a piece of invisible fluff off my shorts. "It's been there about an hour now. Got very sharp teeth. Just ripped a fish's head off."

I neglected to mention that the fish was smaller than a tea bag.

"Wah, really ah," said the combustible auntie. "Where is it, ah? I mus' see. Mus' see. Where is it?"

"Where's what, sorry? Oh, the crocodile? That little thing? It's over by the rocks."

"Oh, yah. There it is. It's on the little island now. A crocodile! Look at its teeth! A crocodile!"

"That's a monitor lizard," I sighed. "The crocodile is still over by the rocks."

But the reptilian cousins did almost cross claws a little later to ensure the wild encounter ended on a memorable note. A prime candidate for a weight-loss diet, the fattest, most cumbersome monitor lizard in Singapore splashed around in the water under the bridge. With a bulging neck and an enormous body, the lizard wobbled and thrashed away, splashing everything around it. Including the crocodile. Mr Bob did not take too kindly to being disturbed by the world's stupidest creature. The sleek swimmer turned his periscope-like snout towards the blubbering embarrassment in front of him and dove under water. There was not even a ripple. Then that brown snout reappeared, just a whisker from the monitor lizard's tail. The stealthy Mr Bob had covered a distance of over 25 metres, undetected, in a matter of seconds. It was breathtaking, but worrying. The dopey lizard took an eternity to clamber onto the riverbank. At one point, the tubby twit stopped, presumably to ask its pursuer, "Now, be honest, Mr Bob. Does my bum look big in this to you? I've tried to exercise I really have but I just don't have the time."

The crocodile had positioned itself just behind the lizard, which had decided that now was the opportune moment to top up its tan. It was unbearable.

"Get out of the water, you silly sod," I found myself shouting. "There's a crocodile behind you and it's going to tear you in half. Move your fat arse!"

The unaware lizard looked up at the noise, as if to say, "What was that? Did someone say something then? Do you know,

I could've sworn someone said 'crocodile'. Silly me, that couldn't be right. This isn't Australia, you know!"

Finally, the dopey sod crawled off into the mangroves. According to the staff at Sungei Buloh, the crocodile was not hunting for its dinner, just protecting its territory. But that was irrelevant. As far I was concerned, Mr Bob pounced on Fatty, bit into its fleshy neck, performed the death roll and dragged it to the murky depths of Sungei Buloh. That is the story I will recount to my grandchildren anyway. I fancy even National Servicemen will have their work cut out trying to eclipse that one.

The Kranji Nature Trail was always going to be an anticlimax after meeting Mr Bob. But that is not to say it was not a splendid amble through grassland, secondary forest and mangroves. Divided into those natural habitats, the 2-kilometre-long trail, which is sandwiched between Sungei Buloh and Kranji Reservoir Park, provides visitors with fascinating examples of the mangroves' importance and subtly points out the damage urbanisation has inflicted upon the island. In the 1820s, when perspiring imperialists with superb sideburns were springing up all over the place, mangroves covered 13 per cent of the island. Now they cover only 0.5 per cent.

It is all a bit depressing really. Mangroves provide an island like Singapore with a natural coastline filter for all the flotsam. That is their purpose. Moreover, mangroves are also believed to absorb carbon dioxide emissions, generally blamed for being the major cause of global warming. According to recent media reports, a marvellous team of scientists from Singapore's National Institute of Education discovered that one hectare of mangrove forest can absorb something like 1.5 tonnes of carbon dioxide a year—the amount produced by one car in the same period of time. Consequently, the scientists appealed to the government to plant more mangroves around the island. I sincerely hope they succeed. And if you do not want to bequeath a lump of charcoal to your children, so should you.

Along the Nature Trail, the amount of crap caught up in the mangroves' roots was astonishing. According to a signboard, much of it is dumped from coastal kampongs along the Johor Straits. What the hell are they doing over there? Apart from the usual plastic bottles and odd shoes, I noticed truck tyres, a windscreen and a car seat. Are people driving their vehicles off the Causeway? It was most disconcerting.

I left the mangroves and took a short stroll down Kranji Way and headed into the reservoir park. It is not much of a park really, just a couple of old concrete benches, a dilapidated children's playground and a reeking toilet used mostly by fishermen to wash their rods. But Kranji Reservoir Park does boast the greatest sign in the country. Nailed to a bit of timber, the whitewashed board simply says "Warning! Beware of Crocodiles". And there is an awful, hand-drawn sketch of a crocodile above the stencilling. Even allowing for artistic licence, it looks more like an armadillo. Mr Bob would be most offended. But I wondered what the equivalent warning sign would be at Parsloes Park, my childhood park in Dagenham. How could it possibly match the exotic beastliness of a crocodile? After several minutes I came up with "Warning! Some kid has crapped in the sandpit". That was always pretty scary. I had suffered more wild encounters with fresh turds in Parsloes Park than with crocodiles in Sungei Buloh. Although they certainly added a spring to your step when you took part in the triple jump.

Kranji also hosted a major event in Singapore's short history that seldom receives the recognition it deserves. Amid the chaotic lack of communication, conflicting defence plans and general military neglect in the first two months of 1942, the sleepy, rural corner of Kranji could proudly claim to have temporarily succeeded where most of Malaya had failed—it scored a rare victory against the invading Japanese forces. On 8 and 9 February 1942, the Japanese Imperial Guard landed here to fight in what became known as the Kranji Beach Battle. But the aggressors landed at low tide and found themselves stuck in the deep mud. The enterprising 27th Australian Brigade, working alongside Singaporean volunteers, had earlier released oil into the sea. The Japanese were stuck in the oil slicks, which were then ignited. As a result, the attack was largely repelled. However, the British military command feared a Japanese landing in Jurong, so the exhausted troops at Kranji were ordered to withdraw south. This decision paved the way for the Japanese to land in greater numbers, take control of Kranji Village and consolidate in the north. It is a tragedy that such a bold stand ultimately proved futile, but that does not mean that it should not be remembered. There is a small, tasteful memorial dedicated to the ingenuity and resilience of the men who successfully defended Kranji in the middle of the reservoir park. But they deserve something more.

I sauntered along the shoreline for a bit, admiring the engineering marvel that is Kranji Dam. Have you ever been to Kranji Dam? It is a charming place. Ignore the dusty trucks bound for the farming estates and pay no attention to the tanned fishermen washing their groins at the public toilets and focus instead on the spectacular views. I stood on a grassy slope on the side that faced Malaysia to take in the stunning vista. The natural, breezy charm of Kranji Reservoir was on my right, the mangrove forest of Sungei Buloh behind me and the Johor Straits on my left. The tide had receded so the sea was a bit smelly, but that certainly did not detract from the splendid image of Malaysia's coastline. It is a familiar statistic, but one well worth repeating. The Johor-Singapore Causeway is only 1,056 metres long. Just 1 kilometre separates the two countries. Yet on a public holiday, it can still take four bloody hours to get across the Causeway.

I sat on a bench and peered over at the next door neighbour. The evening prayers at a coastal mosque drifted across the Straits. Condos, shophouses and the names of the Hyatt Hotel and New York Hotel were all discernible. Being rush hour, the streets were jammed with cars and lorries. From the tranquil setting of Kranji Dam, Johor Bahru was clearly a hive of bustling activity. The world of cheap seafood, discounted petrol and pirated DVDs looked quite inviting. So I decided to pop over.

# CHAPTER 17

I set foot on Malaysian soil. But I was nowhere near the country. I was still in Singapore, in the train station at Tanjong Pagar, which is owned and operated by Malaysian Railways (Keretapi Tanah Melayu Berhad—KTMB). I took a bus to Keppel Road, darted through the dusty, grey building of the railway station and entered Malaysia, thanks to a crumbling empire. In 1918, the British colonial government allowed the grounds around the station and the line that runs through the heart of the island to be sold to the Federal Malay States with one caveat—they were only to be used for train services, not commercial development. Now we are not talking *ulu* land here, we are talking prime real estate: some 40 kilometres of rail track from Keppel in the south to Woodlands in the north, stretching to over 50 metres at its widest point, all owned by Malaysia. Not surprisingly, it remains a contentious issue on both sides of the Causeway. The dogged Singapore government has bought back segments of the land in recent years and asked its Malaysian counterpart to move the station up to Bukit Timah or, better yet, Kranji. But the Malaysians continue to stall on an agreement. I cannot think why.

However, the anomalous station's colonial history makes it a fascinating building. Its high, arched ceilings resembled several train stations in London and had the floor been delicately coated with pigeon shit, it could well have been the Waterloo and Victoria stations of my childhood. Stained glass windows depicted scenes of a nostalgic Malaysia, with men in traditional Malay costume working in a rural world that looked more like an illustration from a children's storybook than an accurate reflection of life over the Causeway. But then, the whole station had a dated, stale air about it. Faded posters of Kinabalu and Sarawak said many things, but visiting either destination was not one of them. There was a drab, Malay coffee shop, a magazine stand cum money changer and a few tatty souvenirs that only the most charitable of travellers would take a fancy to. There were a handful of backpackers and a few foreign workers; otherwise the cavernous station was pretty much empty.

I was nosing through the magazine racks when I realised, to my dismay, that I had less than five minutes to fill out my immigration form, clear Malaysian customs (at a counter positioned beside Keppel Road, it was so bizarre) and make the train before it departed at 10.30am. The immigration officers pointed out that forms could be completed and checked on the train. As that was not the case, I inadvertently spent the entire day in Johor Bahru as an illegal immigrant.

The train itself exceeded my expectations. I had taken a slightly, negative Singaporean view of the Malaysian train and anticipated an antiquated, non-air-conditioned carriage with lowly paid workers hanging out of one window and hens, goats and chickens the other. Instead, the air-conditioned train was modern, clean and comfortable and the wide windows offered expansive views of the journey. The carriage was about a third full with the usual foreign and local blue-collar workers and the omnipresent backpackers.

The train was ready to pull away when another pair of breathless backpackers jumped aboard. The 30-something woman had long, unkempt hair, à la Janis Joplin, and the 40-something man had blond-in-a-bottle hair, à la sad old git. He was one of those ageing, backpacking hippy types who gravitate to Southeast Asia for its bohemian lifestyle, eastern philosophies and naive, olive-skinned women. Less common in Singapore, they are all over the beach resorts of Pattaya, Phuket and Bali. They are usually in their mid-forties, tanned, but craggy from overexposure to the sun. The best ones favour ponytails to cover their bald spots and hang out at (or lease) beach bars and restaurants with Asian women half their age. Locals often view them as exotic, worldly travellers respected for their free-spirited values. Fellow expats often view them as wankers.

But men like the middle-aged hippy on the train have always intrigued me. Why hasn't anyone close to him ever discreetly pointed out that he looks bloody ridiculous? I genuinely do not know how someone in his immediate family has not said, "Shall we call it a day now, John? We recognise that you becoming a beach bum in Thailand is a brave protest against the jackboot of globalisation and the greedy consumerism of Western civilisation, but you're starting to look like Leonardo DiCaprio's grandad. Why don't we spend this summer in the real world, eh? So have a shave, get a job and leave the peroxide in the bottle."

The Malaysian train pulled out of the Malaysian station in southern Singapore and we were off. Well, the journey was delightful. The $2.90 one-way ticket to Johor Bahru provided a glimpse of rural Singapore that is impossible to see any other way. The tracks behind Bukit Merah were dotted with allotments, vegetable patches and handmade shelters and shacks. Knowing that the land on either side of the track cannot be redeveloped for commercial purposes, one or two squatters have moved in. Well, at least someone makes use of the land. We cut through the serious money of Singapore as we passed through the three-storey houses around Holland Road and Sixth Avenue. There were BMWs and overworked maids as far as the eye could see. Somewhere around Bukit Timah, a large sign indicated that KTMB was carrying out extensive renovations to improve the line between here and Woodlands. Then I spotted the industrious workforce—six pot-bellied Malaysian guys sitting on an unfinished track sharing cigarettes. Marvellous. The train raced alongside Bukit Timah Nature Reserve and, at one point, rainforest surrounded the carriage. Foreign visitors entering Singapore on the KTMB train must have an entirely different first impression of the island. The journey was so green. We went over a couple of railway crossings, the one at Ten Mile Junction at Bukit Panjang being the most unusual. For a few fleeting moments, we rejoined the more familiar environment of housing estates and shopping centres before re-entering the countryside once more at Kranji. Darting beneath the snaking queues at Woodlands Checkpoint was worth the $2.90 ticket alone.

Just 10 minutes later, I really had set foot in Malaysia. My passport still had not been stamped. I stood on the scruffy Jalan Tun Abdul Razak in front of the station. The air was stifling and the heat from the traffic almost unbearable. Johor Bahru, or JB, always feels claustrophobic. I scuttled from one shaded spot to another until I ended up in Jalan Wong Ah Fook. Running to the main highway out of Johor Bahru, this is the main street for shopping centres, markets, temples and money changers. I noticed a number of Western backpackers milling around. They have always been an integral part of the JB landscape whenever I have visited. The dusty town provides the perfect launch pad for the beach resorts of Malaysia and a ramshackle, laid-back alternative to the clinical, controlled island across the Straits. At least, that is the impression occasionally suggested in one or two guidebooks. And frankly, I find that hypocrisy abhorrent. Poverty Tourism is one of the most unsavoury by-products of globalisation. Trendy, young Brits or suburban American backpackers called Dwayne Eisenhower Teaspoon III love to come here to sample a little Asian exotica; the poorer, the better. Forget Singapore. It is an Asian city that has dared to emulate Western standards of living. How dare they? Try Cambodia or Vietnam instead. They have got great shanty towns. Some real shitholes. Snap a picture in front of a poverty-stricken auntie washing her clothes in a polluted river and put the framed photograph beside the baseball trophy and the signed 50 Cent album. How totally awesome is that?

But Johor Bahru is changing, even if the progress is slow. Tired of being labelled the poor Causeway cousin, there has been a discernible effort to spruce up the place. I recalled the square between Sri Mariamman Temple and the Sikh Temple being an untidy mix of market stalls selling souvenirs and the usual tat.

Now it boasted a smart town garden, with the usual array of potted plants, paved and covered walkways, mini fountains and a café in the middle. Do not repeat this too loudly but it looked suspiciously like an upgraded HDB town centre. I had a decent lunch in City Square, a shiny shopping centre that summed up JB's identity crisis as it struggles to refashion itself into a modern metropolis and shed its image of being a seedy, but exciting and cheap, coastal shanty town. Beside the impressive City Square was a decaying shopping centre where most of the shopfronts had their shutters down. Across the street was a rundown market and decaying shophouses with rusty zinc roofs. Indeed, in City Square's enormous shadow was a stall selling second-hand shoes and trainers. The footwear had been polished, with newspaper stuffed inside to give that brand new shoe shop look. It all looked rather pitiful really.

And then there were the toilets. If Malaysia's town planners commission the building of a colossal shopping centrepiece like City Square, then they must ensure that the public toilets inside are free. Making my way to the amenities on the third floor, I was stopped at the entrance by a convivial Indian lady who charged me 20 cents. That was acceptable. Then I went inside, locked the cubicle door and realised there was no toilet paper. That was not acceptable.

"Excuse me, but there's no paper," I barked at the poor woman. I went outside first. Please do not think that I shouted from inside the cubicle with my trousers round my ankles.

"It's 20 cents."

"I know it's 20 cents. I already paid the 20 cents. I gave you the money 2 minutes ago. Remember?"

"That was for the toilet. Give me another 20 cents for the tissue paper."

My impatient bowels were in no position to argue, but someone somewhere is taking the piss. When I washed my hands afterwards, I realised there was something unusual about the person at the next sink. She was a woman! And a young attractive one at that. The cleaner pointed her detergent spray nozzle at the sink while an indifferent Malaysian chap pointed Percy at the porcelain just a few feet away. In Singapore, I have occasionally encountered an intrepid auntie mopping the toilet floor while moaning about how long I am taking to tinkle, but I have never witnessed a young woman cleaning the sinks beside the men's urinals. Not a confrontation with the opposite sex one would expect in Malaysia.

I surrendered to the oppressive heat and took a taxi to "Little Singapore" in Jalan Dato Sulaiman, a few kilometres further north. It is nothing more than a shabby, faded shopping centre called Holiday Plaza, but it rivals Toa Payoh Central for the number of Singaporeans shopping there at the weekends. If you are after anything pirated, copied or fake, Holiday Plaza is the place to go. The basement and the first floor are generally populated with shops staffed by *ah bengs* whose outrageously dyed hair suggests they sit blindfolded in a barber's chair and throw darts at a colour chart to determine their latest shade. Each shopfront promises all the latest DVDs. But that is all it is—a front. There will be a handful of copies of the genuine article on dusty shelves, their token gesture of legality for the benefit of officialdom, but the real stuff is found behind a locked door at the back of the shop. Being the only *ang moh* browsing around the basement, I became the prime target for Ah Beng and his Technicolour Haircut.

"Hey, John, come this way," a young Chinese guy said, beckoning me into his illegal emporium. I have been called John a few times and it is a little disconcerting. I know it is only a figure of speech, but it also happens to be my middle name. I am never quite sure if I am dealing with an *ah beng* or a clairvoyant.

"You want DVDs, John?" he continued. "I got the best price in JB."

"And some say Batam?"

He did not laugh either.

"Come, come. I take you into my special VIP room. Only you can come in here, I never open this VIP room to anyone else."

"Only me? You'll open the VIP room just for me? Wow, that's really kind of you."

The same guy had ushered me into the same room on a previous trip to Holiday Plaza six months earlier. Inside the VIP room were floor-to-ceiling shelves of DVDs, including titles not due for cinematic release in Singapore for another three months. I was left in the capable hands of two younger *ah bengs.* They were hilarious. It is not politically correct, but there is something endearing about the incessant sales patter of an *ah beng* selling illegal DVDs in Johor Bahru. They never give up, they never get offended and they will say anything to keep you in the VIP room.

"Hey, do you guys deliver?" I asked, feigning interest.

"Can, no problem. We deliver anywhere. JB, Singapore, anywhere."

"Anywhere? Well, I want to get them delivered to a place called Ramsgate. My mum lives there."

"Can, sure, no problem. Where's that, ah?"

"Where's what?"

"That place ... Ram's Head?"

"Ramsgate? It's in Kent in southern England. About two hours from London."

"Oh, that one, ah? Can, no problem. We deliver to Ram's Head all the time. You buy plenty, we give cheap delivery."

"But what if some of the discs don't work. Then how?"

"No problem, John. Each one got a 10-year warranty."

Although I could have listened to them all day, I pushed on, promising to revisit the VIP room with my mother from Ram's Head.

I discovered for the first time that Holiday Plaza actually had three floors. I had already visited the shopping centre several times but had never gone beyond the first floor. But then, other than pirated software, cheap phone and car accessories, shoe shops and the odd bakery, there is not much else to buy here. Indeed, Holiday Plaza represents a real legal dichotomy for the authorities. Publicly, they are utterly determined to crack down on the rampant piracy and copyright infringement that bedevils the country and makes it the bane of companies like Microsoft. And there are occasional, token raids on warehouses that manufacture pirated discs to pacify Bill Gates and his corporate pals. But the reality is harder to swallow. Crack down too hard on the DVD and software piracy in Holiday Plaza and visitors from Johor and over the Causeway will go somewhere else and the place will die. Indeed, its precarious position was discernible on the almost deserted upper floors, where a number of units that once sold legitimate products had closed down. There were fewer illegal DVD shops on the upper floors, so there was not an incentive for most shoppers to take the escalators. As a result, a blind eye is frequently turned at Holiday Plaza to ensure the customers keep coming back. Indeed, when I walked past the Crocodile menswear shop, I saw two Malaysian policemen trying on shirts. Beneath their feet, *ah bengs* were encouraging browsers to visit their VIP rooms. The cops could have apprehended the lot without breaking into a sweat. Perhaps it was their lunch break.

My next destination was supposed to be Lido Beach. As it faces Kranji Dam across the Johor Straits, I had planned to make poignant comparisons between the two countries. But the taxi driver insisted that was not where I really wanted to go.

"You don't want to go to Lido Beach," he said, as if playing a Jedi mind trick. "There's nothing for you to see. You want to go to Danga Bay. I take you there instead."

In no position to argue, I allowed him to take me to a place I had never heard of. It proved to be a wise move. Danga Bay is a half-finished waterfront city that spreads out over 25 kilometres and will eventually be home to residential and commercial centres, an education hub and sports facilities. Building work started in 2001 and the RM15 billion project promises a cruise terminal, a marina and a spa village, among many other things. The location is not unattractive. Overlooking the sea, it boasted one of the most picturesque food courts I had ever seen and was complemented by a couple of beach bars, a street bazaar and a mini fairground, most of which were closed. But the taxi driver assured me that locals flocked to Danga Bay on weekends and I believed him.

When it is finished, Danga Bay will be a cross between East Coast and Sentosa Cove, with yachts and boats docked at its jetties, children playing beach sports and tourists having a drink by the sea. That is, if it ever meets its 10- to 20-year completion date. Pardon my pessimism, but I have visited several neglected Malaysian beach resorts in the last 10 years. Looking more like ghost towns than a seaside playground for holidaymakers, these sad, peeling relics are dotted all over Malaysia and Indonesia. For Danga Bay to survive, it clearly needs Singaporeans to pop over on the odd weekend with their families to patronise the eateries and play on the beach. There are certainly worse places to have a cold beer and a plate of tasty chicken rice.

When leaving, I noticed a surreal attempt to attract the attention of Singaporean visitors. It was one of those guys who sketched your portrait while you waited. For a few dollars, this artist painted in oils on a half-decent canvas. Normally, these painters display their talents with illustrations of international celebrities such as Brad Pitt or Julia Roberts. Not this guy. No, he had proudly pinned up portraits of Malaysian Prime Minister Abdullah Ahmad Badawi and Singaporean Prime Minister Lee Hsien Loong. Now, PM Badawi I could just about understand, but PM Lee? The painter clearly expects Singaporeans to admire the portrait and say, "Wow, I've never seen such a likeness. It could be my prime minister standing there right now. I'm so overwhelmed by the patriotism that I can almost feel a verse of 'Majulah Singapura' coming on. If the artistic genius can do that for my country's leader, just think what he could do for me. Show me where to sit!"

But most Western tourists, on the other hand, will spend several puzzled minutes staring at the portraits of the two prime ministers before one of them is brave enough to ask, "Excuse me, I don't mean to be rude and I certainly don't wish to denigrate your talents, but who are these two meant to be? I don't think I've seen any of their movies."

Two hours later, I was ready to kill the Marco Polo of Johor Bahru's taxi services. Danga Bay might have been a welcome diversion, but it was also miles from the town centre and the Causeway. I limped along Jalan Skudai beside the Johor Straits as the warm, sea air melted my skin. Buses sped past at regular intervals, but there appeared to be no bloody bus stops. The public transport accessories that I usually take for granted in Singapore are apparently unnecessary in the orderly, functional world of JB, along with public benches and shelters from the merciless sun.

My fractious mood took a turn for the worse when I struggled through the public toilet that was Lido Beach. Being so close to the town centre, this coastal spot has long been a popular picnic spot for locals, but it was difficult to see why now. Drains filled with the most repugnant and smelly sewage imaginable trickled down sandy trenches and into the open sea, much of which will wash up around Kranji's mangroves. The lack of subtlety was almost laughable. There were no discreet pipes or tunnels involved, just puddles of black, treacle-like sludge all over the beach. To complement the putrid smell, there was a dead cat on the pavement, across the road from the Straits View Hotel, which easily won the title for least original hotel name. The poor cat had obviously been knocked down several hours earlier and mini-beasts of all shapes and sizes were gleefully ripping its exposed organs to shreds. And this was on a main street, opposite a hotel, in the middle of a scorching day. In the same week, Malaysia had unveiled a typically ostentatious plan to build a new scenic Causeway bridge on its side of the Straits (the project was eventually halted, even though millions had been spent on the foundation work). But in generating headlines with such grandiose schemes, municipal planners still neglect the very basics of public services, like clean streets and decent sanitation.

Sidestepping the dead cat, I eventually found the spot I was looking for. I took out my binoculars, sat on the concrete wall above Lido Beach, surveyed the horizon line and there it was—Kranji Dam and the very bench I had earlier been sitting on to peer over at Johor Bahru. Staring across at my home for the past 10 years left me with a very sentimental, and very obvious, thought. In geographical terms, Singapore is nothing. It barely qualifies for that little red dot status. From certain angles within Danga Bay, most of the country was obscured and here the miniscule island looked so unremarkable. Singapore really is nothing more than a remote island of four million castaways. It is dislocated from the natural resources of the Malayan hinterland and, apart from its advantageous location for shipping fleets, it has very little else to offer. To call Singapore a mere success borders on an insult. It is a bloody economic miracle and the envy of most of its neighbours, including those who lived behind me. Singapore does not come up with daft, extravagant schemes to rebuild half a bridge, but it keeps its streets clean. For most people, that is more than enough.

But the Malay fisherman who sat beside me at Lido Beach was not impressed. He eyed my binoculars suspiciously, waiting for me to give an explanation.

"Singapore. I live there," I said to the fisherman. He could barely contain his indifference.

"I don't like it."

"Don't like what?"

"Singapore. I don't like it. Everything need a permit. I want to fish, need permit. Want to work, need permit. Drive a taxi, need permit. In Singapore, I need a permit for everything. In Malaysia, if I want to fish, I fish."

The tide was out by at least 100 metres and would not be in for another two hours. My fisherman friend clearly had too much time on his hands.

"Since I got retrenched, I come here to fish," he explained. "At my age, very tough to find work. So I sit here and fish, and I don't need a permit."

"No, that's true. You don't need a permit to do nothing. Well, I've got to get to the Causeway now. It's time to go home."

And I really meant it.

# CHAPTER 18

Few people walk over the Causeway. There is a footpath on the left-hand side of the bridge, if you are entering from the Singapore side, but it is seldom used. That is because only an idiot would stroll across the 1,056-metre-long bridge. You will never hear a sensible Singaporean or Malaysian say, "It looks like it's going to be a lovely day. There's not a cloud in the sky. Let's take a gentle amble across the Causeway and marvel at the sights, sounds and distinct smells of the Johor Straits."

In the interests of authenticity, I thought it might be awfully windswept and debonair to return to my island home on foot. It was not. After spending several minutes explaining to the impatient immigration officer at Johor Bahru why I had entered the country illegally, I was allowed to leave once I had surrendered my train ticket as evidence. Malaysia is a country where dozens of *ah bengs* can illegally peddle pirated products while two coppers try on polo shirts in the same shopping centre, but an overzealous immigration official confiscates a used $2.90 train ticket.

I followed the railway line that brought me into Malaysia and realised I was on the wrong side of the Causeway. I dashed between crawling lorries, reversed around stationary cars and jogged alongside packed No. 170 buses. And those bloody motorbikes are relentless, aren't they? Standing at a small zebra crossing just a few yards from the footpath, I waited impatiently as the army of revving ants refused to stop. Getting across the Causeway is akin to playing a board game. You need to throw a six to start. In the end, I cheated death by marching across with my hands held aloft like a deranged messianic figure. They soon stopped then.

The walk across the Causeway was abominable. Opened officially in 1924, the bridge is drab and colourless and there was little to see other than the corrugated iron fences that some underlings had kindly put up to obscure any vista that might possibly be more arresting than that of a crawling traffic jam. And yes, it is not a myth—the Johor Straits really does stink. The odour from the sea, coupled with the carbon dioxide cocktails served up by the endless stream of zigzagging motorcyclists, created a combustible toxic stench that left me with a headache. The lengthy queues at the Woodlands Checkpoint followed by an even longer wait for the buses to clear customs left me to draw only one incontrovertible conclusion—if you are not driving, always take the train to and from Malaysia.

I found my way to Woodlands Town Park East. Naturally, I staggered around Woodlands Street 13 for a bit, looking in vain for the entrance, before I clambered up a grassy hillside and found a few canoodling couples and some people walking their dogs, who kindly pointed out that I had come up the wrong side of the park. There was a gentle path on the other side that I had missed completely. Annoyed by my myopia, I threw my bag down in a huff, removed my sweaty, sticky shirt with some difficulty, kicked off my shoes and socks and settled down on the grass for a nap. I lasted less than five minutes. Ants had apparently mistaken my hairy chest for a nest of twigs and were setting up base camp. And three foreign domestic workers were now sitting on a nearby bench, giggling at my perspiring, flabby stomach.

I left the park, which provided a wonderful view of the sunset, and cut through the tidy housing estates of Marsiling. The neighbourhood was so open and spacious. This tour was forcing me to stubbornly accept the fact that there were other roomier and more colourful estates than my beloved Toa Payoh. My suspicions were confirmed when I reached the junction of Marsiling Road and Woodlands Centre Road.

Woodlands Town Garden must be a contender for the country's finest town garden. Toa Payoh's pond and green penis tower look woefully inadequate in comparison. An impressive 11 hectares in size, Woodlands' green haven boasted two ponds and cleverly incorporated Sungei Mandai Kecil, a river that ran through the park. The ponds were separated by a tasteful stone bridge and the park also offered a couple of pagodas, good fishing, some great picnicking spots for the family and a middle-aged taxi driver groping a woman half his age on one of the benches. What more could you want? Standing on the stone bridge, I could still make out the Malaysian coastline, but this lovely garden, with its manicured lawns and tidy flowerbeds, seemed a million miles away from the putrid drains on Lido Beach. Not for the first time, I realised I was really going to miss this country.

The next morning I fulfilled a promise to Cliff. When the World War II veteran visited Singapore in 2005, I promised to visit Pulau Blakang Mati and the Sembawang Shipyard, which was once home to the British Royal Navy. Criminally overlooked in many history books and guidebooks here, the old Sembawang Naval Base played host to the British battleship HMS *Prince of Wales* and the battlecruiser HMS *Repulse* as preparations to confront the Japanese fleet off Kota Bahru, Kelantan, were finalised. With the men of Force Z, the vessels left Sembawang on 8 December 1941 and never came back. Like the American ships at Pearl Harbor, which had been pummelled a day earlier, they proved to be sitting ducks in the open sea. Military warfare was changing, with air power triumphing over heavily armoured warships, and over 760 British sailors and dozens of Japanese aircrew were sent to their watery graves off Kuantan.

It is one of many significant events in Singapore's modern history that is sadly neglected. Students can regurgitate facts regarding Stamford Raffles, the battle for independence, the rise of the PAP and the transformation from third world to first almost parrot fashion, but the sinking of the *Prince of Wales* and the *Repulse* gets scant coverage in comparison. It is deplorable. Apart from the loss of life, the decisive air attack had far-reaching consequences for mainland Singapore. With their enemies' major sea vessels destroyed, the Japanese were confident enough to launch a ground assault in the New Year and storm Singapore with a force roughly three times smaller than that of the British. Yet I have met many Singaporeans who have little knowledge of one of the most pivotal moments in the country's history. Fortunately in September 2005, the 60th anniversary of Japan's surrender, a memorial was finally dedicated to the men who lost their lives on both ships. It was unveiled on the very dock where the ships had set sail and I had promised Cliff that I would pay a visit one day.

The only problem was that I had absolutely no idea where the memorial was. I took the MRT to Sembawang and the No. 856 bus to Admiralty Road West. I headed past Sembawang Prison DRC, which is never going to be confused for NTUC holiday chalets. At the top of two watchtowers, soldiers brandishing machine guns observed me wandering down the street, flicking through my street directory. I gave them a cheery wave. Neither waved back. This part of Singapore has long housed the armed forces of Britain, the United States, Australia and New Zealand, among others, and the commodious black-and-white colonial houses and accompanying gardens certainly provide the officers with luxurious living quarters. There are Singaporean CEOs who do not live as well as this. The names of the streets were fascinating: Jamaica Road, Tasmania Road, Fiji Road, Falkland Road and Gibraltar Crescent. It is a dummy's guide to the rise and fall of the British Empire. I propose that if the Union Jack is ever lowered in both the Falklands and Gibraltar, then some street renaming might be in order in Sembawang.

I ambled along Admiralty Road East and passed the Terror Club. Now, isn't that a frightening name? It is a social club for the stationed or visiting naval servicemen of one particular country. There are no prizes for guessing which one. Only straight-faced Americans could come up with a name like the Terror Club and not laugh. At a push, the British might opt for the Slightly Scary

Club and the Canadians may plump for the genuinely applaudable We Never Go to War Club, but only the Americans could conjure something so terrifying and so pitiful at the same time. The young troops that passed me certainly looked scary. I had never seen so many crew cuts and pimples. Bouncing along wearing oversized shorts and baseball caps, some of these guys should not be trusted with a calculator, never mind a gun. A banner above the club's swimming pool read "The Terror Club Welcomes USS *Blue Ridge*". That only meant one thing for Singapore. The working women (and men) of Orchard Towers were in for a busy weekend.

After reading several news reports, I suspected that the memorial was behind the Port of Singapore Authority's (PSA) Sembawang Wharves in Deptford Road, which was a private building with security at the gate. I had neither my passport nor my employment pass with me. My chances of bluffing my way through were slim at best. I figured that I had more chance of eating a hotdog at the Terror Club with one of its dudes.

Well, I have to say, the security guards at PSA were wonderfully helpful and accommodating. They made a call and, within minutes, I was being driven around the extremely private shipyard by a petty officer in the British Royal Navy! A considerate chap by the name of Geoff Fawcett, he went way beyond the call of duty and gave me an informal tour of a place that is not open to Singaporeans, never mind a strange *ang moh* with no formal identification. It was an extraordinary, private world occupied by foreign military. The navies of the United States, Britain, Australia and New Zealand all continue to operate at Sembawang, which serves as a logistic base and an administration centre for visiting vessels. I passed a minimart, a money changer, a tailor's and a hairdresser's, all of which were managed by Singaporeans, yet relied exclusively on the foreign forces for custom. The tailor's shop was over 40 years old and the owner has measured up the same senior-ranking officers since they were teenagers. The local hairdresser is even allowed onto the gargantuan vessels to cut the hair of the rank and file on board. It was quite amazing.

Geoff dropped me off beside the memorial, which is along the west wall of the Sembawang Shipyard. It really was just a few yards from the store basin where the ships had left for the last time all those years ago. It was a simple sombre memorial, with a plaque detailing the events of 8 December 1941, enclosed by three pristine white walls. The plaque was made in Melbourne, significant because so many of the servicemen who died in Singapore or were imprisoned at Changi were Australian. According to Geoff, the British Royal Navy officers stationed in Singapore had long championed the importance of having a memorial to those in Force Z who had perished and that they should be credited for their perseverance. A considerate, respectful guide, Geoff told me he had taken several families to the memorial in the past year, including one who had flown all the way from Plymouth, an area in the southwest corner of England.

I stayed for about half an hour before the genial Geoff dropped me back on Admiralty Road East. I was glad I had visited, for Cliff and my late Uncle Johnny, both of whom had docked at Sembawang and Blakang Mati with the British Royal Navy sometime between 1939 and 1946. But I cannot help but feel that the memorial is a little wasted at the back of Sembawang Shipyard, tucked away beyond the private properties of the PSA. A little later, I visited the nearby Sembawang Park, which offered amazing views of the American vessels stationed at the shipyard next door. Perhaps the park might have been a more suitable location for the memorial. Although it is not the exact spot, the park's jetty does show visitors where the ships left and there is no reason why a simple plaque cannot still be added there by the National Heritage Board. Building such a tribute around Sembawang Park's jetty or beach might not be geographically precise, but it would be far more accessible. And a memorial is only a memorial if people can come to remember.

# CHAPTER 19

Sembawang was really growing on me. The two-storey terraced houses around Jalan Basong that backed onto plant nurseries had a rustic feel about them and the northern town offered a gentler lifestyle more in tune with its Causeway neighbour than the buzzing multitudes around Orchard Road. More importantly, Sembawang is also home to Singapore's most eccentric ice cream vendor. I walked towards the entrance of Sembawang Park beside Kampong Wak Hassan when the ice cream vendor zoomed past and stopped at the lay-by. It was 2pm on Friday afternoon and the park was deserted. Queues of eager customers were out of the question. I took pity on the elderly uncle and treated myself to a raspberry ripple.

"You like a cone?" asked a pair of shoulders. His head was buried in the tubs of ice cream somewhere inside the trolley. He was down there for an inappropriate length of time.

"No thanks. I'll have a wafer," I replied, peering down into the trolley. If the guy resurfaced licking his lips with a face full of raspberry ripple, the dollar coin was going straight back in the pocket. But the robust chap suddenly reappeared holding a raspberry ripple wafer. Only then did I realise he was impressively tanned and had a shocking head of red hair. I had never encountered such an elderly *ah beng* before.

"Hey uncle," I asked, desperate to maintain eye contact and not focus on his red moptop. It was brighter than a baboon's backside. "Why did you stop here? How to get customers?"

"No lah, I come here to go swimming."

"Really? Is there a swimming pool here then?"

"There, lah," he replied, betraying a flash of irritation at the asinine nature of the question. "Can see the sea or not?"

I could indeed see the sea. But having examined the Straits at close quarters on both sides of the Causeway in recent days, I was aghast at the possibility that anyone might fancy a bit of breaststroke around floating turds. I thought only mad dogs and English tourists at Blackpool did that. But the ice cream vendor was obviously an exception. I found a bench that was a discreet distance away from his motorbike and tucked into my raspberry ripple while observing an old man with red hair prepare for a swim. He had a cursory look around and, satisfied that the coast was clear, stripped off in the middle of the street! His shoes, socks and T-shirt were insouciantly discarded and tucked away in the trolley with the tubs of chocolate chip. Then he dropped his shorts to reveal what can only be charitably described as a well-worn pair of Y-fronts. They were pinkish and baggy in all the least flattering places, not helped by the tanned potbelly that protruded over the waistband. Now appropriately attired, I assumed that he would trot down to the seashore. But no, the suave swimmer helped himself to a cornet first. He dove into his trolley holding his neatly folded shorts and re-emerged with a raspberry ripple. Casting aside the traditional notions of public decency, he stood at the end of Sembawang Road in his pink underpants, with one hand nonchalantly leaning on the seat of his motorbike and the other holding his ice cream cornet.

And he did not move. Even when a bus pulled into the Sembawang Road End Bus Terminal beside him, reversed and went back out again, he stayed by his bike in his underpants, licking his raspberry ripple. Only when he had finished the cornet did he finally decide to saunter down to the beach, where he swapped the pink undies for a pair of trunks under the cover of his towel. But he did not swim. Instead, he stretched out on his towel, lit a cigarette and let out a satisfied sigh. His ice cream cornets, it seemed, were better than sex.

I waited at a nearby picnic table for 15 minutes to catch a glimpse of him paddling in the Johor Straits, but he appeared to have dozed off. It then occurred to me that there was something deeply disturbing about loitering around a beach waiting for a near naked uncle to show off his doggy paddle so I wandered off into the park.

Sembawang Park is considered to be one of the country's most *ulu* spots because of its comparative isolation, and it was almost empty. But that suits some people. As I passed a shelter, a breathless Indian couple hurriedly stood up and the man adjusted his zip. There was something about Sembawang Park that made Singaporeans want to take their clothes off. The park also has several monkey puzzle trees, which are stunning Chilean pine trees, with symmetrical branches that make them look like Christmas trees. I only mention them because there is no other tree on the planet that has a better name than the monkey puzzle tree. According to legend, the name derives from some daft Englishman who, in the 1800s, remarked that its scale-like leaves and prickly branches made the tree a puzzle to climb for most monkeys. No one is quite sure what the Englishman had been smoking. The name does not particularly convey a romantic mood though. In *Dr No,* Sean Connery and Ursula Andress sang about being under a mango tree together, but I wonder if the Indian lovebirds were aware that they had shagged under a monkey puzzle tree.

Whistling the tune of "Underneath the Mango Tree", I set off to visit the jewel in Sembawang's comely crown. In 1909, a Chinese merchant by the name of Seah Eng Keong discovered something unique at the heart of the northern kampong—a hot spring. It did not take long for local residents to flock to the natural phenomenon, believing the water's purities tackled common ailments like arthritis and rheumatism. During the Occupation, the Japanese constructed several thermal baths to enjoy the warm water. And by the 1960s, there were plans to transform the area into a spa to rival the world's best resorts. Tourists were expected to come from far and wide to experience the curative benefits of the spring. But nothing happened and, by the 1990s, the spring had fallen into disrepair and most Singaporeans had forgotten about the place.

But a handful of older, wily Sembawang residents, who remembered the hot spring of their kampong childhood, began to quietly return when the opportunity presented itself. In early 2002, the landowners, the Ministry of Defence, cleared the surrounding land to build an extension to the Sembawang Air Base. The story reached the newspapers and suddenly hundreds of Singaporeans were springing up in Sembawang. And they were not amused that the Ministry of Defence intended to fence off the area. Before you could shout "Eureka", community leaders presented a petition to the government, demanding that the spring be preserved.

Singaporeans are certainly a funny lot when it comes to picking their protests. In previous general elections in my Bishan-Toa Payoh constituency, no opposition candidates have stood against the PAP incumbents, which meant a walkover, so voters were denied the chance to troop down to the ballot box. But there were no organised complaints or protests. Threaten to close the island's only hot spring, on the other hand, and the petitions come out. It is most strange. A few months after I visited the hot spring, the 2006 General Election was held and Bishan-Toa Payoh residents were, once again, denied the chance to vote. But in the build-up to the election, the populace was up in arms over a more pressing issue—the price of a cup of coffee had gone up 10 cents. To offset the rising price of coffee, stall owners had been forced to increase their prices. Letter writers to the media suffered an apoplectic fit at the injustice of it all. The message came through loud and clear. Singaporeans will accept a one-party state, but do not take away their hot spring and never mess with their coffee.

But credit must go to those at the Ministry of Defence. Not only did they accede to local residents' demands and keep the hot spring open, they also renovated the compound and replaced the dirt track with a cemented path and some bougainvillea bushes in mid-2002. Hoping to be cured of their various aches and pains, the crowds returned to the revamped spring while the Singapore

Tourism Board examined its potential to attract foreign visitors. And then, nothing happened. Interest from the media and the public waned and the attraction certainly did not end up in STB guidebooks. But it was still open and I was eager to see what had become of Singapore's legendary hot spring.

I bounded off the bus at the junction of Sembawang Road and Gambas Avenue. The spring was just a couple of minutes walk down Gambas Avenue, although it was easy to miss. There was no sign. No mention of the hot spring at all, in fact. Perhaps the Ministry of Defence hopes to downplay the fact that it sits within a restricted area. If that was the intention, it has worked. The Sembawang Hot Spring undoubtedly holds the distinction of having the ugliest entrance to an attraction that I have ever seen. Prisons boast more attractive façades. The fence around the compound stood at least 3 metres high and was topped off by the ubiquitous roll of barbed wire. Although there was no indication of what was actually inside, there was still a sign ordering visitors not to cycle, litter, skateboard, play sports, walk dogs and, best of all, sell ice creams. Guess my swimming friend is screwed then. In addition, the Ministry of Defence could not be held responsible for any injuries sustained and visitors entered at their own risk. I now understood why the coach parties were not queuing up.

The path was also bordered by green fencing and barbed wire. I ambled along for about 25 metres until the path abruptly turned right and there it was, the exotic Sembawang Hot Spring. Now I do not know about you, but when I think of a hot spring, I conjure images of the great Roman baths with their flawless, mosaic floors within magnificent temples that stood several metres high or the religious sanctuary at Lourdes in southern France, with its castles, apparitions and spas. What did the Sembawang Hot Spring offer? A concrete compound and half a dozen taps. I was devastated. I needed a pint of hot spring water just to overcome my sense of disappointment. The unprepossessing concrete square was about 30 metres across and surrounded by the omnipresent high, green fencing. In the middle were four taps, from which the hot spring flowed continuously from 7am to 7pm. There was no religious miracle before and after those hours—the Ministry of Defence turned off the taps. I noticed a few more taps in the corners of the compound, but they were slightly obscured by plastic buckets and chairs that kind souls had left for others to use.

But then, the kampong spirit still prevails here. The moment I entered, an elderly chap told me to help myself to one of the plastic chairs that hung over the fence. I realised later that he was the caretaker; his office nothing more than a tatty old shed. He directed me to an upturned bucket beside the four taps.

"Take, take. Spring, spring," he said, gesturing towards the bucket. But I hesitated. Being even more obtuse than usual, I had foolishly assumed that the hot spring was under the bucket. I was momentarily paralysed by the thought that I would lift up the bucket and unleash a roaring spurt of boiling water into the air, like a geyser at Yellowstone National Park.

"What's underneath?" I asked, taking a couple of tentative steps towards the bucket.

"It's okay. Take, take. Spring, spring."

That is it, I thought. There was a volatile geyser under the bucket just waiting to blow my head off. I flipped the bucket over and jumped back to avoid the thousands of litres of nothing. The bewildered caretaker was offering me an empty bucket to fill at the taps. Now he hesitated. He was clearly not sure whether to hand me a second bucket or call the staff at Woodbridge Hospital.

I filled my bucket, returned to my plastic chair and waited an hour for the boiling water to cool. Aside from the caretaker and myself, I counted four other people. A middle-aged Chinese couple massaged their feet in a bucket beside me while, in the far corner, another Chinese couple, possibly in their early sixties, treated the Hot Spring as a day out. Singing along to the tunes blaring out from a Chinese radio station, the guy relaxed in an old bathtub filled with spring water while the woman washed their clothes in a bucket before stepping into her bathtub—a blue plastic barrel cut in half. Oh, she did look a treat.

I dipped a big toe into my bucket, but the water had not cooled sufficiently. I am not a hypochondriac, just listen to this. In 2002, a 57-year-old carpenter lost six toes here. A desperate diabetes sufferer, he came here looking for a cure but ended up in hospital with gangrenous toes. Unfortunately, his medical condition contributed to his injury. His poor blood circulation meant that he did not feel the water scalding his feet and burning through his skin until it was too late. So I was more than happy to bide my time. Besides, the soothing atmosphere was addictive. There was a real sense of collectivism here. Everyone shared chairs and buckets and talked to each other. The caretaker knew every visitor and even tried to converse with me but my appalling Mandarin let me down. The couple beside me explained the procedure of cooling the water through hand gestures and some quite gifted miming. There might have been a hi-tech airbase next door and a swanky condo complex on the other side of Gambas Avenue, but the socialist kampong spirit had at least survived in here.

After the couple beside me cleaned up and cycled away, I was left with a singing Chinese bathtub and a woman lying in a plastic barrel. It was time to leave. I stood up to wave goodbye to the caretaker and almost knocked my chair over. He was nothing more than a floating head. No one had said that this place was haunted. On closer inspection, the caretaker had somehow contorted his body so it could descend into a barrel smaller than a beer keg. Only his head was visible. The barrel was filled to the brim with steaming spring water, which gave the surreal impression that a dislocated head floated over it. The caretaker's ghostly face appeared through the steam and smiled back at me, the woman in the blue barrel waved and her partner belted out another Chinese ballad from his bathtub.

It had been a fabulous day.

# CHAPTER 20

Anyone who grew up in or around London in the early 1980s will be familiar with the concept of "red bus rovering". Before the uninspiring, all-inclusive travelcard was introduced, London Transport sold a one-day pass called a Red Rover, which essentially allowed you to travel on any red bus in London and its surrounding boroughs, including Barking and Dagenham, for the price of one ticket. It was marvellous. Children travelled out of their Essex housing estates around the city's fringes and into the exciting labyrinth of the nation's capital. Back then, the sun always shone, the buses and telephone boxes were always red and Ross and I could not get anyone to snog us in the school playground. And when you did not have a girlfriend to watch *Rocky III* with, you went "red bus rovering" with your best mate instead. The ticket was a gateway to a hedonistic metropolis that was a million miles away from the monotonous terraces of Dagenham. Any bus, any time, any place and as often as we wanted. Soho, Camden, Petticoat Lane, Tottenham Court Road, Notting Hill and Covent Garden—London called to us. The only problem was that our mums would not let us travel that far.

"Let's go red bus rovering," I would say excitedly as we watched Mickey's funeral in *Rocky III.*

"Yeah, all right, and this time let's go all over London. Even further than last time," Ross would reply as Rocky searched for his eye of the tiger.

"Where did we go last time?"

"Barking."

Barking is the town beside Dagenham. It was like buying a farecard in Toa Payoh and spending the day in Bishan. It was time to stretch our wings. We were almost 12 after all.

"We won't go to Barking again. Only spam heads go there. Let's go somewhere different up London."

So we went "up London". All the way to Upton Park, the home of West Ham United, and waited for Trevor Brooking to catch us kicking a tennis ball around the forecourt, whereupon he would immediately recommend us to the club's scouts. You see, we thought that the players lived in the stadium and we would join them once we had signed professional forms. But Upton Park is only 15 minutes away from Dagenham on the Tube. For all our bluff and bluster, Ross and I only ever went "red bus rovering" to the neighbouring Essex towns of Barking or Romford or to West Ham's Upton Park to demonstrate our ball control. We hardly needed a *London A-Z* as a guide.

And then it happened. We finally realised that we had exhausted every hang-out possibility in Barking and Romford, we were not going to dislodge Tony Cottee and Frank McAvennie from the West Ham first team and, more importantly, we had heard that you only needed to glance at a girl "up London" and her knickers would fall off. So Ross and I ventured into the city. We traipsed along to every major landmark we knew: the Tower of London, Madame Tussauds and the famous cinemas of Leicester Square. We only looked at them, mind you, as we lacked the funds to go inside any of them. Of all of London's landmarks, I loved Piccadilly Circus the most. With its gaudy advertising billboards, the statue of Eros and that roundabout leading to all the major shopping streets, the lively area seemed so glamorous to a 12-year-old. It was like standing on a real Monopoly board. Since then, I have taken every opportunity to visit Piccadilly Circus whenever I have returned to London.

And here I was once again, watching the cars, taxis and buses in Piccadilly Circus. Something was not quite right though. First, I did not have Ross beside me saying, "That girl across the street just winked at me. The one with the twitch. She definitely just winked at me. I reckon I could shag her." Second, I was not in London. I was in Seletar in northern Singapore. But it was Piccadilly Circus nonetheless, a mini-roundabout that was once the gateway to Britain's Royal Air Force and their largest airbase outside of the country in the 1930s. I had taken the MRT to Yio Chu Kang and then the No. 86 bus, which drove past the famous *prata* shops of Jalan Kayu and dropped me at the entrance of what is now the Seletar Camp of Singapore's Armed Forces. The former officers' village is also home to Singapore's oldest airport, 300 colonial properties and a cluster of bizarre street names that stand as a legacy to Britain's former military presence here. From where I stood at Piccadilly Circus, Edgware Road was the first exit, Maida Vale the second and Piccadilly the third. There was also Lancaster Gate, Knights Bridge, Battersea Road, Regent Street, Hyde Park Gate and The Oval, among many others; all in the quiet, remote Singaporean village of Seletar. Before you ask, there were no billboards, giant screens or statues at Piccadilly Circus. There was nothing except a sense of humour. It was just a mini-roundabout with a patch of grass in the middle and a miniscule road sign that cheekily said "Piccadilly Circus". I loved the irony. It was the only mini-roundabout I had ever come across that actually had a name, never mind one so historic and grandiose.

The black-and-white colonial bungalows and two-storey houses were lovely, with many complemented by large, well-tended gardens. Unlike the almost exclusively British community around Dover Road and "Little Kent", the Seletar village had a more cosmopolitan and homely feel. These houses looked like homes, rather than temporary stations for military personnel. The bungalows and gardens around Maida Vale were lived in, varied and inviting, probably due to the estate's eclectic mix of residents. Although there are a number of expatriates living here, there are also a number of Singaporeans, well-known names in some cases, from the arts and academic communities. And it all seemed more genuinely bohemian than the superficial Holland Village.

I strode down Park Lane, hoping to take a short cut to Seletar Airport, but a couple of soldiers at the School of Logistics halted my progress. That was a real Monopoly moment. I had gone round Oxford Street and passed Park Lane, only to be stopped and told to go back to the beginning and start again.

"You can't pass this way," the officer said. "Go back down Park Lane and head up West Camp Road to reach the airport."

"But if I don't pass 'Go', can I still collect $200?"

He had obviously not played Monopoly before. But I took the longer route to the airport, via Bays Water Road, where the houses and gardens were bigger, as were their snarling dogs. For heaven's sake guys, we all get the message. Your houses are palatial fortresses, the envy of Piccadilly and the rest of Singapore, but please, shut those bloody dogs up.

The breezy walk down West Camp Road was wonderful. The road was largely deserted and the welcome silence was only occasionally interrupted by a small private plane coming in to land on the runway to my right. Each flew so low overhead that I could make out the pilot's face. I waved at them as they approached but none of them turned and waved back, the miserable bastards.

Unlike the pilots, however, I almost missed Seletar Airport. Having been inculcated with the mantra "We've got the best airport in the world" so many times, I naively expected something of Changi Airport's proportions. After all, Seletar Airport had once been a magnet for the rich and famous, including actor Douglas Fairbanks and playwright Noel Coward. Today, however, it is almost hidden among old hangars, a roadside canteen and run-down buildings.

Opened in 1929, Seletar Airport consists of a small cluster of attractive single-storey buildings, reminiscent of other smaller airports in the region, such as Lahad Datu in Sabah, where they combine the services of baggage handling and customs. In other words, one man collects the cases from the plane, pushes them across the tarmac on a trolley, opens the doors to the terminal and throws them onto a table. Of course, nothing so slapdash would be tolerated at a Singaporean airport. I watched with not a little admiration as the staff effortlessly guided several shuffling passengers through the appropriate channels before they boarded a plane bound for Tioman Island. Then I went for a pee.

How many countries are there in the world where you can find yourself in a remote, tiny airport and yet the toilets are pristine, cleaned on an hourly basis and, best of all, free? Proudly take one step forward, Singapore. As I relieved myself, a bearded Scottish businessman joined me at the urinal. For reasons best known to themselves, middle-aged Scotsmen tend to favour beards. They also like to respond to every question and comment with the word "fine". This particular Scotsman did both, although he was reluctant to engage in any conversation initially, probably because I had a pen in one hand, my peeing equipment in the other and a notepad in my mouth. I have really got to stop taking notes in public toilets.

"So, er, what ye doin'?" he asked, not looking up.

"Oh, I'm researching a travel book on Singapore."

"Fine."

"So you're off on holiday then?"

"Aye. Well, been here on business. Now I'm off to Tioman for a few days."

"Oh, it's one of the best snorkelling places in the world."

"Fine."

I fancied asking him if, like most tourists, he thought Singapore was a "fine" city but he was bigger than me. I left the quaint Seletar Airport to find a bus stop in West Camp Road. There were a number of private planes parked on Seletar's tarmac. It can still be the airport of choice for those rich or famous enough to warrant a discreet arrival and departure. In 2002, Tom Cruise and his then girlfriend Penelope Cruz landed at Seletar to promote their film *Vanilla Sky* here. Tom and I have actually got quite a lot in common, you know. We have both been to Seletar Airport.

I took a bus back to Piccadilly Circus and meandered over to Baker Street. It was a sentimental journey. My mother was working at Marks & Spencer's old head office in London's Baker Street when she met my stepfather's backside. He was a porter; she was a secretary. He suggested he won her over with his sense of humour; she claimed he came in to empty her bin and provided her with a brief glimpse of his exposed crack. Either way, my youngest brother was the eventual result of that encounter. As one London street had inspired Sherlock Holmes, a fine song by Gerry Rafferty and my little brother, I felt the very least I could do was visit its Singaporean namesake.

Unfortunately, Baker Street could be a contender for the scruffiest street on the island. The untidy weeds gave it an unkempt look that was out of place among the tidy lawns of the neighbouring streets. There were skips full of car scrap and a shack with clothes hanging everywhere that resembled squatting quarters. Two empty boarded-up colonial houses only added to the eerie atmosphere. Even if a porter did come in and stick his backside in your face, you really would not want to live here.

I turned into the optimistically named Hampstead Gardens, which managed to be spookier than Baker Street (an impressive feat in itself) and was home to Singapore's creepiest house. Facing the Seletar Base Golf Course, a boarded-up, derelict property loomed large. The paint was peeling, weeds grew through rusted holes in the roof, the floorboards creaked and cracked and mould covered the walls. If Norman Bates ever bought a holiday home, this would be it.

I waded through the knee-deep undergrowth that bordered the front of the property, climbed over the barbed wire on the top of the fence and peered through a crack in one of the windows. The room was dank, dusty and full of cracked tiles. A filthy plastic chair was in the middle of the room. It looked like an interrogation room for the dead. Even in daylight, there was a sense of trepidation about the place. As I returned to the road to take in the dilapidated shack, I noticed a sizeable monitor lizard's head stick up above the grass beside the fence. It eyed me for a few seconds, then slunk off down the side of the house. In a country famous for its urban density and high-rise living, this crumbling hovel felt entirely incongruous.

I bid farewell to Seletar Village by dancing down a little street and singing a song my nan used to croon to me from her armchair:

"Any time you're Lambeth way
Any evening, any day
You'll find us all
Doin' the Lambeth Walk."

And I did the "Lambeth Walk" in Singapore's Lambeth Walk! London's original Lambeth Walk was known for its street market before World War II but became famous for the song of the same name in the 1937 musical *Me and My Girl.* It was a jaunty, Cockney ditty and its walking dance was nothing more than a cocky, playful strut down the street. My nan always sang it with such panache before finishing with her trademark—a quick flash of her knickers. We were used to her skirt-lifting, but it could get a bit embarrassing, especially when she did it in the supermarket. If my old nan sang "Silent Night" with a church choir on Christmas Eve, she would round it off by lifting her skirt and showing off her bloomers.

So I felt it only right to offer a poignant tribute to my beloved grandmother and one of her favourite songs by "Doin' the Lambeth Walk" in Singapore. So if anyone living there recalls an *ang moh* flashing each house by lifting an invisible skirt, do not worry. It was only me.

I ended up lost in Seletar West Farmway 4. Well, I did not think I was lost. On the contrary, I was enjoying a decent amble around the Jalan Kayu countryside. But when I reached the end of Seletar West Farmway 4, I found myself standing before an unnamed property and was about to turn back when a Malay chap on a bicycle appeared and informed me there was nothing to see here. So I strode irritably back down Farmway 4, blundered through a spider's web, removed the fractious spider from my forehead and ended up outside The Animal Resort in Seletar West Farmway 5. It was a real hidden gem and a fine place to take children. A 2.2-hectare animal farm, The Animal Resort serves as a care centre and a hotel for pets. As soon as I wandered in, some geese ran across my feet. Many of the animals roamed around freely. There were goats, horses, rabbits, dogs and an enormous wood stork that was standing guard over a turtle pond. Now there probably is an uglier bird than the wood stork somewhere on the planet but I have never seen it.

The high point of my brief visit was undoubtedly the School of Pet Grooming. As the title suggests, trainee pet groomers and stylists come here to learn how to give Lassie a ponytail or Rover a tight perm. There were three silver tables similar to a room service trolley, with a pampered dog on each one. Nervous stylists hovered over each dog, snipping, trimming, stroking and brushing. For some inexplicable reason, all the pets were those tiny, mini-me dogs like Chihuahuas and Shih Tzus with bows in their hair. One stylist was in the process of giving a toy poodle what I can only call furry pigtails. It looked preposterous. As she fussed over the yapping midget, I admired the stylist's restraint. She obviously wanted to push Toto off the table. The walls were covered with framed certificates of achievement for pet grooming. The awards included bizarre categories like Best Poodle Perm, Cutest Poofy Tail and Closest Scrotum Shave. I would gladly give out the certificates for that one.

"I've seen some dogs' bollocks in my time," I would say. "But I've never seen a pair shaved this well before. I'm not sure why Fido is whimpering; that's one flawless scrotum he's got there. They look like a couple of fine fish balls."

As I finished the day in Jalan Kayu, I feel it only appropriate to acknowledge the man who supposedly gave the street its name. As the principal building officer for the British Royal Air Force in the Far East in the 1920s, C. E. Woods designed the airbase at Seletar. In recognition of his sterling work, Jalan Kayu, the road that leads to the airbase, shares his name. In Malay, *kayu* means "wood". But in recent years, and particularly since the Malaysia Cup era, the word *kayu* has taken on negative connotations. "Referee *kayu*", for instance, means that the man in black is wooden or dim-witted. So if you translate it literally, Jalan Kayu will always be dedicated to the man who shaped Seletar's airbase and colonial village. A plank.

# CHAPTER 21

I was on a mission. I planned to track down Singapore's last kampong. Somewhere out in Lorong Buangkok there was not just a traditional Malay village of wooden homes, there were the final remnants of a country's past. A world of collective spirit, shared hardships and togetherness. In its race to build a first-world economy in the 1960s and 1970s, Singapore swept away the kampongs of its founding generations without batting an eyelid. *Attap* huts, crumbling timber homes, inadequate sanitation and polluted streams were all systematically bulldozed, cleaned up and drained to make way for the city of concrete we all know and love today.

But one survived. Hidden from public view, the small kampong of fewer than 20 rustic homes escaped the blueprints of the Urban Redevelopment Authority to allow its mostly Malay residents to continue a rural way of life not dissimilar to their great-grandparents. Being an endangered species, the village enjoys an almost mythical status. Singaporeans are vaguely aware of the country's last kampong being somewhere in Lorong Buangkok, but few have actually seen it. I wanted to catch a glimpse of Singapore's past before the future took it away once and for all.

Following a short bus ride from Ang Mo Kio MRT Station, I sauntered past the brand new HDB blocks of Buangkok Link and ventured into the living time capsule in Lorong Buangkok. Little more than a country lane, it was not signposted and a wonky lamp post with a smashed light encapsulated the street's spookiness. I trotted up the slight incline as quickly as I could. With Woodbridge

Hospital to my right and whistling trees to my left, there really was not the inclination to loiter. I came to the end of Lorong Buangkok and discovered, to my consternation, not a kampong but a retirement community called Surya Home. It was a rather run-down establishment, and not the first time I had seen the poor elderly folk of Singapore get the short straw for living in a country that does not subscribe to welfarism. I called out to a couple of Filipino nurses to ask for directions, but an elderly Chinese woman appeared from nowhere and took charge of proceedings.

"You want kampong? I find you kampong," she cackled.

She was certainly a peculiar woman. She held a pink toothbrush aloft like an Oscar, but there was not a single tooth left in her mouth. That made it difficult to concentrate for two reasons. First, I could not work out what she actually used the toothbrush for. And second, it is difficult to understand someone whose organs of speech are limited to a pair of gums.

"Yeah, I'm looking for a kampong. In Lorong Buangkok."

"This is kampong. Kampong is home," she mumbled vaguely through her toothless mouth. "This is my home. This is kampong. Kampong here."

"No, no, I'm looking for the old Buangkok kampong, not too far from Jalan Kayu."

"Wah, Jalan Kayu had a lot of kampongs last time. Wah, so many. Now no more already."

"That's great, thanks. But what about the one in Lorong Buangkok?"

"That one here, look. Kampong here. Surya Home. My kampong, Buangkok kampong."

Clearly medication time, the nurses ushered the poor woman and her toothbrush away and left me none the wiser. I was plodding off back into Lorong Buangkok when a middle-aged Chinese chap chased after me. His unkempt hair had been cut several different lengths and he had only three or four tooth stumps left in his mouth. Were the nurses dipping their patients' toothbrushes in sulphuric acid? His fingers were yellow and he constantly sucked on a cigarette stub that was neither lit nor fresh. The reek of tobacco made me nauseous.

"You want kampong at Lorong Buangkok?" he asked, grinning a toothless smile.

"Yeah, that's right. You know where it is?"

"Yeah, yeah I do. You are very tall," he replied.

"That's true. But do you know where the Buangkok kampong is?"

"Yah, yah, I know where, I know where ... Wah, you very tall, ah." He was mad. Friendly and eager to help, but mad. "My father was tall, you know. You look like my father. Do you know my father? Do you know where my father lives? Where does my father live?"

I thanked him and wished him well but he continued to shout out to me as I marched back down Lorong Buangkok, asking me where his father lived. Poor sod.

I retraced my steps and found another single lane off Buangkok Link. Once again, the dirt track was not signposted and appeared to double up as a coach park and a dumping ground. When the road ended, I went behind it and into the forest. Stone pillars ensured the path was only accessible on foot and a statue of Buddha had been placed on one of the pillars. I squeezed between the pillars and stepped over a man-made barrier of sticks and twigs tied together. The dense foliage was not inviting. The wild elephant grass towered above me in some places while my clomping around triggered slithering noises through the undergrowth every few paces. I was certainly apprehensive. Pythons and cobras are extremely common here. In the distance, I heard chickens and made out the tops of zinc roofs. But they were too scruffy to be part of a kampong and it quickly became clear that I had inadvertently stumbled across a group of squatters. A stray dog picked me out through the grass and started howling. Now, if I have learnt one thing during my tour of Singapore, it is that feral dogs are not solitary creatures. Suddenly, half a dozen of them were running towards me. I did not wait for a formal introduction. I was eager to keep my testicles. I sprinted back through the elephant grass. My arms flapped around in front of me in a vain attempt to see where I was going. I crossed a stream, startled a few lizards, hurdled the man-made barrier and almost knocked over the sacred Buddha before ending up on a muddy path in front of a ramshackle workshop.

At a stroke, I had gone back 40 years. I had found the kampong. The workshop was made of timber, with a sloped zinc roof. There were a number of Chinese deities on shelves in one corner, next to countless tins of Milo. At least half a dozen bicycles were tied to a tree and there was a broken washing machine stuck in the mud. I nervously called out. Although the workshop's owner was not around, his possessions and tools were laid out in front of me. Remember when your parents said that in their day, they could leave their doors and windows open all day long and no one would steal anything? Well, this was their day.

Behind the workshop, I glimpsed a couple of wooden houses and stepped tentatively inside Singapore's last kampong. I realised that I had missed the village earlier because it was almost entirely camouflaged by the forest. Coconut and banana trees served as natural borders for the kampong, along with a few mango trees and the ever-present elephant grass. Some workmen were laying pipes at the entrance of the kampong, providing the only telltale sign of modernity. The first two houses I passed were dilapidated and on the verge of collapse. The roofs had caved in and coconuts from the trees above had performed the role of the Dambusters' bouncing bombs, smashing through the walls and floors. It was a terrible sight.

I crossed a stream via a tiny bridge constructed from two old wooden doors that creaked ominously and had a peek at two intact houses next door. They were enormous. Taking into account the gardens, each property was at least twice the size of my four-roomed flat. And according to one of the residents, they only pay $13 a month in rent. No wonder families are reluctant to move.

As I peered around one of the houses, the owner appeared. And at the risk of making a facile comparison, I have wandered around some of the more upmarket estates and postcodes of Singapore and been greeted with indifference, suspicion and the odd devilish dog specialising in human castration. The kampong owner, however, invited this nosy stranger into his home.

"You want to see how big it is? Come, I'll show you the back garden," the amiable Malay chap said.

Well, his garden was indeed bigger than any other that I have seen in Singapore. It was a veritable menagerie. The guy had a dozen caged birds, five dogs that I counted and other animals that I did not manage to identify. The garden also incorporated a veranda, a table and chairs, two old wells previously used for sanitation, an electricity generator and a stream, all for $13 a month. The guy had been born in the kampong and returned to take care of the property after his parents died. We walked over to the stream where there were hundreds of empty oyster shells on the bank.

"They're not all from this tiny stream, surely?" I asked incredulously. My host did not wait for an answer. Instead he jumped into the ankle-deep stream and fished around in the water for no more than five seconds before producing an oyster. I thought I was in the presence of a native from a forgotten rainforest tribe. He shrugged his shoulders.

"Once a village boy, always a village boy," he said. Two of his dogs then bounded off down the stream.

"They're looking for snakes," said my indifferent host. "That's why I keep them. They've caught two pythons for me in this stream. And I had to cut down all the trees behind the stream to keep out the cobras."

The rustic simplicity of this man's life was difficult to take in. Everything seemed so incongruous. I was only 15 minutes from the air-conditioned modernity of Hougang Green Shopping Mall and his kampong faced the expensive private properties of Gerald Drive on the other side of the canal. And here we were plucking out oysters with our bare hands and chasing snakes down the stream. My pessimism suggested it could not last, but my host was adamant that his way of life would be preserved for at least another eight or nine years.

"Those pipes they're putting in where you came in are to improve the sanitation of all the houses," he said. "They wouldn't bother if they were going to knock us down. We need them though. We've always had problems with flooding."

That is an understatement. During the monsoon season, flood waters reach knee-level here and the kampong is often washed out. In the 1970s, frustrated residents bestowed a new name upon the village, Kampong Selak Kain, which is Malay for "lift up your sarong". I just love that. But my new friend was not going anywhere just yet. As he walked me to the home-made bridge across the stream, he said, "I've got to paint the place and do a lot of work, but I hope to stay. It was my parent's house. I can't let it fall apart."

I admired his optimism and I sincerely hope Kampong Selak Kain is spared the HDB bulldozers. And I am not patronising the residents. Nor do I pity them. They neither need nor crave my pity; they just want to be left alone to live quietly in their family homes. But then, the kampong in Lorong Buangkok is not there for my benefit. Nor should it remain solely to enable tourists to turn up and marvel at the rural simplicity of life in equatorial Asia. The kampong must stay because it is the only one in the country. Through the commendable work of the National Heritage Board, the government is finally accepting that no amount invested in interactive museums and fancy 3-D exhibits can resurrect dead history. There is no substitute for living, breathing history. If those traditional wooden homes ever pay the price for urban redevelopment, then one of the most vibrant, colourful and proud chapters of the Singapore Story closes forever. And the elusive kampong spirit dies with it.

# CHAPTER 22

I left the past and quickly returned to the present when I took the train to the most controversial station in Singapore. When the doors opened at Buangkok Station, I was astonished. The station is an architectural marvel. Flawlessly designed with dazzling local artwork around its fringes, Buangkok feels more like an art gallery than an MRT station. But then, more people probably visit an art gallery. Only nine other people alighted with me. As I passed through the turnstile at the cavernous but deserted station, I noticed one lonely guy manning the information counter. As he looked thoroughly bored, I took it upon myself to cheer him up a bit.

"Excuse me, sir," I asked, gently tapping on the window. "Can you tell me where the white elephants are?"

He was stunned. "You want to see the white elephants?"

"Yeah, of course. They're very famous, you know. They made news all over the world and, as you can see, I've come a long way to see them."

"No, no, they've been taken down already."

"Oh dear. That's tragic. Has the art exhibition finished? Are the white elephants now displayed somewhere else?"

"No. They were taken down almost immediately. They were just cartoon elephants. Nothing serious."

"Oh, I see. Why were they put up here? Outside Buangkok MRT?"

"It was nothing. Just someone playing a joke. It was nothing very serious."

I beg to differ. The white elephant debacle was a joke, but a serious one. In 2005, residents and grassroots leaders in Buangkok had just about had enough. A gleaming, brand new $80 million MRT station sat proudly on the edge of their town, with trains trundling through every few minutes on the North-East Line. But the trains did not stop at the station because it was not open. Train operators had originally suggested Buangkok Station would open in 2008 when there would be enough housing units in the area to justify the expenditure. This did not please residents, to say the very least, many of whom had moved to the new town on the proviso that they would be provided with adequate transportation services. So the empty, ghostly station sat there every day: a giant white elephant in the heart of an expanding community.

Then in late August 2005, eight cardboard white elephants mysteriously appeared around the station's grounds to coincide with a ministerial visit. I loved the impudence and applauded the residents' sense of humour. Others did not. The cardboard cut-outs led to a police probe to find the culprits, who had not obtained the necessary permit. Not for the first time, Singapore threatened to become a laughing stock on the international stage. But on this occasion, common sense prevailed. It was a great day for Singapore. Not because residents had actively engaged in a benign political protest, but because the white elephant furore showed that everyone from the top down was finally taking this business of a sense of humour seriously. A local politician once remarked that Singapore must take this business of a sense of humour seriously; arguably the daftest remark ever uttered by any parliamentarian anywhere in the world. But ironically, the government is trying really, really hard to do just that.

Just a few months later, it was decided that Buangkok Station should be opened after all. At the residents' party to mark the occasion in January 2006, some students sold "Save the white elephant" T-shirts to raise money for charity, which was marvellous. But at the risk of bursting Buangkok's radical bubble, the fact that only nine other people alighted with me at the station may suggest that the station was not ready to be opened. When I exited the station, I was met with a sweeping view of nothing. There was an open field on one side and a half-finished housing estate on the other. It did not look promising.

I had decided to go to Buangkok to sample the Singapore I was leaving behind. If the kampong in Lorong Buangkok represents the country's past, then the new towns of Sengkang, Punggol and Buangkok in the northeast are stepping stones to the future. All three offer modern, luxurious HDB blocks that can easily be passed off as condominiums and the estates have been touted as a 21st-century township. But a house alone is not a home. When residents began moving into Sengkang in the late 1990s, there was a flood of complaints. Aside from the initial teething problems of any housing estate, such as dimly lit lift lobbies, concealed block numbers and leaking roofs, there were more pressing concerns that astounded me. Inadequate public transportation and a lack of linking roads were so serious that the debate reached Parliament. Residents understandably rushed to move into their ultra-modern apartments only to find a lack of community centres, coffee shops, schools, medical facilities and banks. At one point, around 1,000 households moved into their new Sengkang blocks every month in a township that covers over 1,055 hectares. That is almost twice the size of Ang Mo Kio. Eager homeowners were moving in faster than the amenities were being built.

The perceived incompetence was extraordinary. How could the HDB get it so right with Toa Payoh in the 1970s and yet seemingly get it so wrong with the new estates around Sengkang? It intrigued me because my English hometown of Dagenham had suffered the same problems. When the London County Council built the estate in the 1920s to rescue working-class Londoners from the East End's slums, it was lambasted for providing nothing more than red bricks and cement. At the very heart of the so-called British Empire was the world's biggest housing estate, but it failed to provide decent shops, schools and medical facilities for its tenants. There were not even any pubs! How on earth can you transport an entire community of Cockneys and dump them in the Essex marshes without giving them a few pubs? Dagenham still suffers from the after-effects of the town planners' short-sightedness. When town councils break up extended families in their pursuit of urban redevelopment, there must be a trade-off. The public facilities and amenities of the new town should, at the very least, be the equal of the community that has been left behind. Otherwise, what is the point of uprooting a family?

I sauntered down Sengkang Central to see if the town had righted its wrongs and found myself in a huge housing estate off Compassvale Drive. Now the first thing you notice about Sengkang is its sea-shanty, seafaring, "ahoy there, shipmates" architecture. As it was once the town of the seafarer and a port, Sengkang's planners incorporated its past into their designs, hence street names like Compassvale and Rivervale. The marine theme can be seen everywhere, from the metallic sails that hang off most of the blocks at Compassvale to the lighthouses and timber ship that feature inside Compass Point Shopping Mall. It certainly was not subtle but it was quirky, with the highlight being the shark's fin. Have you seen it? There may be several poking out around the estate, but I only found the one and it was freakish. I walked past a badminton court and there it was; a life-sized silver shark's fin sticking out of the grass.

"Hey lads, what the hell is that?" I asked the two teenagers playing on the court. "It looks like a shark's fin."

"It is a shark's fin," one of them replied. "It's part of the fish theme here. Stupid, right?"

Well, I do not know about stupid, but it was certainly bizarre. If a drunk stumbled across it at night, he might think he was drowning. Every time I looked at it, I could hear the primeval sound of John Williams' cello. To me, the architectural feature said "*Jaws*". To many older Chinese, it must say "wedding dinner".

The badminton court was occupied and there were other teenagers waiting to play. I also noticed matches in full swing at the basketball court and the street soccer pitch. In fact, all of the public courts and playgrounds were filled with youngsters. I realised that the designers had pulled off a masterstroke here, not by emulating the superficial features of a condo complex, such as fancy lift lobbies and marble floors, but by fostering a sense of community. The enclosed nature of the estate provided security. Building the blocks around the recreational facilities gave the estate a focal point, in this case the various sports courts, to enable younger residents to come together and play. Because the apartments themselves bordered the facilities, they provided an element of safety, a literal physical barrier from the outside world. I was very impressed. Children cannot play like this in a sprawling estate like Toa Payoh. Aside from the lack of green spaces and sports courts, they would invariably need to cross streets, void decks and roads to find an appropriate venue. Toa Payoh's centrality makes it an ideal location for working parents, but I now wondered what the old town actually offered their children. Compassvale, on the other hand, was a great place for sporty, energetic children to grow up safely. The swanky estate had a real self-contained, communal feel about the place. I will not get carried away and say that the kampong spirit had returned to Sengkang—the days of borrowing a cup of sugar and dashing through muddy streams to catch fish are long gone. But the town's heart is in the right place.

As time was getting on, I found a willing tour guide to show me around the townships of Sengkang and Punggol—the LRT. For those of you who share my utter contempt for all short forms, abbreviations and acronyms, the LRT stands for Light Rapid Transit (LRT), a mini-transportation network set up to serve the far-flung estates of Sengkang and Punggol. The Sengkang LRT, a $302-million driverless system, opened in 2003. It followed the much maligned Bukit Panjang LRT, which opened in 1999 and has since spent much of the time breaking down. Now I like the LRT. It is cute and convenient. But it is not a train. I mean, it is a train in the technical sense, but it is not really a train. The LRT reminds me of little dogs like Chihuahuas, Shih Tzus or, my personal favourite,

Cockapoos (a cross between a Cocker Spaniel and a Poodle). They are dogs in the literal mammal classification sense but, let's face it, they have got far more in common with other four-legged animals. Like hamsters. You will never read the headline "Man mauled by Chihuahua". Or see armed police officers send for the Shih Tzus before a drug bust. They call themselves dogs but, really, they look more like cats with big ears and hormonal issues. Well, the LRT is the public transportation equivalent of a Chihuahua. Those driverless contraptions masquerade as a sleek, steel train but, if the operators painted a face on the front windows, the cuddly carriages could hang out with Thomas, Percy and the Fat Controller. As the automated, single carriage chugged along the track, I kept hearing the dulcet tones of Ringo Starr telling the mischievous Thomas to come back and pick up his driver.

Not that the LRT was not a comfortable ride. On the contrary, the carriage was spotless, as you would expect here, and television screens played movie trailers to while away the time. It just felt like I was being transported from Terminal One to Terminal Two. Furthermore, the skytrain at Changi Airport could stake a valid claim that it provides a more scenic ride than the Sengkang LRT. By the time I had reached Bakau LRT Station, it was difficult to distinguish one side of the track from the other. The blocks on the left were beige with an orange window sill and the blocks on the right beige with a blue window sill. That was the extent of the variation in design. When the sprawling estate in Dagenham opened in the 1920s, there were reports of new tenants going shopping and not being able to locate their home when they returned. How does that not happen here? I would not be surprised if Sengkang resembled the *Village of the Damned* on a full moon, with dozens of lost residents staggering aimlessly around the streets shouting, "Where the fuck's my apartment?"

Toa Payoh, like the neighbouring older towns of Ang Mo Kio and Serangoon, has its faults, but uniformity is not one of them. Tall, short, fat and thin—apartment blocks of all shapes and sizes are welcomed in the Big Swamp. From my window in Lorong 2

Toa Payoh, I could count six blocks that were different in shape and colour and all within walking distance. The view from a window in Rivervale must resemble Huxley's *Brave New World.* I switched over to the Punggol LRT and alighted at Riviera LRT Station because it sounded French and exotic and, according to my street directory, it overlooked the Sungei Serangoon River. I need not have bothered. The amenities at Riviera consisted of an HDB block, a car park and a bus stop. It must be like the Rio de Janeiro Carnival here at weekends.

I took a bus to the jetty at the end of Punggol Road, which once offered seafood restaurants by the sea. Pig farms also dominated the vicinity back then, so heaven knows what the area must have smelt like. Now there was a jetty for fishermen and a small plaque to remember the 300 to 400 Chinese civilians who were executed here on 28 February 1942 by the Japanese military police. They had not done anything of course. The executions were part of the nationwide Sook Ching operation to purge the country of suspected anti-Japanese civilians. The plaque was installed in 1995 by the National Heritage Board, which has redoubled its efforts in recent years to commemorate key incidents in Singapore's short history but rarely gets the credit it deserves.

Apart from some parents making sandcastles with their children, the seafront was deserted. Few people visit Punggol Beach now. It is a shame because the beach was surprisingly clean and the sunset was breathtaking. There were a few kissing couples waiting to get it on after dark, but I barely noticed them. With weary resignation, I accepted the fact that I am destined to stumble upon every shagging couple in Singapore.

I finished the day inside the lift of Block 187 in Punggol Central. I cannot explain it really. I caught a brief glimpse of the HDB apartment block and wandered over. With its underground car park, palm trees, marble floors and cream-coloured apartments with wide, blue-tinted windows, the block easily fitted the dream of a 21st-century township. I had never seen a more attractive HDB apartment block. But best of all, Block 187 had a sexy lift voice.

I travelled up to the top floor accompanied by a seductive, arousing female voice. I pressed the top-floor button and she groaned, "Going up". The woman's pouty voice was straight out of a pornographic movie. I had a quick peek around the top floor but there was not an unblocked view of Punggol. Besides, I was eager to get back to the female orgasm. She did not disappoint. In fact, she even lifted a line direct from a porno movie. "Going down," whispered the woman, clearly quivering with lust. At that moment, an unforgettable scene from the movie *Fatal Attraction,* involving a lift and Glenn Close, suddenly popped into my head. I was not displeased; I had been thinking about Punggol's old pig farms.

# CHAPTER 23

It was not always easy growing up in England. My parents divorced when I was in kindergarten, my mother worked long hours and my younger sister had to eat my sausages and mash. Those burnt bangers just floated in the potato purée and it is no coincidence that she is now a vegetarian. But at the end of every school year, we packed our bags and headed off for our annual caravan holiday in Clacton on the Essex coast. Before outrageous property prices in Britain forced people to take out a second mortgage to buy a doll's house, caravans were the destination of choice for most working-class families. Cheap, homely and easy to maintain, caravans afforded us a little castle by the seaside. We would stay for the entire six weeks of the summer holiday and live on a shoestring. The journeys were always special. As we drove out of Dagenham, my sister and I would tuck into the chocolate goodies provided for the two-hour journey. Twenty minutes later, my sister would reproduce the chocolate goodies all over my A-Team T-shirt. My mother would tell her off and my sister would cry and blame me for complaining when I clearly should have sat in silence for the remainder of the trip covered in vomit. Meanwhile, I would sulk all the way to Clacton because I had to bare my bony, milky-white chest to giggling lorry drivers.

Nevertheless, those caravan holidays were glorious. At our caravan park, there was a swimming pool, a video arcade, a clubhouse and a playground, all ideal locations to target pretty girls. But as my mother gave me a wonky haircut and a red turtleneck to go with my perpetually runny nose, I looked like a heroin addict going cold turkey. So I spent most of my days on the swings listening to the *Rocky IV* soundtrack on my portable tape recorder, which, I seem to recall, was the size of my HDB apartment. We divided our time between the pool, the park and the beach. Evenings were always spent at the cosy clubhouse with the other caravanners, all of whom came together to watch me take part in the annual fancy dress contest. Each year, my giggling mother covered me in green food dye and threw me onto the stage as "the world's skinniest Incredible Hulk". Oh, how we all laughed.

Without a doubt, those caravan holidays were easily the highlight of my childhood, as they have been for countless working-class children growing up in Britain. Singaporean children really do not know what they are missing. I have always believed that the biggest drawback of growing up in a small country is that there are very few places for a child to escape to. There is no space for a caravan park here and even if there was, I suspect it would lose out to a more lucrative shopping centre, condo complex or integrated resort.

Of all the coastal towns in Singapore, only one comes close to simulating the communal, caravan culture of my British childhood: Pasir Ris. I love everything about Pasir Ris and it is easily my favourite town in Singapore. The fact that few tourists or expats visit the place is nothing short of criminal. Once the home of poultry farmers and fishermen, the northeastern coastal town has long been considered an idyllic destination for day trippers and picnicking families.

A holiday town, Pasir Ris is one of the country's newer HDB estates with younger, more active residents favouring a healthier, outdoor lifestyle by the sea. At one time, Pasir Ris MRT Station had more bicycle stands than any other station in Singapore, and the town boasts one of the most scenic cycling trails in the country. They are certainly not couch potatoes in Pasir Ris.

I asked a member of staff at Pasir Ris MRT Station how long it would take to walk to NTUC Lifestyle World-Downtown East.

He looked utterly horrified. "You sure you want to walk?" he asked. "There's a feeder bus, you know. No need to walk."

"It's okay, I want to walk. I know it's not that far."

"It's very far. At least a 15-minute walk."

It took five minutes. That is another drawback that comes with living in such a small country. Distance is relative. On several occasions during my trip around the country, I was advised to take public transportation only to discover that my destination was no more than a couple of streets away or on the other side of a shady park. By and large, Singaporeans do not walk anywhere unless it is on an air-conditioned treadmill. And while we are on the subject, the next time a teenager steps into your HDB lift and casually presses the button to the second floor, pick the lazy bastard up by the scruff of the neck and throw him back out into the lobby. Can't healthy youngsters walk up a couple of flights of stairs anymore? The social and economic ramifications for the country are terrifying. Seriously.

Downtown East is the main reason why most people visit Pasir Ris today. Built by the National Trades Union Congress, the entertainment complex was little more than a couple of public swimming pools beside some holiday chalets when I first arrived. Now the entire facility has been transformed beyond recognition; the swimming pools gave way to the marvellous Wild Wild Wet water theme park, with the usual tunnel slides and wave pools. I have been a couple of times at the weekend and the park is never less than packed. The Escape Theme Park is a poor man's Disneyland, but the few decent rides are reflected in the reasonable admission fee.

Still, there is a certain mocking cynicism when it comes to Downtown East. Like Sentosa, the resort draws unfavourable comparisons to the magical kingdoms of Florida, the Gold Coast and now Hong Kong. It is an unfortunate symptom of the "whacking" culture that permeates society here. As there is very little to complain about in the economic and political arenas, there is a tendency to "just whack" trivial stuff such as minor bus fare increases, taxi drivers and Downtown East. Town planners are damned if they do and damned if they do not. Addressing the age-old gripe that there is nothing to do on this tiny island, NTUC spent $30 million to redevelop Downtown East and then endured further complaints from those unfairly comparing apples with oranges. If those gambling behemoths pencilled in for Marina Bay and Sentosa fail to live up to international standards of an integrated resort, then public criticism will be more than justified. But Downtown East more than adequately meets the needs of its community, NTUC members and the accidental tourist.

I went into Downtown East through the back entrance via Aranda Country Club and encountered a world that bore close similarity to my caravan holidays. There were teenagers shooting and killing things in the video arcades, market stalls that sold sweets, crisps and the usual tat only sold at seaside resorts, a kiddies' play centre and ball pool, a theatre for movies, concerts and the odd circus and the usual fast food outlets. Every time I have visited Downtown East, changes have been implemented and they are always for the better. On this occasion, a stretch of shops leading to the chalets had been upgraded and now sold magazines, hawker food and, rather strangely, VCDs.

Outside the Wild Wild Wet water theme park, I glimpsed four teenage boys flirting with girls as they tottered past. That is what it is all about—getting away from the books and blogs for a little quality time with the opposite sex. With far too many teenagers going to single-sex schools here, they need to savour every opportunity they can get to mingle.

As it was Friday, the weekends-only Escape Theme Park was closed so I hired a bicycle and poked my nose around Pasir Ris Park. Built on reclaimed land, the massive 71-hectare park is a charming, well-maintained retreat for families, fitness fanatics and, well, just about everyone. The Fishermen's Village served up the kind of seafood on the water's edge that once packed them in at Punggol; children had a quaint cycling trail for beginners, a maze garden and an adventurous adventure playground; and the mangrove swamp boasted a new boardwalk for nature enthusiasts. There was even a birdwatching tower that provided some decent graffiti on its top level. Someone had written "You shit on me, I shit on you", which displayed a Corinthian spirit of fair play if nothing else. Another hand had scrawled "No Vandalism!". I loved that.

Convinced I could not embrace Pasir Ris any further, I whizzed past a couple of carpenters who were hammering in the final few nails of a brand new pony stable. The foreman told me that within a month, children would be able to come here for pony-riding lessons followed by dinner at the adjacent café, all within the secluded setting of a breezy park overlooking the sea. Until the glittering doors to those integrated resorts are opened, there is simply no better venue to take your children for a day out, and that includes the half-finished Sentosa. The fad culture makes the pony stable a bit of a risky business venture but I sincerely hope it survives. Singapore can always eke out a little space for an alternative leisure activity and I have long had a soft spot for horses.

When I first met my wife, she was 16 and an accomplished horse rider. She devoted every spare moment to her beloved pony Pepi, attending to his every grooming need. Anyone in the horsey fraternity will tell you that the magnificent sturdy studs are prone to uncomfortable penis scabs. Pepi was no exception, and my wife would clinically pick them off. Now, most teenagers usually spend their puberty years drowning in a maelstrom of hormonal insecurities and self-doubt. So have you any idea what it does to a teenager's self-confidence when he discovers that his girlfriend spends her weekends examining the sexual organ of one of the most prodigiously well-developed mammals on the planet? When she said her favourite companion was hung like a horse, she meant it.

Having returned my borrowed bicycle, I reluctantly left Pasir Ris. I planned to spend the rest of the day in the neighbouring town that still conjures evocative images and scarred memories for people across the Asia-Pacific region by the mere mention of its name: Changi.

Home to both the world's finest airport and the darkest chapter in Singapore's history, Changi generates pride, sadness, anger and bitterness, depending on your age, race and nationality. Younger Singaporeans are proud of their airport; older Singaporeans recall Sook Ching. Australians and Brits think of concentration camps, hardship and brutality. The Japanese do not really talk about the place. And Nick Leeson will always equate the town with a prison cell and colon cancer. It is many things to many people but, for me, it has always been about the history. So I took the No. 89 bus along Loyang Avenue to find Fairy Point Hill. I was going for three reasons. First, the name made me laugh. Second, I knew that there was something vaguely historical about the place. And third, no one I had spoken to had a clue where Fairy Point Hill was or what was actually there.

I alighted beside Hendon Camp, home to some of the finest commandos in Singapore, and almost bumped into a couple of Singapore's military elite. Surely, the buffed, bronzed pair would know where I was going.

"Hey guys, do you know where Fairy Point Hill is?" I asked.

They had no idea. "I've never heard of the place. Oh wait, do you mean the one over at Changi Village beside the hawker centre?" one of them ventured.

"No, that's the ferry point. I mean Fairy Point. It's supposed to be off Cranwell Road, which we're in now."

"Sorry, never heard of it. But I know for sure it's not anywhere around here."

Fairy Point Hill proved to be 200 metres away in the next street. Those commandos have got a wonderful sense of direction, haven't they? Not that I can blame them for being unaware of Fairy Point's whereabouts because, technically, I am not sure if it is even supposed to exist. Besides, they were not alone in their ignorance. After ambling past the government bungalows and reaching the end of Cranwell Road at Changi Beach Club, the security guard there also insisted that Fairy Point Hill did not exist. The road proved to be right behind him.

I turned back down Cranwell Road and noticed a side turning that obviously did not intend, or want, to receive any visitors. A striped barrier and concrete pillars ensured that vehicles could proceed no further. There were no street names, signposts, mailboxes, lamp posts, electricity cables or anything to suggest that the crumbling path was a street. But it clearly led to a grassy hillock and, according to my street directory, the location of Fairy Point Hill so I smothered myself in insect repellent and ducked under the barrier. I followed the cracked, uneven road up the hill, past the overgrown weeds. In the overhanging branches of a tree, a couple of green parrots screeched at me. The heat was insufferable so, after checking that there were no giggling lorry drivers around, I peeled off my drenched T-shirt and invited all the mosquitoes in Changi to attack my flabby nipples. They duly obliged.

I turned a corner at the top of the deserted hill and there it was—the most haunted of haunted houses. On the crest of Fairy Point Hill stood a stately two-storey colonial mansion. The majestic building was cream-coloured with bright, sturdy pillars that have long been popular in military architecture. There was a rusty flagpole on the roof. Several archways, flawlessly carved out of timber, adorned the façade and gave the doors and windows an undeniable elegance. You do not come across historic structures like this in Singapore very often.

Sadly, the house was falling apart. The interior had been gutted, the paint was peeling off every wall, chunks of plaster were strewn across the floors and electricity cables hung out of every crevice. With all the doors and windows either smashed or removed, I peeked into the rooms. They were all empty. I lacked the courage to step inside because signs all over the building warned that trespassers would be prosecuted and, if I am being honest here, the house was spooky, even in daylight. So I wandered around the back instead. Weeds covered the outside toilets and storeroom. I was desperate for a pee but the constant rustling in the undergrowth and the strange surroundings ensured I left Fairy Point Hill cross-legged. The place was just too damned eerie. At the bottom of the slope, I noticed a sign that I had missed earlier. It had been posted up by the Urban Redevelopment Authority to inform interested parties that Fairy Point Hill, now euphemistically named Changi Point Cove, was up for sale as a prime residential and entertainment site.

Now, at what point will all this stop? How many historic sites, sacred grounds or green spaces will be auctioned off, demolished or dug up before someone suggests calling it a day? With every parcel of historic land that is sold off, Singapore sells another piece of its soul to the highest bidder. It really is that simple.

I later discovered that the dilapidated building was originally a command house for British forces. Designed by colonial architects and completed in the 1930s, Fairy Point Hill's strategic location in the island's leafy northeastern corner ensured it played an integral role as a British air- and naval base. After Singapore's independence, the building was taken over by the Ministry of Defence and served as the SAF Command Headquarters. History oozes from every nook and cranny and the National Heritage Board could work wonders with the house. The dying site is crying out to be resuscitated and turned into a World War II museum or archive, a tribute to those imprisoned in Changi, a memorial to those who perished in the Sook Ching operation or even an administrative centre for the Heritage Board. Changi has more than enough hotels and chalets to take care of the future; what it does not have is enough buildings to take care of its past.

# CHAPTER 24

I should point out that Changi is doing many things right. I left Fairy Point Hill and found myself on the exceptional Changi Point Boardwalk. Over 2 kilometres long, the boardwalk begins at the Changi Beach Club, follows the edge of the coastline and finishes at the ferry terminal in Changi Village. When I say the edge of the coastline, I mean just that. At one point, the platform took me above the rocks on the shore and within a couple of feet of the crashing waves. And its information panels are faultless. I learnt that a famously tall "Changi tree" (most likely *Sindora wallichii* and believed to have provided the town with its name) was removed by the British to stop the Japanese using the local landmark as a marker for their guns. I cannot help but feel that if the British had spent less time chopping down historic trees and more time worrying about the tens of thousands of Japanese troops who were making their way towards the Johor Straits, the events of 1942 might have been a little different. I also found out that Changi Village was a popular destination for tigers in the early 1900s. They swam over from Johor, stopped over in Pulau Ubin for a bit of wild boar and then made their way over to Changi. That route is now popular with illegal immigrants.

At the end of the boardwalk, I took a bus to Upper Changi Road North to have a quick peek at something that the National Heritage Board really has got just right. Opened in 2001, the Changi Chapel and Museum is housed inside a gentle, respectful white building and commemorates those who were imprisoned in the vicinity during the Japanese Occupation. Admission was free, as it should be for every museum, and there were excellent storyboards and poignant keepsakes, diaries and clothing that once belonged to the POWs. And the touching replicas of the Changi Murals, sketched by ailing bombardier Stanley Warren, have to be seen to be believed. Warren's story is truly one of the most uplifting accounts of World War II.

Increasingly sick from his incarceration, Warren kept his spirits up by drawing a number of religious murals, such as *The Last Supper* and *The Resurrection*, on the walls of Roberts Barracks, Changi Camp, which was used as a POW hospital, beginning in October 1942. Now, this was one brave man. He had eight kidney stones removed with no anaesthetic, and still worked on the murals. The Japanese were hardly going to provide paintbrushes and easels so Warren improvised. He used clumps of human hair for paintbrushes, brown camouflage paint and crushed-up billiard chalk for blue paint. When the war ended, Warren assumed the paintings had been destroyed by the Allied forces' bombing campaign, returned to England and thought no more about them.

Then the story took a remarkable turn. In 1958, the murals were uncovered, by accident, in Changi Camp Block 151. Stanley Warren was somehow tracked down in England, where he worked as an art teacher, and was invited back to Singapore to restore and finish the Changi Murals. He made several trips back and they were finally completed in 1988. He died in 1992. Due to their sensitive location, the originals are not open to the public, but the replicas at the Changi Museum are respectfully displayed. You must see them.

What I have always liked about the Changi Chapel and Museum is its sombre subtlety. I visited Pearl Harbor several years ago and it felt more like a Disneyland attraction. First, there was the film with the bombastic sound effects, accompanied by the ever-present chest-beating patriotism and bugle blowing. Then came the trip to the viewing platform from which you could peer into the sea and stare at the rusty USS *Arizona,* an experience that

I found rather uncomfortable. But that was only slightly less macabre than the sweaty tourists in floral shirts and knee-high white socks dashing around with their camcorders, ordering their children to pose beside the watery graves of dead servicemen. Americans just cannot do subtle, even when it comes to war memorials. But the quiet, reflective tone at Changi is perfect.

I continued down Upper Changi Road North and stopped outside the new, pristine Changi Prison. Part of the modern complex opened in 2004 to some controversy. Not for the first time, the authorities had not entirely considered the political and historical sensitivities when announcing that the old, decaying prison, built in 1936, would be torn down and replaced. For many war veterans around the world, as well as thousands of elderly Singaporeans who suffered Japanese persecution, the prison was a symbolic reminder of their horrific past. And we are not talking about a handful of aunties and uncles here. Between 1942 and 1945, around 76,000 POWs were interned in the area. Not surprisingly, letters to the press came from Australia and New Zealand, begging the authorities to respect their memories of the dead. But if cemeteries cannot be spared, then an archaic, crumbling prison has got no chance.

The original Changi was demolished, but a sensible compromise was made and I was here to see it. I strode quickly past the shiny Prison Link Centre, which bears more than a passing resemblance to a shopping centre with its gleaming glass frontage. I arrived at the main entrance to the prison and found what I was looking for. I could not miss it. An old, grey, 180-metre stretch of wall facing Upper Changi Road North, with a turret at each end, stood out among the new shiny structures. The stark, depressing façade now provides the only gateway to the site's past as it was rightfully gazetted by the Preservation of Monuments Board as a National Monument. Common sense prevailed as the authorities finally acknowledged the tremendous emotional value of the original Changi Prison. Even the present Australian foreign minister, Alexander Downer, whose father endured three years as a POW in Changi, applauded the decision.

I could not really see much of the old wall from the street so I approached a young Indian woman who was coming through the prison gates at that moment.

"Is there any chance I can go in and have a look around?" I asked.

"Can you go inside? This is Changi Prison." Her tone made it clear that she was dealing with a moron.

"No, sorry, what I meant was, is there a museum or an exhibition inside?"

"Of course not, it's a prison."

She hurried off to the nearest bus stop as a genial guard gently ushered me back towards the street. Security is certainly stringent at Changi Prison. And I do ask some bloody stupid questions at times.

The following morning I returned to the charming Changi Village in a very chirpy mood. The giddy prospect of a little sea travel always gets me excited and I planned to spend a rustic day on Pulau Ubin. I arrived at the new Changi Point Ferry Terminal to find it transformed into a modern, airy building with a bar on its roof overlooking Serangoon Harbour. The only downside was the bumboat drivers are more finicky now. They will not start their engines until there are 12 passengers waiting to travel (or you are willing to charter the entire boat for $24 to match the $2-per-person fee). But I was suitably entertained while I waited. A couple of perspiring, overweight Chinese gentlemen sat on the bench beside me. If you needed a stereotypical profile of two loan sharks, these greasy guys fitted the bill. Three students joined us, one of whom was a tall, attractive Chinese girl. Well, that was it, wasn't it? In a mixture of English, Singlish and Hokkien, the guys remarked how sexy the girl was, what they would like to do to her and in what positions. I have always found these conversations utterly engrossing. Do such guys really believe that all that lustful snorting, guffawing and hand signalling will lead the beautiful young woman to say, "Do you know what? I've succumbed to your irrepressible charm. Come, let's find an empty bumboat. I want to have sex with you both right now."

The nifty journey took 10 minutes and I stepped onto Pulau Ubin's jetty and back to the 1960s. Whatever route you take, whether you walk, cycle or drive, Pulau Ubin is a peaceful, beautiful getaway. Its very charm lies in its simplicity. The island offers a rustic retreat of kampongs, wooden jetties, undisturbed wildlife, old plantations and a traditional agrarian lifestyle, in which residents rely on prawn farms, fishing, provision stores and renting bicycles to survive. Being an island of undulating, granite hills, granite mining once provided work for thousands of settlers in the 19th century. This occupation also gave the island its name; Pulau Ubin means "Granite Island" in Malay. But the quarries are no longer in operation. They are now filled with water and vegetation is recolonising the areas. In fact, I noticed reforestation taking place all over the island, which was most pleasing. Across most parts of the island, the sound of silence is still deafening. Of course, you will still occasionally encounter wearisome types who carp on about there being nothing to do on Pulau Ubin. Shoot them.

I rented a mountain bike from an ebullient woman who had lived on the island for over 40 years, whizzed past the shops, eateries and stray dogs (those buggers could not catch me on a bike) and headed into the countryside. It was delightful. I cycled through old coconut and rubber plantations and around the picturesque Pekan Quarry, stopping twice to allow monitor lizards to swagger across the road, and then headed west along Jalan Endut Senin.

One of the joys of cycling is being part of the secret society of fellow cyclists. It is like the masons. There are secret signals, expressions and comments shared only among cyclists and only when passing each other. A brief downward glance denotes a serious cyclist not to be trifled with. Raising your eyes to the sky followed by a brief sigh and a smile indicates a social cyclist who is not as fit as he should be. Looking down at your pedals suggests a red-faced, panting cyclist who is in no mood to talk to anyone. While open-mouthed, wide-eyed horror insinuates that you are about to collide with your fellow secret society member and you might wish to get out of the way.

There are also the snatches of conversation. The quick "Hello, lovely day" is always practical when cycling downhill. But in Pulau Ubin's unhurried, tranquil setting, there was time for slightly longer exchanges. There were comments like "The countryside here is beautiful", "We must be mad to cycle in this weather", "Hang in there, the jetty's just up ahead", "Gee, that's a nice bike" and "You don't get many of them to the pound, do you?".

I stopped at a kampong where a homeowner sold cold drinks to day trippers. I already had a bottle of water in my bag, but I loved his hand-painted sign which read "Oh yeh, oh yeh, y u so like that? Buy a drink lah!", so I did. Remembering my manners, I stood at the door and called out to the guy. He appeared, but was clearly none too pleased that I had called him out to the front door. He ushered me into his kitchen and left me to pick out a drink from a cool box while he turned his back on me and returned to his washing up. He was not being rude. He trusted me. They still do not feel the need to lock their doors on Pulau Ubin.

I pedalled past the new Marina Country Club, which I must say has been blended in with its rural environment rather well. Partially covered by trees, the simple wooden chalets with their mock thatched roofs were not ostentatious. No one hankers for another concrete jungle on Pulau Ubin, but the sports and adventure retreat actually matches its habitat. If the Urban Redevelopment Authority insists that further construction is required on the island, let's have more of this please.

I was heading towards Jalan Wat Siam and Kekek Quarry when a small sign caught my attention. The sign caught my eye because it was written in English, German and Chinese; a linguistic combination you do not expect to find on Pulau Ubin. The sign said "German Girl Shrine" and an arrow pointed towards a narrow gravel path. Now I do not know about you but I will always make time to visit the shrine of a dead German girl at the end of a country lane in a remote corner of a tiny Asian island. I raced off down the track and soon found myself bouncing over ragged rocks, chipped stones and fallen branches. I puffed my way up a steady incline and found myself in an open field surrounded by *lalang* grass. The gravel track was uneven and slippery. It was like taking part in a motocross race. I swerved down a sharp left slope and stumbled upon a striking yellow hut. It was shaded beneath two trees; other than that, the area was deserted. I peered through the window of the hut and jumped back. There was a lavishly decorated altar at the far end of the room with a large white urn in the centre. This was the dead German girl's shrine. I turned the handle of the bright yellow door and, to my utter disbelief, it opened. The smell of joss sticks was overwhelming and there were half a dozen lit candles scattered around the room. Someone had been here before me. On the altar were a number of pitiful offerings to a teenage girl, including cheap perfumes, soaps and make-up mirrors. There was also a newspaper clipping about the German girl that some kind soul had nailed to the timber.

Her tale was undeniably fascinating. According to local folklore, the dead girl was the daughter of a coffee plantation owner on the island. After World War I, British soldiers did not take too kindly to having Germans making a good living on one of their crown colonies so they marched in to intern the parents. The young girl apparently escaped through the back door, lost her footing at the edge of the quarry and plummeted to her death. Chinese workers carried her remains to the crest of a quarry hill and gave her a proper burial. Then, of course, devotees began turning up to pay their respects and pray for good fortune. One or two must have hit the jackpot because devotees are known to come from as far as Myanmar and Thailand to pray for wealth and happiness. According to folklore, quarry excavation meant that the grave was exhumed in 1974 and the girl's remains were rehoused here. At weekends, devotees still light a candle for the girl, leave a small present and pray for a little something in return.

It is a great story. But there must be an easier way to strike 4D and get rich.

I spent no more than five minutes at the northern beaches of Noordin and Maman. Unlike the packed beaches around Sentosa and the East Coast, the sand was untouched, the sea was reasonably clean and there was not a single tanker on the uncluttered horizon. But all of that was academic, thanks to the bloody awful fences that have been erected just past the water's edge to keep out illegal immigrants. I cannot begin to express how depressing and unsightly it all looked. The immigrants may not be able to get in but snorkelling Singaporeans cannot get out either and heaven knows what detrimental effect the bamboo barricades have had on Ubin's indigenous wildlife.

At the point where Jalan Maman and Jalan Sam Heng meet, I had stopped for a drink when I heard an intense, high-pitched squeal echo through the trees. I nearly fell off my bike. Being the shameless coward that I am, I waddled from side to side and pulled back from the edge of the forest. Although the foliage was thick, I spotted a short, stubby hairy tail wagging through a narrow clearing. It was a wild boar. Satisfied that it was a safe distance away and the road was downhill if I needed a quick getaway, I crept towards the animal. Wild boars are generally harmless, but they will attack with their tusks if they feel cornered. A deep snort followed by a quick rustling through the undergrowth stopped me dead in my tracks. I crouched and peered through the trees again. There were two of them. Grey, heavy and over a metre in length, the boars snorted in my general direction and continued to sniff the ground. As it was getting dark, the nocturnal creatures were foraging for food. It was a priceless moment. But I was not going to test my good fortune by venturing any closer, even if I had paid my respects to the dead German girl. The burly boars continued on their merry way through the forest, grunting at each other in a dismissive fashion that was uncannily reminiscent of my grandparents.

I love Pulau Ubin and I know I will dearly miss its traditional, rustic simplicity when I leave Singapore. Around 300,000 people visit the 1,020-hectare island every year. Of that figure, a substantial number are tourists and there are over four million people living in Singapore. The figure could be much higher and the residents would almost certainly welcome the additional revenue. So go to Pulau Ubin. Find $2 for the bumboat and go this weekend. I cannot promise you anything but peace and quiet, the shrine of a dead German girl and, if you are lucky, the odd glimpse of a wild boar. But the island does provide a temporary escape from that jungle on the other side of Serangoon Harbour.

# CHAPTER 25

And so to Singapore's biggest and most popular park. East Coast Park stretches across some 20 kilometres of reclaimed land in the southeast of the country. Boasting just about every outdoor and indoor pursuit imaginable, the park's theme is one of "Recreation For All" and I do not disagree. At weekends, families enjoy barbecues on the beach under breezy coconut trees while fitness enthusiasts cycle, skate, bowl, swim or smack a few golf balls around a driving range. The only slight problem I have with the East Coast is that it has a higher proportion of wankers than elsewhere.

On any given Sunday, the cycling and skating paths are undeniably swamped with idiots. After gathering at the nearby Idiot Club, these skaters don their wraparound sunglasses and knee and elbow pads and spend the afternoon irritating as many people as possible. The Idiot Club generally accepts two classes of skater: Beginner and Expert.

The beginner's task is simple: totter along the skating path for three steps, then fall over in front of half a dozen cyclists and pedestrians. Repeat. All bloody day long. The expert skater's job, on the other hand, is to define coolness with every effortless stride. With their aviator shades, Lycra shorts, bare chests and hands behind their stooped backs, these guys are so cool it hurts. To everyone else, they look like silly sods with lumbago. But when the two groups come together, as they frequently do at East Coast Park, they form a congested traffic jam of Rollerblades, such that the casual walker cannot cross the path without being poleaxed by a giggling beginner or knocked into a bird sanctuary by a speeding extra from *Starlight Express*.

Taking refuge from a heavy downpour, I stood under a shelter beside the old Big Splash water slide park and waited for my clothes to dry. When the rain stopped, members of the Idiot Club quickly resumed their weekend's activities. A French couple pulled up at a barbecue pit beside me to allow the woman to adjust her skates while her partner perfected his spins. With his slicked back hair and enormous aviator glasses, he had clearly gone for the Alain Delon look. But his appearance suggested that he had just escaped from the early 1980s. Do you remember the TV series *Magnum, P.I.*? Well, this guy looked like the butler. With legs apart and hands on his hips, he performed numerous spins, much to the admiration of his sophisticated companion. Now I know the French believe their European neighbours across the English Channel are an uncouth lot. The Brits might lack fashion sense and stubbornly insist that leggings go with anything. We might drink more beer, swear at football referees and eat chips with everything. But I am proud to say that if an Englishman wore anything Lycra and pirouetted on a pair of roller skates in a public park, his embarrassed partner would say he looked a prat.

I arrived at the Big Splash end of the East Coast because that is where Scott and I first went 10 years ago. Singaporeans had told us that the Big Splash swimming pool was a popular hang-out (times change so quickly, don't they?) and we decided to pay it a visit for no other reason than the name of the water slide park sounded like "dick splash", which is a childish vulgarity in Britain. I wandered along the path near Big Splash for a bit. There was a persistent drizzle in the air but that did not stop a middle-aged Malay couple from insisting that they could defy science and get a barbecue going in the rain. The husband fussed over the satay sticks while his wife held an umbrella over both their heads. Every few seconds, the husband made a futile attempt to light the wet charcoal and the wife shouted at him when the charcoal predictably failed to ignite. This went on for several minutes. It was better than Punch and Judy.

Then I made an impetuous decision. I noticed a sign that offered kayaks for rental and impulsively decided that what I craved in my life at that moment was to sit in a plastic hammock, in damp clothes, in the drizzle, on the sea. I collected my bright yellow kayak from the shop inside Big Splash and felt entirely satisfied with the $6 rental fee. I had to pick up the kayak and, through a combination of lifting and dragging, carry the thing out of Big Splash, across the skating and cycling paths, around the excitable members of the Idiot Club, down the beach and drop it into the sea. By the time I had finished, I was ready to take the kayak back. But I must say it was worth it. The rain took a breather, the heavy clouds parted and the sun peeked through for the first time that day. I felt quite the mariner, rowing along the shoreline, waving at fishermen and disturbing their fish, narrowly missing children's heads with my paddle and generally making a decent stab at joining the Idiot Club. Exhausted after 10 minutes of, quite frankly, ineffective rowing, I decided to lie back for a bit and go wherever the sea took me. Five minutes later, I looked around to find a thick film of oil floating on the surface of the sea around the kayak. It was black, gritty and extremely unpleasant. Just 20 metres away, children splashed around in the sea. The East Coast is a fine place to go kayaking but I am not sure that I would want to swim in it.

After I had dragged the kayak back to the shop, I jumped straight onto a hired bicycle. Big Splash is at the far western end of East Coast Park. Knowing that it is 20 kilometres long, I had plenty of ground to cover and set off for the National Sailing Centre at the opposite end. The number of extended Malay families I passed was remarkable. Children, parents, grandparents, aunts and uncles were gathered around various barbecue pits, cooking, eating, drinking, pitching a tent, listening to music, reading newspapers, kicking a ball or playing board games. I hold the deepest respect and admiration for the Malay community's ability to still appreciate and enjoy the simpler things in life despite living in a frenetic, urban metropolis. Watching the happy children mess around on the beach while their parents prepared their picnic lunch brought back memories of my family's unostentatious beach holidays when I was growing up in Essex. It made me smile.

East Coast Park has always been a curious place because it has not always been there. It is an underwater world brought to the surface. Built on reclaimed land after 1966, East Coast and the Marine Parade estate behind it arose from the seabed. In just over 20 years, over 1,000 hectares of land was reclaimed for recreational and residential development. But there is always a cost. Just past the underpass at Amber Road, I noticed the by-product of rapid land reclamation—erosion. A sizeable area along the coastline had been roped off because it appeared on the verge of collapsing. Huge chunks of the shoreline, riddled with plant and tree roots, lay on the empty beach and, if the unstable ground I stepped on was any indication, more will follow. The very land that was extended, over a period of many years, is receding quite quickly. Apparently, the stone and concrete structures built to protect the new coastline from excessive erosion, known as breakwaters, might not be up to the task. Originally, the sea went between them, which lessened the impact of the waves and explains why you see C-shaped beaches along the East Coast. But stronger, more aggressive waves are now going over the breakwaters and smacking into the reclaimed land. Coastline erosion is a natural phenomenon, of course, but not a popular one here I would have thought. East Coast Park is barely 40 years old, but the number of areas cordoned off is clearly increasing. The next time you visit the East Coast, count the number of benches inside those roped-off zones. There are a lot. And yet Singapore marches towards higher population targets (eight million has been mentioned more than once) by investing billions in land reclamation to eventually house everyone. But the sea is gradually taking the land back, free of charge.

I cycled past the bustling Marina Cove; a football clinic, where two mini-Hitlers barked orders at terrified seven-year-olds; a sandcastle corner; and four teenage boys performing handstands and cartwheels on the beach together. It was certainly an eclectic mix. At the bird sanctuary, I spotted my favourite sign to date. In a swampy area covered with long grass was a sign that read "Long Grass Area". Whatever next? Signs that say "A Really Big Tree" or "An Empty Muddy Field"? I assumed the sign served as a public safety notice. If it were not there, perhaps the sanctuary would be littered with fallen cyclists shouting, "Who forgot to put a bloody sign here? Why didn't someone tell me there was long grass in here? I cycled right into it, couldn't see anything and tumbled over a bird's nest."

The extensive makeover at East Coast Lagoon was amazing. The venue had recently been converted into Singapore's first cable ski park in which wakeboarders are pulled along by cables suspended overhead from pylons in one loop around the lagoon. I watched several skiers somersault and backflip off ramps with begrudging admiration. I cannot even skateboard. A young couple joined me at the lagoon to marvel at the East Coast's latest and, I have to say, most impressive attraction.

"It's great, isn't it?" I said cheerily. "But it looks like they've lost their speedboat, eh?"

The guy stared at me with the utmost seriousness. "No, no, they don't use a speedboat here. No need."

"I know that. It's just as well because that guy's obviously lost his."

"No, he hasn't. He doesn't need one. Look. The cables pull him around."

The couple gave me a blank look. I suspect they give many people blank looks. I reminded them to look both ways when they crossed the road and pedalled off.

It was getting late and I still planned to get over to Katong Park so I upped the pace a bit. As I passed yet another bird sanctuary, one of our feathered friends, and I swear this is true, defecated on my exposed shoulder. That had never happened to me before and I fancy myself as a bit of an amateur ornithologist. But here I was in a public park, travelling downhill on a mountain bike and yet somehow a bird managed to smother my shoulder with something that bore a remarkable similarity to pork rib soup. Optimistic types will intercede at this moment and insist it is lucky to be covered in the excrement of another animal. And do you know something? They are completely wrong.

No more than two minutes later, I cycled purposefully towards Bedok Jetty. Cycling towards me was a chubby Chinese girl who decided at that very millisecond that she fancied a breezy ride down the jetty. Being a junior member of the Idiot Club, she waited until she was certain it was a kinetic impossibility for me to avoid a collision before turning right. As the oblivious girl manoeuvred her bike to ensure maximum impact, I hit the brakes and they squealed like a traumatised pig. Performing a melodramatic emergency stop, my bike skidded in a straight line for an impressive 10 metres. I almost retained my balance but my momentum forced the back wheel to swerve 180 degrees to my right and I landed on that side of my body. For several, not uninteresting, seconds, I continued to slide along the ground, removing much of my skin's outer layer in the process, while still sitting on the bike. It was quite a feat. I eventually came to a halt in front of Bedok Jetty. Eager to milk the sympathy from bystanders, I remained prostrate for a bit with the bike on top of me, nursing my cuts and complaining loudly about "these bloody kids today". The back wheel was still turning slowly, adding a theatrical touch to the scene. One cyclist offered to help me to my feet and another shouted at the girl to stay in her lane. The girl was fine, of course. My sensational emergency stop had permitted her just enough time to move out of the way before I tumbled over. She peered down at me, muttered a brief "sorry" and pedalled off into the sunset.

"Well, at least you're all right," I shouted after her. But the moment had passed. Public sympathy was no longer forthcoming and devoted members of the Idiot Club were hurtling towards me. So I returned the bike to the rental shop, washed my cuts, took the underpass beneath the ECP and found myself at Singapore's original park by the sea.

Before the East Coast, there was Katong Park. In the 1950s, when land reclamation was still a pipe dream, Singaporeans flocked to the park that boasted a coastal swimming bay. Built in the 1930s, Katong Park is one of the oldest parks in the country. Famous for its coconut plantations, the place began life as a fort, protecting what is now Keppel Harbour, then became a Japanese war factory during the Occupation before ending up being the place to be seen by the sea. At weekends, Malays held popular dances and the Peranakans, Eurasians, Jews, Arabs, Ceylonese, Punjabis and the seriously wealthy flocked to Katong Park (the condos and swanky houses around Meyer Road are their legacy). They came for the swimming bay. It is interesting to note that the bay was enclosed by a fence to protect paddlers from the strong currents and the odd stray shark. Similar fences are used around Pulau Ubin's beaches today to keep out illegal immigrants.

Katong Park is also a historic site. On 24 September 1963, the park was bombed as a result of Indonesia's Konfrontasi (Confrontation) campaign against the formation of Malaysia. Two more bombs exploded there in the following two weeks, triggering two years of violence across the country. Then in 1966, land reclamation started on the East Coast and England won the World Cup (the latter has no relevance whatsoever but I thought I would mention it). The construction of East Coast Parkway left Katong Park overshadowed, in every sense. I stood at the edge of the park now and all I could see was a dog-run area and the concrete leviathan of the ECP. Fifty years ago, I could have jumped into the sea from here. It is extraordinary really.

I glanced through the long list of rules and regulations for the dog run, one of which stipulated that "bitches on heat are not allowed in this facility". I have been to Essex nightclubs that had a similar ruling. I wandered past the dog run and noticed a fenced-off area. It was the fort! Partially excavated, it was clearly part of Fort Tanjong Katong, the 19th-century British fort. I was excited. Built in 1879 to protect Singapore from a possible Russian invasion, the fort is one of the oldest in Singapore and is commemorated by the adjacent Fort Road. The military structure appeared to be in the process of being excavated as it was only partially exposed.

The section was made of brick, spoon-shaped and about 10 metres long and 3 metres across at its widest point. Little slats provided spyholes and what must have been a good vantage point to spot incoming vessels off the eastern coast of the island. But the site was extremely odd. I could not find any information panels or plaques; nothing to indicate what the structure was. Dog walkers, joggers and foreign domestic workers all drifted past the archaeological dig without giving the historic gem a second glance. Why should they? It was fenced off, unnamed and offered the curious visitor no information. Without that, it was nothing more than a lifeless lump of dusty rock.

I found out later that the fort had been reburied during the 1960s (the British made a real hash of their original attempt to bury it in the early 20th century) and rediscovered by a Katong resident who spotted some incongruous rocks sticking out of the ground in 2001. Three years later, a community project kicked off a dig to determine the size of the fort. Diggers chipped away at the soil for 10 months and much of the perimeter wall of the 6,000-square metre fort was revealed. But no one was quite sure what to do next. So, and you really could not make this up, a decision was taken to rebury the fort—again—to protect it from the weather. By early 2006, there was just one section left uncovered. The one I stood above now. It was crazy. Having been buried, reburied, dug up and reburied again, the fort's future remains uncertain. It could be declared a national monument but there has been no firm decision because historic sensitivities must, as always, be balanced with economic sensitivities. Katong Park occupies prime real estate and is surrounded by condos, with more to come judging by the noisy construction sites that I saw. Perhaps the government could turn Fort Tanjong Katong into a casino.

I hope something is done to preserve the fort because Katong Park was certainly a comely little spot and deserves more visitors. Not that the park was empty. On the contrary, I was impressed by the number of residents using it. A Caucasian father was organising a game of cricket with his son and some Eurasian lads while Indian

Sikhs, Malays, Chinese and Eurasians played football on the opposite field. It was only a five-a-side game, but just about every race was represented. It is a real melting pot in Katong. I know the areas around Mountbatten Road and Tanjong Rhu Road are more affluent and perhaps more English-educated, but you would not see this in Toa Payoh. It is just not cricket.

I left Katong Park and drifted down Mountbatten Road in the hope that I might discover a minimart hidden among the condominiums. Instead I stumbled upon a street that made me do a cartoon-like double take. Barely discernible in the darkness, I made out the words on the sign from the other side of the street—Ramsgate Road! I had visited "Little Kent" off Dover Road and had hoped to find a Ramsgate Road there, but it had been here in Katong all along. Ramsgate Road, a street named after the English town where my family now lives and the town where I spent several happy holidays as a child. I checked the street directory and discovered that there was also a Margate Road, a Clacton Road and a Walton Road further down the street. Those four roads pretty much incorporated every caravan or chalet holiday I ever had growing up in England. Being a sucker for nostalgia, I called my mother in Ramsgate, England, from Ramsgate Road, Singapore. She informed me she was busy cleaning out the dog's ears and had no time to talk, which took a bit of shine off the serendipity.

But the coincidence crowned an entertaining day by the sea. I had already said goodbye to one country with a place called Ramsgate. And here I was, over 10,000 kilometres away, doing it all over again.

# CHAPTER 26

I had never been to Joo Chiat, a little enclave of Peranakan shophouses and seafood restaurants that separates Geylang and the East Coast and provides some colourful pre-war architecture. However, in recent years, Joo Chiat has taken in the overspill of prostitutes and pimps from Geylang, much to the chagrin of its residents. Always keen to explore a little local nightlife, I took a bus to East Coast Road and ventured down Joo Chiat Road.

The street's tone was set immediately by a poster pinned to a KTV lounge window. It promised "Free Pool, 4.30pm to 7.30pm". The poster was surrounded by photographs of half-naked women crouched on all fours to ensure ample views of their ample charms. How the hell did they play pool in this joint? Not one of the women held a pool cue. I did not want to contemplate where they might have put it. I passed several KTV lounges, bars with blacked-out windows and massage parlours. Then I spotted a shop that had a sign that read "Crabs And More". I thought that was a bit forward. Everyone knows the Joo Chiat stretch offers more than just a massage, but few patrons wish to consider the medical implications. On closer inspection, the shop was a seafood restaurant and appeared to be doing a roaring trade. But if I were a lady of the night, I would avoid standing under a sign that promised "Crabs And More".

Joo Chiat certainly provides an eclectic mix of goods and services. Shops sell Tibetan artefacts, fish tanks and marine supplies, DIY products and spare parts for cars, all of which are sandwiched between family eateries, the omnipresent karaoke bars and short-stay hotels. This diverse range of retailers complicates the efforts of Joo Chiat's working women. Standing outside a bar with the word "angel" in its name may attract the punters, but pouting outside a paint shop offering discounted tins of vinyl is far less appealing.

Just after 8pm, the prostitutes appeared. When they stepped under the street lights, their appearance alarmed, rather than aroused. They wore so much make-up that they looked embalmed. If one or two of them died on the job, as it were, it might be difficult to notice. Within moments of the women tottering along the cracked pavements, the foreign workers were suddenly two strides behind them. It was uncanny. Just half an hour earlier, Joo Chiat had been nigh on deserted. Now, I found myself surrounded by Indian and Bangladeshi workers strolling together arm in arm. That close physical bonding among Asians, particularly Indians, still surprises me. If I returned to England after being marooned on an uninhabited island for 25 years, I would receive nothing more than a hearty handshake from my closest friends. But foreign workers will cuddle each other when they come back from a coffee shop. It is most impressive.

But it is not all hookers and crabs in Joo Chiat. Visitors are drawn to the area, which was once a massive coconut plantation, because of its colonial architecture. The Hotel 81 Joo Chiat might earn much of its living from the women outside but its colourful façade was stunning. It picked up the Singapore Architectural Heritage Award in 1996 and it was not difficult to see why. On the corner of Koon Seng Road and Joo Chiat Road, another two-storey masterpiece, built in 1928 with beautifully carved archways, stood out from the seedier shenanigans on the street. Although the building now houses a KTV lounge, the owners must be credited for respecting the Peranakan architecture.

On the subject of KTV lounges, why are all their doormen ugly? Is it a job requirement? Outside almost every establishment in Joo Chiat stood an individual who appeared to be auditioning for *Richard III*. At most nightclubs, the bouncers are invariably young, buffed-up beefcakes in ill-fitting tuxedos. KTV lounges, however, clearly favour fat, middle-aged, chain-smoking types, whose job description involves leering at the hostesses and greeting them with the occasional grope. That was not a pleasant sight.

Understandably, Joo Chiat residents are tired of the KTV lounges, the massage parlours and the budget hotels offering hourly rates. I wandered behind the main stretch along Tembeling Road and passed many decent, comfortable family homes. These people do not want hookers on their doorsteps, quite literally in one or two cases. In 2004, an expatriate engineer complained to the media that he had heard strange thumping noises outside his Joo Chiat home one night and found a randy pair going at it like rabbits on his car bonnet.

As the hookers were increasingly overshadowing Joo Chiat's proud Peranakan and Eurasian heritage, the locals bravely stepped in and took matters into their own hands. Eleven residents formed the Save Joo Chiat Working Group in 2004 to register complaints about disreputable businesses with the authorities. Their efforts were rewarded quickly. According to media reports, there were 400 arrests for vice-related activities in the neighbourhood in 2004, a marked increase over the 50 arrests made the year before. The Joo Chiat residents' proactive stance can only be applauded. With illegal Chinese immigrants still working the streets here, the residents need all the help they can get.

At the northern end of Joo Chiat, I had originally planned to turn left into Geylang Road and venture into Singapore's infamous red-light district but I took a brief diversion. Geylang has been the heart of the island's ethnic Malay community ever since the British impolitely removed their floating village at the mouth of the Singapore River in the mid-19th century. By the 1930s, distinct Malay districts had formed and evolved into Geylang Serai, where I was now standing. In a bid to replicate the community's proud heritage, the Geylang Serai Malay Village opened here in 1989. The attraction promised authentic cuisine and costumes, traditional dances, museums and galleries.

There is only one problem with the Malay Village—it is monumentally crap. I have visited some lame Singaporean attractions in the last 10 years (Sentosa's Lost Civilisation and the now defunct Clarke Quay Adventure Ride spring to mind) but nothing comes close to the Malay Village. And that is a real tragedy.

Although it was almost 10pm when I popped in, the Malay Village was still open, not that it made any difference. I was the only visitor. Built in the traditional kampong style with sloped roofs and timber frames, its entrance had the misfortune of resembling a ferry terminal at one of the many seaside resorts dotted around the region. Most of the retail units had clearly been closed for some time, the food stalls were out of action and the Kampong Days exhibit was a joke. Apart from a few interesting panels on prominent Singaporean Malays in the art gallery, the ghost town was a faded, peeling mess, a truly shameful tribute to the vibrant heritage of Singapore's indigenous community. I later discovered that a new management team had recently taken over control of the Malay Village, the fifth in 17 years. Although the bosses have promised a new restaurant, a resource centre and shops selling art and traditional clothing, the Malay community is not holding its breath. The Malay Village has been down this road four times before. If this makeover does not work, then the artificial attraction should close its doors for good. It is an embarrassment to the community it claims to represent and offers nothing to tourists. Chinese visitors have Chinatown, Indians gravitate towards Serangoon Road and Westerners head for Orchard Road and the colonial district. But Malaysian and Indonesian coach parties have no compelling reason to leave countries steeped in indigenous tradition to sample this replicated rubbish. The Malays deserve something better.

In some respects, Geylang has not really changed. Historians believe its name is a corruption of *kilang,* the Malay word for "factory". Coconuts and lemon grass were once processed in factories around the area, hence the name. In the alleyways behind Geylang Road today, the factories remain productive after dark although there are marginally fewer coconuts now. Everyone knows the place. Sex websites provide top 10 lists, tourists occasionally visit for a cheap thrill and Singaporean teenagers are guaranteed an easy classroom laugh with the mere mention of its name. In a country famous for its transparency and strait-laced conservatism, Geylang is synonymous with seedy sex. Everyone knows that. But appearances can be deceptive. I sauntered down Geylang Road from the east and the street initially promised nothing more sordid than a new chandelier. Like Balestier, much of Geylang Road is dominated by lighting shops, offering the latest fittings and designs. I know most men harbour ambitions of leaving Geylang glowing in the dark, but not like this.

In fact, Geylang Road provides a subtle route to its red-light district. It sneaks up on you. The odd pub and KTV lounge gradually overtake shops selling fluorescent tubes and household appliances; it is a surprisingly discreet process. By the time I had reached Lorongs 22 and 20, the transition was complete. Neon lights dazzled from overhanging signs, special offers on jugs of beer were scribbled outside every bar, skinny Chinese girls with bad teeth grabbed at my arm to coax me into their drinking dens and sex shops sold terrifying plastic cylinders with pumps that promised to inflate my penis.

I stopped for a drink at a coffee shop and immediately aggravated the beer promoter by occupying an entire table with one can of Coke, thereby depriving her of four potential beer guzzlers. As she treated me with such cold contempt usually reserved for the parasitic pimps operating in the alleys behind, I reciprocated by staying put for an hour, pretending to be completely engrossed in the Chinese drama on TV that had something to do with martial arts and a eunuch.

After dark, Geylang gives you the opportunity to briefly see how the island's invisible people live. Singapore's much maligned foreign workers dominated the vicinity at every turn. On the ground behind me, four Bangladeshis were huddled together in the darkness, passing around a bottle of beer. The ground was filthy. Half-finished containers of take-away food, bags of rubbish and cat excrement cluttered the damp ground around them as they sat, cross-legged, beside an open drain. As it was Friday night, they were obviously wearing their best clothes. It was a pitiful image I will never forget. A little later, another foreign worker, possibly Thai, sneaked between coffee shop tables. Crouching the entire time, the young man hid among the patrons' legs while hawking contraband cigarettes from a plastic bag. I watched him for five minutes and he did not stand up once. His business was illegal but it appeared to be thriving.

I finished my drink, gave the beer promoter a tip (wear less make-up) and followed the throngs of foreign workers and *ah peks* into Geylang's underbelly. The real red-light district runs parallel with Geylang Road in the scruffy alleys that stretch from around Lorong 22 to Talma Road and Lorong 8. Visibility was almost negligible and I could barely make out the women sitting on plastic seats. It was so dark that I am surprised punters do not inadvertently end up having sex with each other in those gloomy alleyways. Being the only white face in the crowd, I stood out like the Raffles Lighthouse and found myself an easy target for the pimps, who had clearly attended the same school of charm and deportment as the Joo Chiat doormen. Standing about 3 metres away from "their" girls, they blocked my path as I passed and occasionally grabbed my arm, all the while gesturing towards the women sitting in front of the drains and some garishly lit shophouses. The pimps' sales patter was usually the same. They emerged from the shadows, appeared at my shoulder and whispered, "Massage, special service, blow job for you?" No matter how many pimps stopped me, their spiel rarely changed. At one point, I contemplated turning back and asking, "Excuse me, can I change the order? What will happen if I have the special service first and the massage last? Will it fall off? Will I get 'crabs and more'?" But squeezed in among the gangs of foreign workers, *ah peks* and pimps, I was a conspicuous figure in the darkness and thought better of it.

Then I was accosted. A slim Indian girl, still in her teens, threw her arms around my waist and held on tightly. She would not let go. Instead, she smiled and shrieked, "Come with me! Come with me!" I was not aroused; I was petrified. Half a dozen Indian men, who had just been talking to the girl, eyed my every move. Rather melodramatically, I threw my arms into the air and kept them there. I marched along in the shadows, arms still aloft, as the girl clung to my waist and her teenage friend followed in hot pursuit. I was desperate for the girl to release me but lacked the inclination and the courage to physically remove her. I was left with no option but to pray she released her grip somewhere after Geylang's Lorong 12 so I could escape the prying eyes of her admirers, but preferably before Toa Payoh. I did not fancy greeting my wife with my hands in the air and a teenage hooker attached to my hips crying, "Come with me! Come with me!" The young girl released me, finally, when she bumped into some washing poles hanging in the alley. They clattered to the floor which ensured we briefly captured the attention of every punter in Geylang. Fortunately, the incident embarrassed my young friend enough to admit defeat and she slunk away into the darkness.

I reached the budget hotels around Talma Road, the heart of the red-light district, and witnessed the very entrepreneurial zeal that Singapore's government now demands of its people. Behind the prostitutes standing outside the hotels, I noticed an ice cream vendor who was doing more business than all of the hookers put together! Whenever the ice cream van stopped near our house in Dagenham, only teenagers and young parents queued up for a cornet. But the ice cream queue at Talma Road comprised four hookers, two of their customers and a pimp. It was marvellous. In Britain, adults light up cigarettes after sex. In Singapore, they lick a chocolate chip cone.

Time was getting on so I took a bus to Jalan Besar, marched purposefully through its empty street and turned into Desker Road. I had been to Desker Road only once before when David played tour guide around Singapore's saucier streets. We stumbled across the finest pair of breasts ever created that night. The only drawback was that they were the work of a gifted plastic surgeon and attached to a man. Older Singaporeans often refer to Desker Road as *Kin Jio*

*Ka*, or "banana foot" in Hokkien. This has no relevance whatsoever, I just think that "banana foot" is a superb name for a street. I am also particularly fond of Kay Poh Road off River Valley Road. It is childish, I know, but before I leave Singapore for good I am determined to tell a taxi driver that I live in a condo there. What a spectacularly brief conversation that would be.

"Where you go?"

"Kay Poh."

"Yeah? Well, balls to you, *ang moh.*"

Like Geylang, Desker Road is internationally recognised for its nocturnal services. Instead of hookers, however, it specialises in transvestites. I wandered down the street just before midnight and the only nightlife I came across was a bustling fruit and vegetable market that reminded me of my short career at Spitalfields Market. I lasted two weeks working with my uncle at East London's famous fruit and vegetable market before someone offered me cannabis behind a lorry and my mother promptly ordered her brother to sack me. No such social concerns in Desker Road though. The most serious threat to public order came from a group of mercurial Indians shouting at a TV in a coffee shop. I thought they were watching a political protest or hearing about news of a natural disaster back in their homeland, but they were watching WWE Wrestling. As they waited for The Undertaker to make his grand entrance, I enquired if Big Daddy or Giant Haystacks was on the bill. I was quickly shooed away.

I ambled over to Syed Alwi Road and found myself in the middle of a shopping maelstrom; Mustafa Centre was packing them in. Desker Road might have been largely deserted, but this 24-hour shopping district had families, couples, singles and tourists queuing up to get in. Midnight had come and gone but a security guard directed traffic into a burgeoning car park while another pedantically checked the bags of every shopper entering the store. Singapore harbours pretensions of becoming a round-the-clock global city. Although it is not there yet, Mustafa's and the coffee shops around Little India are on the right track.

I was ready to call it a night when I reached Serangoon Road but I saw a small crowd of foreign workers gathered around in Rowell Road. I took a peek and realised that the famous transvestites of Desker Road had apparently moved to the next street. As it was still only 1am, they had not yet ventured onto the streets. Instead they sat on the stairwell of the two-storey shophouses behind a locked gate as prospective punters peered through the cracks. This peculiar setting may have been for the prostitutes' own protection, but the scene seemed so desperately sad.

I walked a little further down Rowell Road when a voice beckoned me over. I peered through the gate and thought I had confronted the American rock group Kiss. Five male faces, practically obscured by long, straight hair and startling amounts of make-up, were crouching on the staircase and smiling back at me. As they sat beside, above or below each other on the stairs, they formed a neat circle of talking heads in the shadows. For one fleeting moment, they reminded me of Queen in their "Bohemian Rhapsody" video. One of the transvestites, who bore an uncanny resemblance to the singer Robert Plant, blew me a kiss, licked his lips and asked if I fancied having a good time. I politely declined his offer, wished him well and headed back to Serangoon Road for supper.

I have absolutely no problem with transvestites; I am just not a big fan of Led Zeppelin.

# CHAPTER 27

On a damp November morning in 1996, Scott and I set foot in Singapore's most famous street for the first time. Being enthusiastic tourists, we arrived an hour before the shops opened and shuffled along an empty Orchard Road desperately trying to fathom what all the fuss was about. We reached Ngee Ann City, spotted a monstrous billboard advertising an ongoing *Star Wars* exhibition and immediately concurred that this was the very country for us. Scott was also pleased that Singapore had been courteous enough to name the adjacent shopping street after him, reinforcing the belief that kismet was firmly in our corner. From a historical perspective, it now seems particularly apt. I explored Orchard Road for the first time with Scott, a street that took its name from Captain William Scott's orchards. In the 1830s, Scott was both harbour and post master of Singapore and his plentiful orchards, pepper farms and nutmeg plantations were dotted all along the street, partially concealed by colourful shrubbery and shaded by thousands of breezy trees. Now, Orchard Road boasts several Coffee Beans, a handful of McDonald's and a number of 7-Elevens. Singapore's premier shopping district has come such a long way.

Fortunately, Orchard Road boasts two of the finest city parks in the world at either end: Singapore Botanic Gardens in the north and Fort Canning Park in the south. Being in absolutely no hurry to drift along in a sea of a thousand shoppers on a Saturday afternoon, I happily strayed over to the Botanic Gardens. Originally established by dear old Tommy Raffles in 1822 at Fort Canning to satisfy his naturalistic tendencies and provide his house with a decent view, the first garden closed just seven years later. An agri-horticultural society set up the present one 30 years later and, today, the Botanic Gardens is maintained by the assiduous National Parks Board. It is over 52 hectares of lakes, gardens, heritage trees, rainforest trails, sculptures, fountains and cafés, with a children's garden on the way. Unfortunately, it pissed down when I visited.

As I admired one particular tree, the extraordinary 47-metre-tall *jelawai*, one of the tallest indigenous trees in Southeast Asia, it started to drizzle. I am no botanist but I was desperate for a pee and examined the tree's girth to determine whether it was broad enough for me to nip behind. To my consternation, the low, menacing clouds decided to release their water before I could so I dashed to the bandstand and narrowly escaped the deluge. I have always relished the unexpected equatorial downpours here. In Britain, the incessant drizzle that passes for rain is uncomfortable and irritating, rather like a baby dribbling down your face. It is neither here nor there, just gloomy. But there is nothing remotely babyish about Singapore's rain. Oh no. This is primeval Neanderthal stuff. It roars down from the heavens, thunders along the streets like a Hobbesian brute, beats you around the head for an hour and then swiftly disappears to terrorise another neighbourhood. I will miss it a lot.

I sheltered in the bandstand with four couples. It was like hanging around for the next meeting of the Social Development Unit. To compound matters, a young couple occupied their time by fondling each other. He was discernibly French and she might have been Japanese and they spent the first 15 minutes of the thunderstorm declaring their unfettered love for each other and groping various erogenous zones. When I was young, and this is true, I thought an erogenous zone was part of the London Underground. I knew the Tube network was broken up into zones and just assumed that the erogenous zone was off the map somewhere past Upminster. I have been to Upminster and have since concluded that this might well be the case.

After about an hour of chest rubbing and doe-eyed staring at the relentless rain, however, the Frenchman's patience was clearly wearing thin. His exotic girlfriend continued to expound upon the romantic virtues of a tropical storm and he responded with a forced smile and a nod. But his stiff, fidgety body language really said, "It's just rain, darling. I can no longer feel my legs and I'm desperate for a curry."

I shared his impatience so I took my chances in the blustery conditions, splashed blindly through the puddles and headed for the toilets beside the National Orchid Garden. They were the best that I have ever had the privilege of relieving myself in. Whoever designed the public facilities at the Botanic Gardens must be recognised at the next National Day Awards. The toilets boasted freshly laid tiled floors and ceilings that were cleaner than most hawker centre tables. Tropical plants adorned the three individual basins and every immaculate toilet and urinal had an automatic flush. Not only did the toilet provide a welcome respite from the rain, its open concept, a familiar feature at Singapore's parks, made it breezy and cool. I would live in here. Do not come to the Botanic Gardens for its rainforest trees and free Symphony Stage shows, come for its toilets. The National Parks Board even provided a helpline above the urinals for visitor feedback. I was so impressed that I called and notified the bemused operator that I had never peed in a more welcoming toilet.

I toyed with visiting the National Orchid Garden next door but thought better of it. I know the importance orchid breeding plays in Singapore and, as flowers go, the orchid is one of the most attractive. I even had them at my wedding to give the ceremony a Singaporean flavour. However, the idea of paying $5 to see bunches of flowers in the middle of a free garden covered with all kinds of tropical flora and fauna strikes me as a trifle odd. I would not visit the Sahara Desert and hand over $5 to peer into display cases of sand. Instead I sauntered past the majestic Symphony Lake and watched children feed bread to the ducks. There are far worse ways to spend a Saturday afternoon.

It was here that I encountered one of those anal pet owners who believe that their pets are human beings. When these poor souls are not barking at the moonlight, they are dressing their pets up in human clothes and putting pigtails in Rover's hair. The storm had stopped by now, but this particular woman thundered towards me dragging a yapping sausage dog in a blue rain mac. Only the helpless canine's stumpy legs and perspiring, panting face protruded through its ill-fitting coat. Why do owners bestow such a cruel punishment upon their pets in the tropics? It is a dog. It is already wearing a bloody coat. As the woman marched past me, I registered my displeasure by releasing a distinct odour that the poor dog would have been proud of and headed for the exit.

Orchard Road has never really appealed to me. It has no identity other than being a street full of shops, a characteristic that barely distinguishes the place from Toa Payoh Central. Orchard Road is revered by most tourists, even though it has no central feature to attract those with interests other than credit card abuse. The pagoda-shaped Singapore Marriott Hotel at the junction of Scotts Road and Orchard Road comes close to being a national landmark, but it is hardly the Sydney Opera House. For a road that is namechecked in every guidebook and tourist guide written about the country, Orchard Road offers no iconic building or structure, no vivid history and little in the way of heritage. London's Regent Street and Oxford Street boast glorious histories. New York has Times Square and the Champs Elysées relies on the Arc de Triomphe to fill its Parisian postcards. Singapore has its fair share of famous buildings and tourist attractions: the overrated Merlion, Raffles Hotel, the Padang, the Singapore River, Boat Quay, Clarke Quay, Chinatown and Little India are just a few. But none of them are in Orchard Road.

To borrow the vague language of Scott's favourite shopping centre sign, Orchard Road offers shops, more shops and even more shops. What is more, most of them are the same. It is like a day trip to Toon Town. Do you remember watching older cartoons such as *Scooby Doo* in which the hooded villain always raced past that same nondescript backdrop every few seconds? Well, that is Orchard Road. In *Scooby Doo*, it is tree, grassy knoll, house; tree, grassy knoll, house. In Orchard Road, it is McDonald's, 7-Eleven, Coffee Bean; McDonald's, 7-Eleven, Coffee Bean. Originality is not high on the street's list of priorities. That is why it has plenty of familiar retail outlets behind polished glass frontages, but no identity. It undoubtedly does the all-under-one-roof concept very well. But then, so does Lakeside Shopping Centre, a characterless suburban behemoth on the borders of Kent and Essex that serves the populations of both English counties. And tourists are not clocking up air miles to visit that place.

Orchard Road's only real function is to satisfy one's materialism and the annual Great Singapore Sale is proof of its success. Every year, the Singapore Tourism Board sets higher targets of visitors and the media gleefully reports the record-breaking retail revenues as those tills just keep on ringing. The desire to create a nation of soulless shoppers who flood Orchard Road to upgrade their phones, buy electronic gizmos they do not need and toast their efforts with a well-earned latte is relentless. To help achieve the dream, one of the street's last green lungs, Orchard Turn, was recently sold off for redevelopment with the caveat that the site must house premier residential and retail outlets. The small grassy hillock beside Orchard MRT Station is just 1.8 hectares in size and has long been a popular spot for maids to meet for picnics as well as providing space for the occasional funfair. But the sale of Orchard Turn for over $1 billion dispelled any confusion or ambiguity regarding Orchard Road. The message was unequivocal: fuck 'em. The bulging Boss wallets and Prada purses from China and India are coming and more shops are needed to satisfy demand. So the maids can scurry away to the Botanic Gardens and the funfairs can stay in Chinatown.

I sat on a wall in my least favourite place in Singapore and watched the multitudes shuffle out of the underground exit of Orchard MRT Station. Humming The Kinks' "Waterloo Sunset", I watched as hundreds of youngsters scurried off in every direction to spend a few hours staring into shop windows at branded goods that they either could not afford or planned to throw onto a credit card that they probably should not have. I know they are all doing their national service by boosting their country's GDP, but there must be more fulfilling ways for young Singaporeans to spend their weekends than this.

I have always been fascinated by the design of Orchard MRT Station. I still struggle to comprehend how someone sat down and said, "Let's take a hot country with stifling humidity on the equator and build the exit to its most popular station underground. Then attach the station to a labyrinth of shopping lanes with a myriad of retail outlets selling essentially the same thing and link it all up with slow escalators and an inadequate air-conditioning supply. Now, watch the people come."

And the sad thing is, they do. They come 18 hours a day, 7 days a week. I gloomily observed the shoppers shuffle through the crowds, carrying too many bags, the sharp edges of which banged against people's knees and babies' buggies. No one seemed to smile and no one looked particularly happy.

I fled the retail prison and took a welcome stroll down Orchard Road above ground, which was practically deserted thanks to the grey weather and damp pavements. I may have escaped the shopping hordes but fell into the clutches of the roadshow MCs instead. You cannot walk 10 metres down Orchard Road without being blown under a bus by a booming speaker promising credit cards with lower interest rates, a free car, a condo and sex with the TV artiste of your choice. And those faux-American accents are exasperating, aren't they? It is bad enough that you cannot switch on a radio station here without suffering a 21-year-old giving you tips on how to lead your life in a voice that suggests she was schooled with Forrest Gump; now we also have to endure roadshow MCs convinced that they were raised in Boston rather than Buangkok. A guy selling a ladies' credit card considered approaching me, but checked himself when he noticed the steam coming out of my ears.

Orchard Road does have its plus points though. I ambled up Emerald Hill to admire the beautifully restored Peranakan shophouses. A certain William Cuppage had a nutmeg plantation around here in the 1840s before the Peranakans moved in and built many of the stunning pre-war houses that I now wandered around. Some have been converted to bars, restaurants and office units, but they have been stylishly done and most of the original façades remain intact. Emerald Hill provided a timely breather from the credit card salesmen. It is also home to Chatsworth International School, which I indulgently mention because my wife taught there for five extremely happy years.

At the junction of Orchard Road and Bras Basah Road stands the historic Cathay Building, which, I was delighted to see, had been renovated and reopened. It is the high point at the end of an otherwise drab street. One of Singapore's oldest cinemas, the Cathay Cinema, originally opened here in 1939 and was the focal point for the entire Orchard area. Even my dear war veteran friend Cliff fondly remembers enjoying an ice cream outside the building and watching the girls go by in 1945. After being closed for a few years, the building (now known as The Cathay) has opened its doors again with a new multiplex and renovated art house with, of course, the predictable shopping outlets to follow. More impressively, its original art deco façade was recently declared a national monument and restored. As dusk approached, I stood in front of the building's grand entrance, which once led to Singapore's first skyscraper, and was reminded of the cavernous odeons of my Dagenham childhood. Those eccentric, pre-war gems were eventually converted into bowling alleys or demolished and replaced by generic multiplexes. But The Cathay is still here. Critics have complained that only the original façade remains, but with the construction workers whistling their way over to Orchard Turn, I would be grateful for small mercies.

Just after midnight, I returned to Orchard Road and walked the same route again. There has been plenty of talk in recent years to turn the shopping precinct into a 24-hour playground with a vibrant street life to rival Nanjing Lu in Shanghai. London and New York supposedly never sleep and Orchard Road is eager to join the exclusive club of city insomniacs. It is already a bit of a chameleon. Once the final train has trundled out of Orchard MRT Station just after midnight, the day tripping shoppers go away and the prostitutes, transvestites and rent boys come out to play. Before dark, Orchard Road harbours ambitions of becoming the region's answer to Regent Street. After dark, it bears closer similarity to King's Cross. I stood outside Tanglin Mall and watched several foreign workers scavenge through the dustbins, looking for any gems that might have been thrown away at the flea market earlier in the afternoon. Not a great start. Between Tanglin Mall and Tanglin Shopping Centre, I encountered three people and they were all security guards. Were they bravely protecting their properties from each other? There was more life in Toa Payoh on a Saturday night.

Fortunately, Orchard Towers can always be relied upon to provide the area with a splash of colour and a sense of humour. Often referred to by locals as the "four floors of whores", Orchard Towers supplies alcohol, women and song in ample quantities at the right price. I made my way past the fidgety taxi drivers who were doubling up as pimps, ambled up the steps and brushed past the biggest pair of breasts in Singapore. I felt a right tit, and so did she. The lady of the night momentarily blocked my path until she accepted that I was not going to be her next client and all three of her left.

I climbed the three escalators that had been cheekily turned off by the building's operators. By the time that I had reached the top floor, I needed to lean on a handrail. A plump lady tottered over and enquired if I needed a special service. I asked if she had a defibrillator. As I battled in vain to get my breath back, I watched with nothing but admiration as these working women traipsed up and down the stairs hunting down customers. Occasionally, they got lucky and strode off with their client, arm in arm, to the nearest hotel. I will never know how they manage to have sex after all those stairs. I observed men twice my age climb all three escalators, agree a price with a woman and leave. I have no idea how they got it up in the bedroom. I struggled to get it up the stairs.

If I were going to invest in a Singaporean business, I would open a tattoo parlour on the top floor of Orchard Towers without any hesitation whatsoever. Drunk Americans with close-cropped hair were queuing up to go under the needle in these places. It had never occurred to me before, but setting up a tattoo parlour beside a bar is sound marketing savvy because, as we all know, when you have had a few, those babies sell themselves. When you are sober, a tattoo is for people who believe that collecting semi-automatic weapons is no different to collecting stamps. But when you are drunk, that spider's web on your left buttock is the very thing that has been missing from your life all these years. I walked quickly past one young American who could not decide whether to get an eagle tattooed onto his back or punch his reflection in the shop window. I peered inside another tattoo parlour and saw an *ang moh* who had fallen into the deepest of sleeps while sitting in the waiting room. His video camera was still switched on and recording his crotch while a steady stream of saliva dribbled down his chin.

Unlike Geylang or Joo Chiat, however, I have never regarded Orchard Towers as seedy. Tacky, certainly; unsubtle, definitely; but there is an overriding sense of the tongue being placed firmly in the cheek here. From the taxi drivers and the club doormen to the working women and the guy in the wheelchair selling red roses to drunks at exorbitant prices, everyone knows the score. Orchard Towers offers sex quite openly, but if you do not want it, no one is going to think any less of you. They will still usher you inside to buy a few beers, enjoy the house band and have a good night. Unlike in Geylang, you will seldom find hundreds of greasy men sniffing around filthy back alleys here. Instead, I discerned families, couples and friends of all races and ages eating and drinking at the various restaurants and pubs in the building. Orchard Towers provides the street with a convivial ambience that, with the exception of Emerald Hill, is lacking elsewhere.

I crossed the road and sat outside Forum—The Shopping Mall, near to a Malay motorcycle gang. Clearly going through their James Dean phase, the bikers were stretched out along the steps, sipping spirits from plastic cups and admiring each other's tattooed forearms. To be honest, it was difficult to spot an arm that did not have any ink on it. I had never noticed biker gangs in Orchard Road before. The black-clad group, some of whom had a fawning girlfriend attached to their waist, numbered at least 30. Now and again, they disappeared to race down Orchard Road on their mopeds and scooters. They were neither rowdy nor threatening and I found their homage to The Who's iconic movie *Quadrophenia* fascinating. But one or two of them reminded me of some of my Dagenham peers growing up. That was not necessarily a good thing.

Just after 2am, I took a rest on a bench near Le Meridien Hotel and was quickly joined by an attractive, middle-aged woman. "I've been watching you walk up and down," she said. "Where are you from?"

"Toa Payoh," I replied chirpily. She was the first person that I had spoken to in hours.

"Ah, not too far from me. You want a good time tonight?" She put her hand on my shoulder. The woman was old enough to be my mother. It then occurred to me that I had not been propositioned by a single prostitute under the age of 35. How bloody old did they think I was?

"No, no, it's okay, really. I just came out for the exercise."

"I understand," she said. Her warm, maternal smile betrayed a hint of rejection. I wanted to hug her. It was after 2am, most of Singapore was asleep and here she was talking to a sweaty stranger on a near-deserted, damp street. This was no way to earn a living. "Well, it was nice talking to you," she continued. "But it's getting late, you know. Maybe it's time for you to go home."

She gave me that kind, maternal smile again. So I did as I was told.

# CHAPTER 28

I will never forget the day I discovered what an archaeologist did for a living. I thought it was the most glamorous, and easiest, job in the world. Take a shovel, dig up your front garden and discover the complete skeleton of a *Diplodocus* before lunch. Thus, the following weekend, my best friend Ross and I set to work in my Dagenham side garden with a pitchfork. We had certain advantages. Undisturbed land is an obvious boon for any budding archaeologist and no one in our family had touched the side garden since 1822. We made light work of the sodden soil and recovered a historic gem in less than two hours. The moment the pitchfork hit something metallic, we dove into the dug-up earth and pulled out a round, off-green object caked in mud. Once we cleaned it up, we deduced that it was a military helmet left over from World War II! As Dagenham had suffered some bomb damage during the Blitz, it must have belonged to a soldier in the Home Guard.

I waited impatiently for my mother to return home from work to inform her that she could quit her job immediately as my archaeological discovery guaranteed untold millions from a forthcoming Sotheby's auction. When she walked into the house, I handed her the treasure and told her, with some authority because we had recently covered World War II at school, what it was. She laughed and told me that it was not a military helmet but an old bedpan. I had not dug up part of a valiant serviceman's uniform; I had retrieved a potty from some old dear with incontinence. Despite that minor setback, I have been intrigued by archaeology ever since and decided to spend a morning at the site of Singapore's most productive dig.

I really like Fort Canning Park. Hidden away from the hubbub of Orchard Road, the historic site sits quietly, and most majestically, on a hill away from the maddening crowds. Old Raffles took one look at Bukit Larangan (Malay for "Forbidden Hill", as it was then known), and said, "That'll make a nice back garden." Before you could say "Mind that heritage", the jungle was cleared and animals were shot to facilitate the building of Raffles' bungalow here in 1822. He died four years later, which was a bit of a bummer. After his death, Raffles found it quite difficult to return to the bungalow so Singapore's governors lived there until 1860, when some bright spark realised that the hill's incomparable vistas made it an obvious choice for a military fort.

I mention old Raffles because it is hard not to conclude that Singapore's history was wilfully determined by just two men. I have read several local history books, particularly school texts, and the same two dates take centre stage: 1819, when Raffles first landed in Singapore, and 1959, when the People's Action Party was first voted into power. No one seriously disputes the impact these two events had on Singapore but the country existed, and thrived, before both Raffles and Lee Kuan Yew entered the picture. Fort Canning Park, the history of which can be traced back to Singapore's golden age of the 1300s, is living proof of that.

I planned to have my lunch of sweaty cheese sandwiches at the site of Singapore's oldest known house. In the 1300s, the Mongol rulers of China referred to the island as "Dragon's Tooth Strait", probably due to a large pillar of rock off Labrador Point. How I wish the island still went by that name. Just consider the marketing potential for T-shirts for tourists. In the 1300s, Dragon's Tooth Strait was ruled by a number of Malay kings, the fifth and last of whom, Sultan Iskandar Syah, was driven out of the country but went on to found Malacca before dying around 1413. The royal palace of Iskandar Syah and his predecessors probably stood at Bukit Larangan's summit. There is also the belief that his final resting place is also here as the hill was once a *keramat,* a traditional burial ground for revered Malay leaders. Muslims have prayed here since the 1820s. They are convinced that the area is a 600-year-old tomb and, considering the island is largely starved of juicy history, I am content to agree with them.

The *keramat* that now stands on the site is built in the traditional Malay style. Twenty wooden pillars support a replica of a 14th-century roof. At the centre is a tomb with Iskandar Syah's name inscribed on the side. When I visited, an Indian Muslim was leaning on the tomb and praying so I took my shoes off and sat a respectful distance away. I was starving but refrained from eating my sweaty sandwiches. First, I was not sure if it was disrespectful to eat in a *keramat.* Second, I found myself donating blood by the litre to the local mosquito population. When I was not swiping them away, I tried to make a grab for a sandwich but intimidating pigeons kept hovering fearlessly in my face. And it is not right to punch a pigeon in a *keramat,* is it?

So I had lunch at the wonderfully informative Archaeological Dig & Exhibition. I spent a happy hour there examining the artefacts and playing with the automated fan and lights system. But the exhibition also underlined the lack of understanding about Singapore's history. There just is not enough evidence. When I was growing up in Dagenham, farmers and fishermen frequently stumbled upon ancient Roman relics in the bogs of the Essex marshes beside the River Thames. Coins, pottery and jewellery were often unearthed, to the indifference of the blasé local populace. But at Fort Canning, archaeologists are ecstatic if they find tiny fragments of 13th-century pottery or a piece of an indecipherable coin because it is all that they have got. It is so sad. The information panels even referred to the period of Singapore's golden age as ancient history when, of course, it only took place 700 years ago and falls under the medieval period in the West.

That is not to say that human indifference or neglect is not occasionally at fault. As almost every centimetre of land on this minuscule island has been bulldozed, reclaimed or tunnelled through since the 1960s, archaeologists believe that the only undisturbed sites left that might throw up some historical clues are the Padang, the Armenian Church and St. Andrew's Cathedral. And economic and religious sensitivities are likely to keep the shovels away from all three.

There are also unforgivable stories that highlight the contempt people can have for a country's heritage. Consider the discovery of the Singapore Stone. Now the Singapore Stone should have been a key to the locked door marked the Dark Ages. Discovered at the mouth of the Singapore River in the 19th century by British engineers, the ancient boulder was around 3 metres high and 3 metres wide and contained approximately 50 lines of engraved text. Believed to be a variant of old Sumatran script, the stone has been dated from the 10th to the 14th century. Its scholastic importance to Asean history should have been obvious to all and sundry. The Singapore Stone could have been its country's "Rosetta Stone". (The Rosetta Stone was unearthed in an Egyptian port by invading French forces in 1799 and, because it was written in Hieroglyphic, Demotic Egyptian and Greek, allowed historians to finally decipher hieroglyphs and unlock the language of the pharaohs.) Comparing the Singapore Stone with the Rosetta Stone may smack of hyperbole, but we will never know now. Because in their eternal wisdom, British engineers blew up the Singapore Stone to prepare the ground for Fort Fullerton. Only a few fragments remain today in the National Museum of Singapore and they are either too small or too badly damaged to determine the date of or the language used on the stone. It was a gross error of judgement that can never be rectified. Singapore wields the financial clout to purchase water from Malaysia, rice from Indonesia, fresh milk from Australia and cheap labour from the subcontinent but it cannot buy back its own history.

Fort Canning Park has two trails: the 14th Century Walk of History, which includes the *keramat* and the archaeological dig, and the 19th Century Walk, which focuses on the impact Raffles had on the hill. Strangely, the former felt more authentic than the latter. In

2003, Fort Canning Park opened Raffles Terrace, which showcases reminders of the British Empire's contributions to the vicinity. There was a replica of the flagstaff originally erected by Singapore's first British Resident William Farquhar, a largely pointless time ball and a replica of the old Fort Canning Lighthouse. There was even Raffles House, a replica of the old man's bungalow, which, I believe, is available for private functions and conferences. That is always good to know, I suppose. I found the information panels enlightening, but Raffles Terrace seemed so artificial after spending time at the very real archaeological dig.

But Fort Canning is a remarkable park. I have not even mentioned the Battle Box, where the British made the decision to surrender to the Japanese on the morning of 15 February 1942; or the Sally Port; or the historic cemetery; or the simple fact that the city's green refuge is an ideal spot for a family picnic. More pertinently, Fort Canning provides a little insight into the increasingly forgotten island of Dragon's Tooth Strait, ancient royal palaces and fleeing kings. The sacred hill is a constant, physical reminder that the country was not born in 1819 or reborn in 1959. For that reason alone, the park should be revered as a national treasure.

I left Fort Canning, walked along Hill Street and entered the historical site that gave me the initial idea of writing this book. Sitting at my desk in the *TODAY* office in late 2005, I received an email request to cover the anniversary of a small church that served a tiny community within Singapore. I was not interested. Its name—the Armenian Church of St Gregory the Illuminator—was not familiar so I stopped reading the press release after the first few lines. A couple of days later, my boss asked me when "that Armenian Church story" was coming out so I sighed, reluctantly retrieved the email and read it properly. I was stunned. The church claimed to be the oldest in Singapore and was finalising its 170th anniversary celebrations. Surely that was a typing error? A 70th birthday seemed acceptable, but a building that was 170 years old in Singapore was absurd. This is a country, remember, where a good deal of the history syllabus in schools focuses on events after the

Japanese Occupation of 1942. And here were church volunteers claiming that their particular house of worship was constructed just 12 years after Raffles sailed away from Singapore for the last time and when most of the country was still a swampy jungle. I was not having it.

Of course, it all turned out to be true and it really is a wonderful story of dedication, application and perseverance from a community that has punched above its weight in Singapore for over 180 years. In the 1800s, 12 Armenian families came together to commission the Armenian Orthodox Church. Never a community to take half measures, they employed the services of George Coleman, one of the country's most respected architects and responsible for the Old Parliament House (now The Arts House). Construction began on the Hill Street site on 1 January 1835.

Just to reiterate, that is 1835. There were more Malayan tigers roaming freely around the jungles of Singapore than there were Armenian families. I am not joking. According to the helpful staff at the superb Raffles Museum of Biodiversity Research, one person was killed every day by a tiger in 1835. That is seven deaths a week. That is a lot of tigers.

But nothing stopped those resolute Armenians. The church opened its doors in late 1835 (in those days, they could commission, plan and build a stately neoclassical structure in less than a year. At the time of writing, Wembley Stadium was still not finished.). And those doors have stayed open to the public ever since. In the meantime, the surrounding jungles were cleared, the last of the tigers was shot in Choa Chu Kang in the 1930s, the British were attacked, the Japanese wreaked havoc, the British returned, communism loomed large, race riots threatened social order, HDB flats went up all over the island, reclaimed land was redeveloped just south of Hill Street and the banks at Raffles Place were built to clutter the skyline. Yet a small, unremarkable church still quietly goes about its business, serving the same community after 170 years.

But then the Armenians are a resilient bunch. Ignoring the adage that size matters, the tiny group has certainly left its imprint on the country. The Sarkies brothers conceived Raffles Hotel, which opened in 1887, and the botanist Agnes Joachim cultivated the *Vanda* Miss Joachim, the hybrid orchid that later became Singapore's national flower. When you consider that there are now around 40 Armenians still living in Singapore, their impact is nothing short of extraordinary. There are more people at my local coffee shop on most week nights.

The Armenian Church was everything I expected it to be. An elegant, white-washed building with flawless marble floors under grand porticos, it was neither garish nor ostentatious. It was a charming church with a graceful spire on top. I had walked down Hill Street a dozen times before but had not noticed the historic gem. Perhaps that helps to explain its longevity. Out of sight, out of mind, the Armenian Church has been pretty much left to its own devices by the British, Japanese and now Singaporean governments. A little too much perhaps. A collection box proudly stated that the building sustained itself without government subsidies. Now, if central funds can be allocated to build artificial tourist fluff like Raffles Terrace, then surely a few dollars could be handed out to help preserve one of the island's oldest structures?

I ambled around its manicured garden and discovered the grave of Agnes Joachim. She died in 1899 and the headstone, rather like the church, paid an unpretentious tribute, with a small plaque acknowledging her role in discovering Singapore's national flower. Some kind soul had left a pot of orchids by her grave.

It suddenly started to rain so I took shelter under one of the church's splendid porticos and watched soaked Singaporeans splash their way through Hill Street. The church did not seem to mind. It has been providing shelter for over 170 years.

# CHAPTER 29

This island tour is fast reaching its conclusion so I thought I would recognise the people who made this glorious country what it is today. Revered for their honesty, transparency and lifelong commitment to a common goal, their contribution to society is acknowledged across the world. They helped bring a fledgling nation together to celebrate its independence every year. Indeed, the debt Singapore owes these fine, upstanding citizens can never be repaid.

I am referring, of course, to the Dagenham Girl Pipers. Or more specifically, Peggy Iris, Sheila Nobes and Carole Granfield of the Dagenham Girl Pipers. Those three women helped make Singapore's National Day Parade (NDP) what it is today.

As we all know, Singapore celebrates its independence on 9 August with an extravaganza at either the Padang or the National Stadium. (If you are thinking of attending the next one, the colour scheme tends to be red and white.) These glittering occasions give the country a chance to show off their Chinook helicopters and disturbingly energetic hosts who get paid a dollar every time they screech, "Singapore, make some noise!" They earn an additional 50 cents if they cry "woo", "awesome" or "Are you ready to par-ty?". These well-drilled affairs display a military precision that betrays a year of stringent planning, choreography and rehearsal. I have heard that even the "woos" are rehearsed.

But in 1967, it was a different story. In the first quarter of that year, preparations for the next NDP began in earnest. Having declared its independence in 1965, Singapore staged its first parade in 1966 and the show was an unqualified success. So the word from the top was "The NDP is to become an annual event so make sure that the second one is a marked improvement upon the first." But how do you top an exhilarating first act? How do you make the sequel more entertaining than the original? Simple. You get on the government hotline and call Dagenham.

That NDP organising committee meeting, comprising military bigwigs, political figures and members of the People's Association, must have been mind-blowing:

"We need to top last year's smash at the Padang. Don't think Malaysian standard, Indonesian standard or even Asian standard. The world will be watching so think world standard, people. I'm thinking foreign talent for this one. So where do we go to get world-class foreign talent?"

"Dagenham."

"Dagenham? No way! Out of the question! I don't want anything to do with Australians."

"No, it's in England, sir. In Essex. You know, the world's biggest council housing estate?"

"What? Bigger than our plans for Toa Payoh? Impossible."

"No, it is, really. It's also got the Ford car plant, Dudley Moore, Sir Alf Ramsey, Jimmy Greaves and that singer Sandie Shaw. She's in the charts right now, actually. You know, 'A Puppet on a String'?"

"Oh, that is a catchy song. Is Dagenham anywhere near Cambridge? We like Cambridge."

"Er, yeah, it's close enough."

"Right then. Let's call Dagenham and get them to send over some world-class talent. Who knows? Dagenham could become a veritable factory of foreign talent for this country."

I am milking this, I know, but my hometown and the adjectival "world-class" are seldom found in the same sentence. But in 1967, the Dagenham Girl Pipers was an internationally renowned marching bagpipe band that toured the world. So when *The Straits Times* reported in February 1967 that Singapore must have a 36-member all-girl bagpipe band, Dagenham's Iris, Nobes and Granfield were flown over, on business class I hope, to form the Singapore Girl Pipers and prepare them for the NDP. According to the report, the girls had to play the pipes and the drums and learn to dance the Scottish reel. I have no idea what encompassed the Scottish reel, but I suspect it involved drinking a copious amount of whisky and falling over.

Dagenham's coaches had to work with pipers who had good physiques and shapely legs, according to the government, which took time out from its busy schedule of building a country from scratch to discuss young girls' legs. Dr Goh Keng Swee, the Minister for Defence back then, pointed out that girl pipers are usually attired in tartan skirts so the need for well-formed legs should be obvious to all. In other words, fatties need not apply.

Dagenham's finest delivered the goods. The all-new Singapore Girl Pipers made a spectacular debut at the second NDP in 1967 and, by all accounts, stole the show. The girls went on to become a regular, and popular, feature at subsequent Padang parades. Under the tutelage of the People's Association, the Singapore Girl Pipers evolved into the Singapore Pipe Band, which is still going strong today. And, if I might be permitted to jut out my chest for just a moment, it is all thanks to my tiny hometown.

I sat on the steps of City Hall and looked across at the Padang. It was Sunday morning and there were a handful of tourists snapping pictures with Singapore's skyline as their backdrop. City Hall, a glorious building with its imposing colonnade, is steeped in history. On 12 September 1945, the Japanese climbed these very steps before formally surrendering to the dwindling British Empire. Twenty years later, Lee Kuan Yew announced the country's independence. Again, after climbing these steps. Now, I could pretend that I was pondering the magnitude of these events and their indelible imprint upon Singapore's history, but I was really picturing several pairs of "well-formed legs" marching up and down the Padang. I once watched the players of Liverpool Football Club jog around this hallowed turf and tried to recall which Reds were there that day. But it was no good. I got as far as Robbie Fowler and

Michael Owen before they were swiftly elbowed aside by startling images of the Fat Girl Pipers stomping across the Padang. I had to leave.

After a quick look at the old Supreme Court, a classically designed masterpiece that will soon be wisely converted into a national art gallery, I drifted down the small side street that separates City Hall and the old Supreme Court and was confronted by the new Supreme Court. Now, I have encountered some pitiful erections on this tour; the green penis in Toa Payoh's Town Garden will stay with me forever. But the new Supreme Court is spectacularly awful. Not untypical of modern monstrosities, it is covered in gloomy glass and pales in comparison to the old Supreme Court. That stately structure, with its respectful nod to St Paul's Cathedral via its majestic dome, was preoccupied with a much sillier concern: its appearance. However, its frighteningly functional successor is topped off with a disc-shaped structure that suggests it has just fallen out of a Steven Spielberg film. Irritated that such an incongruous design had ever been commissioned to stand behind two classical buildings, I marched across Anderson Bridge and took a bus down Beach Road to a place where heritage has been treated with a little more respect.

Kampong Glam (or Gelam) existed before Stamford Raffles. Named after the *gelam* tree that grew in the area, the kampong was located at the mouth of the Rochor River and populated by the Malay and Orang Laut, or sea people, communities. In 1822, Raffles beat the People's Action Party to its racial quota policy by carving up the areas around the Singapore River into racial districts. Kampong Glam, rather sensibly, was kept for the Malays and Bugis traders. Arab, Javanese, Boyanese and other Muslim merchants soon joined them. Ironically, the population surge put pressure on the land and Kampong Glam's original occupants moved away to places like Geylang Serai. Today, their descendants are stuck with a crappy Malay Village, so you could argue that they got a raw deal.

But Kampong Glam's new settlers gave the area an exotic feel still discernible today. With road names like Baghdad Street and Muscat

Street, the Arab Quarter is certainly one of Singapore's most unique places. As you leave Beach Road and wander down Arab Street, you enter a Middle Eastern world of two-storey shophouses selling the finest silk, fabrics, handicrafts, rattan, willow and bamboo. Arabs invite you to peruse their Persian rugs, tourists snap up batik shirts, sarongs and saris and locals come to be fitted out in traditional ethnic costumes. I even noticed elderly Malay fishermen haggling with a shop owner over some archaic-looking fishing tackle. But this is nothing new. In the 1950s and 1960s, Kampong Glam was the place to be on balmy nights when shoppers from across the region hunted down the cheapest textiles and hawkers pushed food carts selling *rojak*, *popiah* and, of course, satay. In 1989, the Urban Redevelopment Authority wisely declared Kampong Glam a preservation area and many of the pre-war shophouses around Arab Street, Baghdad Street and Bussorah Street were renovated.

The only problem was that the place was more or less empty when I visited. The pedestrianised Bussorah Mall had a slightly manufactured touristy feel, sprinkled with the usual backpackers' essentials: Internet cafés, cheap egg and bacon breakfasts, postcards and, most important of all, soap. The restored street looked great but, apart from a handful of backpackers, an expat family and some locals eating lunch at a halal coffee shop, I had the street to myself.

I also had the Malay Heritage Centre largely to myself, too. I originally had no intention of visiting the museum. I drifted over only because the building was the former Istana Kampong Glam, built in 1840 by Sultan Ali, the son of Sultan Hussein Shah (Singapore's first sultan). But the girl at the counter stared at me with such imploring eyes that I went in. I had reservations. I suspected that the museum would be nothing more than old kettles, some artificial timber boats and golden artefacts from royal ceremonies. That pretty much summed up the contents of the first floor, but the second floor was superb. The Malay community's cultural contribution to Singapore was its central theme and the gallery displayed Zubir Said's handwritten music and lyrics for "Majulah Singapura", the country's national anthem no less. There they were, right in front of me. I was impressed. One of the other galleries focused on the prodigious work of actor/writer/director/composer P Ramlee, an extraordinarily talented man who dominated Asean cinema in the 1950s and 1960s. Singapore's most recent artistic offering to the region has been Phua Chu Kang. I suppose that is progress.

My favourite exhibition centred upon Malay home life and the evolution from kampong to HDB flat. Although it banged the government drum a bit, the museum had recreated a generic Toa Payoh flat from the 1970s, complete with cheesy furniture, a television the size of a car and a wireless that must have required the services of a crane to get into the flat. I know it is kitschy but I am a sucker for this sort of stuff. With no one around, I sat in one of the dusty armchairs and imagined that I was wearing bell-bottoms and a polyester shirt, drinking warm Anchor beer and watching West Ham's Trevor Brooking knock one in on the *Star Soccer* black-and-white highlights show. It was fabulous.

I returned to Arab Street and had another look around the shops. They were all very exotic, but I did not urgently need a silk scarf, a tablecloth or a wicker basket so I shuffled back to Beach Road. On the way, I spotted a shop sign that read "Oriental Biggest Belly Dancer Boutique". I was intrigued. I had never seen a belly dancer's shop before and was not aware that Singapore had one. But the shop's name was ambiguous. Did the retail outlet promise an extensive range of costumes or did it just cater to fat dancers? Besieged by images of obese belly dancers, I went to Raffles Hotel for a quick pee.

Raffles Hotel is a charming hotel, a national landmark and the birthplace of the Singapore Sling. It is also a great place to have a pee. So let me give you an invaluable tip here. If you are caught short anywhere in the City Hall or Beach Road area, pop over to Raffles Hotel to relieve yourself. If you are going to go, you might as well go in style. A few years ago, I discovered that the toilets that serve the famous Long Bar (where the Singapore Sling was originally concocted) are outside the bar and just down the corridor. They are even air-conditioned, which is rather ironic as some of the bars and restaurants in the courtyard are not. So I sauntered casually along the red carpet at the hotel's grand entrance, took a sharp left past some fountains, perused the meagre selection of books in the hotel's gift shop, climbed the stairs, nipped past the Long Bar and whipped the old willy out in the most luxurious of surroundings. I will only pee in the best. And Raffles Hotel is my kind of toilet.

I stumbled upon the agreeable public facilities beside the Long Bar quite by accident. In 2001, the former Manchester United and England midfielder Bryan Robson was in town for a charity football tournament. His job as Middlesbrough manager was under threat at the time and I, the intrepid sports reporter, was tasked with tracking him down to find out if he intended to resign. A phone call informed me he was enjoying dinner at the Long Bar Steakhouse so off I went in hot pursuit. When I arrived, the head waiter said that I had no right to interrupt Mr Robson while he was eating and ordered me to wait outside. Unperturbed by this setback, I improvised. Captain Marvel had to empty his bladder at some point so I staked out the toilets. I stood at the door and smiled at each patron who entered. My appearance suggested a high-class rent boy. One or two visitors even went to give me money, which I quickly refused. What kind of service did they think they were paying me for?

The more I perspired in the sweltering heat, the more suspicious I must have looked. Ninety minutes passed and we were well into extra time, but old Robbo failed to make a late appearance. His assistant manager Viv Anderson, however, did. When he saw my reporter's notepad, he tried to bloody autograph it. But Captain Marvel steered clear of the Long Bar toilets. He was a combative midfielder in his day, one of the all-time greats, but Bryan Robson's physical attributes extend beyond the football pitch. He can hold his bladder for England.

It was a relatively cool evening so I took a slow walk across Esplanade Drive and watched the festivities below. There was a decent country band giving a free concert outside the Esplanade

Mall. The band played to a full house. The Esplanade's design may leave a lot to be desired but there is no doubt that the Theatres on the Bay concept has brought a much-needed vibrancy back to the Marina area.

The casino should do the rest. After visiting one of Singapore's oldest urban centres at Kampong Glam, I wanted to see the location of a glittering metropolis yet to be constructed. I hurried through the ghostly Clifford Pier, which had recently been closed down and moved to Marina South, and sat at the end of a jetty. Although it was now dark, I could make out the twinkling lights on the cranes across Marina Bay. On the left of the Bay, work has already begun on the Marina Barrage, which will eventually create a 48-hectare reservoir to host water sports events and perhaps even National Day celebrations. On the right, another construction site marked the colossal condo project The Sail @ Marina Bay. Sandwiched between the two, of course, will be the roulette wheels and the blackjack tables.

After years of debate, Singapore's government finally allowed the building of two casinos: a smaller one at Sentosa and a major integrated resort here at Marina Bay. The Bay's complex should be ready by 2010. Apparently, an integrated resort houses conference centres, artistic venues, hotels, galleries, restaurants and high-end retail outlets. That is all window dressing, of course, because if there was not a casino at the heart of the project, bidders from Las Vegas to Genting would not be queuing up to get a piece of the action. Not that the government really had a choice. Singaporean gamblers flood the casino in Malaysia's Genting Highlands and they are not spending their weekends on Star Cruises to spot marine life either.

And, dare I say it, the integrated resort is probably what Singapore needs. If it attracts the right nightlife, Marina Bay promises to be everything that Orchard Road is not. Urban planners are finally recognising that glass and concrete will build towns and shopping centres indefinitely, but they can destroy a country's soul. To avoid this, the National Parks Board recently launched an international competition for planners to come forward with their designs for three waterfront gardens. There will be a 54-hectare garden behind the integrated resort, a 30-hectare water-themed park in Marina East and a 10-hectare park that will neatly line the waterfront of Marina Centre. Now, that is more like it. The gardens should be ready by 2010 to accompany a twisting, 280-metre-long pedestrian bridge that will stretch across Marina Bay. It will be the longest bridge in Singapore. By that stage, the Singapore Flyer, an observation wheel modelled on the popular, if rather overrated, London Eye, should be packing them in. At 170 metres, it is projected to be the world's tallest revolving structure. This is Singapore. I would expect nothing less.

Honestly, it all sounds rather exciting. Singapore has to get the Marina Bay project right and it will. It has no choice. The government now accepts that a five-roomed flat, decent education and pristine trains that always run on time no longer impress younger, restless Singaporeans. They need to have some bloody fun in their own country and should not be forced to travel to California, Queensland or Genting to find it. Singapore may be a tiny country, but it can still accommodate both the history of Kampong Glam and the hedonism of Marina Bay. And as I stood on the edge of an empty, gloomy Clifford Pier, I promised to return to sample a bit of both.

# CHAPTER 30

My Singaporean journey was almost over. In every sense. There was just one gigantic, gaping, green hole in the middle of the country left for me to cover. And I foolishly intended to cover it in a single day. On foot.

I got up at 6am, dressed quickly, kissed my wife goodbye and assured her that I would not die. I strode briskly through the quiet Toa Payoh streets, crossed over the already busy Thomson Road and headed into MacRitchie Reservoir Park. Knowing that a day-long trek was ahead of me, I performed my usual warm-up routine. I stretched my legs half a dozen times, bent over twice, ate half a cheese sandwich and waited for Benjamin Lee to join me. A lovely, accommodating man, the Senior Conservation Officer at the National Parks Board had offered to meet me at MacRitchie to point out the safest route on a map and underscore the importance of sticking to the trails. When he arrived, Benjamin insisted that I would enjoy the walk, but his uncertain body language betrayed his real opinion: the *ang moh's* gonna die.

I had wanted to tackle this walk for a long time. Eager to dispel the stubbornly persistent myth that Singapore is nothing more than an island of concrete, I planned to circumnavigate the Central Catchment Nature Reserve and Bukit Timah Nature Reserve in the middle of the country on foot. Now, that is a pretty daft plan. Comprising the reservoirs of MacRitchie, Peirce and Seletar, the Central Catchment area covers around 3,043 hectares. Bukit Timah is another 163 hectares. So I foolishly intended to trek through rainforest that covered 3,206 hectares. As one hectare (100 metres x 100 metres) is slightly shorter and fatter than the football pitch inside Cardiff's Millennium Stadium (120 metres x 79 metres), you will realise that Singapore's major green lung is a respectable size. It could be bigger of course. Those 3,206 hectares constitute 4.6 per cent of Singapore's total land area, but I have noticed reforestation taking place across the country and those three splendid gardens planned for Marina Bay should ensure that you bequeath a green island to your children, rather than a charred country. That said, 4.6 per cent of Singapore's land area is still a bugger to walk.

I planned to hike around 4.5 kilometres to the TreeTop Walk in MacRitchie, then cover another 6 kilometres or so to reach Bukit Timah Nature Reserve and eat my remaining cheese sandwiches. After lunch, I would follow a biking trail out of Bukit Timah, skirting the fringes of Upper Peirce Reservoir Park and Seletar Reservoir Park, turn right at Mandai Road, my northernmost point, then venture south along Upper Thomson Road, pop into Lower Peirce Reservoir Park, sneak around the Singapore Island Country Club, return to MacRitchie and be back home in time for tea. For some strange reason, Benjamin was not convinced.

"You shouldn't really go on your own, you know," he said, making a mental note to keep a search party on standby. "Have you got enough food and drink, plenty of insect repellent and your mobile phone? Oh, and don't forget to take down our helpline."

I laughed. He did not. So I took out my notepad like a penitent schoolboy and reluctantly jotted down the National Parks Board's helpline. I noticed Benjamin watch me write down every digit. There was no doubt in his mind. He clearly thought that the next time we met, I would be strapped to a stretcher and dangling from a helicopter.

I ventured onto the MacRitchie Nature Trail and was impressed by the number of eager middle-aged trekkers I passed. They powered along, always taking the time to smile, say "hello" or wish me a pleasant morning. I encountered one particular middle-aged group engaged in a bizarre conversation. Peering nervously into the undergrowth, one chap said, "Got a lot you know. I see them all the time. Must be careful."

"Yah, it's true," said a plump woman in a tracksuit with a beach towel round her neck. "The park ranger never talks about it, might scare off visitors."

"Yeah, loh. But the park ranger must take responsibility, right or not?"

"But he bites, right?"

"Of course he bites. Cannot keep secret. Park ranger must tell the public. He's damn fierce. If he bites you, must get antidote or sure die one."

I was not sure if they were discussing a snake or a psychotic park ranger.

I reached the TreeTop Walk remarkably quickly. Not through choice, though. I was pursued mercilessly by a group of expatriate housewives. There were six of them, all armed with walking sticks and one-piece Lycra suits, stomping through the forest at breakneck speed and knocking casual walkers into the reservoir. Then they closed in on me. Now, I should have been a mature grown-up and kindly stepped aside and allowed the Lycra ladies to pass. Instead I decided to race them to the TreeTop Walk. It was not their gender, you understand, it was their inane chattering. They never stopped talking. How did they do it? I panted, wheezed and swore at every chipped rock that stubbed my toes. Yet the far from desperate housewives breezed along and still found the energy to swap jokes and waffle on about the aesthetic value of black Lycra. I was insanely jealous of their fitness and vowed to spread my legs and jump on the nearest tree stump if so much as one of them surged past me.

I paid the price for my puerile behaviour. By the time I had dragged my shaking legs to the entrance of the TreeTop Walk, my vision was blurred and I thought I was hallucinating. Everywhere I turned, the forest was filled with those singing and dancing Ribena berries from the TV commercials. They were everywhere. I sat down, downed an entire bottle of Coke and belched so loudly that several startled birds flew out of the trees. It was just what I needed. The Ribena berries disappeared and I was ready for Singapore's greatest bridge.

On a trip to Western Australia a few years ago, my wife and I took four hours to drive south of Perth to reach the Tree Top Walk in the Valley of the Giants near the town of Walpole. Singapore's TreeTop Walk, on the other hand, was just a brisk 90-minute stroll from my apartment in Toa Payoh. And it was spectacular. In a country that is so small, there is a tendency to overlook things that are on your doorstep. I have met Singaporeans who have been to Australia's Valley of the Giants but would not consider visiting MacRitchie's TreeTop Walk. That is such a shame. Opened in 2004, the free-standing suspension bridge is 250 metres long and stands majestically over the forest canopy, which is about 25 metres below. As the bridge connects MacRitchie's two highest points, its panoramic vistas of the forest are breathtaking.

As I shared the bridge with only a handful of other visitors, I took my time. The bridge reaches 27 metres at its highest point but it was still dwarfed by many of the surrounding trees. It is awe-inspiring stuff and feels more like Sabah than Singapore. Of course, the adorably *kiasu* signs are always on hand to remind you where you are. On a list of dos and don'ts, it was suggested that, in the event of a thunderstorm, visitors must see the ranger on duty to avoid being struck by lightning. Why? Is he on a higher spiritual plane than the rest of us? Does the National Parks Board employ shamans? No disrespect to the young ranger who was sitting in his booth at the edge of the bridge but, if lightning had struck at that particular moment, I would have followed traditional protocol and screamed like a little girl and dashed for the exit.

Halfway across the bridge, I spotted a long-tailed macaque sitting pretty at the top of a tree some 30 metres above ground. I was delighted. It was the first monkey I had seen on the tour, which was rather surprising considering they are one of the more common wild mammals in Singapore. The macaque was certainly the first exotic animal I saw when I arrived in the country. Some colleagues took me to Bukit Timah Nature Reserve and the playful primates were everywhere: on dustbins, car bonnets, house roofs, rest shelters, benches and any other location where they could be guaranteed human interaction, some potato chips and the odd Mars bar. The idea of glimpsing monkeys in their natural habitat was exciting, but it was quite an anticlimax watching a fat kid feed them some Pringles in the car park.

But that is all changing. The monkeys are being forced back into the forest whether they like it not. There has been a discernible shift in attitude towards feral creatures in recent years, both in the media and in public forums. Heavier punishments are being handed down to animal abusers and the National Parks Board is doing a tremendous job in raising public awareness. I noticed massive billboards placed strategically in areas that were once popular with scavenging monkeys that reminded visitors to let the wild animals feed themselves. According to the billboards, offenders can even be fined now for feeding monkeys. NParks is determined to get the message across and the positive results were self-evident. From the bridge, I glimpsed at least a dozen monkeys foraging for fruits and seeds under leaves and branches. A decade ago at Bukit Timah Nature Reserve, a fearless macaque climbed nonchalantly onto a bench and stole a bag of potato chips from my lap. The cheeky bugger then sauntered over to the other end of the bench and ate them in front of me. But that is less likely to happen now. The monkeys are trooping back to the trees. Keep them there.

I embarked upon the long walk along Rifle Range Link and Rifle Range Road. Perhaps understandably, I met a lot of young men carrying weapons. National Servicemen were dotted all over the place: under tents, at checkpoint barriers or marching in single file through the forest in their camouflaged uniforms. To make a rather obvious point, the soldiers were so young. They were just kids. I know it is not politically correct, but I will never be comfortable with teenagers brandishing guns. They should be out chasing young women at Zouk, not chasing inanimate objects in the jungle. When I was their age, I felt uneasy with a pint of cider and blackcurrant in my hand, let alone an assault rifle. They looked bored, too. I knew the way to Bukit Timah Nature Reserve but, to make conversation, I asked one lonely serviceman for directions. He sat alone in the middle of the Central Catchment Nature Reserve and fiddled with his cable. He probably was not the first soldier to do so, of course.

"Hey man, how's it going?" I asked enthusiastically. "Am I going the right way for Bukit Timah?"

"No, you want to go back that way," he replied, gesturing in the opposite direction.

"Are you sure? That's MacRitchie. I've just been there. Bukit Timah should be this way."

"Ah, okay, if you're sure. But I really think Bukit Timah is the other way."

"Well, I'll soon find out. What kind of exercise are you doing out here anyway?"

"Navigation."

I had to look away and cover my mouth. With navigational experts like that in the Singapore Armed Forces, who needs an enemy?

I followed the trail into Rifle Range Road and was overcome by the putrid stench of rotting flesh. It was inescapable. With my T-shirt pulled up over my nose, I saw two scavenging crows pick away at a dead snake in the middle of the road. The snake had not been dead for long and could consider itself unlucky. In the hour that I had plodded along the road, only four military vehicles had passed, one of which had presumably squashed the snake's head into the tarmac. It was a mashed-up, bloody mess. Ignoring my close presence, the birds' beaks poked at the snake's organs like a surgeon's probing scalpel. It was a fascinating scene I had seen many times before, but it was usually through a small screen and accompanied by David Attenborough's narration. Now I understand why smell-o-vision never took off.

I reached Bukit Timah before noon, ate my sandwiches, replenished my water supplies, informed Benjamin that I was still alive, rinsed out my sweaty T-shirt and had a surreal conversation about local politics with a half-naked man in the toilets. Eager to get away, I plunged back into the forest at Senapang Link and trekked north along the biking trail that runs alongside Bukit Timah Expressway.

Now there is one obvious problem with biking trails; they are designed for rugged, all-terrain mountain bikes and not tiring hikers. The path was extremely narrow, with sharp, jagged rocks sticking out of the ground, mischievously camouflaged by thick vegetation to ensure that the soothing songs of the cicadas and the cheerful chirping of the birds was occasionally interrupted by cries of "Argh! Where the fuck did that rock come from?".

Somewhere in the Taban Valley, short bursts of rapid gunfire sent the entire forest running for cover. I am not joking. I was admiring the number of macaques playing in the trees when a series of gunshots exploded into the air like a dozen thunderclaps. I foolishly dove into some grass and grazed my arms and knees on some rocks. But I was not the only petrified primate. Troops of screeching monkeys scattered in every direction and I noticed a few squirrels jump from trunk to trunk in utter panic. The periodic gunshots were deafening. Through a clearing in the forest, I made out a number of targets and realised I was peering down at the Bukit Timah Rifle Range. Every time, the sharp shooters fired, there was pandemonium. The monkeys hopped up and down in the trees and bared their teeth, the birds flew away and the undergrowth moved as various reptiles slunk away. The forest obviously did not like having a rifle range next door. Neither did I.

Coincidentally, Benjamin sent a text message a little later to check that I was still conscious. I was in the process of replying when a helicopter circled overhead and appeared to follow me. It would disappear above trees only to reappear the moment I stepped back into an open clearing. It tracked me for several minutes as I trudged through the Dairy Farm area. You may call me paranoid, but the moment I replied to Benjamin and confirmed that I had not yet passed out, the helicopter disappeared.

Then the rainforest decided to live up to its name and ruin any chance of completing the tour on foot. I was deep inside the forest, on the Chestnut Track just before Bukit Panjang Road, when the heavens opened. I was pleased at first as the blustery conditions blew away the humidity. But it rained. And rained. And rained. Climbing a gentle incline at the time, I struggled to make headway as the soggy path quickly turned into a mudslide and I found myself ankle-deep in water. I found it all rather exciting initially, but the rain refused to relent and my map, street directory and mobile phone were soaked. I left the path and took refuge under some trees, but it made little difference. The contents of my bag were saturated by intermittent big blobs of water rather than a constant shower. There was no shelter anywhere and standing under a tree during an intense electric storm did not really appeal. I had little choice but to return to the flooded track. I ran blindly through the rain, cutting my ankles on jagged lumps of rock and stumbling through trenches of water that occasionally came up to my shin. At least 18 kilometres into my journey by now, my heart pounded and my tired legs were threatening to go on strike.

Fortunately, salvation came in the form of the Zhenghua Flyover of the Bukit Timah Expressway. I took refuge beneath the flyover, along with several motorcyclists, in Bukit Panjang Road. Some renovation work had recently been abandoned and there were tins of paint and bags of cement lying around under the flyover. I found an old pair of paint-spattered trousers and gladly used them to dry myself. I hope the owner did not mind.

The ferocious storm continued for another hour and I could not risk ruining my map, notepad and the rest of the contents of my rucksack by plodding on to Mandai Road. Nor would I entertain the prospect of rambling around Nee Soon Swamp after dark. Hikers do get lost out there and I did not fancy becoming another statistic for the National Parks Board's rescue team. So I dried my clothes and relied on public transport to get to Lower Peirce Reservoir Park. The flesh was just about willing, but the logistics were weak.

I like Lower Peirce Reservoir Park. The reservoir provides a charming backdrop for a picnic and a great place to go skinny-dipping with your mates when you are drunk at 3am. For legal reasons, I cannot say anymore on that particular subject. The park also has a gentle, amiable boardwalk through mature secondary rainforest and, most important of all, provided the location for my daft Stamford Raffles scenes in *Talking Cock, The Movie.*

When I arrived, I had the entire park to myself, but that was probably because it was pissing down on a Wednesday afternoon. I climbed over a gate to take a short cut through the Singapore Island Country Club (SICC) to get back to MacRitchie when Mr Kiasu appeared. That guy is like a bus or a policeman, isn't he? He is always there when you do not bloody need him. My feet had barely touched SICC ground when he descended down an immaculate grassy slope, waving at me frantically. Remembering my manners, I smiled and waved back. My flippancy irritated him.

"Cannot, cannot, cannot," he shouted as he thundered across one of the greens. "Cannot come in here. No, no, no." Mr Kiasu liked to repeat himself.

"It's okay. I'm just going to take a short cut through the golf club to MacRitchie. I've done it before." That was true, albeit with a nature group that had first obtained written permission from SICC.

"Cannot, cannot, cannot," he reiterated, waving a finger near my face. "Must go back to Upper Thomson Road." His authoritarian demeanour and aggressive tone annoyed me.

"Okay mate, calm down. I was just trying to take a short cut."

"Cannot, cannot. This is a private golf course. Cannot. No, no, no."

"All right, don't wet yourself. I'm not going to steal the grass off your bloody greens, am I? "

I will not miss Mr Kiasu when I leave Singapore. I will not miss private golf clubs either.

But there are so many glorious things about this country that I will miss. As I trudged wearily down Upper Thomson Road in the rain, a kindly taxi driver tooted his horn and enquired if I needed a ride. I declined, but his unexpected, benevolent gesture made me smile. I will miss Singaporean taxi drivers and their insistence that I tell them which way to go. Theirs is the only profession where the customer must provide directions to get the job done. I had a tonsillectomy at Singapore General Hospital and the surgeon did not seek my opinion on which way to go in.

I will miss a country where you can call a referee "a plank", "talk cock" and "fuck spider", often at the same time. A country where cheeky children step into a lift and shout "Wah, *ang moh!* So tall, ah" and inquisitive aunties insist on knowing your life story before you reach the ground floor. This is the country that gave the world the chicken chop, the contents of which remain a mystery to me, and Romancing Singapore, a festival of love that offers conclusive proof that the government has finally taken the business of a sense of humour seriously.

In Singapore, I can walk along any street, *lorong*, country lane or forest trail at any time, day or night, without fearing for my personal security. Having been mugged twice in England, I have never taken my safety for granted here. Nor should you. Cherish it. In Singapore, it is possible to have a politician's son, a lawyer's son, a doctor's son, a hawker seller's son, a bus driver's son and a cleaner's son sitting together in the same classroom. I know. I have taught them. In Singapore, aunties and uncles are still revered and treated with respect, quite rightfully, even when they jab a bony elbow in your kidneys to get on a bus. And they still look over their shoulder and speak in hushed tones when discussing the PAP at coffee shops, convinced that Lee Hsien Loong is sitting at the next table.

I know that I will never again live in a country where I can get a decent meal 24 hours a day. Or in a country where food courts, shopping centres, cinemas, hotels, massage parlours, surgeries, schools, train stations, bus stops, taxi stands, libraries, community centres, public swimming pools, parks, reservoirs, primary rainforest, a treetop trail, monitor lizards and wild monkeys are all within walking distance of my apartment. There is even a gynaecologist at the end of my street. I have never needed one, but it was always reassuring to know that there was one on my doorstep.

And to thoroughly dispel that persistent myth, Singapore is a charming, beautiful, green country where I can walk continuously for over eight hours and never leave a forest or park trail. I started my trek at 8am and by the time I had reached the end of the MacRitchie Nature Trail, it was almost 6pm. In total, I had covered approximately 27 kilometres on foot. My hike had included MacRitchie, Rifle Range Road, Bukit Timah, Upper Peirce and the fringes of Upper Seletar, Lower Peirce and Upper Thomson Road before returning to MacRitchie and Toa Payoh. And exotic flora and fauna surrounded me the entire day. The Central Catchment Nature Reserve boasts 1,190 recorded species of plants, 207 birds, 44 mammals and 72 reptiles. I saw a monitor lizard, two squirrels, some monkeys and a dead snake. It was a great day.

I reached home just before dark. I was exhausted. My wife opened the door, curtly informed me that I stank and ordered me to remove my shoes and most of my clothes outside. So I stood in the public corridor in my sweaty boxer shorts and looked out at Toa Payoh. As I craned my neck, I could just about make out my first apartment in Lorong 8, where Scott and I had mistaken a void-deck funeral for a coffee shop the night we arrived in Singapore. It was not that far really. If I walked briskly, I could probably cover the distance in just over 10 minutes. But the journey had taken me almost a decade to complete and I was extremely sad that it was coming to an end. I knew I was not just leaving a great island. It was much more than that. I was saying goodbye to the best 10 years of my life.

# EPILOGUE

And then I left. But I almost didn't, thanks to *Final Notes from a Great Island*. The book exceeded all expectations and the last two months spent in Singapore were among the most memorable. At book talks, aunties dished out the occasional public rebuke, albeit in a humorous fashion, suggesting I should stay. At schools, students insisted that I was mad to say goodbye to Singapore and one particular teenager refused to let me leave the school hall until I'd taught him a passable impersonation of Scott's Yorkshire accent. It wasn't perfect but it wasn't half bad either. Today, there is probably an Indian Singaporean standing at a KFC counter somewhere on the island and saying, "Ello, ken ye ge' meh eh tool piss cliss-beh chickin se' wi chips 'n eh cork?"

Around the coffee shops of Toa Payoh, strangers actually stopped me in the street, shook my hand and wished me well. One particular encounter stands out for its brevity. At Toa Payoh Central, there are two escalators inside the HDB Hub. One ascends beside NTUC Fair Price and the other goes down beside a jewellery store where pushy sales assistants shoved leaflets into my hand, insisting that the one thing missing from my life was a silver pendant with a vomit-green stone in the middle. The escalators are about five metres apart. As I was going down, a voice on the opposite escalator shouted, "HEY, DUMPWEE!" Now, I don't know if you've been called a spittoon in a crowded shopping mall but, as jaw-dropping, attention-grabbing ice-breakers go, it takes some beating. I glanced furtively over at the opposite escalator and noticed an uncle, in his early sixties, waving frantically in my direction. So I did the noble thing and turned away, hoping that my fellow shoppers would deduce that the poor man suffered from a Hokkien version of Tourette's Syndrome and randomly called people 'spittoons'. Toa Payoh Central was packed. He could be shouting out to anyone …

"HEY ANG MOH!" he shouted. That narrowed the odds considerably. I looked around quickly, in the desperate hope that The Flying Dutchman might be standing on the same escalator, but I was the solitary Caucasian. I smiled and waved back at the man, but that only served to encourage him. "Hey, Dumpwee. I knew it was you. Hey, all the bes' ah, Dumpwee! All the bes'!" "… That's Dumpwee over there. See. Look. Dumpwee!" he shouted to the 350 other shoppers within earshot.

I had a lump the size of a dumpling in my throat. When I returned to the apartment, I seriously reconsidered our decision to move on. But my wife put things in perspective.

"That man was really sweet," she said, packing the last of the boxes. "That's a nice memory to have."

"Yeah, but it's making me think we should cancel moving to Australia and stay in Singapore."

"We could do that, I suppose. Our plane leaves in less than a week, all our belongings are on a ship bound for Australia, we've both quit our jobs and we'll be homeless by the end of the month. So we could change our minds at the very last minute and stay. Definitely."

About two weeks later, at approximately 3am, my wife also had second thoughts. We had arrived in Geelong, an hour's drive south of Melbourne, found a place to rent and were gamely attempting to live a more rural, outback-ish lifestyle. And then our new, unfamiliar home got burgled. Or at least we thought it did. At 3am, my wife suddenly sat bolt upright in the bed. She does this a lot. It's like sharing the duvet with Dracula. It usually means she needs to use the toilet or has misplaced a chocolate bar. She encouraged me to wake up by kicking me repeatedly in the shins.

"We're being burgled," she hissed. She wasn't joking. I jumped out of the bed, realised my Hulk boxer shorts were not the appropriate attire to tackle a weapon-wielding housebreaker and fumbled my way around the room in search of my wife's dressing gown. At that particular moment, I wondered what possessed us to leave the sacred security of Toa Payoh. I also wondered why I'd never bothered to buy a dressing gown.

"How do you know we're being bloody burgled?" I whispered back at my wife, who was using a duck feather-stuffed pillow to shield herself from the axe-murdering Aussie she claimed was on the property.

"I heard him walk across the roof," a muffled voice muttered from beneath the pillow.

"Across the roof? Who the fuck's up there? Spiderman? Are you sure it's a burglar?"

And then I heard it—the unmistakable sound of footsteps creeping across the roof. Oh shit. We really were being burgled. Ten years in Singapore—nothing. Two weeks in Australia—our house gets burgled. Terrific. But then I heard more footsteps, several pairs at once, and they sounded almost rhythmic, as if they were skipping rather than creeping. Now, either Dick Van Dyke was up there with his chimney sweeps singing 'Step in Time' or something altogether less human, and possibly much smaller, was scurrying around in the dark. Roadside carrion provided us with the answer the following morning. At the opposite end of our street, a ring-tailed possum was splattered across the tarmac. It was not a pretty sight but a rather common one in Australia. Birds, rabbits, hares, possums and kangaroos—we've spotted them all along the roads since we arrived. In fact, it was over a month before we actually glimpsed a live kangaroo at Anglesea Golf Course; the previous ones had all been dead.

Possums ruled our street after dark. That was an immense relief for both of us. At least tap-dancing burglars were not keeping us awake at night. But the nocturnal partying of hedonistic possums was turning us into sleep-deprived zombies. And, my god, do those boys really know how to party. They also conform to stereotype. They like to play possum, funnily enough, all bloody night long. For an entire month before we moved to another house, it was like living with those singing and dancing animals in the animated movie *Madagascar.* When we were awake, the possums played dead. Not a peep. Complete silence. But as soon as we dropped off, those little bastards pumped up the volume and held hardcore raves on the roof. In my semi-conscious state, I could almost hear them saying, "Shush, the tall one's just falling asleep. Quiet, he's drifting off, get the CD ready … You got it? Okay, good, now we just wait … Right, he's asleep. Hit it! … *I like to move it, move it. I like to move it, move it. Do you like to, MOVE IT!"*

They were up and down the roof, performing a possum chorus line just long enough for me to jump up and shout, "Will you dancing bastards shut up?"

And then complete silence. Not a sound from above. The possums played possum. Blessed sleep beckoned. But the moment I pressed my sleepy head against the pillow … *I like to move it, move it. I like to move it, move it. Do you like to … MOVE IT!*

I soon realised that I'd moved from one young country with a slight inferiority complex (at the official level at least) to another. During my last couple of years in Singapore, I couldn't open a newspaper without being bombarded with all those post-colonial, navel-gazing, hang-ups. The headlines came thick and fast: "Things that make us uniquely Singaporean." "Things that make us proud to be Singaporean." "What makes us Singaporean?" "How Singaporean are we as a nation?" More importantly, "What makes *you* Singaporean?" Surveys were carried out, the usual social commentators were wheeled out and Singaporeans were being asked to quantify their national identity. With all this talk of globalisation and brain drains, paranoia permeated certain corridors. In a post-Sars environment, it was time to bang the nationalist drum again. But it got a little farcical. I came across 'Test your Singapore-ness' multiple choice exercises where you earned extra points if you could recount the back story of the Merlion and a bonus if you could track down the best pork rib soup (it's at Balestier Road, if you're interested). But what is the logical extension of such an exercise? Take away one's citizenship if they can't stomach *rojak*? Issue stern, written warnings to those who turn their nose up at chilli crab? If you can't recall the last verse of 'Majulah Singapura', should you contact the Samaritans and possibly Singapore Airlines? At the risk of stating the obvious, young Singaporeans who've tasted various alternatives overseas—be they cultural, political, artistic or even sexual— will not necessarily dash back to Changi Airport for the crispiest *roti prata*. It's going to take more than a plate of *rojak* and a casino to convince these guys to return to the ties that bind after their overseas studies.

Australia is little different. But rather than feeling threatened by the insider going out, they appear fixated on the outsider coming in. They want to set national tests not to reassert the country's identity but to determine whether foreigners have what it takes to be 'fair dinkum' Aussies. There are plans afoot to devise tests on 'fair dinkum' Australian values that immigrants must pass if they want to swap their poorer, occasionally war-torn, countries for Aussie Rules Football, beer stubbies and endless reruns of *The Simpsons*. But there is only one glaring drawback. Like Singapore, no one is entirely sure what Australian values are. There is the spirited 'mateship', forged on the battlefields at Gallipoli and forever championed on Anzac Day. It is true that aspects of 'mateship' in Australia are special; my neighbours already treat us as extended members of their own family and it is wonderful. But there are other, distasteful elements of 'mateship' Down Under. It is unlikely an immigration officer will sit down a family of Somali refugees and say, "Now, the first thing you need to master is fair dinkum values. And top of the list is 'mateship'. That can be achieved in various ways. You can have a barbeque together and ridicule the poms and convince yourselves that cricket really is a global game and that it means just as much to England as it does to Australia. And then you get pissed. Or, you and your mates can train to become 'hoons,' where you skid down streets in a car that probably isn't yours, without the appropriate insurance or documentation. And then you get pissed. Alternatively, you can do all of the above after you've got pissed. Then you can pass the values of 'mateship' down to your children, reach middle age and shake your head incredulously when you read about the rise of drink-driving convictions and the ridiculously high number of car accident fatalities. Now, sign here, and promise not to plunder our suburbs and turn them into ghettos."

Like a relatively new country, there is that subconscious effort to join the big boys. Singapore can never compete in terms of geography, so it laid down the best carpets, opened up more shops and staked a successful claim for the world's best airport instead. And for many proud years, Changi Airport ruled the skies. But in the 2007 Airports Council International service quality awards, Changi came in fourth in the overall prize of Best Airport Worldwide. That in itself was unfortunate but no disaster. The national calamity came when it was announced that—I can barely bring myself to type it—the Kuala Lumpur International Airport came in third! Malaysia's airport has a better service quality than its Causeway neighbour. How did Singapore allow this to happen? Malta can have a finer airport than Singapore, perhaps, but not Malaysia. The news provoked near hysteria in the media. By the time you read this, Changi Airport will have doubled its shops, retrained its customer service officers and added an extra terminal or two. Gotta stay with the big boys.

Australia holds similar aspirations, but it plays the geography card instead. Recently, my adopted town of Geelong hosted the Head of Schoolgirls Regatta 2007, where Victoria's finest young female rowers locked oars on the nearby Barwon River. The event was an unqualified success. Later that weekend, I was discussing the regatta and the importance of bringing sports events to the region with a colleague. He agreed, before adding, "And do you know this is the biggest regatta in the southern hemisphere."

"It's the biggest where?" I asked, thoroughly confused.

"It's the biggest regatta ever held in the southern hemisphere."

I have heard this claim being made on several occasions in the Australian media since arriving. We've assembled the tallest Ferris wheel in the southern hemisphere. We've cooked the biggest pizza in the southern hemisphere. We've built the ugliest car park in the southern hemisphere. It all sounds rather grandiose, but what does the title actually mean? Geelong's regatta is bigger than any previously staged in New Zealand and the Falkland Islands?

"When you say the best in the southern hemisphere, aren't you just really saying you're better than New Zealand?" I asked a colleague later.

"And South Africa," he replied proudly, clearly miffed that I might have questioned the title's prestige. Intrigued, I checked a map later and noticed that, 'fair dinkum', the southern hemisphere includes the sporting giants of Papua New Guinea, the economic might of Angola and the dense population of Tonga. Of course, the southern hemisphere also includes Brazil and Argentina, but the claim is always strangely absent when it comes to the subject of football. The southern hemisphere is home to only 10–12 per cent of the world's human population, which means this part of the world is far less polluted than the northern half. Now that really is something to brag about. But it also means that the other 88 per cent to 90 per cent of the world's population are making fatter pizzas and organising bigger regattas. So, take heart, Singapore. If you lost out to Malaysia on this occasion, just move the goalposts a little. You're still the proud owners of the Best Airport On The Equator title.

Like Singapore, Australia is a new country largely populated by immigrants. Unlike Singaporeans, who often have fond memories of singing 'God Save The Queen' in the classroom back in the 1950s, Australians are 'true blue' Aussies. I've met one or two who'd gladly lose their reproductive organs before conceding that someone, somewhere down the family line, came from England or 'Over There'. They appear to be the two favoured geographical references in Geelong: England and 'Over There'. England is the country that is mentioned every 15 minutes, usually when one of its natives gets bowled in a cricket fixture of some importance. There are the usual disparaging comments and liberal mentions of the word 'pom' before moving on to more pressing matters of national significance, like the next England wicket. Almost everywhere else on the world map, particularly in neighbouring Asia, is 'Over There'.

Australia is a distant, dislocated country in the southern hemisphere at the toe-end of the planet and the insularity can be extraordinary. I met a lovely woman who was warm and accommodating, but she had a phobia regarding 'Over There'.

"I'm not sure I'd go to Singapore right now," she told me solemnly. "Not with all that rioting you keep reading about in the papers."

Rioting? What rioting? I knew that the IMF/World Bank meetings had been staged peacefully and the Great Singapore Sale was still months away.

"But you keep hearing about all these problems with race and religion 'Over There'."

I presume she meant southern Thailand, but it could've been southern Timbuktu. 'Over There' usually covers Southeast Asia, maybe Japan and Korea, and occasionally India and China. 'Over There' also incorporates Bali, which remains a popular Australian 'mateship' boot camp.

But Australia knows Singapore—partly because the tiny city-state appears to own half of Melbourne, most of its hotels and a major telco company in Australia (a fact I just love sharing with Australians whenever they pick up their mobile phones or make unflattering comments about 'Over There'), but also because most Australians have been to the island at some point. Usually for about an hour. For anyone living in the southern hemisphere, Singapore should probably be renamed 'Transit' because Australians will invariably call from a payphone and say, "I'm in Transit, mum."

I've had lengthy conversations about Singapore's pluses and minuses with Australians whose understanding of the country derives from two hours spent inside Changi Airport.

"I lived in Singapore for 10 years and would recommend the country to anyone," I'd say.

"Yeah, we were in Transit. They had the loveliest toilets. Very clean."

Nude dance revues may come and go, bar-top dancing may be passé and Singapore may eventually fulfil its ambition of becoming the hub of hubs, but to most visitors it will always be 'very clean'. There are certainly worse things to be remembered for.

And there are better. As I mentioned in *Final Notes from a Great Island*, Changi is an emotive word to not only Singaporeans but also Australians. Since I've been here, the epic mini-series *Changi,* which chronicles the hardships suffered by Australian POWs inside the concentration camp during World War II, has been aired on cable TV again. Changi is also the place where Australian drug smugglers go to die. And some Australians do not have a problem with that. My painter certainly doesn't. In the middle of a tea break recently, he kicked off the conversation with an unexpected opener.

"What are Singaporeans like with drugs?" he asked casually, while stirring his tea.

"Well, they don't usually take them."

"No, what's their view on drug-taking?"

"Not good, as a rule."

"Yeah, I heard that. Singapore locks up all the drug smugglers and throws away the key. That's how it should be, mate."

I love that phrase. It has cropped up on more than one occasion when discussing Singapore's penal system. Singapore "locks 'em up and throws away the key."

There must be a private parcel of land on the island that is nothing but a mountain of keys.

Of course, there is one Singapore tidbit that has been devoured across the globe. Everyone knows it, everyone likes to drop it into a conversation to highlight how Draconian life is 'Over There' and demonstrate how au fait they are with the political shenanigans of Southeast Asia. I'm talking about … well, you know what I'm talking about, don't you? You saw it coming as soon as 'Draconian' cropped up, just as I see it coming at the mere mention of the country's name. I could set my watch by it.

"Wow, you were in Singapore for 10 years," a young journalist said shortly after I'd arrived. I could hear the cogs turning. Get ready.

"I went there once. Transit. The airport was very clean. But it's quite a strict country, isn't it?"

Here it comes.

"Some of their laws and fines are crazy. Isn't that the place where it's illegal to …"

"Let me stop you there. Yes, it's true. You won't be able to pick up chewing gum in Singapore stores, unless it's been prescribed. But no, it's not illegal to chew gum there. Hasn't been for a while."

She was crestfallen. I'd taken her tidbit away. She'd clearly exhausted her one fun fact about the island. There's always the hanging drug smugglers stuff, but that's not really fun, is it? Whereas banning something as fundamentally daft as chewing gum is comical, lamentable and dripping in so much excruciating self-parody that it's almost hip, in an ironic, right-on, post-modern kind of way. It was the island's David Brent law. How dare Singapore take away the western world's most amusing anecdote about the city-state?

But I left a 'fine' city for one that is ostensibly keen on bans. The state of Victoria does enjoy implementing a ban or six. Two months after we arrived, there was a big bang in the bedroom. I'd like to say it was of my own making, but I was in the living room waiting for the English Premiership highlights show to start. The TV, the lights and the fridge all stopped abruptly. It was a crisis of monumental proportions. We couldn't get the TV back on. The mid-summer temperature outside was creeping up to 40°C and the town was enveloped in a haze, caused not by Indonesia but by uncontrollable bush fires. I had to go to work, I couldn't entertain the prospect of leaving my wife in darkness, the food in the kitchen was melting and I missed the Premiership highlights show. It was a crisis all right.

But it wasn't just my house, or the street, or the town, or even Greater Geelong. Parts of the entire state of Victoria, including Melbourne, had experienced a massive power cut. Remember, Victoria is roughly the size of Britain. Driving through the town centre, we encountered a dazed, almost apocalyptic world. None of the traffic lights worked, cars crawled through the jams and the malls were all gloomy. From every darkened nook and cranny, confused customers shuffled out onto the streets. Picture a Michael Jackson video with fewer red leather jackets and more shopping bags. A bushfire in northern Victoria had damaged one of the state's major electricity lines. Extreme demand from air-conditioning units (please, please, take note, Singapore) caused an overload that wiped out most of Melbourne and the state. It took several hours to restore the power supply but with the caveat that the state authorities couldn't prevent it from happening again soon. So the Victorian state government came up with a far-sighted, foolproof proposal: a possible statewide ban on residential air-conditioning. Logistics were clearly not on the list of priorities when this master plan was mooted. How does a state the size of Britain enforce a ban within individual households? Does it send out hundreds of surveillance vans to crawl along dimly-lit streets listening out for rattling noises in the master bedroom?

Australia has endured a bit of a battering from Mother Nature since I arrived and its people have been bamboozled with one ban after another. No wet season; hosepipe ban. No rain; car-washing ban. Drought; complete ban of water usage outdoors. Damaged power lines; calls for an air con ban. The state cannot control the rainfall (although it can control its water storage facilities, reservoirs and recycling plants, but that is an entirely different story) so it zooms in on water usage instead. The crisis has reached the stage where I feel guilty pulling the chain after taking a pee. At times, I can almost hear the next-door neighbour shouting, "That's the second time he's pulled the chain in an hour. And I know he didn't have curry last night because I checked his dustbins at dawn." Neighbours are actively being encouraged to 'dob in' (report) their fellow neighbours for using too much water. The water bans are turning some neighbours against each other and it's all rather unpleasant. We all want Good Samaritans for neighbours, not the Gestapo.

There have even been calls to ban men and women from whipping out their dangly bits at the local nudist beach. Okay, that's hardly an Orwellian outburst but it does give me an excuse to tell you about the day I practically bumped into a bare bum. It took me about a week to realise Australians have a penchant for exposing unusual body parts in unexpected places, beginning with their feet. In supermarkets, I kept noticing kids, teenagers and middle-aged adults wandering down the aisles in their bare, often filthy, feet. I was rather indignant at first, consumed by an unsavoury social snobbery. I felt compelled to chase them to the checkout, shouting: "Put some bloody shoes on, man. You're not in a Charles Dickens novel." Now I find it endearing and indicative of a more laidback lifestyle and, yes, I have participated once or twice myself. But only under the cover of darkness, when there are fewer shoppers around and I can meander around the bakery section, snapping up the 'reduced for a quick sale' sliced loaves.

The odd pair of exposed feet, however, does not prepare oneself for coming across an exposed thingy. Still exploring the unfamiliar country, we were driving along the Victorian coastline through a town called Torquay one Saturday afternoon. My wife was about to start teaching there on the Surf Coast so we thought we'd have a wander around. There were several popular routes leading down to various packed beaches and a deserted gravel track that appeared to lead to nowhere. Naturally, we took the gravel track. We trundled along and found a tiny car park with half a dozen vehicles there baking in the sun. Dwarfed by the surrounding sand dunes, the park was so secluded we almost missed it. My wife was reluctant to stop, but I'd already tumbled out of the car and was halfway up a sand dune. They seemed to go on forever. The crashing waves of the Bass Strait were out there. I could hear them in the distance. I just couldn't see them. Then I was confronted by a man's saggy bum. It crossed my path with an insouciant wiggle. Now, this was no ordinary bum. This was a blue bum. Its appearance suggested its owner had spent the day scribbling on his bare behind with a blue crayon.

Then he turned around and we saw his blue crayon. I did the manly thing and expressed my indifference, issuing a dramatic sigh that I desperately hoped provided a clear indication that I was impressed by neither girth nor general presentation. In truth, I wasn't. It was freezing: both the temperature and his limp appendage. My wife did the womanly thing and practically climbed onto my shoulders for a better vantage point.

"Ooh, he's got his thingy out," she said.

"I realise that. And the chilly sea breeze is doing him no favours." We concluded that he was either one of the many surf dudes who frequently drop their towels in car parks (where my wife encountered another taut, younger bottom a few weeks earlier and almost crashed the car), or a man whose bowels had got the better of him. Unperturbed, the naked man strode nonchalantly on into the sand dunes, taking his little chap with him.

After a few more twists and turns around the sand dunes, we reached the crest and peered down at the ocean. The panoramic view was breathtaking. We'd found a little corner of heaven. It was a crisp, flawless spring day bathed in blue, making it difficult to distinguish the clear sky from the pellucid ocean below. Then a pair of exposed boobs jiggled into view and I suddenly forgot all about the picture postcard backdrop. A naked lady had emerged from the sea and was walking briskly across the beach. She was holding hands with a middle-aged guy, who was also nude, but I never really noticed him. I can't even recall what he looked like. I am not sure why. I later learned that Victoria has just two nudist beaches. Somehow, we'd managed to stumble upon one of them and I was genuinely fascinated by the admirable attempts to return to Man's natural state. Not fascinated enough to actually participate, of course. There are several species of shark in the Bass Strait. In the previous weeks, the Great White had made a fleeting appearance and there had been a couple of reported attacks in the area so I had no intention of offering my sausage on a stick as an hors d'oeuvre.

I had been to a nudist beach before. About two years earlier, my mother had dragged me to one near her English hometown of Ramsgate. I'm sure there are many psychologically damaging reasons why patients are reluctantly drawn to therapists. But watching your mother pick out naked men on a nudist beach has to be somewhere near the top of the list. Nevertheless, I feel qualified to make a rather unkind observation about nudist beaches: those who participate probably shouldn't. To use an appropriate analogy, you wouldn't turn up at the Bukit Timah Rifle Range with a kid's water pistol, would you? Particularly if the water pistol was designed some time after Hitler invaded Poland but before colour television was introduced. The Torquay beach was like *Baywatch* for the over sixties. If you bore a passing resemblance to Angelina Jolie or Brad Pitt, you were out. But if you were overweight, under-exercised, shrivelled up and last touched your toes in 1974, you were in. I suspect there is an anatomical explanation why some of the men had lost all inhibition when it came to displaying their private parts: they hadn't seen them for years.

A little research later informed me that the beach was called Point Impossible and the local nudist group, which was called something like Get 'Em Out For The Locals, planned annual ball games to raise awareness. The games never went ahead in the end. There were complaints in the local media and calls for all sorts of 'bans'. Ban the boobs. Ban the bums. Ban the willies. The letter writers to *The Geelong Advertiser* had a field day. But I must say a tournament that raises awareness about nudism does seem a trifle redundant. It's not like the leisure pursuit requires any formal training. Participants turn up, strip off and wave their bits around. Job done. And what sports are benefited by their participants being naked? The javelin brings a tear to the eye just thinking about it, and I wouldn't take part in the tug of war with anyone.

We didn't hang around at Point Impossible for too long. We were clearly overdressed for the occasion. But as we headed back towards the car, we realised we'd come full circle. From Singapore to Australia, we still can't escape middle-aged women flashing their boobs.

Neil Humphreys
Geelong, Australia 2007

# ABOUT THE AUTHOR

In 1996, Neil Humphreys turned down a chance to become Dagenham's answer to Nick Leeson. The young Brit rejected a London stockbroker's lucrative offer to train as a floor trader and decided to travel the world instead. He ended up in Singapore and settled in Toa Payoh. By 2001, he was one of the country's best-selling authors. His first book, *Notes from an even Smaller Island,* became an immediate best-seller and travelled across Southeast Asia, Australia and Britain. The book appeared on the Singapore best-seller list for over four years. BBC World said it was "a warts and all view of the city-state and celebrates many of the things most often criticised". Humphreys' travelling companion, Scott, said it was "a load of bollocks". In 2003, his second book, *Scribbles from the Same Island,* a compilation of his popular humour columns in *WEEKEND TODAY,* was launched in Singapore and Malaysia and also became an immediate best-seller. In 2006, *Final Notes from a Great Island: A Farewell Tour of Singapore* completed the trilogy. The book went straight to No.1 and decided to stay there for a few months. Having run out of ways to squeeze 'island' into a book title, Humphreys moved to Geelong, Australia. He now writes for several magazines and newspapers in Singapore and Australia and spends his weekends happily looking for echidnas and platypuses. But he still really misses *roti prata.*